OXFORD MONOGRAPHS IN INTERNATIONAL LAW

General Editor: Professor Ian Brownlie CBE, QC, FBA
Chichele Professor of Public International Law in the University of Oxford and Fellow of All Souls College, Oxford

INTERNATIONAL MANAGEMENT OF HAZARDOUS WASTES: THE BASEL CONVENTION AND RELATED LEGAL RULES

OXFORD MONOGRAPHS IN INTERNATIONAL LAW

The aim of this series of monographs is to publish important and original pieces of research on all aspects of public international law. Topics which are given particular prominence are those which, while of interest to the academic lawyer, also have important bearing on issues which touch the actual conduct of international relations. None the less the series is wide in scope and includes monographs on the history and philosophical foundations of international law.

RECENT TITLES IN THIS SERIES

The Human Rights Committee: Its Role in the Development of the International Covenant on Civil and Political Rights
DOMINIC McGOLDRICK

Human Rights in States of Emergency in International Law
JAIME ORAÁ

China's Practice in the Law of the Sea
JEANETTE GREENFIELD

The International Law of Maritime Boundaries and the Practice of States in the Mediterranean Sea
FARAJ ABDULLAH AHNISH

Human Rights in the Private Sphere
ANDREW CLAPHAM

INTERNATIONAL MANAGEMENT OF HAZARDOUS WASTES

The Basel Convention and Related Legal Rules

KATHARINA KUMMER

CLARENDON PRESS · OXFORD
1995

This book has been printed digitally and produced in a standard specification in order to ensure its continuing availability

OXFORD
UNIVERSITY PRESS

Great Clarendon Street, Oxford OX2 6DP

Oxford University Press is a department of the University of Oxford.
It furthers the University's objective of excellence in research, scholarship, and education by publishing worldwide in

Oxford New York

Auckland Cape Town Dar es Salaam Hong Kong Karachi
Kuala Lumpur Madrid Melbourne Mexico City Nairobi
New Delhi Shanghai Taipei Toronto
With offices in
Argentina Austria Brazil Chile Czech Republic France Greece
Guatemala Hungary Italy Japan South Korea Poland Portugal
Singapore Switzerland Thailand Turkey Ukraine Vietnam

Oxford is a registered trade mark of Oxford University Press in the UK and in certain other countries

Published in the United States
by Oxford University Press Inc., New York

Reprinted 2007

ISBN 978-0-19-825994-7

Editor's Preface

Dr. Kummer, working at Queen Mary and Westfield College in the University of London, under the supervision of Professor Alan Boyle, has produced an important study of the legal aspects of the management of hazardous wastes. The significance of her work is elaborated upon in the Foreword furnished by Mr. Flavio Cotti. It is expected that other studies relating to the protection of the environment will be added to the *Monograph Series* in the near future.

All Souls College,
Oxford

IAN BROWNLIE
6 July 1995

Acknowledgements

I would like to express my gratitude to the many people who contributed to this book in various ways. First and foremost, thanks are due to Professor Alan Boyle (University of Edinburgh, formerly Queen Mary and Westfield College, University of London) for his constructive and critical advice, which involved many hours of discussing concepts and ideas. Professor Francesco Francioni (University of Siena) made valuable comments and suggestions on parts of this work, and helped me in numerous practical ways during my research in Siena in 1992. I am also indebted to Jennifer Clapp and Susanne Rublack for interesting discussions on waste-related issues, and to Ursula and Rolf Ganz-Blättler for technical as well as moral support.

Numerous institutions and individuals provided me with essential information and documentation. In this context, special thanks are due to Pierre Portas and Ahmed Fathalla of the Secretariat of the Basel Convention (Geneva) for responding to my frequent requests for pertinent information and updates, and for giving me access to their files. I am also grateful to the staff of the Secretariat of the London Convention (IMO, London), the Documents Section of IMO, and the OECD Secretariat, for extensive information and documentation. On various occasions, Albert Mumma of Simmons & Simmons (London) and Alier Deng of the Sudanese Mission to the UN (Geneva) provided me with documents and information that would otherwise have been difficult to obtain within a reasonable period of time.

I am particularly grateful to Queen Mary and Westfield College, and to the Janggen-Pöhn Foundation (St. Gallen, Switzerland) for the research scholarships awarded to me, as well as to the Committee of Vice-Chancellors and Principals of the Universities of the United Kingdom for awarding me an Overseas Research Studentship (ORS) for the duration of my research. Without the generous financial support of these institutions, this book could not have been written.

Last but not least, I wish to thank the staff of the Department of Law and the Centre for Commercial Law Studies (Queen Mary and Westfield College) as well as the Institute of Public and International Law (University of Siena) for considerably facilitating my task by giving me access to photocopying, telefax, and printing facilities. I would also like to thank the Research Centre for International Law (University of Cambridge) for hosting me during the final months of my research.

K.K.

Contents

Abbreviations

ACP States	African, Caribbean and Pacific States
ACOPS	Advisory Committee on the Pollution of the Sea
ADN	European Agreement Concerning Transport of Dangerous Goods by Inland Navigation
ADNR	Regulations on the Carriage of Dangerous Substances on the Rhine
ADR	European Agreement Concerning the International Carriage of Dangerous Goods by Road
AJIL	American Journal of International Law
AMCEN	African Ministerial Conference on the Environment
Am. U. J. Int'l. L. & Pol'y	American University Journal of International Law and Policy
ASEAN	Association of South-East Asian Nations
BC Code	Code of Safe Practice for Solid Bulk Cargoes
BCH Code	Code for the Construction and Equipment of Ships Carrying Dangerous Chemicals in Bulk
BYIL	British Yearbook of International Law
CCAMLR	Convention on the Conservation of Antarctic Marine Living Resources
CITES	Convention on International Trade in Endangered Species
Colum. J.Transnat'l. L.	Columbia Journal of Transnational Law
Colum. J. Env. L.	Columbia Journal of Environmental Law
CRAMRA	Convention on the Regulation of Antarctic Mineral Resource Activities
CRISTAL	Contract Regarding an Interim Supplement to Tanker Liability for Oil Pollution
CRTD Convention	Convention on Civil Liability for Damage Caused during the Carriage of Dangerous Goods by Road, Rail and Inland Navigation Vessels
CYIL	Canadian Yearbook of International Law
D/R	Decision and Recommendation (OECD)
EC	European Community
ECJ	European Court of Justice
ECOWAS	Economic Community of West African States

Ed.	Editor / Edition
Eds.	Editors
EEC	European Economic Community
EELR	European Environmental Law Review
EEZ	Exclusive Economic Zone
EFTA	European Free Trade Association
EIA	environmental impact assessment
Env. L. Rep.	Environmental Law Reporter
EPA	United States Environmental Protection Agency
EPL	Environmental Policy and Law
Europ. J. Int'l. L.	European Journal of International Law
EU	European Union
FAO	United Nations Food and Agriculture Organization
GATT	General Agreement on Tariffs and Trade
GESAMP	Joint Group of Experts on the Scientific Aspects of Marine Pollution
GYIL	German Yearbook of International Law
Harv. Int'l. L. J.	Harvard International Law Journal
HNS Convention	Draft International Convention on Liability and Compensation for Damage in Connection with the Carriage of Hazardous and Noxious Substances by Sea
IAEA	International Atomic Energy Agency
IBC Code	International Code for the Construction and Equipment of Ships Carrying Dangerous Chemicals in Bulk
ICC	International Chamber of Commerce
ICJ	International Court of Justice
ICJ Rep.	International Court of Justice Reports
ICLQ	International and Comparative Law Quarterly
IDI	Institut de Droit International
IGO	inter-governmental organization
IJMCL	International Journal of Marine and Coastal Law
ILA	International Law Association
ILC	International Law Commission
ILM	International Legal Materials
ILR	International Law Reports
IMDG Code	International Maritime Dangerous Goods Code
IMF	International Monetary Fund
IMO	International Maritime Organization
Int'l. J. Est. & Coastal L.	International Journal of Estuarine and Coastal Law

IOPC Fund	International Oil Pollution Compensation Fund
IWIC	International Waste Identification Code (OECD)
J. Env. L.	Journal of Environmental Law
MARPOL Convention	International Convention for the Prevention of Pollution from Ships
NAFTA	North American Free Trade Agreement
Nat. Res. J.	Natural Resources Journal
NGO	non-governmental organization
NYIL	Netherlands Yearbook of International Law
OAU	Organization of African Unity
ODIL	Ocean Development and International Law
OECD	Organization for Economic Co-operation and Development
OJ	Official Journal of the European Communities
OPPRC	Convention on Oil Pollution Preparedness, Response and Co-operation
PrepCom	Preparatory Committee for the UN Conference on Environment and Development (Rio 1992)
PBB	polybrominated biphenyl
PCB	polychlorinated biphenyl
PCT	polychlorinated terphenyl
PIC	prior informed consent
repr.	reproduced / reprinted
RGDIP	Revue Générale de Droit International Public
RID	International Regulations Concerning the Carriage of Dangerous Goods by Rail
SEA	Single European Act
SOLAS Convention	Convention on the Safety of Life at Sea
Swiss YIL	Swiss Yearbook of International Law
Tex. Int'l. L. J.	Texas International Law Journal
TOVALOP	Tanker Owners Voluntary Agreement Concerning Liability for Oil Pollution
UNCED	United Nations Conference on Environment and Development
UNCUEA	United Nations Centre for Urgent Environmental Assistance
UNCLOS	United Nations Convention on the Law of the Sea
UNCTAD	United Nations Conference on Trade and Development
UNCTDG	United Nations Committee of Experts on the Transport of Dangerous Goods
UNEP	United Nations Environment Programme
UNGA	United Nations General Assembly

UNHCR	United Nations High Commissioner for Refugees
UNITAR	United Nations Institute on Training and Research
UN/DHA	United Nations Department of Humanitarian Affairs
UN/ECA	United Nations Economic Commission for Africa
UN/ECE	United Nations Economic Commission for Europe
UN/ECLAC	United Nations Economic Commission for Latin America and the Caribbean
UN/ECOSOC	United Nations Economic and Social Council
UN/ESCAP	United Nations Economic and Social Commission for Asia and the Pacific
U. Brit. Colum. L. Rev.	University of British Columbia Law Review
Vol.	Volume
WACAF	West and Central African Action Plan (UNEP)
WCED	World Commission on Environment and Development ('Brundtland Commission')
WHO	World Health Organization
WMO	World Metereological Organization
WTO	World Trade Organization
Yale J. Int'l. L.	Yale Journal of International Law
YBIEL	Yearbook of International Environmental Law

Foreword

by Flavio Cotti, Federal Councillor, Switzerland

The adoption of the Basel Convention on the Control of Transboundary Movements of Hazardous Wastes and their Disposal, in March 1989, was a landmark in the struggle against the dumping of hazardous wastes from industrialized nations in countries with less advanced technical capacities and less stringent environmental laws. As president of the Ministerial Conference that adopted the Convention, and as representative of the country which hosted it, I was closely associated with the efforts made by the international community for solving this problem through international law.

The legal regulation of hazardous waste management has been of particular interest to the Swiss government for over a decade. Indeed, in the aftermath of the Seveso accident in 1983, Switzerland, in consultation with other countries, initiated the elaboration of a treaty aiming at restricting and controlling the transportation of hazardous wastes. In these early days, such a treaty was contemplated within the framework of the OECD, but in 1987, as work was advancing, it became evident that its scope should be extended to all countries if it were to be truly effective. With the support of Senegal and Hungary, my government therefore proposed to the Governing Council of UNEP to elaborate a global convention on the control of international movements of hazardous wastes. This proposal was well received. Less than two years later, the Ministerial Conference I was honoured to chair, adopted the treaty. As the adoption took place in Basel, that city gave its name to the new convention.

Work, however, did not halt there. The Basel Convention entered into force in 1992, and a number of regional agreements on waste management have been adopted. Under the guidance of the Geneva-based Convention secretariat, Parties to the Convention explore further ways of eliminating illegal traffic in hazardous wastes, and strengthening the capacity of less industrialized countries to deal with their own wastes. Furthermore, political opinion has evolved from recognizing the need to control the movements of hazardous wastes to enforcing a ban on all exports of such wastes from OECD to non-OECD countries. This trend is reflected in a growing number of regional conventions and international instruments on hazardous waste management. It has further been endorsed by the 2nd meeting of the Conference of the Parties to the Basel Convention, held in Geneva in March 1994.

Such developments and their pace call for the harmonization of the various international legal rules. The present study focuses on this necessity. It was carried out by a former UNEP staff member who could draw both on practical experience and theoretical analysis. After outlining the problems that call for international legal regulation, the author recounts the elaboration history of the Basel Convention and analyses its provisions. The study goes on to investigate the relationship between the Basel Convention and regional agreements on hazardous waste management, including the OAU-sponsored Bamako Convention, as well as the rules elaborated by the European Union and the OECD. After examining ways to harmonize the Basel Convention with established international instruments on pollution control, the study addresses the enforcement of such instruments through international mechanisms. The author concludes that the Basel Convention, together with other international legal rules, provides an important starting point for a truly comprehensive global waste management regime.

Switzerland is, in many ways, associated with these efforts. I therefore welcome the present analysis of the Basel Convention and related international legal rules. The study sheds a new light on waste-related issues. It constitutes an important contribution to an innovative and holistic perspective and a welcomed addition to the ongoing academic discussion on the legal aspects of hazardous waste management.

TABLE OF CASES

EUROPEAN COURT OF JUSTICE

INTERNATIONAL COURT OF JUSTICE/INTERNATIONAL ARBITRATION

TABLE OF LEGAL INSTRUMENTS OF THE EU AND THE OECD

TABLE OF TREATIES AND OTHER INTERNATIONAL LEGAL INSTRUMENTS

Introduction

During the past decade, the problem of transboundary transport of toxic and dangerous wastes, and their disposal far from the place of generation, has become a major environmental issue acknowledged by the international community. A number of widely publicized incidents of uncontrolled dumping of hazardous wastes from industrialized nations in Third World countries created world-wide awareness of the dangers connected with this practice. The amount of hazardous wastes shipped across national borders has increased dramatically in recent years. On a global scale, thousands of transboundary movements of hazardous wastes take place every year, some in accordance with national and international law but others illegally.

Accordingly, from the mid-1980s, various international organizations initiated the elaboration of international legal instruments to address this issue. Among these legal instruments, the Basel Convention on the Control of Transboundary Movements of Hazardous Wastes and their Disposal, negotiated under the auspices of UNEP, is the first to attempt comprehensive regulation of transboundary movements and the disposal of hazardous wastes on a global scale. The Basel Convention is the outcome of 18 months of difficult negotiations. It was adopted in early 1989 and entered into force in May 1992 after an initially slow ratification process. Celebrated by some as one of UNEP's major successes in promoting the development of international environmental law, it was harshly criticized by others for allegedly legitimizing 'garbage imperialism' i.e. the use of developing countries as cheap dumping grounds for hazardous wastes from the rich countries of the North. At the time of its adoption, the new convention was thus surrounded by controversy, and its future was uncertain. While its supporters optimistically expected it to enter into force within a year after adoption, its critics predicted that due to its inherent weaknesses, it would never receive the necessary number of ratifications, and would therefore remain an ineffective declaration of intentions.

The position of the Basel Convention within the body of existing and emerging international legal rules addressing the same and related fields was equally uncertain. After a lengthy debate, a provision was incorporated into the convention which was designed to establish its role as an 'umbrella' for regional waste management systems. The negotiators also considered it important that the future convention secretariat should co-operate with other organizations engaged in similar codification efforts. In addition, the need to harmonize the new treaty with established legal rules in related fields, namely marine pollution, transport of dangerous goods by sea, and the management of radioactive wastes, was repeatedly stressed during the negotiation process. As the implications of these issues were beyond the scope of the treaty negotiations, the task of following them up was delegated to UNEP.

Events since 1989 have enhanced the significance of these issues. Not only is the Basel Convention now operational and subject to continuous review and update in accordance with changing policies and priorities, but a number of potentially important regional agreements and other legal instruments of regional scope have been adopted that cover the same or similar areas as the convention, and additional ones are being negotiated. In the field of marine pollution, several new treaties have been concluded, and existing ones developed and strengthened. UNCED has developed the basis of new strategies to address environmental protection, including the management of hazardous substances and wastes. In view of these developments, the need to ensure that the Basel Convention is in harmony with other relevant international legal rules is even more acute than at the time of its adoption, if it is to fulfil its role as a starting point for further efforts to protect the environment against the ill-effects of hazardous wastes. The Basel Convention could provide the basis of an emerging global regime which would ensure systematic and comprehensive regulation of the management, transboundary movement, and disposal of hazardous wastes. It has also the potential, by virtue of its global scope, to further the development of international law in this field. The investigation of these options will be the focus of this study.

The introductory chapter outlines the problem of transboundary movements and disposal of hazardous wastes, and examines traditional international legal rules applicable to hazardous waste management. Based on this examination, it establishes the need for a comprehensive global regulatory system in this field. In Chapter 2, the Basel Convention is analysed and assessed. Chapters 3 and 4 examine the role of the Basel Convention as an umbrella for existing regional waste management systems, concluding that the Basel Convention and the regional systems can complement each other to form a flexible regime for wastes subject to transboundary movement, here termed the 'Basel Convention regime'. In Chapter 5, the relationship between this regime and environmental treaties addressing forms of discharge of hazardous wastes and substances other than by international transfer is analysed. Means to harmonize the relevant treaties with the Basel Convention regime are proposed, which would lead to the emergence of a global waste management regime covering all wastes, not merely those subject to transboundary movement. Chapter 6 evaluates the strengths and weaknesses of existing and emerging enforcement mechanisms in the achievement of the aims of the waste management system provided by the Basel Convention and related rules. In the final chapter, the characteristics of the emerging global waste management regime are analysed, and its contribution to the further development of fundamental international legal rules in this field is examined.

A number of issues must, for practical reasons, be excluded from the scope of this study, even though their significance may be equal to that of the issues addressed. This applies to the area of transboundary transfer and management of radioactive wastes, which is subject to a discrete international legal regime under the auspices of the IAEA. The study being limited to wastes, the international transport and management of toxic chemicals intended for commercial, agricultural or domestic use is also excluded, although it displays characteristics similar to those of the issue under discussion. Finally, problems at the interface of international transfer of hazardous wastes and international trade will be addressed only marginally, as will the relationship between the international rules on transport of hazardous wastes by sea and the rights and duties established by the Law of the Sea.

The study generally covers relevant developments up to December 1994, and takes into account materials and documentation available at that time. In a number of instances, it was possible to include later developments and documentation. Conversely, in a few cases information was readily available only up to mid-1994.

I

Transboundary Movements of Hazardous Wastes in International Law

TRANSBOUNDARY MOVEMENTS OF HAZARDOUS WASTES: QUANTITIES AND CAUSES

A. *Quantities of Hazardous Wastes*

Growing amounts of wastes containing hazardous substances are generated world-wide, particularly in the industrialized nations. World production of chemicals has multiplied in the past decades: according to one estimate, the total volume of organic chemicals produced globally went from approximately 7 million metric tons in 1950 to over 250 million metric tons in 1985.[1] The amount of hazardous wastes is believed to have increased accordingly. Faced with the problem of disposal, holders of hazardous wastes have in recent years increasingly chosen the option of exporting them to an area outside the jurisdiction of the state in which they were generated, either for further treatment or disposal in another country, or for dumping or incineration at sea. The practice of shipping hazardous wastes over long distances for disposal far from the place of generation constitutes a serious threat to human health and the environment.

It is very difficult to estimate the quantities of hazardous wastes involved. Not only do numerous hazardous waste transactions take place without the knowledge or beyond the control of state authorities,[2] which means that the actual quantities probably exceed official estimates by far, but systematic monitoring and data collection does not exist in many states. Where it does exist, the methods used are far from uniform. Also, national definitions of 'wastes' and 'hazardous wastes' differ widely, and states accordingly monitor different types of wastes in different ways and to a different extent.[3] Many contemporary laws and regulations base the definition of wastes on the subjective notion that a substance is subject to disposal by its

[1] United Nations, (1989), p. 6 (quoting an estimate by UNEP's International Register for Potentially Toxic Chemicals). See also Tolba and El-Kholy, (1992), p. 249; Richter, (1989), p. 11 et seq.

[2] Cf. United Nations, (1989); *World Resources Report 1990–91*, p. 328; also Grefe and Bernstorff, (1991); Kiss and Shelton, (1991), p. 313.

[3] UNEP, (1993), p. 330; OECD, (1993b); *World Resources Report 1990–91*, pp. 315, 328; Bureau de la gestion des déchets, (1993); Hackett, (1990), p. 313 et seq.; Richter, (1989), p. 111 et seq.; Porteous, (1985), p. 2 et seq.

holder. The hazard potential is often defined by lists of characteristics which render the substance hazardous.[4] Despite various attempts at elaborating international definitions, a generally recognized, sufficiently detailed and practical definition of 'waste' or 'hazardous waste' does not as yet exist.[5] As far as industrialized states are concerned, the rules and standards developed by the OECD and the EU do give some guidance for national legislation (see Chapter 4).

Given these difficulties, available figures are far from exact and must be considered with caution. They can only give a rough indication of the scope of the problem. Estimates of the global volume of hazardous wastes generated each year range from 300 to 500 million tons. According to statistics compiled by the OECD and other organizations, OECD member states generated around 300 million tons of hazardous wastes per year in the late 1980s, of which the USA produced between 260 and 275 million tons and EU member states between 20 and 35 million tons. Eastern European states produced around 19 million tons, while the rest of the world generated about 16 million tons.[6] The share of the USA appears particularly high because in that country large quantities of dilute waste waters are managed as hazardous wastes. In Europe, these are managed under water protection regulations and do not appear in the hazardous waste statistics.

According to statistics of the late 1980s and early 1990s, approximately 10 per cent of all hazardous wastes are shipped across international boundaries. A cargo of hazardous wastes is believed to cross a frontier within the OECD area every 5 minutes. Within Europe, approximately 2.2 million tons of hazardous wastes are estimated to make a total of 100,000 border crossings per year; the number of waste movements within North America has been estimated at 6–9000 tons annually. Several thousand tons of hazardous wastes are believed to be moved between OECD and non-OECD states every year. These figures refer to legal transactions only. The statistics contained in the World Resources Report as well as those of the OECD show that exact data are unavailable for most countries.[7]

[4] See the compilation of pertinent national legislation of some thirty countries, carried out by the Secretariat of the Basel Convention in 1993 (Basel Convention Series/SBC No. 94/002, Geneva, January 1994). For a discussion of problems pertaining to national definition see Kummer, (1994a); Spitalnik, (1992); Kiss and Shelton, (1991), p. 313; Atkinson, (1991), p. 265 et seq.

[5] For a detailed analysis of current international definitions, as well as pertinent problems, see Smith, (1993); also Strohm, (1993), p. 131; Jones, (1993), p. 330.

[6] UNEP, (1993), p. 332; *World Resources Report 1990–91*, p. 328; OECD, (1993b); OECD, (1991); World Bank, (1989), Vol. I p. 5; Hilz, (1990), p. 31 et seq. (quoting figures obtained from the OECD, the EU, and UNEP). An overview of the generation and management of different types of wastes in selected Eastern and Western European countries is given by Sander and Küppers, (1993).

[7] For an overview of exports and imports at the global level see *World Resources Report 1990–91*, p. 325. For exports and imports of OECD countries see OECD, (1993b); OECD Waste Management Policy Group, *Working Paper No. 3 for the 37th Meeting*, March 1993

According to reports submitted to the IMO, between 6 and 17 million tons of industrial wastes were dumped at sea by industrialized states between 1980 and 1985, even though the amount is reported to be decreasing.[8] Between 1980 and 1988, an estimated annual average of 100,000 tons of wastes, particularly organic materials in liquid form, were incinerated at sea.[9]

B. *Causes of the Increase in Transboundary Movements of Hazardous Wastes*

The causes of the increase in the quantities of hazardous wastes disposed of abroad are diverse,[10] but can be divided roughly into three categories.

1. Wastes following the 'path of least resistance'

First, export of hazardous wastes destined for final disposal takes place along the 'path of least resistance'.[11] The holders of the waste in the state of generation are faced with an increasing scarcity of disposal facilities, growing public opposition to the establishment and operation of such facilities as a result of what has been termed the 'NIMBY (Not In My Back Yard) syndrome', a tightening of environmental rules and standards, and escalating disposal costs as a result of these developments.[12] Dumping or incineration at sea provides an easier and less costly alternative.[13] Likewise, potential target countries offer disposal options at prices that are often a mere fraction of the equivalent costs in the state of origin: according to a study carried out in the late 1980s, the average disposal costs for one ton of hazardous wastes in Africa was between US $ 2.50 and US $ 50, with equivalent costs in industrialized nations ranging from US $ 100 to US $

(estimated annual hazardous wastes exports and imports of selected OECD member states). For waste imports and exports of the EU member states see DG XI, Office Statistique des Communautés Européennes, *Mouvements des déchets et résidus selon les statistiques douaniers (juin 1991)*. See also UNEP, (1993), p. 333 et seq.; OECD, (1993a), p. 9 et seq.; United Nations, (1989).

[8] IMO, (1989); UNEP/GESAMP, (1990), p. 13. On dumping of wastes in the Oslo Convention area between 1976 and 1986, see *World Resources Report 1990–91*, p. 341 et seq. On dumping of wastes in the North Sea in the 1980s, see Hohmann, (1989), p. 524; and idem, (1990), p. 50.

[9] UNEP/GESAMP, (1990), p. 14.

[10] For a discussion see among others OECD, (1993a), p. 9 et seq. (quoting a 1984 study of the OECD Waste Management Policy Group); Kiss and Shelton, (1991), p. 320; Lang, in Lang, Neuhold, and Zemanek, (1991), p. 149; Hilz, (1992).

[11] US Congressman Florio, 1984; quoted by Gade, (1989) at p. 327.

[12] *World Resources Report 1990–91*, p. 325. These phenomena have been discussed by numerous authors, including Richter, (1989); Hilz, (1992); Grefe and Bernstorff, (1991); Donald, (1992); Clapp, (1994).

[13] See Kiss, (1991), p. 523.

2,000.[14] This discrepancy in costs is usually the result of lower environmental standards, an absence of public opposition due to lack of information, less stringent or non-existent laws and regulations, and a lack of control over compliance.

Transboundary movements of hazardous wastes carried out for the above reasons frequently take place in contravention of such legal rules as do exist.[15] Unscrupulous waste traders from the generating states stand to make huge profits, and will induce uninformed individuals or corrupt government officials in the importing states to accept waste shipments by substantial financial offers. Also, governments of poor countries are often willing to accept foreign hazardous wastes in exchange for hard currency—in amounts that sometimes exceed the countries' GNP—despite the risks to human health and the environment.

These are the commonest reasons for hazardous waste traffic taking place between the industrialized states of the North, on the one hand, and the developing countries of the South and the countries with transitional economies of Eastern Europe, on the other. According to a Greenpeace estimate, almost 5.2 million tons of hazardous wastes were exported from industrialized states to Eastern European and developing countries between 1986 and 1990, many of them illegally. This figure is believed to represent only the tip of the iceberg. A later Greenpeace estimate gives the amount of hazardous waste exports from OECD to non-OECD countries between 1989 and early 1994 as 2.6 tons. Numerous developing countries have either received hazardous waste shipments or have been proposed as importing states since the 1980s. Within Europe, about 200,000–300,000 tons per year are believed to have been exported from the more heavily industrialized West to the East in the late 1980s.[16] Moreover, waste transfers also take place between industrialized countries of the EU and the OECD for the same reasons, i.e. where there is a discrepancy in legal and technical standards and disposal costs.[17]

It is this situation, in which the economic and regulatory imbalance between the generating and importing states is exploited for financial

[14] Richter, (1989), p. 20–1; see also the Preface by Tolba in Kwiatkowska and Soons, (1993), estimating average disposal costs in Africa as 4–25 times lower than equivalent costs in Europe, and 12–36 times lower than in the USA; also Long, (1990), p. 199 et seq.

[15] Cf. United Nations, (1989); *Note of the Executive Director of UNEP on Illegal Traffic in Hazardous Wastes to the 1st Meeting of the Conference of the Parties to the Basel Convention*, 15 September 1992, (UNEP/CHW.1/19).

[16] Greenpeace, (1990), Preface, and *World Resources Report 1990–91*, p. 328; Greenpeace, (1994), p. II–3. See also Richter, (1989), giving a comprehensive analysis of hazardous waste shipments to twenty seven African countries in the mid- and late 1980s; also Clapp, (1994); Ndi, (1993); OECD, (1993a), p. 9; Hilz, (1990), p. 28; and United Nations, (1989), quoting *World Resources Report 1987*.

[17] Long, (1990), p. 199; EU, *Community Strategy for the Management of Hazardous Wastes*, September 1989, (SEC(89)934 final).

reasons, that poses the gravest threat to the environment and human health. Typically, the importing country will not have adequate facilities to treat and dispose of the wastes safely, nor the technical, legal and institutional capacities to monitor the transactions. A number of well-publicized cases such as that of the 'Philadelphia fly ash' deposited on Kassa Island (Guinea), the illegal deposit of Italian hazardous wastes in the port of Koko (Nigeria), and the epic voyage of the vessel *Khian Sea* provoked an international outcry against such practices, and led to global public awareness of the issue in the late 1980s.[18] Numerous writers have since highlighted the issue of developing countries targeted for illegal hazardous waste imports, analysed its causes, and outlined ways to address this problem.[19] It is notable, however, that in contrast to the public scandals involving the illicit deposit of hazardous wastes in developing and transitional countries, hazardous waste transfers between industrialized countries have received scarce attention, despite the fact that they are much more significant in terms of quantity: of the hazardous wastes exported from OECD states, a vast majority is moved to other OECD members. Of the hazardous wastes generated in the USA, around 1 per cent is exported; in 1988, 85 per cent of this went to Canada and 8 per cent to Mexico.[20]

2. Wastes exported on a regional scale

Second, export of hazardous wastes destined for disposal takes place on a regional scale for more ecologically sound reasons. Hazardous wastes may be exported to a neighbouring country if superior technology for treatment or disposal is available in that state; if the nearest facility appropriate for a specific type of waste is located across an international frontier; if several countries have established a joint disposal facility because the small quantities of wastes generated by each of them do not justify the operation of a separate facility in each state; or if a multinational enterprise operates a subsidiary specialized in waste treatment in a country other than the country of generation.[21]

[18] An extensive compilation of information on illegal hazardous waste export schemes, including the cases mentioned, is given in Greenpeace, (1990), pp. 21–380. See also United Nations, (1989).

[19] See among many others Clapp, (1994); Jones, (1993); Kwiatkowska and Soons, (1993), Editors' Introduction; Strohm, (1993); Donald, (1992); Watts, (1992); Grefe and Bernstorff, (1991); Abrams, (1990); Cusack, (1990); Montgomery, (1990); Hilz, (1990); Richter, (1989); Wynne, (1989). See also Greenpeace, *Toxic Trade Update* (providing regular reports on activities involving hazardous wastes).

[20] OECD, (1993a), p. 9; also Hackett, (1990), p. 295, and n. 16; Kummer and Rummel-Bulska, (1990), p. 35; Long, (1990), p. 199; Montgomery, (1990), pp. 316–17 and n. 16, quoting EPA sources.

[21] See OECD, (1993a), p. 10; Birnie and Boyle, (1992), p. 302; Handl, (1989), pp. 368–9; also *ICC Statement on the Basel Convention*, repr. in EPL 19/6(1989), p. 238.

This type of regional hazardous waste transfer currently takes place primarily among neighbouring industrialized states with comparable technical and environmental standards (e.g. within the EU or the OECD), accounting for a significant amount of hazardous waste transfer among the countries in question. In the future, however, it may represent a feasible option also for less industrialized countries as their economies develop and the quantities of hazardous wastes they generate increase. Regional hazardous waste management schemes set up by developing countries, or countries with economies in transition, would entail a certain number of transboundary waste movements between the countries concerned. In this context, a South African scholar made the interesting suggestion that his country, as the most economically advanced state in the southern African subcontinent, might in the future offer to import hazardous wastes from its neighbouring countries, thus attempting to provide the subcontinent with environmentally sound and adequate disposal options.[22]

3. Wastes with value as secondary raw materials

A third reason for the international transfer of hazardous wastes is the potential value as secondary raw materials of certain wastes. Hazardous wastes with an economic value (e.g. heavy metals) are treated as a tradeable commodity and are exported in order to be subjected to operations leading to resource recovery, recycling, reclamation, re-use, or alternative use.[23] This accounts for a significant proportion of the movement of hazardous wastes across national borders: there is a substantial trade in hazardous wastes destined for recycling or recovery. Of the hazardous wastes moved between OECD member states in 1990, about 50 per cent on average were subjected to recovery operations in the state of destination.[24] According to OECD estimates, around 95 per cent of the hazardous wastes that were legally exported from the OECD area to non-OECD countries between 1989 and 1991 were destined for recycling or recovery. Most of these wastes were metals or metal compounds subjected to resource recovery. According to OECD estimates, the amount of recoverable metals or metal-bearing wastes subject to international trade in 1989 was 40 million tons, valued at US $ 16 billion.[25]

[22] Glazewski, (1993), p. 247.

[23] These terms are defined in OECD Council Decision C(88)90, and Annex IV of the Basel Convention, as well as other relevant international legal instruments. For greater simplicity, the operations in question are referred to collectively as 'recycling or recovery operations'.

[24] OECD, (1993b). See also OECD, (1986b), and the background document prepared by the OECD Secretariat for the OECD Workshop on Wastes Destined for Recovery Operations (Vienna, June 1991), giving an overview of types and quantities of wastes moved within the OECD for recycling or recovery operations.

[25] OECD Waste Management Policy Group, *Working Paper No. 3 for the 37th Meeting*, (March 1993); Doc. UNEP/CHW.2/12 (17 December 1993).

Transboundary movements of hazardous wastes for the purpose of recycling or recovery has been the subject of increasing controversy in the last few years. While the benefits of international trade in waste materials, including hazardous wastes, are widely recognized, there is also widespread awareness of the dangers connected with it.

On the one hand, by achieving re-use of potentially valuable substances that would otherwise be discarded, recycling can slow down the depletion of limited natural resources and reduce the quantity and hazard potential of wastes going to final disposal. Provided the country of destination has more environmentally sound facilities and higher environmental standards than the country of origin, export of hazardous wastes for recycling can ultimately lead to an overall reduction of air and water pollution. From an economic viewpoint, recycling of certain wastes leads to the recovery of valuable raw materials. In this case, there usually is an established market for the wastes in question, and the relevant trade has substantive economic significance. As noted above, the most important example is that of scrap metals, subject to a multi-billion-dollar international trade.

On the other hand, recycling must take place under conditions meeting certain environmental criteria if it is to have the environmental and economic benefits mentioned, and not to provide a source of environmental hazard equal to that of disposal operations. This is often impossible in practice, especially in countries with little technical and infrastructural capacities. The factors that influence the international market for recyclable wastes do not necessarily correspond to the requirements of environmentally sound waste management. Subjecting the export of hazardous wastes for recycling to less strict rules than the export for disposal might provide a disincentive to the promotion of waste reduction in the country of origin. It could also encourage fake recycling schemes, i.e. the use of the label of recycling for disposal operations that would otherwise be prohibited. Uncertainties concerning the current national and international definitions of the relevant operations contribute further to the ambiguity of the issue.[26]

C. *Hazardous Waste Generation in the Future*

In general, the problem of hazardous wastes is still largely a problem of the industrialized world, which currently generates over 90 per cent of all hazardous wastes. This may however change in the not too distant future. Of

[26] For a further discussion of the problems connected with international trade in hazardous wastes destined for recycling or recovery see e.g. Kummer, (1994a); Fluck, (1994); Donald, (1992), p. 449 et seq.; *Note by the Secretariat of the Basel Convention on the Implementation of Decision I/16 of the 1st Meeting of the Conference of the Contracting Parties on Transboundary Movements of Hazardous Wastes Destined for Recovery Operations*, 17 December 1993, (UNEP/CHW.2/12).

the seventy two country reports submitted in the course of the preparatory process for UNCED, forty two indicated that states have waste management problems of a magnitude that concern them now or will do so in the immediate future. The problems are linked with the use of agrochemicals (in almost 40 per cent of the countries), household waste (35 per cent), and industrial waste including toxic waste (30 per cent). Some reports from Central and Eastern European countries described alarming waste management problems, and identified several 'disaster areas' with transboundary effects.[27]

While it is unlikely that the least developed countries will soon produce large amounts of hazardous wastes, even the small quantities they do generate constitute a danger to the environment and to human health if not properly managed and disposed of. Moreover, the quantities produced are generally on the increase.[28] In the least developed countries, diverse kinds of hazardous wastes are produced in varying quantities by small-scale industries. These are difficult to monitor, and appropriate treatment is usually not available.[29] More significantly, a group of states commonly considered developing countries are rapidly industrializing. According to a 1993 economic forecast of the IMF, a relatively large number of newly industrialized countries are currently experiencing economic growth of over 5 per cent per year.[30] Some of these countries are beginning to have problems with the management and disposal of hazardous wastes on a larger scale.[31] In a number of countries of South and South-East Asia, for example, massive industrial development as a result of trade liberalization has led to a corresponding increase in pollution, including the generation of large amounts of hazardous wastes. According to one estimate, 1.9 million tons of hazardous wastes were generated in Thailand in 1990, and a fourfold increase of this figure is expected by the year 2001.[32] In many countries, the development of the technical and regulatory infrastructure necessary for proper management and disposal of the wastes has not kept pace with industrialization. As a result, proper facilities for receiving wastes are often unavailable.[33] In this sense, the situation is in some respects more difficult than in OECD countries, where a certain—albeit not always perfect—infrastructure usually exists.

[27] *Preparations for UNCED on the Basis of General Assembly Resolution 44/228 and Taking into Account other Relevant General Assembly Resolutions: Overview of National Reports* (Report of the Secretary-General of the Conference (Doc. A/CONF.151/PC/98)).

[28] Ydhego, (1993), p. 37 et seq.

[29] Tolba and El-Kholy, (1992), pp. 264, 273.

[30] International Monetary Fund, (1993), p. 7 et seq.

[31] Tolba and El-Kholy, (1992), ch. 10, give an overview of the increase in the generation of industrial waste in some developing countries (p. 342 et seq.). Cf. also Spitalnik, (1992), p. 3, quoting individual country studies on hazardous waste generation in Asian countries.

[32] Repetto, (1994), p. 4.

[33] Repetto, (1994), p. 3 et seq.; see also Tolba and El-Kholy, (1992), p. 264 et seq. (giving figures for Thailand, Malaysia, and Singapore).

This overview may give some indication of the complexity of the problems confronting any attempt to adopt and implement legal rules to control international trade in hazardous wastes. The difficulty lies not only in the elusiveness of the hazardous waste trade, but also in the diversity of situations to be taken into account. The problem is rendered more complex by the absence of sufficiently detailed, universally agreed definitions of important concepts, namely those of hazardous wastes and recycling or recovery operations.

THE NATURE OF THE PROBLEM: CRITERIA FOR LEGAL REGULATION

Prior to examining existing and emerging international legal rules addressing transboundary movements of hazardous wastes, it will be useful to identify some characteristics of this activity which should be taken into account by such legal rules.

D. *The Hazardous Waste Cycle as an International and Multi-sectoral Issue*

The process of management and transboundary movements of hazardous wastes constitutes a cycle, consisting of a sequence of activities:

(a) generation of the hazardous wastes in the state of origin as a by-product of industrial activity;
(b) transport to or through one or more states or the global commons;
(c) possibly treatment and/or temporary storage at some point during the journey; and
(d) treatment and/or disposal at the place of final destination, either in the recipient state or the global commons.

This cycle is often fairly complex, with hazardous wastes being handled by numerous operators, collected from various sources, or undergoing repackaging, mixing, or transformation in the course of the cycle.[34] The geographical scale of these operations, and the fact that most stages of the cycle take place beyond the jurisdiction of the generating state, render the issue inherently international. The diversity of the operations involved means that every stage of the cycle has to be controlled if legal regulation is to be effective.

The hazardous waste cycle constitutes a risk of detrimental effects to

[34] For an analysis of the hazardous waste cycle see Wynne, (1989), p. 130 et seq.; also Kiss, (1989a), p. 275 et seq.; Birnie and Boyle, (1992), p. 300.

practically every sphere of the environment: land, air, continental waterways, and seas. These effects can be produced within every sphere, possibly passing from one into another. Of the commonly available disposal options, landfill affects the geosphere, incineration affects the atmosphere, and release into the sea or continental waterbodies affects the hydrosphere. Transport over long distances prior to disposal substantially increases the risk to every sphere of the environment: accidents can occur during transport, and the treatment or disposal in a recipient country with low environmental standards and lack of control mechanisms increases the risk of detrimental effects on the environment and human health. Unsound management of the wastes at any point in the process equally affects every sphere. Legal rules on the issue must therefore address the protection of every sphere of the environment at every stage of the cycle in order to be effective.

E. *Transboundary Movements of Hazardous Wastes as an Aspect of Transboundary Pollution*

The detrimental effects of the hazardous waste cycle on the environment can be described by reference to the concept of pollution. This concept was subject to international policy and law long before the emergence of the more specific issue of transboundary waste traffic.[35] The legal rules that have evolved to address pollution may be relevant for the regulation of the waste cycle. An early definition of pollution is given in the Principles Concerning Transfrontier Pollution, adopted by the OECD in 1974: 'Pollution means the introduction by man, directly or indirectly, of substances or energy into the environment, resulting in deleterious effects of such a nature as to endanger human health, harm living resources and ecosystems, and impair or interfere with amenities and other legitimate uses of the environment.'[36]

A study by Allen Springer sets out four key elements of pollution:

(a) the source of pollution, defined as 'the range of human activities that can give rise, directly or indirectly, to detrimental environmental effects';
(b) the polluting agent, defined as a 'substance or energy that is created or displaced by the source and that produces the detrimental effect';
(c) the medium by which the polluting agent is transmitted, including

[35] See e.g. Principles 6, 7, 21 and 22 of the 1972 Stockholm Declaration; para. 12 of the *1982 World Charter for Nature* (UNGA Resolution 37/7, 1982), and UNEP's Montevideo Programme of 1981 (discussed in Chapter 2 below). See also OECD, (1986a); OECD, (1977).

[36] *Recommendation of the OECD Council on Principles Concerning Transfrontier Pollution*, C 74(224), 14 November 1974, Title A; repr. in OECD, (1977). For a discussion and analysis of this definition, see among many others Kiss and Shelton, (1991), p. 116.

natural media such as the atmosphere, the hydrosphere, and food chains within ecosystems, but also man-made media such as international trade; and

(d) the detrimental effects of pollution on the environment, which must reach a certain level of gravity in order to be legally relevant.[37]

The elements of this definition appear in most legal instruments which address aspects of pollution, although some of the newer definitions are more specific.[38]

Applying this definition to the hazardous waste cycle, it can be said that the activities constituting the cycle conform to the notion of the source of pollution. Some of these activities (e.g. disposal) can directly lead to pollution, while others (e.g. transport or temporary storage) merely create a risk of pollution. The hazardous wastes themselves can be described as polluting agents. The medium is primarily international trade, but this can be supplanted by any other medium (e.g. air or water) once the wastes have been released into the environment. The effects of the pollution are the contamination of one or more spheres of the environment. As the hazardous waste cycle thus conforms to the notion of pollution, international rules on pollution control are in principle applicable. Alexandre Kiss considers the generation of wastes a significant aspect of pollution:

Au sens le plus large, la majeure partie des pollutions consiste à introduire dans l'environnement des substances dont on veut se débarasser, qu'il s'agisse de rejets de matières liquides ou solides dans la mer ou dans les eaux continentales, voire de fumées ou de poussières dans l'atmosphère provenant ou non de l'incinération de matières à éliminer, aussi bien que du dépôt de telles matières sur le sol ou dans le sous-sol. Toutefois, le sens technique du terme «déchet» ne comprend que cette dernière hypothèse (sic!)'.[39]

[37] Springer, (1983), in particular p. 5 et seq., p. 63 et seq. Cf. also Magraw, (1991).

[38] For an overview of contemporary definitions cf. van Heijnsbergen, (1979), pp. 11–13; also Kiss, (1989a), p. 68 et seq.; Rest, (1991), p. 38. Treaty provisions incorporating similar definitions include the following: 1982 UNCLOS (Article 1(4)); 1976 Barcelona Convention for the Protection of the Mediterranean (Article 2); 1981 Abidjan Convention for the Protection of the Marine Environment of the WACAF Region (Article 2); 1992 Oslo/Paris Convention for the Protection of the Marine Environment of the North-East Atlantic (Article 1(d)); 1992 Helsinki Convention for the Protection of the Baltic Sea (Article 2(1)); 1979 Geneva Convention on Long-Range Transboundary Air Pollution (Article 1(a)); 1988 CRAMRA, Article 1(15) (strongest definition). See also OECD Council Recommendation for the Implementation of a Regime of Equal Right of Access and Non-Discrimination in Relation to Transfrontier Pollution, C(77) 28, 1977 (repr. in OECD, (1977)); 1982 ILA Montreal Rules of International Law Applicable to Transfrontier Pollution (repr. in Hohmann, (1992), Vol. 1, p. 249); 1987 Cairo Guidelines (Chapter 2 above; principle 1(h)); 1972 Stockholm Declaration, Principles 6 and 7.

[39] 'In the widest sense, a major proportion of pollution consists of introduction into the environment of substances of which one wishes to rid oneself. This may take the form of discharge of liquid or solid materials into the sea or continental waters, or even the release of fumes and dust—which may or may not be derived from incineration of materials subject to disposal—into the atmosphere, as well as deposit of materials onto land or into the sub-soil.

Due to its international nature, it can be argued that the hazardous waste cycle constitutes a form of 'transboundary' or 'transfrontier' pollution. This is generally defined as pollution originating within the area of jurisdiction of one state, and affecting other states or the global commons.[40] Transboundary pollution has also been subject to international policy and law longer than the issue of transboundary movements of hazardous wastes. A large number of legal rules addressing this issue, based on both customary law and treaties, are thus potentially applicable to the hazardous waste cycle.

It must be noted, however, that the traditional concept of transboundary pollution, which underlies most relevant legal rules, presupposes that the source of pollution is located in the territory of one state and is therefore subject to its exclusive jurisdiction, whereas the effects of the pollution are incidentally produced in another state which has no influence or control over the source of pollution.[41] Conversely, in the case of transboundary movements of hazardous wastes, the activities that constitute the source of pollution—i.e. the management and disposal of the wastes—take place to a large extent outside the territory of the generating state. Although initiated under its jurisdiction, they are carried out in the territory of the recipient state, and are subject to control by that state; or in an area beyond the jurisdiction of any state. In other words, the source of pollution, instead of being located in the state of origin, is deliberately transferred into another state or into the global commons. This situation, which encompasses transboundary movements of hazardous wastes as well as transfers of hazardous chemicals or technology, will be referred to in this study as 'pollution source transfer'. The conceptual difference between the two situations may be relevant in the application of existing legal rules on transboundary pollution to the hazardous waste cycle. In practical terms, the exporting state often has no factual control over technologies, substances or wastes once they are in the

However, the technical meaning of the term "waste" covers only the last case.' Kiss, in *La réparation des dommages catastrophiques*, p. 301. Cf. Magraw, in Magraw, (1991), p. 5, listing specific instances of pollution; these include 'water and soil pollution following the export of hazardous wastes'. See also Porteous, (1985), pp. 18–19; Springer, (1983), p. 79.

[40] See e.g. the definitions in OECD Council Resolution C(77)28 (Final), Annex (repr. in OECD, (1986a)), in the ILA's 1982 Montreal Rules of International Law Applicable to Transfrontier Pollution, and more recently in the 1992 Convention on Transboundary Effects of Industrial Accidents, Article 1(d) (repr. in ILM 31(1992), p. 1333 et seq.). See also the definition of 'transboundary air pollution' in Article 1(b) of the 1979 Geneva Convention on Long-Range Transboundary Air Pollution, and the definition of 'transboundary impact' in Article 1(VIII) of the 1991 UN/ECE Convention on Environmental Impact Assessment in a Transboundary Context (repr. in Hohmann, (1992), Vol. 1, p. 345). Cf. Magraw, in Magraw, (1991), distinguishing further between 'transboundary pollution' and 'commons pollution'.

[41] On the traditional concept of transboundary pollution, and its limitations, see Iwama, in Brown Weiss, (1992b), ch. 4.

state of destination. Moreover, sovereignty considerations can prevent any influence by the state of export.[42] The need to specifically address pollution source transfer as an issue separate from transboundary pollution is implicitly recognized in Principle 14 of the Rio Declaration on Environment and Development, adopted by UNCED in June 1992, which provides that states shall 'effectively co-operate to discourage or prevent the relocation and transfer to other states of any activities and substances that cause severe environmental degradation or are found to be harmful to human health'.

EXISTING AND EMERGING INTERNATIONAL LEGAL RULES RELEVANT TO THE HAZARDOUS WASTE CYCLE

The growing awareness of the risks posed by transboundary movements of hazardous wastes led to the adoption, between the mid-1980s and the early 1990s, of a large number of binding and non-binding international legal instruments that specifically address one or more aspects of the issue.[43] The 1989 Basel Convention on the Control of Transboundary Movements of Hazardous Wastes and their Disposal, constituting the first attempt at comprehensive global regulation of the issue, entered into force in 1992. The Basel Convention will be analysed in Chapter 2 below. In addition, several regional regimes for transboundary movements of hazardous wastes were adopted; these will be discussed in Chapters 3 and 4 below. These efforts to deal with this problem are fairly recent; the issue was previously addressed by more general international legal rules relating to environmental protection, in particular pollution control.[44]

F. *Customary Law Related to Pollution Control*

4. The limitation on the 'freedom to pollute' and the concept of due diligence

The sovereignty of states over the use of their territory and resources is a

[42] For a detailed analysis of legal problems pertaining to the transboundary transfer of environmental risks see Rublack, (1993), p. 132 et seq.; also Magraw, in Handl and Lutz, (1989a), ch. 10.

[43] For a comprehensive overview of international legal instruments, both binding and non-binding, that address one or more aspects of the hazardous waste cycle, cf. Kwiatkowska and Soons, (1993), Editors' Introduction, pp. XVII–XCIV.

[44] For an overview of customary law relevant to pollution control cf. Birnie and Boyle, (1992), ch. 3; Dupuy, in Magraw, (1991), p. 61 et seq.; idem, in *La réparation des dommages catastrophiques*, (1990), p. 219 et seq. An overview and analysis of older customary law rules, i.e. shortly after the adoption of the 1972 Stockholm Declaration, is given by Dupuy, in OECD, (1977).

[45] See e.g. Sohn, (1973), p. 486 et seq., for an outline of the history of this principle; also Schneider, (1979), p. 30.

fundamental concept in international law.[45] Customary law, however, provides for limitations on the exercise of the rights pertaining to state sovereignty. Thus, every state has the obligation to ensure that activities within its area of jurisdiction or under its control do not cause serious harm to other states.[46] The concept of 'control' in this context is fairly ambiguous, being accorded different meanings in various legal instruments and academic writings.[47] For the purpose of this study, 'control' is understood to mean a state's internationally recognized right and duty to exercise control over an activity taking place outside its territory, notably any activity taking place in marine areas over which it has jurisdiction, or involving ships flying its flag and aircraft registered in its territory.

This rule was established in general terms by the *Trail Smelter Arbitration* and the *Corfu Channel Case*, which are considered to have laid the foundations of international environmental law in the field of transboundary pollution.[48] Principle 21 of the Stockholm Declaration, adopted by the UN Conference on the Human Environment in 1972, codifies this rule in a way that specifically addresses environmental protection: 'States have, in accordance with the Charter of the United Nations and principles of international law, the sovereign right to exploit their own resources pursuant to their own environmental policies, and the responsibility to ensure that activities within their jurisdiction do not cause damage to the environment of other States or of areas beyond the limits of national jurisdiction.'[49]

In this form, the principle has become one of the most fundamental customary law rules relevant to environmental protection. It is re-iterated in Principle 2 of the 1992 Rio Declaration, as well as in many treaties and non-binding legal instruments. A. O. Adede notes that a provision reflecting the substance of Principle 21 of the Stockholm Declaration has become

[46] See generally Boyle, (1989), p. 269 (and sources quoted in n. 88); Verdross and Simma, (1984), p. 646 (and sources quoted there); OECD, in OECD, (1977), p. 380 et seq.; also Caldwell, (1990), p. 68. On the concept of jurisdiction cf. Bowett, in MacDonald and Johnston, (1983), p. 553 et seq.

[47] For a discussion see McCaffrey, in Magraw, (1991), p. 95 et seq.; Brownlie, ibid, p. 123; Handl, (1980), p. 529 et seq.; Tomuschat, in Francioni and Scovazzi, (1991), p. 40; Koh, in Handl and Lutz, (1989a), p. 181; Brownlie, (1983), p. 180 et seq.

[48] *Trail Smelter Arbitration*, UN R. Int'l. Arb. Awards 1905, (1941); *Corfu Channel Case*, ICJ Rep. 4(1949) 4–28. For a discussion see among many others Kiss and Shelton, (1991), p. 122 et seq.; Dupuy, in Magraw, (1991), pp. 63–4; Schneider, (1979), p. 48 et seq.; OECD, in OECD, (1977), p. 382 et seq.

[49] On Principle 21 of the Stockhom Declaration cf. among many others Sohn, (1973); Brownlie, (1973), p. 188; Kiss, (1989a), pp. 59, 80, 289; idem (1989b), p. 245 et seq.; Birnie and Boyle, (1992) pp. 91 et seq.; Kiss and Shelton, (1991), p. 119 et seq.; Boyle, (1989), p.269 et seq.; Koh, in Handl and Lutz, (1989a), p. 174 et seq.; OECD, (1977), pp. 380–1 (noting also that the word 'responsibility' in Principle 21 does not refer to the defined legal term of state responsibility, but indicates a general obligation).

[50] Adede, (1992), p. 95. See also Kiss, (1989b), pp. 246–7; Schneider, (1981); Handl, (1990), p. 20; Orrego Vicuña, in Brown Weiss, (1992b), p. 130 et seq.; Dupuy, in Magraw, (1991),

almost a standard clause in environmental treaties.[50]

Whereas the rule was originally limited to an obligation to prevent unreasonable harm to other states, the evolution of international environmental law pursuant to the adoption of the Stockholm Declaration has led to the acceptance that states have a customary obligation to refrain from activities within their territory which result in serious harm to the environment, regardless of whether or not another state is directly affected.[51] The rule is thus extended to areas beyond the jurisdiction of any state.[52] According to some authors, it also applies to the territory of the generating state itself, insofar as the interests of the world community as a whole are affected. This can be the case where an activity, even if not necessarily affecting transboundary interests, has negative effects on the global commons.[53] With regard to pollution, two Principles of the Stockholm Declaration reaffirm the obligation to protect the environment independently of national interests: Principle 6 establishes a general duty to protect the environment from the ill-effects of the discharge of dangerous substances, and Principle 7 reiterates this with respect to the marine environment in particular. These duties are also incorporated in Articles 192–4 of the 1982 UNCLOS, which entered into force on 16 November 1994. A large number of the provisions of that treaty, including many of the environmental provisions, are widely accepted as customary law rules.[54]

The rule has further evolved to specify the duties of states in the context of pollution control. With few exceptions—such as the disposal of high-level radioactive materials at sea, and atmospheric nuclear tests—activities

pp. 64–5. International legal instruments incorporating this rule include the 1992 UN Convention on Biological Diversity (Article 3); the 1985 Vienna Convention and the 1987 Montreal Protocol; the 1974 Helsinki Convention (Article 3(1)); the 1974 Paris Convention (Article 1(1)); the UNEP Regional Seas Conventions; the 1982 UNCLOS (Article 192(2)); the UNEP Principles on Shared Natural Resources (Principle 3(1)); and UNGA Resolution 44/207 (1989).

[51] Stockholm Declaration (Principle 21); UNGA Resolution 43/212 (1988); Cairo Guidelines (Principle 2). Cf. Boyle, (1989), p. 270 et seq.; Birnie and Boyle, (1992), p. 92; Kiss, (1989a), p. 81; Schneider, (1979), p. 47; Sohn, (1973), p. 492.

[52] Article 21(d) of the 1982 World Charter for Nature embodies the same principle. Cf. Kiss and Shelton, (1991), p. 130; Boyle, in Churchill and Freestone, (1991), p. 4; Sohn, (1973), p. 493; Caldwell, (1990), p. 122; Orrego Vicuña, in Brown Weiss, (1992b), p. 129 et seq.; Bothe, in Handl and Lutz, (1989a), pp. 168–9 (also discussing the limitations of the rule).

[53] Kiss, (1989a), p. 93 et seq. (outlining the elaboration of this rule by the 1982 World Charter for Nature, UNCLOS, and the Brundtland Report *Our Common Future*); OECD, in OECD, (1977), p. 392. See also the declaration of Peru, Chile, and Ecuador in 1947, proclaiming that 'it is therefore the duty of each Government to ensure the conservation and protection of its natural resources and to regulate the use thereof to the greatest possible advantage of its country' (quoted in the *North Sea Continental Shelf Case* (ICJ Rep. (1969) 3 et seq.), *Separate Opinion of Judge Ammoun* at 108).

[54] See Introductory Note to Part V: The Law of the Sea, 2 Restatement Third of the Foreign Relations Law of the United States, 5(1987) (quoted by Könz, in Brown Weiss, (1992b), p. 161); also Boyle, (1992a), p. 24, and idem, (1992b), p. 80. Cf. Caflisch, (1983), p. 39 et seq., giving an overview of the status of relevant customary law prior to UNCLOS.

which lead to pollution or pose a risk to the environment are not prohibited by customary law. States do have an obligation to exercise due diligence in the regulation and control of such activities within their territories or under their control.[55] The concept of due diligence is, however, very unspecific.[56] The threshold which determines whether or not the impact of an activity on the environment calls for legal response has, to some extent, been specified by treaties and non-binding guidelines. Particularly in the field of marine pollution, technical annexes to treaties as well as technical guidelines and 'codes of conduct' determine the acceptable level of pollution.[57] However, these standards apply only to the particular activity addressed by the rule in question. Even if some of the relevant rules, e.g. the MARPOL Convention and the 1972 London Convention (see Chapter 5 below), can be considered universally accepted, this does not apply to all of them.[58]

In examining the significance of this fundamental rule for the issue of transboundary movements of hazardous wastes, we have to bear in mind that it originally evolved to address situations such as the one which gave rise to the *Trail Smelter Arbitration*, and is thus based on the traditional concept of transboundary pollution. Accordingly, the significance of this rule for transboundary transport of hazardous wastes, which constitutes an aspect of pollution source transfer, is limited.[59] The rule makes it clear that there is no unlimited 'freedom to pollute', and requires the state of generation to adopt and enforce national legislation with respect to the management of hazardous wastes within its territory or under its control, in accordance with the principle of due diligence.[60] It does not, however, resolve the problem of the rights and obligations of the states involved in transboundary waste traffic since it does not extend to situations where the source of pollution is transferred to an area beyond the jurisdiction of the state of origin. That state cannot be required to observe the duty of due diligence if it does not have jurisdiction or control over the relevant activity. An interesting exception is Article X of the ILA's Helsinki Rules on international rivers, which provides that a basin state shall take measures

[55] Cf. Birnie and Boyle, (1992), chs. 3, 8, 9; Handl, (1990), p. 21. For a detailed discussion of the concept of due diligence see Dupuy, in OECD, (1977), p. 396 et seq.; OECD, ibid, p. 381 et seq.

[56] Gündling, in Lang, Neuhold, and Zemanek, (1991), pp. 93, 99; Boyle, (1989), p. 272 et seq.; idem, in Churchill and Freestone, (1991), p. 14 et seq.; Springer, (1983), p. 89 et seq.; OECD, in OECD, (1977), p. 387.

[57] Cf. Chapter 1(G) and (H) below. Relevant rules include the MARPOL Convention the SOLAS Convention; the 1972 London Convention and regional treaties on dumping, and the numerous codes of conduct for transport of hazardous substances elaborated by the IMO and other relevant organizations. Cf. also Dupuy, in OECD, (1977), p. 363.

[58] Birnie and Boyle, (1992), p. 93 et seq.

[59] Cf. Bothe, in Handl and Lutz, (1989a), p. 160.

[60] OECD, in OECD, (1977), p. 384 et seq.

to control water pollution originating within its territory, as well as pollution originating outside it, if it is caused by the state's conduct. There is as yet, however, little evidence of state practice supporting the extension of the requirement of due diligence to the exporting state in the case of pollution source transfer.[61] In fact, the importing state may itself have a duty to manage imported hazardous wastes in such a way as to prevent serious harm to third states or to the global commons.[62]

5. The right of states to control activities within their area of jurisdiction

An important aspect of the sovereign right of states over the use of their territory is the right of every state to exploit its own resources in accordance with its national environmental policies, and to control activities within its area of jurisdiction.[63] This rule, which is also reaffirmed and specified in Principle 21 of the Stockholm Declaration and in Principle 2 of the Rio Declaration,[64] provides more guidance with respect to the issue of pollution source transfer than the limitation of the 'freedom to pollute'. Whereas there is as yet no customary obligation to obtain the prior consent of a neighbouring state that may be affected by transboundary pollution in the traditional sense—customary law merely obliges the source state to negotiate in good faith with the state affected by the harmful activity[65]—the existence of such an obligation in the case of pollution source transfer can be deduced from the above rule: the right to give or refuse permission for a potentially dangerous activity to be carried out within its area of jurisdiction is part of a state's right to control activities within its own territory.[66] This means that a state has the right to prohibit, in general or under specific conditions, the import of hazardous wastes for transit or disposal.[67] If such import does take place, it may only be with the recipient state's con-

[61] In support of this view see generally Bothe, in Handl and Lutz, (1989a), p. 158 et seq. (basing his assessment on an analysis of relevant legal instruments and state practice). Cf. also Nanda and Bailey, in Handl and Lutz, (1989a), pp. 21–2; McCaffrey, in Magraw, (1991), p. 102. For a differing opinion cf. Kiss, in *La réparation des dommages catastrophiques*, (1990), p. 305.

[62] See Koh, in Handl and Lutz, (1989a), p. 175.

[63] Caldwell, (1990), p. 22; Birnie and Boyle, (1992), p. 334.

[64] Cf. Caldwell, (1990), p. 22; also Koh, in Handl and Lutz, (1989a), p. 175.

[65] *Lac Lanoux Arbitration* (ILR 24 (1957) 101). See also Springer, (1983), p. 150; Birnie and Boyle, (1992), p. 336.

[66] Kiss and Shelton, (1991), p. 323. For an interesting extension of this concept cf. Timoshenko, in Brown Weiss, (1992b), p. 435 et seq. The author proposes a 'principle of equal ecological security' based on the sovereign equality of states, prohibiting interference by one state with another state's ecological well-being. This includes a prohibition of transferring wastes and other hazardous substances into another state to the detriment of that state's environment.

[67] For a similar view cf. Gündling, in Handl and Lutz, (1989a), p. 82.

sent and in accordance with its relevant national legislation. There seems, therefore, to be a strong argument in favour of an evolving customary law rule obliging the state of origin to obtain the recipient state's prior consent to a transboundary movement of hazardous wastes. This requirement has been incorporated into a number of recent treaties and other legal instruments; their role in consolidating the rule will be examined in the following chapters.

In the context of the protection of the marine environment against pollution, the above rule has developed further. In accordance with the recognition in customary law of coastal states' rights over their adjacent sea areas,[68] a rule has evolved to the effect that a coastal state has the sovereign right to adopt measures for the protection of the marine environment, and to exercise jurisdiction in these matters, within its territorial sea. In accordance with Article 56 of the 1982 UNCLOS, coastal states also have jurisdiction over their Exclusive Economic Zone (EEZ) with regard to the prevention and control of marine pollution. There is some disagreement, however, as to whether this is an existing or merely an emerging rule of customary law.[69] The coastal state may adopt and enforce measures to prevent marine pollution—or to minimize the risk of such pollution—by foreign vessels, including ships exercising the right of innocent passage through its territorial sea.[70] Thus the prohibition of hazardous waste imports without the consent of the recipient state extends to deliberate disposal of wastes (dumping) within the territorial sea and the EEZ. This rule has been reaffirmed in treaty law.[71] The customary right of innocent passage may, however, not be impeded by such regulation.[72] Article 19 of the 1982 UNCLOS attempts to clarify that right by laying down a list of activities which render the passage non-innocent. These activities include 'any act of wilful and serious pollution contrary to this convention'. The significance of this provision seems to be unclear. In particular, it is not clear whether loss of innocence can only result from an activity, or whether transit in itself can render the passage non-innocent.[73] The further evolution of this rule will determine the important question whether the transit passage of a hazardous

[68] Churchill and Lowe, (1988), pp. 73–4, 139–40, 252–6.

[69] For a discussion see among others Churchill and Lowe, (1988), pp. 139–40; O'Connell, Vol. I, (1982), pp. 995–7; Kiss, (1989a), p. 58; Birnie and Boyle, (1992), p. 326. For an overview of states' rights and duties in the different maritime zones, and the evolution of these rules, see Plant, (1993).

[70] UNCLOS (Articles 21(1.d) and (1.f), 210, 211(4)). Cf. Kiss, (1989a), p. 58; Birnie and Boyle, (1992), p. 326, n. 100 (quoting the *Libya-Malta Continental Shelf Case*, ICJ Rep., (1985) 13; and the *North Sea Continental Shelf Case*, ICJ Rep (1969) 3); also Plant, (1993).

[71] UNCLOS (Article 210(5)); Noumea Protocol for the Prevention of Pollution of the South Pacific Region by Dumping (Article 3(2)). See Chapter 5 below.

[72] 1958 Convention on the Territorial Sea (Article 14); UNCLOS (Article 17 et seq.); *Corfu Channel Case* (see n. 48 above). See Churchill and Lowe, (1988), pp. 71–2, 253; Birnie and Boyle, (1992), p. 337.

[73] Churchill and Lowe, (1988), p. 72.

waste shipment can be considered innocent passage. An examination of this question being beyond the scope of this study, reference is made to works devoted to this issue.[74]

Another consequence of the right of the importing state to control activities within its own territory is that the state of origin does not have the authority to adopt measures with respect to those stages of the hazardous waste cycle over which it has no jurisdiction, without the recipient state's permission. This applies in particular to the disposal of hazardous wastes in the country of import: the generating state may not, for example, carry out a prior environmental impact assessment (EIA) of a proposed waste disposal facility against the wishes of the recipient state. From an environmental viewpoint, this might be considered a slightly problematic aspect of the rule, especially if the national environmental policy of the exporting state is more stringent than that of the importing state. It can be argued, however, that there is evidence of an emerging customary obligation to carry out a prior EIA for potentially hazardous activities, although this is not as yet universally recognized.[75] This obligation is consistent with the rule that no state has unlimited 'freedom to pollute', discussed above. The function of an EIA is to determine the hazard potential of an activity, and to provide a basis for determining whether or not it would lead to an unacceptable level of pollution, and thus whether or not it should be permitted. If this obligation is recognized, the recipient state will have to co-operate with the generating state, as appropriate, in carrying out an EIA for hazardous waste disposal facilities.

[74] See e.g. Pineschi, in Francioni and Scovazzi, (1991); van der Mensbrugghe, (1990), p. 267 et seq.; idem, (1989), p. 360 et seq.; Nollkaemper, (1991), p. 428 et seq.; Weinstein, (1994). The issue is also under discussion in the Legal Committee of the IMO in the context of the elaboration of the HNS Convention, discussed in Chapter 6 below (cf. the report on the Legal Committee's discussions, in EPL 22/5/6(1992), p. 311).

[75] For an analysis of this emerging rule cf. Wirth, in Handl and Lutz, (1989a), p. 83 et seq.; also Handl, (1990), p. 21; Kiss and Shelton, (1991), p. 147; Birnie and Boyle, (1992), p. 97; Kwiatkowska and Soons, (1993), Editors' Introduction, p. XXX; Timoshenko, in Brown Weiss, (1992b), p. 442; Adede, (1992), p. 95. See also Dupuy, in Magraw, (1991), pp. 66–7 (arguing that there is not as yet sufficient grounds for the recognition of EIA as a customary law rule). The 1991 UN/ECE Convention on Environmental Impact Assessment in a Transboundary Context (repr. in ILM 30/3 (1991), p. 802) is likely to accelerate the recognition of this rule. Other legal instruments incorporating EIA include the 1982 UNCLOS (Article 206); the 1992 UN Convention on Biological Diversity (Article 14); the 1992 Helsinki Convention (Article 7); the more recent UNEP Regional Seas Conventions; the 1988 CRAMRA; the 1985 EU Directive on the Assessment of the Effects of Certain Public and Private Projects on the Environment (OJ L 175, (1985), p. 40); OECD Council Recommendations C(79)116 and C(85)104 (repr. in Hohmann, (1992), Vol. 1, p. 400 et seq.); Principle 17 of the Rio Declaration; Chapter 17 of Agenda 21 (marine pollution); the 1991 Declaration on the Protection of the Arctic Environment (repr. in YBIEL 2(1991), p. 582); and the UNEP Goals and Principles of Environmental Impact Assessment (GC Decision 14/25, 17 June 1987).

6. Duties of co-operation and information[76]

As a procedural corollary to the prohibition of causing unreasonable harm to the environment of other states, customary law provides for a duty of co-operation in the control of transboundary pollution and environmental risks.[77] The obligation of prior notification of and consultation with states likely to be affected by a potentially harmful activity, as established by the *Lac Lanoux Arbitration*, is a concrete expression of this concept.[78] Another expression of the concept, established by the *Corfu Channel Case*, is the duty to immediately inform other states which are likely to be affected by any situation causing environmental damage, e.g. accidents.[79] Principle 24 of the Stockholm Declaration extended the duty of co-operation in the field of transboundary pollution to the more comprehensive obligation of international co-operation between all states in the field of environmental protection.[80] This duty is reiterated in Principles 7, 18 and 19 of the Rio Declaration. It was expanded and given more precise content by a multitude of soft law rules and treaties addressing pollution control. Thus it now encompasses co-operation in scientific research and monitoring of the state of the environment, and exchange of relevant information.[81]

[76] For an overview cf. Thacher, in Brown Weiss, (1992b), ch. 3; Dupuy, in Magraw, (1991), p. 69 et seq.; Kiss and Shelton, (1991), p. 132 et seq. See also Kiss, in Brown Weiss, (1992b), pp. 337–8; Gündling, in Lang, Neuhold, and Zemanek, (1991), ch. 3.

[77] Boyle, (1989), p. 278; OECD, in OECD, (1977), p. 385.

[78] *Lac Lanoux Arbitration* (see n. 65 above). See also the ILA 1982 Montreal Rules of International Law Applicable to Transfrontier Pollution (Articles 7–8), and the 1991 ILC draft Articles on the Non-Navigational Uses of International Watercourses (Article 12) (both repr. in Hohmann, (1992), Vol. 1); WCED, *Our Common Future*, (1987), p. 350. For a discussion see Orrego Vicuña, in Brown Weiss, (1992b), p. 137; Iwama, ibid, pp. 119–21; Handl, (1990), p. 21; Kiss and Shelton, (1991), p. 133 et seq.; Kwiatkowska and Soons, (1993), Editors' Introduction, p. XXX.

[79] *Corfu Channel Case* (see n. 48 above). These rules are codified in a number of international legal instruments, including the following: UNEP Principles on Shared Natural Resources (UNEP/GC. 6/14, 19 May 1978); 1974 OECD Council Recommendation on Principles Concerning Transfrontier Pollution C(74)224 (repr. in ILM 42 (1975)); and the 1992 Helsinki Convention (Article 13). Cf. Birnie and Boyle, (1992), ch. 8; Boyle, (1989), p. 278 et seq.; Kiss, (1989a), p. 59; idem, (1989b), p. 246; Schneider, (1979), p. 50 et seq.; Handl, (1990), p. 21; idem, in Handl and Lutz, (1989a), p. 119 et seq.; Iwama, in Brown Weiss, (1992b), p. 121–2.

[80] See also Principle 20. Cf. Kiss and Shelton, (1991), p. 133.

[81] Relevant legal instruments include the following: 1982 World Charter for Nature; 1979 UN/ECE Declaration on Low- and Non-Waste Technology and Re-utilization and Recycling of Wastes (repr. in Hohmann, (1992), Vol. 1, p. 338); 1992 UN Framework Convention on Climate Change; 1992 UN Convention on Biological Diversity; 1982 UNCLOS (Articles 63 et seq., 197 et seq.); 1992 Oslo/Paris Convention (Articles 8, 9); 1992 Helsinki Convention (Article 14 et seq.); UNEP Regional Seas Conventions; regional conventions on marine pollution from land-based sources (cf. Chapter 5 below); 1988 CRAMRA (Article 6); 1985 Vienna Convention for the Protection of the Ozone Layer; 1979 Geneva Convention on Long-Range Transboundary Air Pollution; statement of the 1989 Tokyo Conference on the Global Environment; 1978 UNEP Principles of Conduct on Shared Natural Resources; OECD Council Recommendations C(74)224, C(77)115, C(77)28, and C(78)77. See Thacher, in Brown

In the context of transboundary movements of hazardous wastes, the duties of co-operation and information are significant. The transfer of hazardous wastes from the state of generation to another state for transit or disposal can undoubtedly be considered an activity which is potentially harmful to the environment of the recipient state. If the state of origin is required by customary law to give prior information to, and enter into consultations with, neighbouring states that are potentially affected by hazardous activities carried out in its own territory, it follows, *a fortiori*, that this duty applies equally to a hazardous activity initiated or authorized within the state of origin but planned to be carried out within the recipient state. The recipient state's right to be notified is essential in that it provides the basis for the exercise of its right to prohibit or control the activities in question. For these reasons, it can justifiably be argued that the duty of prior information and consultation in the case of pollution source transfer is based in customary law. The role of relevant international legal instruments adopted in the late 1980s and early 1990s in consolidating this rule will be examined in the following chapters.

If both the duty of prior information and the duty to obtain prior consent are thus considered to have a basis in customary law, this lends considerable weight to the argument that the principle of prior informed consent (PIC) for pollution source transfer is also an emerging customary law rule.[82] This principle, which will be discussed in more detail in Chapter 2(F) below, makes the permissibility of a hazardous activity contingent on the prior express consent of a potentially affected state, based on information provided to it by the perpetrating state.

The above arguments for according the status of customary law rules to the duties of prior notification and PIC in the context of pollution source transfer are not universally accepted, some scholars arguing that there is not as yet sufficient state practice to justify such an assumption. This view was predominant in the mid-1980s, i.e. prior to the adoption of the most important legal instruments that embody these concepts.[83] The recent inclusion of PIC in a number of legal instruments addressing different aspects of pollution source transfer is likely to accelerate its acceptance as a customary law rule. This will be discussed in the following chapters.

Weiss, (1992b), ch. 3; Iwama, ibid, ch. 4; Timoshenko, ibid, p. 439 et seq.; Dupuy, in Magraw, (1991), p. 71 et seq.; Adede (1992). See also WCED, *Our Common Future* (1987), p. 349 et seq.

[82] For similar arguments see among others Birnie and Boyle, (1992), pp. 334, 336; Kiss and Shelton, (1991), p. 323; Orrego Vicuña, in Brown Weiss, (1992b), p. 151.

[83] Cf. Gündling, in Handl and Lutz, (1989a), p. 81; Handl and Lutz, ibid, pp. 53–5; Bothe, ibid, pp. 158–62.

7. An assessment of the relevant customary law rules

The above overview shows that the rules of international customary law on pollution control give some guidance with respect to the regulation of transboundary movements of hazardous wastes, and provide a basis for further regulation by laying down the fundamental principles. Nevertheless, it is clear that these rules do not set sufficiently precise standards of behaviour to ensure effective pollution control.[84] Due to the rapid development of international environmental law, it is difficult to define the exact content of relevant customary law rules at any given time, and to draw a line between customary law and soft law rules.[85] Customary rules are also subject to differing interpretations concerning their content and implications for pollution control.[86]

Apart from these general shortcomings, the customary rules do not take sufficient account of the specific characteristics of pollution source transfer insofar as it differs from transboundary pollution in the traditional sense. Where rules specifically addressing the hazardous waste cycle (such as PIC) are emerging, their status as customary rules remains doubtful. The recent adoption of specific treaty and soft law rules addressing the hazardous waste management cycle is likely to accelerate the evolution of customary law in this field, and to provide more precision as to the contents of the rules. This issue will be examined further in Chapter 7 below.

G. *Sectoral Pollution Control Regimes*

In addition to customary rules, a large number of treaties address the pollution of individual spheres of the environment. In accordance with the sectoral approach to environmental protection, still predominant in international law, most of these treaties address the protection of one particular medium against pollution: the oceans, the air, or continental waters. These treaties commonly set more or less detailed standards determining the acceptable threshold of pollution, and oblige states to control the sources of pollution. They also establish obligations of exchange of information, international co-operation, and monitoring the condition of the relevant sphere of the environment.

[84] See e.g. Gündling, in Lang, Neuhold, and Zemanek, (1991), ch. 3; Springer, (1983), p. 31 et seq., and sources quoted there; Rublack, (1994), p. 61 et seq.

[85] Dupuy, in Magraw, (1991), p. 61 et seq.; Watts, (1992), p. 254. See also para. 6 of the conclusions of the 1990 Siena Forum (repr. in EPL 20/6(1990), p. 232), noting that customary law in the environmental field is still at an early stage of development; Springer, (1983), pointing out that customary law is 'slow to evolve and vague in the obligation it imposes'.

[86] Cf. Magraw, in Magraw, (1991), pp. 13–14 (giving the Chernobyl accident as an example); Springer, (1983), p. 31 et seq. (noting that customary law rules can be modified to support the interests of states in *not* protecting the environment).

The role of sectoral pollution control treaties in the international regulation of transboundary movement of hazardous wastes will be examined in more detail in Chapter 5 below. For the present purpose, it is sufficient to note that they contribute to the regulation of the issue insofar as they directly or indirectly address the disposal of hazardous wastes in a particular sphere of the environment. They generally establish more detailed standards than the customary norms, and thus contribute to the development of internationally accepted thresholds for the different forms of pollution. Clearly, however, the sectoral pollution control treaties do not in themselves constitute an adequate regulatory framework for the hazardous waste cycle. They address at best only the final stage of the cycle, namely disposal, leaving the other stages unregulated. Moreover, as each regime is designed to protect only one particular sphere of the environment against pollution, and the different regimes do not necessarily correspond with each other, they do not provide a harmonious regulation even for the stage of disposal.

H. *International Rules on the Transport and Management of Hazardous Substances*

There exists a large body of non-binding international rules, e.g. guidelines and codes of conduct, that establish safety standards and uniform procedures for the international transport of dangerous substances.[87] A comprehensive set of rules is provided by the Recommendations of the UN Committee of Experts on the Transport of Dangerous Goods (UNCTDG Recommendations, commonly referred to as the Orange Book).[88] The Recommendations are addressed to governments and international organizations, and are widely used. They are updated biennially to take into account new developments. Covering all modes of transport, they set out a classification system for dangerous goods and provide rules on packaging, testing, labelling and placarding, and shipping documents.

Transport by sea is covered by numerous rules adopted under the auspices of the IMO. Chapter VII of the 1974 SOLAS Convention (as amended) provides the framework for extensive international regulation of the carriage of dangerous goods by sea. Annexes I–III of the 1973/78

[87] For a list and an analysis of the international regulations on the transport and management of dangerous goods and wastes see EU Commission, *Final Report on Transport of Dangerous Goods and Wastes*, 16 June 1987, (COM(87)182 final); IMO, (1991); Kwiatkowska and Soons, (1993), Editors' Introduction. On the legal nature of codes of conduct see Lutz and Aron, in Handl and Lutz, (1989a), p. 129 et seq.; Kiss, in Brown Weiss, (1992b), p. 319 et seq.

[88] UN Doc. ST/SG/AC.10/1/Rev. 9, 1995; cf. also the report of the UN Secretary-General on the work of UNCTDG, 7 May 1991, Doc. E/1991/68, (repr. in Kwiatkowska and Soons, (1993), no. 4.2).

MARPOL Convention regulate the prevention of pollution by hazardous substances carried by sea: oil, noxious liquid in bulk, and harmful substances carried in packaged form, respectively. A number of codes of conduct regulate in great detail the modalities of sea transport of dangerous substances. Among the most important is the International Maritime Dangerous Goods Code (IMDG), elaborated pursuant to a 1960 resolution of the conference of parties to the SOLAS Convention and adopted in 1965. It applies to a wide range of substances subject to sea transport, which are divided into nine classes. The IMDG Code gives detailed guidance on marking, identification, consignment procedures, labelling and placarding, documentation, and packing of dangerous goods. It also regulates emergency procedures, and reporting procedures under the SOLAS and MARPOL Conventions. In 1985, the IMDG Code was amended to extend to 'marine pollutants', which for the purposes of the Code are substances harmful to the marine environment even if they do not have adverse effects on human health. This amendment is designed to assist states in the implementation of Annex III of the MARPOL Convention. The IMDG Code is periodically updated in accordance with a flexible amendment procedure, which allows quick response to new developments. The national legislation of individual states determines whether the Code is mandatory or merely used as a guideline. At present, the IMDG Code is applied by some fifty states, accounting for 85 per cent of the world's gross tonnage. A number of codes of conduct regulate the carriage of dangerous materials in bulk. The Code of Safe Practice for Solid Bulk Cargoes (BC Code) has as its primary aim the promotion of safe stowage and shipment to counter the special hazards posed by bulk cargoes of solid chemicals. Two codes for the Construction and Equipment of Ships Carrying Dangerous Chemicals in Bulk (BCH Code and IBC Code) apply to ships carrying chemicals in liquid form. Other IMO Codes deal with a wide range of additional issues, including accident response, use of chemicals aboard ships, packing of cargo, and handling of dangerous substances in port areas.[89]

Under the auspices of the UN/ECE, a number of regional agreements covering modes of transport of dangerous goods other than by sea were elaborated: the 1957 European Agreement Concerning the International Carriage of Dangerous Goods by Road (ADR);[90] the 1985 International Regulations Concerning the Carriage of Dangerous Goods by Rail (RID), Annex I to the 1970 Berne Convention Concerning the Carriage of Goods by Rail (CIM)); the 1970 Regulations on the Carriage of Dangerous Substances on the Rhine (ADNR); and the European Agreement Concerning Transport of Dangerous Goods by Inland Navigation (ADN).

[89] For a comprehensive overview see IMO, (1991); also Gold, (1986), pp. 185–91.

[90] UN Doc. ECE/TRANS/80, Vols. I and II (E. 89 VIII.2). Cf. also Kwiatkowska and Soons, (1993), p. 819; Lang, in Lang, Neuhold and Zemanek, (1991), p. 158.

These agreements, providing classification systems and setting safety standards for the transport of dangerous goods, form a regime which also includes the 1989 CRTD Convention (discussed in Chapter 6 below). They are harmonized with each other and updated at regular intervals. The latest revision became effective on 1 January 1995.[91]

The rules on transport of dangerous goods are for the major part highly technical and detailed. Whereas they primarily address substances other than wastes, many of them were amended to include hazardous wastes subsequent to the adoption of the Basel Convention, as we will see in Chapter 2. The rules thus provide technical standards for the management of hazardous wastes subject to transport. Like the sectoral pollution control treaties, they therefore offset one of the principal weaknesses of customary law, and may play a role in the emergence of internationally recognized 'ecostandards'. They are regularly updated in accordance with a predetermined procedure, and therefore provide the necessary flexibility for constantly keeping up with new requirements and technical developments.[92] However, with the exception of the UN/ECE agreements, the technical rules on international transport of dangerous substances are non-binding, and adherence is thus left to the discretion of states. Also, like sectoral pollution control treaties, they address only one stage of the hazardous waste cycle, namely transport. In addition, they focus on the establishment of safety standards, and do not provide much guidance with respect to the permissibility of waste shipments, or the mutual rights and obligations of states in this context.[93]

THE NEED FOR A GLOBAL WASTE MANAGEMENT REGIME

The above overview shows that while the rules discussed make a contribution to the regulation of various aspects and stages of the hazardous waste cycle, none of them provides an adequate regulatory framework for the issue as a whole. The rules address the individual issues in an incomplete and piecemeal fashion. If the hazardous waste cycle is to be effectively controlled, there is a need for a global regime to address the issue in a comprehensive manner. The term 'regime' is defined in various ways; for present purposes, it should be understood as referring to a comprehensive

[91] Cf. Kwiatkowska and Soons, (1993), Editors' Introduction, p. LXIII et seq.; also Sand, in YBIEL 2, (1991) pp. 400–1; Kiss and Shelton, (1991), p. 320.

[92] On the role of non-binding technical rules in international law-making, cf. Sand, (1990), p. 17.

[93] This was also the conclusion of the IMO's Ad Hoc Group of Legal Experts on Dumping which examined the relationship between the Basel Convention and the London Convention, discussed in Chapter 5 below (see Doc. LDC/LG 4/WP.1, p. 2). For a differing view cf. Lang, in Lang, Neuhold, and Zemanek, (1991), p. 148 et seq.

set of international legal rules generated by international negotiations and designed to govern a particular issue subject to international law.[94] It is submitted that the Basel Convention, to date the most advanced attempt at comprehensive global regulation of this issue, has the potential to form the basis on which to build this regime. The other rules, which effectively address some aspects of the hazardous waste cycle, have a useful and important role in complementing and enhancing the Basel Convention. As will be discussed in Chapter 2 below, this idea was first expressed by the diplomatic conference that adopted the Basel Convention, and was subsequently taken up within various international fora.

A future waste management regime should offset the weaknesses of the individual rules of which it is composed, and combine their strengths. The specific characteristics of the hazardous waste management cycle should be taken into account. The regime should also incorporate the fundamental concepts of international law and policy related to environmental protection which have evolved over the past decades, as well as changes in the perception of the role of international law in the protection of the environment.[95] The following paragraphs will seek to establish the main characteristics of a future global waste management regime. The elements of the regime will then be discussed in more detail in subsequent chapters.

I. *Uniform Global Standards and Regional Rules*

Unlike some other aspects of environmental degradation, the cycle of transboundary movements and management of hazardous wastes is not limited to specific regions, but often takes place on a world-wide scale. For this reason, the concept of regulation on a purely regional level, as adopted for the protection of enclosed and semi-enclosed seas, pollution from land-based sources, or the use of international lakes and rivers (see Chapter 5 below), is inappropriate. On the other hand, the issue does not necessarily require universal regulation in every respect: regional peculiarities do exist and should be taken into account. As discussed in para. 2 above, a group of industrialized states with generally high technical standards, and suffering from a scarcity of disposal options due to a high density of population, may contemplate the establishment of joint disposal facilities for certain types of hazardous wastes; on the other hand, a group of developing countries may want to adopt joint measures to prevent the use of their territories as cheap disposal sites for foreign hazardous wastes. An acknowledged advantage of regional regulation is the possibility of a group of states situated in a

[94] Cf. List and Rittberger, in Hurrell and Kingsbury, (1992), p. 86 et seq.; also Lang, in Lang, Neuhold, and Zemanek, (1991), p. 148 et seq.; Gehring, (1990), pp. 36–7; Handl, (1990), p. 3 et seq.

[95] For an outline of these changes cf. Kiss, in Brown Weiss, (1992b), p. 317 et seq.

particular region, and linked through similar problems and concerns, adopting specific rules which take into account their common needs. In addition, the usually relatively small number of states involved and the similarity of their interests make it easier to reach agreement at the regional than at the global level.[96]

In attempting to combine the advantages of regional regulation with the need for a global regime, an obvious option is a global 'umbrella' treaty, providing a framework of general obligations, under which regional agreements laying down more precise rules may be concluded.[97] This approach would allow specific regional situations to be taken into account. One author in fact gives transboundary movements of hazardous wastes as an example of an issue requiring a 'multi-layered approach', i.e. regulation at national, regional and international levels simultaneously.[98] This technique has been used in other treaties, notably in Article VIII of the London Convention, which will be discussed in Chapter 5(A) below, and Articles 197 and 210(4) of UNCLOS. It is being considered by the ILC in the context of the regulation of international waterways, which will be addressed in Chapter 5(D) below.

In the case of the hazardous waste cycle, however, this solution has problematical aspects, due to the inherent danger of differing regional standards facilitating waste exports to regions where the regulations are least strict.[99] In order to avoid this, an 'umbrella' treaty would need to provide more than a framework; it would have to regulate the fundamental aspects of the issue, setting sufficiently high and detailed global standards, from which the regional treaties should not be allowed to derogate.[100] This option will be examined in Chapters 3 and 4 below.

J. *Sectoral and Integrated Regulation*

As discussed above, the vast majority of the existing treaties on pollution control, as well as many of the non-binding texts issued by international organizations, adopt the sectoral approach, which aims for separate protection of the different spheres of the environment against pollution. The integrated approach, on the other hand, aims for regulation of all aspects of a particular polluting activity, including deleterious effects on every sphere of the environment.[101] The rules of customary law reflect this

[96] On the characteristics and respective advantages and disadvantages of regional regulation cf. Caldwell, (1990), p. 129 et seq.; Handl, (1990), pp. 13–15; Kiss, (1989a), p. 51; Sand, (1990), p. 9 et seq.

[97] For a definition of an 'umbrella' treaty see Kiss, in Brown Weiss, (1992b), p. 323.

[98] Magraw, in Magraw, (1991), p. 8, n. 26.

[99] A similar view is expressed by Sand, (1990), p. 9.

[100] Cf. Ando, in Zacklin and Caflisch, (1981), p. 351.

[101] For a discussion of the sectoral and integrated approaches see among others Kiss, in Brown Weiss, (1992b), ch. 10; Kiss and Shelton, (1991), p. 155 et seq.; Adede, (1992), p. 90; Hohmann, (1990), p. 55 et seq.; Teclaff and Teclaff, (1991), pp. 187–211; OECD, (1987).

approach to a certain extent: the majority of them address every form of pollution and are not restricted to a particular sphere. There is also a notable trend towards an integrated approach in international environmental policy, most particularly in the areas of management of hazardous and nuclear wastes.[102] As early as 1976, an OECD Council Recommendation called for 'comprehensive waste management policies', to be developed 'in such a way that they aim at the protection of the entire environment and not of one of its constituent sectors'.[103] The concepts of 'cleaner production', 'integrated pollution control', and 'cradle-to-grave monitoring' of hazardous substances and wastes, increasingly supported in environmental policy and law, are concrete expressions of the integrated approach. They are reflected in a number of recent policy statements on environmental protection.[104] They also receive increasing support from the relevant international organizations, notably UNEP,[105] IMO,[106] UN/ECE,[107] OECD,[108] and the EU.[109] Chapters 20 and 21 of UNCED's Agenda 21, proposing an integrated action programme on waste manage-

[102] See e.g. para. 4. of the conclusions of the 1990 Siena Forum on International Law of the Environment (repr. in EPL 20/6(1990), p. 232). See also Kiss, (1989a), p. 275 et seq.; Caldwell, (1990), p. 67; Ando, in Zacklin and Caflisch, (1981), p. 351; OECD, (1987), p. 46; Kummer, in YBIEL 3(1992), p. 288.

[103] OECD Council Recommendation on a Comprehensive Waste Management Policy, 28 September 1976, (C(76)155/final). See also Chapter 4(E) below.

[104] For an overview see UNEP Governing Council Decision 16/39, 31 May 1991, operational para. 7. See also OECD Council Recommendation on Integrated Pollution Prevention and Control, C(90)164, 1991; Article 35 of the Lomé IV Convention (see Chapter 3(H) below).

[105] Cf. the 1987 Cairo Guidelines (discussed in Chapter 2(A) below); Governing Council Decisions SS/II/4 B (3 August 1990) and 16/30 (31 May 1991) on a comprehensive approach to hazardous waste; the Recommendations of the 1991 Rio Meeting for the Review of the UNEP Montevideo Programme (repr. in Kwiatkowska and Soons, (1993), no. 6.1.3); and the elements of a waste management strategy and the draft technical guidelines elaborated within the framework of the Basel Convention (discussed in Chapter 2 below).

[106] Cf. the waste management strategy currently elaborated under the auspices of the IMO (discussed in Chapter 5 below).

[107] Cf. the 1979 UN/ECE Declaration on Low- and Non-Waste Technology and Re-utilization and Recycling of Wastes (repr. in Hohmann, (1992), Vol. 1, p. 338); the 1988 UN/ECE *Regional Strategy for Environmental Protection up to the Year 2000 and Beyond*, which includes principles on waste management (repr. in Kwiatkowska and Soons, (1993), p. 855), and the *General Concept for a Regional Strategy for Integrated Waste Management*, 26 August 1991, (Doc. ENWA/WP.2/R.3, Annex). For a discussion see Kwiatkowska and Soons, (1993), Editors' Introduction, p. LXIII.

[108] Cf. the OECD Council Recommendation on Integrated Pollution Control, C(90)164/final, 31 January 1991; and the 1976 Waste Management Strategy. See also OECD, (1986a), and documents reproduced there. The waste management policy of the OECD will be dicussed in Chapter 4 below.

[109] Cf. the Third Action Programme for the Environment (1982–86, discussed in Johnson and Corcelle, (1989), p. 12); Article 130r of the Single European Act; and the 1989 Waste Management Strategy. For a discussion of the EU's waste management policy see Chapter 4 below.

ment, also endorse these concepts, as does Chapter 17 on marine pollution.[110]

As we have seen, the hazardous waste cycle is one of the most obvious illustrations of the inadequacy of a purely sectoral approach. In accordance with the relevant policy recommendations issued by the organizations concerned, the future waste management regime should therefore be based primarily on the integrated approach. This does not mean, however, that existing sectoral rules have no part to play: sectoral rules, especially those which are long established and provide detailed 'ecostandards', can be very useful in addressing a particular stage of the cycle. The rules must, however, be incorporated into the regime in such a way as to complement and enhance the integrated approach. Thus they must be harmonized not only with rules addressing the waste cycle as a whole, but also with each other, in order to prevent stricter regulation of the protection of one sphere from leading to increased pollution of a less regulated sphere.[111] As we will see in Chapter 5 below, this concept is already embodied in numerous sectoral treaties, notably in the field of marine pollution. The role of sectoral treaties in the emergence of a global waste management regime will be examined in more detail in Chapter 5 below.

K. *'Sovereignty-based' and 'Holistic' Rules*

In the traditional view, pollution was considered a form of harm inflicted by one sovereign state upon another. It was accordingly treated as what will be referred to in this study as a 'sovereignty-based' issue, i.e. an issue concerning the mutual rights and duties of two or more sovereign states. In accordance with this approach, pollution was only relevant in international law if it emanated from a 'polluter' state and produced damaging effects in a 'victim' state, thus infringing the sovereign rights of the latter.[112]

Following the adoption of the Stockholm Declaration, the development of international environmental policy and law progressed towards what will be termed here a 'holistic' approach, i.e. the recognition of the need to address environmental protection in terms of protecting the earth as a whole. Pollution came to be seen as a form of harm to the environment as such, and the idea of a collective responsibility of the world community to

[110] Report of UNCED, Doc. A/CONF.151/26/Rev.1, Vol. I, p. 238 et seq. (Chapter 17), p. 335 et seq. (Chapter 20), p. 353 et seq. (Chapter 21). See also *Environmentally Sound Mangement of Hazardous Waste: Options for Agenda 21*, UNCED PrepCom III, September 1991, Annex I; *Environmentally Sound Mangement of Solid Wastes and Sewage-Related Issues: Options for Agenda 21*, UNCED PrepCom III, September 1991, Annex II.

[111] See Kwiatkowska and Soons, (1993), Editor's Introduction, p. XXXIII; Birnie and Boyle, (1992), p. 300; Teclaff and Teclaff, (1991), pp. 187–211; OECD, (1987), pp. 46–7.

[112] Kiss, (1989a), pp. 71, 93; idem, (1989b), pp. 245, 261–2; van Heijnsbergen, (1979), p. 12; Müller and Wildhaber, (1977), p. 405 et seq.; Handl, (1990), p. 10; Springer, (1983), p. 33.

protect the environment from such harm began to evolve.[113] One of the more far-reaching consequences of this idea is the concept of 'common concern of humankind', which implies that all states share a legal interest in the protection of the global environment. This principle, although frequently advocated in the negotiations on the 1992 UN Framework Convention on Climate Change, has yet to gain universal recognition.[114] Nevertheless, pollution can be subject to international regulation even in cases where it does not directly affect the interests of a particular state, as we have seen in the context of customary law rules. Günther Handl notes that 'international competence is inexorably expanding at the cost of national jurisdiction.'[115] Contemporary international environmental law does not address the problems related to pollution in a uniform way in this respect. Both the sovereignty-based and the holistic approaches are reflected in the relevant legal sources governing pollution control. Principles 6 and 7 of the Stockholm Declaration, for example, reflect both approaches, as does Article 194 of UNCLOS: paragraph 1 of that provision contains an obligation to protect the environment in general, while paragraph 2 obliges states to 'take all measures to ensure that activities under their jurisdiction or control are so conducted as not to cause damage to other states and their environment, and that pollution arising from incidents under their jurisdiction or control do not spread beyond the areas where they exercise sovereign rights in accordance with this Convention'.[116]

Unlike wholly holistic issues such as the depletion of the ozone layer and global climate change, the risk of pollution posed by the hazardous waste cycle has both sovereignty-based and holistic aspects, and should therefore be addressed by both types of rules. On the one hand, the transfer of hazardous wastes from one state to another does raise questions of sovereignty. It is for this reason that the traditional sovereignty-based rules of customary law are to a certain extent applicable to the issue, as we have seen above. There exists a real need to protect the national interests of recipient states against the dangers emanating from foreign hazardous wastes, especially where there is an economic and regulatory imbalance between the states involved. On the other hand, the risk posed by hazardous wastes must also be seen independently of frontiers, and there is a shared interest to protect the globe as a whole against their ill-effects. The future waste

[113] For an overview of the transition from the sovereignty-based to the holistic approach see Kiss, in Brown Weiss, (1992b), p. 331 et seq.; Kiss and Shelton, (1991), p. 115 et seq.; also Caldwell, (1990), p. 55 et seq.; Springer, (1983), p. 80.

[114] Cf. e.g. Boyle, in Churchill and Freestone, (1991), ch. 1; Kiss, in Brown Weiss, (1992b), p. 334 et seq.; also Rest, in EPL 22/1(1992), p. 32 et seq.; Stocker, (1993); Bodansky, (1993).

[115] Handl, in Handl and Lutz, (1989a), p. 126 et seq. See also Kiss, in Brown Weiss, (1992b), p. 325; Caldwell, (1990a), p. 68; Springer, (1983), pp. 13–15; Magraw, in Magraw, (1991), ch. 1.

[116] See also Kiss, (1989a), pp. 80–103.

management regime should therefore strike a useful balance between the two approaches.

L. *The Preventive and the Remedial Approach*

An essential problem that needs to be addressed by the future waste management regime is the application and enforcement of relevant rules. In this respect, there has been a shift in international policy and law from the traditional mechanisms focusing on remedy after the event to mechanisms that aim for prevention of the damage.[117] This so-called preventive approach, advocating a replacement of the imperative 'react and correct' with the imperative 'forecast and prevent', is strongly supported in recent academic discussion.[118] It is increasingly recognized that in the context of environmental damage, prevention is usually more effective and less costly than remedy. In more extreme cases, damage can be irreparable, or the harmful processes irreversible.

A growing number of binding and non-binding international legal instruments specifically advocate the preventive approach.[119] Methods of regulation which are indicative of the preventive approach are increasingly used in environmental treaties. These include the absolute or conditional prohibition of certain activities; the requirement of PIC or prior authorization of activities; requirements of prior EIA and evaluation; requirements of exchange of information, consultation, co-operation, and technical and financial assistance; requirements of emergency preparedness and elaboration of emergency plans; the adoption and application of technical norms setting qualitative and quantitative standards; and the establishment of specialized institutions with the functions of policy formulation, facilitation of international co-operation, and compliance monitoring.[120]

[117] For a discussion cf. Springer, (1983), pp. 123 et seq., 141 et seq.; Caldwell, (1990); Kiss, (1989a); Carroll, (1988).

[118] The need for a preventive approach is spelled out, for example, in the Declaration of the 1st World Climate Conference, 1979 (repr. in EPL 5(1979), p. 65); and in para. 4 of the Conclusions of the Siena Forum (see n. 85 above). See Brown Weiss, (1992b), especially the chapters by Iwama, Orrego Vicuña, Könz, and Timoshenko. See also Koh, in Handl and Lutz, (1989a), p. 192; Magraw, ibid., p. 242; Hohmann, (1990), p. 49 et seq.; idem, (1989), p. 538 et seq.; Kiss, (1989a), p. 131.

[119] For an overview see UNEP Governing Council Decision SS.II/4/B (3 August 1990), operational para. 4. Relevant legal instruments include the 1992 UN/ECE Convention on the Protection and Use of Transboundary Watercourses and International Lakes, (discussed in Chapter 5(D) below); the 1992 UN/ECE Convention on the Transboundary Effects of Industrial Accidents (repr. in 31 ILM, (1992), p. 1333); Article 130r of the Single European Act and the EU's Action Programmes for the Environment (discussed in Johnson and Corcelle, (1989), p. 12, and Krämer, (1990), p. 61 et seq.); the 1982 World Charter for Nature adopted by the UNGA; the 1982 Nairobi Declaration adopted by the UNEP Governing Council; Article 35 of the Lomé IV Convention; and Chapters 17, 20 and 21 of UNCED's Agenda 21. See also WCED, *Our Common Future*, (1987), p. 349.

[120] Cf. Könz, in Brown Weiss, (1992b), p. 163 et seq.; Koh, in Handl and Lutz, (1989a), p. 192; Springer, (1983), p. 145 et seq.

A specific expression of the preventive approach is the precautionary principle, providing that action to protect the environment against potentially harmful activities should be taken even where there is no scientific certainty regarding the effects of that activity, or regarding the causal link between the activity and the effects.[121] This principle has recently gained wide recognition in environmental policy and law.[122] Its significance for the hazardous waste cycle is probably not as great as it is for environmental issues such as climate change, where much research remains to be done on the causal link between activity and effect. In the case of hazardous wastes, the ill-effects on human health and the environment appear to a large extent known and undisputed. Nevertheless, the precautionary principle should be reflected in the future waste management regime, as was pointed out in the relevant Chapters of UNCED's Agenda 21.

In the context of the issue of hazardous waste management in particular, the preventive approach has widespread support. Waste prevention was designated by UNEP's Montevideo Programme of 1981 (see Chapter 2(A) below) as the main objective of waste-related activities. Chapters 20 and 21 of Agenda 21 define the overall objective of any waste-related activities as the prevention or minimization of the generation of hazardous wastes, and their management in a way that does not cause harm to human health and the environment. The achievement of this objective is seen as part of an integrated 'cleaner production' approach. Chapter 20 identifies and elaborates four programme areas, all of which reflect the preventive approach:

(a) promoting the prevention and minimization of hazardous wastes;
(b) promoting and strengthening institutional capacities in hazardous waste management;
(c) promoting and strengthening international co-operation in this field; and
(d) preventing illegal traffic in hazardous wastes.

[121] For an extensive discussion of the precautionary principle and its interpretation cf. Gündling, in *Int'l. J. Est. & Coastal L.* 5 (1990), p. 23 et seq.; Freestone, in Churchill and Freestone, (1991), ch. 2. Cf. also the study prepared by OECD for submission to the 14th Consultative Meeting of the Contracting Parties to the London Convention (IMO Doc. LDC14/INF.9); and the study by Hey, commissioned by the Secretariat of the London Convention (IMO Doc. LDC 14/4).

[122] The legal instruments advocating the precautionary principle include most of the recent sectoral pollution control treaties discussed in Chapter 5 below, as well as the 1990 OPPRC; the 1988 CRAMRA (Article 4); the 1992 Framework Convention on Climate Change (Article 3(3)); the 1987 Montreal Protocol on Substances that Deplete the Ozone Layer (preamble); the 1992 UN/ECE Convention on the Protection and Use of Transboundary Watercourses and International Lakes (Article 4(5)); and a large number of non-binding legal instruments, including the 1992 Rio Declaration (Principle 15). The environmental policies of the EU and the OECD (discussed in Chapter 4 below) also support the precautionary principle, as does the 1992 Maastricht Treaty (Article 130r).

The waste management strategies that are being formulated under the auspices of UNEP, IMO and UN/ECE, as well as the environmental policies of the EU and the OECD, embody the same approach. It appears obvious, therefore, that a future hazardous waste management regime should rely primarily on measures that reflect the preventive approach.

While emphasizing the importance of the preventive approach, remedial mechanisms should nevertheless not be neglected. On the one hand, they can act as deterrents. On the other hand, where preventive measures fail and environmental harm is caused, mechanisms must be in place to ensure that steps are taken to restore the affected parts of the environment and compensate the victims.[123] The hazardous waste cycle, especially if it involves transport over long distances, is prone to accidents that can cause severe environmental damage. In this context, the so-called 'polluter pays principle' must be taken into account. This principle calls for the allocation of the financial consequences of a harmful activity not to the victims, to uninvolved states or individuals, or to the international community as a whole, but to the person who has control over the polluting activity. This is usually also the person who benefits from it economically. The polluter pays principle was first developed by the OECD, but has recently received more widespread support.[124] The future waste management regime should therefore take into account both the preventive and the remedial approaches, aiming to achieve a useful balance between the two. The means of achieving this aim will be discussed more fully in the context of mechanisms ensuring compliance in Chapter 6 below.

M. *Conclusions*

In summarizing the conclusions to be drawn from the above, we can submit that a future global waste management regime, in order to be effective, should be primarily global, holistic and integrated, and should focus on the preventive approach. It should, however, make allowance for the adoption of regional rules—provided that they conform to specifically defined global

[123] Cf. Könz, in Brown Weiss, (1992b), p. 168 et seq.; Magraw, in Magraw, (1991), p. 8.

[124] See Boyle, in Francioni and Scovazzi, (1991), p. 368 et seq.; Springer, (1983), p. 18 et seq. The polluter pays principle is reflected in OECD Council Recommendation C(74)223 on the Implementation of the Polluter Pays Principle (repr. in OECD, (1986a), p. 26), and in Council Recommendation C(89)88 on Application of the Polluter Pays Principle to Accidental Pollution (repr. in Hohmann, (1992), Vol. 1, p. 382). It is also embodied in Article 130r of the Single European Act (for a discussion cf. Krämer, (1992), p. 244 et seq.; Gautier, in *La réparation des dommages catastrophiques*, (1990), p. 391 et seq.). Other legal instruments expressly incorporating the polluter pays principle include the more recent of the sectoral pollution control regimes discussed in Chapter 5 below, as well as the 1990 OPPRC; Principle 16 of the Rio Declaration; and Chapter 17 of Agenda 21. The principle is also supported by a number of international legal instruments addressing civil liability for environmental damage (cf. Chapter 6(J) below).

standards—and for the application of existing sectoral rules that are in line with its objectives and provisions. It should take sufficient account of sovereign rights of states, particularly those which are at a disadvantage in controlling the waste streams, and provide remedial measures to offset any failings of the preventive rules. The following chapters will examine the feasibility of building such a regime, with the Basel Convention as a basis and related international rules on pollution control and waste management as constituent elements.

2

The Basel Convention: an Analysis and Assessment*

THE ELABORATION OF THE BASEL CONVENTION

A. *Preliminary Work within UNEP: The Montevideo Programme and the Cairo Guidelines*

UNEP's concern with the hazardous waste cycle dates from the early 1980s. The issue was not included as a priority area in the original Action Plan adopted by the Governing Council of UNEP at its first session in 1973.[1] It did not receive much attention until 1981, when the Governing Council mandated a group of senior government officials expert in environmental law to determine major subject areas suitable for increased global and regional co-operation in the elaboration of environmental law.[2] The Montevideo Programme for the Development and Periodic Review of Environmental Law, which sets out the conclusions and recommendations of the experts and constitutes a fundamental policy document for UNEP, identified the transport, handling and disposal of toxic and dangerous wastes as one of these major subject areas. It recommended the preparation of guidelines and principles which could lead to a global convention on hazardous wastes, within the framework of UNEP and in co-operation with other competent organizations. This priority was reaffirmed and strengthened by the second meeting of the senior government officials, convened in Rio de Janeiro in 1991 to review the Montevideo Programme.[3]

Based on the Montevideo Programme, the Governing Council in 1982

* An earlier version of this chapter appeared in ICLQ 41/3(1992), p. 530 et seq., entitled 'The International Regulation of Transboundary Traffic in Hazardous Wastes: The 1989 Basel Convention'.

[1] Decisions of the Governing Council of UNEP at its 1st session: *Action Plan for the Human Environment: programme development and priorities*, 3 July 1973, (UNEP/GC/10), reprinted in ILM 12 (1973) p. 1183 et seq.

[2] UNEP Governing Council Decision 9/19A of 26 May 1981 (UNEP/GC. 9/19A), recalling Decision 8/15 of the previous year (UNEP/GC.8/15) and UNGA Resolution 35/74 of 5 December 1980.

[3] UNEP, Montevideo Programme (Nairobi 1982); *Report of the Ad Hoc Meeting of Senior Government Officials Expert in Environmental Law to the Governing Council of UNEP*, 7 December 1981 (UNEP/GC.10/5/Add. 2); UNEP, *Review of the Montevideo Programme 1981–1991* (Nairobi 1991); *Conclusions and Recommendations of the Rio Meeting of the Senior Government Officials*, repr. in EPL 22/2(1992) p. 123. Cf. also Caldwell, (1990), p. 121.

authorized the convening of a working group of experts to develop guidelines or principles on the environmentally sound transport, management and disposal of hazardous wastes.[4] The Cairo Guidelines and Principles for the Environmentally Sound Management of Hazardous Wastes, elaborated by this working group, set out the major principles of hazardous waste management in rather broad and general terms. As a non-binding legal instrument, they are primarily designed to assist governments in the development and implementation of their national management policies for hazardous wastes.[5]

The Cairo Guidelines incorporate a number of fundamental principles related to the management of hazardous wastes, whether or not subject to transboundary movement. Their declared aim is to ensure the protection of human health and the environment against the ill-effects of hazardous wastes. The Guidelines embody the principles of waste minimization, promotion of new low-waste technologies, exchange of information, and transfer of technology. They recommend specific measures to be taken by states to ensure the environmentally sound management of hazardous wastes under their jurisdiction. These include the establishment of national authorities with the competence and expertise to monitor waste disposal activities, and of an authorization system for waste brokers.

The Cairo Guidelines contain a definition of 'pollution by hazardous wastes', thus specifically designating the effects of hazardous wastes on the environment as pollution. They also affirm existing customary law rules on transboundary pollution in the context of waste disposal facilities (see Chapter 1(F) above): they set out the principles of prior notification to states likely to be affected by such facilities, consultation in good faith with potentially affected states, and equal access for nationals of a potentially affected state to relevant administrative and judicial proceedings in the state of origin. They call for the elaboration of safety standards, and for contingency planning. The Cairo Guidelines also address the issue of transboundary movements of hazardous wastes, laying down the principles of non-discrimination,[6] and prior notification to the prospective states of import and transit. They recommend that no export of hazardous wastes should be permitted unless subject to the prior consent of such states.

[4] UNEP Governing Council Decision 10/24 (31 May 1982).

[5] UNEP, Environmental Law Guidelines and Principles no. 8: *Environmentally Sound Management of Hazardous Wastes*, Nairobi 1987. For a discussion cf. Kiss and Shelton (1991), p. 326. See also the reports of the Ad Hoc Working Group of Experts on the Environmentally Sound Management of Hazardous Wastes on its three sessions, March 1984 (UNEP/WG.95/5); December 1984 (UNEP/WG.111/3); December 1985 (UNEP/WG.122/3).

[6] For an outline and discussion of the principle of non-discrimination cf. Dupuy, in Magraw, (1991), pp. 67–8.

B. *The Basel Negotiation Process*

1. The Working Group and the Basel Conference

In June 1987, the Governing Council of UNEP approved the Cairo Guidelines. At the same time, based on a joint proposal by Switzerland and Hungary, it mandated the Executive Director of UNEP to convene a working group with the task of elaborating a global convention on the control of transboundary movements of hazardous wastes, drawing on the Cairo Guidelines and the relevant work of national, regional and international bodies. The Council also authorized the Executive Director to convene, in early 1989, a diplomatic conference to adopt and sign the convention.[7] This decision and the resulting negotiations were subsequently endorsed by the Governing Council, and by the UN General Assembly.[8]

The schedule determined by the Governing Council allowed for a period of less than two years for the drafting and negotiation of the convention. The Ad Hoc Working Group of Legal and Technical Experts with a Mandate to Prepare a Global Convention on the Control of Transboundary Movements of Hazardous Wastes 'Working Group' began its deliberations at an organizational meeting in October 1987. The discussions proceeded on the basis of a first draft convention prepared by the UNEP Secretariat. Subsequently, five sessions of the Working Group were held between February 1988 and March 1989. Experts from ninety-six states participated in one or more of the sessions, and representatives of over fifty international organizations and NGOs attended as observers.[9]

The Conference of Plenipotentiaries on the Global Convention on the Control of Transboundary Movements of Hazardous Wastes, convened at the invitation of the Swiss government from 20–22 March 1989 in Basel (Basel Conference), and in which 116 states were represented, considered the final draft of the Convention submitted to it by the Working Group. The Basel Convention was adopted unanimously by the Conference on 22 March 1989. The Conference also adopted eight resolutions related to the

[7] UNEP Governing Council Decision 14/30 (17 June 1987).

[8] UNEP Governing Council Decisions 15/33 (25 May 1989), SS.II/4/A (3 August 1990), and 16/30 (31 May 1991); UNGA Resolutions 42/183 (11 December 1987), 43/212 (20 December 1988) and 44/226 (22 December 1989) (repr. in Kwiatkowska and Soons, (1993), p. 81 et seq., p. 192 et seq).

[9] See the Reports of the Working Group meetings as follows: organizational meeting, Budapest (Hungary), 27–29 October 1987 (UNEP/WG.180/3); 1st session, Geneva (Switzerland), 1–5 February 1988 (UNEP/WG.182/3); 2nd session, Caracas (Venezuela), 6–10 June 1988 (UNEP/WG.186/3); 3rd session, Geneva, 7–16 November 1988 (UNEP/WG.189/3); 4th session, Luxembourg, 30 January–3 February 1989 (UNEP/WG.190/4); 5th session, Basel (Switzerland), 13–17 March 1989 (*Final Report of the Working Group* with *Report on the Fifth Session* as Annex I: UNEP/IG.80/4); First Draft Convention on the Control of the Transboundary Movements of Hazardous Wastes, 15 October 1987 (UNEP/WG. 180/2).

further development and the implementation of the Basel Convention.[10] 105 states and the EU signed the Final Act of the Basel Conference. On 22 March 1990, when the Basel Convention was closed for signature in accordance with Article 21, fifty three states and the EU had signed it.[11] It entered into force on 5 May 1992 upon deposit of the 20th instrument of accession (Article 25). As of 9 February 1995, eighty one states and the EU had ratified or acceded to the Basel Convention, and it had entered into force for seventy two states and the EU. Regional distribution of the Basel parties was as follows: twelve parties from Africa, twenty from Asia, twenty four from the group referred to as Western Europe and others, ten from Eastern Europe, and fifteen from Latin America.[12]

In accordance with Article 15(1), the Conference of the Parties to the Basel Convention met for the first time in Piriapolis (Uruguay) in December 1992, seven months after the entry into force of the Convention. The second meeting of the Conference was convened in Geneva in March 1994. Both Conferences, as well as the preparatory sessions immediately preceding them, were well attended by parties and by observers representing non-parties, international organizations, and NGOs. In accordance with its functions as laid down in the Convention, the Conference at both meetings considered procedural and substantive matters related to the further development and the implementation of the Convention, and adopted pertinent decisions. The ground for this work was prepared by numerous working group and inter-agency meetings convened in the intersessional

[10] *Final Act of the Conference of Plenipotentiaries on the Global Convention on the Control of Transboundary Movements of Hazardous Wastes*, 22 March 1989.

[11] The following states signed the Basel Convention: Afghanistan; Argentina; Austria; Bahrain; Belgium; Bolivia; Canada; Chile; China; Colombia; Cyprus; Denmark; Ecuador; El Salvador; Finland; France; Federal Republic of Germany; German Democratic Republic; Greece; Guatemala; Haiti; Hungary; India; Ireland; Israel; Italy; Jordan; Kuwait; Lebanon; Liechtenstein; Luxembourg; Mexico; Netherlands; New Zealand; Nigeria; Norway; Panama; Philippines; Poland; Portugal; Saudi Arabia; Spain; Sweden; Switzerland; Syria; Thailand; Turkey; USSR; United Arab Emirates; UK; USA; Uruguay; and Venezuela (information received from the Interim Secretariat of the Basel Convention, April 1991). In some cases, newly founded states have in the interim succeded to the original signatories.

[12] The following states are parties: Antigua and Barbuda; Argentina; Australia; Austria; Bahamas; Bahrain; Bangladesh; Belgium; Brazil; Canada; Chile; China; Comoros; Croatia; Cuba; Cyprus; Czech Republic; Denmark; Ecuador; Egypt; El Salvador; Estonia; Finland; France; Greece; Hungary; India; Indonesia; Iran; Ireland; Israel; Italy; Ivory Coast; Japan; Jordan; Kuwait; Latvia; Lebanon; Liechtenstein; Luxembourg; Malawi; Malaysia; Maldives; Mauritius; Mexico; Monaco; Netherlands; New Zealand; Nigeria; Norway; Oman; Pakistan; Panama; Peru; Philippines; Poland; Portugal; Republic of Korea; Romania; Russian Federation; St. Kitts and Nevis; St. Lucia; Saudia Arabia; Senegal; Seychelles; Slovak Republic; Slovenia; South Africa; Spain; Sri Lanka; Sweden; Switzerland; Syria; Tanzania; Turkey; Trinidad and Tobago; United Arab Emirates; UK; Uruguay; Zaire; and Zambia. Germany informed the Secretariat in October 1994 that it was about to deposit its instrument of ratification (information received from the Secretariat of the Basel Convention, March 1995).

periods. The third meeting of the Conference of the Parties is scheduled for September 1995 in Geneva, and the fourth meeting for 1997.[13]

2. Background to the negotiations

An account of the negotiation process leading to the adoption of the Basel Convention and the discussions of the Conference of the Parties is, however, incomplete without an outline of the background, and the general difficulties which emerged during the deliberations of the Working Group, and continued to some extent after the adoption of the Convention. The Basel negotiations proved to be extremely difficult and contentious. This was mainly due to the great political sensitivity of the issue, which intensified the difficulty of accommodating the aims of states with widely diverging situations and interests. The negotiations accordingly provoked considerable interest, which in turn resulted in numerous academic writings analyzing the negotiations themselves as well as the provisions of the Convention.[14]

During the mid-1980s, the political discussion of the issue of international transport of hazardous wastes in general, and that of illegal transboundary traffic in such wastes in particular, had gathered momentum, reaching its culmination in 1988 in widely publicized media reports on incidents involving the illegal dumping of toxic wastes from industrialized nations in Third World countries (see Chapter 1 above). The problem was taken up by governments and intergovernmental agencies, as well as non-governmental environmental groups, at national and international levels. The growing interest in the issue is reflected in the number of states represented at the sessions of the Working Group, which increased from twenty four at the organizational meeting to almost eighty at the last session, and

[13] See the reports of the Conference of the Parties on its 1st meeting, 4 December 1992, (UNEP/CHW. 1/24) and on its 2nd meeting, 25 March 1994, (UNEP/CHW.2/30). The Decisions adopted by the Conference at the two meetings are reproduced in Basel Convention Series/SBC No 94/008 (Geneva, June 1994). An overview of the intersessional work is given in the relevant reports of the Executive Director and the Secretariat to the Conference: Doc. UNEP/CHW.1/2 of 7 July 1992 for the 1st meeting (*Executive Director's Report to the 1st Conference of the Parties*); Docs. UNEP/CHW.2/2–2/23 for the 2nd meeting (for detailed references see the list of documents before the Conference at its 2nd meeting, Doc. UNEP/CHW.2/INF.3).

[14] See among many others Wynne (1989); Bartram and Engel (1989); Clerc, (1990); Gröbl, (1989); Bernstorff, (1989); Handl, (1989); Huntoon, (1989); Moisé, (1989); Rublack, (1989); Bothe, (1990); Cusack, (1990); Abrams, (1990); Hackett, (1990); Kummer and Rummel-Bulska, (1990); Sebek, (1990); de Villeneuve, (1990); van der Mensbrugghe, (1990); Montgomery, (1990); Lang, in Lang, Neuhold, and Zemanek, (1991); Kiss, (1991); Kiss and Shelton (1991), p. 315 et seq.; Hilz and Radka, (1991); Birnie and Boyle, (1992), p. 332 et seq.; Rosencranz and Eldridge, (1992); Walsh, (1992). Kempel, (1993), gives a detailed analysis of the negotiation process.

in a similar increase in the number of organizations participating in the proceedings as observers.[15]

Due to these developments, the focus of public opinion during the negotiation process on the Basel Convention was almost exclusively on the 'North–South' aspect of the problem: the threat posed to the environment of ill-equipped developing countries by the illegal import of hazardous wastes from industrialized nations. The fact that the vast majority of international waste transport takes place between industrialized nations (see Chapter 1 above) was widely ignored. This added a political dimension to the negotiation process, which had considerable influence on the direction of the discussions.[16] The elaboration of the Basel Convention was seen by many primarily as an opportunity to put a stop to illegal international waste traffic from North to South. A substantial number of developing countries, led by member states of the OAU, regarded the deliberations as an opportunity to demonstrate their solidarity in refusing to tolerate the use of their territories as dumping grounds for toxic wastes from the rich states of the industrialized world. Their demand for a complete ban of all transboundary movements of hazardous wastes world-wide was strongly supported by a number of environmental NGOs.[17] On the other hand, many developed countries, focusing on the option of controlled waste traffic, were not prepared to agree with any proposed measures that would put too many restrictions on the trade in wastes—especially recyclable materials with an economic value—amongst industrialized states. UNEP adopted the position that a complete ban of international hazardous waste transport was not the best solution from an environmental viewpoint, since it would preclude such transport even in cases where waste disposal in a country other than the country of origin was more environmentally sound (see Chapter 1 above).[18] This position attracted harsh criticism from developing countries as well as environmental NGOs, who saw it as a betrayal of their struggle against illegal traffic, and as an active support of the interests of

[15] Cf. the reports of the Working Group, see n. 9 above.

[16] *Note from the Executive Director of UNEP to the Working Group*, 23 May 1988 (UNEP/WG. 186/2); *Report of the Working Group on its 2nd session* (UNEP/WG.186/3), p. 2; *Report of the Meeting of the Legal Experts Sub-Working Group*, 10–12 August 1988, (UNEP/WG.189/2), p. 2.; *Report of the Working Group on its 3rd session* (UNEP/WG.189/3), in particular p. 5.

[17] See e.g. the statement of the representative of Jamaica at the 2nd session of the Working Group (UNEP/WG.186/3, p. 5), the statement of the representative of Nigeria at the 3rd session (UNEP/WG.189/3, p. 5), and the statement of the observer from Greenpeace International at the 2nd session (UNEP/WG.186/3, p. 9). See also Greenpeace *Waste Trade Update*, Vol. 2, Issue 2, 1 March 1989; *New Scientist*, 19 November 1988; *Time Magazine*, 3 April 1989; *New York Times*, 23 March 1989.

[18] Cf. e.g. *Ending the Commerce in Poison*, statement by Dr. M.K. Tolba, Executive Director of UNEP, to the Basel Conference (Basel, 20 March 1989). Cf. also Tolba, (1990), p. 205; Bartram and Engel, (1989), p. 117.

the industrialized world. Disagreement between developed and developing countries also arose on other key issues.

As the negotiations progressed, the rift between industrialized and developing countries deepened. Following the adoption by the Council of Ministers of the OAU, in May 1988, of a resolution on dumping of nuclear and industrial wastes in Africa, which condemned the import of such wastes into the African continent as 'a crime against Africa and the African people' (see Chapter 3(F) below), the OAU member states consolidated their position in the negotiations, demanding the incorporation of strong safeguards against waste traffic from developed to developing countries into the draft Convention, as well as far-reaching provisions for financial and technical assistance to developing countries in the field of waste management.[19] An African ministerial conference, convened in Dakar in January 1989 by the government of Senegal in co-operation with UNEP as a forum for discussion of the contentious issues by representatives of African states and a small number of Western states, led to open disagreement between the two sides. The only result of the conference was a very broadly worded appeal for active participation by African states in the Basel negotiations.[20] At the fourth session of the Working Group, held shortly afterwards, disagreement was so strong that the Group failed to produce a further amended version of the draft Convention, as had been planned originally; instead, agreement was only reached on a limited number of provisions. At this point, doubts emerged concerning the feasibility of elaborating an agreed draft for submission to the Basel Conference, and therefore concerning the success of the Conference itself. In an attempt to redeem the situation, the Executive Director of UNEP convened, at short notice, a round of informal negotiations of the Working Group, where the most contentious issues were discussed.[21] Based on the results of these talks, which took place in early March 1989, the Working Group was able to resume its work at its fifth session, which immediately preceded the Conference of Plenipotentiaries.[22]

[19] UNEP, (1989a).

[20] *Revised Draft Final Joint Declaration of the Dakar Ministerial Conference on Hazardous Wastes*, 6 January 1989 (UNEP/IG.81/L.1); *Draft Report of the Dakar Ministerial Conference*, 27 January 1989 (UNEP/IG. 81/L.2 and 81/L.2/Add.1). Neither document was taken beyond the draft stage. Of the draft declaration prepared by UNEP, only the first paragraph was adopted.

[21] Cf. *Report of the Working Group on its 4th session* (UNEP/WG.190/4), in particular pp. 11–12. See also the *Note by the Executive Director on some points of the Hazardous Wastes Convention which were not resolved at the 4th session of the Ad Hoc Working Group*, 10 February 1989 (UNEP/WG.191/2) (*Executive Director's Luxembourg Note*); also Greenpeace *Waste Trade Update*, Vol. 2, Issue 2, 1 March 1989.

[22] *Final Report of the Working Group*, 22 March 1989 (UNEP/IG.80/4), Annex I: *Report of the Working Group on its 5th session*, p. 7. For the proposals put forward as a result of the informal discussions, see *Proposals by the Executive Director for consideration by the Ad Hoc*

At the Basel Conference, the same difficulties presented themselves. They were aggravated by the fact that due to the tight schedule, only 3 days were available in which to reach agreement. In addition, a substantial number of countries were represented that had not participated in the previous negotiations, which meant that the discussion on many issues had to be reopened. After the first day of the negotiations, the success of the Conference was again uncertain. Parallel to the discussion in the plenary session, another informal round of talks was convened by the Executive Director of UNEP between a limited number of representatives of each group of states supporting the various conflicting viewpoints. Based on the conclusions reached in this informal discussion, the plenary session finally reached an agreement on the text of the Convention in the early hours of the last day of the Conference.

At the opening of the adoption ceremony, a statement was made on behalf of the President of Mali, then Chairman of the OAU, to the effect that the African states were not prepared to sign the Convention, as they considered it too weak, and that they had agreed to decide on their final position after further discussions within the framework of the OAU.[23] This came as a considerable surprise to the other delegations. A number of other states, including important industrialized states such as the Federal Republic of Germany, the USA, the UK, and Japan, also deferred their decision on signature, for exactly the opposite reason. This meant in effect that there was considerable danger of the Basel Convention remaining an ineffective declaration of intentions, should all these states ultimately decide against becoming parties to it. It also shows how precarious the agreed compromise was. On the key issue of a complete ban on international hazardous waste transport, the outcome was considered mainly by developing countries and environmental NGOs (as well as a number of academic writers) to be less than satisfactory: a prohibition of transboundary movements of hazardous wastes in general, or from developed to developing countries in particular, was rejected due to the opposition voiced by industrialized states. At the suggestion of Greenpeace International, a provision was introduced by way of compromise which mandated the Conference of the Parties to reconsider the issue at regular intervals.[24]

Working Group at its 5th session, 12–13 March 1989 (UNEP/WG.191/3, 191/3/Add.1–7) (*Executive Director's Basel Proposals*).

[23] See UNEP, (1989a), for a summary of the OAU representative's address to the Basel Conference.

[24] On the pertinent discussion see: *Report of the Working Group on its 3rd session* (UNEP/WG. 189/3), pp. 10, 37; *Report on its 4th session* (UNEP/WG. 190/4), p. 20. See also the statements of various delegates to the Working Group (UNEP/WG.186/2, p. 5, UNEP/WG.189/3, p. 5), and the proposal by Nigeria at the Basel Conference (UNEP/IG.80/CRP.1/Rev.1); also the *Note by the Executive Director on the Further Development of a Global Convention on the Control of Transboundary Movements of Hazardous Wastes*, 2 August 1988; *Executive Director's Basel Proposals* (UNEP/WG.191/3), p. 5.

An analysis and critical assessment of the provisions of the Basel Convention has to take into consideration the difficulties faced by its drafters, as outlined above. As we will see, a number of the Convention's provisions, particularly in areas which were subject to substantive disagreement during the negotiation process, are the result of last-minute compromise. This accounts for the complexity of the wording or the lack of precision in some provisions.

3. Subsequent developments

Developments subsequent to the adoption of the Basel Convention show an increased acceptance of its fundamental concepts by states. The activities of the Secretariat and the various bodies established under the Convention, subsequently endorsed by the Conference of the Parties, contributed to the implementation and further development of the Convention. The ratification process, initially slow, has accelerated dramatically: whereas accession by the twenty states required to bring the Convention into force took three years, the number of parties had increased to thirty six one year after entry into force, and to sixty four at the time of the second meeting of the Conference of the Parties, just under two years after entry into force. The OAU has since withdrawn its opposition to the Basel Convention, and twelve African states have so far acceded to it. The EU and a large majority of the OECD member states—including the states that had voiced the strongest reservations at the time of the adoption of the Convention—have also become parties. Chapter 20 of Agenda 21 adopted by UNCED in 1992 promoted many of the Convention's principles, and endorsed activities already undertaken by the Secretariat. The Commission on Sustainable Development in July 1994 supported the actions that were consequently taken, and set out guidelines for further activity.[25] With a fairly large number of parties and an established infrastructure, the survival of the Convention is obviously no longer in question.

The further development of the Basel Convention within the framework of the Conference of the Parties and its auxiliary bodies has given rise to a number of new controversies. The long-standing issue of a ban on exports of hazardous wastes from industrialized to non-industrialized countries was also followed up; it occupied a central position in the discussion at both meetings of the Conference of the Parties held to date.[26] Heated debates

[25] Cf. *Note of the Executive Director of UNEP to the Conference of the Parties on Issues Raised in Agenda 21 which have Relevance to the Basel Convention*, 15 September 1992, (Conference Doc. UNEP/CHW.1/7/Add.1); *Report of the Commission on Sustainable Development on its 2nd session*, 12 July 1994, (Doc. E/CN.17/1994/20).

[26] See *Report of the Ad Hoc Meeting of Government-Designated Experts on a Draft International Strategy for the Environmentally Sound Management of Hazardous Wastes*, December 1991, (UNEP/CHW/WG.2/1/3); *Note by the Executive Director to the Conference of the Parties*, 30 November 1992, (Conference Doc. UNEP CHW.1/21).

and extensive pressure from Greenpeace and a number of developing country parties, supported by the Nordic states, led first to a compromise decision in December 1992, requesting developed countries to refrain from exporting hazardous wastes for disposal to developing countries, and submitting the question of export of wastes destined for recycling or recovery to further study by the Technical Working Group established under the Convention.[27] In March 1994, the Conference adopted Decision II/12, which bans immediately all traffic in hazardous wastes destined for final disposal from OECD to non-OECD countries, and provides for phase-out of traffic in hazardous wastes destined for recycling or resource recovery from OECD to non-OECD countries by the end of 1997.[28] This constitutes the one substantive change to the policy to be followed under the Convention thus far introduced by the Conference of the Parties.

The debate is continuing. In March 1995, the four Nordic states (Denmark, Finland, Norway, and Sweden) submitted to the Secretariat of the Basel Convention a formal proposal for the inclusion of a new Article 4a, in accordance with Article 17. The proposed provision would incorporate the substance of Decision II/12, thus making the ban formally binding. An alternative amendment was proposed by the Commission of the EU. According to the EU proposal, the export ban from OECD to non-OECD states would cover only wastes destined for final disposal. A decision on both proposals will have to be taken by the third Conference of the Parties in Geneva, which is likely to be dominated by the pertinent debate. The issue has given rise to procedural and substantive controversy within the EU: whereas the Commission contests the competence of its members to submit an amendment proposal, the three Nordic countries which are EU members are not prepared to withdraw their proposal in favour of that submitted by the Commission.

STRUCTURE AND CHARACTERISTICS OF THE BASEL CONVENTION

Taking into account Decision II/12 of the Conference of the Parties, the fundamental principles of the Basel Convention, as it stands, can be summarized as follows:

(1) The generation of hazardous wastes should be reduced to a minimum (principle of waste minimization).
(2) Where it is unavoidable, the wastes should be disposed of as close as possible to the source of generation (principle of proximity of disposal).

[27] Conference Decision I/22, 4 December 1992.
[28] Conference Decision II/12, 25 March 1994.

(3) In a number of instances, the export of hazardous wastes is prohibited absolutely: hazardous wastes may not be exported from OECD to non-OECD countries, or from any party state to Antarctica, or to a state not party to either the Basel Convention or a treaty establishing equivalent standards, or to parties which have banned the import of hazardous wastes.

(4) In all other cases, transboundary hazardous waste movements must conform to the provisions of the Convention: they are permissible only if they present the best solution from an environmental viewpoint; if the principles of environmentally sound management and non-discrimination are observed; and if they take place in conformity with the regulatory system established by the Convention.

(5) The cornerstone of this regulatory system is the prior informed consent (PIC) of the prospective states of import and transit.

(6) Hazardous wastes that have been exported illegally, as well as legally exported hazardous wastes that cannot be safely disposed of in the state of destination, must be re-imported into the state of origin.

Due to disagreement on some points during the negotiation process, these principles are not followed consistently throughout the Convention: they have been weakened or modified in some instances. On the other hand, they have to some extent been followed up and developed further by the Conference of the Parties.

C. *The Scope of the Basel Convention*

4. Wastes covered by the Basel Convention

The question which wastes should be included in the scope of the Basel Convention generated considerable debate during the negotiations, and is subject to ongoing controversy. The Convention adopts the concept of the 1985 OECD draft agreement on hazardous wastes (never finalized, see Chapter 4(E) below) which defines the wastes to be covered by reference to a set of technical annexes, supplemented by a provision that allows every party to determine, by national legislation, additional hazardous wastes. The relevant annexes to the Basel Convention are closely modelled on the corresponding annexes to the relevant legislation of the EU and the OECD, discussed in Chapter 4 below.[29]

4.1 *The definition of wastes and the 'recycling dilemma'* 'Wastes' are defined by the Basel Convention as substances which are subject to disposal (Article 2(1)). The notion of 'disposal' in turn is defined by reference to Annex IV, listing the disposal operations covered by the Convention (Article

[29] For an analysis of this definition and its implications for the application of the Convention see Smets, (1991), p. 141 et seq.

2(4)). In addition to operations which lead to final disposal of the wastes, such as landfill, incineration on land and at sea, release into a continental waterbody, and release into seas, including sea-bed insertion (Annex IV A), the definition also includes the recycling and recovery operations listed in Annex IV B. With one minor exception (Article 4(9.b), see para. 6 below), the provisions of the Basel Convention thus apply equally to wastes destined for recycling and wastes destined for final disposal.[30] The Convention does not, in principle, take account of the different reasons for exporting wastes, discussed in Chapter 1 above. This absence of a distinction between 'recyclable' and 'non-recyclable' wastes has long been the object of criticism. The question has significant practical implications in view of the acknowledged benefits and dangers of recycling, briefly discussed in Chapter 1 above: while some feel that the special characteristics of recyclable wastes necessitate the adoption of less stringent rules, others fear that this would encourage fake recycling schemes. At the request of the Conference of the Parties, the Technical Working Group established within the framework of the Convention (see para. 7 below) prepared a fairly extensive analysis of this problem in 1993. The study was endorsed by the Conference, which also mandated the Group to continue to pursue the issue.[31] The problem can be expected to remain on the agenda for some time to come. It is gaining new significance in connection with the attempt to give the prohibition on export of hazardous wastes destined for recycling and disposal from OECD to non-OECD states a legally binding form.

4.2 *Classification of hazardous wastes and hazardous characteristics* A waste is included in the scope of the Basel Convention if it belongs to one of the following two types:

(1) Hazardous wastes. A waste is defined as 'hazardous' if it belongs to any category contained in Annex I to the Convention, unless it does not possess any of the characteristics listed in Annex III (Article 1(1.a)). A waste not covered by Annexes I and III is also considered hazardous for the purposes of the Convention if it is defined as hazardous by the national legislation of one or more of the parties involved in any given movement of the waste in question (Article 1(1.b)). States must inform each other, within six months of becoming parties, through the Convention Secretariat, of the additional wastes they define as hazardous (Article 3).

[30] During the negotiations a distinction between the two categories was briefly considered (Fourth Revised Draft Convention, Article II para. 4, Alternative I, 6 September 1988 (UNEP/WG.189/L.2), but subsequently rejected.

[31] Conference Decision I/16 (1992); *Draft Paper on Transboundary Movement of Hazardous Wastes Destined for Recovery Operations*, prepared by the Technical Working Group, 17 December 1993, (UNEP/CHW.2/12); Conference Decision II/14 (1994).

(2) 'Other wastes'. Annex II lists two types of wastes—household wastes, and residues arising from the incineration of household wastes—which are not defined as hazardous wastes but are also included in the scope of the Convention (Article 1(2)).

This distinction is purely terminological. There is no substantive difference between the two types of wastes in the provisions of the Convention (for this reason, unless stated otherwise, the term 'hazardous wastes' will be used in this study to cover both types of wastes). The latter type was included during the final stages of the drafting process, as a compromise between two opposing groups of negotiating states. The first group insisted on the inclusion of household waste and incinerator ash in the scope of the Convention; the second objected to defining these types of wastes as hazardous, arguing that they are not generally recognized as such.[32]

The Basel Convention's system of classifying hazardous wastes and hazardous characteristics by reference to technical annexes has been subject to criticism: many consider it too wide, allowing a disproportionate range of substances to be included. In fact, one of the key problems with the efficient implementation of the Convention concerns the use of Annex III, which lists hazardous characteristics. There is a lack of criteria to define some of these characteristics, namely the last four classes in the list (H10–H13), whereas others are fairly well defined. Pursuant to a Decision of the Conference of the Parties at its second meeting, UNEP and other interested international organizations are co-operating to develop appropriate criteria.[33] For similar reasons, there are difficulties with the application of some of the categories of wastes listed in Annex I (e.g. Y18: 'residues arising from industrial waste disposal operations').

Another shortcoming of the Basel classification system is that it does not establish minimum values of concentration, so that a substance with a quantitatively insignificant hazardous component may be considered a hazardous waste. This problem is indirectly addressed in a note to Annex III referring to the need for further research into testing methods to determine the hazard potential of the wastes in question. The OECD draft convention of 1985, referred to above, would have established a generic definition of hazardous wastes while placing the burden of proof for the absence of hazardous characteristics on the holder of the wastes.[34] The holder would thus have had

[32] *Report of the Working Group on its 5th session* (UNEP/IG.80/4), Annex I, p. 9; Doc. UNEP/CRP.6, 13 March 1989. See also the *Explanatory Notes with Recommendations for Amending Annexes I–IV of the Fifth Revised Draft Convention*, submitted by the Sub-Group of Technical Experts to study the Annexes, 13 January 1989, (UNEP/WG.190/3 Add.1).

[33] See the relevant report of the Secretariat (UNEP/CHW. 2/22), and Conference Decision II/24 (1994).

[34] Article 1(2) of the OECD draft Convention provided that either the generator or the disposer, depending on the circumstances, 'shall bear the responsibility for establishing that a particular waste is not subject to this agreement . . .'. On this point see also Abrams, (1990), p. 820.

the option of proving that a given waste was not hazardous: he could show, for example, that the hazardous component was so small as to render the whole substance non-hazardous. This concept has not been explicitly included in the Basel Convention. Indeed, the Basel Convention leaves open the question of the burden of proof for the inclusion of a substance in its scope. The inclusion of a pertinent provision was briefly discussed during the negotiations, but agreement was not reached.[35] This may in future prove to be a major loophole.

4.3 *Exclusion clauses* Paragraphs 3 and 4 of Article 1 exclude certain types of wastes from the scope of the Basel Convention. The exclusion of all radioactive wastes (para. 3) was proposed by the UNEP Secretariat in the first draft Convention, the reason being that such wastes are subject to control by the IAEA.[36] At the time of the Basel negotiations, work on the IAEA Code of Practice on transboundary movements of nuclear wastes, adopted in September 1990, had already been initiated (see below). This proposal was, however, contested by some of the negotiating states, and others proposed modified versions.[37] The final text excludes 'wastes which, as a result of being radioactive, are subject to other international control systems, including international instruments, applying specifically to radioactive materials' (Article 4(3)). This wording is open to interpretation, in particular the term 'international control systems': depending on the definition of that term, certain types of radioactive wastes may be included in the scope of the Basel Convention.[38] It has also been argued that radioactive wastes excluded from the scope of pertinent regulatory systems should be subject to the Basel Convention. In response to an enquiry from the Basel Convention Secretariat, the IAEA in 1993 confirmed that some radioactive wastes are not subject to relevant IAEA or IMO control systems due to their low level of radioactivity. The Secretariat formed the opinion that such wastes should be covered by the Basel Convention. Another open question is whether radioactive wastes resulting from military activity, also not covered by IAEA control systems, come within the purview of the Basel Convention. The discussion on these questions is continuing.[39]

[35] See e.g. the proposal made by the Executive Director of UNEP, in *Points identified by the Executive Director for further consideration at the Informal Negotiations on Hazardous Wastes*, 4–6 January 1989, p. 3.

[36] First Draft Convention on the Control of the Transboundary Movements of Hazardous Wastes, 15 October 1987, (UNEP/180/2), p. 4.

[37] See for example Doc. UNEP/CRP.24, 17 March 1989.

[38] Cf. the *Final report of the working group on liability* (discussed in Chapter 6 para. 16 below), p. 6, n. 1; also the statement of the respresentative of the USA at the 4th session of the Basel Working Group (UNEP/WG.190/4/Corr.1), and the statement of the representative of the IAEA at the 5th session (UNEP/IG.80/4), Annex I, p. 9.

[39] *Note of the Basel Convention Secretariat to the Conference of the Parties on the scope of the Basel Convention in relation to its applicability to radioactive wastes*, December 1993,

Article 1(4), excluding 'wastes which derive from the normal operation of a ship, the discharge of which is covered by another international instrument', was included during the final stages of the drafting process. It is based on a proposal by the representative of the IMO, and its objective is to make a clear distinction between the substances regulated by the Basel Convention and those regulated by the MARPOL Convention.[40] There has recently been some discussion about the scope of this exclusion clause, as individual operators proposed to interpret it to cover wastes generated by de-sludging of tankers at sea. The term 'wastes derived from the normal operation of a ship', although not formally defined, is generally understood to refer to wastes generated in the course of activities directly related to the purpose of the ship. An unduly wide interpretation of this clause would obviously pose the danger of creating a loophole for hazardous residues resulting from cleaning operations on board a ship.

Apart from generally prohibiting waste exports to Antarctica, the Basel Convention only addresses hazardous wastes subject to 'transboundary movement' (Article 1(1)). This is defined as movement from the area of jurisdiction of one state to or through that of another, or to or through an area beyond national jurisdiction, provided at least two states are involved in the transaction (Article 2(3)). This definition conforms to the traditional understanding of 'transboundary' in the context of pollution, excluding what Magraw terms 'commons pollution'.[41] Thus, the direct transfer of hazardous wastes from the generating state to the high seas as part of the global commons is not covered by the Basel Convention.

5. Territorial scope

During the negotiations, there was considerable disagreement concerning the territorial areas to which the provisions of the Basel Convention should apply. This was particularly important for the position of transit states in the context of the Convention's regulatory system (para. 14 below). States which did not want to see that system applied to transit of hazardous wastes through the airspace or territorial sea of third states objected to the use of the term 'territory', since they feared that it might be interpreted to include those areas.[42] The resulting compromise language is not very clear.

(UNEP/CHW.2/26); Conference Decision II/11 (1994); *Report of the Secretariat to the Ad Hoc Committee on Implementation*, 27 September 1994, (UNEP/CHW/C.1/2/4).

[40] *Report of the Working Group on its 5th session* (UNEP/IG.80/4) Annex I, p. 10. A similar exclusion clause is contained in Article III(1.b) of the London Convention, discussed in Chapter 5 below.

[41] Magraw, in Magraw, (1991); also Kiss, (1989a), pp. 70–1.

[42] Cf. *Report of the Working Group on its 2nd session* (UNEP/WG.186/3), pp. 7, 8; also the summary of the discussions at the 4th session of the Working Group (UNEP/WG.190/4, pp. 5, 8), and of the discussions at the 5th session (UNEP/IG.80/4, p. 11); as well as the

In the final text of the Convention, the term 'territory' is replaced throughout with 'area under the national jurisdiction of a State', which is defined as 'any land, marine area or airspace within which a State exercises administrative and regulatory responsibility in accordance with international law in regard to the protection of human health or the environment' (Article 2(9)). This term, though precisely defined, is not used in the definitions of the states of export, import and transit. 'State of transit', for example, is defined in Article 2(12) as 'any State, other than the State of export or import, *through which* a transboundary movement of hazardous wastes is planned or takes place'. Equivalent wording is used in the definitions of the states of export and import (Article 2(10) and (11)). It was adopted after the experts failed to reach agreement on a specification of the parts of each state's territory to which the regulatory system should apply.[43] The wording of Article 2 therefore leaves open the question whether or not the regulatory system applies to hazardous waste transport through the territorial sea and the airspace of transit states, or to activities in other areas over which a state exercises control, such as the EEZ and the continental shelf.[44] An attempt at addressing this issue was made with the inclusion of Article 4(12), adopted as a last-minute compromise,[45] which reads as follows:

> Nothing in this Convention shall affect in any way the sovereignty of States over their territorial sea established in accordance with international law, and the sovereign rights and the jurisdiction which States have in their exclusive economic zones and their continental shelves in accordance with international law, and the exercise by ships and aircraft of all States of navigational rights and freedoms as provided for in international law and as reflected in relevant international instruments.

This provision does little more than reaffirm the customary rights of states over the component parts of their territory and with respect to parts of the sea and airspace, outlined in Chapter 1, para. 5 above. It does appear to give priority to these rights over any rule established by the Basel Convention, by inferring that a transit state's rights may be exercised only to the extent that they are not in conflict with the international law of the sea and other relevant international rules.[46] It does not, however, make a substantive contribution to the complex issue of the relationship between a transit state's rights and innocent passage, briefly mentioned in Chapter 1,

declaration of Japan made at the time of the adoption of the Basel Convention (attached to the Final Act of the Basel Conference).

[43] See the Fifth Revised Draft Convention (UNEP/WG.189/3) Annex I, p. 6; the Luxembourg Revision of the Preamble and Articles I–XII of the Fifth Revised Draft Convention (UNEP/WG.190/4) Annex I, p. 17; *Executive Director's Basel Proposals* (UNEP/WG.191/3/Add. 1); and the Draft Convention as submitted to the Conference of Plenipotentiaries by the Working Group, 19 March 1989, (UNEP/IG.80/L.4).

[44] For a discussion of this point see van der Mensbrugghe, (1990), pp. 275–7.

[45] *Executive Director's Basel Proposals* (UNEP/WG.191/3/Add. 1).

[46] See e.g. the declaration of the UK at the time of deposit of the instrument of ratification (7 February 1994). A similar view was expressed by Lukasik, *Report on Resolution 2 of the*

para. 5 above. A similar view is expressed by Lang and van der Mensbrugghe, the latter remarking somewhat ironically that 'the problem has been left to Providence' by the Convention.[47] The need to re-address this problem was discussed at the first meeting of the Conference of the Parties, but no concrete action was decided.[48] A further examination of this issue is beyond the scope of this study.

The inclusion of a provision was discussed which would have extended the obligations of a party state to vessels flying its flag and aircraft registered in its territory, and prohibited the export of wastes from a party on vessels or aircraft registered in a non-party.[49] This provision was intended to eliminate the use of flags and registrations of convenience for the purpose of avoiding the application of the Basel Convention's regulatory system. Agreement could not, however, be reached on the inclusion of this article, and it was eventually deleted on the grounds that due to the Convention's adherence to the concept of a limited ban (para. 10 below), it was not necessary to address the issue of flags of convenience.[50] This argument is indeed convincing if both the exporting and the importing state are parties to the Convention. In that case, the provisions of the Basel Convention apply to the movement, regardless of the status of the flag state. If, however, a shipment of hazardous wastes generated in non-party state A is transported from that state to non-party state B, by a ship flying the flag of party state C, then the provisions of the Basel Convention are not applicable, despite the fact that C is a party to the Convention. The inclusion of the provision on flags of convenience would have covered this situation: state C would have had the obligation to prohibit the transport of hazardous wastes between two non-parties by a ship flying its flag. It remains to be seen to what extent this omission will provide a loophole.

1989 Basel Conference, (unpublished consultant's report submitted to the Environmental Law and Institutions Unit of UNEP in 1989; on file with the author). See also Birnie and Boyle, (1992), p. 337 (giving an overview of different interpretations of this provision by maritime and coastal states).

[47] Lang, Neuhold, and Zemanek, (1991), p. 155, and Commentary, p. 161 et seq. See also van der Mensbrugghe, (1990), pp. 274–5.

[48] *Report of the Conference of the Parties on its 1st meeting* (UNEP/CHW.1/24), p. 9.

[49] The relevant draft provision, as proposed by a sub-working group, read as follows: '1. Each Contracting Party shall prohibit vessels flying its flag or aircrafts registered in its territory to carry out a transboundary movement of hazardous wastes if the movement would not be permitted under Article [Z] of this Convention had it commenced within its own territory.' (*Report of the Working Group on its 4th session* (UNEP/WG.190/4)), p. 6)). An earlier proposal by the Executive Director of UNEP added the following paragraph: 2. 'Each Contracting Party country of export shall prohibit export of hazardous wastes from its territory on vessels registered or flying the flag of or on aircraft registered in the territory of non-Contracting Parties . . .' (UNEP/WG. 190/3, p. 4). Cf. also the proposals made at the 3rd session of the Working Group (UNEP/WG.189/3) Annex I, p. 8.

[50] Cf. *Executive Director's Luxembourg Note* (UNEP/WG.191/2), p. 3; *Report of the Working Group on its 4th session* (UNEP/WG.190/4), pp. 16–17; Proposal by the OAU, *Article 0—Obligations of Flag States and States of Registration* (informal Conference room paper).

The inclusion of a provision regulating the position of dependent territories, in the event that a party has not ratified the Convention on behalf of such a territory, was also discussed.[51] Again, agreement was not reached, and the draft provision was deleted by the Working Group on the basis that precedents had shown that countries with dependent territories consistently ratified international environmental treaties on behalf of such territories.[52] Notwithstanding this pronouncement, Denmark later made a declaration to the effect that its signature of the Convention does not apply to Greenland and the Faroe Islands.[53]

D. *General Obligations*

6. Minimization of generation and transboundary movement of hazardous wastes

Under the provisions of the Basel Convention, parties are required to take appropriate measures to ensure the reduction of the generation of hazardous wastes to a minimum. This obligation is, however, not absolute; sociological, technological and economic aspects may be taken into account (Article 4(2.a)). Parties must co-operate in the development and implementation of new low-waste technologies with a view to eliminating, as far as practicable, the generation of hazardous wastes (Article 10(2.c)). This was reaffirmed by the Conference of the Parties, which also specified that parties should promote cleaner production and technology transfer to further this aim.[54]

Each party must endeavour to ensure the availability of disposal facilities located within it; exports must be minimized (Article 4 (2.b) and (d)). Hazardous wastes may be exported only if the state of export does not have the technical capacity and facilities to dispose of them in an environmentally sound and efficient manner, or if the wastes are required as raw material for recycling or recovery industries in the state of import, or in accordance with additional criteria, to be determined by the party states (Article 4(9)).

These exceptions, reflecting a reluctance to put too many restrictions on hazardous waste exports, are somewhat problematic. The impossibility of

[51] *Report of the Working Group on its 3rd session* (UNEP/WG.189/3) Annex I, p. 8; *Proposals by the Executive Director for consideration by the Ad Hoc Working Group at its 4th Session* (UNEP/WG.190/3), p. 4.

[52] *Report of the Working Group on its 4th session* (UNEP/WG.190/4), p. 6; *Executive Director's Luxembourg Note* (UNEP/WG.191/2), pp. 3, 16–17.

[53] Declaration made at the time of the adoption of the Basel Convention (text attached to the Final Act of the Basel Convention).

[54] Conference Decisions I/17 (1992) and II/25 (1994).

environmentally sound *and efficient* disposal has in fact been interpreted to encompass any circumstance that makes disposal abroad easier: one author argues that the use of the term 'efficient' means that lower disposal costs abroad may justify export, provided that minimum environmental standards are observed.[55] The exemption applying to hazardous wastes required for recycling or recovery in the country of destination may encourage fake recycling schemes: recycling may be used as a mere label for exports that would otherwise be prohibited under the Convention. Another concern that has been raised is that the exporting state's assessment of whether a waste is required as raw material in the state of import may pose the danger of interference with the internal affairs of the importing state. Indeed, this problem arises in the context of all provisions requiring an assessment of conditions in the state of import by the export state (see also para. 7 below).[56] In partial acknowledgement of these concerns, Article 4(13) obliges parties to review periodically the possibilities of reducing the amount and/or the hazard potential of hazardous wastes which are exported, especially to developing countries.

It should be pointed out that many of the concerns arising here are of particular relevance for transboundary movements of hazardous wastes from developed to developing countries, and were voiced in that context. With the adoption of Conference Decision II/12 which bans such movements (para. 12 below), the points raised above obviously lose some of their significance.

7. Environmentally sound management of hazardous wastes and the principle of non-discrimination

Parties must require that hazardous wastes subject to transboundary movement are managed in an environmentally sound manner, whatever the place of their disposal (Article 4(8)). Thus, in accordance with the principle of non-discrimination, the same rules and standards must be applied to hazardous wastes moved out of the state of generation as to those disposed of domestically. Article 4(10) prohibits the transfer, 'under any circumstances', of the generating state's obligation to ensure environmentally sound management of hazardous wastes to the states of import or transit. By implication, the duty to ensure environmentally sound management is thus allocated primarily to the generating state. That state may not allow the export of hazardous wastes if it has 'reason to believe' that their environmentally sound management and disposal would not be guaranteed in

[55] Lang, in Lang, Neuhold, and Zemanek, (1991), p. 153.

[56] See de Villeneuve, (1990), p. 537; also Greenpeace, (1991a), p. 15 et seq.; Abrams, (1990), p. 833.

the prospective state of import (Article 4(2.e)).[57] The Basel Convention does not specify the manner or the extent to which the state of export must verify this. It does not give the exporting state the right of active verification, e.g. by means of prior EIA of a disposal facility,[58] nor is this right recognized by customary law, as we saw in Chapter 1(F) above. Any such initiative might thus come up against claims to sovereignty by the importing state. Therefore, except where the lack of proper facilities is notorious, the term 'reason to believe' must be interpreted to refer to the exporting state's conclusion based on relevant information received from the importing state.[59] The prospective state of import has the parallel obligation to prohibit the import of hazardous wastes into its territory if it has reason to believe that they would not be managed in an environmentally sound manner (Article 4(2.g)).

The Basel Convention itself defines the crucial notion of 'environmentally sound management' only in very general terms (Article 2(2) and (8)), a fact that has been criticized extensively.[60] For the purposes of the Convention, this term means 'taking all practicable steps to ensure that hazardous wastes or other wastes are managed in a manner which will protect human health and the environment against the adverse effects which may result from such wastes'. A number of provisions, although not elaborating the definition, give some guidance for the management of hazardous wastes in accordance with the Convention's aims. Each party is required to establish an authorization system for persons handling hazardous wastes (Article 4(7.a)), and to ensure that every hazardous waste transport is accompanied from start to finish by a movement document containing the information specified in Annex VB, to be signed by each person who takes charge of the wastes (Articles 4(7.c) and 6(9)). In order to encourage the use of a standardized document, the Secretariat drafted a movement document in accordance with the requirements of the Convention, which was subsequently considered by the open-ended Ad Hoc Committee on Implementation (see para. 18 below) and provisionally adopted by the Conference of the Parties. States were encouraged to use it

[57] A proposal made by Nigeria during the Basel negotiations to replace the phrase 'if it has reason to believe . . .' with 'unless it is established that the wastes in question will be managed in an environmentally sound manner' was not accepted (Doc. UNEP/WG.190/3, p. 7).

[58] A proposal by the Executive Director to consider the need for prior authorization of disposal sites (*Note to the Working Group at its 3rd session*, October 1988, Na.88–6251 0553) was not considered by the Working Group. On this issue see Rublack, (1989), p. 375 et seq.

[59] On this point cf. Abrams, (1990), p. 828 et seq.; Smets, (1991), p. 142; and Lang, in Lang, Neuhold, and Zemanek, (1991), p. 153 (noting that the relevant obligation requires a higher degree of insight into the internal situation of a state than is usually possible under the current notion of state sovereignty).

[60] See e.g. Abrams, (1990), p. 828; Birnie and Boyle, (1992), p. 342; Handl, (1989); Montgomery, (1990), p. 321; Rublack, (1989), p. 376 et seq.; Rosencranz and Eldridge, (1992), p. 321; Schmidt, (1992), p. 76.

and to submit their comments to the Secretariat.[61] Parties must also establish requirements for packaging, labelling and transport in conformity with relevant international rules, standards and practices (Article 4(7.b)). Recognized international standards in these fields exist, as discussed in Chapter 1(H) above, and efforts were made by UNEP in co-operation with other international organizations to incorporate the requirements of the Basel Convention into the pertinent legal instruments, as we will see below.

After the adoption of the Convention, additional efforts were made to give more concrete content to the notion of environmentally sound management of hazardous wastes. In accordance with Article 4(8) and Resolution 8 of the Basel Conference, work on a set of technical guidelines for the environmentally sound management of hazardous wastes has made significant progress over the past years. An informal consultative meeting of experts in October 1991 developed a set of principles, parameters and matrices intended to help states with the assessment of the environmental soundness of disposal options, and with decisions on intended transboundary movements of hazardous wastes. Subsequently, the Executive Director of UNEP convened a Technical Working Group, which now forms part of the infrastructure established under the Convention (see para. 18 below). Based on the work of the informal consultative meeting, and with input from the Convention Secretariat, the Technical Working Group has to date prepared two sets of Technical Guidelines. The first covers the four following waste streams, accorded priority by the Group: wastes from the production and use of organic solvents (Y6 in Annex I of the Convention); waste oils from petroleum origins and sources (Y8); wastes comprising or containing PCBs, PCTs and PBBs (Y10); and wastes collected from households (Y46 in Annex II). The second set addresses one recycling and two disposal operations, i.e. specially engineered landfill (D5 in Annex IVA); incineration on land (D10); and used oil re-refining (R9 in Annex IVB). The sets of guidelines form a part of the Framework Document on the Preparation of Technical Guidelines, which also provides guidance on their preparation.[62] The main purpose of the Technical Guidelines is to provide governments and organizations with elements, criteria and principles which, applied together, constitute environmentally sound management of hazardous wastes.

The Framework Document and the first four sets of guidelines were adopted by the Conference of the Parties, while the second set was provisionally adopted. Following the instructions of the Conference, the Group

[61] Conference Docs. UNEP/CHW.1/12, Annex II (1 September 1992) and UNEP/CHW.2/14, Annex I (14 December 1993); Conference Decisions I/21 (1992) and II/16 (1994).

[62] The Technical Guidelines and the Framework Document are reproduced in Basel Convention Series/SBC No. 94/005 and 94/006 (Geneva, May 1994). See also Conference Docs. UNEP/CHW.1/2, 1/20, 2/10, and 2/10/Add.1. For a summary of the relevant work see Rummel-Bulska, in YBIEL 2 (1991), p. 388; Kummer, in YBIEL 3 (1992), p. 289.

will elaborate additional Technical Guidelines. With the approval of the Conference, it has accorded first priority to the following waste streams and disposal options: physio-chemical treatment (D9 in Annex IVA); recycling and reclamation of metals and metal compounds (R4 in Annex IVB); and wastes resulting from surface treatment of metals and plastics (Y17 in Annex I). Second priority was given to the following: clinical wastes (Y1 in Annex I); biological treatment (D8 in Annex IVA); use as a fuel (R1 in Annex IVB); and solvent reclamation or regeneration (R2 in Annex IVB).[63]

A related initiative is the elaboration of an 'International Strategy and Action Programme for the Environmentally Sound Management of Hazardous Wastes'. This goes back to a request by the UNCED Preparatory Committee (PrepCom) in 1990, re-iterated by the UNEP Governing Council in 1991.[64] A meeting of government-designated experts, convened under UNEP auspices in December 1991, elaborated elements of a strategy, based on a draft prepared by the (then) Interim Secretariat in consultation with other organizations.[65] The elements were submitted to the UNCED PrepCom at its fourth session in March/April 1992, and influenced the discussion on the relevant Chapters of Agenda 21. They were also submitted to the first meeting of the Conference of the Parties to the Basel Convention, and are to be submitted to the first Conference of the Bamako Convention after its entry into force (see Chapter 3(F) below). The Governing Council of UNEP invited governments and international organizations to use the strategy elements, and asked the Executive Director to promote their application.[66] In common with the Technical Guidelines, the strategy elements reaffirm and develop further the fundamental principles of environmentally sound waste management embodied in the Basel Convention. These are summarized comprehensively in the objectives of the strategy: 'Within the framework of integrated life-cycle management, prevent to the extent possible and minimize the generation of hazardous wastes, treat and dispose of the wastes in such a way that they do not cause harm to health and the environment, and eliminate or reduce transboundary movements of hazardous wastes'. The strategy document enumerates basic concepts which are consistent with these principles, such as the precautionary principle and the polluter pays principle. It sets out strategic

63 Conference Decisions I/19 (1992) and II/13 (1994).

64 PrepCom Decision 1/22 (Section I, para. 3), 31 August 1990 (*Official Records of the UN General Assembly, 45th Session*, Supplement No. 46(A/45/46), Annex I); UNEP Governing Council Decision 16/30 (31 May 1991).

65 Report of the experts meeting on an international waste management strategy, 12 December 1991, (UNEP/CHW/WG. 2/1/3, with elements of a strategy as Annex). See also Doc. UNEP/CHW/WG.2/1/2 (7 November 1991); Conference Doc. UNEP/CHW.1/15, pp. 5–6. For a summary see Kummer, in YBIEL 2 (1991), p. 176, and eadem, in YBIEL 3 (1992) p. 291.

66 UNEP Governing Council Decision on the control of transboundary movements of hazardous wastes and their disposal, 21 May 1993, (repr. in EPL 23/3/4(1993), p. 171).

guidelines and strategic elements which are designed to give concrete content to the relevant concepts.

Other efforts to give content to the concept of environmentally sound waste management include the joint elaboration by IMO and UNEP of the Global Waste Management Survey (see Chapter 5 below), and the preparation of the Manual for the Implementation of the Basel Convention. On the recommendation of the open-ended Ad Hoc Committee on Implementation, the Conference of the Parties at its first meeting instructed the Secretariat to undertake this task. The Manual was approved by the second meeting. Its purpose is to facilitate implementation by setting out in a transparent way the provisions and requirements of the Convention.[67]

8. Nature of the general obligations

The provisions of Article 4 have the character of a general framework. While providing guidance for the conduct of states in the context of hazardous waste management, they do not contain absolute obligations. States are required to take 'appropriate measures' to achieve these aims; the exact nature and extent of such steps is left open.[68] In addition to the definition of environmentally sound management, the provisions also leave open a number of other important questions, such as the extent of the generating state's duty to ascertain the adequacy of disposal facilities in the prospective state of import, and the allocation of the burden of proof for the inclusion of a waste in the scope of the Convention and for the permissibility of export. Nevertheless, they do set important global standards for the protection of the environment against adverse effects of hazardous wastes, which are open to further development.

The above overview of the follow-up work pursuant to the Convention's adoption shows that efforts to clarify and further elaborate the general principles laid down in its provisions are thus far successful, namely in the areas of clarifying the definitions of wastes and giving more concrete content to the notion of environmentally sound management. These efforts may to some extent counter the early criticism of the Basel Convention for failing to provide clear definitions and unequivocal obligations. However, these efforts are still at a fairly early stage. They are neither intended nor likely to lead to the adoption of binding rules in the near future.

[67] Basel Convention Series/SBC 94/004 (Geneva, April 1994). See also Conference Decisions I/3 (1992) and II/26 (1994), Conference Doc. 2/7 (1994), and Doc. UNEP/CHW/WG.3/1/4.

[68] The same opinion is expressed by Lang, in Lang, Neuhold, and Zemanek, (1991), p. 152: 'Frequently parties are only called upon to achieve a certain result, whereas they are free to choose the means to attain this objective, usually by taking "appropriate measures." '

E. *Restrictions on Transboundary Movements of Hazardous Wastes*

9. Hazardous waste traffic between parties

The sovereign right of every state to ban the import of hazardous wastes for transit or disposal—recognized, as we have seen, by customary law (see Chapter 1 para. 5 above)—is referred to in the preamble to the Convention (operational para. 6). Any party exercising this right must inform the other parties, through the Convention Secretariat, of its decision (Articles 4(1.a) and 13(2.c)). No party state may permit hazardous wastes to be shipped to a party which has prohibited their import (Article 4(1.b)). The parties must also prohibit the export of hazardous wastes to a group of states, belonging to an economic and/or political integration organization, which prohibit such imports by their legislation (Article 4(2.e), first sentence). Hazardous waste exports to party states which have not adopted an import ban are permitted only in accordance with the general obligations outlined above, and subject to the prior consent of the states concerned, in accordance with the Convention's regulatory system (Articles 4(1.c) and 9(1); see para. 13 below).

10. Hazardous waste traffic between parties and non-parties

After a lengthy and arduous debate, the negotiators agreed on the adoption of the concept of a 'limited ban', which prohibits parties to the Basel Convention from trading in hazardous wastes with non-parties. Article 4(5) of the Convention stipulates that parties may not permit the export of hazardous wastes to a state which is not a party to the Convention, or the import of hazardous wastes from a non-party state. Transit of hazardous wastes through non-party states is not included in this prohibition; if carried out in accordance with the relevant provisions of the Convention, it is therefore not prohibited (Article 4(5), by implication; Article 7).

The objective of the concept of a limited ban is twofold. First, it is designed to prevent party states from engaging in hazardous waste trade with states that, as non-parties, do not adhere to the rules and standards established by the Basel Convention. Thus the first objective of the concept is to ensure the application of the Convention's rules and standards by its parties in all their transactions. Second, by excluding non-parties from trade with parties, the concept provides an incentive for non-parties to accede to the Convention. The larger the number of parties, and the greater their collective significance as potential partners in trade, the more important this incentive becomes. In the case of the Basel Convention, it is obviously more relevant for countries seeking trade in certain wastes amongst each other than for some developing countries having no interest in participating in the waste trade. One author, urging ratification of the Basel Convention by the USA, puts forward this argument in no uncertain terms: 'Those countries which have not ratified will find themselves increasingly isolated as regards countries with which they may trade in the Basel-covered wastes . . . all other waste trade (i.e. except that covered by bilateral agreements compatible with Basel) is at risk of being shut down if the country at the other end of the waste movement is a Basel party'.[69] The same reasoning underlies the ban on trade in ozone-depleting substances and techniques between parties and non-parties imposed by the Montreal Protocol on Substances that Deplete the Ozone Layer (Article 4). Due to the fact that the current parties to the Montreal Protocol account for approximately 95 per cent of the world's consumption of substances controlled by the Protocol,[70] the concept of a limited ban is particularly effective in that case. Similar measures have been adopted under CITES (Articles II(4) and X), and the London Convention (Resolution 29(10) of the Consultative Meeting of Contracting Parties, discussed in Chapter 5 below).

In the Basel Convention, the concept of a limited ban is modified by Article 11, which accords parties the right to enter into multilateral, bilateral or regional agreements or arrangements on transboundary movements of hazardous wastes with other parties, and also with non-parties, provided that such agreements conform to the requirement of environmentally sound management stipulated by the Basel Convention. If this condition is met, the provisions of the Basel Convention do not affect transboundary movements carried out in accordance with such agreements. The Secretariat of the Basel Convention must be informed of any such agreement entered into by a party either before or after the entry into force of the Basel Convention. The inclusion of Article 11, and its wording, were subject to disagreement. After the introduction of the concept of a limited ban, a number of states proposed the deletion of Article 11, since they saw it as a weakening of that concept.[71] Consensus could not, however, be reached on this point, nor on a proposed requirement for agreements concluded under Article 11 to be consistent with the provisions of the Basel Convention.[72] The requirement of conformity with environmentally sound management of hazardous wastes was therefore adopted as a compromise solution. A full analysis of the provisions of Article 11, its implications for separate

[69] Murphy, (1992), p. 13.

[70] UNEP/WMO, *Fact Sheets on Climate Change*, no. 224 'Phasing Out CFCs: The Vienna Convention and its Montreal Protocol' (UNEP/WMO Information Unit on Climate Change, Geneva 1991, updated periodically).

[71] *Report of the Working Group on its 5th session* (UNEP/IG.80/4), Annex I, p. 12, and draft report (UNEP/WG. 191/L.1).

[72] Proposal by the African Group (UNEP/WG.191/CRP.29); cf. also the proposed wording in the Luxembourg revision of the draft Convention (UNEP/WG.190/4).

agreements on transboundary movements of hazardous wastes, and its role in combining global and regional regulation of the issue as advocated in Chapter 1(I) above, is the subject of Chapter 3 below.

11. Absolute prohibition of hazardous waste exports to Antarctica

The Basel Convention prohibits hazardous waste exports to the area south of 60° South latitude, whether or not such wastes are subject to transboundary movement as defined by the Convention (Article 4(6)).

12. Prohibition of hazardous waste traffic from OECD to non-OECD countries

As mentioned above, this issue was among the most contentious both during the negotiations on the Basel Convention as well as in the follow-up process. The preamble recognizes an 'increasing desire for the prohibition of transboundary movements of hazardous wastes and their disposal in other states, especially developing countries' (operational para. 7), and Article 15(7) requests the Conference of the Parties to re-evaluate the effectiveness of the Convention periodically and to consider the adoption of a complete or partial ban on transboundary movements of hazardous wastes in the light of the latest scientific, environmental, technical and economic information.

Decision II/12 of the Conference of the Parties, adopted on 25 March 1994, prohibits all transboundary movements of hazardous wastes destined for final disposal from OECD to non-OECD states with immediate effect. This had already been agreed in principle by the Conference in December 1992, and corresponds to a virtual consensus within environmentalist, industrial and governmental circles, which had emerged in the last few years. The same Decision prohibits transboundary movements of hazardous wastes destined for recycling or recovery from OECD to non-OECD states as of 31 December 1997. Non-OECD states which continue to allow the import of hazardous wastes for recycling from OECD states until that date must inform the Secretariat accordingly. The relevant statement must specify the categories and quantities of hazardous wastes accepted, the specific recycling processes to be used, and the disposal options for residues derived from the recycling process. A number of non-OECD countries subsequently provided the relevant information to the Secretariat at its request.[73]

This Decision remains extremely controversial as it raises very complex and contentious issues, some of which have already been mentioned. They

[73] *Report of the Secretariat to the Ad Hoc Committee on Implementation*, 30 September 1994, UNEP/CHW/C.1/2/5.

include the need for a more detailed and practicable distinction between disposal and recycling or recovery operations; the need for a clearer definition of hazardous wastes which are subject to the ban and wastes to be exempted on the basis of their low hazard potential and their economic value; the need for a more accurate definition of the groups of countries between which the ban should be effective (taking into account the current changes in OECD membership and the fact that the group of non-OECD members is amorphous in more than one way); and—in more general terms—potential conflicts between environmental protection and industrial development in all groups of countries. The ambiguity of this issue was reflected in the discussions at the second meeting of the Conference of the Parties to the Basel Convention, where a number of countries agreed to this measure only reluctantly. Some industry circles subsequently predicted serious consequences for the recycling industries concerned, both in developed and developing countries. A more detailed examination of this problem is beyond the scope of this study; reference can be made to a paper by the author which is specifically devoted to this issue.[74]

The rules outlined above have not as yet been given the form of an amendment to the Convention in accordance with the relevant procedure (Article 17), but that of a Conference decision. The legal value of such a decision is not clearly defined. In the strictest sense, it is not legally binding on the parties to the Convention. On the other hand, it is clearly intended to be more than a mere non-binding recommendation. The legal value and status of such rules have been subject to discussion for many years, but there is as yet no clear agreement on this issue.[75] Without entering into this discussion, some guidance might be obtained in this particular case by referring to the wording of the decision: in the preamble, it states that 'transboundary movements of hazardous wastes from OECD to non-OECD States have a high risk of not constituting environmentally sound management of hazardous wastes as required by the Basel Convention'. It can be argued that the decision adds an element to the definition of this term by establishing a presumption that hazardous waste transfer to non-OECD countries will not be in conformity with environmentally sound management. Thus, the obligation under the Basel Convention to ensure environmentally sound management can be interpreted to include the prohibition of hazardous waste movement to non-OECD countries, unless proof is provided of its environmental soundness.

Independently of its legal status, however, the decision has great political significance, as it represents a formal consensus of the numerous states and organizations involved in the hazardous waste debate: politically, it

[74] Kummer, (1994a), p. 46 et seq. See also Donald, (1992), p. 444, pointing out the vast differences among states commonly defined as developing countries.

[75] For a discussion see Aust, (1986), p. 786 et seq.

would be very difficult for any state party to the Basel Convention to justify a contravention of the ban on the grounds that the decision is not legally binding. Continuous application of this rule by states is likely to enhance its acceptance. As noted above, the Nordic proposal for a formal amendment to the Convention is designed to clarify the legal status of the ban. A parallel development can be observed in the London Convention, discussed in Chapter 5 below: that Convention was further developed over the years by numerous decisions of the Consultative Meetings of the Contracting Parties, which have gained widespread acceptance. One of the pertinent rules, prohibiting the dumping at sea of radioactive wastes, has recently resulted in an amendment to the Annexes of the London Convention, and other amendments are likely to follow.

The adoption of Conference Decision II/12 constitutes a significant innovation. It has also led to a shift in the relative importance of the other provisions of the Convention: since transboundary movements of hazardous wastes are now permissible only within the group of OECD member states, on the one hand, and within the group of non-members of the OECD, on the other, provisions designed to restrict transboundary movements of hazardous wastes between developed and developing countries, or to mitigate their negative effects, have lost much of their relevance. This applies, for example, to the restrictions discussed in the preceding paragraphs, as well as to the prior informed consent procedure discussed below.

F. *The Prior Informed Consent (PIC) Procedure*

As noted above, any transboundary movement of hazardous wastes which is not, in principle, prohibited, and which is in conformity with the general obligations, must be carried out in accordance with the Convention's regulatory system (Article 4(1.c) and (2.f)). This system, generally referred to as the PIC procedure, is regulated in Articles 6 and 7 and in Annex VA of the Convention.[76] Party states must designate at least one competent authority responsible for administering the PIC procedure (see para. 18 below). The duties of the states involved, as outlined below, are to be carried out by their competent authorities.

13. The position of the states of export and import

The state of export has the duty to notify the prospective states of import and transit of any intended transboundary movement of hazardous wastes. The state of export can either provide this information itself or require the generator or exporter to do so, through the channel of its competent

[76] For a critical analysis of the PIC procedure see Abrams, (1990), p. 824 et seq.

authority. The information to be provided must be sufficiently detailed to enable the authorities of the states of import and transit to assess the nature and the risks of the intended movement; the content of the information is specified in Annex VA. Among other things, the reason for the export; the exporter and the generator; the site and process of generation; the nature of the wastes and their packaging; the intended itinerary; the site of disposal; the disposer; and the method of disposal as per Annex IV must be specified (Article 6(1)). In accordance with Article 6(6)–(8), the exporting state may, with the prior approval of the states of import and transit, allow the use of a general notification for shipments of wastes having the same characteristics and the same transport route, for a maximum period of 12 months.

In order to promote uniformity in this regard, the (then) Interim Secretariat of the Basel Convention prepared a form to be used for the notification of transboundary movements of hazardous wastes, which is based on the above requirements. Following a consideration of this form by the open-ended Ad Hoc Committee on Implementation, the Conference of the Parties provisionally adopted it, and recommended that states use it and provide comments to the Secretariat.[77]

The state of import must respond to the notifier in writing, consenting to the movement with or without conditions, denying permission for the movement, or requesting further information. In its reply, the state of import must also confirm the existence of a contract between the exporter and the disposer, which specifies the environmentally sound disposal of the wastes. Copies of the importing state's final response must be sent to the competent authorities of all states involved in the transaction (Article 6(2) and (3.b)). The state of export may not allow the movement to commence until the notifier has received the importing state's written consent, along with the confirmation of the existence of the contract (Article 4(1.c)), Article 6(2) and (3)). The Convention gives no time limit for the response by the importing state. Since the consent of the importing state has to be explicit and unconditional, a movement may not be permitted to commence if *no* response is given by that state. After the completion of the disposal operation, the exporter and the exporting state must be informed accordingly (Article 6(9)).

This regulation is very detailed; however, some points are again left open. Thus, there is no requirement for the state of export to verify the contents of the contract concluded between the exporter and the disposer; the transaction may commence on the basis of mere confirmation of its existence. The requirement for the contract to specify the environmentally sound dis-

[77] Conference Doc. UNEP/CHW.1/12, Annex I and 2/14, Annex I; Conference Decisions I/21 (1992) and II/16 (1994).

posal of the wastes may be problematic, since that term is elaborated only in non-binding guidelines, as mentioned above.

Earlier drafts of the Basel Convention contained an obligation to send copies of all notifications and the final responses to the Convention Secretariat. Since a number of countries did not agree to that provision, it was finally replaced by Article 15(4), which constitutes a carefully worded compromise. That Article requires the provision of copies to the Secretariat only upon request by a party which considers that its environment may be affected by the movement in question.[78] This last-minute change has led to a considerable restriction of the Secretariat's monitoring function in the context of the PIC procedure.

14. The position of the state of transit

The rights of transit states in the context of the PIC procedure were one of the most contentious issues during the negotiation process (see para. 10 above). One group of states, composed mainly of developing countries, wanted to accord transit states the same rights as are given to import states. They were opposed mainly by industrialized states, who maintained that this would contradict the navigational rights and freedoms guaranteed in international law, in particular the right of innocent passage and the right of overflight (see para. 5 above). The conflict of views is reflected in the declarations made by various delegations at the time of the adoption of the Convention, or with their signature: some coastal states asserted their right to control activities taking place in their adjacent sea areas, while some maritime states asserted the right of innocent passage. Numerous proposals were put forward and discussed in an effort to reconcile these two conflicting aims.[79] The relevant provisions are based on a last-minute compromise. The wording is accordingly involved and complex, and does not in fact resolve this particular conflict (see also para. 5 above). Since the Convention generally permits transit of hazardous wastes through the territory of non-parties (see para. 10 above), different rules apply to party and non-party transit states.

[78] Draft Convention on the Control of Transboundary Movements of Hazardous Wastes (as submitted to the Working Group at its 5th session), 11 March 1989, (UNEP/WG.191/4), Articles VI(10), XV(4); *Executive Director's Basel Proposals* (UNEP/WG.191/3), p. 4; Doc. UNEP/WG.191/CRP.10 (15 March 1989); Doc. UNEP/IG.80/CRP.4, (21 March 1989).

[79] *Report of the Working Group on its 2nd session* (UNEP/WG. 186/3), p. 8; *Report of the Meeting of the Legal Experts Sub-Working Group*, 22 August 1988, (UNEP/WG.189/2), p. 4; *Report of the Working Group on its 3rd session* (UNEP/WG.189/3), p. 18; *Report of the Working Group on its 5th session* (UNEP/IG.80/4), Annex I, pp. 10–11. See also *Executive Director's Luxembourg Note* (UNEP/WG.191/2), p. 2; *Proposals on transit states made at the 5th session* (UNEP/WG.191/CRP.2,7,15); *Executive Director's Basel Proposals* (UNEP/WG. 191/3/Add.1). For a discussion see Gröbl, (1989), p. 8; van der Mensbrugghe, Commentary, in Lang, Neuhold, and Zemanek, (1991), p. 162; Birnie and Boyle, (1992), p. 337.

14.1 *Party transit states* After receiving the notification, a party transit state must 'promptly acknowledge to the notifier receipt of notification' (Article 6(4), first sentence). No deadline is given, but the term 'promptly' indicates a short time limit. Since no assessment, decision making or major administrative procedure is necessary, it is reasonable to assume that the acknowledgement should be provided within a few days. The transit state must then respond to the notifier within 60 days, on the same terms as the importing state, and the movement of hazardous wastes may not be allowed to commence before the written consent of the transit state has been received (Article 6(4)).

Unlike the state of import, a transit state which is a party can waive the requirement of prior written consent, either generally or under specific conditions. Notice of such a decision must be given to the other parties through the Secretariat. If a party state has waived the requirement of prior written consent for transit movements, the state of export may allow the movement to proceed through that state if it has received no response within 60 days after the receipt of notification from the state of transit (Article 6(4)). Thus, the concept of tacit consent applies in the case of a party state having waived its right to explicit consent for transit movements.

14.2 *Non-party transit states* Curiously, the Basel Convention's regulation of the rights and duties of non-party transit states is only fragmentary. Article 7, which addresses this issue, merely provides that paragraph 1 of Article 6, regulating the notification of the states concerned, applies *mutatis mutandis* to non-party transit states.[80] The Convention thus requires notification to prospective non-party transit states, but is otherwise silent on these states' position in the transaction. Various authors have commented on the lack of clarity of this provision.[81] The circumstances of the adoption of Article 7 point to the conclusion that it was adopted in this fragmentary form because no agreement could be reached on a more comprehensive provision.[82] This is often the case in treaties on highly polit-

[80] The English text of Article 7, as adopted, erroneously referred to para. 2 instead of para. 1 of Article 6. The UN Secretary-General in his capacity as despository, on the proposal of the government of Japan, has since corrected this error in accordance with the applicable procedure (cf. *Report of the Conference of the Parties on its 1st meeting* (UNEP/CHW.1/24), p. 7 et seq.).

[81] See de Villeneuve, (1990), p. 574, describing this provision as 'perfectly incomprehensible'; also Lang, in Lang, Neuhold, and Zemanek, (1991), p. 154, noting that insufficient cross-referencing between Articles 6(4) and 7 does not allow a clear conclusion on the position of non-party transit states.

[82] The corresponding article of the Fifth Revised Draft Convention contained a total of five paragraphs. Para. 1, which corresponds to the final version of Article 7, referred to para. 1 of Article 6. In addition, two substantive paragraphs regulated the rights and duties of non-party transit states. Agreement had, however, not been reached on either of them (Fifth Revised Draft Convention (UNEP/WG.189/3), Annex I, p. 20). In a note addressed to the Working Group at its 4th session, the Executive Director proposed the deletion of these two

ical issues, when the negotiators expressly or tacitly avoid clear wording in the interest of reaching an agreement in spite of considerable differences of opinion. Interpretation of the provisions in question is not easy, since the rules of Article 31 of the Vienna Convention on the Law of Treaties cannot readily be applied to a situation were no clear meaning was *intended* by the negotiating parties. An analysis of the subsequent practice of party states will give the most conclusive indication of how the provisions are being interpreted.[83] However, since the Basel Convention only recently entered into force and relevant state practice has not yet developed, such an analysis is not yet possible.

As an alternative approach, an attempt can be made to apply the teleological interpretation method.[84] In the light of the fundamental aims of the Convention, as outlined above, what would be the most reasonable regulation of the position of non-party transit states? In accordance with the aims of the Convention, any form of transboundary waste traffic between parties and non-parties should be considered the exception. If it does take place, standards no lower than those of the Basel Convention should apply. Accordingly, we can conclude that the position of non-party transit states should correspond at least to that of the party states involved. In this context, the requirement of express consent is the rule, and mere tacit consent the exception. Article 7 does not refer to paragraph 4 of Article 6 giving party transit states the option of tacit consent, which would mean that non-party transit states had the same option. Bearing in mind also the Convention's restrictive attitude towards traffic with non-parties, it is therefore reasonable to assume that the requirement of express consent applying to importing states rather than the requirement of tacit consent applying to party transit states should apply to non-party transit states. This means that transit of hazardous wastes through a non-party, unlike transit through a party, is not permissible under the Basel Convention based on mere tacit consent: the state of export must always gain the express consent of the non-party state concerned. In this context, Bartram and Engel refer to the rule *pacta tertiis nec nocent nec prosunt* ('agreements neither harm nor benefit third parties'), codified in Article 34 of the Vienna Convention. Pointing out that the Basel Convention cannot impose obligations on non-party states,

paragraphs, but did not suggest a viable alternative. The exact wording of the proposal is as follows: 'The Executive Director believes that paragraph 1 is the most straightforward and therefore proposes the deletion of paragraphs 2 and 3' (*Proposals by the Executive Director for consideration by the Ad Hoc Working Group at its 4th session* (UNEP/WG.190/3), p. 7). This proposal was adopted, but no alternative was discussed by the Working Group or the Basel Conference (*Report of the Working Group on its 4th session*, (UNEP/WG.190/4), pp. 10, 25). The reason, presumably, was the inability to reach an agreement.

[83] See generally Verdross and Simma, (1984), p. 482.

[84] See Brownlie, (1990), p. 631 et seq.; Reuter, (1989), p. 75 et seq.; Ott, (1987), p. 195 et seq.; Verdross and Simma, (1984), p. 492.

they note that Article 7 must be interpreted to mean, not that a non-party transit state has a duty to give prior consent, but that an exporting state acts in contravention of its obligations if it authorizes transit through a non-party without prior consent.[85]

15. Wastes defined as hazardous by national legislation

The Convention specifies modifications of the PIC procedure in cases where the wastes in question are not defined as hazardous by all party states involved in the movement (Article 1(1.b)). In that case, every state which considers the wastes to be hazardous is in principle accorded the rights and duties pertaining to its position in the transaction, even if other party states concerned do not define the wastes as hazardous (Article 6(5.a)–(5.c)).[86]

G. *Illegal Traffic and the Duty to Re-import*

Transboundary movements of hazardous wastes carried out in contravention of states' obligations stipulated by the Basel Convention are termed 'illegal traffic' (Article 2(21), Article 9). Article 4(3) contains the—fairly rhetorical—statement that the parties consider illegal traffic to be criminal. Paragraphs 1(a)–(d) of Article 9 list specific contraventions of the PIC procedure which render a movement illegal, and paragraph 1(e) contains the general clause '[any transboundary movement] that results in deliberate disposal (e.g. dumping) of hazardous wastes or other wastes in contravention of this Convention and of general principles of international law'.

The definition of illegal traffic and the allocation of responsibility to states in this context was one of the very contentious issues during the negotiation process. Some states generally opposed the concept of placing responsibility for illegal traffic on the state itself, while others insisted on its inclusion. Developing states in particular maintained that the state of export should always bear exclusive responsibility for illegal traffic, a viewpoint considered unacceptable by some industrialized states.[87] As with

[85] Bartram and Engel, (1989), p. 119 et seq. See also Brownlie, (1990), p. 622 et seq.; Verdross and Simma, (1984), p. 482 et seq.

[86] For a critical assessment of this provision cf. Smets, (1991), p. 141, noting that it could oblige a state to restrict the movement of a waste it does not consider hazardous, thus indirectly forcing it to apply national legislation other than its own.

[87] See the *Report of the Working Group on its 3rd session* (UNEP/WG.189/3), p. 5; the *Report on its 4th session* (UNEP 190/4 and 190/4/Corr. 1); and the *Report on its 5th session* (UNEP/IG.80/4), Annex I, pp. 11–12; also Docs. UNEP/WG.190/CRP.8 and CRP.8/Rev.1 (2 February 1989); *Executive Director's Luxembourg Note* (UNEP/WG.191/2), p. 3; Docs. UNEP/WG.191/CRP.9 and UNEP/WG.191/CRP.21 (March 1989); Kenyan proposal to amend Article 8bis—illegal traffic (informal Conference room paper). On the allocation of the management responsibility for hazardous substances to developing and developed countries cf. Handl and Lutz, in Handl and Lutz, (1989a), pp. 49–51.

other contentious issues, the wording as adopted is the result of a compromise.

The Basel Convention obliges its parties to adopt and enforce national legislation for the prevention and punishment of illegal traffic (Article 4(4), Article 9(5)), i.e. states must adopt and implement legislative measures to ensure compliance with the restrictions on hazardous waste traffic, the PIC procedure, and other relevant provisions, by persons under their national jurisdiction or control. The Convention goes on to regulate the duties of states in the event that illegal traffic does occur (Article 9(2)–(4)). It allocates the responsibility for illegal movements to the states involved, and obliges the state responsible to ensure the disposal of the wastes in an environmentally sound manner, if necessary by re-importation into the state of origin. The obligations of the states concerned in this context will be discussed more fully in Chapter 6(E) below. Finally, Article 9(5) obliges parties to co-operate in the implementation of the illegal traffic provisions. Since illegal traffic mostly involves persons operating under the jurisdiction of more than one state, this may prove very important.

The parties may also request the Convention Secretariat to assist them in identifying cases of illegal traffic. This is one of the few Secretariat functions that go beyond mere co-ordinating and monitoring (see para. 18 below). In addition to providing the requested assistance, the Secretariat must immediately circulate any information it has received on illegal traffic to the parties concerned (Article 16 (1.i)). Efforts to combat illegal traffic have emerged as one of the priorities since the entry into force of the Convention. The Conference of the Parties, based on recommendations of the open-ended Ad Hoc Committee on Implementation, outlined a strategy to control illegal traffic. Accordingly, the Secretariat is working with governments and regional organizations to assess the illegal traffic situation and to assist in the enactment of national legislation and mechanisms. It is also liaising with specialized international organizations, including the International Customs Co-operation Council and Interpol. The Commission on Sustainable Development supported these actions and made further suggestions on their continuation.[88]

Article 8 obliges the state of export to accept back hazardous wastes the transfer of which has commenced in compliance with the provisions of the Convention, but cannot be completed in accordance with the terms of the contract between the exporter and the disposer. The adoption of this Article was also subject to disagreement during the negotiations: some states opposed the concept of imposing a duty to re-import in a case where

[88] See *Note by the Secretariat on Illegal Traffic*, December 1993, (UNEP/CHW.2/8), giving an overview of activities in this field; Decision I/6 of the open-ended Ad Hoc Committee on Implementation; Conference Decisions I/15 (1992) and II/4 (1994); *Report of the Commission on Sustainable Development*, 12 July 1994, (E/CN.17/1994/29), p. 43.

the relevant rules were adhered to. This provision, which is a concrete expression of the allocation of primary responsibility for the environmentally sound management of hazardous wastes to the generating state, will also be discussed in Chapter 6(E) below.

Both Article 8 and Article 9 provide that the state concerned 'shall not oppose, hinder or prevent the return of those wastes to the State of export'. There remains the question whether the PIC procedure applies in such cases, especially in the case of Article 9, where no valid consent was given by the states concerned, and, in the case of Article 8, if the return transport takes place through a state which was not previously involved in the movement. This question was not addressed during the negotiations. The wording of the provision seems to point to the conclusion that the states concerned may not withhold their consent to the return movement, although, in accordance with the aims of the Convention, it must be assumed that they have to be informed of it.[89]

H. *Liability and Compensation*

The issue of liability and compensation for damage caused by hazardous wastes was left open by the Basel Convention, mainly due to lack of sufficient time to address so complex and contentious an issue. This was the subject of extensive criticism both before and after the adoption of the Convention.[90] A mandate to deal with this issue at a later stage was, however, included in the Convention (Article 12). This was given concrete content by Resolution 3 of the Basel Conference, which called for the convening of a working group to draft elements which could be included in a future protocol on liability and compensation. The need for rapid elaboration of a liability protocol was stressed by a number of subsequent policy statements.[91] As a result, work on the elaboration of a protocol on liability and compensation is progressing, and the establishment of an international hazardous waste compensation fund and an emergency fund is under consideration. These issues will be addressed in Chapter 6 below.

[89] This is the solution adopted by the 1993 EU Council Regulation on transboundary waste shipments (see Chapter 4 para. 1 below). In accordance with the relevant provisions, a further notification must be made, and the states concerned may not oppose the return of the waste 'at the duly motivated request of the competent authority of destination and with an explanation of the reason' (Articles 25, 26).

[90] Cf. e.g. the statement by the representative of Nigeria to the Working Group at its 3rd session, to the effect that without substantive provisions on liability, the future convention would at best provide a code of conduct (UNEP/WG.189/3, p. 7); and the statement of the representative of Ghana (ibid.). See also Cusack, (1990), p. 422; Hackett, (1990), p. 320; Handl, (1989), p. 376; Montgomery, (1990), p. 323; Greenpeace, (1990), p. 16.

[91] e.g. UNGA Resolution 44/226 (22 December 1989); Manaus Declaration of the Amazonian States, 24 February 1992, (Doc. A/CONF.151/PC/123, excerpts repr. in Kwiatkowska and Soons (1993), p. 1077).

I. *International Co-operation and Exchange of Information*

16. International co-operation

Article 10 of the Basel Convention sets out comparatively far-reaching and detailed duties of co-operation. Aimed primarily at the need to assist developing countries in technical fields, it was adopted in response to the concern—expressed frequently during the negotiation process—that due to lack of technical capacity and know-how, developing countries would not be able to implement the provisions of the Convention, and the regulatory system would therefore fail in its objective of protecting those countries against illegal imports of hazardous wastes.[92]

In accordance with the aim of reducing the generation and transboundary movement of hazardous wastes to a minimum at the global level, the Basel Convention calls for co-operation between its parties in areas related to environmentally sound waste management, such as harmonization of technical standards and practices; monitoring of the effects of waste management on human health and the environment; development of low-waste technologies and environmentally sound waste management systems; transfer of technology; and development of technical guidelines and codes of practice (Article 4(2.h), Article 10(1) and (2)). Assistance is to be given to developing country parties in the implementation of their general obligations as set out in Article 4 (Article 10(3)). The importance of such assistance was re-iterated by the Governing Council of UNEP in 1993.[93] Co-operation between parties and competent international organizations is also encouraged (Article 10(4)).

Article 14(1) calls for the establishment of regional training centres for waste management and related issues, again with the primary aim of enhancing developing countries' capacities in this field. In accordance with a 1992 Decision of the Conference of the Parties, the Ad Hoc Committee on Implementation has developed guidelines to be used in considering the setting up of one or more pilot centres. The Conference of the Parties at its second meeting asked the Committee to follow up on this work.[94]

17. Exchange of information

The Basel Convention's requirements for exchange of information are also comparatively extensive. In addition to the information exchange required

[92] *Report of the Working Group on its 1st session* (UNEP/WG.182/3), p. 4; *Report on its 2nd session* (UNEP/WG.186/3), p. 5. The issue is also addressed in the Preamble to the Convention (operational paras. 20 and 21).

[93] UNEP Governing Council Decision on the control of transboundary movements of hazardous wastes and their disposal, 21 May 1993, (repr. in EPL 23/3/4(1993), p. 171).

[94] *Note of the Secretariat* (UNEP/CHW.2/19); Conference Decisions I/13 (1992) and II/19 (1994, with Decision I/5 of the open-ended Ad Hoc Committee on Implementation as Annex).

by the PIC procedure, Article 13 calls for exchange of information between party states on a broad range of issues. Transmission of information is channelled mainly through the Convention Secretariat (Article 13(2) and Article 16). In order to facilitate the exchange of information and the access to relevant data, the Secretariat is in the process of developing an electronic information management system of the Basel Convention in response to a request by the Conference of the Parties.[95]

Accidents occurring during a transboundary movement of hazardous wastes must be reported immediately to any potentially affected state (Article 13(1)). Article 13(2) calls for transmission of specific information related to the regulatory system. In addition, states are required to prepare, for submission to the Conference of the Parties, annual reports on substantive issues, such as particulars of transboundary waste movements in which they have been involved, accidents occurring during transboundary movements, disposal facilities operated by them, and measures adopted to implement the Convention (Article 13(3.a–i)). These reports are to be made available to every party by the Convention Secretariat (Article 16(1.b)). Only a small number of parties submitted reports prior to the first meeting of the Conference of the Parties. The Conference accordingly urged states to meet this requirement, and also asked the Secretariat to prepare an analysis of any reports it had received, and submit this to the Ad Hoc Committee on Implementation for evaluation. Response from parties was somewhat better prior to the second meeting. The Secretariat was asked by the Conference to distribute all information it had received to parties as well as non-parties and organizations.[96]

J. *Institutional and Financial Mechanisms*

Following is a brief overview of existing institutional and financial mechanisms established within the framework of the Basel Convention. These mechanisms, as well as their role in the implementation of the Convention, will be examined more fully in Chapter 6 below.

18. Institutional mechanisms

Article 15 of the Convention establishes the Conference of the Parties with overall policy-making powers. The Conference periodically reviews the Convention's effectiveness. It adopts amendments to the Convention and

[95] Conference Decision II/18 (1994).

[96] *Note by the Executive Director of UNEP on the implementation of Article 13 of the Convention*, 28 September 1992, Conference Doc. UNEP/CHW.1/18; *Report of the Secretariat to the 2nd meeting of the Conference of the Parties*, 1 December 1993 (UNEP/CHW.2/15); Conference Decisions I/11 (1992) and II/17 (1994).

any subsidiary legal instruments, and establishes additional institutions as required (Article 15(5)).

Article 16(1) establishes a Convention Secretariat with comparatively wide-ranging competences. In addition to administrative, co-ordinating, and clearing-house functions, most of which are related to facilitating information exchange and international co-operation as required by Articles 10 and 13 (Article 16(1.a–h)), these include two substantive duties: the Secretariat assists parties in identifying cases of illegal traffic, and helps parties to secure equipment and experts in the event of an emergency (Article 16(1.i and 1.j). During the negotiation process, the inclusion of additional substantive Secretariat functions, mainly related to the provision of technical assistance, was proposed by some developing countries; the more far-reaching of these proposals were opposed by industrialized nations, and by UNEP, for practical and financial reasons.[97] In accordance with Article 16(2), an Interim Secretariat was set up in Geneva (Switzerland) under the auspices of UNEP in November 1989. The focus of its activities was on promoting the entry into force of the Convention and preparing for the first meeting of the Conference of the Parties. This body now serves as the permanent Convention Secretariat, the first Conference of the Parties having designated UNEP as the organization responsible for carrying out the Secretariat functions on a permanent basis in accordance with Article 16(3).[98] As we saw, the Secretariat has assumed a very important and active role in the promotion of the implementation and further development of the Convention.

Additional bodies have been set up by the Conference of the Parties at its first meeting, including the Technical Working Group and the open-ended Ad Hoc Committee on Implementation referred to above, and the Working Group of Legal Experts to develop a protocol on liability and compensation. All of these mechanisms are so far working on an ad hoc basis, their mandates being periodically extended and modified by the Conference of the Parties.[99]

At the national level, each party is required to establish two pertinent agencies: a 'focal point' responsible for the exchange of information with other parties and the Secretariat, and a 'competent authority' for handling the PIC procedure (Article 2(6) and (7), Article 5(1)). Parties must inform each other, through the Secretariat, within 3 months of entry into force of

[97] See UNEP, (1989a), pp. 7–8, 10; *Report of the Working Group on its 3rd session* (UNEP/WG.189/3), pp. 7–8, 38–40; *Executive Director's Luxembourg Note* (UNEP/WG.191/2); *Executive Director's Basel Proposals* (UNEP/WG.191/3/Add.7).

[98] Conference Decision I/7 (1992); cf. also *Note of the Executive Director of UNEP on the Designation of the Secretariat*, 7 September 1992, (UNEP/CHW.1/17).

[99] Cf. Conference Decisions I/2, I/4, I/5, I/9, I/13, I/15, I/19 (1992); Decisions II/1–3, II/13–15 (1994). For a summary of the 1992 Decisions see Kummer, in YBIEL 3 (1992), p. 288 et seq.

the Convention for them, about the agencies they have entrusted with these functions, and subsequently about any changes in this designation (Article 5(2) and (3), Article 13(2.a)). About half of the parties had not complied with this requirement prior to the second meeting of the Conference of the Parties, and were accordingly requested by the Conference to do so.[100]

19. Financial mechanisms

Whereas the infrastructure established by the Basel Convention relied chiefly on voluntary contributions from signatories and parties and the UNEP Environment Fund during its interim period of operation,[101] the main financial mechanisms were determined subsequent to entry into force. The Conference of the Parties regularly approves the budget for the Secretariat and the scale of contributions from parties. At its first meeting, it asked the UN Secretary-General to establish a trust fund for the Basel Convention, and a technical co-operation trust fund for assistance to developing countries. Since many states have failed to make their contributions to the funds in a timely manner, the financial status of the Basel infrastructure remains precarious.[102] The proposed establishment of a fund for emergency response in accordance with Article 14(2), and an international hazardous wastes compensation fund, both under consideration by the Conference of the Parties, will be discussed in Chapter 6 below.

K. Compliance Monitoring and Settlement of Disputes

During the negotiations, numerous proposals for the verification of compliance and action against parties found to be acting in breach of the Convention's provisions were put forward, including the establishment of a 'watchdog agency' with the competence to actively verify states' compliance with their obligations. The proposals put forward included a duty of the Secretariat to investigate alleged contraventions of the Convention and to convene a Conference of the Parties to adopt the necessary countermeasures (Nigeria); the right of every party to verify, through inspection, the activities of other parties (Nigeria); the treatment of parties found to act in breach of the Convention as non-parties (Australia); and the estab-

[100] Conference Docs. UNEP/CHW.1/13, UNEP/CHW.2/17; Conference Decisions I/10 (1992), II/6 (1994).

[101] Cf. the relevant *Report of the UN Secretary-General to the General Assembly of 4 June 1991* (Doc. A/46/214–E/77, repr. in Kwiatkowska and Soons, (1993), p. 124 et seq.) and the *Executive Director's Report to the 1st Conference of the Parties* (UNEP/CHW.1/2), pp. 9–10.

[102] Conference Decisions I/7 (1992); II/25 (1994). Cf. also Conference Docs. UNEP/CHW.1/9 and 1/9/Corr.1 on financial provisions (21 August 1992); Governing Council Decision on the control of transboundary movements of hazardous wastes and their disposal, 21 May 1993, (repr. in EPL 23/3/4(1993), p. 170), urging states to meet their financial obligations.

lishment of a task force charged with actively assisting parties in implementing the Convention, and carrying out waste surveys (Egypt).[103]

Some of the proposed mechanisms might have provided effective control; however, none of them were accepted. Article 19 of the Basel Convention merely provides that any party which has reason to believe that another party is acting in contravention of the Convention shall inform the Secretariat, and the party in question, accordingly. The Secretariat must then relay 'all relevant information' to the other parties. The Secretariat is thus given a rather limited monitoring function. Although this mechanism may constitute a basis for compliance monitoring through transparency, an institutionalized verification procedure, including, in particular, performance supervision by an independent body, would have been more effective.[104] On a more modest scale, the first Working Group charged with the elaboration of elements of a future protocol on liability and compensation considered the establishment of an international commission with exclusive jurisdiction for the assessment of clean-up and remedial action costs, and the valuation of environmental damage.[105] The relevant provision was subsequently deleted by the Second Working Group, however. These issues will be discussed more fully in Chapter 6 below.

Article 20 deals with the settlement of disputes concerning alleged non-compliance or interpretation of the Convention's provisions. Such disputes should be resolved primarily by negotiation or other peaceful means, or, if this proves impossible, by agreement on submission either to arbitration in accordance with the procedure set out in Annex VI, or to the International Court of Justice.

AN ASSESSMENT OF THE BASEL CONVENTION

The above examination of the Basel Convention shows its support of most of the major concepts on which a future global waste management regime should be based, as submitted in Chapter 1 above. The Convention's fundamental principles of waste minimization, proximity of disposal, environmentally sound waste management, and 'cradle-to-grave' monitoring by means of an international control system, indicate a tendency towards an integrated approach to pollution control. This tendency is enhanced by the Technical Guidelines and the Waste Management Strategy elaborated

[103] Doc. UNEP/WG.191/CRP.14; Proposal by Nigeria (informal Conference room paper); Doc. UNEP/WG.189/3, Annex I, p. 31, Annex II.

[104] See Handl and Lutz, in Handl and Lutz, (1989a), p. 60; Abrams, (1990), p. 831; Rublack, (1993), p. 31; and Lang, in Lang, Neuhold, and Zemanek, (1991), p. 155. Cf. Sebek, (1990); Handl, (1990), p. 16 et seq. (discussing examples of supervisory mechanisms established by other conventions).

[105] *Report of the Ad Hoc Working Group on liability on its 2nd session*, 9 March 1991, (UNEP/CHW/WG.1/2/3), p. 7.

within the framework of the Convention. By addressing the necessity of protecting the global environment against the adverse effects of hazardous wastes, establishing global standards for waste management, and calling for exchange of information between states and mutual assistance in technical fields, the Basel Convention contains elements of a holistic approach towards environmental protection. On the other hand, some of its cornerstone provisions are indicative of the sovereignty-based approach.[106] This is best illustrated by the Convention's definition of the term 'transboundary', which, by requiring the involvement of at least two states in any operation covered by the Convention, effectively excludes the protection of the global commons against contamination by hazardous wastes—with the exception of Antarctica—from its scope of application. Another indication of a sovereignty-based approach is the express recognition of the sovereign right of states to decide whether or not they accept hazardous waste imports. This right is enhanced by the PIC procedure, though modified by the principle of non-discrimination, by restrictions of transboundary movements of hazardous wastes based on objective criteria, and by obligations to abide by the international standards established by the Convention. The Basel Convention strongly supports the preventive approach to environmental protection. This is evident in all of its fundamental principles, as well as in the strong emphasis on international co-operation and provision of assistance to states in the implementation of the Convention. The work on the Technical Guidelines, the Waste Management Strategy, and the Manual on Implementation point towards a continuation of this trend.

With regard to the quality of the legal regime established by the Basel Convention, one of the most common criticisms until recently was that it did not ban transboundary movements of hazardous wastes and was therefore bound to fail entirely in its objective to curb international waste traffic; instead, it legitimized such traffic.[107] On the other hand, it was pointed out that a total ban would not be appropriate since it would prevent transboundary hazardous waste disposal even in cases where this represents the best solution from an environmental viewpoint. It would, for example, preclude the establishment of joint disposal facilities by neighbouring industrialized countries.[108] Despite the new problems it raises, the 1994 Decision

[106] See also Handl, (1989), p. 369 et seq.

[107] See among many others Greenpeace *Waste Trade Update*, Vol. 2, Issue 2, 1 March 1989; Greenpeace, (1990), p. 12 et seq.; Bernstorff, (1989); Cusack, (1990), p. 420; Handley (1989), p. 10171 et seq.; Jones, (1993), p. 341.

[108] See UNEP: First Revised Draft Convention on the Control of the Transboundary Movements of Hazardous Wastes (UNEP/180/2), Comments, p. 10; Tolba, (1990), p. 205 et seq.; *ICC Statement on the Basel Convention* (repr. in EPL19/6 (1989), p. 238); Huntoon, (1989), p. 268; Kummer and Rummel-Bulska, (1990), p. 35; Birnie and Boyle, (1992), p. 302; Kwiatkowska and Soons, (1993), Editors' Introduction, p. XXIX, and sources quoted there; Schmidt, (1992), p. 76 et seq. For a discussion of advantages and disadvantages of the ban see Donald, (1992), p. 445 et seq.

banning hazardous waste exports from OECD to non-OECD countries has in principle addressed both these criticisms: it provides a basis for affording stronger protection to countries not sufficiently equipped to deal with foreign hazardous wastes, but does not preclude the establishment and operation of joint disposal facilities by countries with similar situations and needs. The definition of the group of countries to be protected against the influx of foreign hazardous wastes in terms of their non-membership of the OECD instead of as 'developing countries'—despite its problematic aspects mentioned above—acknowledges the need for protection of countries with economies in transition, an issue that was not on the political agenda at the time of the elaboration of the Basel Convention.

L. *Perceived Strengths of the Convention*

In the first few years following the adoption of the Basel Convention, there seemed to emerge a consensus among most writers addressing the issue that even though the Convention was far from providing a perfect solution to the problem of transboundary movements of hazardous wastes, it did address most of the relevant issues and was therefore a step in the right direction. Its future effectiveness depended on the effective and timely regulation of the issues still left open, as well as on adherence by as many states as possible, and on strict implementation and enforcement by party states.[109]

This seems a fair assessment. It might be added that the Basel Convention, as adopted, represented the maximum degree of consensus that was politically possible at that time. As illustrated above, the negotiators' willingness and capability to compromise had to be stretched to the limit in order to reach agreement. Thus the adoption of a treaty providing more than minimum standards had to be considered an achievement in itself. With the incorporation of the PIC procedure, the concept of a limited ban, the allocation of responsibility to states for illegal transactions, the duty to re-import, and the duty to provide technical assistance to developing countries, the Basel Convention goes far beyond the minimum commitment to monitor the state of the environment and exchange scientific information, found in many of the older environmental treaties. The Convention also contains commitments and directives for its further elaboration, many of which are currently being implemented by the subsidiary bodies and the Secretariat under the guidance of the Conference of the Parties, as we have seen.

[109] See among others Abrams, (1990), pp. 844 et seq., 923; Bartram and Engel, (1989), p. 121; Birnie and Boyle (1992), p. 341 et seq.; Donald, (1992), p. 457; Gröbl, (1989), p. 8; Hackett, (1990), p. 322; Handl, (1989), p. 367; Kiss, (1991), p. 539; van der Mensbrugghe, (1990), p. 277; Moisé, (1989), p. 906; Montgomery, (1990), p. 325 et seq.; Rublack, (1989), p. 391; Sebek, (1990), p. 295; Walsh, (1992).

The adoption of the 1994 Decision on a ban on hazardous waste traffic from OECD to non-OECD countries is a striking illustration of a change of attitude among the main international actors within a relatively short period of time, which made it possible for them to agree on a measure that was the object of extensive controversy only a few years previously. In addition, work on equally important but less politically fraught issues is contributing to the further development and implementation of the Convention: this includes the clarification of the definition of hazardous wastes and the notion of 'environmentally sound management'; the elaboration of a protocol on liability and compensation; the consideration of international funds for emergency assistance and compensation; the proposed establishment of regional training centres; the assignment of additional functions to the Convention Secretariat; and the establishment of the Technical Working Group, the Working Group on Liability, and the open-ended Ad Hoc Committee on Implementation. The active role of the Secretariat and the subsidiary bodies in many fields justifies hope that the Convention may provide the basis for the continuous elaboration of new and more stringent rules.[110] The simplified procedure for amending the Annexes provides the necessary flexibility for changing the lists of wastes to be controlled by the Convention in accordance with new scientific findings, should this become necessary.[111] The Basel Convention could therefore follow the pattern of the 1979 Geneva Convention on Long-Range Transboundary Air Pollution and the 1985 Vienna Convention for the Protection of the Ozone Layer: it could provide the first stage of a more stringent and detailed regime.[112] Thus it provides a sound basis for the further development of international law in this field.

M. *Perceived Weaknesses of the Convention*

Nevertheless, a number of weaknesses of the Convention should be pointed out. One is the use of many imprecise and vague terms which are open to differing interpretations. Another problem is the fact that a number of points on which agreement could not be reached at the Basel Conference were left open, thus deferring the decision on their regulation.[113] However, developments subsequent to the Convention's adoption show that both these deficiencies can be remedied. We may refer to the work on the liability protocol, and to the development of the concept of environmentally

[110] See Handl, (1989), p.372.

[111] See Kiss, in Brown Weiss, (1992b), pp. 324–5; and idem, (1989a).

[112] See the *Statement by the Executive Director of UNEP to the 1st Conference of the Parties* (excerpts repr. in EPL 23/1(1993), p. 13). See also Kiss, in Brown Weiss, (1992b), p. 320 et seq.; Sand, (1990), p. 12; Hurrell and Kingsbury, in Hurrell and Kingsbury, (1992), p. 16 et seq.

[113] For a discussion of this point see Handl, (1990), p. 6.

sound management of hazardous wastes by the Technical Guidelines and the Waste Management Strategy.

A significant practical problem is the potential inability of states, especially developing and transitional countries, to comply with the Convention's fairly complex system of control, monitoring, and exchange of information. As we saw, many parties had not complied with the requirements of submitting reports to the Secretariat, and designating competent authorities and focal points, in time for the second Conference of the Parties. The successful application of the PIC system in particular depends on a sophisticated national infrastructure. This presents even the majority of the industrialized states with a problem, and borders on the unrealistic in the case of developing or transitional countries. The point is illustrated by the shipment of 18 tons of wastes containing PCBs from Australia to France on board the vessel *Maria Laura* in September 1992: reportedly, Australia did not obtain the prior consent of France (or that of the transit countries) to this transaction, even though both states had by that time acceded to the Basel Convention.[114]

Despite the Convention's attempt to mitigate this problem by stressing the need for international co-operation and giving relevant support functions to the Secretariat, this remains a potential weakness. Notwithstanding the optimism of some its supporters, the ban adopted in 1994 is not likely to dispose of this concern entirely: in common with the application of the PIC procedure, the successful enforcement of the ban requires an effective infrastructure. One argument that was put forward in this context is that compliance with the ban will be difficult to monitor and therefore easy to circumvent, whereas the PIC system, however difficult to apply effectively, at least ensures transparency, thus allowing 'cradle-to-grave' monitoring of waste transactions as well as rapid intervention in the event of an accident.[115] Some fear that the adoption of the ban, by eliminating the option of legal hazardous waste transactions between the two groups of countries, will in effect force the relevant hazardous waste trade into illegality. This seems to be borne out in part by observations which indicate that illegal schemes for the transfer of hazardous wastes have tended to become more ingenious and elaborate since the inception of the Basel Convention, and thus more difficult to spot: where the hazardous wastes were once transported straightforwardly, there is now more camouflage to circumvent the mechanisms of the Convention. Some illegal schemes take on the

[114] See the report in EPL 22/5/6(1992), p. 337. On this point see also Wirth, in Handl and Lutz, (1989a), p. 98; Kwiatkowska and Soons, (1993), Editors' Introduction, p. XXIX; Schmidt, (1992), p. 75 et seq.

[115] Cf. Schmidt, (1992), p. 77, referring to the parallel discussion in the context of the ban on ivory trade under CITES.

characteristics of organized crime, and some are carried out in conjunction with humanitarian aid or the illicit transfer of money.[116]

It is at this point in time difficult to decide whether the PIC procedure or the ban is more difficult to apply and enforce. To a certain extent, this problem is in the nature of the issue and cannot be considered a weakness of the Basel Convention as such: the fact remains that persons who stand to make millions of dollars through illegal traffic will not be easily deterred.[117] In any event, it is undisputed that the national mechanisms for control and prevention of hazardous waste traffic will have to be strengthened considerably, not only through adoption of criminal legislation as required by the Basel Convention, but also through development of the relevant national infrastructures.

A related problem is that—contrary to the intentions of some negotiating states—the Convention Secretariat was given very limited substantive supervisory functions, as we have seen. With few exceptions, its function is limited to co-ordinating and monitoring. The absence of supervisory authority in the PIC procedure, for example, may prove a major weakness.[118] The effectiveness of the PIC procedure will thus depend all the more on the extent and quality of its implementation at the national level. It is therefore too early to decide whether it will provide effective control, or merely additional bureaucracy, as claimed by some.[119]

In addition, the diversity of the situations leading to transboundary movements of hazardous wastes, discussed in Chapter 1 above, has not as yet been sufficiently taken into account. The adoption of the 1994 Decision did provide the basis for different sets of rules governing the relationship within the OECD, among non-OECD members, and between the two groups, thus creating a 'two-world system': this goes some way towards addressing the justified concern that the same rules were applicable under the Basel Convention to all countries, regardless of their different situations.[120] On the other hand, the same rules are still applicable to wastes with a high level of toxicity destined for disposal and wastes with a low hazard potential destined for recycling. This inadequacy may be mitigated to some extent by resorting to regional regulation, as we will see in Chapters 3 and 4 below. Nevertheless, the elaboration of a more sophisticated system of classifying hazardous wastes, and recycling and disposal operations, will be an important step forward. These issues are currently being examined by the Technical Working Group in accordance with the mandate given to it by the Conference of the Parties.

116 Informal information received from the Secretariat of the Basel Convention, May 1994. See also Kummer, (1994a), p. 58 et seq. Cf. Louka, (1994), p. XIV.

117 See also Donald, (1992), p. 456.

118 See also Abrams, (1990), p. 835.

119 Greenpeace *Waste Trade Update*, Vol. 2, Issue 3, 15 July 1989; Strohm, (1993), p. 140.

120 See Donald, (1992), p. 458.

Finally, Article 11—allowing separate agreements with non-parties to the Basel Convention—entails the danger of weakening the concept of a limited ban or even jeopardizing the aim to ensure compliance with the Convention's standards by all parties, in particular since it is difficult to determine the quality of such agreements and states' compliance with them.[121] On the other hand, Article 11 opens the possibility of the adoption, under the umbrella of the Basel Convention, of regional agreements which are more stringent than the Basel Convention.[122] These issues will be examined in the next chapter.

THE NEED FOR CO-ORDINATION WITH OTHER RELEVANT LEGAL INSTRUMENTS

The significance of other sources of international law which are relevant to the issue of transboundary movements of hazardous wastes, already addressed in the Montevideo Programme and the 1987 Governing Council Decision adopting the Cairo Guidelines, was discussed throughout the negotiation process on the Basel Convention. Accordingly, it is reflected in the preamble of the Convention (operational paras. 12–16, 22).

Relevant international legal sources were important in two respects. First, a number of existing legal rules served as models for the Convention's provisions. The first two drafts of the Convention, prepared by the UNEP Secretariat, were based to a large extent on the Cairo Guidelines, but also drew on other pertinent legal instruments, namely the EU Council Directive on transfrontier shipments of toxic and dangerous wastes, the OECD's draft Agreement on Control of Transfrontier Movement of Hazardous Wastes (see Chapter 4 paras. 2, 8 below), and the UNCTDG's Orange Book (see Chapter 1(H) above).[123] Accordingly, the relevant rules had considerable influence on the final shape of the Convention. In addition, representatives of these and other international organizations continued to provide relevant input during the deliberations.[124]

Second, it was recognized that a number of pertinent issues were regulated by existing international legal sources, as we saw in Chapter 1 above.

[121] See Abrams, (1990); Hackett, (1990), p. 322; Kwiatkowska and Soons, (1993), Editors' Introduction, p. XLVIII; Lang, in Lang, Neuhold, and Zemanek, (1991), p. 155.

[122] Kummer and Rummel-Bulska, (1990), p. 35; also Handl, (1990), p. 13 et seq.

[123] First Draft Convention on the Control of the Transboundary Movements of Hazardous Wastes (UNEP180/2), pp. 4, 20; First Revised Draft Convention (UNEP/WG.182/2). See also the report of the Working Group on its organizational meeting (UNEP/WG.180/3), p. 4; and the *Explanatory Memorandum to the 1990 Proposal of the EU Commission for a Regulation on waste shipments*, 26 July 1990, (Doc. COM(90)362 final).

[124] See the *Final Report of the Working Group* (UNEP/IG.80/4), p. 4; also the *Report on its 2nd session* and *the Report on its 3rd session* (UNEP/WG.186/3, p. 2; UNEP/WG.189/3, p. 5 et seq.)

This meant that, to prevent duplication, the relevant instruments should be taken into account by the new Convention, and conflicts and overlaps should be avoided.[125] The Basel Convention addresses this problem in a number of different ways. In the area of packaging, labelling and transport of hazardous wastes, for instance, the Convention regulates only the basic principles, and refers to the 'accepted international practices and standards' in the field (Article 4 (7.b)); see para. 7 above), thus providing for application of the non-binding rules discussed in Chapter 1(H) above. Other provisions, in addition to regulating an issue, call for compliance with 'relevant rules of international law', or state that such rules shall not be affected by the Convention, without, however, identifying these sources, or addressing the possibility of contradictions. This approach is adopted with respect to navigational rights and freedoms, and in the definition of illegal traffic (Article 4(12) and Article 9(1.e)). In some areas, where the possibility of conflict is evident, the Basel Conference referred the question to the appropriate international body. These areas include the transport of hazardous wastes by sea, the protection of marine and coastal areas against pollution by discharge or disposal of hazardous substances, and the management of radioactive wastes. The Basel Conference adopted three resolutions calling upon UNEP to co-operate with IMO and IAEA, respectively, to harmonize the Basel Convention and the legal instruments in question.[126]

Following the adoption of the Basel Convention, the need for its harmonization with other legal instruments was re-iterated by a number of international organizations.[127] Subsequently, numerous initiatives were taken at the international and regional levels to achieve this harmonization.[128] These efforts were subsequently endorsed, and their continuation encouraged, by the Conference of the Parties to the Basel Convention.[129]

Of the transport rules discussed in Chapter 1(H) above, the IMO Codes of Conduct on the transport of dangerous goods by sea have been adjusted

[125] *Reports of the Working Group on its 1st and 5th sessions* (UNEP/WG. 182/3, p. 5; UNEP/IG.80/4, Annex I, pp. 9–10); see also the summary of the Executive Director's opening statement to the Working Group at its 3rd session (UNEP/WG. 189/3), p. 2.

[126] Resolutions 2, 5 and 7 of the Basel Conference, 22 March 1989 (attached to the Final Act of the Conference).

[127] e.g. the UN General Assembly (UNGA Resolution 44/226 (22 December 1989), repr. in Kwiatkowska and Soons, (1993), p. 82); the UNCED PrepCom (see Kwiatkowska and Soons, (1993), p. XXXIII); the UN/ECE's Inland Transport Committee (Kwiatkowska and Soons, (1993), p. LXIV; Sand, in YBIEL 2(1991), p. 401), and the IMO (see Chapter 5 below).

[128] For an overview of this work cf. the *Executive Director's Report to the 1st Conference of the Parties* (UNEP/CHW.1/2); Secretariat paper on relations with other international organizations (Conference Doc. UNEP/CHW.1/7).

[129] Conference Decisions I/4 (1992) and II/7 (1994) (co-operation between UNEP and IMO on dumping of wastes at sea); I/6 (1992) and II/8 (1994) (co-operation between UNEP and IAEA); I/18 (1992) and II/24 (1994) (co-operation between UNEP and IMO on transport of dangerous goods by sea); I/8 (1992) and II/23 (1954) (co-operation between UNEP and other international organizations); I/23 (1992) and II/21 (1994) (implementation of Agenda 21).

to the requirements of the Basel Convention. In response to Resolution 7 of the Basel Conference and a 1989 Resolution of the IMO Assembly,[130] the Maritime Safety Committee and the Marine Environment Committee of the IMO amended the IMDG Code and the BC Code in May 1991, and the BCH and IBC Codes in November/December 1992, to include provisions on hazardous wastes.[131] In particular, relevant revisions were made to the sections dealing with prior notification of waste shipments. The UNCTDG's Orange Book was amended in 1990 to ensure alignment with the classification of hazardous wastes by the Basel Convention.[132] The Conference of the Parties to the Basel Convention endorsed these amendments as being consistent with the requirements of the Convention.[133]

The issue of transboundary movement of nuclear waste was recognized from the beginning as being within the sphere of competence of the IAEA, and it was accordingly agreed to exclude nuclear wastes from the scope of the Basel Convention (see para. 4 above). UNEP's contribution, in implementation of Resolution 5 of the Basel Conference, consisted in participation in the negotiations on the non-binding Code of Practice on the International Transboundary Movement of Radioactive Waste, adopted by the General Conference of the IAEA in September 1990,[134] which embodies most principles of the Basel Convention, albeit in weaker form. In October 1993, the General Conference of the IAEA decided to initiate preparations for a convention on the safety of nuclear waste management, even though the timing of this preparatory work was left open.[135] The Conference of the Parties to the Basel Convention welcomed this decision and mandated the Secretariat to cooperate with the IAEA on this issue.[136]

[130] IMO Assembly Resolution on Transboundary Movement of Hazardous Wastes, 19 October 1989, (A 16/Res. 676).

[131] Cf. *Executive Director's Report to the 1st Conference of the Parties* (UNEP/CHW.1/2); IMO Docs. MSC/Circ.558 (20 June 1991), MSC/Circ.555 (20 June 1991), A/17/12/2+Add.1 (26 September 1991). See also Kwiatkowska and Soons, (1993), p. 491 et seq.; IMO Sub-Committee on the Carriage of Dangerous Goods, 42nd session, *Report to the Maritime Safety Committee*, 9 November 1990, (CDG 42/22), pp. 23–5; IMO Sub-Committee on Containers and Cargoes, 31st session, *Report to the Maritime Safety Committee*, 28 January 1991, (BC 31/14), p. 22. For an outline of this work cf. Kwiatkowska and Soons, (1993), Editors' Introduction, p. XLI; Kummer, in YBIEL 2(1991), p. 177, and eadem, in YBIEL 3(1992), p. 291.

[132] Cf. *Executive Director's Report to the 1st Conference of the Parties* (UNEP/CHW.1/2); Kwiatkowska and Soons, (1993), Editors' Introduction, p. XL. See also the account of the 15th session of the UNCTDG in EPL 19/1(1989), p. 8.; and the account of the 16th session by Sand, in YBIEL 2(1991), p. 401.

[133] Conference Decision I/18 (1992). Cf. also *Executive Director's Report to the 1st Conference of the Parties* (UNEP/CHW.1/2).

[134] Repr. in Kwiatkowska and Soons, (1993), p. 71 et seq. See also IAEA General Conference Resolution GC(XXXIV)/RES/530 (21 September 1990), repr. ibid., p. 69; IAEA *News Features* no. 9, December 1990. Cf. Lang, in Lang, Neuhold, and Zemanek, (1991), p. 159; Kwiatkowska and Soons, (1993), Editors' Introduction, p. XXVII et seq.

[135] IAEA General Conference Resolution GC(XXXVII)/RES/615, (October 1993).

[136] Conference Decisions I/6 (1992), II/8 (1994).

The more substantive of the efforts to harmonize the Basel Convention with related legal instruments will be the subject of the following chapters. They include the adjustment of the EU and OECD legislation to the requirements of the Basel Convention (Chapter 4 below), and the joint efforts of UNEP and the IMO to harmonize the Basel and London Conventions in response to Resolution 2 of the Basel Conference (Chapter 5 below).

3
The Basel Convention as an Umbrella for Regional Hazardous Waste Treaties

Initially, the intention of the drafters of the Basel Convention was to elaborate a global 'framework treaty' on transboundary movements and management of hazardous wastes, which would regulate only the fundamental principles, and within which detailed regional agreements could be concluded. This approach is reflected in the following provision, contained in the early drafts of the Basel Convention:[1] 'The Contracting Parties are encouraged to enter into bilateral, multilateral and regional agreements with a view to implementing and further developing the provisions of this Convention.' This concept was abandoned at an early stage in favour of a high degree of detailed regulation at the global level, combined with a fairly restrictive approach towards regional treaties.[2] As mentioned in Chapter 2 above, the Basel Convention, while setting uniform global standards, makes provision for the adoption of separate agreements or arrangements on transboundary movements of hazardous wastes under its umbrella. Article 11 of the Convention determines the conditions of adherence to such legal instruments by Basel parties, and the relationship between the Basel Convention and these agreements. Article 30 of the Vienna Convention on the Law of Treaties applies as a subsidiary rule.[3] Chapter 20 of UNCED's Agenda 21 endorses the formulation of regional agreements on transboundary movements of hazardous wastes.[4] A number of regional treaties that could come within the purview of Article 11 already exist, while others are in the process of elaboration.

The same concept underlies the 1992 UN/ECE Convention on the protection of international waterways, discussed in Chapter 5 below: in addition to providing uniform global standards, it calls on parties to adopt bilateral or regional agreements or arrangements, for which it gives detailed guidelines. These extend even to the institutional framework to be set up under regional systems.

[1] Third Revised Draft Convention on the Control of Transboundary Movements of Hazardous Wastes (UNEP/WG.186/3), Annex A, p. 17.

[2] See *Report of the Working Group on its 3rd session* (UNEP/WG.189/3), Annex I, draft Article XII; also the First Draft Convention (UNEP/WG.180/2), pp. 4, 9, 22; *Report of the Working Group on its organizational meeting* (UNEP/WG.180/3), p. 4; *Report on its 1st session* (UNEP/WG.182/3), p. 4.

[3] See Sciso, (1986), p. 63; Sinclair, (1984), p. 97.

[4] UNCED Agenda 21, ch. 20 para. 20.15. Cf. also Basel Convention Conference Doc. UNEP/CHW.1/7/Add.1 (15 September 1992), p. 2.

The aim of this chapter is to analyse the relationship between the Basel Convention and the existing regional treaties addressed by Article 11, and to examine the question whether the Basel Convention and the relevant legal instruments can supplement and enhance each other as submitted in Chapter 1 above.

ARTICLE 11 OF THE BASEL CONVENTION

A. *Overview*

As mentioned in Chapter 2 para. 10 above, the inclusion and wording of Article 11 were subject to considerable debate during the elaboration of the Basel Convention. This accounts for some imprecision and a number of inconsistencies in its wording. Prior to examining the treaties that could come within the scope of Article 11, this provision needs to be analysed in more detail. Article 11 of the Basel Convention reads as follows:

1. Notwithstanding the provisions of Article 4 paragraph 5, Parties may enter into bilateral, multilateral, or regional agreements or arrangements regarding transboundary movement of hazardous wastes or other wastes with Parties or non-Parties provided that such agreements or arrangements do not derogate from the environmentally sound management of hazardous wastes and other wastes as required by this Convention. These agreements or arrangements shall stipulate provisions which are not less environmentally sound than those provided for by this Convention in particular taking into account the interests of developing countries.
2. Parties shall notify the Secretariat of any bilateral, multilateral or regional agreements or arrangements referred to in paragraph 1 and those which they have entered into prior to the entry into force of this Convention for them, for the purpose of controlling transboundary movements of hazardous wastes and other wastes which take place entirely among the Parties to such agreements. The provisions of this Convention shall not affect transboundary movements which take place pursuant to such agreements provided that such agreements are compatible with the environmentally sound management of hazardous wastes and other wastes as required by this Convention.

The provision addresses two types of legal instruments, termed 'agreements' and 'arrangements', respectively. The present analysis is limited to those legal instruments which are denoted by the term 'agreements'. This term obviously refers to a convention or treaty concluded between two or more states, as defined by the Vienna Convention on the Law of Treaties (Article 2(1.a)).[5] Legal instruments denoted by the term 'arrangements' will be discussed in Chapter 4 below.

[5] Cf. ILC, Commentary on the Final Draft Articles on the Law of Treaties, *Yearbook of the ILC* II (1966), pp. 204–7 (*ILC Commentary*), giving examples of the variety of terms used to designate a treaty—including the term 'agreement'. On the distinction between agreements

Article 11 does not limit the adoption of relevant treaties to the regional scale: treaties of global as well as bilateral scope may also be concluded in conformity with this provision. In order to come within the purview of Article 11, the relevant agreements must specifically address transboundary movements of hazardous wastes as defined by the Basel Convention, i.e. pollution source transfer involving at least two states (see Chapter 2 para. 4 above). The relationship between the Basel Convention and treaties that address any other aspect of the hazardous waste cycle is not governed by Article 11. It will be discussed in Chapter 5 below.

Article 11(2) requires parties to notify the Secretariat of any separate agreement on transboundary movements of hazardous wastes they have entered into either before or after the entry into force of the Basel Convention for them. The Conference of the Parties at its first meeting requested the open-ended Ad Hoc Committee on Implementation to examine such agreements and to present a report on their compatibility with the Basel Convention to the Conference at its second meeting. In complying with this request, the Committee side-stepped the implications of making a pronouncement on the compatibility of individual agreements with the Convention. Instead, it decided to focus on assisting states in making their own assessment, and drew up a list of questions to be used for this purpose. The Conference endorsed this course of action.[6]

In the further analysis of Article 11, the following questions must be answered:

(1) What environmental standards must the relevant treaties establish in order to be in conformity with the requirements of Article 11?

(2) Does the requirement for relevant treaties to govern hazardous waste movements '*entirely between parties to such agreements*' apply only to pre-Basel agreements, or to post-Basel agreements as well?

(3) What is the relationship between the Basel Convention and the treaties concluded under Article 11, in particular in the event of incompatibility between them?

and less formal international legal instruments cf. Aust, (1986), p. 787 et seq. On the Vienna Convention cf. also Reuter, (1989), pp. 22–7; Rosenne, (1985); Sinclair, (1984); Sciso, (1986); Verdross and Simma, (1984), p. 432 et seq. and sources quoted there; Brownlie, (1990), p. 630 et seq. and sources quoted there.

[6] See Conference Decisions I/9 (1992), II/10 (1994); *Report of the Ad Hoc Committee on Implementation on its 1st meeting*, October 1993, (UNEP/CHW/C.1/1/9, with Decision I/3 as Annex); and Conference Docs. UNEP/CHW.1/16 and UNEP/CHW.2/9.

B. *Compatibility of Separate Agreements with the Provisions of the Basel Convention*

1. Interpretation of Article 11 based on the requirement of 'environmentally sound management'

The first question concerns the extent to which legal instruments addressed by Article 11 must conform to the provisions of the Basel Convention. In this respect, the wording of Article 11 is at the same time verbose and vague. The provision attempts to express the relevant requirement in three different ways. Paragraph 1 stipulates that such agreements are permissible provided that they 'do not derogate from the environmentally sound management of hazardous wastes and other wastes as required by this Convention', and that they 'shall stipulate provisions which are not less environmentally sound than those provided for by this Convention'. Paragraph 2 provides that the Basel Convention shall not affect transactions taking place pursuant to such agreements provided that they are 'compatible with the environmentally sound management of hazardous wastes and other wastes as required by this Convention'. In addition, paragraph 1 requires the interests of developing countries to be taken into account in the conclusion of such agreements.

Earlier drafts of this provision required relevant agreements to be 'compatible with the aims and purposes' of the Basel Convention.[7] A draft provision requiring that such agreements 'shall not be inconsistent with the provisions of this Convention' was rejected, as was a proposal by the African Group to require such agreements to be 'in conformity with the provisions of the present Convention'.[8] Such wording would have prohibited Basel parties from entering into any agreement which was in any respect less stringent than the Basel Convention. It was opposed mainly by certain industrialized states who feared that their existing regional legal instruments would not meet this requirement.[9]

Since more stringent proposals were rejected, we must conclude that the relevant legal instruments need not conform in detail to the provisions of the Basel Convention. Instead, they must be in conformity with the Convention's requirements related to the 'environmentally sound management' of hazardous wastes. One approach to the interpretation of this

[7] Cf. the Third Revised Draft Convention on the Control of Transboundary Movements of Hazardous Wastes (UNEP/WG.186/3); and the Fifth Revised Draft Convention on the Control of Transboundary Movements of Hazardous Wastes (UNEP/WG.189/3).

[8] Luxembourg revision of the Fifth Revised Draft Convention on the Control of Transboundary Movements of Hazardous Wastes (UNEP/WG.190/4); Doc. UNEP/WG.191/CRP.29 (March 1989). See also Article VIII of the London Convention and Article 197 of UNCLOS, both of which require relevant regional agreements to be 'consistent' with the corresponding global convention.

[9] Cf. Rublack, (1989), p. 386.

requirement would be to refer to Article 2(8) of the Basel Convention, which defines the term 'environmentally sound management'. As we saw in Chapter 2 para. 7 above, that definition, as it stands, is very unspecific. Efforts to give it more precise content have yet to be completed, and will in any case result in non-binding guidelines rather than a formal amendment of the Convention. Therefore, an interpretation based solely on Article 2(8) would lead to the conclusion that almost any legal instrument providing restrictions for transboundary movements of hazardous wastes, however vague, could satisfy the criterion of 'environmentally sound management'.[10] It seems doubtful that this is the intention of Article 11.

In the absence of a clearly defined and binding standard of 'environmentally sound management' against which to measure separate agreements on transboundary movements of hazardous wastes, an interpretation of the requirement under discussion should rely primarily on the spirit and fundamental objectives of the Basel Convention, in accordance with the teleological interpretation method. As discussed in Chapter 2, the Convention establishes uniform global rules based on a number of fundamental principles, and aims to restrict transactions taking place outside its framework—and therefore not adhering to its fundamental rules—through the concept of a limited ban. The same reasoning underlies CITES and the Montreal Protocol, neither of which allows its parties to circumvent this concept by entering into separate agreements that do not meet its fundamental standards.[11] The relevant Resolution of the Consultative Meeting of the Parties to the London Convention adopts the same approach (see Chapter 5(A) below).[12] The result of an interpretation of Article 11 based solely on the vague definition of 'environmentally sound management' offered by Article 2(8) would therefore clearly be incompatible with the spirit of the Basel Convention.[13]

[10] This view seems to be supported by Murphy, (1992), p. 13, claiming that Article 11 represents a 'grandfathering in clause', which 'allows trade to continue as it existed under prior bilateral and multilateral agreements'. No arguments are offered to substantiate this view.

[11] CITES does not prohibit trade with non-parties, but provides that standards comparable to those established by its provisions must apply to such trade (Articles II(4), X). The Montreal Protocol (as amended) permits trade with non-parties on a very limited scale if the non-party in question has been determined by the meeting of the parties to be in full compliance with the requirements of the Protocol (Article 4(8)).

[12] Resolution 29(10) of the Consultative Meeting calls for a prohibition on waste export for sea disposal to non-parties to the London Convention or a compatible regional agreement, unless there are 'both compelling reasons for such export and clear evidence that the wastes should be disposed of in compliance with the requirements of the London Convention and such regional conventions'.

[13] A similar argument is put forward in Greenpeace, (1992), p. 4, in the context of the compatibility of the 1992 OECD Decision with the Basel Convention (see Chapter 4 below).

2. Suggested broader interpretation of Article 11

It is submitted, therefore, that the requirement of 'environmental soundness' established by Article 11, instead of being derived solely from Article 2(8), should be defined in broader terms. It should be interpreted to mean that the relevant legal instruments must be based on environmental considerations, and that they must, as a minimum, adhere to the fundamental principles of the Basel Convention, as outlined in Chapter 2 above, with respect to the issues they address.[14] In particular, they should establish objective environmental standards. The adoption of such standards may not be left to be determined solely by the national legislation of the states involved. This interpretation is also consistent with the ongoing work to further develop the definition of 'environmentally sound management' through the Technical Guidelines, which support and clarify the fundamental principles of the Convention. A similar reasoning underlies the EU's 1993 Regulation on waste shipments (see Chapter 4 para. 2 below), which includes a provision inspired by Article 11 but giving more specific content to the requirement of 'environmental soundness' (Article 16(2)).

In more concrete terms, the requirements of Article 11 should thus be specified as follows. A separate agreement which establishes a regime for the transboundary movement and management of hazardous wastes should, firstly, promote the minimization of the generation of hazardous wastes, and their disposal as close as possible to the source of generation (principle of proximity). Thus, the instrument in question should not merely provide a 'tracking system' for hazardous waste transports, but must include incentives for their reduction. Secondly, the agreement should adhere to the principle of non-discrimination: it should establish environmental standards for the management of the wastes, whatever their place of disposal. This also means that it should prevent the export of hazardous wastes for the purpose of less environmentally sound, and therefore cheaper, disposal, e.g. by establishing environmental requirements for permissible exports. Thirdly, if the agreement does not in principle prohibit transboundary movements of hazardous wastes, it should adopt a control system for such movements, under which all potentially affected states take an informed part in the decision on a given transboundary movement. Lastly, provision should be made for the environmentally sound disposal of the wastes in the event of an illegal transaction, or a transaction that

[14] Similar reasoning appears to underlie the equivalent provision of UNCLOS: Article 311(3) permits the conclusion of separate agreements between parties, applicable solely to the relationship between them, 'provided that such agreements do not relate to a provision derogation from which is incompatible with the effective execution of the object of this Convention, and provided further that such agreements shall not affect the application of the basic principles embodied herein . . .'. For a discussion of this provision and its elaboration history see Rosenne, (1985), p. 85 et seq.

cannot be completed as foreseen. If the agreement does not establish a regime, but addresses only a particular stage or aspect of the transboundary transfer of hazardous wastes, it must adhere to standards similar to those of the Basel Convention with regard to that aspect.

The requirement for the interests of developing countries to be taken into account adds another aspect. Agreements governing waste transactions that involve developing countries should take special account of the limited capacity of those countries for monitoring the transport and ensuring the environmentally sound management of hazardous wastes, by imposing stricter mechanisms for the control of hazardous waste transactions than agreements applying exclusively to industrialized countries. Contrary to the views expressed by a number of writers, this should not, however, be interpreted to mean that agreements adhered to only by industrialized countries may establish significantly laxer standards than the Basel Convention. Such interpretation reflects the position adopted by some industrialized countries during the Basel negotiations. It implies that lower international standards can be justified in this case based on the assumption that appropriate standards exist at the national level.[15] Such delegation of standard-setting to national legislation is, in the author's view, incompatible with Article 11.

Article 11 has been interpreted by some as establishing different environmental requirements depending on whether the agreement in question was concluded before or after the entry into force of the Basel Convention: in this interpretation, paragraph 1, applying to 'post-Basel' agreements, is understood to establish more stringent rules than paragraph 2, applying to 'pre-Basel' agreements.[16] Although the elaboration history of Article 11 does show an initial distinction between pre- and post-Basel agreements, subsequent developments point towards the application of the same standards to both (see the analysis below). In addition, the wording does not indicate a clear distinction between the environmental requirements in the two cases.

The proposed interpretation of the requirement of 'environmental soundness' in Article 11 set out above appears at least in part to be supported by the Ad Hoc Committee on Implementation: a number of the points made here are reflected in the list of questions drawn up by the Committee, mentioned above. The questions are as follows (emphasis added):[17]

(1) Does the agreement *address the control of the transboundary movement* of hazardous wastes and other wastes subject to the Basel Convention?

[15] See Gröbl, (1989); de Villeneuve, (1990), p. 576.

[16] See e.g. the statement of the representative of UNEP to the 13th Consultative Meeting of the Contracting Parties to the London Convention, November 1990, (Report of the meeting, Doc. LDC13/15), p. 42; also Greenpeace, (1992).

[17] Decision I/3 of the Committee, October 1993, (UNEP/CHW/C.1/1/9), Appendix III.

(2) Taking all practicable steps, will the management of hazardous wastes under the agreement or arrangement be such that it will *protect human health and the environment against adverse effects*?

(3) How does the agreement or arrangement take into account the *interests of developing countries*?

(4) Does the agreement or arrangement *require prior notification*?

(5) Does the agreement or arrangement *require prior consent*?

(6) Does the agreement or arrangement provide for the *tracking of the wastes*?

(7) Does the agreement or arrangement provide for alternative *measures for wastes which cannot be managed as planned*?

(8) Does the agreement or arrangement provide for the *identification of authorities responsible for the implementation* of such agreement?

(9) Are the obligations of the Article 11 agreement or arrangement *consistent with the control measures* related to transboundary movements of hazardous wastes *as provided for by the Basel Convention*?

(10) Are the wastes covered by the Article 11 agreement or arrangement *consistent with the scope of the Basel Convention*?

C. *Limitation of the Scope of the Agreements Addressed by Article 11*

Article 11 of the Basel Convention appears at first glance to make a distinction between agreements concluded prior to the entry into force of the Basel Convention, and those concluded subsequent to its entry into force, in one respect. Paragraph 1 of this provision clearly refers to agreements entered into by parties—with other parties or non-parties—*after* the entry into force of the Basel Convention for them. Paragraph 2 requires parties to 'notify the Secretariat of any bilateral, multilateral or regional agreements or arrangements referred to in paragraph 1 *and those which they have entered into prior to the entry into force of this Convention for them, for the purpose of controlling transboundary movements of hazardous wastes and other wastes which take place entirely among the Parties to such agreements*' (emphasis added).

Read in conjunction with paragraph 1, paragraph 2 must thus be understood to introduce the rule that agreements entered into under Article 11 by parties to the Basel Convention take precedence over the Convention only if they govern waste transactions taking place exclusively between the parties to the agreement in question. The wording of paragraph 2 makes it clear that this rule applies to 'pre-Basel' agreements, i.e. agreements concluded prior to the entry into force of the Basel Convention. It is not clear, however, whether it also applies to 'post-Basel' agreements, i.e. agreements concluded after the entry into force of the Basel Convention. The English text of paragraph 2 could be interpreted either way, whereas the French text seems to point towards a distinction between pre-Basel and post-Basel agreements in this respect.[18]

In order to clarify this point, it is useful to look first at the elaboration history of Article 11 as a whole. In the early drafts of the relevant provision, paragraph 1 set out the rules applying to post-Basel agreements, whereas paragraph 2, already containing the requirement under discussion, applied to pre-Basel agreements only. In a later draft, a reference to post-Basel agreements was inserted into paragraph 2; this was upheld in the final version.[19] It therefore seems reasonable to conclude that this addition means that paragraph 2 as a whole now applies to post-Basel as well as pre-Basel agreements. In this case, the requirement that relevant agreements must regulate only transactions among their parties applies equally to all agreements addressed by Article 11, whether concluded before or after entry into force of the Basel Convention.

This interpretation is supported by the teleological method. As mentioned repeatedly, one of the fundamental aims of the Basel Convention is to restrict transboundary movements of hazardous wastes to a minimum. In accordance with the concept of a limited ban, the Convention also aims to restrict transactions between parties and non-parties. The objective of the provision of Article 11(2), which gives precedence over the Basel Convention solely to those agreements concluded by Basel parties and governing transboundary movements of hazardous wastes between parties to the relevant agreements only, is obviously to reduce the scope of transactions which parties to the Basel Convention are allowed to regulate outside the framework of the Convention. Basel parties may enter into separate agreements in areas addressed by the Convention, but such agreements may not extend to transactions with countries which are neither parties to the Basel Convention nor to the separate agreement in question, and do not therefore necessarily adhere to the standards established by the Convention. This is a logical consequence of the concept of a limited ban.

In accordance with the teleological interpretation method, we must ask next whether the application of this rule to pre-Basel but not to post-Basel agreements would serve a useful purpose, and whether a distinction between the two types of agreements would be in line with the spirit and objectives of the Convention. The ratio of a distinction is difficult to see. It would not be consistent to declare a pre-Basel agreement covering

[18] The French wording of paragraph 2 is as follows: 'Les Parties notifient au Secretariat tout accord ou arrangement bilatéral, multilatéral ou régional visé au paragraphe 1, ainsi que ceux qu'ils ont conclus avant l'entrée en vigeur à leur égard de la présente Convention aux fins de contrôler les mouvements transfrontières de déchets dangereux et d'autres déchets qui se déroulent entièrement entre les Parties auxdits accords . . .'.

[19] See Fifth Revised Draft Convention on the Control of Transboundary Movements of Hazardous Wastes (UNEP/WG.189/3); Luxembourg Revision of the Fifth Revised Draft Convention (UNEP/WG.190/4).

transactions with non-parties to it incompatible with the Basel Convention, and at the same time consider an agreement covering transactions with non-parties concluded subsequently—in the light of the Basel Convention—to be in line with the Convention.

It can be concluded, therefore, that Article 11 generally requires that all agreements which come within its purview must apply to transactions between parties to such agreements only.

D. *The Relationship between the Basel Convention and Legal Instruments Addressed by Article 11*

Paragraph 2 of Article 11 states that 'the provisions of this Convention *shall not affect* transboundary movements which take place pursuant to such agreements . . .' (emphasis added). Thus, agreements which conform to the requirements of Article 11 as discussed above take precedence over the Basel Convention. This applies equally to agreements concluded before and after the entry into force of the Basel Convention, as Article 11 does not make a distinction between the two in this respect. Article 11 of the Basel Convention is consistent with Article 30(2) of the Vienna Convention on the Law of Treaties, which provides that if the provisions of a treaty give preference to an earlier or later treaty, that other treaty prevails. For the modalities, the general rules of the law of treaties, as codified by the Vienna Convention, are applicable.[20] If and insofar as a relevant agreement between parties to the Basel Convention, or between parties and non-parties, is compatible with the Basel Convention, it takes precedence over the Convention as between parties to both the Basel Convention and the agreement in question. As between parties to both treaties and parties to one of the treaties only, the treaty to which all states involved are parties takes precedence (Vienna Convention, Article 30(4)). It seems logical that the separate agreement takes precedence over the Basel Convention as a whole only if it establishes a comprehensive regime for transboundary movements of hazardous wastes, comparable in scope to that of the Basel Convention. If, on the other hand, the agreement addresses only certain specified aspects of transboundary movements of hazardous wastes, it takes precedence, as between parties to both treaties, only in that particular area; the Basel Convention remains applicable in all other areas.

The Basel Convention does not spell out the consequences of incompatibility of an agreement concluded under Article 11 with the Convention's

[20] The arguments in this chapter are based on the premise that the relevant rules of the Vienna Convention represent customary international law and are therefore applicable even where not all states concerned are parties to the Vienna Convention. On this problem cf. Brownlie, (1990), p. 604; Cassese, (1986), p. 189; Verdross and Simma, (1984), p. 433. The preamble of the Basel Convention (operational para. 16) expressly refers to the Vienna Convention.

requirements. The general rules of the law of treaties must therefore be applied. In applying these rules to separate agreements on transboundary movements of hazardous wastes which do not, or only in part, comply with the requirements of Article 11 of the Basel Convention, three cases can be distinguished.

The first concerns an agreement, concluded prior to the entry into force of the Basel Convention, exclusively between states which are also parties to the Convention.[21] In this case, unless it is the intention of the parties to terminate or suspend the earlier agreement in accordance with Article 59 of the Vienna Convention, the rule *lex posterior derogat legi priori* ('a later law supersedes an earlier law'), spelled out in Article 30(3) of the Vienna Convention, applies, i.e. the Basel Convention takes precedence over the earlier agreement to the extent that the provisions of that agreement are incompatible with those of the Basel Convention. Provisions of the agreement in question which address issues not covered by the Basel Convention are, however, not affected by that Convention.[22]

The second case is that of an agreement concluded prior to the entry into force of the Basel Convention between parties and non-parties to the Convention. In this case, the provisions of the Basel Convention prevail only in relationships involving exclusively parties to both treaties. In relationships between parties to both treaties and parties to the earlier treaty only, the earlier treaty prevails in accordance with the rule *pacta tertiis nec nocent nec prosunt* ('agreements neither harm nor benefit third parties').[23] This means that, notwithstanding Article 11 of the Basel Convention, it is possible for an incompatible pre-Basel agreement to take precedence over the Basel Convention if it governs transactions between Basel parties and non-parties.

The third case concerns agreements concluded after the entry into force of the Basel Convention, between Basel parties only or between parties and non-parties to the Basel Convention. With regard to agreements concluded after the entry into force of the Basel Convention, the ratio of Article 11 is clearly to prevent Basel parties from entering into agreements that govern the same issues as the Basel Convention, but are intrinsically incompatible with the Convention and thus defeat its fundamental objectives. Such a clause has legal significance under the general rules of the law of treaties if the treaty in question establishes an exclusive regime for a certain issue.[24]

21 For a detailed analysis of this case cf. Sciso, (1986), pp. 145–81.

22 Sciso, (1986), pp. 115–21, 176; Verdross and Simma, (1984), p. 412 et seq.; Brownlie, (1990), p. 625; Cassese, (1986), pp. 169, 180; Sinclair, (1984), pp. 184–5; *ILC Commentary*, p. 234 et seq.

23 Vienna Convention, Articles 30(4), 34. Cf. *ILC Commentary*, pp. 234–5; also Brownlie, (1990), p. 622; and the detailed analysis by Sciso, (1986), pp. 103–15, 116–18, 182 et seq.

24 *ILC Commentary*, p. 235 (quoting a number of conventional rules which meet this requirement).

This is obviously true in the case of the Basel Convention: as discussed in Chapter 2 above, the Convention aims to establish a global and comprehensive regime for the environmentally sound management, transboundary movement, and disposal of hazardous wastes. In addition, the conclusion of a later treaty which defeats the fundamental objectives of the preceding Basel Convention would be contrary to the maxim *pacta sunt servanda* ('agreements must be adhered to'), codified in Article 26 of the Vienna Convention, which obliges states to fulfil international obligations in good faith.[25] It can be concluded, therefore, that Basel parties may not enter into later agreements, whether with parties or with non-parties, if and to the extent that these are incompatible with its requirements. The conclusion and application by parties to the Basel Convention of such agreements, in contravention of this prohibition, would constitute a breach of the obligations imposed by the Basel Convention. The consequences of this are not addressed by the Vienna Convention. It could either be concluded that the later treaty would be void to the extent of its incompatibility with the Basel Convention, or alternatively, if its validity were not affected, that its conclusion and implementation in contravention of the Basel Convention would entail state responsibility in accordance with the applicable rules of international law.[26] This question seems as yet unresolved. An examination of the legal consequences of the conclusion of a non-compatible agreement by parties to the Basel Convention is beyond the scope of this study. As we will see below, it is at this point academic, since all currently existing regional agreements come within the category of 'pre-Basel' agreements.

E. *Conclusions*

Based on the above considerations, the following interpretation of Article 11 of the Basel Convention can be proposed. In order to be considered compatible with the Basel Convention, an agreement concluded under Article 11 must explicitly address transboundary movements of hazardous wastes as defined by the Convention. Furthermore, it must adhere to the fundamental principles of the Convention, namely the minimization of waste generation and the principle of proximity, the principle of non-discrimination, the application of a control system for hazardous waste movements involving all states concerned, and the environmentally sound disposal of the wastes in the event that a transaction is illegal or cannot be completed as foreseen. In addition, such an agreement must govern waste

[25] On the obligation to act in good faith cf. Verdross and Simma, (1984), p. 280 et seq.; Müller, (1971).

[26] For a detailed analysis of this problem see Sciso, (1986), pp. 93–103, 145–50, 185–200, 210–19. See also Reuter, (1989), p. 101; Rosenne, (1985), p. 88 et seq.; Sinclair, (1984), pp. 6, 94; *ILC Commentary*, p. 237.

transactions that take place exclusively between parties to the relevant agreement. If these requirements are met, the agreement in question takes precedence over the Basel Convention in accordance with the international rules on the law of treaties. In the following paragraphs, the relationship between the Basel Convention and existing separate agreements will be examined in the light of the above considerations.

THE BASEL CONVENTION AND THE 1991 BAMAKO CONVENTION

F. *Outline of the Elaboration History and Provisions of the Bamako Convention*

The issue of transboundary movements of hazardous wastes (including nuclear wastes), in particular the import of such wastes from industrialized countries into Africa, was the subject of various statements issued by African organizations and conferences,[27] and of a number of resolutions of the Council of Ministers of the OAU. The first relevant OAU Council of Ministers resolution, adopted in 1988, condemned the import of industrial and nuclear wastes into Africa as 'a crime against Africa and the African people'. It called upon member states to introduce import bans, and to adhere to the Cairo Guidelines.[28] Subsequent resolutions, re-iterating this position, were concerned with the adoption of a common African position in the Basel negotiations, and the elaboration of a regional African convention on hazardous wastes, which would address the continent's common concerns.[29]

Under the auspices of the OAU, work on an African convention on hazardous wastes began shortly after the adoption of the Basel Convention, in response to a general feeling among African states that their needs had not been adequately taken into account in Basel (see Chapter 2(B) above). Nevertheless, the working group charged with the drafting of the African convention relied heavily upon the Basel Convention as a model. The drafting process took place over a period of nearly 2 years; it was somewhat delayed by inconsistencies in the intentions of the participating states. The

[27] ECOWAS Resolution A/RES.1/6/88 Relating to the Dumping of Nuclear and Industrial Waste (June 1988); *Report of the 2nd Meeting of the Committee on Seas of AMCEN*, 22 December 1988, (UNEP/AEC/B4/COMM.4/9, excerpts repr. in Kwiatkowska and Soons, (1993), p. 975); statements of the African preparatory Conferences for UNCED held under the auspices of UN/ECA in Cairo (July 1991) and Abidjan (November 1991), respectively (repr. in Kwiatkowska and Soons, (1993), p. 979 et seq.). See also Richter, (1989), p. 49 et seq.; Greenpeace, (1990).

[28] OAU Council of Ministers Resolution on Dumping of Nuclear and Industrial Waste in Africa, 23 May 1988, (CM/Res.1153(XLVIII), repr. in 28 ILM 567 (1989)).

[29] OAU Council of Ministers Resolutions CM/Res. 1199(XLIX), February 1989; CM/Res. 1225(L), July 1989; CM/Res. of February 1990.

two main aims of the proposed African convention were determined as, firstly, a common commitment by African states to prohibit the import of hazardous wastes into the continent, and secondly, the establishment of a regime for the management of hazardous wastes generated within Africa.[30]

The Bamako Convention on the Ban of the Import into Africa and the Control of Transboundary Movement of Hazardous Wastes within Africa (Bamako Convention) was adopted by the Pan-African Conference on Environment and Sustainable Development in Bamako (Mali) on 30 January 1991. The Conference was attended by twenty nine African states. A number of intergovernmental organizations including UNEP, WMO, and FAO, attended as observers, as did Greenpeace International.[31] The Bamako Convention is structured in accordance with the aims outlined above.[32] At the same time, it is modelled to a large extent on the Basel Convention. For this reason, it shares many of the Basel Convention's strengths and weaknesses discussed in Chapter 2 above. In some areas, however, it deviates from the Basel Convention in accordance with its specific aims, and introduces stronger provisions. As the drafting of the Bamako Convention shows some imperfections, the interpretation of some of its provisions is difficult. Some of the difficulties result from the fact that the basis of the provisions is taken from the Basel Convention, and the changes necessary for the introduction of the specific aims of the Bamako Convention have not been made consistently.

Twenty five African states have signed the Bamako Convention.[33] It is open for ratification or accession to all OAU member states, and will enter into force on the 90th day after the deposit of the tenth instrument of ratification (Articles 22, 25). As of November 1994, eight states had ratified the Bamako Convention.[34]

[30] OAU Council of Ministers Resolution on Control of Transboundary Movements of Hazardous Wastes and their Disposal in Africa, July 1989, (CM/Res. 1225(L)). This resolution provided the legal basis for the drafting of the Bamako Convention. For an outline of the drafting process see Jones, (1993), p. 336; Donald, (1992), p. 429 et seq.; and the report in EPL 20/4–5(1990), pp. 136–7.

[31] For an outline of the proceedings of the Conference see the report in EPL 20/4–5(1990), pp. 65–7. The Bamako Convention is reproduced in ILM 30/3(1991), p. 775 et seq.

[32] For a discussion and analysis of the Bamako Convention see Jones, (1993); Glazewski, (1993); Donald, (1992); Kiss, (1991), p. 532 et seq.; Kwiatkowska and Soons, (1993), Editors' Introduction, p. LXX et seq.; Kummer, in YBIEL 2(1991) p. 178; Lang, in Lang, Neuhold, and Zemanek, (1991), pp. 159–60; Rublack, (1993), p. 46 et seq.; Rosencranz and Eldridge, (1992), p. 319.

[33] The following states signed the Bamako Convention: Benin; Burkina Faso; Burundi; Cameroon; Central African Republic; Chad; Djibouti; Egypt; Guinea; Guinea-Bissau; Ivory Coast; Lesotho; Libya; Mali; Mauritius; Niger; Rwanda; Senegal; Somalia; Sudan; Swaziland; Tanzania; Togo; Tunisia; and Zimbabwe (information received from the OAU Office (Addis Ababa) via the Permanent Mission of Sudan to the United Nations (Geneva), November 1994).

[34] The following states have ratified the Bamako Convention: Ivory Coast; Libya; Mauritius; Senegal; Sudan; Tanzania; Tunisia; and Zimbabwe (information received from the

3. Scope of the wastes covered

The Bamako Convention adopts the Basel system of defining hazardous wastes by a set of annexes listing categories of wastes and hazardous characteristics; the annexes are to a large extent copied from those of the Basel Convention. However, the Bamako Convention provides that a waste *either* listed in Annex I *or* having one of the characteristics listed in Annex II is considered hazardous. Thus the scope of wastes covered is considerably broadened in comparison with the Basel Convention, under which the characteristics listed in the two relevant Annexes are cumulative requirements for the designation of a waste as hazardous. As under the Basel Convention, party states may define additional wastes as hazardous by domestic legislation (Articles 2(1.b), 3). Unlike the Basel Convention, however, the Bamako Convention extends the definition of hazardous wastes to radioactive wastes subject to international control systems, and to all hazardous substances (whether or not defined as wastes) that have been banned in the country of manufacture. The inclusion of the latter was inspired by the GATT draft Decision on Products Banned or Severely Restricted in the Domestic Market, the elaboration of which was initiated by African states, and by the UNEP London Guidelines for the Exchange of Information on Chemicals in International Trade, as amended.[35] The Bamako Convention adopts the Basel Convention's exclusion of wastes covered by the MARPOL Convention (Article 2). Like the Basel Convention, the Bamako Convention does not provide different rules for wastes destined for recycling and those destined for final disposal.

4. Ban on imports of hazardous wastes into Africa

The Bamako Convention requires parties to prohibit the import, for any reason, of all hazardous and nuclear wastes from non-contracting parties (Article 4(1)). As only OAU member states may become parties to the Convention (Articles 21, 22), this amounts to a ban on imports of hazardous wastes generated outside the African continent. However, it also prohibits Bamako parties from importing hazardous wastes from OAU member states which have not acceded to the Bamako Convention. The prohibition of hazardous waste imports 'for any reason' emphasizes the intention to make no distinction between recyclable and non-recyclable wastes, and not to allow for less stringent rules to apply to wastes destined

OAU Office (Addis Ababa) via the Permanent Mission of Sudan to the United Nations (Geneva), November 1994).

[35] GATT draft Decision, 2 July 1991, (Doc. L/6872); amended London Guidelines, 25 May 1989, (UNEP Governing Council Decision 15/30) (both repr. in Kwiatkowska and Soons, (1993)).

for recycling.[36] The Convention is silent on the issue of exports of hazardous wastes from parties to non-party states. Since the chapeau of Article 4(3.i.–l.) reads 'Obligations in the Transport and Transboundary Movement of Hazardous Wastes from Contracting Parties' (sic!), it can be argued that such exports are not prohibited if carried out in accordance with the obligations imposed by the paragraphs in question, which are similar to those of the Basel Convention.[37] On the other hand, the provisions on the PIC procedure (Articles 6, 7) clearly address movements taking place between parties only, which could be interpreted to indicate that the Convention does not cover exports to non-parties.

Parties may enter into separate agreements with other parties and with non-parties regarding transboundary movements of hazardous wastes generated in Africa (Article 11(1), (2)). This provision, modelled on Article 11 of the Basel Convention and sharing its inconsistencies, reflects the concept of a limited ban, but its scope is much narrower: as the agreements in question may only cover wastes generated in Africa, the prohibition of importing hazardous wastes into Africa remains absolute.

The Bamako Convention prohibits hazardous waste exports to Antarctica, as does the Basel Convention. It also imposes a ban on every form of sea disposal of hazardous wastes, be it discharge into marine areas under the jurisdiction of party states, or dumping and incineration on the high seas by party states (Article 4(2)). In this it goes further than the Basel Convention, which does not afford specific protection to the global commons with the exception of Antarctica, as we have seen. Another improvement on the Basel Convention is the requirement for a state to apply the Bamako Convention's provisions to vessels flying its flag and aircraft registered in its territory (Article 11(3); see Chapter 2 para. 5 above).

5. Transboundary movements and management of hazardous wastes generated in Africa

For transboundary movements and management of hazardous wastes among party states, the Bamako Convention imposes restrictions virtually equivalent to those of the Basel Convention. These include a PIC procedure, specified in Articles 6 and 7, which are taken almost verbatim from the relevant provisions of the Basel Convention and thus share its inconsistencies. However, the requirements of this procedure are stronger in some respects than those of the Basel Convention. Thus, a copy of each

[36] This provision may lead to conflicts with Article 39 of the 1989 Lomé IV Convention, which allows ACP-generated hazardous wastes processed in an EU country to be re-imported into the country of origin (see para. (H) below).

[37] This view is supported by van der Mensbrugghe, Commentary, in Lang, Neuhold, and Zemanek, (1991), p. 162, and Glazewski, (1993), p. 239.

notification, and the response to it, must be sent to the Convention Secretariat (Article 13(4)); this requirement enhances the Secretariat's monitoring function. A party transit state may not waive the requirement of PIC, and the use of a general notification for multiple shipments of wastes with the same characteristics and following the same transport route is not allowed. Parties must designate a limited number of points of entry for hazardous waste shipments, which must be notified to the Convention Secretariat.

The general obligations regarding waste management imposed on states are along the lines of the Basel Convention, but are more far-reaching (Article 4(3)). Thus, the Bamako Convention enshrines the precautionary principle: parties are required to promote clean production methods, preventing the release of harmful substances into the environment without waiting for scientific proof regarding their hazardous qualities (Article 4(3.f, g)). This point is elaborated in a provision requiring that 'the issue of the transfer to Africa of polluting technologies shall be kept under systematic review by the Secretariat of the Conference and periodic reports made to the Conference of the Parties' (Article 4(3.h)).

The Bamako Convention's provisions on the duty to re-import and on illegal traffic (Articles 8, 9) closely resemble the relevant provisions of the Basel Convention. Article 9 on illegal traffic is, however, somewhat stronger in that it provides for the wastes to be returned to the state of origin in every case, and places a stronger emphasis on states' duties to adopt relevant criminal legislation of a punitive and deterrent character.

6. Other provisions

The Bamako Convention's provisions on inter-African co-operation (Article 10) and exchange of information (Article 13) are virtually the same as the relevant provisions of the Basel Convention. Along with that Convention, the Bamako Convention delegates the elaboration of a protocol on liability and compensation to a working group, to be set up by the Conference of the Parties (Article 12). The Convention does, however, require parties to impose, by national legislation, unlimited liability as well as joint and several liability on waste generators (Article 4(3.b)). The regulation of the financial aspects of the implementation of the Bamako Convention is left to the Conference of the Parties (Article 14), as in the Basel Convention.

The Convention establishes a Conference of the Parties (Article 15) and a Secretariat (Article 16), the functions of which are virtually equivalent to the corresponding bodies under the Basel Convention. In addition, the Convention Secretariat is required to carry out hazardous waste audits, based on information submitted to it by the parties (Article 4(3.a)). The

Bamako Convention also gives its Secretariat the competence to actively verify alleged breaches of the Convention, reported to it by a party (Article 19); this is a significant improvement on the Basel Convention. Interestingly, the Basel Convention's requirement for a periodical consideration, by the Conference of the Parties, of the introduction of a complete ban on hazardous waste movements (within Africa) has not been included in the Bamako Convention. The Convention requires parties to appoint, in addition to focal points and competent authorities having the same functions as those of the Basel Convention, a national body which shall act as 'dumpwatch' (Article 5). The wording of the provision does not, however, make it clear what the duties of this agency should be.[38]

Despite weaknesses similar to those of the Basel Convention, and some inconsistencies in the drafting, the Bamako Convention provides a highly detailed and ambitious regime, incorporating a number of innovative and potentially effective concepts. Its implementation, however, will require significant technical, personnel, and financial resources.[39] In view of the limited capacities of most African states in this respect, the question of successful implementation imposes itself even more strongly than in the case of the Basel Convention. The IMO's Global Waste Survey, discussed in Chapter 5 below, shows African states' capacities in this respect in the field of waste management as ranging from limited to non-existent.[40] In addition, the ratification process has been slow to date: in November 1994, nearly 4 years after its adoption, the number of parties was still two short of the number needed to bring the Convention into force.

G. *The Bamako Convention as a Regional Agreement Within the Meaning of Article 11 of the Basel Convention*

Following the adoption of the Basel Convention, some of the African complaints regarding alleged shortcomings of that treaty were countered with the argument that the Basel Convention, being global in scope, was not designed to accommodate specific regional concerns, but that in Article 11, it provided the appropriate framework for the adoption of regional agreements which would take into account such concerns (see Chapter 1 above). This position was adopted in particular by UNEP, which also offered its

[38] See Kwiatkowska and Soons, (1993), Editors' Introduction, p. LXXII, noting that a 'dumpwatch' system was also advocated by ECOWAS in 1988 and subsequently introduced by that organization in 1990, and that similar systems were established by inter-regional bodies comprising African states.

[39] See Kwiatkowska and Soons, (1993), Editors' Introduction, p. LXXIII, for an overview of the efforts of the UN/ECA to promote the monitoring of hazardous wastes in Africa; Rublack, (1993), p. 49.

[40] Kwiatkowska and Soons, (1993), Editors' Introduction, p. LXXIII. See also Rosencranz and Eldridge, in EPL22/5/6(1992), p. 319; Louka, (1994), p. XIV.

assistance to the OAU in the drafting of a regional African convention within the framework of Article 11 of the Basel Convention.[41]

The Bamako Convention was never formally designated as a regional agreement within the meaning of Article 11 of the Basel Convention, although its preamble contains an explicit reference to that provision. Nevertheless, the adoption of the Bamako Convention was formally notified to the (then) Interim Secretariat of the Basel Convention as provided by Article 11 of that Convention.[42] The Bamako Conference did not go as far as to recommend accession to the Basel Convention by African states. It did adopt a resolution calling upon OAU members to ratify the Bamako Convention *before* ratifying any other treaty on hazardous wastes (clearly envisaging the Basel Convention), and inviting African states to take a sovereign decision on the Basel Convention. This shows a shift from the OAU's previous opposition to Basel (see Chapter 2(B) above),[43] but the African position regarding the Basel Convention remains ambiguous. Nevertheless, more African states have by now ratified the Basel Convention than the Bamako Convention, although both Conventions have been ratified by a comparatively small number of African states. Although Articles 21–25 of the Basel Convention—unusually—provide for the accession of political as well as economic integration organizations, which envisages the OAU,[44] the possibility of the OAU's becoming a party has not to date been seriously considered.

In practical terms, the Bamako Convention can only come within the purview of Article 11 of the Basel Convention if there are states which are parties to both treaties. In this sense, the question is at this point almost academic: of the eight OAU member states that have thus far ratified the Bamako Convention and the twelve OAU members which are parties to the Basel Convention (see Chapter 2(B) above), only Ivory Coast, Mauritius, Senegal and Tanzania have acceded to both. In the event that more African states accede to both Conventions, however, the qualification of the Bamako Convention as a regional agreement in the sense of Article 11 must be analysed in the light of the points considered under para. 1. above.

Such analysis shows that the Bamako Convention establishes a compre-

[41] UNEP's position on this issue is outlined in Kummer and Rummel-Bulska, (1990), and in a UNEP paper entitled *Hazardous Wastes: Why Africa Must Act Now* (Nairobi, December 1989).

[42] Resolution on the African Common Position on the Basel Convention on the Transboundary Movements of Hazardous Wastes and their Disposal (OAU/CONF/PAN-COOR/ENV/EXP/DFT/Res.1(1) Rev.1), adopted by the Bamako Pan-African Conference on 30 January 1991 (repr. in EPL21/2(1991), p. 100).

[43] Resolution on the African Common Position on the Basel Convention (see n. 42 above). See also the report in EPL21/2(1991), pp. 65–7, 100.

[44] See the records of the negotiations on the Basel Convention quoted in Chapter 2 above. The term 'economic integration organization' refers to the EU (cf. Chapter 4 below). The relevant provisions were included on the proposal of the two organizations in question.

hensive regime for transboundary movements of hazardous wastes. It must be considered a pre-Basel agreement, having been concluded prior to the entry into force of the Basel Convention for any state. Since, as discussed above, it is modelled on the Basel Convention but also contains provisions which afford stronger protection to the environment than that treaty, it is in line with the Basel Convention's fundamental principles. The requirement of Article 11 that separate agreements be concluded for the purpose of controlling hazardous waste movements entirely between parties to such agreements is also met: the Bamako Convention bans the import of hazardous wastes from non-parties and provides a control system for transboundary movements between parties. It does not regulate the export of hazardous wastes to third countries, even though it does not expressly prohibit it.

Thus the Bamako Convention appears to be the typical example of a regional agreement within the meaning of Article 11 of the Basel Convention. In accordance with the rules discussed above, it therefore takes precedence over the Basel Convention where parties to both treaties are involved, or where parties to both treaties and parties to the Bamako Convention only are involved. In a relationship between parties to both treaties and parties to the Basel Convention only, the Basel Convention prevails. This, however, does not interfere with the aims of the Bamako Convention, since the Basel Convention provides that its parties may 'not allow the export of hazardous wastes or other wastes to a State or group of States belonging to an economic and/or political integration organization that are Parties (i.e. to the Basel Convention), particularly developing countries, which have prohibited by their legislation all imports' (Article 4(2.e) of the Basel Convention). Thus the Basel Convention obliges its parties to respect the import ban imposed by the Bamako Convention.[45] Those provisions of the Basel Convention which relate to transboundary movements of hazardous wastes therefore do not apply in a relationship between a Basel party and an OAU member state which is a party to both treaties. It must be noted, however, that only those wastes which are within the scope of the Basel Convention are expressly covered by the provision of Article 4(2.e) of the Basel Convention. That provision cannot, therefore, be interpreted to include a prohibition on the export of nuclear wastes not covered by the Basel Convention to Bamako parties.

The precedence of the Bamako Convention does not affect those provisions of the Basel Convention which are not related to the permissibility of waste traffic and the control system: they remain applicable even in relationships between parties to both treaties and parties to the Basel Convention only. These provisions include Article 10, on international

[45] On this issue cf. Smets, (1991), p. 141; Donald, (1992), p. 434.

co-operation in fields such as transfer of technology and development of low-waste technologies; Article 13, on exchange of information; and Article 16, determining the Secretariat's function of channelling the flow of information between parties, supporting their co-operation, and assisting them in particular areas. These provisions primarily envisage assistance from industrialized countries to developing states which are Basel parties, as we saw in Chapter 2(I) above. Their applicability is therefore to the advantage of those states that are parties to both treaties, all of which are developing countries. To a certain extent, the possibility of OAU members which are parties to Basel receiving technical assistance under the terms of the Basel Convention, and their reliance on its institutional framework, may offset the absence of sufficient expertise, resources, and capacities among OAU states which would otherwise be likely to hamper the effective implementation of the Bamako Convention. The Basel Convention's provision on illegal traffic (Article 9) applies in the event that a waste transport to a party to both treaties has been carried out in contravention of the prohibition in Article 4(2.e) of the Basel Convention.

These reflections show that in the case of the Bamako Convention, the Basel Convention has a strong potential for serving as global umbrella to a regional treaty. Whereas the specific needs of the African region, and its internal relations with regard to hazardous waste management, are addressed by the regime of the Bamako Convention, the Basel Convention governs the relationship with third states in fields such as mutual assistance, while at the same time obliging all its parties to respect the regional import ban imposed by the Bamako Convention.[46] As the functioning of this mechanism is contingent on the party status of the countries concerned, the accession to both the Bamako and Basel Conventions by African states seems highly desirable. It is therefore to be hoped that the ratification process of the Bamako Convention will accelerate, and that additional African states accede to the Basel Convention.

THE BASEL CONVENTION AND ARTICLE 39 OF THE LOMÉ IV CONVENTION

H. *Outline of the Provisions of Article 39 of the Lomé IV Convention*

In December 1989, the EC and its member states, and the sixty nine African, Caribbean and Pacific (ACP) states, concluded the Fourth Convention of Lomé (Lomé IV).[47] In accordance with Article 360 of Lomé

[46] For a similar conclusion see Donald, (1992), p. 434. An opposing view is expressed by Glazewski, (1993), p. 237, and Jones, (1993), p. 341.

[47] Adopted at Lomé (Togo) on 15 December 1989; repr. in 29 ILM (1990) p. 783 et seq. (also briefly outlining the elaboration history). For a discussion see Abrams, (1990), p. 840 et

IV, it entered into force on 1 September 1991, after the EC, its member states, and two thirds of the ACP states had acceded to it.[48] By 20 November 1991, virtually all ACP states had become parties.[49] Unlike its predecessors, Lomé IV devotes a chapter to environmental protection. Article 39 deals specifically with the issue of transboundary movements of hazardous wastes. Paragraph 1 of this provision obliges the contracting parties 'to make every effort to ensure that international movements of hazardous waste and radioactive waste are generally controlled'. More specifically, it obliges the EC (now the EU) and its members to ban direct or indirect exports of such wastes to ACP states, and the latter to prohibit direct or indirect imports from the EU or from any other state. This provision creates an imbalance between the two groups of states: whereas ACP states must prohibit imports from the EU *and* from any other states, EU members must prohibit exports to ACP states only, but may continue to export to third states.[50] It also creates a conflict with the Bamako Convention by prohibiting waste movements between African ACP and non-ACP states that are permissible under Bamako.[51] An exception to the prohibition is made where an ACP state has sent wastes for processing to an EU member state: the processed wastes may be returned to the state of origin. Since the Convention as a whole governs the relationship between the EU and its members, on the one hand, and the ACP states as a group, on the other, Article 39 cannot be interpreted to prohibit waste transports among the ACP states themselves.[52] Waste movements within the EU and among the ACP states are not addressed by the provision.

seq.; Kwiatkowska and Soons, (1993), Editors' Introduction, p. LXVIII et seq.; Mathijsen, (1990), pp. 295–9; Marin, (1990), p. 14 et seq.; Ndi, (1993), p. 28 et seq.; Rublack, (1993), p. 49; Schmidt, (1992), p. 64 et seq. The ACP states are Angola; Antigua and Barbuda; Bahamas; Belize; Benin; Botswana; Burkina Faso; Burundi; Cameroon; Cape Verde Islands; Central African Republic; Chad; Comoros; Congo; Djibouti; Dominica; Equatorial Guinea; Ethiopia; Fiji; Gabon; Gambia; Ghana; Grenada; Guinea; Guinea-Bissau; Guyana; Haiti; Ivory Coast; Jamaica; Kenya; Kiribati; Lesotho; Liberia; Madagascar; Malawi; Mali; Mauritania; Mauritius; Mozambique; Namibia; Niger; Nigeria; Papua New Guinea; Rwanda; St. Kitts and Nevis; St. Lucia; Dominican Republic; St. Vincent and the Grenadines; Sao Tomé and Principe; Senegal; Seychelles; Sierra Leone; Solomon Islands; Somalia; Sudan; Surinam; Swaziland; Tanzania; Togo; Tonga; Trinidad and Tobago; Tuvalu; Uganda; Vanuatu; Western Samoa; Zaire; Zambia; and Zimbabwe.

[48] OJ No. L 229/287, 17 August 1991.

[49] List of parties reproduced in Kwiatkowska and Soons, (1993), p. 887 et seq.

[50] Kwiatkowska and Soons, (1993), Editors' Introduction, p. LXIX.

[51] Kwiatkowska and Soons, (1993), Editors' Introduction, p. LXIX; van der Mensbrugghe, Commentary, in Lang, Neuhold, and Zemanek, (1991), p. 163.

[52] See the Final Act of the Lomé IV Convention, and Article 1, providing that 'The Community and its Members, of the one part, and the ACP states, of the other part (hereinafter referred to as the Contracting Parties), hereby conclude this cooperation Convention . . .'. Such interpretation would also be contrary to the wording of Article 39, which prohibits waste imports 'from the Community *or any other country*', whereas the term 'ACP States' is used throughout Lomé IV where those states are addressed. 'Other country' must therefore be understood to indicate a third country. Cf. Marin, (1990), p. 14.

Article 39(3) of Lomé IV defines as 'hazardous wastes' all wastes covered by Annexes I and II of the Basel Convention, but omits the Basel Convention's additional requirement that the wastes must have one of the hazardous characteristics listed in Annex III. Like the Bamako Convention, the Lomé IV provision thus covers a broader range of wastes than the Basel Convention. On the other hand, the Lomé IV provision, unlike the Basel Convention, does not provide for states to define additional wastes as hazardous by national legislation. The most significant difference between the scopes of the two treaties, however, is the inclusion of radioactive wastes in the scope of the Lomé IV provision. For the definition of radioactive wastes, the Lomé IV provision refers to ongoing work within the IAEA (Annex VIII to the Lomé IV Convention), subsequently completed with the adoption of the 1990 Code of Practice on the International Transboundary Movement of Radioactive Waste (see Chapter 2 above). Prior to the completion of that work, the definition followed the relevant EU legislation (i.e. Directive 80/836 EURATOM as last amended by Directive 84/467 EURATOM, Article 4(a), (b)).[53] The scope of wastes covered by the Lomé IV provision is thus very similar to that of the Bamako Convention.

The contracting parties adopted a joint declaration to the effect that they would 'make every effort to sign and ratify as quickly as possible' the Basel Convention (Annex IX). In 1990, a Resolution of the ACP-EU Joint Assembly recommended, among other things, the establishment of a working group to monitor procedures and instruments in the environmental fields addressed by Lomé IV.[54] This was reaffirmed, with special regard to hazardous and radioactive wastes, by a 1991 Resolution of the Joint Assembly, which also urged speedy ratification of the Bamako Convention by OAU states, and of the Basel Convention by the OAU, by the EU and its members, and by the ACP states.[55]

Article 39 of Lomé IV is the first binding agreement between developed and developing countries prohibiting North-South traffic in hazardous and nuclear wastes. It is in line with the Bamako Convention, Decision II/12 of the Conference of the Parties to the Basel Convention, the many non-binding declarations adopted in the last few years within international fora, and the national import bans enacted by numerous developing countries, all of which are indicators of a growing consensus on the need for a ban on North–South hazardous waste traffic (see Chapter 7 below). Adopted only months after the Basel Convention, the Lomé IV provision went beyond

[53] See Kwiatkowska and Soons, (1993), Editors' Introduction, p. LXIX.

[54] Resolution on the Environment, 22 March 1990, OJ No. C 218/46 (1990), repr. in Kwiatkowska and Soons, (1993), p. 902.

[55] Resolution on the Ratification of the Basel Convention, 28 February 1991, repr. in Kwiatkowska and Soons, (1993), p. 904; see also ibid., Editors' Introduction, p. LXX.

that treaty with respect to the scope of the wastes it covers and the stringency of the measures it imposes.

I. *Article 39 of the Lomé IV Convention Within the Framework of Article 11 of the Basel Convention*

As mentioned in Chapter 2(B) above, the EU and all but one of its member states are parties to the Basel Convention. Fifteen of the sixty nine ACP states have thus far ratified the Basel Convention, all of which are also parties to Lomé IV,[56] and one other ACP state (Haiti) has signed it. Thus the number of states for which both Conventions are applicable has increased to twenty nine. The issue of the qualification of the Lomé IV provision as a regional agreement under Article 11 of the Basel Convention is therefore gaining practical significance.

The relationship between the two treaties will be analysed in the light of the considerations discussed above. Lomé IV can doubtless qualify as an agreement within the meaning of Article 11 of the Basel Convention, concluded between an organization and its member states, on the one hand, and a group of states, on the other. As required by Article 11, the relevant provision of Lomé IV addresses waste transactions exclusively between its contracting parties. Like the Bamako Convention, Lomé IV was concluded prior to the entry into force of the Basel Convention. Unlike the Bamako Convention, Article 39 of Lomé IV does not attempt to establish a comprehensive regime for the transboundary movement of hazardous wastes. In a single provision, it provides one basic rule. Therefore, as submitted above, its relationship with the Basel Convention is relevant only with respect to the issue addressed by that rule. We must therefore ask whether the rule in question is compatible with the Basel Convention.

This question can easily be answered in the affirmative. By generally banning transboundary movements of hazardous as well as nuclear wastes from a group of developed to a group of developing countries, the provision in question is in line with the fundamental concepts of that treaty, as specified and enhanced in this instance by Decision II/12 on the ban of hazardous waste export from OECD to non-OECD countries. In fact, by giving a legally binding form to the ban, it goes further than the Basel Convention's requirements in the relevant matter.

In relationships between parties to both treaties, the general ban imposed by the Lomé IV provision therefore takes precedence over the Basel Convention's control system for transboundary waste movements, and any other provision related to the permissibility of such movements. As the ban

[56] Antigua and Barbuda; Bahamas; Comoros; Ivory Coast; Malawi; Mauritius; Nigeria; Senegal; Seychelles; St. Kitts and Nevis; St. Lucia; Tanzania; Trinidad and Tobago; Zaire; and Zambia.

is one-sided, the Basel provisions are, however, applicable to transboundary movements from ACP states which are Basel parties to EU states which are Basel parties. They also apply to wastes processed in an EU member state and being returned to the ACP state of origin, provided both states are Basel parties. The Basel Convention's provisions pertaining to the control system also apply in relationships between parties to both treaties and parties to the Basel Convention only. However, in accordance with Article 4(1.b) of the Basel Convention, even its non-EU parties must respect the general national import bans adopted pursuant to Lomé IV by ACP states which are Basel parties. Article 4(2.e) of the Basel Convention does not apply in this case (unlike the case of the Bamako Convention) because it envisages only bans adopted under the auspices of political or economic integration organizations as defined by the Basel Convention (Article 2(20)). The ACP group of states does not conform to this definition. The distinction is, however, academic, as the content of the two provisions is virtually identical. Any import ban enacted pursuant to Lomé IV must be notified to the Secretariat of the Basel Convention (Articles 4(1.a), 13). As in the case of the Bamako Convention, this does not extend to wastes covered by the scope of the Lomé IV provision but not the Basel Convention (e.g. nuclear wastes). Transactions between EU states which are Basel parties, and Basel parties which are not parties to Lomé IV, are governed exclusively by the Basel Convention.

Since the Lomé IV provision does not replace the Basel Convention as a regime, those of its provisions which do not relate to the permissibility of hazardous waste movements or to the control system are not affected by Lomé IV. They apply as between parties to both treaties, and in relationships between Basel parties and parties to both treaties, but not between parties to both treaties and parties to Lomé IV only. These provisions include the general obligations concerning environmentally sound management of hazardous wastes (Article 4 of the Basel Convention). They also include the provisions envisaging assistance to developing countries, i.e. Articles 10 and 13 on international co-operation and exchange of information (indirectly referred to in Article 39(1) of Lomé IV); and Article 16, governing the Basel Secretariat's functions as a monitoring and assisting body. As in the case of the Bamako Convention, this is of interest to those Lomé IV parties which are developing countries, i.e. all ACP states. The Basel provision on illegal traffic (Article 9) is applicable in the event that a movement takes place in contravention of the ban imposed by Lomé IV.

As in the case of the Bamako Convention, the Basel Convention can thus provide a useful framework for the Lomé IV provision, provided the Lomé IV parties are also parties to the Basel Convention, as recommended by the 1991 Resolution of the ACP–EU Joint Assembly. Since Lomé IV is already in force, and nearly all African ACP states, constituting the vast majority of OAU members, have acceded to it, this provision has the potential to protect Africa against waste imports from Basel parties even if the entry into force of the Bamako Convention with its more detailed regulation is further delayed.

The example of Lomé IV shows, moreover, that the Basel Convention can be supplemented by fairly simple means: it is not strictly necessary to adopt a separate comprehensive regime at the regional level in order to ensure the protection of a particular group of developing or transitional countries against imports of foreign hazardous wastes. As illustrated by the Lomé IV provision, a group of states parties to the Basel Convention can achieve this aim through the stipulation of a collective import ban within the framework of the Basel Convention, while relying on the Basel regime for the general rules related to hazardous waste management. The regional import ban must be respected by Basel parties in accordance with that Convention's provisions, and any breach of this obligation entails the consequences envisaged by the Basel Convention's provision on illegal traffic. The control system of the Basel Convention is applicable to any exports from the states in question to Basel parties that have not prohibited imports, e.g. industrialized states which have the proper facilities. Moreover, the 'Lomé IV approach' allows the states in question to benefit from the Basel Convention's provisions on technical co-operation, technical and financial assistance, and exchange of information, which are to a large extent aimed at the needs of developing countries, as we have seen. In addition, these states can rely on the Basel Convention's institutional mechanisms. Accordingly, lack of resources and expertise among a group of developing or transitional countries with similar aims and needs is not necessarily an obstacle to regional regulation, as under this approach, the establishment of complex and costly institutional mechanisms to service the regional convention, though desirable, is not strictly necessary.

For these reasons, the Lomé IV provision could provide a useful model for other relevant agreements involving developing or transitional countries that wish to ban imports of hazardous wastes, but do not envisage a separate waste management regime amongst themselves. This model character remains valid even after the adoption of Basel Conference Decision II/12, which bans hazardous wastes exports from OECD to non-OECD countries: besides wishing to give legally binding form to regional import bans, some groups of developing countries may opt for a general import ban into their region, not only from OECD member states. Incidentally, the adoption of such regional bans by groups of developing or transitional countries parties to the Basel Convention, with or without the participation of developed countries, might be politically more feasible at present than the proposed formal amendment of the Basel Convention to incorporate a global ban on waste exports to developing countries. The end result, however, would be the same.

THE BASEL CONVENTION AND THE NORTH AMERICAN BILATERAL AGREEMENTS ON TRANSBOUNDARY MOVEMENTS OF HAZARDOUS WASTES

In 1986, the USA concluded two bilateral agreements on transboundary movements of hazardous wastes with Canada and Mexico, respectively.[57] The two agreements, adopted within a few days of each other, have common features but differ in some respects.[58] The conclusion of NAFTA in 1992 may have some impact on these agreements, even though they are expressly given preference over NAFTA to the extent of any incompatibility and provided the principle of proportionality is adhered to (see Chapter 4 para. 5.3 below).

J. *Outline of the Provisions of the Agreements*

7. The agreement between Canada and the USA on transboundary movements of hazardous waste

This agreement, which entered into force on 8 November 1986, is particularly significant as the vast majority of the hazardous wastes exported from the USA goes to Canada, as mentioned in Chapter 1 above. It was amended by exchange of notes between the two parties in November 1992. The agreement lays down the principles of hazardous waste movements taking place across the common borders of the two contracting parties. For the modalities, it refers to the national legislation of the parties. In the preamble, reference is also made to a number of pertinent international legal instruments. The scope of wastes covered is to be determined by the national legislation of the parties; the agreement does not set out guidelines for such definition. The agreement provides for notification of exports of hazardous and other wastes, whether in single or multiple shipments, from one party to the other, and adopts the concept of prior consent of the importing state. This consent may be express or tacit, and may be withdrawn or modified 'for good cause'. Each party has to be notified by the other of hazardous wastes transit through its territory, but the permissibility of such transit is not contingent

[57] Agreement between the Government of Canada and the Government of the United States of America Concerning the Transboundary Movement of Hazardous Waste, adopted in Ottawa, 28 October 1986 (Canadian Treaty Series 1986 No. 39); Agreement of Co-operation between the United States of America and the United Mexican States regarding the Transboundary Shipments of Hazardous Wastes and Hazardous Substances (Annex III to the 1983 Agreement between the USA and Mexico on Co-operation for the Protection and Improvement of the Environment in the Border Area), adopted in Washington D.C., 12 November 1986 (ILM. 26(1987)); both also repr. in Kwiatkowska and Soons, (1993), pp. 877, p. 1081.

[58] For a discussion see Handley, (1990); Kiss, (1991), p. 530; Kwiatkowska and Soons, (1993), Editors' Introduction, pp. LIII, LXXV et seq., and sources quoted there; Mounteer, (1991), p. 10087 et seq.; Rublack, (1989), p. 389; eadem (1993), p. 39 et seq.

on the transit country's express consent. The parties are required to co-operate in the application of the agreement, which includes monitoring and spot-checking of waste shipments, and to adopt any regulations necessary to this end. The country of export must re-admit any waste shipment which has been refused by the importing country. Either party can require that a waste shipment be covered by insurance or other guarantee. This is, however, not compulsory.

8. The agreement between the USA and Mexico on transboundary movements of hazardous wastes and hazardous substances

The bilateral agreement between the USA and Mexico, which entered into force on 29 January 1987, covers not only hazardous wastes, but also hazardous substances which are banned or severely restricted in either country. Like the Canada–USA agreement, it lays down the principles of transboundary movements of such wastes and substances, and refers to the domestic legislation of the parties for the modalities. Under a 1987 Decree, Mexico prohibits the import of foreign hazardous wastes for disposal. Therefore, hazardous wastes from the USA can be legally exported to Mexico under the bilateral agreement for recycling only.[59]

As under the Canada–USA agreement, hazardous wastes are to be defined by national legislation. The agreement requires notification of transboundary waste movements to the country of import; the modalities of this notification are largely to be determined by the national legislation of the state of export. The country of import may, however, impose additional requirements regarding the notification. It must respond within 45 days, consenting or objecting to the proposed movement. It can withdraw or modify this consent at any time. No provision is made, in this agreement, for tacit consent. As regards transit, the requirements are much less stringent: each party must merely notify the other party of any transit movement through that country's territory, that it is aware of. As under the Canada–USA agreement, the exporting state must re-admit waste shipments which are returned for any reason. The agreement contains a general obligation of co-operation, including spot-checking of waste shipments. The agreement also provides a notification scheme for hazardous substances other than wastes. As such substances are not within the scope of the Basel Convention, there is no incompatibility in this field.

In its final provisions, the agreement sets out the terms of exchange of information and mutual assistance in the management of hazardous wastes and substances. These include assistance to be provided under any international treaty or other arrangement to which the USA and Mexico are par-

[59] Mounteer, (1991), p. 10088, quoting relevant sources; Greenpeace, (1990), Appendix C.

ties. The agreement also provides a basis for later additions and amendments in the light of new, more stringent national laws adopted by the parties. It provides the possibility of insurance coverage, and sets out fairly extensive and detailed rules on reparation of damage caused by hazardous wastes or hazardous substances in the country of import. Thus, in the event of an illegal transaction, or if the wastes cause damage to public health, property or the environment, the person responsible must return the wastes to the exporting country, restore the affected ecosystem to the extent practicable, and pay compensation for the damage. The exporting state must co-operate with the importing state in seeking the satisfaction of these matters in its courts.

Lastly, the agreement expressly states that its provisions shall not affect the rights and obligations of the parties under other international agreements to which they are parties.

K. *The North American Bilateral Agreements Within the Framework of Article 11 of the Basel Convention*

9. General considerations

Both Mexico and Canada have ratified the Basel Convention, and the USA has signed it and is in the process of elaborating implementing legislation (see Chapter 2(B) above; Chapter 7 below). The question therefore arises whether the two bilateral treaties come within the purview of Article 11 of the Basel Convention. This question was in fact addressed by the United States delegation during the elaboration of the Basel Convention, when it stated that it was the understanding of the USA that its agreements with Canada and Mexico came within the scope of Article 11 and would therefore take precedence over the Basel Convention.[60] Taking into account the considerations discussed above, we can conclude that both treaties can be defined as agreements as understood in Article 11, both concluded prior to the entry into force of the Basel Convention for the states in question. They also fulfil the requirement of governing transactions taking place entirely between the parties to the agreements in question. Both agreements establish a regime for transboundary movements of hazardous wastes. The issue which needs to be examined in more detail is whether or not they conform to the requirement of 'environmentally sound management' established by the Basel Convention, discussed above.

[60] *Final Report of the Working Group to the Basel Conference* (UNEP/IG.80/4), p. 12.

10. Environmental standards established by the Canada–USA agreement

The agreement between Canada and the USA adopts some of the same concepts which also underlie the Basel Convention: prior notification of transboundary movements of hazardous wastes, prior consent by the importing state, general duty of co-operation, duty to re-import hazardous wastes. From an environmental viewpoint, however, it falls short of the Basel Convention in a number of respects. Thus, general notification can be given for multiple shipments of wastes taking place over a period of 12 months, without any additional requirements and without the consent of the state of import. The concept of prior consent is considerably weaker that the PIC procedure of the Basel Convention. Information to be provided on notification is not specified. The agreement provides the possibility of tacit consent by the state of import, and does not require the prior consent of the state of transit.[61] Insurance coverage of waste shipments is optional, to be provided only if requested by a party in a particular instance.

Since an agreement accorded precedence over the Basel Convention does not have to conform in detail with the provisions of that Convention, as argued above, these differences in themselves do not necessarily mean that the Canada–USA agreement is incompatible with Article 11 of the Basel Convention. There is, however, a more fundamental discrepancy. Although the need to prevent environmental damage resulting from hazardous wastes is recognized in the preamble, the agreement contains no general obligations relating to the minimization of generation and transboundary movement of hazardous wastes, and to their environmentally sound management and disposal, nor does it uphold the principle of proximity. It does not establish environmental standards to determine whether or not the export of hazardous wastes is permissible. Instead, it leaves this to be determined solely by the national legislation of the parties. Likewise, no reference is made to the environmental soundness of the final disposal option in the state of import, or to the principle of non-discrimination. The exporting state, when giving notification to the state of import, does not have to specify environmental reasons which make the export desirable or even acceptable.

Therefore, most of the Basel Convention's fundamental principles are not supported by the agreement, which in fact does little more than establish the basis of a control mechanism or 'tracking system', leaving the determination of its requirements almost entirely to the discretion of the parties.

[61] On this point cf. Kwiatkowska and Soons, (1993), Editors' Introduction, p. LIII, noting that criticism of the insufficient control system led to proposals for revision of the agreement to include a full PIC system. These proposals were not followed up, however.

If we follow the interpretation of Article 11 proposed above, we must therefore conclude that the agreement does not meet the environmental requirements of that provision.[62] In accordance with the rules discussed above, the Basel Convention will therefore take precedence over the bilateral agreement if the USA also accedes to the Convention, unless the relevant amendments are made to it. If, however, Canada alone is party to the Basel Convention, the bilateral agreement remains applicable and will take precedence over the Basel Convention.

11. Environmental standards established by the USA–Mexico agreement

The basic requirements of this agreement are similar to those of the Canada–USA agreement. At the same time, the USA–Mexico agreement reflects, to some extent, the difference between the two party states with respect to technical standards and capacities, and takes into account the most frequent situation in which the USA is the exporting and Mexico the importing state.[63] Thus, its provisions on prior consent are somewhat stronger than those of the Canada–USA agreement as regards the rights of the importing state, even though the national legislation of the state of export is given disproportionate weight.

Nevertheless, it falls short of the requirements of the Basel Convention and deviates from its fundamental concepts in much the same respects as the Canada–USA agreement; reference can therefore be made to para. 10 above. An exception must be made, however, in two fields. Firstly, the obligations of co-operation and assistance are fairly detailed and far-reaching. In this field, the agreement also refers to obligations set out by other treaties to which the states are parties. These would include the obligations of the Basel Convention should the USA also become a party to it. Secondly, the provision on the mitigation of damage caused by hazardous wastes in the country of import is quite extensive; it goes beyond the requirements of the Basel Convention in some respects. In these two areas, the agreement can therefore be considered compatible with the Basel Convention. In accordance with the rules outlined above, the USA–Mexico agreement as it stands would therefore take precedence over the Basel Convention only in those two areas in the event that both states were parties to it. In all other fields, the obligations imposed by the Basel Convention would prevail.

Unlike the Canada–USA agreement, the USA–Mexico agreement contains specific reference to other agreements to which the two states are

[62] See Rublack, (1989), p. 389, reaching the same conclusion based on similar observations, with respect to both the Canada–USA and the USA–Mexico agreements. See also Abrams, (1990), p. 815; Mounteer, (1991), p. 10087.

[63] On this point cf. Rublack, (1993), p. 39.

parties, and expressly provides for amendments to be made in the light of new developments. These provisions might serve as a basis for the adjustment of this agreement in line with the environmental requirements of the Basel Convention.

THE BASEL CONVENTION AND OTHER EXISTING AND EMERGING REGIONAL AGREEMENTS ON TRANSBOUNDARY MOVEMENTS OF HAZARDOUS WASTES

Pursuant to the adoption of the Basel Convention, the concept of regional regulation of the hazardous waste cycle was taken up within various international and regional fora.[64] In some cases, this has led to efforts to develop pertinent agreements; in others, the relevant statements are not designed to promote the adoption of binding legal instruments, but merely to endorse the concept.[65] The legal instruments examined above currently constitute the most important examples of regional regulation, both in terms of their content and with regard to the number and importance of their actual or potential parties, or due to their function as models for similar efforts. Additional legal instruments may come within the purview of Article 11 of the Basel Convention. For reasons which will be discussed below, these do not merit a full analysis under that aspect at this stage.

L. *Post-Basel Agreements on Transboundary Movements of Hazardous Wastes*

A number of bilateral agreements have been concluded subsequent to the inception of the Basel Convention. Some of these were adopted on a transitory basis, pending entry into force of the Basel Convention for one of the partners. Others take into account particularly close ties between the parties.[66]

The Central American Regional Agreement on the Transboundary Movement of Hazardous Wastes, signed in Panama City in December 1992 by Costa Rica, El Salvador, Guatemala, Honduras, Nicaragua and Panama

[64] For an extensive overview see Kwiatkowska and Soons, (1993), Editors' Introduction, p. XLVII et seq.

[65] For a summary of the provisions of agreements notified to the Basel Convention Secretariat by late 1993 see the *Note of the Secretariat to the Conference of the Parties*, March 1994, (UNEP/CHW.2/9), Annex. The texts are reproduced in Doc. UNEP/CHW/C.1/INF.2 (October 1993). See also Conference Doc. UNEP/CHW.1/7 (1992).

[66] E.g. Austria–Germany; Finland–Germany; Finland–Ireland; Romania–Germany; Croatia–Germany; Switzerland–Germany. See *Note by the Secretariat* (UNEP/CHW.2/9); *Report of the Secretariat to the Ad Hoc Committee on Implementation*, 30 September 1994, (UNEP/CHW/C.1/2/3).

(Central American Agreement),[67] adopts an approach similar to that of the Bamako Convention: it obliges its parties to prohibit the import of hazardous wastes from states not parties to the agreement into the Central American Region. Likewise, it prohibits the dumping of hazardous wastes in the marine areas of the region. Parties are required to adopt the necessary measures to prevent and punish contravention of these prohibitions, including the establishment of competent national authorities. They must also promote clean production and prevention of pollution. Unlike the Bamako Convention, the Central American Agreement does not address the issue of transboundary movements of hazardous wastes among the parties themselves. It does prohibit parties from exporting hazardous wastes to third countries which have banned such imports, as does the Basel Convention. In common with the Lomé IV provision, it does not establish an institutional infrastructure.

As this Agreement clearly has the same purpose as the Bamako Convention and the Lomé IV provision, namely to establish a regional import ban for hazardous wastes, the conclusions reached in the context of the said treaties apply *mutatis mutandis*. The regional import ban must be respected under the provisions of the Basel Convention in relationships between parties to both treaties, or between a party to both treaties and a party to the Basel Convention only. The absence of an independent infrastructure under the Central American Agreement indicates adherence to what has been termed the 'Lomé IV approach'. To the extent that the parties to the Agreement adhere to the Basel Convention, they can rely on the infrastructure of that treaty, as discussed. At present, only El Salvador and Panama are parties to the Basel Convention.

M. *Hazardous Waste Agreements Currently Under Discussion*

Various additional regional agreements on transboundary movements of hazardous wastes are currently at different stages of negotiation, but their elaboration is not sufficiently advanced to predict their final shape and their future relationship with the Basel Convention.

In this context, mention must be made of the hazardous waste protocols currently being elaborated within the framework of a number of regional marine protection conventions adopted as part of UNEP's Regional Seas Programme (discussed in Chapter 5 below). Of these efforts, the relevant work undertaken within the Mediterranean Action Plan is at the most advanced stage. In accordance with a 1989 request of the Conference of the Contracting Parties to the Barcelona Convention for the Protection of the Mediterranean Sea against Pollution, a first draft protocol on transboundary

[67] Repr. in Doc. UNEP/CHW/C.1/INF.2 (October 1993), see n. 65 above.

movements of hazardous wastes in the Mediterranean region was submitted to the Conference at its 7th meeting in October 1991.[68] This draft had been prepared by Greenpeace International and reviewed by the competent UNEP institutions. Following the instructions of the Conference of the Parties, a working group of experts is in the process of reviewing and finalizing the draft. The protocol is scheduled to be ready for adoption in 1995. In its present form, the draft protocol incorporates aims and provisions similar to those of the Basel and Bamako Conventions. It calls for prohibition of hazardous waste export from developed to developing countries within the Mediterranean region, but does not explicitly ban the import of hazardous wastes from non-parties into the region.[69]

Work has also started on a hazardous waste protocol to the Lima Convention on the protection of the marine environment in the South-East Pacific. On the basis of the conclusions of a legal experts group convened in Quito (Ecuador) in October 1992, the Secretariat of the South-East Pacific Action Plan prepared a revised draft protocol, to be finalized by a further meeting of the legal experts. In its current form, the draft protocol also largely follows the format of the Basel and Bamako Conventions (and that of the Mediterranean draft protocol), to which frequent references are made in the annotations. It includes a prohibition of hazardous waste imports into the region covered by the Lima Convention, a prohibition of waste traffic among parties, and a prohibition of exports to states having adopted an import ban.[70]

Plans for the elaboration of regional hazardous waste protocols have also been made within the framework of the Regional Seas Conventions covering the Caribbean,[71] the Gulf,[72] and the Black Sea.[73] Relevant efforts are at different stages of development.

[68] Draft Protocol for the Prevention of Pollution of the Mediterranean Sea by Transboundary Movements of Hazardous Wastes and their Disposal, 31 July 1991, (UNEP(OCA)/MED IG.2/3/Add.1).

[69] *Report of the 7th Ordinary Meeting of the Conference of the Contracting Parties to the Barcelona Convention*, Cairo, 11 October 1991, (Doc. UNEP(OCA)/MED IG.2/4), and *Report of the 8th meeting*, Antalya, Turkey, October 1993, (Doc. UNEP(OCA)/MED IG.3/5); *Report of the Working Group on the preparation of a protocol on its 1st meeting*, Cervia, Italy, April 1993, (Doc. UNEP(OCA)/MED/WG.64/3, with draft protocol as annex). See also IJO *Newsletter*, December 1993, p. 7. For a discussion see Kwiatkowska and Soons, (1993), Editors' Introduction, p. LXVII et seq.; Boyle, Freestone, Kummer, and Ong, in Sand, (1992), p. 206.

[70] Proyecto de protocolo sobre prohibición y control de los movimientos transfronterizos de desechos peligrosos y su elminiación en el Pacífico Sudeste; texto revisado por la Secretaría, Julio de 1993 (text as provided to the Secretariat of the Basel Convention). Cf. Kwiatkowska and Soons, (1993), Editors' Introduction, p. LXXV.

[71] Resolution no. 1 of the 5th Intergovernmental Meeting on the Caribbean Action Plan and the 2nd Meeting of Contracting Parties to the Cartagena Convention on protection of the marine environment in the Caribbean, Annex IX to the Report of the two Meetings (Doc. UNEP(OCA)/CAR IG.6/6 (14 February 1990)). See also Docs. UNEP(OCA)/CAR IG.8/5 (June 1991), and UNEP CET Technical Report No. 7 (1991); all repr. in Kwiatkowska and

Similar work is ongoing within other international fora. The member states of the Association of South-East Asian Nations (ASEAN), i.e. Malaysia, Indonesia, the Philippines, and Singapore, are considering the adoption of a regional hazardous waste convention. A draft prepared by the Philippines, based to a large extent on the Bamako Convention, was discussed at a ministerial meeting in April 1994. In addition to a ban on imports of foreign hazardous wastes into the ASEAN region, the draft also calls for reduction of hazardous waste generation and sets out rules for transboundary movement within the ASEAN region.[74]

Within the South Pacific Forum, work on a regional hazardous waste convention was initiated by Papua New Guinea. The draft in its current form is modelled to a large extent on the Basel Convention, and provides for a ban on imports of hazardous wastes to the developing island states of the region. Negotiations are at an advanced stage; the convention is scheduled to be adopted within the framework of the South Pacific Forum in September 1995.

This brief overview shows that the concept of regional regulation of transboundary movements of hazardous wastes has taken root since the beginning of the 1990s. Although most draft agreements discussed have not yet assumed their final shape, numerous common features are already evident. Chief among these is the establishment of a regional import ban and the adoption of principles along the lines of the Basel and Bamako Conventions. The latter, although not in force, has thus attained an important pioneering role, which may in the long term surpass its significance as a binding legal instrument. The model role of the Bamako Convention was endorsed by the Commission on Sustainable Development in July 1994.[75]

In order to qualify as regional agreements within the meaning of Article 11 of the Basel Convention, future regional agreements on hazardous wastes will have to meet the environmental requirements outlined in paragraph (B) above, and govern transboundary waste movements taking place exclusively among parties, as discussed in paragraph (C) above. Judging by

Soons, (1993), p. 1021 et seq. Cf. also ibid, Editors' Introduction, p. LXXIV; Boyle, Freestone, Kummer, and Ong, in Sand, (1992), p. 233.

[72] Cf. Kwiatkowska and Soons, (1993), Editors' Introduction, p. LXXX; Boyle, Freestone, Kummer, and Ong, in Sand, (1992), p. 211.

[73] Resolution 1 of the Diplomatic Conference on the Protection of the Black Sea against Pollution (attached to the Final Act of the 1992 Bucharest Convention), reaffirmed in the Ministerial Declaration on the Protection of the Black Sea, Odessa, 7 April 1993, (repr. in EPL23/5(1993), p. 235 et seq. Cf. also the report by Hey and Mee, ibid, p. 215 et seq.; Kwiatkowska and Soons, (1993), Editors' Introduction, p. LXVII.

[74] Draft ASEAN Convention on the Management and Control of Transboundary Movements of Hazardous Wastes within the ASEAN Region (text as submitted to the Basel Convention Secretariat, 1994).

[75] *Report of the Commission on Sustainable Development*, 12 July 1994, (Doc. E/CN.17/1994/20).

their current status, the agreements discussed are fairly likely to be in conformity with these requirements. Where this is not the case, a state for which the Basel Convention has already entered into force may not become a party to such agreement, as discussed in paragraph (D) above.

N. *Agreements on Wider Environmental Issues*

In addition to agreements specifically addressing transboundary movements of hazardous wastes, there are agreements that deal with a wider issue, but devote an individual provision to one or more aspects of the hazardous waste cycle. The Lomé IV Convention, discussed above, may be seen as the prototype of such agreements. In some such treaties, the relevant provision contains a programmatic statement, but does not establish detailed rules. An example is the 1986 Noumea Convention for the Protection of the Natural Resources of the South Pacific Region, Article 11 of which obliges parties to 'prevent, reduce and control pollution in the Convention Area resulting from the storage of toxic and hazardous wastes', and to prohibit the storage of radioactive wastes in the region.[76] A few recent bilateral agreements also come within this category.[77] A potentially important example is Article 59 of the 1991 Abuja Treaty Establishing the African Economic Community.[78] That provision reflects the aims of the Bamako Convention and the Lomé IV provision, discussed above: 'Member states undertake, individually or collectively, to take every appropriate step to ban the importation and dumping of hazardous wastes in their respective territories. They further undertake to co-operate in the transboundary movement, management and processing of such wastes produced in Africa'.

This type of provision is indicative of the 'Lomé IV approach': it provides for a collective import ban by a group of developing countries, without establishing a separate regime for transboundary movements and management of hazardous wastes, or indeed an independent infrastructure. We may therefore refer to what was said in the context of the relationship between the Basel Convention and the Lomé IV provision.

[76] Cf. Kiss and Shelton, (1991), p. 322.

[77] e.g. the agreement on environmental co-operation between Brazil and Uruguay, 28 December 1992; cf. the *Report of the 1st Conference of the Parties to the Basel Convention* (UNEP/CHW.1/24), p. 11; and the 1991 Environmental Protection Treaty between Argentina and Chile (see Kwiatkowska and Soons, (1993), Editors' Introduction, p. LXXVII).

[78] Adopted at Abuja (Nigeria), 3 June 1991 (repr. in ILM 30(1991) p. 1241; Article 59 also repr. in Kwiatkowska and Soons, (1993), p. 953).

CONCLUSIONS

The examination of the relationship between the Basel Convention and existing regional treaties in the relevant field shows that the Basel Convention has a strong potential for serving as a global umbrella for regional agreements on transboundary movements of hazardous wastes. If Article 11 is interpreted as proposed above, i.e. to the effect that regional agreements entered into by Basel parties must be based on environmental considerations and may not derogate from the fundamental principles of the Basel Convention, the Convention can be said to prescribe objective standards that constitute a minimum requirement for separate agreements concluded by its parties. This means that the Basel Convention goes well beyond a mere 'framework treaty' as defined above. As we saw, not all currently existing regional treaties on transboundary movements of hazardous wastes meet its standards. At the same time, the Convention leaves sufficient leeway for regional treaties concluded under its umbrella to adopt the measures necessary for dealing with specific regional situations. It therefore strikes an adequate balance between global and regional regulation of the issue under discussion, as advocated in Chapter 1(I) above.[79]

The proposed interpretation of Article 11 would also serve to eliminate the misuse of that provision to conclude agreements with non-parties that fall short of the standards established by the Basel Convention, thus circumventing the Convention and jeopardizing the concept of a limited ban. This problem was addressed in Chapter 2 above. Even so, the difficulty of verifying the contents and adequate application of relevant regional agreements remains.

By setting objective standards which constitute a minimum requirement for regional agreements, the Basel Convention has an important pace-setting function: every regional agreement, one or more parties to which are also Basel parties, must adhere to its standards. Consequently, if the standards in question are supported by a sufficiently large number of regional treaties, they may eventually gain widespread recognition and be accepted as customary law rules. A parallel development can be observed in the case of the London Convention (discussed in Chapter 5 below) as well as MARPOL and UNCLOS, all of which set global standards that are supported by pertinent regional rules.[80]

[79] A diagonally opposed view on this point is expressed by van der Mensbrugghe, Commentary, in Lang, Neuhold, and Zemanek, (1991), p. 163; the claim is made that the adoption of regional treaties such as the Bamako Convention, providing rules that differ in some respects from those of the Basel Convention, is likely to seriously hamper the global approach of the Basel Convention, notwithstanding the fact that Basel allows its parties to adopt more stringent measures, and to conclude separate agreements under Article 11. This line of thought seems difficult to follow, and it is not substantiated by argument.

[80] Cf. Boyle, (1985), p. 355 et seq.

The Basel Convention moreover has the potential of supporting and enhancing regional waste management agreements which adopt higher standards or stricter control systems. This could ultimately lead to some of the Basel Convention's rules being supplanted by more stringent regional standards. A parallel development can again be observed in the context of the London Convention: many regional treaties on ocean dumping now go further than the global London Convention in that they prohibit all dumping at sea (see Chapter 5(A) below).

As we have seen, the hazardous waste agreements under discussion illustrate two different approaches to regional regulation, of which the Bamako Convention and the Lomé IV provision can be considered the respective prototypes. The first approach is adhered to, apart from the Bamako Convention, by the two North American agreements; the hazardous waste management agreements currently elaborated under the Regional Seas Conventions and within ASEAN and the South Pacific Forum; and, to some extent, the Central American Agreement of 1992. It provides for the establishment of a comprehensive waste management regime separate from that of the Basel Convention, and in some cases for an independent institutional mechanism. The alternative—and possibly simpler—approach is taken by the provisions of Lomé IV and the Abuja Treaty, and related provisions, which address only the points in which their parties wish to differ from the Basel Convention, relying on the global regime in all other respects.

Based on the considerations in this chapter, we may conclude that the Basel Convention and the relevant existing and emerging regional agreements that meet its requirements form the basis of a regime for the control of transboundary movements of hazardous wastes in the narrow sense defined by the Basel Convention. This regime will be referred to in this study as the 'Basel Convention regime'. The combination of global and regional regulation ensures that the issue may be addressed in a manner that is both comprehensive and flexible. The development of this regime, still at a very early stage at the time of the adoption of the Basel Convention, has accelerated in the 1990s. Given the current efforts towards regional regulation of hazardous waste management in a fairly large number of regions of the world, it may be assumed that the Basel Convention regime will continue to develop as it is supplemented by additional regional rules in the relevant field. Appropriate amendments to those regional treaties that are not yet in conformity with the Basel Convention would also be desirable. As discussed above, the success of the Basel Convention regime depends on adherence to the Basel Convention and the relevant regional treaties by a sufficiently large number of states.

For an examination of the role of the Basel Convention regime in the development of recognized fundamental concepts in the field of transboundary movements of hazardous wastes, reference is made to Chapter 4 below. The relationship between the Basel Convention regime and rules addressing aspects of the hazardous waste cycle that do not come within the purview of Article 11 will be discussed in Chapter 5 below.

4

The Relationship Between the Basel Convention and the Waste Management Systems of the EU and the OECD

Two regional waste management systems that do not constitute agreements within the meaning of Article 2(1.a) of the Vienna Convention on the Law of Treaties are of potential relevance for the Basel Convention: the pertinent secondary legislation of the EU (previously the EC),[1] and the waste management policy and legislation of the OECD. Both these systems played a significant part in the elaboration of the Basel Convention, as already mentioned (see Chapter 2 above). They will be examined in this chapter in the light of their relationship with the Basel Convention, and their possible role as component elements of the Basel Convention regime discussed in Chapter 3.

THE BASEL CONVENTION AND THE EU RULES ON THE MANAGEMENT OF HAZARDOUS WASTES

A. *The Management of Hazardous Wastes in EU Policy and Law*[2]

1. The waste management policy of the EU: fundamental concepts

The EU's waste management policy evolved in the 1970s. Since 1973, five Action Programmes on the Environment have been adopted, each constituting the fundamental reference charter for EU environmental policy for a given period of time.[3] The second and third Action Programmes estab-

[1] For greater simplicity, 'EU' is used throughout this chapter, even when applying to the period prior to the entry into force of the Maastricht Treaty in 1993.

[2] For a detailed overview of the EU's waste management policy and legislation, see Johnson and Corcelle, (1989), pp. 187–219; Schmidt, (1992), p. 57 et seq.; de Villeneuve, (1990), pp. 568–77. See also Abrams, (1990), p. 812 et seq.; Cusack, (1990), p. 401 et seq.; Hackett, (1990), p. 304 et seq.; Huntoon, (1989), p. 252 et seq.; Kelly, (1985), p. 98 et seq.; Kiss, (1991), p. 531 et seq.; idem, in *La réparation des dommages catastrophiques*, (1988), pp. 301–17; Kiss and Shelton, (1991), pp. 316–17; Kwiatkowska and Soons, (1993), Editors' Introduction, p. LIV et seq.; Ripa di Meana, (1990), p. 271 et seq.; Rublack, (1989), p. 386; idem, (1993), p. 33 et seq.

[3] OJ No.C112, 20 December 1973; OJ No.C139, 13 June 1977; OJ No.C46, 17 February 1983; OJ No.C328, 7 December 1987. For an overview of the first four Action Programmes and their significance for waste management see Johnson and Corcelle, (1989), pp. 11–19, 158–9.

lished three main objectives for waste management, which were confirmed and elaborated in subsequent Programmes: the prevention and reduction of non-recoverable waste; the recovery, recycling or re-use of waste where possible; and the proper management and safe disposal of non-recoverable waste. The fifth Action Programme, adopted on 18 March 1992, contains innovations to the environmental policy in general and the waste policy in particular.[4] Covering the period from 1993 to 2000, it will be implemented under the new environmental provisions of the 1992 Maastricht Treaty on European Union, which entered into force on 1 November 1993.[5] One of its primary aims is the enhanced integration of environmental considerations into other EU policies. The Programme thus confirms and develops further the elevation of environmental policy to the same importance as the EU's traditional policies, already asserted in the 1986 Single European Act (SEA)[6] and the 1992 Maastricht Treaty. With regard to waste management, the fifth Action Programme also contains a number of innovations, the most important being a phase-out of exports of hazardous and other wastes from the EU to third countries by the year 2000.[7] In addition, the Action Programme confirms and elaborates the aims of the waste management policy established by the earlier programmes.

In 1989, the Commission elaborated a Community strategy for waste management, which was endorsed by a Council Resolution on waste policy in May 1990, and on which the section on waste management of the fifth Action Programme is based.[8] Referring to Article 130r of the SEA, the strategy re-iterates and elaborates the three main aims for waste management established by the earlier Action Programmes, and determines an order of priority between them. Waste prevention is defined as the primary aim, recycling or recovery of wastes once produced as the second, and environmentally safe disposal of non-recoverable wastes as the third aim.

[4] *Towards Sustainability: A European Community Programme of Policy and Action in relation to the Environment and Sustainable Development*, 27–30 March 1992, (COM(92)23 final, Vol. I and II). Cf. in particular Vol. II p. 54 et seq.

[5] See in particular Title XVI: Environment. For a discussion of the impact of the Maastricht Treaty on EU environmental policy and law see Wilkinson, (1992), p. 221 et seq.; also Greenpeace, (1991b), for a critical view.

[6] SEA amending the Treaty of Rome of 1958, signed in February 1986 and entered into force on 1 July 1987; repr. in Cartier and Trimble, (1991). See in particular Title VII: Environment. For an overview and discussion of the environmental provisions see Krämer, (1992), p. 62 et seq. On the significance of the SEA for EU environmental policy see Johnson and Corcelle, (1989), p. 342 et seq.; Gautier, in *La réparation des dommages catastrophiques*, (1990), p. 379 et seq. On the elevation of environmental protection to the importance of other EU policies under the SEA, see Krämer, (1990), p. 63.

[7] A ban on waste exports from the EU was already advocated repeatedly by the European Parliament; see Parliament Resolution on export of toxic wastes to the third world, 25 May 1989, (OJ No.C158/239); Parliament Resolution on a Community strategy for waste management, 19 February 1991, (OJ No.C72/34, 18 March 1991).

[8] Document SEC(89)934 final (14 September 1989); Council Resolution on waste policy, 7 May 1990, (OJ No.C122/2, 18 May 1990). See also Schröder, (1991), pp. 910–15.

The strategy document also addresses the question of waste management within the EU after the completion of the internal market, pointing out the probability of increased 'waste tourism' towards member states with less developed environmental standards and low-cost disposal options, in an area without internal frontiers. The document notes that this danger can be reduced but not entirely overcome by the establishment of common environmental standards in all member states. Even if uniform standards are introduced, regional differences in the cost of waste disposal operations will continue to provide an incentive for moving wastes to those member states with the cheapest disposal options (see Chapter 1 above). The strategy document therefore concludes that, in order to protect the environment effectively, it may be necessary to introduce restrictions on waste movements in addition to uniform standards. At the same time a coherent network of disposal facilities has to be established within the EU, and the principle of disposal in the nearest adequate facility (principle of proximity) has to be adhered to.

According to the strategy document, a special situation exists with regard to recyclable wastes having positive economic value. Management of those wastes should in principle be subject to free competition. An exception to the principle of proximity may therefore be made in the case of recyclable wastes. Nevertheless, control measures are also necessary to safeguard environmental interests in the context of the management of recyclable wastes.

With regard to the export of wastes to third countries, the document refers to the principles established by the Basel Convention, and calls for adjustment of the relevant EU legislation to that treaty. Through the strategy document, the Commission also expressed its willingness to assist third states in technical and administrative fields through exchange of information.

2. EU legislation on the management of hazardous wastes

Three important Directives relevant to the management of hazardous wastes have been adopted in the past two decades: the 1975 framework Directive on waste; the 1978 Directive on toxic and dangerous waste; and the 1984 Directive on transfrontier shipment of hazardous waste, amended in 1986. In accordance with the evolution of EU waste management policy, all of these instruments have been revised or replaced in the past few years. In 1991, the 1975 framework Directive was amended and the 1978 Directive replaced by a new Directive on hazardous waste. The changes reflect the principles of the 1989 waste management strategy, and contain provisions designed to facilitate monitoring by the Commission of member states' compliance with the Directives. A new Council Regulation, designed to implement the Basel and Lomé IV Conventions, was adopted in February

1993 to replace the 1984 Directive. In addition, a recent Directive addresses packaging waste, and a number of Directives cover particular categories of wastes, such as waste oils, and PCBs and PCTs.[9] A Directive on the incineration of hazardous wastes was adopted by the Council in December 1994, and a Commission proposal for a Directive on the landfill of wastes is under consideration.[10]

2.1 *The 1975/1991 framework Directive on waste* The 1975 framework Directive on waste, as amended in 1991, elaborates the general principles of waste management within the EU, as established by the 1989 Community strategy.[11] The amendment considerably extends the range of waste products and operations covered by the original 1975 Directive. It is not limited to wastes with hazardous characteristics, and applies to wastes destined both for final disposal and for recycling or recovery operations. These operations are defined in two annexes which are closely modelled on the relevant annexes to the Basel Convention. Based on Annex I, the Commission in December 1993 drew up a 'European Waste Catalogue' to be covered by the Directive.[12] The Directive requires member states to promote measures for waste minimization, and for the recycling and reprocessing of wastes the generation of which is unavoidable. In accordance with the principle of proximity and the aim of achieving self-sufficiency in waste disposal within the EU (and as far as possible within each member state), members are required to establish, in co-operation with each other as appropriate, a network of authorized waste disposal installations. This network must guarantee the disposal of each type of waste in the nearest appropriate disposal facility, to be determined on the basis of high environmental and human health standards. The nearest facility need not be located within the national boundaries of the generating state. Transboundary transport of wastes to neighbouring states will therefore not necessarily be reduced. The disposal network should, however, lead to a minimization of long-distance transport of wastes.

[9] Council Directive 94/62/EC of 20 December 1994 on packaging and packaging waste (OJ No.L365/10); Council Directive 75/439/EEC of 16 June 1975 on the disposal of waste oils (OJ No.L194, 25 July 1975), amended by Directive 87/101/EEC (OJ No.L42, 12 February 1987); Council Directive 76/403/EEC of 6 April 1976 on the disposal of PCB and PCT (OJ No.L108, 26 April 1976).

[10] Council Directive 94/67 of 16 December 1994 on the incineration of hazardous waste (OJ No.L365/34); *Commission Proposal for a Council Directive on the landfill of waste* (COM(91)102 final, 1991), as amended (COM(93)275 final–SYN335). See also the *Report of the Committee on the Environment, Public Health and Consumer Protection*, 30 November 1992, (Doc. EN/RR/217/217979).

[11] Council Directive 75/442/EEC of 15 July 1975 on waste, as amended by Directive 91/156/EEC of 18 March 1991, (OJ No.L78/32, 26 March 1991). For an analysis see Schröder, (1991), pp. 913–14.

[12] Commission Decision 94/3/EC, 20 December 1993 (list of wastes repr. in EELR (1994) p. 65 et seq).

To further this aim, the Directive requires member states to draw up detailed waste management plans. They may prohibit transfer of wastes that is not consistent with these plans. Members must also introduce permit systems for disposal operations and installations; exemption from the permit requirement is, however, permissible in some cases. States must provide for regular inspection of disposal and recycling installations. They must periodically submit reports on their implementation measures to the Commission, which must publicize this information. In accordance with the polluter pays principle, the Directive provides for disposal costs to be borne by the holder of the wastes or of the product from which the wastes are derived.

2.2 *The 1991 Directive on hazardous waste* This Directive replaces the 1978 Directive on toxic and dangerous waste as from the date member states are requested to implement it; this was originally 12 December 1993, but it has been delayed by amendment to 27 June 1995. The Directive's objective is the approximation of the laws of member states on the controlled management of hazardous wastes.[13] Adopted within the framework of the 1975/1991 waste Directive, it contains a general reference to that Directive, subject to the special rules established in some areas. It introduces the term 'hazardous waste' as being more comprehensive than the term 'toxic and dangerous waste' used in the 1978 Directive. The annexes contain a general definition of hazardous wastes covered by the Directive. As in the case of the framework Directive, the Commission is to specify this definition by drawing up a list of hazardous wastes at least 6 months before the date of implementation. Such definition may include limit values of concentration. The mixing of different categories of hazardous wastes, and of hazardous and other types of wastes, is to be prohibited by member states. The permit system of the framework Directive, and its provisions on inspection and keeping of records, apply to hazardous wastes with some alterations. International and EU standards on packaging and labelling must be applied. Member states must adopt management plans for hazardous wastes, which must be made public. The Commission, to whom these plans must be submitted, must compare them; this should contribute to approximation of standards in the different states. Finally, the Directive establishes a requirement for extensive mandatory reports by member states to the Commission on disposal companies and plants.

[13] Council Directive 78/319/EEC of 20 March 1978 on toxic and dangerous waste (OJ No.L84/43, 31 March 1978); Council Directive 91/689 of 12 December 1991 on hazardous waste (OJ No.L377/21, 31 December 1991), as amended by Directive 94/31/EC (OJNo. L168/28, 2 July 1994). See also the proposals by the Commission (COM(88)399 final–SYN165 (OJ No.C295/8, 1988); COM(89)560 final–SYN145 (OJ No.C42/19, 1990)), discussed by von Lersner, (1990), p. 214.

2.3 *The 1984 Directive on transfrontier shipment of hazardous waste* This Directive, which is the precursor of the 1993 Regulation discussed below, regulated transboundary movements of toxic and dangerous wastes as defined by the 1978 Directive, as well as PCBs. Originally covering transfrontier waste movements within the EU only, it was extended in 1986 to waste traffic with third states.[14] Since it was repealed only recently, it retains a certain significance in the context of the present analysis, as we will see.

For waste movements between EU member states, the Directive adopted the system of prior notification to prospective importing and transit states, to be given by means of a consignment note. The contents of this note were laid down in detail in an annex to the Directive. The competent authority of the recipient state could object to the proposed transaction within one month of receiving the notification; the Directive thus incorporated the concept of tacit consent. For traffic with third states, the concept of prior informed consent (PIC) was adhered to. The generator of the wastes had the primary responsibility of ensuring their environmentally sound disposal. A simplified procedure applied to wastes intended for recycling operations.

2.4 *The 1993 Regulation on the supervision and control of shipments of waste within, into and out of the European Community* The 1993 Regulation was adopted by the Council after nearly 3 years of intensive and difficult negotiations within the competent EU institutions.[15] In accordance with its Articles 43 and 44, it replaces the 1984 Directive as of 5 May 1994. The legal form of Regulation, establishing rules that are directly applicable in the member states,[16] was chosen in order to overcome the difficulties experienced in the application of the earlier Directives.[17] Although the need to incorporate the requirements of the Basel and Lomé IV Conventions into EU law was generally recognized, there was substantive disagreement

[14] Council Directive of 6 December 1984 on the supervision and control within the EEC of the transfrontier shipment of hazardous waste (84/631/EEC), as amended by Directives 85/469/EEC, 86/279/EEC, and 87/112/EEC. For a discussion see Williamson, (1989), p. 347 et seq.; Johnson and Corcelle, (1989), p. 173.

[15] Council Regulation 259/93 of 1 February 1993, (OJ No.L30/1, 6 February 1993). For a summary of its provisions see EC Press Release 9042/92 (Presse 179), 20 October 1992; 'Waste: Environment Ministers Approve Waste Shipments Regulation', in *Europe Environment* no. 397, 5 November 1992, p. 4 et seq. (*Europe Environment*, (1992)). For a discussion see von Wilmowsky, (1993), p. 562 et seq.

[16] Treaty of Rome, Article 189. Cf. Mathijsen, (1990), pp. 113–14; Louis, (1990), p. 119 et seq.; Krämer, (1992), p. 156 et seq.

[17] Explanatory memorandum to the 1990 Commission Proposal (see n. 18 below), p. 3. The record of implementation is indeed poor: the 1978 Directive had only been implemented by one member state in 1989, the 1984 Directive had been implemented by two states in 1987, and the 1991 framework Directive had been implemented by three states in August 1994. See EELR (1994) p. 234; Krämer, (1992), pp. 197–8; Schmidt, (1992), p. 61; Kwiatkowska and Soons, (1993), Editors' Introduction, p. LV et seq.; de Villeneuve, (1990), p. 570 et seq.

on the concrete form of the prospective provisions. The most contentious issues included the compatibility of control mechanisms for waste traffic within the EU with the free movement of goods, the nature and extent of such control measures, and the right of EU member states to prohibit unilaterally the import of wastes from other member states.

The Commission first put forward a proposal for a Regulation on waste shipment to replace the 1984 Directive in 1990. In November 1991, the European Parliament proposed some hundred amendments, most of which were aimed at strengthening the environmental requirements. The majority of these were not taken into account by the Commission in its revised proposal of March 1992. Most of the important concepts proposed by Parliament were, however, incorporated into the final version adopted by the Council.[18]

Initial hopes were that the Regulation could be finalized by May 1992, providing the basis for accession to the Basel Convention by the EU and its member states in time for the first meeting of the Conference of the Parties in December 1992. However, relevant negotiations at the Council's May session broke down, and it was not until October of the same year that political agreement on the major issues was reached.[19] The Council subsequently adopted the Regulation on 1 February 1993, and by the same token approved the Basel Convention on behalf of the EU.[20] The instrument of approval was deposited on 7 February 1994; the Convention thus entered into force for the EU on 7 May 1994.[21] Virtually all EU member states have also acceded to the Basel Convention (see Chapter 2(B) above).

The declared aim of the 1993 Regulation is to take into account the 1989 waste management strategy, and to implement the Basel Convention and Article 39 of Lomé IV.[22] The Regulation now also incorporates the principles of the 1992 OECD Decision on recyclable wastes, the EU Commission and its members having participated actively in the elaboration of that Decision (see para. 9 below).

[18] *Commission Proposal for a Council Regulation*, 26 October 1990, (COM(90)415 final–SYN305) (*1990 Commission Proposal*); *Opinion of the Economic and Social Committee* (OJ No.C269/10, 14 October 1991); *Amendments proposed by the European Parliament* (OJ No.C326/130, 16 December 1991); *Amended Commission Proposal for a Council Regulation*, 23 March 1992, (COM(92)121 final–SYN 305) (*1992 Commission Proposal*). For a discussion see Schröder, (1991); Greenpeace, (1991a).

[19] 'France Blocks EU Bid to Agree Waste Trade Rules', Reuter, (Brussels, 26 May 1992); 'France Prevents EU Accord on Waste Trade Rules', Reuter, (Brussels, 27 May 1992); EC Press Release, 20 October 1992; *Europe Environment*, (1992), see n. 15 above. For an overview of the negotiations see also Kummer, in YBIEL 2(1991) pp. 179–80, and eadem, in YBIEL 3(1992) pp. 292–3.

[20] Council Decision 93/98 of 1 February 1993 on the conclusion, on behalf of the Community, of the Basel Convention, (OJ No.L39/1, 16 February 1993).

[21] OJ C211/2 February 1994.

[22] *Explanatory memorandum to the 1990 Commission Proposal*, p. 2 et seq.

Scope of the Regulation

The scope of wastes covered by the 1993 Regulation is broadened considerably in comparison with the 1984 Directive. With few exceptions, it encompasses not only hazardous wastes but all wastes covered by the 1975/1991 framework Directive (Article 1). Unlike the Basel Convention and the regional treaties discussed in the preceding chapters, the Regulation provides for different rules and different levels of control for transboundary movements of wastes intended for disposal and those intended for recycling or recovery. The two categories of operations are defined by reference to the relevant Annexes to the framework Directive. In classifying the wastes covered, the Regulation adopts the three-tier system of the pertinent OECD Council Decision of 1992 (see para. 9 below), according to which a waste is allocated to the 'green', 'amber' or 'red' list based on its hazard potential. The 'red list' wastes listed in Annex IV are subject to the rules applying to disposal. The rules on recycling apply to wastes listed in Annex III, which corresponds to the 'amber list' of the OECD Decision. Annex II sets out a 'green list' of recyclable wastes, which is a replica of the pertinent list of the OECD Decision. With a number of exceptions (Articles 1, 11, and 17), wastes figuring on this list are not subject to the provisions of the Regulation, but are governed by the rules of the framework Directive. The 'green list' comprises wastes considered comparatively harmless, such as certain scrap metals, solid plastic, paper, glass, textiles, and food wastes. In accordance with the provisions of the Regulation, the three lists were amended in October 1994 to incorporate equivalent amendments to the annexes of the OECD Decision.[23]

Taking into account the completion of the internal market under the terms of the Maastricht Treaty, the 1993 Regulation establishes different procedures for the control of internal waste traffic (i.e. within the EU), and external traffic (i.e. with third states). Member states must establish one or more competent authorities with the function of administering these procedures (Article 36). Wastes transported within a member state are not subject to the Regulation, which requires only that the members must provide an appropriate national control system, taking account of the need for coherence within the EU (Article 13).

Waste shipments within the EU

Shipments of wastes destined for final disposal in another member state are subject to PIC. The person proposing a shipment of wastes must notify the competent authority of destination by means of a consignment note, the basic contents of which are set out in the Regulation. The Commission has

[23] Commission Decision of 21 October 1994, (OJ No.L288/36 (9 November 94)).

been mandated to draw up a standard consignment note in accordance with the relevant provisions. Copies of the note must be sent by the notifier to the competent authorities of dispatch and transit. The notifier must conclude a contract with the consignee, a copy of which must be submitted to the competent authorities on request. Among other things, the contract must stipulate the notifier's obligation to take the waste back in the event of illegal traffic or impossibility of proper disposal (Article 3). The authority of destination must acknowledge receipt of notification within 3 working days. Each competent authority may raise objections to the shipment, within a given time-frame, on the basis of the reasons stated in the Regulation. The authorities of dispatch and destination may, for example, object if the shipment does not conform to a rule established by the framework Directive. The shipment may proceed only after express authorization by the competent authority of destination, within 30 days following the dispatch of the acknowledgement. This may be given only in the absence of objections by any authority concerned (Article 4).

Member states may, in accordance with the Treaty, generally or partially prohibit the import of wastes for disposal from other member states, if such a measure serves to implement the main principles of the framework Directive. Agreed at the insistence of France after considerable debate, this is one of the most important additions made by the Council.

Movements of wastes listed in Annex III and intended for recovery or recycling are subject to notification under basically the same terms as wastes destined for disposal. The consignment note must again provide detailed information, including the planned method of disposal for residual waste after the operation has taken place (Article 6). However, in this case the principle of tacit consent applies, i.e. the transaction may take place if none of the competent authorities has raised a reasoned objection within 30 days. A state may choose to give express consent or refusal. Acceptable grounds for objection, listed in the Regulation, do not in this case include non-conformity with the principle of proximity (Articles 7, 8). The right of tacit consent may be waived for specific facilities. Any such decision must be notified, through the Commission, to all competent authorities and to the OECD Secretariat. Waiver of the right of tacit consent does not affect the obligation and requirements of notification (Article 9). States do not have the right to ban unilaterally the import of wastes destined for recycling or recovery. Transit of waste moving between member states may take place through non-member states. In this case, the state in question must be given the option of PIC, and the authority of destination may only authorize the movement 'where appropriate' (i.e. if all other requirements are met), once the transit state has consented (Article 12).

Waste shipments between EU members and third states
Unlike the Commission proposal, the Regulation in its final form prohibits the export of wastes for disposal except to EFTA states which are parties to the Basel Convention. Even those exports are prohibited if the intended state of destination has banned waste imports, or if the competent authority has 'reason to believe' that the wastes would not be managed in an environmentally sound manner. This term is taken from the Basel Convention and thus poses the same problems of interpretation (see Chapter 2 para. 7 above). Any such transaction is subject to authorization by the competent authority of dispatch, which may only be given in the absence of objections by other competent authorities, and if the notifier has obtained the prior consent of the states of import and transit in conformity with the rules of the Regulation. The transaction itself must also be carried out in accordance with the requirements of the Regulation (Articles 14–15). These rules are carefully adjusted to the Basel Convention.

Wastes destined for recovery are prohibited except to OECD member states that have accepted the 1992 OECD Decision (i.e. all except Japan), or to states parties to the Basel Convention and/or an agreement concluded under Article 11 of that Convention. The transactions must be carried out in conformity with the requirements of the applicable legal instrument (Basel Convention, OECD Decision, or separate agreement). The Regulation contains a provision similar to Article 11 of the Basel Convention, specifying the requirements to which separate agreements must conform (Article 16(2)). Special rules are applicable to wastes figuring on the 'green list', and to wastes in transit through third states (Article 17). In accordance with the Lomé IV Convention, waste exports to ACP states are prohibited (Article 18).

Equivalent rules apply to the import of wastes into the EU: wastes intended for disposal may only be imported from EFTA states which are Basel parties (Articles 19–20), and wastes intended for recovery only from OECD states to which the 1992 Decision applies, or from Basel parties and/or in accordance with a separate agreement, and must be carried out in accordance with the applicable rules (Articles 21–2). It is interesting that special provision is not made for the import of wastes from ACP states, which would be permissible under the Lomé IV provision (see Chapter 3(H) above). It could be argued that the Lomé IV provision constitutes a separate agreement under Article 16 outlined above. However, it seems doubtful that it would conform to Article 16 in this context, as it does not directly address waste traffic from ACP to EU states and sets out no environmental requirements for such traffic. PIC of the last competent authority in the EU is required for transit through the EU from and to third states, and tacit consent is required for transit from and to OECD states to which the 1992 Decision applies (Articles 23, 24).

Provisions common to all transactions

The Regulation includes provisions on the duty to re-import wastes which cannot be disposed of in the state of destination in accordance with prior arrangements (Article 25), and on the responsibilities of states in the event of illegal traffic in waste (Article 26). These are modelled on the Basel Convention's relevant rules but address a few points left open in the Convention, e.g. the duty to notify any state to or through which the return movement takes place (see Chapter 2(G) above). All waste subject to transboundary movement, whether destined for recycling or final disposal, must be covered by financial security (Article 27). In the case of waste destined for recycling, a general notification procedure is provided (Article 28). The Regulation also specifies that wastes subject to different notifications may not be mixed (Article 29), and that member states must adopt supervisory mechanisms which may include inspection of facilities and undertakings, and spot-checking of shipments (Article 30). Other provisions concern administrative matters, including specifications of the consignment note and other documentation; the allocation of costs of measures adopted under the Regulation; and the designation of competent authorities and other national bodies (Article 31 et seq). Member states are required to comply with the international transport conventions listed in Annex I (Article 32). Primary responsibility for proper treatment or disposal is allocated to the notifier (Article 34). The Commission and the member states are asked to co-operate with the Basel Convention Secretariat (Article 40).

3. An assessment of EU policy and legislation

With the two 1991 Directives and the 1993 Regulation in place, the waste management system established by EU policy and law is very elaborate and sophisticated, as the above overview shows. It covers all types of wastes, not only those defined as hazardous, and establishes and elaborates such fundamental principles as waste minimization, proximity, and environmentally sound management. With the requirements of inspection of facilities and operations and spot-checking of shipments, and the extensive reporting requirements, it also provides for stronger implementation and supervisory measures than any of the other legal instruments discussed so far (see also Chapter 6 below). The 1993 Regulation in particular establishes a highly complex regulatory system for all types of wastes, addressing practically every conceivable case of transboundary disposal or recycling. The differentiation between the various causes for transboundary waste traffic is thus more advanced than in the Basel Convention. Efforts have clearly been made to take account of the requirements of that Convention. In numerous instances, the provisions go beyond those requirements, or provide clarifications or specifications which are missing in the Convention. This is an astonishing advance on the earlier Commission proposals, which were considerably less stringent and contained a number of loopholes.[24] The most important substantive difference between EU policy and law and the Basel Convention is that the former establishes dual standards in favour of wastes destined for recycling and recovery operations, including hazardous wastes. This is based on the perception of trade in recyclable materials as an economically beneficial activity, and of recycling as an environmentally sound waste management option generally encouraged by the EU.[25]

B. *The EU Rules Within the Framework of the Basel Convention*

In common with a number of other recent international environmental treaties, the Basel Convention expressly provides for adherence by the EU: Articles 21–25 regulate the accession of 'political and/or economic integration organizations'. The term 'economic integration organization' denotes the EU.[26] The EU's recent accession in accordance with these provisions raises a number of questions, which will be addressed in the following paragraphs. Two interrelated problem areas can be distinguished: firstly, the respective competence of the EU and its members in the areas governed by the Basel Convention, in particular with respect to the conclusion and implementation of the Convention; and secondly, the modalities of the application of the Basel Convention's principles and provisions within the EU, on the one hand, and between the EU and third states, on the other, in the context of the completion of the internal market. Although the adoption of the two 1991 Directives and, more specifically, the 1993 Regulation, has contributed to the clarification of a number of points in these contexts, all problems are not yet resolved.

4. The competence of the EU and its members with regard to the conclusion and implementation of the Basel Convention

4.1 *International competence of the EU in the field of hazardous waste management* The EU's capacity to enter into international agreements is recognized by the international community as well as within the EU itself.[27]

[24] For a critical assessment of the *1990 Commission Proposal* see Greenpeace, (1991a), pointing out numerous weaknesses.

[25] e.g., the Commission has drawn up proposals for compulsory recovery or re-use of 90 per cent of all packaging waste; cf. the report in EPL 22/5/6(1992) p. 338 et seq.

[26] Cf. the records of the negotiations on the Basel Convention, quoted in Chapter 2 above. The term 'political integration organization' refers to the OAU (see Chapter 3 para. 2 above). The relevant provisions were included on the proposal of the two organizations in question.

[27] Mathijsen, (1990), p. 282, and sources quoted there; Nollkaemper, (1987), p. 63 et seq.;

Since the member states also have this capacity, it must be determined in each instance whether a given treaty should be concluded and implemented by the EU, by its member states, or by both. EU doctrine and case law acknowledge the possibility of 'mixed agreements', i.e. international treaties to which both the EU and its members are parties, exercising their rights and obligations toward third parties within their respective spheres of competence. Mixed agreements may, however, be concluded only if the member states have residual competence in the areas governed by the agreement in question.[28] In the field of environmental protection, mixed agreements have become a common feature.[29]

The Basel Convention, by allowing for accession by both the EU and its member states, provides a basis for a mixed agreement. In common with a number of other recent international treaties, it contains a so-called participation clause,[30] addressing the extent of the exercise of the respective rights and duties of the EU and its members in the event that both are parties. Article 22(2) provides that 'the organization and its member states shall decide on their respective responsibilities for the performance of their obligations under the Convention', and that they may not exercise their party rights concurrently. The organization must declare the extent of its competence in its instrument of accession (Article 22(3)). On approving the Basel Convention, the EU made the following declaration:

As provided for in the EEC Treaty and in the light of existing Community legislation in the field covered by the Basel Convention, more particularly Council Regulation (EEC) No 259/93 and Council Directive 84/631/EEC on the supervision and control within the European Community of the transfrontier shipment of hazardous waste (as amended), the Community possesses competence at an international level in this field. The Member States of the European Economic Community

Cameron, (1992), p. 3; Louis, (1990), p. 63 et seq. The EU's capacity to enter into international agreements was established by the *ERTA Case* (*Commission* v. *Council*, Case 22/70, ECR 1971 p. 263). The supremacy of international law over the secondary legislation of the EU, and the EU's duty to implement international treaties to which it is a party, has been affirmed by ECJ case law pursuant to the *Third International Fruit Co. Cases* (Joined Cases 21–24/72, ECR 1972 p. 1219).

[28] On mixed agreements see Cremona, (1982), pp. 393–428, in particular the analysis of relevant ECJ cases (p. 413); Gaja, (1988), pp. 605–6; Nollkaemper, (1987), pp. 65–6; Louis, (1990), pp. 65, 96–7.

[29] Haigh, (1991), p. 173 et seq. (and revised version of this paper in Hurrell and Kingsbury, (1992), p. 228 et seq.); Nollkaemper, (1987), pp. 65–6 (noting that nearly all currently existing agreements on environmental matters to which the EU is a party are mixed, and analysing a number of mixed agreements in this field); Krämer, (1990), p. 18 (discussing seven environmental treaties concluded as mixed agreements by the EU and its members); Brusasco-MacKenzie and Kiss, (1989), p. 704.

[30] See Haigh, (1991), pp. 174–75; Nollkaemper, (1987), p. 67; Brusasco-Mackenzie and Kiss, (1989), p. 704 (discussing participation clauses of a number of environmental treaties). For a detailed analysis of the participation clause of UNCLOS, see da Fonseca-Wollheim, (1992). A participation clause virtually identical to that of the Basel Convention is contained in the 1992 UN/ECE Convention on international waterways (Article 25(3)).

also have competence at the international level, including certain matters which are covered by the Basel Convention.[31]

Thus the intention was clearly to conclude the Basel Convention as a mixed agreement. In order to determine whether this is the correct approach, the respective external competence of the EU and its members under EU law in the relevant subject area must be examined.

The issue of external powers of the EU is addressed by some provisions of the Treaty of Rome, in particular Article 130(5) of the SEA. EU doctrine and the case law of the ECJ on the subject is quite extensive. The issue is complex and has become even more so after the entry into force of the SEA, which introduced new legislative powers for the EU in some fields, but contains only fragmentary rules on the exercise of external powers.[32] The pertinent problems are not generally resolved; in fact, they have given rise to arduous debates in the context of a number of mixed agreements in the environmental field. An analysis of this issue is beyond the scope of this study, which is limited to aspects directly relevant to the Basel Convention. Reference can be made to the numerous works devoted to the analysis of the problem.[33]

It is generally recognized by doctrine and by the case law of the ECJ that if the EU has internal competence in a specific field, it has the same competence in relations with third states. Such competence need not be explicitly allocated to the EU by the Treaty of Rome; it is sufficient for the EU to have adopted pertinent legislation.[34] Even if legislation has not yet been adopted, it is sufficient for the EU to have the acknowledged internal power to do so.[35] The EU's legislative activity in the field of management of wastes, including transboundary movements of hazardous wastes, has been extensive, as the above overview shows. The EU therefore obviously has international competence in this field.

4.2 *Legal basis of EU legislation in the field of hazardous waste management* We have to ask next whether the EU's international competence in the areas governed by the Basel Convention is exclusive, or whether the

[31] Corrigendum to Council Decision 93/98/EEC of 1 February 1993 on the conclusion of the Basel Convention (OJ No.L74/52, 17 March 1993).

[32] For a general discussion cf. Barents, (1993), p. 85 et seq.; Krämer, (1992), p. 70 et seq.; idem, (1990), p. 81 et seq. For an outline of the changes introduced by the SEA with regard to the relations of the EU and its members with third countries see Hilf, (1990), p. 89 et seq.; Krämer, in Common Market Law Review 24 (1987), p. 659 et seq.

[33] See among many others Cremona, (1982), p. 393 et seq.; Francioni, (1983), p. 53 et seq.; Haigh, (1991); Hilf, (1990), p. 89 et seq.; Brusasco-MacKenzie and Kiss, (1989); and Nollkaemper, (1987), p. 55 et seq.

[34] *Commission* v. *Council* (*ERTA*), Case 22/70, ECR 1971 p. 273. See also the discussion by Francioni, (1983), p. 65 et seq.; also Nollkaemper, (1987), p. 59.

[35] *Opinion 1/76 on the draft Agreement establishing a European Laying-up Fund for Inland Waterway Vessels*, ECR 1977 p. 741. See also Francioni, (1994); Haigh, (1991), p. 171 et seq.; Nollkaemper, (1987), p. 63 et seq.; Cremona, (1982), p. 394.

member states retain residual powers. In order to answer this question, the legal basis in the Treaty of Rome for the EU legislation in the field of waste management must first be determined.[36]

Even before the adoption of the SEA, the ECJ had affirmed the EU's competence in the field of environmental protection.[37] All waste directives adopted prior to the entry into force of the SEA are based on Articles 100 and 235 of the Treaty, as are most of the older directives in environmental fields.[38] The SEA introduced more specific legal bases for measures concerning both the protection of the environment, and the furtherance of the internal market; these have been further elaborated by the Maastricht Treaty. Measures concerning the management and transboundary movement of wastes—located in a borderland between environmental protection and trade policy—can now be based either on Article 130r et seq. (environment), or on Article 100a (internal market). Each of these solutions entails different procedural and substantive consequences.[39] The most important consequence in the present context is that, if the EU's competence is based on Article 130r et seq., member states have the right to adopt more stringent national rules in accordance with Article 130t,[40] whereas if the Treaty basis is Article 100a, they merely have the option of 'contracting out' in accordance with paragraph 4 of that provision.[41] Some aspects, in particular control measures for transboundary transport of wastes having economic value, affect the EU's commercial policy. They may therefore come within the purview of Article 113 of the Treaty, which gives exclusive competence to the EU.

The problem of the Treaty basis for waste management legislation is by no means resolved.[42] In the elaboration of the recent legal instruments addressing wastes, it was the subject of an extensive—and continuing—debate between the competent EU institutions.[43] In the case of the two 1991

[36] On this issue see Barents, (1993), p. 91 et seq.

[37] *Procureur de la République* v. *Association de défense des brûleurs d'huiles usagées* (*ADBHU*), Case 240/83, ECR 1985 p. 531 et seq., and discussion by Francioni, (1994).

[38] Johnson and Corcelle, (1989), p. 4; Gautier, in *La réparation des dommages catastrophiques*, (1990), p. 380 et seq.; Kelly, (1986), p. 90 et seq.; Nollkaemper, (1987), p. 58.

[39] For an extensive discussion of these provisions, their elaboration history, and their relationship in this context see Krämer, (1990), p. 31 et seq., p. 87 et seq.; and idem, (1992), p. 79 et seq. See also Nollkaemper, (1987), p. 58 et seq. On changes introduced by the Maastricht Treaty see Wilkinson, (1992), p. 227 et seq.

[40] For a discussion cf. Krämer, (1990), p. 93 et seq.

[41] See Krämer, (1990), p. 93 et seq.; idem, (1992), p. 79 et seq.; idem, (1993), p. 115; Nollkaemper, (1987), p. 82 et seq.

[42] Cf. Barents, (1993) p. 105; Francioni, (1994); Schröder, (1991) p. 911 et seq.; Krämer, (1990), p. 44 et seq.; Schmidt, (1992), p. 69 et seq.

[43] Cf. the *Commission Proposal for a Directive on hazardous waste* (COM(88)399 final,OJ No. C295/8 (1988)), and *Proposal for amending Directive 75/442/EEC on wastes* (OJ No.C295/3 (1988)); the *Opinion of the Economic and Social Committee* on these two Proposals, 14 December 1988; Parliament Resolution on the legal basis of the Proposal for a Council

Directives on wastes and hazardous wastes, respectively, the Commission proposed Article 100a as Treaty basis. The Council, however, opted for Article 130s as a basis for both Directives. The Commission consequently referred both cases to the ECJ, requesting annulment of the Directives on the grounds that they were adopted on the wrong legal basis.[44] In its March 1993 decision concerning the framework Directive on wastes, the Court upheld the Council's choice of Treaty basis.[45] The 1993 Regulation was also adopted on the basis of Article 130s by the Council, this time with the (reluctant) approval of the Commission.[46] In this case, the matter has now been referred to the ECJ by the European Parliament, again challenging the choice of legal basis.[47]

Prior to the above events, the discussion mainly centred around a 1991 decision of the ECJ in a case concerning the legal basis for a directive on the harmonization of national plans to reduce pollution caused by wastes resulting from the production of titanium dioxide.[48] In this case, the Court concluded that the objective and the contents of the directive in question comprise both the protection of the environment and the prevention of distortion of market conditions. Based on the argument that in accordance with Article 130r(2), environmental protection is considered a component of other EU policies, and that Article 100a(3) provides a sufficient basis for the consideration of environmental concerns in the adoption of measures aimed at harmonization of market conditions, the Court held that Article 100a should serve as a legal basis for the measure in question. This argument does not seem very convincing.[49] However, even if the Court's conclusion is accepted in this particular instance, it cannot be applied to every case of conflict between environmental and market aims. As pointed out by Francesco Francioni, the ECJ decision in the *Titanium Dioxide Case* cannot be construed to support a general subsidiarity of Articles 130r et seq.

Council Directive on hazardous waste (A3–0166/91, OJ No.C240/63, 16 September 1991). For a discussion see Krämer, (1990), p. 45.

[44] Case C 155/91 (OJ No.C189, 20 July 1991), p. 12, and Case C/86/92 (OJ No.C97, 1992), p. 7. See Krämer, (1993), p. 116; Kromarek, in YBIEL 2(1991) p. 338; and the report in EPL 22/5/6(1992) p. 337.

[45] *Commission* v. *Council*, Case C 155/91, 17 March 1993, not yet published in ECR. Cf. ENDS Report 221, June 1993.

[46] The Commission had originally proposed Articles 100a and 113 as a legal basis, whereas the Economic and Social Committee expressed preference for Article 130s. See the *Explanatory Memorandum to the 1990 Commission Proposal*, p. 6; and the *Opinion of the Economic and Social Committee on the 1990 Commission Proposal* (OJ No.C269/10, 14 October 1991), p. 6. See also the report in *Europe Environment*, (1992), p. 6, see n. 15 above.

[47] *Parliament* v. *Council*, Case C 187/93. Cf. also the report 'Environment: Waste Shipment Regulation Could End Up In Dock', in *European Report* no. 1839, 27 February 1993, p. 20 et seq.

[48] *Commission* v. *Council*, Case 300/89, 11 June 1991; see also Kromarek, in YBIEL 2(1991) p. 338. For a discussion see Barents, (1993), p. 94 et seq.; Robinson, (1992), p. 112 et seq.

[49] Cf. Schröder, (1991), p. 911.

in the case of a conflict between the two objectives. Such an approach, which would significantly reduce the scope of Articles 130r et seq., has no textual basis in the Treaty. Instead, the respective importance of environmental and market aims should be balanced in each case. Article 100a should only prevail if in fact the primary objective of the measure is to secure the internal market, and environmental considerations are incidental to that aim. Likewise, Articles 130r et seq. should prevail if the primary objective is the protection of the environment, even if the measure has incidental implications for the internal market. This corresponds to the theory of the 'principal objective', supported by the Council in this context.[50]

In analysing the relevant EU legislation on the transport and management of hazardous wastes in the light of these considerations, we therefore have to consider its main objectives. It aims for the establishment of a harmonized Community-wide system for the environmentally safe management, transport and disposal of wastes, including hazardous wastes. Its main objectives are the minimization of generation and transport of wastes, disposal in the nearest appropriate disposal facility, environmentally sound management of wastes regardless of the place of disposal, and control of all activities related to the transport and management of hazardous wastes.

On the one hand, the relevant measures undoubtedly have implications for the internal market. The harmonization of national legislation applicable to waste management, and the setting of Community-wide standards for the handling and transport of hazardous wastes, contribute to the harmonization of market conditions in the field of waste management. In addition, control measures for waste transport have effects on trade, especially in the case of recyclable wastes having positive economic value.[51] On the other hand, the protection of human health and the environment against adverse impacts of the management, transport and disposal of hazardous wastes has an important place in the relevant EU legislation. Uncontrolled handling and unrestricted movements of hazardous wastes, especially in an area without internal frontiers, would pose great risks to human health as well as to the environment. A lack of control of waste movements, and different environmental standards within the EU, would encourage 'waste tourism' to the less developed regions of the EU and put at greater risk the populations of those areas.

We may conclude that the relevant legislation does indeed encompass both environmental and market objectives; an order of priority must therefore be established.

Hazardous wastes are basically unwanted by-products of industrial activ-

[50] Francioni, (1994). Cf. Schröder, (1991), p. 911; Barents, (1993) pp. 100–1.

[51] On recyclable wastes cf. *Vessoso and Zanetti*, Joined Cases 206/88 and 207/88, 23 March 1990, reaffirming that recyclable wastes can be considered 'wastes' within the meaning of the 1975 and 1978 Directives.

ity; any economic value is incidental. It is their significance as a source of serious pollution and a danger to human health and the environment that calls for the adoption of relevant measures, rather than their significance as a tradeable commodity. All hazardous wastes, whether recyclable or not, pose a grave danger to human health and the environment. The risk of disastrous accidents is increased if the wastes are transported over long distances prior to disposal or re-use (see Chapter 1 above). The main consideration in adopting legislation to control and harmonize their management and transport must therefore be the minimization of that risk, and market considerations are a secondary consequence. The main objectives of the waste legislation are all environmental in nature. For this reason, even though legislation on hazardous wastes has implications for the completion of the internal market, environmental protection must be considered the primary aim of legislation on hazardous wastes.

This interpretation, though by no means uncontested,[52] is supported by the ECJ's recent decision in the case of the 1991 framework Directive on wastes, based on the same arguments. While accepting that wastes are goods as understood in EU law and practice,[53] and that some provisions of the Directive affect the internal market, the Court held that—in contrast to the directive under discussion in the *Titanium Dioxide Case*—its principal objective is environmental protection, and effects on the internal market are ancillary. The incorporation into the 1993 Regulation of the right to enact unilateral import bans even within the EU also seems to point towards a recognition of the supremacy of environmental concerns over market considerations in waste management,[54] as does the ECJ's 1992 decision in the *Wallonia Case* (discussed in para. 5.3 below). The 1989 Community strategy for the management of wastes, while recognizing the close connection between environmental and market aims in the context of waste management, refers to the three fundamental

[52] A number of scholars argue that waste-related measures must be based on Article 100a: see e.g. de Villeneuve, (1990), p. 574; Schmidt, (1992), p. 69 et seq.; Robinson, (1992), p. 116 et seq.; Barents, (1993), p. 100 et seq., rejecting the theory of primacy of the objective, and concluding that Article 100a applies in all matters affecting the common market, while Article 130s is limited to so-called 'habitat protection' measures. See also the detailed analysis by Krämer, (1990), p. 40 et seq., and idem, (1992), p. 80 et seq., proposing to replace the criterion of respective importance of the environmental and market aims with that of 'objective closeness' of the measure to the completion of the internal market or the environment, and arguing that waste-related measures are objectively closer to market aims.

[53] For a definition of 'goods' for the purposes of Article 9 of the Treaty cf. *Commission* v. *Italy*, Case 7/68, ECR 1968 p. 428 et seq.: 'By goods . . . there must be understood all products which can be valued in money and which are capable, as such, of forming the subject of commercial transactions.' Wastes having economic value can thus be considered goods in accordance with this definition.

[54] Cf. the report in *Europe Environment*, (1992), p. 4 (see n. 15 above), interpreting this to indicate a shift in policy towards the precedence of environmental concerns over market considerations in the field of waste management.

objectives of the EU's environmental policy set out in Article 130r of the Treaty, and declares the avoidance and reduction of the quantity and hazard potential of wastes as the fundamental aim of the EU's waste management policy; secondary aims are the reprocessing and environmentally sound disposal of the wastes (see para. 1 above).[55] These aims, intended to guide the elaboration of EU legislation on the issue, are clearly environmental.

In view of these considerations, there is a strong basis for the argument that the EU's competence in the field of the management of hazardous wastes should be based on Article 130s rather than on Article 100a, as decided by the Council and confirmed by the ECJ in the case of the framework Directive.

The controversy surrounding the Treaty basis for measures on the control of management and transport of hazardous wastes is not limited to the question of prevalence of Article 100a or Articles 130r et seq. Since some of the measures adopted for the control of waste traffic result in trade restrictions, it is sometimes argued that the EU's competence in the areas addressed by the Basel Convention should not be based on either Articles 100a or 130r et seq., but on Article 113 of the Treaty, governing the common commercial policy.[56] EU competence based on Article 113 is exclusive, leaving no room for national measures to be adopted by member states. If EU legislation in the field of waste management were based entirely on Article 113, member states would have no residual competence in the field, and the Basel Convention could not be concluded as a mixed agreement by the EU and its members.

It is true that some of the measures adopted under relevant EU legislation amount to trade restrictions and should therefore be based on Article 113. This can be said notably for the restrictions on import and export, and the PIC procedure. However, it can again be pointed out that the primary aims of such measures are of an environmental nature, and market considerations are only a secondary consequence. Apart from this, areas addressed by the Basel Convention and requiring the adoption of measures by its parties also include issues which are clearly not within the scope of the commercial policy, such as the general obligations with regard to environmentally sound waste management (Article 4); the need for international co-operation in technical and scientific fields (Article 10); the need for transmission of information (Article 13); and the financial aspects

[55] Cf. the analysis by Schröder, (1991), p. 911.

[56] See de Villeneuve, (1990), pp. 575–6. The Commission, while agreeing to Article 130s as a Treaty basis for the EU Regulation, expressed the view that Article 113 should be added as a second basis (*Europe Environment*, (1992), p. 6, see n. 15 above). Cf. however Krämer, (1990), p. 48, pointing out that Articles 130s and 113 are mutually exclusive.

(Article 14).[57] This makes it difficult to sustain the argument that the EU's competence in all areas addressed by the Basel Convention should be based on Article 113 of the Treaty.

If the relevant legal instruments are thus based on Article 130s, the member states have, in accordance with Article 130t, the competence to adopt additional, more stringent measures in the fields governed by the Basel Convention.[58] The competence of the EU is therefore not exclusive. The concept of residual competence of the member states is in fact strongly supported in the 1993 Regulation on waste shipments.[59] This is expressed especially in the recognition of member states' right to enter into separate agreements with third states, and to adopt unilaterally general or partial waste import bans—a right that had already been exercised by some members prior to its acceptance by the Council, e.g. by Belgium in the situation that gave rise to the *Wallonia Case* discussed in para. 5.3 below, and by France in adopting a unilateral import ban for wastes (see also Chapter 1 para. 5 above).

If residual competence of the member states is thus accepted, the Basel Convention may be concluded and implemented by the EU and its member states as a mixed agreement.

5. The modalities of the implementation of the Basel Convention within the EU, and between the EU and other states

The problem of applying a treaty in the relationship between the EU member states, on the one hand, and between the EU as a whole and third states, on the other, arises in the context of treaties adhered to by the EU and its members which have two distinct characteristics: (a) they cover transactions between the member states, and (b) they do not allow states to derogate substantially from their rules. Apart from the Basel Convention, this is the case with CITES and the Montreal Protocol.

5.1 *The legal nature of the EU for the purposes of the Basel Convention*

With the accession of both the EU and virtually all its members to the Basel Convention, the question arises to what extent EU law has to conform to

[57] This view was also expressed by the Commission in its earlier proposal for a Council Decision on the conclusion of the Basel Convention, 26 July 1990 (COM(90)362 final). Cf. Cremona, (1982), pp. 414–16.

[58] Article 130r(4), establishing the principle of subsidiarity in this area, was deleted in Maastricht. The principle of subsidiarity has been attributed a more general scope by incorporation into the new Article 3b (for a discussion see Wilkinson, (1992), p. 225).

[59] A similar approach underlies Article 15 of Council Regulation 3626/82 implementing CITES (OJ L384/1, 31 December 1982, amended in 1986 (Reg. 2295/86), 1987 (Reg. 3143/87), and 1990 (Reg. 197/90). CITES addresses an area on the borderline between environmental and market considerations, as does the Basel Convention, and the implementing regulation expressly allows member states to adopt more stringent measures in some instances.

the Convention in the internal relationship. In order to answer this question, the legal nature of the EU for the purposes of the Convention needs to be examined. The EU could either be regarded as a legal entity to which the provisions of the Convention apply—in a similar way as to a state—only with respect to its relationship with other states, not affecting the internal relationship; or as an organization composed of individual states, to which the Basel Convention applies in the internal as well as the external relationship. Two opposing positions could be adopted on this issue, with opposing consequences for the implementation.

If the EU were attributed a quasi-state quality for the purposes of the Basel Convention, its position would be similar to that of a state under the Convention. The Basel Convention would have to be implemented at EU level, through EU legislation, in the same way as a state has to implement it. In this case, the residual competences of the member states would be similar to those of cantons or equivalent entities in a federal state. This would mean that the general obligations imposed by the Convention, e.g. the principle of proximity, would apply to the EU as a whole rather than to each member state. The issue of transboundary movements of hazardous wastes among member states would be governed by EU law rather than by the Basel Convention. In the internal relationship, the EU would have to comply with the Basel Convention only insofar as it would have to meet the Basel requirements of a holistic nature, i.e. those obligations that relate to the protection of the environment regardless of whether or not other states are directly affected (see Chapter 1(K) above). Only in relation to third states would the Basel Convention be fully applicable. The most important consequence of this would be the right of the EU to adopt its own internal control system for transboundary movements of hazardous wastes, which would not need to be in line with the Basel Convention. Thus, the EU could in theory even provide for freedom of hazardous waste movements within its boundaries as long as the external obligations, and the obligations of a holistic nature, were respected. Waste transactions between the EU as a whole and third states would be permissible, in accordance with the Basel Convention, if the states in question were parties to the Convention, and the transactions were carried out in conformity with the Convention. This approach is advocated by some authors, substantiated by a reference to the requirements of the completion of the internal market and the abolition of internal frontiers in accordance with the Maastricht Treaty, or—less convincingly—by the argument that the EU's competence in this field is exclusive and that there is therefore no room for the application of the Basel Convention in the internal relationship. This approach also inspired the original Commission proposal for a Regulation on waste shipments.[60]

[60] *Explanatory Memorandum to the 1990 Commission Proposal*, p. 4; de Villeneuve, (1990), p. 575; Schmidt, (1992), p. 73.

The other possibility is to approximate the EU to an international organization. This would mean that the Basel Convention would, in principle, be implemented—and the relevant rights and duties exercised—at the level of the member states. The fact that the EU has a legal system determining the respective rights and duties of the member states and the EU, as well as its own detailed waste management system, would then have to be taken into account by resorting to a regional agreement between the EU member states under Article 11 of the Basel Convention. Such an agreement, incorporating the concepts of EU legislation, would have to conform to the requirements set out in Article 11 (see Chapter 3 above). This means that internal as well as external rules on waste management would have to comply with the fundamental principles of the Basel Convention. Unlike a state, the EU thus would not be free to regulate internal waste transactions as long as the external obligations, and the obligations of a holistic nature, were met. The most important consequence of this approach would be that a control procedure for waste movements, in line with the fundamental aims and concepts of the Basel Convention, would have to be established within the EU by means of the regional agreement. As under the first approach, relations between the EU and third states would be governed by the relevant provisions of the Basel Convention in accordance with Article 11. This second approach appears to be implicitly supported by the Greenpeace demand that EU law be in full conformity with the provisions of Basel.[61]

It seems obvious, from the outset, that neither of these extreme solutions would be entirely satisfactory. Both are incompatible with the parallel external competence of the EU and its members, outlined above, and with the special legal nature of the EU. Indeed, the 1993 Regulation in its final form seems to settle for a compromise between these two positions: while establishing requirements that are to be implemented at EU level, thus treating the EU as a whole, it also gives member states the option of adopting their own rules at the national level, namely by adopting unilateral import bans and by concluding separate agreements with third states on transboundary movements of recyclable wastes.[62] Such a compromise is justified on the basis of objective criteria. It is generally recognized that the EU is neither a state in the traditional sense, as it lacks some of the basic attributes of state nationhood, nor an international organization, since it creates a close union between its members, well beyond the mutual rights and obligations usually established by organizations. Instead, the EU

[61] Greenpeace, (1991a), p. 23 et seq.

[62] A similar approach is adopted by the Regulation implementing CITES (see n. 59 above). Most EU member states are parties to the CITES Convention, although the EU itself is not. However, the EU does have recognized competence in the areas addressed by CITES. Cf. Nollkaemper, (1987), p. 70 et seq.

constitutes a novel and separate legal order under which the member states have renounced a part of their sovereignty in favour of a legal entity of a higher order.[63] The secondary legislation of the EU is distinct both from national legislation, and from an international treaty creating rights and obligations between states;[64] in the hierarchy of legal norms it stands between the two.[65]

Accordingly, special criteria have to be established to determine the status of the EU in the context of the Basel Convention, and the modalities of its application in the internal relationship. On the one hand, an important point is that the abolition of internal frontiers in the course of the completion of the internal market must be understood above all in an economic and fiscal sense.[66] The ever closer union of the EU members does not entail the disappearance of state boundaries in the legal sense. Despite having given over some parts of their sovereignty to the EU, the members do not cease to exist as states in the recognized legal sense;[67] as has been argued above, the EU members also retain the capacity to accede to the Basel Convention concurrently with the EU. This fact cannot be disregarded in the context of the implementation of the Basel Convention within the EU; it is, indeed, an important argument against the 'quasi-state' approach. In addition, it can be argued that the attribution of quasi-state quality to the EU, leading to the non-application of the Basel Convention's concepts in the internal relationship, would defeat the basic aims of the Convention. It is evidently not the intention that a block of fifteen states can be parties to the Basel Convention and yet exempt themselves, for whatever reasons, from the application of some of its most fundamental provisions in their internal relationship. Such an interpretation would be contrary to the obligation of the EU and its members as parties to the Basel Convention to fulfil their obligations under the Convention in good faith. On the other hand, it would be incompatible with the close union of the EU members and the

[63] See *Van Gend en Loos* v. *Netherlands Fiscal Administration*, Case 26/62, ECR 1963 I p. 5 et seq. For a discussion see Cameron, (1992), p. 5 et seq.; Haigh, (1991), p. 163 et seq.; Krämer, (1992), p. 1 et seq.; idem, in *La réparation des dommages catastrophiques*, (1990), p. 399; Louis, (1990), p. 11 et seq., p. 63 et seq.; and Mathijsen, (1990), p. 1 et seq., p. 304 et seq.

[64] See Case 38/69, ECR 1970, in particular p. 47: 'An act which has the characteristics of a Community decision because of its objective as well as of the institutional framework within which it has been drawn up, cannot be described as an "international agreement" '. Cf. Reuter, (1989), pp. 24–5, in particular n. 71.

[65] See Cremona, (1982), pp. 398, 403, 425, and Louis, (1990), p. 92 et seq., both discussing the *Third International Fruit Co. Cases* (Joined Cases 21–24/72, ECR 1972 p. 1219), and noting that in a conflict between EU legislation and an international agreement concluded by the EU, the latter will prevail, since in accordance with the widely accepted doctrine of the ECJ, international law takes precedence over secondary EU legislation. Cf. Hilf, (1990), p. 94.

[66] Cf. Hilf, (1990), p. 96, referring to 'the disappearance of physical, technical, financial and fiscal frontiers between the Member States'.

[67] Francioni, (1983), p. 55.

legal order established by the EU to require the conclusion of a separate treaty under Article 11 between the EU members in order to guarantee the recognition of EU law and policy under the Basel Convention.

An indication of a possible solution, providing both the recognition of EU legislation by the Basel Convention and the application of the Convention's fundamental concepts in the internal relationship, can be found in the Basel Convention itself: its provisions address this point, albeit indirectly. Besides providing for the EU to become a party, and giving an indication as to the exercise of party rights and obligations by the EU and its members, the Convention in Article 11 provides for multilateral, bilateral or regional agreements *and arrangements* to be established within its framework. The question therefore arises whether the secondary legislation of the EU can be considered a regional arrangement within the meaning of that provision, and if so, what consequences this entails. An interesting parallel can be seen in the 1992 UN/ECE Convention on the protection of international waterways, discussed in Chapter 5(D) below. Like the Basel Convention, this treaty provides for the adoption of 'bilateral or multilateral agreements or other arrangements' within its framework, while at the same time providing for the EU to become a party alongside its member states.

5.2 *The EU waste management legislation as a regional 'arrangement' within the meaning of Article 11 of the Basel Convention* As discussed in Chapter 3 above, the term 'agreement' in Article 11 denotes a treaty concluded between two or more states, as defined by the Vienna Convention on the Law of Treaties. On the other hand, the meaning of the term 'arrangement' is not clear from the outset. Does its inclusion indicate that legal instruments which are *not* treaties can also come within the scope of Article 11, and if so, what is their legal nature?

The wording of the Basel Convention gives no ready answer to this question, nor does the history of the provision provide much guidance. The initial drafts of the present Article 11 included only the word 'agreements'. The term 'arrangements' was introduced by a subgroup of legal experts in August 1988,[68] but there is no indication in the records of the negotiations as to the reason for this addition.

The application of the teleological interpretation method may therefore again be useful. It must be assumed that the term 'arrangements' is not synonymous with 'agreements'; if that were the case, the introduction of the term 'arrangements' would add nothing to the provision. The fact that the term 'arrangements' was introduced in addition to 'agreements' indicates that a separate legal source, different from 'agreements', is meant to be

[68] Fourth Revised Draft Convention on the Control of Transboundary Movements of Hazardous Wastes, 6 September 1988, (UNEP/WG.189/L.2).

addressed. The same idea is expressed in a more explicit way in the UN/ECE Convention on the protection of international waterways, which provides for the conclusion of 'agreements or other arrangements'. However, since Article 11 accords agreements as well as arrangements precedence over the Basel Convention if they are compatible with its fundamental aims, it cannot be assumed that 'arrangement' denotes a non-binding legal instrument. It is reasonable to conclude that the term 'arrangements' in Article 11 denotes legal rules on the management of hazardous wastes which do not have the legal form of a treaty, but are of a higher order than national legislation, and impose legal obligations on states. If this definition is accepted, it can be argued that the secondary legislation of the EU, on the basis of its special legal nature, should qualify as a 'regional arrangement'.[69]

This supposition is supported by the fact that at the time of the negotiations on the Basel Convention, the EU's policy and legislation in the field of waste management was already extensive. It had considerable influence on the final shape of the Convention, as we saw in Chapter 2 above. The work of the EU and the OECD is implicitly referred to in operational paragraph 13 of the preamble to the Basel Convention ('Taking into account . . . the work and studies done within other international and regional organizations').[70] At the time when the term 'arrangements' was introduced into Article 11, the provisions allowing the EU to become a party to the Basel Convention (Articles 21–25) had already been incorporated into the draft Convention. It is clearly not intended that the EU's waste management system should be superseded by the Basel Convention, but that it should have a place within the framework of the Convention.

If the relevant EU legislation is thus considered an arrangement under the Basel Convention, its relationship with that treaty is in principle governed by the rules of Article 11, which were discussed extensively in Chapter 3 above: the relevant EU rules take precedence over the Convention if they meet the environmental requirements of Article 11. They need not conform to the Convention in detail, but they must embody its fundamental principles. Furthermore, as a regional arrangement, they may govern only waste transactions taking place exclusively between member states. For this reason, EU rules constitute an arrangement only insofar as they address the internal relationship. In the relationship with third states, any rules adopted by the EU must implement the Basel Convention's provisions, or be in line with separate agreements between the EU or its members (or both) and third states, in conformity with Article 11 of the Convention. The latter possibility is expressly provided for in the 1993 Regulation. This conclusion would, in fact, be the same if the EU were

[69] For a similar view see Rublack, (1989), p. 372; cf. also Greenpeace, (1991a), pp. 16–17. An opposing view is expressed by Schmidt, (1992), p. 72 et seq.

[70] Cf. de Villeneuve, (1990), p. 572.

considered a quasi-state for present purposes, as discussed above. Under neither approach can the EU as a party to the Basel Convention be considered free to regulate, by its own legislation, waste traffic with third states without taking into account the requirements of the Convention.

In the event of incompatibility of EU legislation with the Basel Convention, unlike the case of agreements within the meaning of Article 11, the relevant rules of the law of treaties as laid down in the Vienna Convention on the Law of Treaties are not applicable. These rules apply only to treaties in the legal sense. Unlike two conflicting treaties, which constitute legal instruments of the same order requiring a special set of rules to govern their relationship in the event of incompatibility, the secondary legislation of the EU is below a treaty in the hierarchy of legal norms, as noted above. Therefore, in the event of a conflict between relevant EU legislation and the Basel Convention, the Convention takes precedence. The EU legislation must be amended to the extent that it is incompatible with the Basel Convention.[71]

5.3 *The fundamental concepts of the Basel Convention and the free movement of goods* In the light of the above, EU legislation in the field of management of hazardous wastes, in particular their transboundary movements, must conform to the fundamental concepts of the Basel Convention. These concepts require the establishment of a control system, as well as other measures restricting traffic in hazardous wastes. Prior to examining the relationship of the existing EU rules and the Basel Convention's requirements in the light of the above considerations, the question will therefore be addressed whether the principle of free movement of goods within the EU does not inherently preclude accession to the Basel Convention by the EU and its members. As mentioned above, the relationship between the proposed control measures for wastes and the free movement of goods was one of the contentious issues that delayed the adoption of the 1993 Regulation.[72] It appears to have been settled in that particular context, but the issue remains highly controversial, and will be addressed by the ECJ in the near future: three French and Luxembourg-based waste management companies have filed a case with the ECJ, challenging the incorporation, in the 1993 Regulation, of the right of member states to adopt unilateral bans on waste traffic as being incompatible with the free movement of goods.[73]

[71] The same opinion is expressed by Greenpeace, (1991a), p. 16 (without, however, being substantiated by a legal argument).

[72] Cf. e.g. the *Opinion of the Economic and Social Committee on the Commission's 1990 Proposal*, criticizing the proposed control system (which did not then include bans on waste traffic) as an 'authorization system in disguise' and proposing that it should be changed to a mere notification system. See also Kwiatkowska and Soons, (1993), Editors' Introduction, p. LIX.

[73] Case C 145/93 (1993).

The free movement of goods within the EU, embodied in Article 30 of the Treaty of Rome, is one of the fundamental freedoms guaranteed by the Treaty. Recent decisions of the ECJ have confirmed that hazardous or non-hazardous wastes have positive (recyclable wastes) or negative (wastes subject to disposal) commercial value and are therefore considered goods.[74] The introduction of rules to control the movement of hazardous wastes, such as those required by the Basel Convention, constitutes a limitation of this freedom. This statement must, however, be qualified in two respects. Firstly, as was argued above, the predominant characteristic of hazardous wastes—even those subject to recycling operations—cannot be seen as their commercial value, but their potential for endangering human health and the environment. They are therefore subject not only to the principle of free movement of goods, but to a more important extent to the principles of environmental protection recognized by the EU. Secondly, as affirmed by the ECJ in the *Cassis de Dijon Case* in 1979, and again in the *ADBHU Case* in 1985, the free movement of goods is not absolute: it is subject to such limitation as may be justified by the scope of general interests pursued by the EU, which include environmental considerations.[75] The 1985 case concerned the validity of a directive introducing an authorization system for the disposal of waste oil. The Court stated that 'The principle of freedom of trade is not to be viewed in absolute terms but is subject to certain limits justified by the objectives of general interest favoured by the Community, provided that the rights in question are not substantially impaired. There is no reason to conclude that the directive has exceeded those limits. The directive must be seen in the perspective of environmental protection, which is one of the Community's essential objectives.'[76]

It could be pointed out that the ECJ in 1983 declared a national measure adopted pursuant to a Council directive, which in effect amounted to a prohibition of the export of waste oil for the purpose of consignment to an authorized disposal or recovery facility in other member states, as incompatible with the free movement of goods.[77] However, waste oil undoubtedly does not possess the same hazard potential as some of the substances defined as 'hazardous wastes' by the relevant EU legislation and the Basel

[74] Case 7/68 (see n. 53 above); *Commission* v. *Belgium*, Case C-2/90, 9 July 1992, and the *Opinion of Advocate General Jacobs*, 19 September 1991 (not yet published in ECR; see ENDS Report 210, July 1992, p. 38); *Commission* v. *Council*, Case C-155/91, (ENDS Report 221, June 1993). For a discussion of this issue see Kummer, (1994a), p. 40 et seq.; von Wilmowsky, (1993); Schmidt, (1992), p. 71 et seq.; Krämer, (1993), p. 116.

[75] *Cassis de Dijon*, Case 120/78, ECR 1979 p. 649 et seq.; *Procureur de la République* v. *Association de défense des brûleurs d'huiles usagées* (*ADBHU*), Case 240/83, ECR 1985 p. 531 et seq. For an extensive discussion of the relationship between the free movement of goods and environmental protection cf. Krämer, (1993), p. 120.; idem, (1990), p. 34 et seq. (also examining the above cases).

[76] *ADBHU Case*, Case 240/83, p. 548.

[77] *Inter-Huiles Case*, Case 172/82, ECR 1983 p. 555.

Convention; moreover, with the adoption of the 1989 waste management strategy, the upgrading of environmental aims by the SEA and the Maastricht Treaty, and the fifth Action Programme on the Environment, it can be suggested that the priorities have changed since then. As far back as 1988, in the well-known *Danish Bottles Case*,[78] the Court affirmed that the relationship between market considerations and environmental aims had to be considered in the light of the principle of proportionality, with a considerable margin being given to environmental considerations. The issue was addressed again in 1992 in the *Wallonia Case*.[79] The Commission had sought a declaration to the effect that a Belgian law prohibiting the storage or disposal in Wallonia of waste from other member states, or from Belgian regions other than Wallonia, constituted a trade barrier and was therefore incompatible with the relevant Treaty provisions and with the existing EU waste legislation. In its July 1992 decision, the Court held that the 1984 Directive did not give member states the power to adopt unilateral import prohibitions for toxic wastes, and that the legislation in question was therefore not in conformity with it. On the question of the compatibility of the Belgian measure with the free movement of goods, however, the Court rejected the argument of the Advocate General that the measure was discriminatory. It stated that while wastes are considered goods, their special nature must be considered in the light of Article 130r, providing that environmental damage should be rectified at source. This interpretation seems to suggest that authorities have a duty to ensure waste treatment and disposal at source. Although the implications are not very clear, the decision does seem to give weight to the argument that environmental considerations should be predominant in the case of movement of wastes. The ECJ's 1993 decision in the case of the 1991 framework Directive gives additional support to this argument by stating that the new directive was intended to reinforce the concept of derogation from Article 30 in the interests of the environment.[80]

A strong tendency to give substantive weight to environmental considerations is also evident, as noted above, in the more recent EU legislation in the field of waste management (para. 2 above). The 1989 waste management strategy expressly mentions the need for a control system for movements of waste within the EU if the danger of 'waste tourism' to the poorer and less equipped regions is to be avoided (para. 1 above). Restrictions on free movements of hazardous wastes within the EU were already provided

[78] *Commission* v. *Denmark*, Case 302/86, ECR 1988 p. 4627. Cf. Krämer, (1990), p. 35; idem, (1993), p. 121 et seq.

[79] *Commission* v. *Belgium*, Case C-2/90, (see n. 74 above). See also ENDS Report 210, July 1992, p. 38, and the report in EPL 22/5/6(1992) p. 337 et seq. For an extensive discussion see von Wilmowsky, (1993).

[80] Case C-155/91 (see n. 74 above); ENDS Report 221, June 1993, p. 45.

by the 1984 Directive, and to a greater extent by the 1993 Regulation. The strongest expression of this concept to date is the Regulation's recognition of the right of member states to ban unilaterally waste imports even within the EU, repeatedly referred to above. A parallel can be seen in the Regulation implementing CITES: although expressly affirming the free movement of goods, it also gives member states a limited right to impose trade restrictions, even in the internal relationship.[81]

In the light of these considerations, there is no basis for the argument that the principle of the free movement of goods is opposed to the introduction of control measures for movements of hazardous wastes within the EU in line with the requirements of the Basel Convention.[82] An interesting parallel can be observed in the provisions of the 1992 NAFTA, which also provides for the abolition of trade barriers (Article 102).[83] In this instance, existing environmental agreements, including the Basel Convention and the two North American bilateral agreements, are expressly given priority over the provisions of NAFTA, to the extent of the inconsistency, provided that the principle of proportionality is respected (Article 104, Annex 104.1).

C. *Is the Existing and Emerging EU Waste Management Regime Compatible with the Requirements of the Basel Convention?*

An examination of the compatibility of relevant EU legislation with the requirements of the Basel Convention in the light of the criteria established above, should be based primarily on the 1993 Regulation, which is designed to implement the Basel Convention. However, it has to be seen in close connection with the other relevant legal instruments discussed above; in order to determine its compatibility with the Basel Convention, the body of relevant EU law has to be considered as a whole.

As noted above, the obligations imposed by the 1993 Regulation are similar in many respects to those of the Basel Convention, the latter having served as a model for a number of its provisions.[84] Due to the additions made by the Council, the Regulation now goes further than the Convention in a number of points, establishing rules that are both more stringent and more precise. The rules of the 1991 Directives addressing waste management are also more far-reaching in some respects.

The two fundamental differences between the Convention and the EU legislation are that the latter extends to wastes not defined as hazardous, and that it establishes less stringent rules for wastes destined for recovery or recycling. The fact that the scope of the wastes covered by the Regulation is thus much broader than that of the Convention means that

[81] See n. 59 above.

[82] Cf. Schmidt, (1992), p. 74 et seq.

[83] NAFTA, adopted in December 1992, repr. in ILM 32(1993) p. 289 et seq., p. 605 et seq.

[84] Cf. the *Explanatory Memorandum to the 1990 Commission Proposal.*

only rules applying to wastes covered by both must conform to the principles of the Basel Convention. Thus the exclusion of wastes figuring on the 'green list' from most rules of the 1993 Regulation will not render the Regulation incompatible with Basel, nor will the application of less stringent rules to recyclable wastes figuring on the 'amber list', if and to the extent that these wastes are not defined as hazardous under the Basel Convention. A study by Greenpeace concludes that some of the wastes figuring on the 'green list' do in fact meet the Basel Convention's criteria for hazardous wastes.[85] With respect to any such wastes, the EU rules should adhere to the Basel Convention's principles.

As we have seen, the pertinent problems are different with respect to rules governing waste movements within the EU and those governing the relationship with third states. The two situations are addressed separately by the 1993 Regulation, as we have seen, and will also be discussed separately below.

6. Transboundary movements of hazardous wastes within the EU

As noted above, the rules governing waste management and transport within the EU do not have to comply in detail with the Basel Convention. They must, however, be based on environmental considerations, and incorporate the fundamental concepts of the Basel Convention, discussed in Chapters 2 and 3 above: the minimization of hazardous waste generation and the principle of proximity; the environmentally sound management of hazardous wastes and the principle of non-discrimination; the control of hazardous waste movements based on environmental considerations; and the appropriate disposal of hazardous wastes subject to illegal movement, or to transactions which cannot be carried out in accordance with prior arrangements.

6.1 *Minimization of waste generation and proximity of disposal facilities*

In accordance with the 1989 waste strategy, both the aim of waste minimization and that of proximity of disposal facilities have been incorporated into the 1975/1991 framework Directive. The first aim is to be achieved by the promotion of clean technologies (Article 3), and the second by the establishment of a EU-wide network of authorized disposal installations (Article 5), the drawing-up of waste management plans (Article 7(1), (2)), and the provision allowing member states to prohibit waste movements which are not in accordance with these plans (Article 7(3)). The Directive envisages minimization of waste transport not only in terms of avoiding waste movements across national frontiers, but in absolute terms, thus

[85] Greenpeace, (1992). A further investigation of this issue is beyond the scope of this study.

endorsing the principle of proximity. The incorporation of the polluter pays principle into the Directive (Article 15) is likely to provide a strong incentive for the minimization of generation and transport of wastes.

The 1993 Regulation allows the authorities of dispatch and destination to raise objections against a movement of wastes destined for disposal, on the grounds of proximity (Article 4(3.b)). However, the authority is under no obligation to raise such an objection. In addition, this objection may not be raised in the case of wastes figuring on the 'amber list' and destined for recycling or recovery (Article 7(4)). These two points weaken the principle: in accordance with the aims of the Basel Convention, the principle of proximity, like the principle of waste minimization, should be followed consistently so as to provide an effective disincentive to the movement of hazardous wastes. These rules are therefore compatible with the fundamental principles of the Basel Convention only to the extent that the wastes in question are not considered hazardous under the terms of Basel.

6.2 *Environmentally sound waste management and the principle of non-discrimination* The 1975/1991 framework Directive contains fairly detailed obligations regarding the environmentally sound management and disposal of wastes, including supervisory and enforcement mechanisms which go beyond the Basel Convention in some respects: waste disposal installations must be authorized, registered with the competent authority, and inspected regularly. Additional requirements applying especially to hazardous wastes are introduced by the 1991 Directive on hazardous waste. Article 34 of the 1993 Regulation provides that '. . . irrespective of the point of disposal or recovery of the waste, the producer of that waste shall take all necessary steps to dispose of or recover . . . the waste so as to protect the quality of the environment in accordance with Directives 75/442/EEC and 91/689/EEC . . .'. The Regulation thus incorporates the principle of non-discrimination. Unlike the principle of proximity, this applies to recyclable wastes as well as those destined for disposal. Thus, the Basel Convention's requirements of environmentally sound waste management and non-discrimination are met by the EU legislation.

6.3 *Establishment of a control system for waste transport based on environmental considerations* The 1993 Regulation establishes a control system for waste movements within the EU which is considerably stronger than that of the preceding 1984 Directive, being based on the principle of PIC. This system incorporates a number of the concepts of the Basel Convention, e.g. the coverage of every stage of a waste transport by the notification procedure ('cradle-to-grave' monitoring), the involvement of all competent authorities concerned in the control procedure, the requirement of a contract between the notifier and the disposer, and the requirement of financial security for waste transport. In some respects, the control system established by the Regulation is stronger and more detailed than that of the Basel Convention, as we have seen above.

On the other hand, the fundamental concepts of the Convention are diluted in two respects. First, the 1993 Regulation does not establish objective environmental criteria on the basis of which waste movements are prohibited. As already noted, the competent authorities *may* refuse waste movements on the basis of certain environmental considerations, but they are not under an obligation to do so. This weakens the control system's function of providing a disincentive for transporting wastes. Secondly, the exemption of recyclable hazardous wastes from the principle of proximity, the subjection of their transport only to the tacit consent of the competent authority, and the exemption of installations carrying out recycling operations from the requirement of authorization under the Directives on waste and hazardous waste, are not compatible with the Basel Convention's aims. The transport and management of hazardous wastes destined for recycling operations as defined in Annex IIB to the framework Directive and Annex IVB to the Basel Convention, pose the same dangers to the environment as the transport and management of wastes intended for final disposal, and should therefore be subject to the same controls.[86] Exemption of these wastes from parts of the control procedure could undermine the environmental aims. Therefore, these rules are compatible with the requirements of the Convention only to the extent that the wastes in question are not considered hazardous under the Basel definition.

6.4 *Provisions on illegal traffic and the duty to re-import* Articles 25 and 26 of the 1993 Regulation, dealing with waste movements that cannot be completed in accordance with the contract between the notifier and the disposer, and with states' duties in the context of illegal traffic in hazardous wastes, respectively, are modelled on the Basel Convention but go further in some respects, as discussed. The provisions apply to all wastes covered by the Regulation, whether destined for recycling or disposal, but their application is optional in the case of wastes figuring on the green list. This last provision again is compatible with the Basel Convention only to the extent that the wastes concerned are not defined as hazardous by the Convention. Otherwise, the 1993 Regulation meets the requirements of the Convention in this field.

7. Transboundary movements of hazardous wastes between the EU and third states

As noted above, the secondary legislation of the EU has the status of a regional arrangement within the meaning of Article 11 only in the internal

[86] Cf. Greenpeace, (1991a), in particular p. 19 et seq.

relationship. Any provisions governing the relationship with third states must implement the relevant provisions of the Basel Convention: they must not merely be compatible with the Convention's fundamental aims, but conform to its provisions.

In accordance with the terms of the 1993 Regulation, permissible traffic in wastes with non-EU states is drastically limited. For those transactions that are permitted, the Regulation either establishes rules modelled on those of the Basel Convention (in the case of export for disposal), or refers to the Basel Convention, the 1992 OECD Decision, or a separate agreement concluded in conformity with the Basel Convention (in the case of exports for recycling). The 1993 Regulation, however, does not as yet adhere to the ban of hazardous waste exports to states not members of the OECD, decided by the Conference of the Parties to the Basel Convention in 1994: this is an issue that will need to be addressed in the near future. The control system for permissible waste traffic with third states is based on the concept of PIC, as in the Basel Convention. The provisions on illegal traffic and the duty to re-import are the same as for internal waste movements.

In the elaboration of the 1993 Regulation's system for external traffic, efforts have clearly been made to align it with the provisions of the Basel Convention. The reference to the 1992 OECD Decision is based on the assumption that this instrument meets the requirements of the Basel Convention—an issue that will be considered below. Otherwise, the external rules are in conformity with the Basel Convention. The inconsistencies that existed in the Commission Proposal were eliminated by the Council.

D. *Conclusions*

The above reflections may be summarized as follows. From a formal point of view, the conclusion and implementation of the Basel Convention by the EU and its member states as a mixed agreement is possible, the member states having residual competence in the areas addressed by the Convention. Under this approach, the existing and emerging legal rules of the EU on the relevant issues have a clearly defined place within the framework of the Basel Convention: in the internal relationship, EU law can be considered a regional 'arrangement' within the meaning of Article 11 of the Convention. As such, it must be compatible with the fundamental aims of the Convention. In the relationship with third states which are parties to the Basel Convention, EU law must implement the provisions of the Convention. The recently adopted amendment to the framework Directive on waste and the new Directive on hazardous waste, as well as the new Regulation on internal and external waste movements, generally meet these requirements. The one discrepancy is the introduction of rules for the management of recyclable wastes that dilute the principles of the Basel

Convention, at least to the extent that the wastes in question are considered hazardous under the Basel definition.[87] Although some progress has recently been made in this area, the conflict in EU policy and law between environmental and market aims in the management of hazardous wastes destined for recycling has yet to be resolved in a satisfactory manner. This conclusion should not, however, detract from the shortcomings of the Basel Convention in this respect, pointed out in Chapter 2(M) above: it could be argued that in failing to conform to the Basel Convention in this respect, the EU legislation takes better account of the differences between hazardous wastes destined for recycling and those destined for disposal than does the Convention.

THE BASEL CONVENTION AND THE WASTE MANAGEMENT SYSTEM OF THE OECD

E. *Outline of Existing OECD Rules Addressing the Hazardous Waste Cycle*

The OECD's work in the field of waste management is extensive.[88] In 1974, the Environment Committee established the Waste Management Policy Group, which has since become the OECD's principal body for dealing with the issue. Its main aim is to develop and promote international policies for waste management. Its work provided the basis for the adoption of the relevant legal instruments by the OECD Council.

In 1976, the Council adopted a Recommendation outlining a comprehensive waste management policy, which advocated an integrated and holistic approach to the problem (see Chapter 1(J), (K) above).[89] It emphasized the importance of both the reduction of wastes at source and the promotion of recycling or re-use of wastes. The policy recommended a coherent system of measures for monitoring the design, distribution and use of products as well as the re-use or disposal of the resulting waste products. Member states were called upon to incorporate these principles into their national waste management policies, and the Environment Committee was instructed to elaborate them further.

[87] For a discussion of the 'recycling loophole' cf. Schmidt, (1992), p. 78 et seq.

[88] For an overview see OECD, (1993a); OECD, (1986a); also Abrams, (1990), p. 812 et seq.; Cusack, (1990), p. 405 et seq.; Hackett, (1990), p. 308 et seq.; Kelly, (1986), pp. 115–19; Kiss, (1991), p. 530; Kiss and Shelton, (1991), pp. 316–17; Kwiatkowska and Soons, (1993), Editors' Introduction, p. IL et seq.; Rublack, (1989), p. 386, and eadem, (1993), p. 36 et seq.; Smets, (1985), p. 16 et seq., and idem, (1991), p. 141 et seq.; Williamson, (1989), p. 353 et seq.

[89] OECD Council Recommendation on a comprehensive waste management policy, 28 September 1976, (C(76)155(final), repr. in OECD, 1986(a)).

8. Legal instruments elaborated prior to the adoption of the Basel Convention

Subsequent legal instruments adopted by the OECD adhere to the principles of the 1976 policy. In 1984, the OECD Council adopted a Decision and Recommendation (1984 D/R) addressing in particular the issue of transboundary movements of hazardous wastes.[90] It imposes a binding obligation on OECD member states to control transfrontier movements of hazardous wastes, and recommends a set of principles to be applied by states in implementing this requirement. These principles include the environmentally sound management of hazardous wastes and the imposition of concrete duties on the waste generator in this context; the principle of non-discrimination; full co-operation between all countries involved, including notification of competent authorities and the right of the importing state to oppose any waste movement; and the duty to re-import. The 1984 D/R contains definitions of important terms, many of which were later incorporated into the Basel Convention and other relevant legal instruments. It also introduces the concept of 'cradle-to-grave' monitoring of hazardous wastes.

In 1985, the OECD sponsored a Policy Conference on International Co-operation Concerning Transfrontier Movements of Hazardous Wastes.[91] In addition to reaffirming the principles laid down in the 1984 D/R, this Conference recommended the elaboration by the OECD of an effective international system for the control of transfrontier movements of hazardous wastes. Pursuant to this recommendation, the OECD Council in the same year instructed the Environment Committee to do the necessary work for the development of such a system, which should include a legally binding agreement between OECD member states.[92] Accordingly, the Waste Management Policy Group drafted an international agreement on control of transfrontier movements of hazardous wastes, to be concluded between OECD member states.[93] This draft agreement provided a detailed and fairly comprehensive control system for transboundary waste traffic. Many of its provisions were subsequently taken over by the drafters of the Basel Convention, for which the OECD draft agreement served as a primary basis (see Chapter 2 para. 4 above).

Parallel with the work on the draft agreement, additional Council acts

[90] OECD Council Decision and Recommendation on Transfrontier Movements of Hazardous Wastes, 1 February 1984, (C(83)180(final), repr. in OECD, (1993a)). For a discussion see Smets, (1985), p. 16 et seq.

[91] Held in Basel, Switzerland, 26–27 March 1985. Cf. Conclusions and Recommendations of the Conference (Annex to OECD Council Resolution C(85)100, 20 June 1985).

[92] Council Resolution on International Co-operation Concerning Tranfrontier Movements of Hazardous Wastes, 20 June 1985, (C(85)100, repr. in OECD, (1993a)).

[93] OECD Draft International Agreement on Control of Transfrontier Movements of Hazardous Wastes, 27 October 1988, (ENV(87)9(5th Revision)).

were adopted. Inspired by awareness of the problems resulting from exports of hazardous wastes from the OECD area to third countries, especially those with less strict control systems, the Council in 1986 adopted a D/R (1986 D/R) dealing with this issue.[94] In respect of hazardous waste movements to non-OECD members, it requires member states to adhere to the principle of non-discrimination, to provide for prior notification and consent, and to prohibit exports unless the wastes are directed to an appropriate disposal facility. In a 1988 Decision, the Council established a system for defining hazardous wastes subject to control under the various Council acts.[95] This system is composed of a series of lists setting out the controlled substances, their properties, and disposal operations. It introduces a classification system based on codes, known as the International Waste Identification Code (IWIC). This system was subsequently introduced into the draft international agreement. It can be used as a way to designate wastes subject to the PIC procedure under the Basel Convention.

In early 1989, when the UNEP-sponsored work on the Basel Convention was nearing its completion, the OECD Council decided to suspend the elaboration of the draft agreement, pending the outcome of that work.[96] This decision was confirmed after the adoption of the Basel Convention: since nearly all the provisions and principles of the draft agreement had in fact been incorporated into the Convention, which, unlike the OECD draft, was global in scope, the OECD considered that there was no longer any need for an equivalent agreement covering the OECD region only. The Council instructed the appropriate bodies to give their support to UNEP for implementing the Basel Convention, and to continue work in the technical fields.[97]

9. The 1992 Decision concerning the control of transfrontier movements of wastes destined for recovery operations

Subsequently, the OECD concentrated on the issue of transboundary traffic in recyclable wastes. The inclusion in the scope of the Basel Convention of wastes destined for recovery operations has been a concern to some industrialized states, who perceive the Convention's control mechanisms as being unduly restrictive towards trade in certain recyclable wastes. In

[94] Council Decision and Recommendation on Exports of Hazardous Wastes from the OECD Area, 5 June 1986, (C(86)64(final), repr. in OECD, (1993a)).

[95] OECD Council Decision on Transfrontier Movements of Hazardous Waste, 27 May 1988, (C(88)90(final), repr. in OECD, (1993a)). For a discussion see Smets, (1991), p. 141 et seq.

[96] OECD Council Resolution on Control of Transfrontier Movements of Hazardous Wastes, 30 January 1989, (C(89)1(final), repr. in OECD, (1993a)).

[97] OECD Resolution on the Control of Transfrontier Movements of Hazardous Wastes, 18–20 July 1989, (C(89)112(final), repr. in OECD, (1993a)); see also ibid, p. 23.

January 1991, the OECD Council adopted a D/R (1991 D/R) which instructed the Environment Committee to develop the basis of a multilateral agreement, pursuant to Article 11 of the Basel Convention, which would govern transfrontier movements of recyclable wastes exclusively among OECD member states.[98]

In response to the 1991 D/R, an advisory panel set up by the Waste Management Policy Group elaborated a Council Decision Concerning the Control of Transfrontier Movements of Wastes Destined for Recovery Operations. This Decision was adopted by the Council on 30 March 1992 (1992 Decision).[99] It was accepted by all OECD members except Japan. The 1992 Decision applies to all wastes (as defined in Decision C(88)90 of 1988) that are destined for recovery operations (as defined in the same Decision) and subject to transboundary movement within the OECD area. The scope of the 1992 Decision encompasses both hazardous wastes and those not defined as hazardous under the 1988 Decision or the Basel Convention. The 1992 Decision establishes a 'three-tier system': in accordance with their nature and hazard potential, wastes are allocated to one of three lists to which different levels of control apply. The 1992 Decision establishes a procedure and a set of criteria to be used in the allocation of a waste to one of these lists. In accordance with the review mechanism, the lists were revised in July 1993 and again in May 1994.[100]

The 'green list' of recyclable wastes perceived as comparatively harmless (such as certain metals and metal alloys in non-dispersible form; solid plastic; paper; glass; textiles; food waste), is subject only to controls 'normally applied in commercial transactions' (a term not defined in the 1992 Decision), provided that the wastes do not have any of the hazardous characteristics listed in Table 5 of the 1988 Decision and are not contaminated with more hazardous substances. Recyclable wastes contained in the 'amber list' are subject to a control system established by the 1992 Decision. It requires a written contract between the private parties involved, which must include provisions for financial security and allocation of responsibility for the shipment; prior notification to and tacit consent of the competent authorities of the states concerned, which can be waived under certain circumstances; a movement document accompanying the shipment; and the duty of the person responsible to arrange for the safe disposal or return of the waste if the shipment cannot be carried out in accordance with the arrangements. States may adopt stricter requirements by national legislation. The 'amber list' is quite extensive. It includes wastes such as ashes and

[98] OECD Council Decision and Recommendation on the Reduction of Transfrontier Movements of Wastes, 31 January 1991, (C(90)178(final), repr. in OECD, (1993a)).

[99] OECD Council Decision Concerning the Control of Transfrontier Movements of Wastes Destined for Recovery Operations, 30 March 1992, (C(92)39(final), repr. in OECD, (1993a)). For a critical analysis see Greenpeace, (1992).

[100] OECD Council Decisions C(93)74, 23 July 1993; C(94)153, 28 July 1994.

residues of various metals; waste oil and petrol; wastes from production of certain chemicals; explosive wastes not covered by specific other legislation; chlorofluorocarbons and halons; sewage sludge; and household wastes. Wastes may not be included in this list if contaminated by more hazardous substances. The 'red list' of wastes is subject to the same controls as those in the 'amber list', but requires compulsory PIC in every case. This list, comprising recyclables considered intrinsically hazardous, is quite short. It includes substances consisting of or containing PCBs, PCTs, or PBBs at a concentration level of 50 mg/kg or more; waste tarry residues arising from refining, distillation and pyrolytic treatment of organic materials; asbestos and similar fibres; wastes containing or contaminated with any congenor of polychlorinated dibenzo-furan or polychlorinated dibenzo-dioxin; leaded anti-knock compound sludges; and peroxides other than hydrogen peroxide. The 1992 Decision also requires wastes subject to its provisions to be shipped to an authorized recovery facility, and transport to be carried out in accordance with relevant international transport agreements.

10. An assessment of the waste management system of the OECD

To an even greater extent than the pertinent legislation of the EU, the waste management policy of the OECD has major significance in that it provides a framework for the relevant policies of the world's industrialized nations, which account for nearly the total of global hazardous waste generation (see Chapter 1 above). The OECD policy sets the pace for the elaboration of relevant rules in these countries. Apart from elaborating legal and policy rules, the various sub-bodies of the OECD also have an important role in the technical field, developing detailed technical standards, guidelines, and codes of conduct. The degree of commitment expressed in OECD acts is an indicator of the attitudes prevailing in the industrialized world. In the 'two-world system' established under Decision II/12 of the Conference of the Parties to the Basel Convention, which allows hazardous waste traffic only between OECD states on the one hand and non-OECD states on the other, the management of hazardous wastes within the former group is given a fairly comprehensive framework by the applicable OECD rules.

As a result of the close involvement of the EU Commission and the EU member states in the OECD's work, the EU policy and legislation on hazardous wastes has developed largely in parallel with that of the OECD.[101] This accounts for the high level of similarity in the relevant EU and OECD instruments. The latest example is the inclusion of the 'green' and 'amber'

[101] Cf. Article 13 of the Convention establishing the OECD, Paris, 14 December 1960, (repr. in UN Treaty Series Vol. 888 (1973), p. 173 et seq.). This provision endorses participation of the EU Commission in the activities of the OECD. Cf. OECD, (1993a), p. 18; de Villeneuve (1990), p. 571.

lists of the 1992 OECD Decision into the EU's 1993 Regulation on waste shipments, as we have seen above. OECD acts in the field of hazardous waste management have also had a strong influence, directly or indirectly, on the relevant developments at the international level, including the Basel Convention.

Like the relevant secondary legislation of the EU, the OECD Council acts set out fundamental rules and principles on waste management. They embody concepts similar to those underlying the EU's policy instruments: proximity of disposal, minimization of waste traffic within and outside of the OECD area, and recycling where possible. In contrast to the EU legislation, the binding OECD rules tend to set policy objectives rather than concrete standards of behaviour. Many of the more detailed rules adopt the non-binding form of Recommendation, discussed in the next paragraph below. In addition, member states have the option of not accepting a given Decision. As a consequence, the compulsory nature of the OECD rules is much less pronounced than that of the EU rules.

In common with EU legislation, the OECD acts establish dual standards for recyclable and non-recyclable wastes, aiming to support recycling as an environmentally sound management option. However, whereas in the EU this aim is embedded in the general system, the OECD creates a separate regime for recyclable wastes.

F. *The Relationship Between the OECD Waste Management System and the Basel Convention*

11. General considerations

A decision of the OECD Council is binding on the member states, with the exception of those that have abstained from voting on its adoption. It must be incorporated into national legislation.[102] The existing acts of the Council in the field of waste management frequently adopt the mixed form of 'Decision and Recommendation' (D/R). The obligations, often assuming a general form, are contained in the binding 'Decision' part of the act, and the non-binding 'Recommendation' part sets out guidelines to states for the implementation of these obligations. The following binding obligations are set out in the existing D/Rs: the minimization of the generation of hazardous wastes; the adoption of the principles of proximity and non-discrimination; the environmentally sound management of hazardous wastes, especially through promotion of the establishment of adequate disposal facilities; the control of transport of hazardous wastes, in particular export outside the OECD area; the prohibition of waste exports from the OECD

[102] Convention establishing the OECD (see n. 101 above), Article 5 et seq. Cf. Audretsch, (1987), p. 845; Smets, (1985), p. 17.

area unless directed to an adequate disposal facility; and the application of the principle of PIC in waste trade with non-members of the OECD. All these concepts also constitute fundamental principles of the Basel Convention.

There are two exceptions to the above approach: the two Council Decisions of 1988 and 1992 set out detailed binding obligations. The 1988 Decision provides a system of defining hazardous wastes by a set of lists, which must be adhered to by its members. As already noted, this system was taken over by the Basel Convention, and there is therefore no room for conflicts. The 1992 Decision sets out the requirements for trade in recyclable wastes within the OECD area.

Unlike the relevant legislation of the EU, the legal acts adopted by the OECD Council prior to the adoption of the Basel Convention do not attempt to provide a regime distinct from the global Basel regime. The OECD Council expressed as much when deciding to suspend the work on the draft agreement on transfrontier movements of hazardous wastes, after the successful conclusion of the Basel negotiations (para. 8 above). As already mentioned, the concepts and principles adhered to by the OECD draft agreement and the relevant Council acts have been incorporated to a large extent into the Basel Convention, which was recognized by the OECD as a furtherance and extension of its own efforts. The pre-Basel rules of the OECD do not, therefore, come within the ambit of Article 11 of the Basel Convention, and the fact that the Basel Convention goes further, in some respects, than the OECD rules, will not lead to conflicts with the Convention.

The situation is, however, different in the case of OECD Council Decision C(92)39 on recyclable wastes (1992 Decision). Unlike previous acts of the OECD Council, this legal instrument was intended as 'an agreement or arrangement under Article 11' of the Basel Convention,[103] establishing a special regime for transboundary movements of recyclable wastes. Its conformity with the Convention must therefore be determined on the basis of the rules set out by Article 11, examined in Chapter 3 above and in para. 5.2 above.

12. The Basel Convention and the 1992 OECD Decision on recyclable wastes

As is the case with EU legislation, legal acts of the OECD cannot be considered 'agreements' within the meaning of Article 11 of the Basel

[103] cf. Council Decision C(92)39, Preamble: '. . . Having regard to the Basel Convention . . ., and noting that most Member Countries and the European Economic Community have become signatories to this Convention; Desiring to conclude an arrangement or agreement under Article 11 of that Convention . . .'.

Convention. However, if we follow the definition proposed in para. 5.2 above of an 'arrangement' within the meaning of the Basel Convention as a legal instrument of a higher order than national legislation, not having the form of a treaty but imposing binding obligations on states, an OECD Council Decision can be considered a regional arrangement under the Convention if some or all of the states adhering to it are also Basel parties. In order to take precedence over the Basel Convention, it must conform to the requirements of Article 11, examined in Chapter 3 above: first, it must regulate waste movements exclusively between states adhering to it; and second, it must be based on environmental considerations and comply with the fundamental principles of the Basel Convention. In the event of incompatibility between the Decision and the Basel Convention, the Decision must be adjusted to the Convention. The 1992 Decision obviously meets the first requirement, as its scope of application is restricted to OECD member states having accepted it. Conformity with the second requirement must be examined in the light of the criteria developed in Chapter 3 above. As in the case of the EU's 1993 Regulation, the 1992 Decision should be considered within the context of the whole body of relevant OECD legislation.

Like the EU's 1993 Regulation on waste shipments, the 1992 Decision differs in scope from the Basel Convention. Not all wastes covered by the 1992 Decision are 'hazardous wastes' by the definition of the 1988 Decision, which corresponds to the definition of the Basel Convention. Wastes included in the 'green list' may not have any of the hazardous characteristics under the OECD and Basel definitions. This means that they are not 'hazardous' in terms of the Convention. As this element of the definition is lacking in the EU's 1993 Regulation, the 'green list' concept is more restrictive in the 1992 Decision. Nevertheless, the Greenpeace study mentioned above considers a number of 'green list' wastes to be hazardous by Basel standards. By contrast, wastes figuring on the 'amber' and 'red' lists may or may not have hazardous characteristics as set out in Table 5 of the 1988 Decision. The respective control systems do not expressly take into account the presence or absence of such characteristics. As Article 11 of the Basel Convention extends only to arrangements on transboundary movements of hazardous wastes, the 1992 Decision, like the EU's 1993 Regulation, needs to conform to its requirements only to the extent that it regulates transactions involving wastes having hazardous characteristics within the meaning of the Basel Convention. This applies to wastes under the amber and red control systems, but only if and to the extent that they do display such hazardous characteristics. The regulation of the management of wastes figuring on the green list, to the extent that they are not hazardous in terms of the Basel Convention, is exempt from its requirements.

The preamble of the 1992 Decision refers to earlier OECD legislation, which incorporates the fundamental principles of hazardous waste minimization, proximity, environmentally sound management, and non-discrimination, as discussed above. By implication, these principles are therefore applicable to the transactions governed by the 1992 Decision. In establishing a regime for transboundary movements of recyclable wastes, however, it provides little obligation or incentive to states to abide by these principles. It provides primarily a 'tracking system' for the recyclable wastes which are subject to control. It does make some provision for environmentally sound management by calling for conformity with international transport agreements, and processing of the wastes at authorized recovery facilities. On the whole, however, these principles are not very strongly supported by the 1992 Decision.

The 1992 Decision establishes a control system for transactions included in its scope, and provides that all states concerned must take an active part in the decision concerning permissibility of the transaction. The controls applying to the red list of wastes are very similar to those called for by the Basel Convention, including PIC of all states concerned, a movement document, financial guarantee, and a contract between the private parties involved. Those applying to the amber list are less stringent. As in the case of the EU's 1993 Regulation, they include merely tacit consent instead of PIC, which, in addition, can be waived under certain conditions. Therefore, the procedure applying to red list wastes is in conformity with Basel requirements, but the amber list procedure is more problematic.

The 1992 Decision does not address the problem of environmentally sound disposal of wastes in the event of a transaction having taken place in contravention of its provisions. It does indirectly address the situation where the wastes cannot be processed as foreseen in the country of destination: in the case of green list wastes, the relevant responsibilities under applicable international agreements are transferred from the exporting to the importing state (which is contrary to Article 4(10) of the Basel Convention as far as hazardous wastes are concerned); in the case of the amber and red lists, the Decision merely provides that the relevant responsibilities shall be allocated to one of the operators involved by means of the contract. In this respect, the requirement that the relevant situations must be adequately regulated in the arrangement is therefore not met.

In conclusion, it can be said that while the 1992 Decision meets some of the requirements of the Basel Convention, it falls short of them in other respects. In fact, the ratio of the 1992 Decision differs substantially from that of the Basel Convention: its main objective is not to reduce waste traffic and to ensure environmentally sound waste management, but to establish a tracking system for trade in a potentially dangerous but valuable commodity.[104] It is not intended to reduce the volume of such trade. The same concern appears to have inspired the Report of the Basel Convention Secretariat to the first Conference of the Parties on its relations with other organizations. With regard to the 1992 OECD Decision, the Secretariat noted that 'Basically, the Council Decision adopts a system which provides industry with flexibility for the movement of wastes for recovery that could imply that hazardous wastes subject to full control under the Basel Convention could, within the OECD area, move under less stringent control procedures than those required under the Convention. The Conference of the Parties may wish to take up this issue at its First Meeting, (p. 6).[105]

In its present form, the 1992 Decision can therefore hardly qualify as a regional arrangement compatible with the Basel Convention. As in the case of the EU's 1993 Regulation, discrepancies result mainly from the fact that the contentious issue of the balance between environmental and economic aims in the regulation of transactions involving recyclable wastes has not yet been resolved in a satisfactory manner. The discrepancies appear more substantive than in the case of the EU legislation. As in that case, however, the approach taken by the OECD in the 1992 Decision can be seen as an attempt to take into account the special situation of wastes destined for recycling operations and subject to transboundary movement, which the Basel Convention fails to address in a satisfactory manner.

In practical terms, any discrepancy between the 1992 Decision and the fundamental aims of the Basel Convention is not likely to give rise to serious controversy, as the 1992 Decision currently applies to industrialized states that in general possess reasonable legal and technical infrastructures for hazardous waste management. This situation could, however, change rapidly due to the planned accession of transitional and newly industrialized countries to the OECD, briefly addressed in Chapter 2 para. 12 above.[106]

CONCLUSIONS

The above analysis shows that the Basel Convention has the potential to serve as an umbrella for the waste management systems of the EU and the OECD. Under the interpretation proposed above, these systems conform to the concept of regional 'arrangements' in Article 11 of the Convention.

[104] In this context, see the Preamble to Decision C(92)39: '. . . Noting that recovery of valuable raw materials from wastes has been an integral part of the international economic system and that well established international markets exist for the collection and processing of such wastes . . .'.

[105] Conference Doc. UNEP/CHW.1/7, (7 July 1992). The matter was not addressed by the Conference.

[106] Kummer, (1994a), p. 55.

Apart from formal differences relating to the consequences of incompatibility, the Convention's relationship with the EU and OECD systems is therefore the same as with the regional 'agreements' on transboundary movements of hazardous wastes examined in Chapter 3 above.

If the interpretation of the environmental requirements of Article 11 proposed in Chapter 3 above is accepted, the waste management systems of the EU and the OECD do not meet these requirements in every respect, and appropriate amendments would therefore need to be made. Nevertheless, the EU and OECD systems undoubtedly constitute an element of the emerging 'Basel Convention regime' discussed in Chapter 3 above. Since between them they determine the approach to the hazardous waste cycle taken by the major waste generating states of the world, they constitute a particularly significant addition to this regime.

The examination of the legal instruments constituting the Basel Convention regime, in this chapter and Chapter 3 above, shows that they form the basis of an emerging global approach to the regulation of transboundary movements of hazardous wastes. All relevant systems, having emerged within the last two decades, especially since the mid-1980s, have had considerable influence on each other. The waste management systems of the EU and the OECD, together with the Cairo Guidelines, formed the basis for the elaboration of the Basel Convention and contributed the starting point for some of its fundamental concepts. The Basel Convention, going beyond these instruments and further elaborating their fundamental concepts, has in turn had a strong influence on subsequent developments. This influence has two aspects. On the one hand, the Convention's concepts were incorporated into other international legal instruments with the aim of bringing them in line with its requirements. In this process, the Basel concepts were in some instances strengthened and developed further. This is true for some aspects of the new EU Directives on waste and hazardous waste and the Regulation on waste shipments, as well as many of the provisions of the Bamako Convention. The same approach is likely to be taken in the elaboration of the waste protocols to the Barcelona and Lima Conventions, and equivalent agreements to be adopted within UNEP's Regional Seas Programme, the South Pacific Forum, and ASEAN. On the other hand, the outcome of the Basel negotiations has prompted some states and organizations, who were not satisfied on all counts with the Basel Convention, to elaborate diverging rules. This applies to those provisions of the EU's 1993 Regulation and the 1992 OECD Decision which are aimed at the establishment of less stringent control systems for recyclable wastes. It also applies to the Bamako Convention and the pertinent provisions of Lomé IV and the Abuja Treaty Establishing the African Economic Community, as well as the draft regional protocols currently under negotiation, all of which provide for a complete ban on hazardous waste movements from developed to developing countries. These legal instruments have in turn influenced the discussions within the EU that have led to the virtually general prohibition of exports of hazardous wastes to non-OECD countries. They also influenced the discussions within the framework of the Basel Convention which led to the 1994 Decision II/12 concerning the ban between OECD and non-OECD states. The Bamako Convention in particular created a strong precedent for the other regional hazardous waste management systems currently being elaborated.

As a result of this closely interdependent development of the relevant legal instruments, they form an equally interdependent framework of legal rules. This has a formal and a substantive aspect.

From a formal point of view, the similarities in the fundamental rules and concepts of the relevant legal instruments, resulting from the mutual influence of the respective negotiations, mean that the overall level of conformity of the regional rules with the Basel Convention's requirements is comparatively high. This facilitates the formation of the Basel Convention regime considerably, since few adjustments will be necessary.

From a substantive point of view, the analysis of the relevant legal instruments shows the emergence of a number of fundamental concepts which are common to almost all of them. We may refer to the concepts of waste minimization, proximity of waste disposal installations (reduction of waste movements), environmentally sound management of wastes, and non-discrimination. These concepts are embodied in the Basel Convention, as well as, in varying forms, in the Bamako Convention, the EU legislation, the OECD waste management system, the Cairo Guidelines, and the regional hazardous waste management systems currently being negotiated. All these instruments, as well as the two bilateral agreements between the USA and Canada and the USA and Mexico, also incorporate or advocate a control system for hazardous waste movements based on PIC. It can be assumed that the relevant instruments will contribute significantly to the eventual incorporation of these concepts into customary law in the field of waste management.

A concept that has gained rapid acceptance in the past few years is the need for a prohibition on exports of hazardous wastes from industrialized to developing or transitional countries. Until the end of the 1980s, a number of international legal instruments directly or indirectly advocated some form of prohibition or restriction on hazardous waste exports, but there was no general consensus on the issue. By 1994, the prohibition on hazardous waste transfer for any purpose between the two groups of countries had attained virtually universal consensus, as we have seen: embodied first in the Lomé IV provision and the Bamako Convention, it was taken up by the EU, and will in all probability be introduced into the regional legal instruments addressing hazardous waste that are currently under discussion. It was also introduced into the framework of the Basel Convention, 5 years after its adoption, and was proposed for formal inclusion into the Convention in March 1995.

Another concept is followed less consistently, although it constitutes, in principle, a logical consequence of the principle of environmentally sound management of hazardous wastes: the need for recycling or recovery of hazardous waste the generation of which is unavoidable. Although recycling has an established place in the so-called waste management hierarchy, also endorsed by the relevant Chapters of Agenda 21, it is expressly incorporated only into the legal rules adopted by the EU and the OECD. Since recyclable wastes are a tradeable commodity, there is as yet no general consensus with regard to the application of the principle of proximity, or on the level of control appropriate for wastes subject to these operations. The absence of such rules can in turn have adverse effects on the incentives for waste prevention and environmentally sound management.

The contribution of the Basel Convention regime and of the international rules addressing other aspects of the hazardous waste cycle to the development of customary law in the above areas will be considered in Chapter 7 below.

5
The Basel Convention Regime and Sectoral Pollution Control Treaties

INTRODUCTION

As mentioned in Chapter 1 above, there are numerous global and regional treaties dealing with various forms of release of noxious substances into the environment. In accordance with the sectoral approach to environmental protection, they aim to protect a particular sphere of the environment against such discharges: the oceans, the air, or international lakes and rivers (see Chapter 1(J) above). Since the disposal of hazardous wastes usually means the discharge of the wastes or residues derived from their treatment into the environment, there is a connection between the two issues. The relationship between the Basel Convention regime and the sectoral pollution control treaties is therefore worth an examination.

Of the spheres affected by discharge of noxious substances, the most extensively regulated is the marine environment.[1] Part XII of the 1982 UNCLOS attempts to establish a general framework for the protection of the oceans against pollution. In addition, a substantive number of treaties of global as well as regional scope address the different sources of marine pollution.[2] In 1974, UNEP launched the Regional Seas Programme which now covers eleven regions, most of which are in the developing world. The regions covered are the Mediterranean, the West and Central African region (WACAF), the East African region, the East and South Asian regions; the Gulf, the Red Sea and Gulf of Aden region, the South and South-East Pacific regions, the Caribbean, and—most recently—the Black Sea. The development of an Action Plan is also underway in the North-West Pacific region. Under this programme, regional conventions for the protection of the marine environment and related protocols have been adopted, and additional ones are under preparation.[3] Several regional con-

[1] See generally Churchill and Lowe, (1988); Birnie and Boyle, (1992), ch. 8; Boyle, (1985), p. 347 et seq.; Teclaff and Teclaff, (1991), p. 187 et seq.; Hohmann, (1990), p. 49 et seq.; idem, (1989), p. 518 et seq.; Schneider, (1981), p. 243 et seq. For an analysis of the pertinent treaty regimes see Boyle, Freestone, Kummer, and Ong, in Sand, (1992) pp. 149–255.

[2] Birnie and Boyle, (1992), ch. 8; Johnston, in Carroll, (1988), p. 200 et seq.; Edwards, ibid, ch. 15. On UNCLOS see Caflisch, (1983), pp. 39–104; Boyle, (1985), p. 350; Schneider, (1981), p. 243 et seq.

[3] UNEP, (1989b), and IMO Doc. LDC 14/7/5 (24 October 1991); UNEP, (1988); UNEP, (1991).

ventions on marine pollution have also been adopted in the industrialized world. The sources of marine pollution subject to treaty regulation include deliberate disposal of wastes and other hazardous substances at sea (dumping), marine pollution from land-based sources, marine pollution incidental to shipping, airborne pollution of the sea and accidental discharges in connection with the exploration and exploitation of the sea-bed.[4] Numerous regional conventions address the pollution of international continental waterbodies. Transboundary air pollution is also subject to international regulation. More recently, a legal instrument has been adopted that addresses the protection of the Antarctic environment against pollution. UNCED's Agenda 21 sets out priorities and proposes actions in all these fields.

Unlike the regional waste management systems forming the emerging Basel Convention regime, the sectoral treaties do not address transboundary movements of hazardous wastes in the narrow sense as defined in the Basel Convention, i.e. pollution source transfer involving at least two states (see Chapter 1(E) above, Chapter 2 para. 4 above). Their aim, in general, is to restrict the pollution of parts of the environment shared by more than one state, or by the world community as a whole, from sources situated in one state. With the exception of the treaties that address dumping at sea, they focus on transboundary pollution rather than pollution source transfer. Therefore, none of the sectoral pollution control treaties come within the purview of Article 11 of the Basel Convention, and they do not constitute elements of the emerging Basel Convention regime discussed in the preceding chapters.[5]

Nevertheless, there is a link between the Basel Convention regime and some of the sectoral pollution control treaties. As mentioned in Chapter 1(G) above, the sectoral treaties address activities which are part of the hazardous waste cycle, as does the Basel Convention regime. The sectoral treaties address primarily disposal. The Basel Convention regime covers all stages of this cycle, including disposal, although it focuses on transboundary transfer. In more concrete terms, some of the disposal operations listed in Annex IV to the Basel Convention and the equivalent annexes of regional treaties are also addressed by sectoral conventions. This applies to the release of hazardous wastes into the ocean and into continental waterways, their incineration at sea, and their insertion into the sea-bed. Thus

[4] Cf. Churchill and Lowe, (1988), p. 242 et seq. For an overview of the sources of marine pollution and the scope of the problem see UNEP/GESAMP, (1990); *World Resources Report 1990–91*, p. 179 et seq.; also Nurmi, in Carroll, (1988), p. 212 et seq.

[5] See the discussions on this point by the IMO Ad Hoc Group of Legal Experts on Dumping, and by the 13th Consultative Meeting of the Contracting Parties to the London Convention (IMO Docs. LDC/LG4/WP.2/Rev.1 (26 October 1990), p. 14 et seq.; LDC/LG 5/10 (7 August 1991), p. 3.; LDC 13/15, (18 December 1990), p. 43; and LDC13/8 (2 August 1990)).

the same or related activities may be subject to both the Basel Convention regime and a sectoral convention.

The relationship between the Basel Convention regime and sectoral treaties addressing the discharge of noxious substances can be analysed under two aspects.

First, the relevant sectoral pollution control treaties have the potential of complementing the Basel Convention regime, and vice versa. If this potential is realized, a comprehensive regime might emerge for the management and discharge into the different spheres of the environment of all hazardous wastes, not only those subject to transboundary movement in the narrow sense, as submitted in Chapter 1 above. The Basel Convention regime could thus become part of a wider 'global waste management regime'. In order to achieve this, the component elements of the Basel Convention regime must be harmonized with the relevant pollution control treaties. Otherwise, gaps in the system could be exploited. The inclusion of stronger provisions in any one of the relevant treaties, or the adoption of a new regime such as that of the Basel Convention, may lead to an increase in hazardous activities to the detriment of other, less protected spheres of the environment.[6] For example, the restriction of hazardous waste exports under the Basel Convention regime could incidentally provide an incentive for increased discharges into the ocean; or the phase-out of ocean dumping under the relevant treaties could induce the promotion of land-based disposal options. The aim of the analysis of the relationship between the Basel Convention regime and sectoral conventions under this aspect will be to identify areas in which harmonization is necessary, and the measures needed to achieve it.

Secondly, in cases where the Basel Convention regime and a sectoral pollution control treaty address the same activities, there may be conflicts and overlaps between them. In this case, as in the case of regional waste management treaties which are incompatible with the Basel Convention, the rule of Article 30 of the Vienna Convention on the Law of Treaties will determine the modalities of the application of the conflicting treaties (see Chapter 3 above). At another level, the amendment of the conflicting treaties should be considered in order to adjust their provisions to each other and thus contribute to a comprehensive regime as outlined above. Under this aspect, areas of conflict and overlap should be identified, and pertinent amendments proposed.

In the light of these considerations, the strongest link exists between the Basel Convention regime and the treaties on dumping of wastes and other noxious substances at sea. In common with the Basel Convention regime,

[6] For an extensive discussion of this problem see Teclaff and Teclaff, (1991), p. 187 et seq. See also Lukasik, *Report*, (1989); *Conclusions of a Meeting of the Vice Presidents of ACOPS* (repr. in Doc. LDC12/INF.12 (18 October 1989)).

the dumping conventions address the deliberate transfer of hazardous wastes to an area outside the state of generation, i.e. a case of pollution source transfer as defined in Chapter 1(E) above. What distinguishes the two regimes from each other is the fact that the dumping conventions do not deal with transboundary movements of hazardous wastes in the narrow sense, i.e. between more than one state, but with the transfer of hazardous wastes from the state of generation to part of the global commons. In addition to addressing a form of disposal also covered by the Basel Convention regime, the dumping conventions thus also cover the stage of transfer. There are accordingly two stages of the hazardous waste cycle that come within the purview of both systems.[7] As the regulation of the movement of hazardous wastes constitutes the core of the Basel Convention regime, there is not only a potential for the regimes to supplement each other, but also a possibility of conflicts and overlaps. The relationship between the Basel Convention regime and the dumping conventions therefore has to be analysed under both aspects mentioned above. This will be the subject of paragraph (B) below.

Other sectoral pollution control treaties have a less strong link with the Basel Convention regime: they address disposal options which are also covered by the Basel Convention regime, but they do not address the management or transport of hazardous wastes or substances prior to disposal. Unlike the Basel Convention regime, they deal exclusively with transboundary pollution, not touching upon any aspect of pollution source transfer. As the Basel Convention regime does not contain many substantive rules relating to disposal, overlaps or conflicts are unlikely. The need to harmonize these treaties and the Basel Convention regime is, however, worth an examination under the first aspect outlined above. This applies to the conventions dealing with marine pollution from land-based sources, and pollution of continental waterways. It also applies to the regime addressing the disposal of wastes in the Antarctic region, although this is not a sectoral regime in the present sense. The relationship between these legal instruments and the Basel Convention will be examined in paragraphs (C), (D) and (E) below.

A third group of sectoral treaties have no direct link with the Basel Convention regime. This category includes those conventions that deal with forms of release of toxic substances into the environment that are not a part of the hazardous waste cycle and are therefore not covered by the Basel Convention regime, e.g. pollution of the marine environment resulting from sea-bed activities. It also includes activities that constitute merely a secondary consequence of activities covered by the Basel Convention regime. This applies to transboundary air pollution, or airborne pollution of the

[7] Cf. Lang, in Lang, Neuhold, and Zemanek, (1991), p. 148 et seq.

sea, as a consequence of incineration of hazardous wastes subsequent to their removal from the state of generation. The international legal instruments dealing with these activities are therefore excluded from the present analysis.

THE BASEL CONVENTION REGIME AND EXISTING TREATIES ON OCEAN DUMPING AND INCINERATION OF WASTES AND OTHER NOXIOUS SUBSTANCES

A. *Outline of the London Convention and Other Relevant Rules*

The issue of the dumping of wastes and other noxious substances at sea is regulated, at the global level, by the London Convention on the Prevention of Dumping of Wastes and Other Matter.[8] This Convention was universally referred to as the 'London Dumping Convention' until the fifteenth Consultative Meeting of the Contracting Parties in 1992 decided to change its name to 'London Convention, 1972': this change was intended to avoid the impression of a treaty facilitating dumping.[9] The London Convention was adopted under the auspices of the IMO in 1972, and entered into force in 1975. Its global significance is enhanced by its widespread ratification: as of 5 May 1994, seventy two states had acceded to it, including those industrialized states that have in the past subscribed to the practice of dumping, or are doing so currently. It can be assumed that the London Convention represents the internationally accepted rules and standards for dumping referred to in Article 210 of UNCLOS.[10]

In the spirit of Article VIII of the London Convention, a number of regional treaties and protocols were adopted to regulate and control ocean dumping in specific geographical areas: the 1972 Oslo Dumping Convention,[11] to be replaced by the 1992 Oslo/Paris Convention for the Protection of the Environment of the Northeast Atlantic upon its entry into force;[12] the 1976 Barcelona Protocol for the Prevention of Pollution of the

[8] Repr. in 11 ILM, (1972) p. 1294. For a discussion of the London Convention and related rules see IMO, (1989); Birnie and Boyle, (1992), ch. 8; Kiss and Shelton, (1991), p. 180 et seq.; Kiss, (1991), p. 522 et seq.; Lang, in Lang, Neuhold, and Zemanek, (1991), p. 156 et seq.; Hohmann, (1989), p. 524 et seq.; Schneider, (1981), p. 249 et seq.; Iljstra, in YBIEL 1(1990) pp. 132–7; idem, in YBIEL 2(1991) pp. 146–50; Lumsdaine, (1976), p. 733 et seq.

[9] *Report of the 15th Consultative Meeting*, 12 November 1992, (Doc. LDC 15/WP.3).

[10] Birnie and Boyle, (1992), p. 320. Cf. Boehmer-Christiansen, (1986), p. 121, for an opposing opinion.

[11] Convention for the Prevention of Marine Pollution by Dumping from Ships and Aircraft, and Protocols of 1983 and 1989 (repr. in *Selected Multilateral Treaties*, Vol. I, p. 266). See also IMO Doc. LDC13/INF.32 (2 October 1990). For a discussion see Skjaerseth, (1992).

[12] Adopted in Paris, 22 September 1992 (repr. in ILM 32(1993), p. 1069 et seq.); signed by all contracting parties to the old Oslo and Paris Conventions, and by Luxembourg and

Mediterranean Sea by Dumping from Ships and Aircraft;[13] the 1986 Noumea Protocol for the Prevention of Pollution of the South Pacific Region by Dumping;[14] the 1989 Paipa Protocol for the Protection of the South-East Pacific against Radioactive Pollution;[15] and the 1992 Bucharest Protocol on the Protection of the Black Sea Marine Environment against Dumping.[16] The structure and provisions of the regional dumping conventions are similar to those of the London Convention, being modelled on that convention to a large extent. However, the regional treaties tend to be more stringent than the London Convention in some respects.

In addition to regional treaties devoted to dumping, a few treaties addressing the broader issue of marine pollution also contain relevant provisions. The 1992 Helsinki Convention on the Protection of the Marine Environment of the Baltic Sea Area, which will replace the old Helsinki Convention of 1974 upon its entry into force,[17] addresses dumping at sea in Article 11. The 1991 Bamako Convention, discussed in Chapter 3 above, is considered by the IMO's Ad Hoc Group of Legal Experts on Dumping to be a regional agreement within the meaning of Article VIII of the London Convention, since it addresses the dumping of hazardous wastes at sea (Articles 4(2), 11(3)).[18]

In view of the above, it could be said that the London Convention and the relevant regional treaties form a 'London Convention regime' for the control of ocean dumping and incineration, in much the same way as the Basel Convention and the regional waste management systems form the Basel Convention regime.

As the London Convention is the only global and the most widely accepted convention on ocean dumping, its relationship with the Basel Convention regime is especially important. This was recognized by the 1989 Basel Conference, which adopted a resolution requesting UNEP and the IMO to co-operate in examining the need for harmonization between the two Conventions (see Chapter 2 above). In view of the importance of the London Convention, the present analysis will focus on that Convention; additional reference to regional dumping conventions will be made where necessary. The provisions of the London Convention are, in

Switzerland (cf. Doc. LDC15/INF.11 (October 1992)). As of November 1994, it had not entered into force.

[13] Repr. in *Selected Multilateral Treaties*, Vol. I, p. 454. See also LDC14/INF.15. For a discussion see Haas, (1990); Raftopoulos, (1992), p. 27 et seq.

[14] Repr. in *Selected Multilateral Treaties*, Vol. 2, p. 381 et seq.

[15] *Law of the Sea Bulletin* 15(1990) pp. 41–6.

[16] Adopted in Bucharest, 21 April 1992 (repr. in ILM 32(1993), p. 1101 et seq.). Cf. also Doc. LDC14/INF.16.

[17] Adopted in Helsinki, 9 April 1992. For an extensive discussion of the protection of the marine environment in the Baltic see Fitzmaurice, (1992).

[18] *Report of the Ad Hoc Group of Legal Experts on Dumping on its 5th Session*, 7 August 1991, (Doc. LDC/LG 5/10).

themselves, not very specific in many respects. However, the Convention has been further developed by informal means, mainly by numerous resolutions of the Consultative Meetings of the Contracting Parties held under the auspices of the IMO. Its implementation and further development is also supported by opinions and advice of the technical and scientific bodies of the IMO. Much reporting and consultations between contracting parties is done on an informal basis, even where this is not expressly required.[19] For these reasons, the London Convention has been referred to as a 'living organism'.[20]

While declaring the protection of the marine environment against pollution from all sources as its overall aim, the London Convention specifically addresses the prevention of marine pollution caused by dumping of wastes and other matter. Dumping at sea is defined as deliberate disposal from vessels, aircraft, platforms or other man-made structures, or of the structures themselves, in any part of the sea with the exception of internal waters of states.[21] An addendum to Annex I, adopted by the third Consultative Meeting of the Contracting Parties in 1978, introduced regulations for the control of incineration of wastes and other matter at sea, which is to be considered a subsidiary option to other disposal methods addressed by the Convention. In this indirect way, incineration at sea was included in the scope of operations covered by the London Convention.[22] There are ongoing discussions in the Consultative Meetings of the Contracting Parties as to the interpretation and expansion of the definition of dumping.[23] The 1992 Helsinki Convention and the Oslo/Paris Convention of the same year expressly include incineration at sea in their scope.

The core of the London Convention is a mechanism for restricting dumping of hazardous substances and wastes in accordance with a 'black' and 'grey' list approach. The same approach is adopted by those regional conventions that do not ban dumping outright. The wastes and other substances covered by the London Convention are divided into three

[19] Cf. *Note by the Secretariat on Transboundary Movements of Hazardous Wastes to the 12th Consultative Meeting of the Contracting Parties to the London Convention*, 5 October 1989, (Doc. LDC12/INF.7, p. 23 (*Note by the Secretariat*, LDC12/INF.7, (1989)).

[20] Lang, in Lang, Neuhold, and Zemanek, (1991), p. 156.

[21] Based on a recommendation of the Ad Hoc Group of Legal Experts on Dumping, the 11th Consultative Meeting of Contracting Parties in 1988 agreed that, in accordance with the relevant rules of international law, parties could apply the London Convention in their territorial sea, their EEZ and their continental shelf; a respective amendment of the Convention would be considered at a later stage (Doc. LDC11/5, para. 2.3); also *Note by the Secretariat*, LDC12/INF.7, (1989), p. 14, and Lukasik, *Report*, (1989), p. 14.

[22] Cf. IMO, *World Maritime Day 1992*, IMO Publication 211/92; also Birnie and Boyle, (1992), p. 325.

[23] Questions under discussion concern the inclusion in the definition of insertion of wastes into sub-seabed repositories, and of the disposal of offshore installations and platforms at sea. Cf. Iljstra, in YBIEL 1(1990), p. 133 et seq.; idem, in YBIEL 2(1991), pp. 148–9; Birnie and Boyle, (1992), p. 325; Lukasik, *Report*, (1989), p. 8; Boehmer-Christiansen, (1986), p. 119.

categories, set out in the annexes to the Convention. Annex I contains a 'black list' of substances, the dumping of which is prohibited. It includes organohalogen compounds, mercury, cadmium, persistent plastics, crude oil, radioactive wastes and other radioactive matter, and materials produced for biological or chemical warfare. The dumping of substances listed in Annex II ('grey list') requires a prior special permit. These substances include arsenic, lead, copper, zinc, organosilicon compounds, cyanides, fluorides, and pesticides. All other substances may be dumped subject to a prior general permit. Annex III establishes criteria to be taken into account by state authorities when issuing the permits. Among other things, a permit for dumping should be issued only if a comparative assessment of alternative options (e.g. disposal on land) has been carried out (Article VI(3), Annex III, and pertinent guidelines).[24] Exceptions to the permit system are made in the event of emergency or distress resulting in danger to human life.

The London Convention originally aimed for the restriction and control of dumping at sea rather than outright prohibition, but did expressly recognize the right of states to adopt stronger measures, including the absolute prohibition of dumping. In recent years, however, there has been an overall tendency towards phasing-out dumping as well as incineration at sea.[25] In a 1983 resolution, the Consultative Meeting of the Contracting Parties to the London Convention agreed on a 2-year moratorium on the dumping of all radioactive wastes; in 1985 this was extended to an unlimited moratorium.[26] A 1990 resolution included in this moratorium the disposal of low-level radioactive wastes in sub-seabed repositories accessed from the sea.[27] In 1993, low-level radioactive wastes were moved by amendment from Annex II to Annex I, which amounts to a formal prohibition of dumping of all radioactive wastes.[28] In 1990, the Consultative Meeting adopted a resolution on phasing-out the dumping of industrial wastes by 31 December 1995.[29] Incineration at sea was the subject of two resolutions of the Consultative Meeting: in 1988, the eleventh Meeting agreed to evaluate the status of marine incineration of noxious liquid substances with a view to a phase-out by 1994, in cases where it can be demonstrated that environmentally sound land-based alternatives are available world-wide. This was reconfirmed in 1990. In 1992, the Consultative Meeting agreed to

[24] See *Note by the Secretariat*, LDC12/INF.7, (1989), p. 15.

[25] See Birnie and Boyle, (1992), p. 321; Boehmer-Christiansen, (1986), p. 119 et seq.

[26] Resolution LDC14(7) (1983) and Resolution LDC 21(9) (1985). See IMO, (1989), pp. 18–19; Iljistra, in YBIEL 1(1990), p. 133; Lang, in Lang, Neuhold, and Zemanek, (1991), p. 157.

[27] Resolution LDC41(13) (1990).

[28] Resolution LC51(16) (1993).

[29] Resolution LDC43(13) (1990).

prohibit incineration at sea by 31 December 1992.[30] The sixteenth Consultative Meeting in 1993 adopted relevant amendments to the Convention, formalizing both these prohibitions: a new paragraph 11 to Annex I prohibits dumping of industrial wastes as of 1 January 1996, and an amendment to paragraph 10 prohibits incineration of industrial waste at sea with immediate effect.[31] This corresponds to the recommendation made in Chapter 17 of UNCED's Agenda 21 in 1992.

The same tendency is evident in other relevant legal instruments. In some regional treaties, the commitment to phase out dumping emerged earlier and in stronger form than under the London Convention. The Oslo Commission in 1988 adopted a Decision to phase out incineration at sea by December 1994. This was replaced by a 1990 Decision on phasing-out of such incineration by December 1991 and a reduction by 65 per cent by January 1991.[32] In a 1989 Decision, the Oslo Commission agreed to terminate dumping of industrial wastes in the North Sea by December 1989, and in other waters covered by the Oslo Convention by December 1995. Exceptionally, it could be permitted on the basis of a prior justification procedure.[33] The termination of dumping of sewage sludge by 1998 was agreed in 1990.[34] These decisions were incorporated into the 1992 Oslo/Paris Convention, which prohibits dumping and incineration at sea in principle (Article 4 and Annex II). The 1992 Helsinki Convention prohibits all incineration at sea (Article 10) as well as the dumping of all substances with the exception of dredged materials, other than in cases of emergency (Article 11). Under the Barcelona Protocol, the introduction of a ban on incineration of wastes at sea and on dumping of industrial wastes is planned.[35] The 1991 Bamako Convention obliges parties not to carry out dumping and related operations in any part of the ocean, and prohibits every form of sea disposal of hazardous wastes in African waters by non-parties (Article 4(2.b)). The 1989 Protocol for the Protection of the South-East Pacific against Radioactive Pollution prohibits the dumping of all radioactive wastes or other substances (Article 2). A ban on dumping of radioactive wastes at sea was also agreed under the Black Sea Convention in 1993.[36] These developments give an indication of an emerging customary law rule

[30] Resolution LDC35(11) (1988); Resolution LDC39(13) (1990); Resolution of the 15th Consultative Meeting, November 1992 (repr. in Doc. LDC15/WP.3/Rev.2). See also IMO, (1989), p. 15 et seq.

[31] Resolutions LC49(16) (1993) and LC50(16) (1993).

[32] OSCOM Decisions 88/1, 90/2. See IMO, (1989); Iljstra, in YBIEL 1(1990), p. 135.

[33] OSCOM Decision 89/1 (repr. in Oslo Commission, *Procedures and Decision Manual*).

[34] OSCOM Decision 90/1, repr. in YBIEL 1(1990), p. 693. Cf. also Iljstra, ibid. p. 135.

[35] *Report of the 7th Ordinary Meeting of the Contracting Parties to the Barcelona Convention and the related protocols*, 11 October 1991, (UNEP(OCA)MED IG.2/4), and *Report of the 8th meeting*, Antalya, Turkey, October 1993, (Doc. UNEP(OCA)MED IG.3/5).

[36] Declaration of the Ministerial Meeting on the Protection of the Black Sea, Odessa, 6–7 April 1993.

prohibiting dumping and incineration at sea as a practice incompatible with the protection of the marine environment. The prohibition of dumping of radioactive wastes has generally received earlier and stronger support than the prohibition of dumping of other types of hazardous wastes.[37]

In cases where dumping is not prohibited under the London Convention, the dumping permit must be issued by the competent authority of the state in which the substances are loaded, or of the flag state or state of registration of the loading vessel or aircraft, if the state of loading is not a contracting party (Article 7(1)). This provision appears also in a number of regional conventions.[38] States other than the state of loading or the flag state do not play a part in the decision on dumping operations under the London Convention. There is no formal provision for prior notification of other states, although they are often notified on an informal basis.[39] A 1986 Resolution of the Consultative Meeting of the Contracting Parties does call upon parties to inform the states concerned and obtain their prior consent.[40]

In Chapter 1 para. 6 above it was argued that there is an emerging customary law rule requiring prior notification and prior consent of the target state in the case of pollution source transfer. This is supported, in the context of dumping, by Article 210(5) of UNCLOS, which provides that: 'Dumping within the territorial sea and the exclusive economic zone or onto the continental shelf shall not be carried out without the express prior approval of the coastal State, which has the right to permit, regulate and control such dumping after due consideration of the matter with other States which by reason of their geographical situation may be adversely affected thereby.'[41] Notification of and prior consent from the states concerned is compulsory under the Noumea Protocol for dumping in the territorial sea, EEZ or continental shelf (Article 3(2)). This protocol, going beyond the requirements of the London Convention, already incorporates the UNCLOS requirement. With the entry into force of UNCLOS, dumping without prior notification or consent is now prohibited not only in the territorial sea of a state, but also in its EEZ or onto its continental shelf.[42]

Under the London Convention as well as under the regional treaties, and under Article 216 of UNCLOS, states are requested to enforce the provisions in their areas of jurisdiction, and against ships flying their flag and

[37] Birnie and Boyle, (1992), p. 322; Boehmer-Christiansen, (1986), p. 119 et seq. See e.g. UNGA Resolution 45/58 on General and Complete Disarmament, 14 December 1990 (repr. in Kwiatkowska and Soons, (1993), p. 87).

[38] e.g. 1992 Oslo/Paris Convention, Annex II, Articles 4, 6; 1976 Barcelona Protocol, Articles 10 para. 2, 11 para. 1; 1992 Bucharest Protocol, Article 3; 1992 Helsinki Convention, Article 11, Annex V.

[39] *Note by the Secretariat*, LDC12/INF.7 (1989), p. 17.

[40] Resolution LDC 29(10) (1986).

[41] For a discussion cf. *Note by the Secretariat*, LDC12/INF.7 (1989), p. 15.

[42] Cf. Birnie and Boyle, (1992), p. 326.

aircraft registered in their territory. The London Convention calls on party states to enter into regional agreements compatible with the Convention in order to further its aims. It requires them to assist those parties that request it in the areas of training, provision of equipment, and in the adoption of measures to mitigate pollution caused by dumping.

The functions of the Secretariat of the London Convention cover mainly administrative and co-ordinating duties. They are carried out by the IMO. A Consultative Meeting of the Contracting Parties, held at least every 2 years, acts as governing and supervisory body. The institutional mechanisms of the relevant regional conventions are similar, with the notable exception of the Oslo/Paris Convention (Article 10). The role of the Commission established under that treaty in the monitoring of compliance by parties goes beyond that of most similar institutions (see Chapter 6 para. 9 below).

B. *The Relationship Between the Basel Convention and the London Convention*

By addressing the export of hazardous wastes from the state of generation for the purpose of disposal on the high seas, even where no other state is directly affected, the London Convention and relevant regional treaties protect an important part of the global commons and thus close a significant gap left open by the Basel Convention regime (see Chapter 2(M) above). In this respect, the two regimes already complement each other. Nevertheless, discrepancies exist. Some of these have been recognized and addressed by the respective Secretariats.

In 1986, when the elaboration of a treaty on the international traffic in hazardous wastes was already under discussion both within the OECD and UNEP, the tenth Consultative Meeting of the Contracting Parties to the London Convention adopted a Resolution which recommended that wastes not be exported to non-parties to the London Convention for subsequent dumping, and calling on parties to provide prior notification to and obtain the prior consent of states which are to receive wastes intended for dumping, or which 'may exercise authority over their transport or disposal'.[43] The resolution thus incorporated several of the principles that were later to be included in the treaties constituting the Basel Convention regime. It did not, however, specify the notification procedure or the position of transit states. Two other resolutions addressed the need to restrict or prohibit the export of wastes destined for incineration at sea to non-parties.[44]

[43] Resolution LDC29(10), Export of Wastes for Disposal at Sea (repr. in *Note by the Secretariat*, LDC12/INF.7, (1989), Annex 2). Cf. also the discussion of the resolution in the *Note*.

[44] Resolutions LDC11(V) (25 September 1980), and 35(11) (7 October 1988) (relevant

After the adoption of the Basel Convention in 1989, the issue of the relationship between the Basel Convention and the London Convention was discussed extensively by the Consultative Meeting of the Contracting Parties to the London Convention, and by the IMO's Ad Hoc Group of Legal Experts on Dumping,[45] in accordance with Resolution 2 of the Basel Conference (see Chapter 2 above). That resolution had requested the Executive Director of UNEP to bring to the attention of the Contracting Parties to the London Convention the need for a review of the London Convention in the light of the Basel Convention, with a view to recommending possible changes to the London Convention. Subsequently, the IMO took the lead in examining this issue, with UNEP co-operating.[46] As a result of these discussions, the Consultative Meetings adopted two relevant resolutions in 1990 and 1991, respectively. The first requests all parties to the London Convention to become parties to the Basel Convention. It also calls on parties to minimize the generation of hazardous wastes and their export for disposal at sea; to ban completely the export of such wastes to states not parties to the London Convention; and to consider amending the Convention accordingly. Lastly, it recommends the elaboration of standards compatible with those of the Basel Convention for the export of wastes intended for dumping to London Convention parties. This list of recommended actions reflects the views of the Legal Experts Group on the areas in which the London Convention should be adjusted to the Basel Convention.[47] The second resolution, adopted in 1991, concludes that the area of possible overlap between the two Conventions is relatively small, and that few cases of conflict are likely to occur in practice. Therefore, the resolution limits itself to reaffirming the London Convention's primary importance as the relevant regime to control ocean dumping, and calling upon Basel Convention parties to take adequate account of the London Convention when developing the Technical Guidelines for the environmentally sound management of hazardous wastes, and to adhere to the London Convention.[48]

paras. repr. in the *Report of the Secretariat of the London Convention to the 15th Consultative Meeting on the implementation of the Basel Convention* (Doc. LDC15/INF.12 (14 October 1992)), Annex, p. 2 (*Report of the Secretariat*, LDC15/INF.12, (1992)).

[45] Cf. the *Reports of the 12th, 13th and 14th Consultative Meetings* (Docs. LDC12/16, (1989), LDC13/15, (1990), LDC14/16, (1991)), and the discussions at the 4th and 5th Meetings of the Ad Hoc Group of Legal Experts on Dumping (Docs. LDC/LG4/WP.2/Rev.1 (26 October 1990); LDC/LG5/2 (9 May 1991), LDC/LG5/10 (7 August 1991)).

[46] An overview of this work is given in the relevant *Report of the Executive Director of UNEP to the 1st Conference of the Parties to the Basel Convention*, 7 July 1992, (UNEP/CHW.1/2,), and in the *Report of the Secretariat* (LDC15/INF.12, (1992)). See also Kwiatkowska and Soons, (1993), Editors' Introduction, p. XLII et seq.

[47] Resolution LDC42(13) (1990) (repr. in the *Report of the 13th Consultative Meeting* (Doc. LDC13/15), Annex 8).

[48] Resolution LDC45(14) (repr. in the *Report of the 14th Consultative Meeting*, 30 December 1991, (Doc. LDC14/16)). Cf. also the *Report of the Executive Director of UNEP to the 1st Meeting of the Parties to the Basel Convention* (UNEP/CHW.1/2, (1992)).

Thus the problems of the relationship and possible conflict between the two Conventions were only partially addressed by the relevant resolutions. This probably resulted from an inability of the experts as well as the state representatives to reach agreement on the crucial points. The fourth meeting of the Legal Experts on Dumping and subsequently the thirteenth Consultative Meeting, while addressing all the important points, reached no definite conclusions. The question was consequently referred back to the Legal Experts Group for further discussion at their fifth meeting, but the results were still inconclusive. Consensus was eventually reached to the effect that the issue was of limited practical relevance, but that co-operation between UNEP and the IMO would be needed in the development of Technical Guidelines for both Conventions. Only after the adoption of such guidelines under the Basel Convention would it be appropriate to consider the need for additional standards under the London Convention.

Based on a report by the Executive Director of UNEP on these developments, the first Conference of the Parties to the Basel Convention in 1992 endorsed all pertinent resolutions of the Consultative Meeting, and invited the sixteenth Meeting and the Amendments Conference scheduled to be held in 1996 (see para. 3 below) to consider their formal incorporation into the Convention.[49] The Conference Decision also re-iterated the call to states to adhere to both Conventions, and requested the Basel Secretariat to ensure that the technical standards of the London Convention are taken into account in the work on the Technical Guidelines on waste management, as proposed by the Consultative Meeting. Co-operation between UNEP and the IMO is continuing. The sixteenth Consultative Meeting referred substantive issues related to amendments to the 1996 Conference, a course of action endorsed by the Conference of the Parties to the Basel Convention at its second meeting.[50]

1. Areas of conflict and overlap

For greater simplicity, the following analysis of the relationship between the Basel Convention and London Convention regimes will focus on the two global conventions. Due to the similarities in the structure and provisions of the regional agreements to that of the pertinent global treaty, the relationship between component elements of either regime is likely to be the

[49] *Report of the Executive Director* (UNEP/CHW.1/2, (1992)); Decision I/4 of the 1st Conference of the Parties to the Basel Convention (1992).

[50] *Report of the 16th Consultative Meeting of the Contracting Parties to the London Convention*, 15 December 1993, (IMO Doc. LC.16/4; Decision II/7 of the Conference of the Parties to the Basel Convention (1994), and *Report of the Secretariat* (Doc. UNEP/CHW.2/23 (December 1993)).

same as that between the global treaties. The analysis will also be limited to cases in which all states involved in a given transaction are parties to both Conventions. In these cases, the London Convention provides that the dumping permit must be issued by the state where the loading takes place; the flag state does not take part in the proceedings. Overlaps and conflicts between the Basel Convention and the London Convention can only occur in situations where the provisions of both Conventions are applicable. Prior to an analysis of conflicts, we have to establish the relevant situations.

The scopes of wastes covered by the Basel Convention and by the London Convention coincide only partially. In general, the scope of the London Convention is broader than that of the Basel Convention, covering 'any waste or other matter in whatever form or condition' (Art. IV(1)), whereas the Basel Convention covers only hazardous wastes as defined in Article 1 and the Annexes. However, the more stringent rules of the London Convention apply only to the wastes listed in Annexes I and II, many of which are also covered by the Basel Convention.[51] Overlaps can occur only in situations where wastes covered by both Conventions are managed or disposed of.

The scope of the activities covered by the Basel Convention also differs from that of the London Convention.[52] As noted in the preceding chapters, the Basel Convention encompasses all aspects of the hazardous waste cycle, including disposal (Annex IV covering the release of wastes into the ocean, incineration at sea, and sea-bed insertion), but applies only to transactions in which two or more states are involved. An exception is the export of wastes to the Antarctic region, which is covered even if only one state is involved. The London Convention, on the other hand, addresses only final disposal at sea (deliberate release into the ocean and incineration at sea), but applies also to operations in which only one state is involved.[53] Overlaps between the two Conventions can therefore occur in two situations: first, in the case of transboundary movement of hazardous wastes for the purpose of subsequent dumping or incineration at sea; and second, in the case of shipment of hazardous wastes to the Antarctic region for the

[51] On the difference between the scope of wastes covered by the Basel Convention and the London Convention cf. *Note by the Secretariat* (LDC12/INF.7 (1989)); *Report of the Ad Hoc Group of Legal Experts on Dumping on its 4th session* (LDC/LG4/WP.2/Rev.1), p. 17; *Note by the Secretariat to the Ad Hoc Group of Legal Experts on Dumping on the Review of the Provisions of the Convention in Light of the Basel Convention*, 9 May 1991 (LDC/LG 5/2) (*Note by the Secretariat to the Legal Group* (LDC5/2(1991)); IMO, (1989), p. 16 et seq.; Lukasik, *Report*, (1989), p. 16 et seq.

[52] Cf. *Note by the Secretariat* (LDC12/INF.7, (1989)), p. 7 et seq.

[53] On the difference between the situations covered by the two Conventions see Lukasik, *Report* (1989), p. 3; cf. the First Draft Convention on the Control of the Transboundary Movements of Hazardous Wastes, 15 October 1987, (UNEP/WG.180/2), p. 18.

purpose of dumping or incineration at sea.[54] Transboundary movements of hazardous wastes for disposal other than by dumping or incineration at sea are covered by the Basel Convention only, and the shipping of hazardous wastes from the country of generation directly to a dumping or incineration site on the high seas is covered by the London Convention only (see Fig. 1).

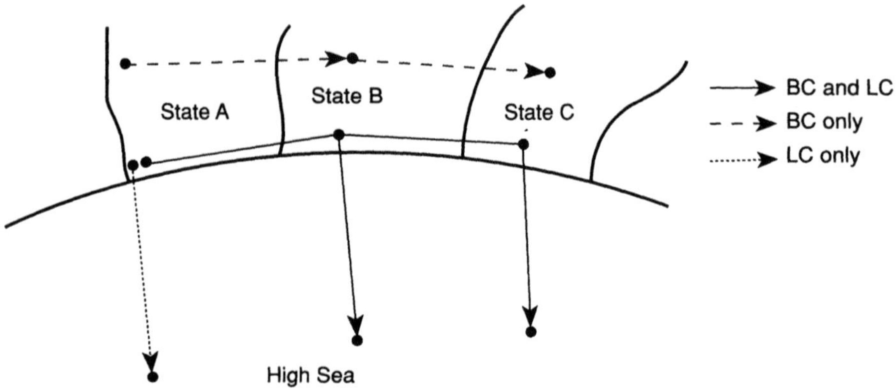

FIG. 1 Applicability of Basel Convention (BC) and London Convention (LC)

These two situations will be analysed in the next paragraphs, with a view to determining potential conflicts, and proposing possible amendments to the two Conventions.

1.1 *Transboundary movements of hazardous wastes for the purpose of dumping or incineration at sea* According to the London Convention Secretariat, there are few known cases of transboundary movements of hazardous wastes for the purpose of dumping at sea, but transboundary movements for the purpose of incineration at sea occur frequently.[55] The following two cases can be distinguished.

[54] This was also the conclusion of the IMO Ad Hoc Working Group of Legal Experts on Dumping (see Docs. LDC/LG4/WP.1 (1990) and LDC/LG4/WP.2/Rev.1 (1990), p. 17), which is reflected in the preamble to Resolution 45(14) of the 14th Consultative Meeting of the Contracting Parties to the London Convention: 'Considering that the question of the applicability of the Basel Convention to dumping at sea arises only with regard to:

.1 a transboundary movement of hazardous waste, as these terms are defined by the Basel Convention, or

.2 Article 4, paragraph 6 of the Basel Convention which provides that the export of hazardous wastes or other wastes for disposal within the area south of 60° South latitude, whether or not such wastes are subject to transboundary movement, is not allowed'.

[55] *Note by the Secretariat* (LDC12/INF.7, (1989)), p. 23; Resolution LDC45(14), Preamble.

(a) *The movement of hazardous wastes from State A to State B for the purpose of subsequent dumping or incineration at a site on the high seas* (see Fig. 2(a)). In this case, State A is the exporting State under the Basel Convention. Accordingly, it may permit the export only if it has obtained the PIC of State B and of any transit State (although the question of PIC of the transit State in the case of transport through its territorial sea remains unresolved under the Basel Convention, as we saw in Chapter 2 above); and if it has received confirmation of a contract specifying the environmentally sound disposal of the wastes. State A has no responsibility under the London Convention. State B is the importing State under the Basel Convention. In fact, the Basel Convention's definition of the State of import in Article 2(11) addresses this situation: it includes a State to which wastes are sent 'for the purpose of loading prior to disposal in an area not under the national jurisdiction of any State'.[56] State B may give or deny its consent to State A after having received the notification. Under the London Convention, State B as the loading State must issue the dumping permit in accordance with the provisions of that Convention.

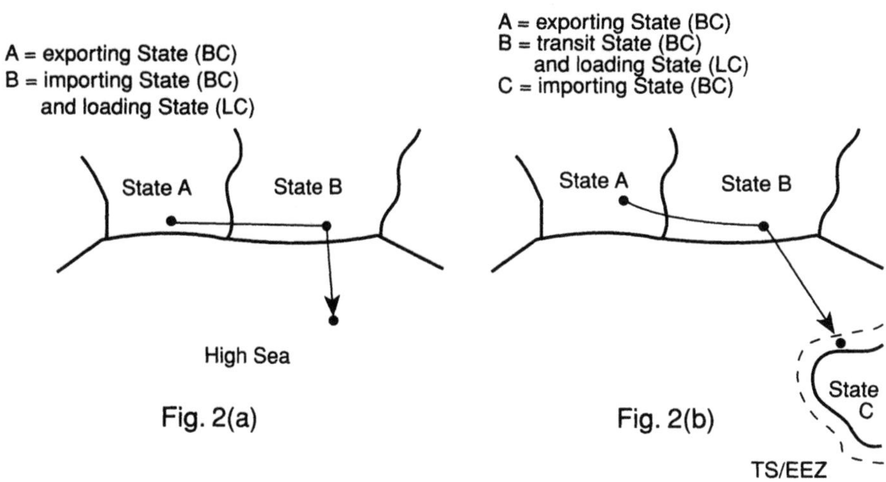

FIG. 2(a) Movement of wastes from State A to State B for dumping or incineration on the high seas
Fig. 2(b) Movement of wastes from State A to State B for subsequent dumping or incineration in the territorial sea (TS) or EEZ of State C

The situation is basically the same if the wastes are moved from State A to State B for the purpose of subsequent dumping or incineration in the territorial sea or EEZ of a third State C (see Fig. 2(b)). The position of State A remains unchanged, except that it must also notify, and obtain the

[56] Cf. de Villeneuve, (1990), p. 573.

consent of, State C under the Basel Convention. State B as the transit State under the Basel Convention has to consent to the movement; its position under the London Convention remains the same. State C as the importing State must also consent to the movement under the Basel Convention (see also Article 4(12) of the Basel Convention). This corresponds to Article 210(5) of UNCLOS, as mentioned above. State C has no responsibilities under the London Convention.

(b) *The movement of hazardous wastes from State A to a dumping or incineration site in a marine area subject to the jurisdiction of State B* (See Fig. 3). In this case, State A is the exporting State under the Basel Convention and the loading State under the London Convention. State B is the importing State under the Basel Convention but has no responsibilities under the London Convention. Accordingly, State A must notify State B and obtain its prior consent to the dumping in its marine waters; it must also obtain the PIC of any transit State. Only if PIC has been given may State A allow the transaction to take place in accordance with the Basel Convention. At the same time, State A must issue a dumping permit under the London Convention.

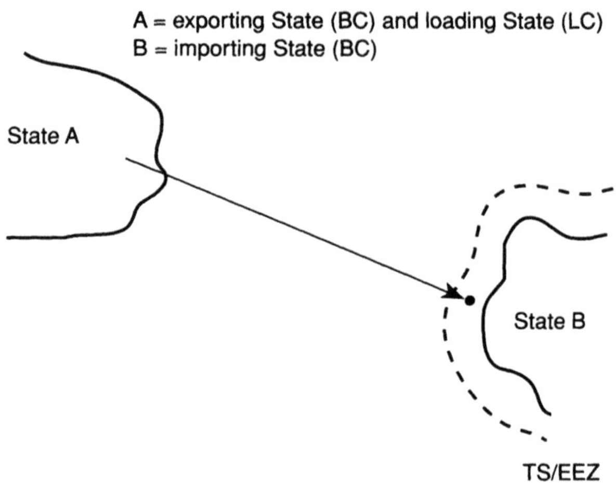

FIG. 3 Movement of wastes from State A for dumping or incineration in a marine area under the jurisdiction of State B

In both the cases outlined, the requirements of the Basel Convention and the London Convention have to be met concurrently if all States involved are parties to both Conventions. The above overview shows that the respective responsibilities of the States involved coexist rather than actually conflict. The conferences of the parties to both the London and Basel Conventions, recognizing the necessity of applying both control systems to the relevant situations, responded by calling on the parties to each Convention to adhere to the other one as well.[57] This would doubtless be a first step towards the aim of obtaining harmonization between the two Conventions.

To strengthen both regimes, however, the respective requirements should in addition be combined and harmonized. The fundamental requirements and concepts of the Basel Convention should be included in the London Convention if the wastes to be dumped or incinerated at sea are subject to transboundary movement. This was in fact proposed by the observer from UNEP at the fourth meeting of the Ad Hoc Group of Legal Experts on Dumping in November 1990; the proposal met with the opposition of some delegates, who objected to the idea of indirectly obliging states not parties to the Basel Convention to abide by its rules.[58] Likewise, the standards established by the London Convention for dumping operations should be incorporated into the Basel Convention if the wastes subject to transboundary movement are to be disposed of by dumping or incineration at sea. If the main requirements of each Convention were thus incorporated into the other, they would be applicable even where one or more States involved in a given transaction are parties only to one of the Conventions.

From a formal point of view, a possible alternative to the incorporation of the fundamental provisions of one Convention into the other is illustrated by the 1988 Joint Protocol to the 1960 Paris Convention on Third Party Liability in the Field of Nuclear Energy and the 1963 Vienna Convention on Civil Liability for Nuclear Damage: the aim of this protocol is the application of the provisions of each convention to the parties of the other, i.e. in fact an extension of their memberships (Article II(a), (b)), and the elimination of conflicts between them (Article III).[59]

In accordance with the former approach, the following paragraphs outline suggestions for changes to be made to the two Conventions, based on the premise that the need for introducing the fundamental aims of the one into the other is, in principle, recognized.

Suggested amendments to the Basel Convention

In the event that hazardous wastes subject to transboundary movement are intended for dumping or incineration at sea, the Basel Convention's requirement that the wastes should be managed in an environmentally sound manner, whatever the place of disposal (see Chapter 2 para. 7 above), can be interpreted to mean that the intended dumping or incineration must

[57] Resolutions LDC42(13) (1990) and LDC45(14) (1991) of the Consultative Meeting of the Contracting Parties to the London Convention; Decisions I/4 (1992) and II/7 (1994) of the Conference of the Parties to the Basel Convention.

[58] Cf. the *Report of the Legal Group on its 4th session* (LDC/LG 4/WP.2/Rev.1), p. 16.

[59] Cf. Politi, in *La réparation des dommages catastrophiques*, (1988), pp. 319–37.

take place in accordance with the provisions of the London Convention, which can be regarded as representing the relevant environmental standards in this field. This could be clarified by adding a new provision to Article 4 of the Basel Convention (General Obligations), along the lines of the following: *If hazardous wastes subject to transboundary movement are intended for disposal by dumping or incineration at sea, the recognized international rules and standards in the field of dumping shall be taken into full account.*' A similar proposal was made by the Secretariat of the London Convention in a background document submitted to the twelth Consultative Meeting of the Contracting Parties in 1989.[60] The Secretariat pointed out that the Basel Convention should have included a reference to the London Convention, in the same way as it refers to recognized international rules and standards in the field of packaging, labelling and transport (Basel Convention, Article 4 (7.b)). The document suggests that this omission be rectified through the adoption of a relevant resolution by the Conference of Parties to the Basel Convention.

Such an amendment would cover case (a) discussed above, requiring that the exporting/loading state A, when authorizing the transboundary movement to take place in accordance with the relevant provisions of the Basel Convention, should take into account the criteria established by the London Convention for issuing a dumping permit. In case (b), it would be useful to introduce the additional requirement that the exporting state A may only authorize the transboundary movement after having received confirmation from the importing/loading state B that the dumping will take place in accordance with the rules set out by the London Convention. State B could be required to provide this information together with PIC. In this way, state B could consider the issuing of a dumping permit in accordance with the provisions of the London Convention on the basis of an assessment of the information provided to it by state A in accordance with the Basel Convention. This requirement cannot be deduced from the wording of the Basel Convention. It would therefore be useful to amend that Convention to include a pertinent provision. This could be done, for example, by adding a new subparagraph c) to Article 6(3) of the Basel Convention, which could be along the lines of the following: 'The State of export shall not allow the generator or exporter to commence the transboundary movement until it has received written confirmation that *c) The notifier has received from the State of import the written confirmation that the operation will take place in conformity with the relevant international rules, in the event that the wastes are intended for dumping or incineration at sea.*'

[60] *Note by the Secretariat* (LDC12/INF.7, (1989)), p. 23. The proposal was supported by the USA delegation at the 13th Consultative Meeting; cf. discussion paper submitted by the USA (Doc. LDC13/8).

Suggested amendments to the London Convention

Under the London Convention, new provisions incorporating the principle of PIC should be included to address cases where the wastes are subject to transboundary movement prior to dumping or incineration at sea. This was already stated in Resolution LDC 29(10), which calls on states to '.1 provide advance notification of any intended movement of such wastes to the receiving country and any other country which may exercise authority over their transport or disposal in sufficient time for an informed assessment; .2 obtain the prior consent of the appropriate national authorities in any country receiving wastes and issuing the required permit for sea disposal'.

In case (a), the importing/loading state B should be required to issue the dumping permit only after having received prior notification of the intended movement as specified in Annex VA of the Basel Convention, having assessed the implications of the proposed dumping operation, and having given its consent to the import. This could be done by adding a new paragraph 2bis to Article IV of the London Convention, which could read as follows: '*If the wastes are imported from a third state, the state in which the wastes are loaded shall issue the dumping permit only if it has received prior notification from that state, and given its consent to the movement, in accordance with the relevant international rules.*'

In case (b), a similar obligation should be imposed on the exporting/loading state A. That state should be required to obtain the PIC of the importing state B prior to issuing a dumping permit. This could be done through inclusion of a new paragraph 2ter in Article IV of the London Convention, along the lines of the following: '*If the dumping takes place within a marine area in which another state exercises jurisdiction or control, the loading state may issue a dumping permit only if it has notified the state in question and obtained its prior consent in accordance with the relevant international rules*'.

Suggested Basel Convention requirements which could be included in the London Convention

In addition to the PIC procedure, three more important requirements of the Basel Convention should be considered for inclusion into the London Convention.

First, the London Convention should expressly prohibit the export of hazardous wastes for the purpose of dumping or incineration at sea to states that have, by national legislation or through conclusion of an international treaty, prohibited the import of such wastes. This would be in line not only with the Basel Convention and relevant regional agreements and arrangements discussed in Chapters 3 and 4 above, but also with the recognized customary rule that every state has the right to control or prohibit hazardous activities taking place in its own territory (see Chapter 1 para. 5 above).

Secondly, exports for the purpose of dumping or incineration at sea should be prohibited if the authorities of the exporting state have reason to believe that the management and eventual disposal at sea of the wastes would not be carried out in accordance with the environmental standards established by the London Convention. This is in line with Article 4(2.e) of the Basel Convention. The purpose of such a provision, as in the Basel Convention, would be to prohibit the export of wastes to countries that are not sufficiently equipped to carry out the sea disposal in accordance with the standards established by Annex III of the London Convention, and the numerous non-binding guidelines adopted under the Convention.[61]

Thirdly, the concept of a limited ban should be incorporated into the London Convention, i.e. the Convention should expressly prohibit transboundary movements of hazardous wastes, for the purpose of dumping or incineration at sea, to or from non-party states.[62] Such a rule would prevent the movement of wastes to or from states that do not adhere to the London Convention and therefore do not apply its standards for sea disposal. The need for this was in fact recognized by the Contracting Parties to the London Convention: it is incorporated in Resolution LDC 29(10) of 1986 as well as, in stronger form, in Resolution LDC 42(13) of 1990. The latter resolution requests parties to consider a relevant amendment to the Convention. If the concept of a limited ban were adopted, the inclusion of a similar exception clause to the one contained in Article 11 of the Basel Convention could be considered, namely that such transports are also allowed to states which are parties to regional agreements establishing equivalent or stronger standards than the London Convention. In the case of the London Convention, such a clause seems justified in view of the fact that most existing regional conventions on dumping are in fact stronger than the London Convention, as noted above. The wording should, however, be more stringent than that used in the Basel Convention, which allows considerable room for interpretation (see Chapter 3 above). This approach was proposed implicitly in Resolution 29(10), which recommended that parties do not export hazardous wastes 'to States not Party to the Convention or to an appropriate regional convention unless there are both compelling reasons for such export and clear evidence that the wastes would be disposed of in compliance with the requirements of the London Convention and such regional conventions'. It was dropped, however, in Resolution 42(13).

If the Basel Convention and the London Convention were brought in line with each other by incorporation of the same fundamental provisions, as proposed above, it would be possible to go one step further and extend the concept of a limited ban to both Conventions, i.e. each Convention could

[61] For an overview cf. *Note by the Secretariat to the Legal Group* (Doc. LDC5/2(1991)).

[62] Cf. Lukasik, *Report* (1989), p. 11.

stipulate that transboundary movements of wastes for the purpose of subsequent dumping or incineration at sea are prohibited to or from states that are not parties to either the Basel Convention or the London Convention. There would no longer be a need for each Convention to limit permissible transactions to its own parties if both Conventions established the same standards.

If the proposed changes were made to both Conventions, the combined systems would complement each other rather than merely coexist. The export of hazardous wastes for the purpose of dumping or incineration at sea would be reduced, and limited to states adhering to appropriate standards, and all states concerned would take an informed decision in any given transaction. In addition to the Basel Convention and the London Convention, the proposed amendments could also be considered for incorporation into the relevant regional treaties concluded under both global Conventions.

The scope and practical significance of the suggested changes has diminished due to the overall tendency under the London Convention and other dumping conventions towards phasing-out dumping and incineration at sea, on the one hand, and the increasing restriction of transboundary movements of hazardous wastes under the Basel Convention regime, on the other: as the scope of permissible operations under both Conventions becomes smaller, so does the number of situations in which the rules proposed above are necessary.[63] Should both Conventions ban all removal of hazardous wastes from the territory of the generating state for any purpose, the above suggestions would become obsolete. In practical terms, a complete ban under both Conventions is unlikely in the foreseeable future: the London Convention will, in all probability, still allow dumping of certain substances under certain circumstances, and the Basel Convention will permit transboundary waste traffic within the OECD and among non-OECD members in certain cases. In any event, it is important that the relevant tendencies in each Convention be reflected in the other. This could be achieved, for example, through the proposed reference to 'internationally accepted rules and standards' in the relevant fields: if the rules of the London Convention develop towards a general prohibition on dumping and incineration at sea, the Basel parties would have to take them into account by not permitting transboundary movements resulting in the relevant operations. Likewise, the London parties would have to prohibit the issuing of a dumping permit if the wastes were subject to a transboundary movement from an OECD member state to a non-OECD member prior to dumping.

[63] Cf. *Report of the 5th Meeting of the Ad Hoc Group of Legal Experts on Dumping* (Doc. LDC/LG5/10, (1991)), p. 3; Resolution LDC45(14) (1991), Preamble.

1.2 *Shipment of hazardous wastes to the Antarctic region for the purpose of dumping or incineration at sea* As mentioned above, the second situation covered by both the Basel Convention and the London Convention concerns dumping or incineration at sea in the Antarctic region. Article 4(6) of the Basel Convention, along with Article 4(3.l) of the Bamako Convention and most draft regional agreements discussed in Chapter 3 above, prohibit any movement of hazardous wastes to Antarctica for the purpose of any form of disposal, whether or not these wastes are subject to transboundary movement as defined by the Convention. In accordance with the internationally accepted definition, Antarctica includes any area south of 60° South latitude.[64] The London Convention, on the other hand, does not prohibit the dumping of wastes in Antarctic waters, which is therefore technically in conformity with that Convention. Unlike the issue of transboundary movements of hazardous wastes for subsequent disposal at sea, this issue has not so far been the subject of resolutions of the Consultative Meetings of the Contracting Parties to the London Convention, nor are there non-binding IMO guidelines addressing it.[65] Nevertheless, the trend towards a general phasing-out of dumping and incineration at sea under the London Convention and other dumping regimes extends to the Antarctic. Unless and until the phase-out becomes more universal under the London Convention, the two Conventions will, however, continue to contain conflicting provisions on this issue. In accordance with the rules of Article 30 of the Vienna Convention on the Law of Treaties, only those London Convention parties which are also parties to the Basel Convention have to respect the Basel prohibition. States which are parties to the London Convention but not to the Basel Convention are technically still allowed to dump or incinerate hazardous wastes in Antarctic waters, provided that this conforms to the rules of the London Convention.

The formal inclusion into the London Convention of a general prohibition on dumping and incineration of hazardous wastes in Antarctic waters would lead to its alignment with the Basel Convention in this field. It would also be in line with the tendency to eliminate dumping and incineration at sea under the London Convention as well as other dumping regimes. Likewise, it would support and strengthen the recognition of Antarctica as an area worthy of special protection in view of its unique characteristics and value. Evidence of this can be seen not only in the relevant provisions of the Basel and Bamako Conventions, but also in the recent designation of Antarctica as a special area under the MARPOL Convention; in the

[64] This definition is adhered to in the Antarctic Treaty system (see 1959 Antarctic Treaty, Article VI). It was taken over by other treaties addressing issues related to Antarctica (e.g. Article 4(6) of the Basel Convention, Article 4(3.1) of the Bamako Convention. Cf. Watts, (1992), p. 148; Kiss and Shelton, (1991), p. 252.

[65] Cf. *Note by the Secretariat to the Legal Group* (LDC5/2(1991)).

1991 Protocol on Environmental Protection to the Antarctic Treaty, the objective of which is to 'designate Antarctica as a natural reserve, devoted to peace and science' (Article 2); and, to a somewhat minor extent, in the 1988 CRAMRA.[66]

2. Areas requiring harmonization

In some areas there are no actual overlaps between the Basel Convention and the London Convention, but harmonization of the relevant rules and active co-operation between the two Convention administrations would strengthen both regimes. The fundamental concepts of the Basel Convention which do not specifically refer to the transboundary movement of wastes should be incorporated into the London Convention. These include notably the minimization of the generation and transboundary movement of hazardous wastes, and the environmentally sound management of wastes whatever their place of disposal. As was pointed out in the relevant resolutions of the thirteenth and fourteenth Consultative Meetings of the Contracting Parties to the London Convention, and reiterated in Decision I/4 of the Conference of Parties to the Basel Convention, the co-ordinated development of technical guidelines for the management and disposal of hazardous wastes under both Conventions would be important for ensuring adherence to similar standards and giving a concrete content to these obligations (see para. (B) above). As numerous technical guidelines already exist under the London Convention,[67] it can be very useful for the Basel Convention's Technical Working Group to build upon the experience gained in their application in the further development and application of the Basel guidelines. Indeed, the Secretariat of the London Convention participates actively in the work of the Technical Group.[68]

Other areas requiring harmonization include the development of rules on liability, which is under way for both Conventions in accordance with the relevant provisions (see Chapter 6 below); the exchange of information, for which the Basel Convention requirements are more far-reaching than those of the London Convention, even though informally London Convention parties are asked to provide the IMO with information similar to that requested under the Basel Convention; the transfer of technology and know-how, and training; and the monitoring of the state of the

[66] 1991 Protocol on Environmental Protection, repr. in YBIEL 2(1991), p. 533 et seq.; 1988 CRAMRA (not in force) (repr. in ILM 859(1988)). See Kiss and Shelton, (1991), p. 251 et seq.; Sands, in Verhoeven, Sands, and Bruce, (1992), p. 54 et seq.; Watts, (1992), p. 253 et seq.

[67] For an overview cf. *Note by the Secretariat to the Legal Group* (LDC/LG 5/2, (1991)).

[68] See the *Report of the Secretariat* (LDC15/INF.12, (1992)); also the *Report of the Executive Director* (UNEP/CHW.1/2, (1992)); and the *Report of the Technical Working Group on its 4th session*, 4 June 1993, (UNEP/CHW/WG.4/4/6), p. 2.

environment.[69] Illegal traffic, which is only regulated in the Basel Convention, could be addressed also in the London Convention. Likewise, the London Convention's rules on emergency response could be incorporated into the Basel Convention, which does not yet address this issue.

3. Outlook

Some or all of the issues discussed in the preceding paragraphs are likely to be addressed in the near future. In order to take into account the developments during its nearly 20 years of operation, the fifteenth Consultative Meeting of the Contracting Parties in November 1992 decided to subject the London Convention to general review with the aim of adopting the necessary amendments. An Amendment Group met in July 1993 to examine proposals for amendment. Based on the recommendations of this group, the sixteenth Consultative Meeting in 1993 decided on a two-track approach, by which only a limited number of amendments which were considered urgent were adopted at the sixteenth Meeting (see above). The remaining issues will be addressed by a specially convened Amendments Conference, scheduled for 1996 at the latest. In preparation for this conference, the Amendment Group will continue to meet, subjecting the Convention to a thorough review. Among other things, the incorporation of the contents of the resolutions of previous Consultative Meetings, outlined above, is under discussion.[70] As these resolutions address many of the points discussed here, this would be a very important step towards harmonizing the London Convention with the Basel Convention.

THE BASEL CONVENTION REGIME AND TREATIES ON THE CONTROL OF OTHER FORMS OF POLLUTION

C. *The Basel Convention Regime and Conventions on Marine Pollution from Land-Based Sources*

4. Outline of the relevant rules

Marine pollution from land-based sources constitutes by far the most significant source of marine pollution in terms of quantity. It accounts for roughly 70 per cent of all marine pollution and poses the most serious long-

[69] See *Note by the Secretariat of the London Convention* (LDC12/INF.7, (1989)), p. 18; Lukasik, *Report*, (1989), p. 19 et seq.

[70] *Report of the 16th Consultative Meeting*, December 1993, (Doc. LC16/14), p. 10 et seq.; Resolution LC.48(16); *Report of the Amendments Group*, July 1993, Doc. LC/AM I/9. See also the *Reports of the 14th and 15th Consultative Meetings* (LDC14/16; LDC15/WP.8/Add.1).

term threat to the marine environment.[71] Unlike dumping at sea, it is not as yet subject to regulation by a global treaty.[72] The Governing Council of UNEP in 1985 adopted the non-binding Montreal Guidelines for the Protection of the Marine Environment against Pollution from Land-Based Sources, which are, however, merely intended to assist governments in the regulation of the problem.[73] Article 207 of UNCLOS sets out a number of general obligations of states in the context of land-based marine pollution, including the obligation to 'endeavour to establish global and regional rules, standards and recommended practices and procedures' for its prevention and control. The existing treaties in this field are all regional in scope. Most of the regional seas agreements adopted under UNEP's Regional Seas Programme impose a very general obligation on party states to control land-based sources of pollution. However, the 1980 Athens Protocol for the Protection of the Mediterranean Sea against Pollution from Land-Based Sources; the 1983 Quito Protocol for the Protection of the South-East Pacific against Pollution from Land-Based Sources; the 1990 Kuwait Protocol for the Protection of the Environment against Pollution from Land-Based Sources; and the 1992 Bucharest Protocol on Protection of the Black Sea Marine Environment against Pollution from Land-Based Sources do regulate this issue in more detail. The relevant provisions of the 1992 Oslo/Paris Convention cover the North-East of the Atlantic and Arctic Oceans. The issue is also addressed in the 1992 Helsinki Convention, which covers the Baltic sea area.

The treaties generally define pollution from land-based sources as the discharge of noxious substances from any source located in the territory of a contracting party, including coastal establishments, watercourses, pipelines, and offshore installations. Airborne pollution is also covered.[74] Like the dumping conventions, some of the treaties on the control of pollution from land-based sources allocate the substances to be controlled to a set of lists annexed to the conventions.[75] Persistent, toxic or bioaccumulative sub-

[71] For an extensive analysis see UNEP/GESAMP, (1990). See also UNCED Agenda 21, Chapter 17, para. 17.19; *World Resources Report 1990–91*, p. 181; Hohmann, (1989), p. 532; Birnie and Boyle, (1992), p. 300; Schneider, (1981), p. 257 et seq.

[72] On international legal regulation of marine pollution from land-based sources see generally Boyle, (1992a), p. 20 et seq.; idem, (1992b), p. 79 et seq.; idem, (1990a), p. 151 et seq.; Birnie and Boyle, (1992), p. 300 et seq.; Meng, (1987); Hohmann, (1989), p. 531 et seq.; Kiss and Shelton, (1991), p. 189 et seq.; Nollkaemper, in YBIEL 1(1990), p. 116 et seq.; and idem, in YBIEL 2(1991) p. 132. For an analysis of the pertinent treaties see Boyle, Freestone, Kummer, and Ong, in Sand, (1992), pp. 149–255.

[73] Montreal Guidelines for the Protection of the Marine Environment against Pollution from Land-Based Sources, UNEP Governing Council Decision 13/18/II, 24 May 1985.

[74] Oslo/Paris Convention, Article 1 (giving a wider definition than most other treaties); Helsinki Convention, Article 2(2); Bucharest Protocol, Article 1; Athens Protocol, Article 1; Quito Protocol, Article II.

[75] UNEP/GESAMP, (1990), p. 91.

stances included in a 'black list' must be progressively eliminated in accordance with relevant programmes and measures to be adopted by states.[76] A 'grey list' contains substances the discharge of which must be controlled and reduced where feasible.[77] Others provide that all steps must be taken to reduce and eliminate progressively the pollution from land-based sources, and establish criteria to be applied in achieving this, such as 'best environmental practice' and 'best available technology'.[78] In contrast to the more advanced dumping conventions, the conventions on land-based pollution do not completely prohibit the discharge of these substances. In some cases, discharge of certain substances is made contingent upon prior authorization by the competent national authority.[79] In addition, the treaties set out general obligations to party states to formulate common guidelines and standards for the control of pollution from land-based sources; to assess the level of pollution along their coasts and evaluate the effects of measures taken to reduce it; to co-operate in scientific research and in the provision of assistance to states in need of it; and to inform each other of measures taken, results achieved, and difficulties encountered. Treaties adhered to by both developed and developing countries allow for the need for economic development to be taken into account, thus establishing dual standards.[80] A dual standard based on different levels of economic development is also incorporated into Article 207 of UNCLOS. For the North Sea region, non-binding rules have been adopted to strengthen the relevant regimes.[81]

The international regulation of the control of pollution from land-based sources is considerably weaker than the rules addressing other sources of marine pollution. In this field, there are no accepted global standards comparable to the London Convention, the MARPOL Convention, or the Basel Convention, and the stringency of the regional agreements varies considerably. Internationally recognized rules in this field do not go beyond the general duties to prevent appreciable harm to the environment of other states or the global commons, and to co-operate in monitoring the state of the marine environment, accepted under customary law (see Chapter 1 above). In addition to calls for strengthening existing regional conventions, there have been plans for the elaboration of a global convention on the control of marine pollution from land-based sources. An intergovernmental

[76] Athens Protocol, Article 5; Quito Protocol, Article IV; Kuwait Protocol; Bucharest Protocol, Article 4.

[77] Athens Protocol, Article 6; Quito Protocol, Article V; Kuwait Protocol; Bucharest Protocol, Article 5.

[78] Oslo/Paris Convention, Article 3, Annex I; Helsinki Convention, Article 6, Annex III.

[79] Helsinki Convention, Article 6(3); Oslo/Paris Convention, Article 2, Annex I; Athens Protocol, Article 6(3); Kuwait Protocol.

[80] Athens Protocol and Kuwait Protocol. For a discussion see Boyle, (1990a), p. 153 et seq.; Edwards, in Carroll, (1988), p. 270 et seq.

[81] Declarations of the International North Sea Conferences and Recommendations of the (old) Paris Commission. See Boyle, (1992a), p. 29 et seq.; Pallemaerts, (1992), p. 1 et seq.

meeting of experts on land-based sources of marine pollution was convened in Halifax (Canada) in May 1991, and a UNEP-sponsored meeting to develop a global strategy to combat land-based marine pollution was held in Nairobi in December of the same year. In 1993, the Governing Council of UNEP authorized the Executive Director to convene a conference for the development of an action programme on marine pollution from land-based sources, including a revision of the Montreal Guidelines. The elaboration of a convention is not envisaged at this point, however. The preparatory process for this conference, which is to be held in Washington DC in November 1995, is currently under way.[82]

The differences in the level and quality of international regulation of ocean dumping and transboundary movements of hazardous wastes, on the one hand, and pollution from land-based sources of the marine environment in coastal areas, on the other, are largely the result of the greater complexity of the issue of land-based marine pollution. Despite the problems of definition and the diversity of the situations to be taken into account in the context of transboundary waste traffic (see Chapter 1 above), the scope of activities and the number of substances to be controlled are still fairly limited. This can also be said in the case of dumping and incineration at sea of wastes. By contrast, land-based marine pollution flows from a wide range of sources, including diffuse sources which are difficult to trace and therefore difficult to control,[83] and involves a great variety of activities. Due to the number and characteristics of the sources of land-based marine pollution, any measures taken are likely to be complex and therefore expensive. Since the larger part of land-based pollution is the direct result of agricultural, industrial and domestic activity in coastal areas, the conflict between economic development and environmental protection is more acute than in the cases of ocean dumping and hazardous waste transfer. Whereas industrialized countries are responsible for practically all transboundary traffic and ocean dumping of wastes, land-based pollution of the marine environment in coastal areas is serious also in developing countries, where economic development has high priority, and financial and technical resources to combat land-based pollution are scarce. The problem is likely to increase as economic development progresses. This is another fac-

[82] Conclusions of the Halifax meeting (repr. in Doc. LDC14/INF.13+Add.1.). On the Nairobi meeting see UNEP/GC. Decision 16/26.A., and the reports in YBIEL 1(1990) and 2(1991). On the Washington Conference see UNEP Governing Council Decision on the protection of the marine environment against pollution from land-based sources, 21 May 1993, (repr. in EPL23/3/4(1993), p. 171), and the *Report of the Meeting of Government-Designated Experts focusing on the Montreal Guidelines*, 10 June 1994, (UNEP/MG/IG/1/5).

[83] For a definition see Springer, (1983), p. 6 et seq.

[84] For a discussion of these problems see UNEP/GESAMP, (1990), in particular p. 91 et seq. See also Birnie and Boyle, (1992), p. 308 et seq.

tor complicating the issue.[84] The deficiencies of the legal instruments addressing the issue of marine pollution from land-based sources are the result of their having to take account of all of these factors in order to be acceptable to states.[85]

5. The relationship between the Basel Convention regime and treaties on land-based sources of marine pollution

There are a few operations that are covered by both the Basel Convention regime and the conventions on land-based marine pollution. The release of hazardous wastes into the ocean, including sea-bed insertion, is one of the disposal options addressed by the Basel Convention (Annex IV), and it is also covered by the relevant treaty definitions of marine pollution from land-based sources outlined above. In addition, the disposal of hazardous wastes in inadequate land-based facilities or their discharge into rivers and lakes can ultimately result in marine pollution from land-based sources. As in the case of ocean dumping, the Basel Convention (or a regional waste management agreement) and a regional convention on marine pollution from land-based sources would be simultaneously applicable in situations where hazardous wastes covered by both regimes are transported from one state to another for the purpose of subsequent discharge into the ocean from a land-based source.

In theory, therefore, there is a possibility of overlaps or conflicts between the relevant rules. In practice, however, even if such situations occur, overlaps between the rules seem unlikely. As already noted, the conventions on pollution from land-based sources—unlike the dumping conventions—do not address the transport of the wastes to the site of disposal. They regulate only the disposal itself, and the rules they establish are very unspecific. The Basel Convention, on the other hand, focuses on transboundary movement, but beyond requiring that it be carried out in an 'environmentally sound' manner and establishing general principles, it does not contain many substantive rules on the disposal of hazardous wastes.

In this situation, it would not be very useful to include into the Basel Convention an obligation to adhere to 'relevant international rules and standards' for the discharge of wastes from land-based sources, as such standards are virtually non-existent. From the point of view of the conventions on pollution from land-based sources, the inclusion of a general obligation to manage wastes subject to transboundary movement in accordance with recognized international rules and standards, as reflected in the Basel Convention regime, might be considered. However, as the conventions on pollution from land-based sources—unlike the dumping conven-

[85] Boyle, (1992a), p. 35.

tions— do not address the transport of wastes to the site of disposal, there is no need to incorporate the Basel Convention's fundamental principles referring to transboundary movements, such as the concept of a limited ban or the PIC procedure, into these conventions.

More relevant than the possibility of conflicts and overlaps is the danger that the adoption of the Basel Convention and related regional waste management systems, as well as the progressive strengthening of the London Convention regime, could lead to an increase in the discharge of hazardous wastes from land-based sources, since that field is considerably less well regulated. In order to avoid this, the introduction of generally stronger rules into the existing conventions on marine pollution from land-based sources, which would meet the standards established by the Basel Convention and the London Convention regimes, should be considered. In addition, a global convention should be adopted to provide an umbrella for the regional treaties. The need to strengthen the regimes for marine pollution from land-based sources is widely recognized, even though relevant action has been slow, as noted above. Necessary amendments would include an obligation to phase out the discharge of certain substances within a specified period of time, and the establishment of stringent standards for the minimization and environmentally sound management of the pollutants subject to the conventions. To give these obligations concrete content and to ensure harmonization with other relevant conventions, the development of technical guidelines in co-ordination with the competent bodies established under the Basel Convention regime and the dumping regime would constitute a useful approach to this task. The elaboration of a global strategy on land-based marine pollution, as proposed by the Halifax Meeting and the Governing Council of UNEP, may provide a good starting point.

D. *The Basel Convention Regime and International Rules on the Pollution of Continental Waterways*

In this field, the situation is similar to that discussed above in the area of marine pollution from land-based sources. While numerous bilateral and regional treaties as well as non-binding guidelines address the use of watercourses shared by more than one state, including the control of pollution, there are as yet no recognized international rules and standards comparable to those governing ocean dumping.[86] Thus the international approach

[86] For an overview and analysis of existing relevant treaties and guidelines see Ando, in Zacklin and Caflisch, (1981), (with an Appendix setting out a list of treaties); Lammers, in Lang, Neuhold, and Zemanek, (1991), p. 115 et seq. (with an Annex listing relevant legal instruments); Bourne, (1971), pp. 115–36; Teclaff and Teclaff, (1985), p. 589 et seq.; Kiss and Shelton, (1991), pp. 202–27; Birnie and Boyle, (1992), ch. 6; Boyle, (1990a); Cano, in Sand, (1992), p. 302 et seq. The non-binding rules adopted by the ILA, the IDI, and the UN/ECE are repr. in Hohmann, (1992), Vol. 1.

to this issue is determined mainly by customary law rules on pollution, which are reflected in the ILA's 1966 Helsinki Rules and supplementary rules elaborated by the ILA.[87] These rules call for equitable utilization of the waters of international drainage basins. Consistent with this principle, they require states to take all reasonable measures to prevent new forms of pollution, and abate existing forms, in order to prevent substantial damage to other states. Substances that are generally considered highly dangerous should not be discharged into the aquatic environment. A state that fails to comply with these obligations must cease the wrongful conduct and compensate the injured state. Remedies should be provided to persons who are or may be adversely affected by water pollution. The rules also establish general obligations of co-operation, consultation and mutual information between states sharing an international drainage basin.[88] These rules are very general: they do not establish specific environmental standards. Moreover, the obligation to prevent pollution applies only insofar as other states are affected, in accordance with the traditional sovereignty-based approach discussed in Chapter 1(K) above. The ILC's draft rules on the Law of the Non-Navigational Uses of International Watercourses[89] do not achieve much more than a codification of these customary principles.

Regional agreements differ widely as to stringency and level of detail. An example of a fairly advanced agreement is the 1978 Canada–USA Agreement on Great Lakes Water Quality.[90] A more recent example of a regional convention that goes beyond the reiteration of general principles is the 1992 UN/ECE Convention on the Protection and Use of Transboundary Watercourses and International Lakes.[91] It expressly advocates the precautionary principle, the polluter pays principle, and the concept of prevention of pollution at source. It defines hazardous substances as 'substances which are toxic, carcinogenic, mutagenic, teratogenic, or bioaccumulative, especially when they are persistent', but gives no further specification. In addition to extensive requirements for international co-operation, consultation, research, and monitoring, it also obliges its parties to apply EIA; to establish a prior licensing system for point source pollution[92] (which must include emission limits based on 'best available technology'); and to develop contingency planning. Where appropriate, parties should develop water quality objectives and criteria. Criteria for 'best avail-

[87] Helsinki Rules on the Uses of the Waters of International Rivers, 1966 (repr. in Hohmann, (1992), Vol. 1, p. 227 et seq.). See also the 1982 ILA Rules on Water Pollution in an International Drainage Basin (repr. in Hohmann, (1992), Vol. 1, p. 227 et seq.).

[88] See Bourne, (1971), pp. 115–36; Lester, (1963) pp. 828–53; Utton, (1973), pp. 282–313.

[89] Draft Articles as adopted in first reading by the ILC at its 43rd session, July 1991 (UN Doc. A/46/10, (1991), Chapter III, repr. in EPL21/5/6, (1991), p. 247). See also the report by McCaffrey in EPL22/2 (1992), pp. 66–7; and idem, in Magraw, (1991), p. 104 et seq.

[90] As amended by the 1987 Protocol (repr. in Hohmann, (1992), Vol. 2, p. 1167 et seq.).

[91] Adopted in Helsinki in March 1992 (repr. in ILM 31(1992), p. 1312).

[92] For a definition see Springer, (1983), p. 6 et seq.

able technology' and 'best environmental practices' are set out in the annexes. Even though the Convention does not set out detailed standards, and many of its requirements are contingent on feasibility, it may constitute a useful precedent for future developments in this field. A similarly advanced approach is adopted by the working group charged with the elaboration of a convention for the protection of the Danube Basin.[93]

The issue of transboundary water pollution shares most characteristics of the issue of marine pollution from land-based sources, discussed above. In this case, the conflict of economic and environmental interests is exacerbated by the fact that the water of shared rivers and lakes is used as a vital resource as well as a disposal option for wastes and other pollutants.[94] For these reasons, the regulatory problems are similar to those encountered in land-based marine pollution (see para. 4 above), and the resulting weakness of the international legal instruments are basically the same.

The Basel Convention covers the release of hazardous wastes into waterbodies other than the ocean (Annex IV), as do most regional waste management treaties. In this sense there is a link between the Basel Convention regime and the rules on pollution of international watercourses. However, as in the case of marine pollution from land-based sources, the question of harmonization with the Basel Convention regime does not arise at this point, due to the weakness of the rules in question. Moreover, there is no direct overlap with the Basel Convention regime as the rules on international waterways do not address the movement of the wastes prior to disposal. Nevertheless, as in the case of the regimes for marine pollution from land-based sources, it will be important to develop stricter general standards for the control of pollution of international watercourses, in order to avoid an increase in the discharge of wastes into international rivers and lakes as a result of restrictions on waste disposal abroad, imposed by the Basel Convention regime. In this context, as in the context of the regulation of land-based marine pollution, the adoption of obligations of waste minimization and environmentally sound waste management, supported by relevant technical guidelines elaborated jointly for the watercourse regimes and regimes for protecting other spheres of the environment as well as the Basel Convention regime, would provide a useful starting point.

E. *The Basel Convention Regime and the 1991 Protocol on Environmental Protection to the Antarctic Treaty*

Although the environment of the Antarctic cannot be considered a 'sphere'

[93] Danube Basin Ecological Convention (4th Draft, Budapest, July 1994).

[94] Cf. the *Keynote Papers prepared for the International Conference on Water and the Environment: Development Issues for the 21st Century* (Dublin, 26–31 January 1992), published 1992. Cf. in particular the contributions by Horchani, Kindler, and Falkenmark and Lundqvist.

of the environment as outlined in Chapter 1(J) above, the relevant legal instrument governing its protection against adverse effects of waste generation and management and its relationship with the Basel Convention will be briefly considered here since the relevant problems are similar.

In addition to the Basel Convention and the London Convention, the issues of reduction, management, and discharge of wastes and other noxious substances in Antarctica is addressed in the 1991 Protocol on Environmental Protection to the Antarctic Treaty, in particular in its Annexes III (Waste disposal and waste management) and IV (Prevention of marine pollution).[95] Unlike the Basel Convention, the Protocol does not, however, specifically address the question of the import of hazardous wastes into the Antarctic area for disposal. It is primarily concerned with wastes generated in Antarctica. Annex III restricts the disposal of wastes in Antarctica, but does not prohibit it in general. The Annex obliges the generator to remove from the Antarctic region those wastes which are considered particularly noxious, including radioactive materials; solid or liquid fuel; substances containing heavy metals or acutely toxic or persistent compounds; and harmful plastic wastes. It sets out rules for the disposal of other wastes on land or at sea, or by incineration. In order to reduce the impact of wastes on the Antarctic environment, parties are required to establish a waste disposal classification system and waste management plans, which will be reviewed by the Committee for Environmental Protection established under the Protocol (Articles 11, 12). Annex IV prohibits the discharge of oil except in compliance with the MARPOL Convention. The discharge of noxious liquid substances and of certain solid wastes is also prohibited. Sewage may be discharged only in accordance with MARPOL. Annex IV is generally in line with the MARPOL Convention.

Neither Annex contains direct references to other legal instruments on marine pollution or waste management, although Annex III does require that wastes removed from the Antarctic should be returned to the country from which the waste-generating activity was organized, there to be disposed of 'in accordance with relevant international agreements'. This can be understood to indicate the Basel Convention and pertinent regional treaties, as well as sectoral treaties addressing the disposal of waste into specific parts of the environment, such as the London Convention or the conventions on marine pollution from land-based sources. The rules of these treaties, in particular those of the Basel Convention regime, should therefore be adhered to when wastes are transferred to the state organizing the hazardous activity in accordance with the requirements of the Protocol.

[95] Repr. in YBIEL 2(1991), p. 533 et seq. See generally Watts, (1992), p. 276 et seq.; Bruce, in Verhoeven, Sands, and Bruce, (1991), p. 175 et seq.; Kimball, in YBIEL 2(1991), p. 190; and Blay, (1992), p. 377 et seq.

Prior to the adoption of the Protocol, the fifteenth Antarctic Treaty Consultative Meeting adopted Recommendation XV–3 (1989), which set out rules for the management of wastes in Antarctica and provided that any dumping of wastes should be carried out in accordance with the London Convention.[96] Similar references to the London Convention were also included in drafts of Annex III to the Protocol. However, these were deleted at the second Session of the eleventh Special Consultative Meeting of the Antarctic Treaty Parties in June 1991, with the intention that specific rules on the protection of the Antarctic marine areas against dumping should be elaborated by the parties at a later stage.[97] In the absence of such rules, ocean dumping in Antarctica is not as yet regulated in the Protocol, beyond a provision permitting the discharge of sewage under certain conditions. The 1989 Recommendation might not now be implemented due to being superseded by the Protocol. In 1991, the fourteenth Consultative Meeting of the Contracting Parties to the London Convention discussed the relationship between the London Convention and the Antarctic Protocol and concluded that the application of the London Convention in Antarctica is not within the exclusive competence of the Antarctic Treaty parties.[98]

As the Basel Convention regime prohibits all shipments of hazardous wastes to the Antarctic, and the Protocol on Environmental Protection does not directly address this issue, there are no actual conflicts between the two regimes. The Antarctic Protocol does, however, fall short of the Basel Convention in that it does not explicitly prohibit the import of hazardous wastes into Antarctica. As in the case of the London Convention, the adoption of a prohibition on waste imports along the lines of Article 4(6) of the Basel Convention should be contemplated.[99] It would also be useful to require parties to the Protocol to take account of the general obligations on waste management established by the Basel Convention, not only in the case of the removal of wastes, but in the management and disposal of wastes generated in the Antarctic in general. This could be done through the insertion of a clause requiring parties to 'take full account of the relevant international rules on the management and disposal of hazardous wastes'.

[96] IMO Doc. LDC14/INF.34 (25 November 1991), with Recommendation XV–3 as Annex. Cf. Kiss and Shelton, (1991), p. 319.

[97] Cf. *Report of the 5th Meeting of the Ad Hoc Group of Legal Experts on Dumping*, 7 August 1991, (IMO Doc. LDC/LG5/10), p. 5.

[98] Cf. Iljstra, in YBIEL 2(1991), p. 148, and IMO Docs. LDC/LG5/10 (7 August 1991), pp. 4–6; 14/INF.34, (1991).

[99] See the *Report of the 5th Meeting of the Ad Hoc Group of Legal Experts on Dumping*, 7 August 1991, (IMO Doc. LDC/LG5/10).

CONCLUSIONS

The above overview shows that the possibility of actual conflicts between the Basel Convention regime and sectoral pollution control treaties is very small. On the other hand, overlaps requiring the adjustment of the Basel Convention and the relevant treaties with each other do exist, but only in the fields of ocean dumping and—to a minor extent—waste disposal in Antarctica. These inconsistencies could be rectified through incorporation of pertinent provisions into the treaties in question, as proposed above. In these fields as well as in the fields of land-based marine pollution and pollution of international waterways, however, the major challenge is the harmonization of the rules and standards of the different regimes. The weaker of the relevant regimes should be strengthened by incorporation of the concepts found in the more advanced regimes, notably the Basel Convention and London Convention regimes. Relevant concepts include the minimization of waste generation at source, the treatment and disposal of wastes close to the source of generation (principle of proximity); the environmentally sound management of wastes whatever their place of disposal; and the prohibition or phasing-out of unsound operations and disposal options within a specific time-scale. All of these concepts are incorporated, to varying degrees, in the component elements of the Basel Convention regime, as we saw in Chapters 2–4 above. They are indicative of the precautionary principle, which receives growing support in international law and is reflected in the Basel Convention and London Convention regimes, but is not generally supported as yet by the regional conventions addressing land-based marine pollution and pollution of international waterways.[100] In order to achieve a harmonized approach to the discharge of wastes and other noxious substances into the environment in general, these fundamental concepts should be incorporated into all sectoral pollution control regimes.

Since the main weakness of some sectoral treaties, especially those governing land-based marine pollution and pollution of continental waterways, is the generality of the obligations they impose, the proposed alignment should not stop at the inclusion of the relevant concepts in the form of general obligations, but should specify the content of such obligations. A useful approach to this task would be the development of a common strategy for the management and disposal of hazardous wastes, including technical guidelines which set out exact and detailed standards for operations involving hazardous wastes, regardless of the sphere in which they are ultimately disposed of. Similar reasoning underlies the proposal by GESAMP that an integrated and comprehensive strategy for the protection of the marine

[100] See Hohmann, (1990), p. 55 et seq.; Boyle, (1992a), p. 22 et seq.

environment be developed, based on common principles, agreed goals, and scientific methods.[101] Pertinent guidelines already exist under the London Convention. Technical Guidelines are also being elaborated under the Basel Convention, as we saw in Chapter 2 para. 7 above, and efforts are under way within the UN/ECE and other bodies to elaborate regional waste management strategies.[102] A global strategy for marine pollution from land-based sources is under discussion. The ongoing co-operation between the institutions concerned to ensure harmonized development of their respective guidelines is a promising step towards the achievement of this aim. In addition to guidelines pertaining to one specific waste management or pollution control regime, guidelines could also be adopted that encompass all activities related to the management and disposal of hazardous wastes and governed by any one of the relevant regimes. In this, the organizations administering the different conventions should co-operate. As discussed in Chapter 1(H) above, similar guidelines and standards already exist in the field of transportation of dangerous substances and wastes.

An interesting initiative that goes in this direction is the development of an 'International Strategy and Action Programme for the Environmentally Sound Management of Hazardous Wastes' under the auspices of UNEP, and with the participation of competent international organizations (see Chapter 2 para. 7 above). Fairly general in character, the elements of the strategy, as presented by the relevant working group, endorse concepts such as the management or design of substances in a way that attains the longest possible life and causes the least possible harm (principle of integrated life cycle); and the principle of integrated pollution control. They also support the principle of waste minimization, the precautionary principle, the polluter pays principle, and the principles of proximity and self-sufficiency. As we saw in Chapter 2 para. 7 above, they influenced the action programme on hazardous wastes included in UNCED's Agenda 21: Chapters 20 and 21 reflect the same principles (see Chapter 1(K) above).[103]

A related initiative was taken under the auspices of the IMO. The thirteenth Consultative Meeting of the Contracting Parties to the London Convention in 1990 instructed the Secretariat to initiate, in co-operation with other UN agencies, a Global Waste Survey with the aim of assessing the implications of a ban on the incineration of liquid noxious substances and the dumping of industrial wastes at sea. This involved a global evaluation of the quantity and types of wastes generated and of existing waste management practices, and the identification of clean technologies and

[101] UNEP/GESAMP, (1991), in particular p. 26. See also Hohmann, (1990), p. 55 et seq.; idem, (1989), p. 538 et seq.

[102] Kummer, in YBIEL 3(1992), p. 293; Kwiatkowska and Soons, (1993), p. LXIII.

[103] Decisions of the UNCED PrepCom on its 1st four sessions (repr. in Kwiatkowska and Soons, (1993), nos. 7.2–7.5). See also ibid., Editors' Introduction, p. XXXI et seq.

processes for waste reduction. The Survey should lead to the elaboration of an Action Plan, with the ultimate goal of helping states with the transition from sea disposal of wastes to environmentally sound land-based disposal options. A Steering Committee sponsored by the IMO and UNEP started work on the Survey in October 1992. This work was due to be completed in November 1994.

The first phase of the project resulted in the development of the Global Waste Inventory and Database System, which currently provides information on industrial and hazardous waste management in 102 countries. The second phase involves the elaboration of National Waste Management Profiles, which assess existing waste management practices as well as the assistance needed to improve such practices. Eighteen countries have prepared such profiles within the framework of the Survey. On the recommendation of the sixteenth Consultative Meeting of the Parties to the London Convention in 1993, the second Meeting of the Conference of the Parties to the Basel Convention agreed to transfer the main responsibility for the Survey to the Basel Convention Secretariat as the appropriate forum, after the completion of the initial phase. The IMO and other interested UN agencies will continue to co-operate with the Secretariat in this field.[104]

The harmonization of obligations and standards under the Basel Convention regime and the relevant sectoral pollution control conventions, supported by uniform and detailed technical guidelines, would contribute towards ensuring the uniform management of hazardous wastes regardless of the fact that their disposal in different spheres of the environment is addressed by different international rules. This would be in line with the call for a 'comprehensive approach to hazardous waste', issued by various international organizations and supported by UNCED's Agenda 21. It would facilitate the emergence of a single regime for the control of the discharge of noxious wastes into all spheres of the environment, and would thus be consistent with the integrated approach to the protection of the environment against pollution, advocated in Chapter 1(J) above. Such an approach would reduce the danger of wastes subject to disposal following the 'path of least resistance', and of stronger rules in one field leading to an increase in polluting activities in less protected spheres. This could be supported by adhering to the principle that measures adopted under one treaty regime should not lead to increased pollution in spheres addressed by another regime. Numerous existing sectoral treaties, notably in the field of

[104] Decision II/23 of the Conference of the Parties to the Basel Convention, (1994). For an overview see *Report by the Secretariat of the Basel Convention to the 2nd meeting of the Conference*, 13 December 1993, (Doc. UNEP/CHW.2/24). See also the *Reports of the 13th, 14th and 16th Consultative Meetings of the Contracting Parties to the London Convention* (IMO Docs. LDC13/15, (1990), LDC14/16, (1991), and LC16/14, (1993)).

marine pollution, already contain provisions obliging parties to ensure that the rules of the treaty in question do not lead to an increase in polluting activities elsewhere.[105] Equivalent provisions should be included into every relevant legal instrument.

To ensure the success of any attempt at harmonization, the creation of links and co-operation between the institutions administering the relevant treaties will be important.[106] This co-operation is already well advanced in practice, as the joint efforts by UNEP and the IMO to harmonize the two Conventions illustrate. An important step is the concerted action in the elaboration of waste management strategies and action programmes. If the relevant legal instruments are developed along the lines proposed above, a global waste management regime could emerge, composed of the Basel Convention regime and those sectoral pollution control treaties that address one or more aspects of the hazardous waste cycle. The characteristics of this prospective regime will be discussed in Chapter 7 below.

[105] E.g. UNCLOS, Article 195; 1992 Helsinki Convention, Article 3(6); 1992 Oslo/Paris Convention, Article 2(4); 1978 Kuwait Convention, Article III(e); 1981 Abidjan Convention, Article 4(5); 1985 Montreal Guidelines on pollution from land-based sources, Guideline 6; 1991 Protocol Treaty on Environmental Protection to the Antarctic, Annex IV, Article 8; 1992 UN/ECE Convention on the Protection and Use of Transboundary Watercourses and International Lakes, Article 2(4). Cf. also the *Statement of the 1988 World Conference on the Changing Atmosphere*, Toronto (repr. in Churchill and Freestone, (1991)). For a discussion of this concept see Teclaff and Teclaff, (1991), p. 187 et seq.; Adede, (1992).

[106] Cf. Teclaff and Teclaff, (1991), p. 187 et seq.; Birnie and Boyle, (1992), ch. 8.

6

Ensuring Compliance: Relevant Concepts and Mechanisms

The preceding chapters have examined the international obligations pertaining to the management, transboundary movement and disposal of hazardous wastes, as set out in the Basel Convention, the regional waste management systems, and some sectoral pollution control regimes. It has been established that a global waste management regime, composed of the Basel Convention, regional waste management systems concluded under its umbrella, and applicable sectoral pollution control regimes, is emerging, and that this could be strongly supported through the harmonization of the relevant legal rules with each other. The emerging global waste management regime provides a standard of behaviour that must be adhered to in the context of the management and disposal of hazardous wastes. This standard is determined by the following fundamental primary obligations: the minimization of hazardous waste generation at source; the disposal of hazardous wastes as close to the source as possible (principle of proximity); the environmentally sound management of hazardous wastes—in accordance with relevant technical guidelines and applicable transport rules—whatever the place of disposal (principle of non-discrimination); the cessation or gradual phasing-out of environmentally unsound disposal options, such as ocean dumping and incineration at sea; the prohibition of exports of hazardous wastes under certain circumstances; the requirement of PIC for transboundary movements of hazardous wastes which are not in principle prohibited; the obligation to arrange for adequate disposal of wastes in the event of illegal transactions, and those that cannot be completed as foreseen; and the exchange of information and technical co-operation.

In order to make this regime effective, mechanisms must be set up which induce compliance with the relevant rules, and regulate the consequences of their breach. Such mechanisms have three main objectives: first, the prevention of environmental damage resulting from hazardous wastes; second, reparation of damage once it has occurred; and third, the equitable allocation of the costs of remedial measures. The objectives of a future liability protocol to the Basel Convention (discussed in para. 16 below) were identified by some members of the Working Group charged with its elaboration in a similar fashion: 'The victim should be protected; the person who created a risk should, in all fairness, be held liable for the consequences of that risk; a good liability regime should in general provide an incentive to prevent waste generation; [and] last but not least, such a regime would enable industry to know where it stood'.[1] These mechanisms are hereafter referred to as 'enforcement mechanisms'.

International policy and law has created a number of enforcement mechanisms, and others are emerging. Their legal nature, focus, and degree of acceptance is very diverse.[2] The traditional enforcement mechanism is state responsibility administered through international adjudication or inter-state diplomatic claims. This mechanism relies on the role of the state as guarantor of compliance with international obligations, and is principally confrontational. Due to inherent practical and theoretical difficulties with state responsibility, alternative mechanisms have evolved or are in the process of evolving. Institutional supervision, shifting the focus from individual states to intergovernmental entities, places the emphasis on multilateral compliance monitoring and supervision, while still relying on states as guarantors of compliance with international rules by individuals. Instead of confrontation between 'polluter' and 'victim' state, however, this mechanism relies on negotiation and public pressure. Another tendency is to transfer the problem from the state level to the private level by referring to the civil liability rules of individual states. This is usually supported and facilitated by international conventions which amount to a unification of civil liability rules, and which provide a guarantee of equal access for foreign victims to judicial institutions in the 'polluting' state. Finally, a mechanism already known at the national level and beginning to emerge also at the international level, is the establishment of a fund, financed by levies or contributions from potential polluters in accordance with a predetermined assessment system. Its function is the compensation of victims of pollution, on the one hand, and the financing of emergency response measures, on the other.

In addition to these mechanisms of international control, enforcement mechanisms adopted at the national level play an important part in the implementation of international obligations. Some conventions expressly oblige their parties to adopt national measures. Since this chapter is concerned with international enforcement mechanisms only, national measures will be discussed only summarily.

[1] *Report of the Working Group on its 1st session* (UNEP/CHW/WG.1/3), p. 5. See Dupuy, in *La réparation des dommages catastrophiques*, (1990), p. 242; also the *Draft Report of the ILC on its 44th session* (UN Doc. A/CN.4/L.476, quoted by Boyle, in YBIEL 3(1992), pp. 202–5); Handl and Lutz, in Handl and Lutz, (1989a), p. 58.

[2] For a concise overview of the relevant mechanisms and the problems inherent in their application, see Birnie and Boyle, (1992), chs. 4 and 5. See also Kummer, (1994b).

THE OBJECTIVES OF ENFORCEMENT MECHANISMS IN THE CONTEXT OF HAZARDOUS WASTE MANAGEMENT

A. *Ensuring Compliance with Relevant Rules in Order to Prevent Environmental Damage Caused by Hazardous Wastes*

In accordance with the preventive approach, the primary objective of the enforcement mechanisms discussed in this chapter must be to ensure that the obligations imposed by the emerging global waste management regime are respected. As discussed in Chapter 1(L) above, there is a strong trend in environmental policy and law to place primary importance on prevention instead of remedy. In order to achieve this, the mechanisms must provide an incentive to states and private operators to act in conformity with the relevant rules. Furthermore, they must facilitate and support compliance, and provide a means of monitoring and verifying the conduct of states and individuals.

B. *Restoration of the Environment and Adequate Compensation of the Victims in the Event of Damage Caused by Hazardous Wastes*

Even if relevant mechanisms are in place, the first objective as outlined above cannot always be attained, as discussed in Chapter 1(L) above. There remains the possibility of environmental damage being caused by the transboundary transport and management of hazardous wastes, either despite compliance with the rules by all parties, or as a result of contravention of the rules.

Where environmental damage is caused, the secondary objective of enforcement mechanisms must therefore be to restore the situation as it would have been had the damage not occurred. This objective has two aspects. First, the mechanisms must help to minimize the damage. To this end, they should encourage and facilitate rapid action in case of environmental emergencies, and support any so-called 'preventive measures', i.e. action taken in order to prevent a deterioration of the situation. This is consistent with the requirement for 'accident preparedness and response', endorsed by international policy and incorporated in a number of legal instruments.[3] Secondly, they should aim at reparation of the damage. This includes restoration of affected parts of the environment as far as possible, on the one hand, and compensation of the victims in the widest sense, to the fullest extent possible and with the least possible delay, on the other.

[3] e.g. the 1990 OPPRC (repr. in ILM 30/3(1991), p. 735)); the 1990 Agreement on Co-operation for Combating Pollution in the North-East Atlantic; and the 1992 UN/ECE Convention on the Transboundary Effects of Industrial Accidents (repr. in ILM 31(1992), p. 1333 et seq.). For a discussion see Handl, in Handl and Lutz, (1989a), p. 107 et seq.

Ideally, this aim should be achieved even in cases where the polluter cannot be identified, or is unable to meet the costs of compensation.

C. *Equitable Allocation of the Costs of Minimization of Risks and Redress of Environmental Damage*

In accordance with the polluter pays principle discussed in Chapter 1(L) above, the costs of minimizing the damage as well as restoring the affected parts of the environment and compensating the victims should be borne by the person who controls the hazardous activity and benefits from it economically. This must therefore be the third objective of the enforcement mechanisms. More specifically, the mechanisms should provide for a transfer of these costs from the victims to the actual or potential polluter. They should also enable the risk created by the transport and management of hazardous wastes to be spread among various polluters, in order to avoid the situation where the costs are so high that a single polluter cannot meet them, and compensation is therefore not available.

STATE RESPONSIBILITY AND STATE LIABILITY

State responsibility and state liability are subject to an extensive theoretical discussion both in the academic world[4] and within international bodies, in particular the ILC.[5] This involves a varying and sometimes confusing use of terminology and definitions to denote the different concepts. In this chapter, no attempt will be made to contribute to this discussion. The following analysis is limited to questions directly relevant to the role of state responsibility and liability in the achievement of the above objectives, in the context of the control of transboundary movements of hazardous wastes as addressed by the rules constituting the emerging global waste management regime. The use of terminology and definitions generally follows the system set out in an excellent paper by Riccardo Pisillo-Mazzeschi, which

[4] See among others Brownlie, (1983); idem, (1990), p. 432 et seq.; Jiménez de Aréchaga, (1978); idem, (1968), ch. 9; Boyle, (1990b) p. 1 et seq. On state responsibility in the context of environmental protection in particular see Birnie and Boyle, (1992), p. 139 et seq., and literature quoted there; Handl, (1975), pp. 156–94; Dupuy, in OECD, (1977); *La réparation des dommages catastrophiques*, (1990), in particular the chapter by Dupuy (p. 219 et seq.); Francioni and Scovazzi, (1991), in particular ch. 2 by Pisillo-Mazzeschi (p. 15 et seq.).

[5] ILC, Draft Articles on State Responsibility, Pt. 1, (in *Yearbook of the ILC* 1980 Vol. II Pt. 2 p. 30 et seq.), Pt. 2, (in *Yearbook of the ILC* 1985 Vol. II Pt. 1 p. 3 et seq.); ILC Draft Articles on Liability for Injurious Consequences of Acts Not Prohibited by International Law (Doc. A/CN.4/428 (1990)). For an overview of ongoing work on the codification of state responsibility and liability see Rosenne, (1991), Editor's Introduction, pp. 1–31; Springer, (1983), p. 123 et seq.; McCaffrey, in Magraw, (1991), ch. 4; idem, (1990), p. 940; Magraw, in Handl and Lutz, (1989a), p. 248 et seq.; Rest, (1991), p. 135 et seq.; and idem, (1992), p. 36 et seq.

corresponds largely to that used by the ILC and the UN/ECE.[6] Thus the term 'responsibility' denotes all duties incumbent on states as a result of the breach of a primary international obligation. The term 'liability' is used only in the context of the controversial concept of obligations pertaining to the reparation of damage caused by acts not prohibited in international law.

D. *Existing and Emerging Rules on State Responsibility and Liability Relevant to Transboundary Movements of Hazardous Wastes*

Existing rules on the responsibility of states for environmental damage are to a very large extent based on customary law.[7] Even though various environmental treaties as well as non-binding international legal instruments contain exhortations to states to develop relevant international rules, only very few substantive conventional rules exist to date, the most important including Article 235 of UNCLOS and Article 8(3) of CRAMRA. The 1972 Convention on International Liability for Damage Caused by Space Objects, although establishing detailed rules on state responsibility and liability, does not expressly encompass damage to the environment. Even very recent environmental treaties do not go beyond exhortatory provisions, e.g. the 1992 UN/ECE Convention on Transboundary Effects of Industrial Accidents (Article 13), and the 1992 UN/ECE Convention on the protection of international watercourses and lakes (Article 7). Treaty rules establishing secondary obligations in the context of environmental damage are practically non-existent.[8] The elaboration of international rules on this issue by the ILC is making little progress, and no pertinent rules have as yet been adopted under the auspices of the IMO or the IAEA.[9] In fact, the general lack of progress in this field in the 20 years following the Stockholm Conference[10] is emphasized by Principle 13 of the 1992 Rio Declaration, which calls upon states to 'co-operate *in an expeditious and more determined manner* to develop further international law regarding liability and compensation for adverse effects of environmental damage caused by activities

[6] Pisillo-Mazzeschi, in Francioni and Scovazzi, (1991), ch. 2. See also Boyle, (1990b), p. 1 et seq.; UN/ECE 1990 Guidelines on Responsibility and Liability Regarding Transboundary Water Pollution (repr. in Hohmann, (1992), Vol. 1 p. 310 et seq.); Rest, (1991), p. 136.

[7] For an analysis of state responsibility and liability in the context of the transfer of hazardous substances, technologies and wastes, cf. Magraw, in Handl and Lutz, (1989a), p. 240 et seq.

[8] On UNCLOS see Schneider, (1981), p. 243 et seq.; on CRAMRA see Orrego Vicuña, in Brown Weiss, (1992b), pp. 147–9, also p. 128. For a discussion of the issue see also Timoshenko, in Brown Weiss, (1992b), p. 451; Spinedi, in Francioni and Scovazzi, (1991), pp. 76–7; Pisillo-Mazzeschi, ibid. p. 17 et seq.; Kiss, (1989a), pp. 116–18; Boyle, (1989), p. 287; Adede, (1992), p. 95.

[9] Cf. Handl, in Magraw, (1991), p. 150; Politi, in *La réparation des dommages catastrophiques*, (1990), p. 331 et seq.

[10] Cf. Fathalla, (1991), p. 25 et seq.; Kiss, (1989a), p. 117.

within their jurisdiction or control to areas beyond their jurisdiction' (emphasis added).

1. Forms of state responsibility and state liability

Even though there seems to be general acceptance of a distinction between responsibility based on subjective criteria pertaining to a state's conduct, and responsibility based on objective criteria, there is a diversity of definitions of these categories. The most convincing approach appears to be that supported among others by Pisillo-Mazzeschi, according to which the form of state responsibility is determined not on the basis of a subjective concept of fault, but on the basis of the nature of the primary obligation that has been breached.[11] The terminology and categories relied upon in this chapter will follow this approach. In this view, 'fault' responsibility is defined as responsibility for the breach of an obligation of due diligence, which in turn is an obligation of conduct. Accordingly, a 'polluting' state may exonerate itself by proving that it observed the required standard of due diligence. This type of responsibility is commonly recognized as the only concept of state responsibility for environmental damage supported by customary international law.[12] This is consistent with the general recognition of due diligence as the form of primary obligation related to environmental protection supported by customary law (see Chapter 1 para. 4 above). The majority of the primary obligations set out in environmental treaties are also based on the standard of due diligence.[13] The emerging global waste management regime is no exception to this: obligations pertaining to 'environmentally sound management' of hazardous wastes reflect the due diligence approach, as do the obligations of promoting the minimization of generation and transboundary movements of hazardous wastes (see Chapters 2 and 3 above). The concept of due diligence is expressed especially in the recurrent use of terms such as 'as far as practicable' in the Basel Convention and the related treaties.

On the other hand, the concepts of 'strict' and 'absolute' responsibility, as defined by Pisillo-Mazzeschi, are understood to mean responsibility

[11] See Pisillo-Mazzeschi, in Francioni and Scovazzi, (1991), p. 16. Cf. generally Jiménez de Aréchaga, (1978), p. 270; Brownlie, (1983), p. 38 et seq.; Birnie and Boyle, (1992), p. 141 et seq.; Boyle, (1990b); idem, (1989), p. 289 et seq.; idem, in Francioni and Scovazzi, (1991), p. 365; Orrego Vicuña, in Brown Weiss, (1992b), p. 133 et seq.; Könz, in Brown Weiss, (1992b), p. 171.

[12] See n. 11 above; also Dupuy, in *La réparation des dommages catastrophiques*, (1990), pp. 223–30; idem, in Magraw, (1991), p. 78 et seq.; Francioni, in Francioni, (1992); Handl, (1975); idem, (1980), pp. 539–40. Cf. Zemanek, in Lang, Neuhold, and Zemanek, (1991), p. 188, arguing that no form of state responsiblity for environmental damage has attained the status of customary law.

[13] Pisillo-Mazzeschi, in Francioni and Scovazzi, (1991), pp. 18–20 (quoting examples); Boyle, (1989), p. 294.

resulting from the breach of an absolute prohibition of an activity, which constitutes an obligation of result.[14] Unlike 'fault' responsibility, this type of responsibility does not permit exoneration of the perpetrating state by virtue of the observance of a standard of conduct determined by due diligence. Whereas 'absolute' responsibility knows practically no grounds for exoneration, the more common form of 'strict' responsibility allows exoneration for a limited number of reasons, including *force majeure*, and wrongful conduct or consent of the victim state. A number of existing environmental treaties establish obligations of result.[15] The emerging global waste management regime also contains such obligations, namely the prohibition of waste exports to Antarctica, to states not parties to a pertinent treaty, and to states which have prohibited waste traffic. Additional obligations of result are emerging, in particular the prohibition of hazardous waste exports from developed to developing and transitional countries, and of disposal of hazardous wastes at sea. However, even though a limited number of treaties addressing environmental issues do provide for 'strict' or 'absolute' responsibility in this sense, neither concept can be considered as generally recognized in customary and treaty law relating to environmental protection.[16]

In addition to state responsibility for the breach of international obligations, there is some support for the concept of state liability for damage caused by activities which are not prohibited in international law.[17] According to some interpretations, this concept underlies the 1972 Convention on International Liability for Damage Caused by Space Objects.[18] The ILC is in the process of developing rules on the subject.[19] In view of the aims outlined above, in particular the polluter pays principle

[14] Pisillo-Mazzeschi, in Francioni and Scovazzi, (1991), p. 16.

[15] Cf. e.g. Brownlie, (1990), pp. 465–6; also Pisillo-Mazzeschi, in Francioni and Scovazzi, (1991), pp. 20–1.

[16] Cf. Handl, in Magraw, (1991), p. 162 et seq.; and idem, (1988), p. 237 et seq. (arguing, however, that strict liability for nuclear harm is a general principle of law in the sense of Article 38 of the ICJ Statute). An exception in treaty law is the 1972 Convention on International Liability for Damage Caused by Space Objects, which expressly provides for absolute responsibility (Article 2). For a detailed analysis see Condorelli, in *La réparation des dommages catastrophiques*, (1990), p. 263 et seq.; also Kiss, in MacDonald and Johnston, (1983), p. 1079; idem, (1989), p. 111.

[17] For an extensive overview and analysis of this concept, as well as the ILC's work on its codification, cf. Tomuschat, in Francioni and Scovazzi, (1991), p. 37 et seq. See also Akehurst, (1985), p. 3 et seq.; Magraw, (1986), p. 305 et seq.; Handl, (1985), pp. 49–79; Boyle, (1990b), p. 1 et seq.

[18] Spinedi, in Francioni and Scovazzi, (1991), pp. 76–7, in particular n. 4 (reviewing the interpretations of the relevant provision by different scholars in the light of their support or rejection of the concept of state liability); also Verdross and Simma, (1984), p. 854; Akehurst, (1985), p. 10.

[19] ILC Draft Articles (n. 5 above). The concept is also included in the UN/ECE 1990 Guidelines on Responsibility and Liability Regarding Transboundary Water Pollution, discussed by Rest, (1991), p. 135 et seq.; and idem, (1992), p. 31 et seq. See also n. 17 above.

and the provision of remedies, there is an argument in favour of such a concept. However, the content and significance of this concept is far from clear, and it is not supported by customary law.[20] Some authors express doubt about the necessity of state liability as a category separate from state responsibility, arguing that existing concepts of state responsibility are sufficient for the achievement of the aim envisaged by the concept of state liability.[21]

2. Attribution to states of acts entailing responsibility

A state is held responsible for acts carried out by its organs in violation of international law. More important in the present context, it is also responsible for such acts carried out by private operators acting within its area of jurisdiction or under its control, if the state has breached its obligation to control or prevent such acts. This presupposes that the state has the effective ability to control the activity and thus meet its obligations.[22] Such attribution appears to be supported by customary and treaty law, and is implicit in Principle 21 of the Stockholm Declaration.[23] In the context of hazardous waste subject to transboundary movement, a state can thus be held responsible for damage caused by persons acting under its jurisdiction or control if the damage is the result of that state's failure to prevent the transaction, or to ensure that it is carried out in accordance with the relevant rules.[24] On the other hand, the state cannot be held responsible for activities taking place beyond its jurisdiction or control, e.g. in the territory of another state.[25]

As the concept of effective control is not entirely clear, it can be difficult to establish the causal link necessary for attribution of an act to the state, especially if the activity is carried out by private parties in exercise of their economic freedom.[26] However, it seems clear that no responsibility attaches

[20] Brownlie, (1990), pp. 444–6; idem, (1983), p. 49 et seq.; Jiménez de Aréchaga, (1978), p. 273; Boyle, (1990b), p. 15; Spinedi, in Francioni and Scovazzi, (1991), p. 77.

[21] Brownlie, (1983), p. 50; Boyle, (1990b), p. 1 et seq.; idem, in Francioni and Scovazzi, (1991), p. 366; Zemanek, in Lang, Neuhold, and Zemanek, (1991), ch. 7, and Commentary by Springer. In support of this concept see Handl, (1985), p. 49 et seq.

[22] McCaffrey, in Magraw, (1991), p. 99.

[23] For a discussion see Verdross and Simma, (1984), p. 863 et seq.; Brownlie, (1983), p. 133 et seq.; Handl, (1975), pp. 158–9; Boyle, (1989), p. 288; Kiss, in Macdonald and Johnston, (1983), p. 1077; Francioni, in Francioni and Scovazzi, (1991), pp. 279–80 (quoting relevant treaties and precedents).

[24] Cf. Bothe, in Handl and Lutz, (1989a), p. 158 et seq.; Koh, ibid, p. 169 et seq. See also Könz, in Brown Weiss, (1992b), p. 171 et seq.

[25] On a state's responsibility for acts of its nationals abroad see Bothe, in Handl and Lutz, (1989a), p. 168, concluding that there is no legal basis for such responsibility, despite the fact that it is contained in various codes of conduct. See also McCaffrey, in Magraw, (1991), p. 103, reaching the same conclusion.

[26] Francioni, in Francioni, (1992).

to environmental risks of which the state authorities were not and could not have been aware[27]; and that conversely, an activity can be attributed to a state if it has been expressly authorized by its competent authorities.[28]

This last observation leads to an interesting conclusion in the context of transboundary movements of hazardous wastes as addressed by the Basel Convention regime. In the case of transboundary pollution in the traditional sense, where the source of pollution is located in one state and harm occurs in another state not having control over the harmful activity, there can, by definition, be only one state responsible. In the case of pollution source transfer, on the other hand, several states may have the authority to authorize or prohibit various stages of the transaction taking place under their jurisdiction or control, and a legal obligation to prevent or control them in accordance with existing and emerging primary rules. Accordingly, all states concerned can potentially be held responsible for damage occurring as a result of the activity.[29] The state of export can be held responsible for damage sustained in another state if the damage is due to the exporting state's failure to prevent or control, in accordance with its legal obligations, the transfer of hazardous wastes out of its area of jurisdiction. At the same time, the state of import can be held responsible for damage to a state of transit, or to a state not involved in the movement, if it authorized the import in contravention of applicable rules, or failed to control the manner in which the wastes were disposed of in accordance with relevant rules (see Chapters 1 and 2 above). Depending on the attribution of the acts to the states involved, responsibility may be allocated to any of them. If more than one state has failed to apply the relevant rules to activities attributable to them, they are jointly responsible. The ensuing duties of reparation may be apportioned between them.[30] This situation resembles that of multinational enterprises with subsidiaries in different countries. In his analysis of state responsibility in that case, Francioni concludes that if the 'host' country has accepted the subsidiary in its territory, it should be held responsible for its activities along with the 'home' country of the company.[31]

[27] Birnie and Boyle, (1992), p. 143, also p. 96.

[28] Brownlie, (1983), p. 161; Francioni, in Francioni, (1992); Kiss, in *La réparation des dommages catastrophiques*, (1990), p. 306.

[29] See Kiss, in *La réparation des dommages catastrophiques*, (1990), pp. 304–7.

[30] On joint responsibility see Magraw, (1986), p. 305 et seq. Cf. the *Nauru Case* (ILM 32(1993), p. 46, ICJ Rep. 1992 p. 240), in particular the separate *Opinion of Judge Shahabuddeen*, (p. 71 et seq.); and Orrego Vicuña, in Brown Weiss, (1992b), p. 136.

[31] Francioni, in Francioni and Scovazzi, (1991), p. 275 et seq. Cf. Koh, in Handl and Lutz, (1989a), pp. 172–3.

3. Forms of reparation

The breach of an international obligation entails a duty of reparation of damage sustained. The concept of damage in this context is not limited to material damage, but extends to the infringement of non-material interests of states.[32] Increasingly, purely ecological damage is also recognized as entailing a duty of reparation.[33] The primary objective of reparation is *restitutio in integrum*, i.e. restoration of the situation as it would have been had the damage not occurred.[34] In the case of damage caused by hazardous wastes, the removal and adequate disposal of the wastes constitutes an important aspect of the duty of restoration. There is increasing recognition of the duty of the state of export to accept back illegally exported wastes.[35] In addition, the duty of restoration includes clean-up of contaminated sites or polluted waterways. In cases where *restitutio in integrum* is impossible or impracticable, the state responsible has a duty of financial compensation; this is in practice the most frequent form of reparation. Other obligations to states in the context of reparation include the cessation of the harmful act, and the provision of satisfaction.[36]

E. *Conventional Rules Established by the Emerging Global Waste Management Regime*

4. Article 9 of the Basel Convention: a basis of state responsibility for illegal traffic in hazardous wastes

As discussed in Chapter 2(G) above, the Basel Convention defines 'illegal traffic' as any movement of hazardous wastes taking place in contravention of its provisions, in particular of the restrictions on waste export, and of the PIC procedure. It provides that states must adopt national measures to

[32] Jiménez de Aréchaga, (1968), p. 534; Verdross and Simma, (1984), p. 849. Cf. Orrego Vicuña, in Brown Weiss, (1992b), pp. 134–5.

[33] Spinedi, in Francioni and Scovazzi, (1991), pp. 103–4; Orrego Vicuña, in Brown Weiss, (1992b), p. 134; Francioni, in Francioni, (1992). Purely ecological damage is expressly recognized in the UN/ECE 1990 Guidelines on Responsibility and Liability Regarding Transboundary Water Pollution, Article 1(m); in the 1988 CRAMRA, Article 1(15); in the 1991 Environmental Protocol to the Antarctic Treaty, Article 3(2); and in the ILC draft Articles on international watercourses, Article 21.

[34] *Chorzów Factory Case*, PCIJ Series A No. 17, p. 47. Cf. Brownlie, (1983), p. 247 et seq.; Spinedi, in Francioni and Scovazzi, (1991); Koh, in Handl and Lutz, (1989a), pp. 178–9.

[35] Handl and Lutz, in Handl and Lutz, (1989a), pp. 44–8; Birnie and Boyle, (1992), p. 334 (maintaining that the duty to accept back illegally exported hazardous wastes had a basis in customary law even prior to the adoption of the Basel Convention and related legal instruments).

[36] For a detailed and comprehensive analysis of this problem see Spinedi, in Francioni and Scovazzi, (1991), p. 75 et seq.; also Brownlie, (1983), ch. XIII; Magraw, in Handl and Lutz, (1989a), p. 241 (on hazardous transfers in particular).

prevent and punish illegal traffic. Especially interesting in the present context, Article 9 obliges states to take specific remedial action whenever a case of illegal traffic has come to their attention. This may be construed as an attempt to codify certain aspects of state responsibility for illegal traffic in hazardous wastes.

From the wording of the provision, it is not clear what form of responsibility is intended. One can argue, however, that Article 9 envisages strict responsibility, as there is no evidence of a standard of conduct the contravention of which entails responsibility. On the contrary, *any* conduct that results in a failure to comply with the PIC procedure entails responsibility, as does *any* conduct resulting in a failure to respect export prohibitions.

Even though the transactions addressed by Article 9 are usually carried out by private operators, the allocation of responsibility to states has a firm basis in the Convention: each party state must introduce an authorization system to which all waste brokers operating within its territory are subject (Article 4(7.a)). Furthermore, all parties are required to establish national authorities which are responsible, 'within such geographical areas as the Party may think fit', for the handling of the PIC procedure, i.e. for controlling and monitoring the activities in question (Article 2(6), Article 5). Responsibility for the actions of private operators is thus based on the state authority's failure to comply with these obligations of control.

The situation where more than one state is potentially responsible for an illegal waste transaction is addressed in paragraphs 2 to 4 of Article 9. The Convention attempts to resolve this problem by allocating responsibility for the actions of each of the principal operators to the state with which the operator in question has the closest link. Thus the state of export is responsible for the actions of the exporter and the generator (paragraph 2), and the state of import is responsible for the actions of the importer and the disposer (paragraph 3). Where the action cannot be attributed to either of these operators, the Convention establishes a form of joint responsibility of all states involved in the transaction (paragraph 4). The situation where both the exporter (or generator) and the importer (or disposer) have contributed to the illegality of the transaction is not directly addressed by Article 9, nor is the situation where the action is attributed to another operator (e.g. the carrier), or where the operator cannot be determined. It can, however, be assumed that these cases are covered by paragraph 4, assigning responsibility jointly to all states concerned. An earlier proposal to allocate exclusive responsibility to the exporting state except in cases where the importer (or disposer) alone is at fault, was rejected during the negotiations (see Chapter 2(B) above).[37]

[37] *Report of the Basel Working Group on its 4th session*, February 1989 (UNEP/WG. 190/4), p. 27; Doc. UNEP/WG.190/CRP.11; *Executive Director's Luxembourg Note*, February 1989 (UNEP/WG. 191/2); *Executive Director's Basel Proposals*, (UNEP/WG.191/3/ Add.2). See also Lang, in Lang, Neuhold, and Zemanek, (1991), p. 154.

Article 9 spells out only one duty pertaining to reparation.[38] The state responsible for the action leading to an illegal movement must ensure the disposal of the wastes in question, in accordance with the provisions of the Convention, by re-importation into the state of export or otherwise, within 30 days of receiving information about the illegal movement. The state must ensure that the disposal is arranged by the operator(s) at fault, or failing that, by itself (paragraphs 2, 3). If several states are jointly responsible, they must co-operate in ensuring the environmentally sound disposal of the wastes. In this case, third states are also called upon to participate in any joint action, although this cannot be construed to entail responsibility of third states beyond the general duty of international co-operation (Article 9(5)). No specific time limit is given; the disposal must be arranged 'as soon as possible' (paragraph 4).

Article 9 does not make the obligations of re-import or alternative disposal of hazardous waste subject to illegal traffic contingent on damage having been sustained. The mere fact of the waste having been moved illegally, according to the definition of that term under the Convention, is sufficient to entail the state's duty to ensure environmentally sound disposal. It can be argued that such illegal movement constitutes in itself an infringement of non-material rights of the state concerned, for which the perpetrating state is responsible (see para. 3 above. This interpretation is consistent with the argument supported by Kiss, that the existence of damage is irrelevant where a treaty rule has been breached.[39]

Even though Article 9 arguably addresses some important points pertaining to state responsibility for illegal traffic, its greatest weakness is undoubtedly the absence of an obligation to provide other forms of reparation, in particular restoration of the affected ecosystem, and payment of compensation. In this instance, it is necessary to resort to the customary law duties of cessation of the illegal activity, *restitutio in integrum*, and payment of compensation, discussed above.

5. Article 8 of the Basel Convention: duty to re-import wastes that were legally exported

Article 8 is an interesting provision in that it imposes a duty of remedial action on a state in a case where no illegal act has been committed.[40] This constitutes an innovative approach which does not as yet seem to be supported by customary law, or have precedents in treaty provisions,[41] even though the related concept of liability for injurious consequences of acts

[38] Cf. Hackett, (1990), p. 321.

[39] Kiss, in Brown Weiss, (1992b), pp. 330–1.

[40] For a critical assessment see Gröbl, (1989), p. 8.

[41] Cf. Magraw, in Handl and Lutz, (1989a), pp. 255–62; also Orrego Vicuña, in Brown Weiss, (1992b), p. 141.

not prohibited in international law is being discussed by the ILC (see para. 1 above). Article 8 applies where a transboundary movement of hazardous wastes has commenced in compliance with the PIC procedure, but cannot be completed in accordance with the terms of the contract between the exporter and the disposer. In this case, the state of export must ensure the re-importation of the wastes by the exporter, if alternative arrangements for their environmentally sound disposal cannot be made, within 90 days from the time the exporting state and the Convention Secretariat have been informed. The states concerned can agree on a different time schedule.

The duties of the exporting state as provided by Article 8 are less stringent than those of Article 9. Article 8 merely obliges the exporting state to ensure re-importation of the wastes by the exporter; the state does not have a subsidiary obligation to arrange the re-import itself.[42] This seems a reasonable approach, since in the cases covered by Article 8, the exporter can always be identified. The time limit for the re-importation is 90 days, as opposed to only 30 days in the case of illegal traffic.

Article 8 does not specify the cause of the impossibility of compliance with the contract. The wording 'cannot be completed in accordance with the terms of the contract' is open to interpretation. Clearly, any action which renders the movement illegal in accordance with Article 9 is excluded from this definition. It is, however, not clear whether Article 8 is limited to cases of *force majeure*, or whether it also covers impossibility due to errors on the part of persons or state authorities involved (e.g. prior consent given on the basis of an erroneous assumption), or changes in the relevant circumstances after consent was given, or unforeseen action by a third party.[43] Since Article 4(10) of the Convention prohibits transfer of the exporting state's fundamental obligation to ensure environmentally sound management of the hazardous wastes to the importing state, one can argue that the main duty to ensure safe disposal remains with the exporting state in the event of impossibility, whatever its cause. Article 8 must then apply to every case of impossibility which is not covered by Article 9.

As in Article 9, no provision is made for remedial measures beyond ensuring re-import or alternative disposal of the wastes. Unlike the case of illegal traffic, however, a customary law basis for additional obligations of reparation incumbent on the state of export (*restitutio in integrum*, payment of compensation) cannot be found here, since no breach of obligation is involved: as discussed above, a duty of reparation for damage caused by actions that are not illegal is not recognized in customary law.

[42] Cf. *Report of the Basel Working Group on its 5th session*, March 1989, (UNEP/IG.80/4), Annex I, p. 11.

[43] Cf. Lang, in Lang, Neuhold, and Zemanek, (1991), p. 154.

6. Related provisions in regional waste management systems and sectoral pollution control treaties

The component elements of the Basel Convention regime discussed in Chapters 3 and 4 above provide similar rules. Articles 8 and 9 of the Basel Convention provided a model for the relevant provisions of the 1991 Bamako Convention and the 1993 EU Regulation on the control of transboundary waste shipments. The Bamako provisions are taken almost verbatim from the Basel Convention, while those of the EU Regulation are based on the same principles. Their interpretation is therefore the same as that of the Basel provisions. The relevant rules of the 1986 agreement between the USA and Mexico are similar. Article IV obliges the state of export to re-admit any shipment of hazardous wastes that may be returned for any reason. In the case of illegal traffic, or if the wastes cause damage to public health, property, or the environment, the state of export must take all practicable measures and legal actions to ensure that the person responsible returns the waste to the state of export, restores the affected ecosystem 'as much as practicable', and pays compensation for damage caused by the waste (Article XIV). Thus the duty of reparation goes beyond that of the Basel Convention, even though weakened by the proviso 'as much as practicable'. On the other hand, the exporting state is not required to actively arrange for the re-import, or take any remedial measures itself. The 1986 agreement between the USA and Canada similarly obliges the state of export to re-admit wastes that are refused for any reason (Article 6), but does not impose any obligations beyond that. The 1992 Central American Agreement declares all transboundary movement of hazardous waste to be illegal, and obliges states to enact pertinent criminal legislation (Article 4). It does not impose further duties on the parties, however.

By contrast, the sectoral pollution control treaties discussed in Chapter 5 above do not contain equivalent provisions. Apart from exhortations to states to develop relevant rules, even the very recent treaties addressing marine pollution and pollution of international waterways do not in fact address the issue of responsibility or state remedies at all.[44] A notable exception can be seen in the ILA's 1982 Rules on Water Pollution in an International Drainage Basin, which provide that a state that fails to comply with the obligations set out in the Rules must cease the wrongful conduct and compensate the injured state (see Chapter 5(D) above). The Rules do not, however, provide a binding obligation.

[44] Cf. the 1992 Helsinki Convention (Article 25); the 1992 Oslo/Paris Convention (which does not contain even an exhortation); the 1992 Bucharest Convention (Article XVI); the 1992 UN/ECE Convention on international waterways (Article 7); the 1972 London Convention (Article X); the 1976 Barcelona Convention (Article 12); the 1978 Kuwait Convention (Article 13); the 1981 Abidjan Convention (Article 15); and the 1983 Cartagena Convention (Article 14).

7. An emerging basis for state responsibility and liability in the context of waste management?

Articles 8 and 9 of the Basel Convention, together with similar regional provisions, contain rules pertaining to state responsibility and state liability which, although still at an incomplete stage of development, are considerably more far-reaching than those found in most other environmental treaties. Surprisingly, Articles 8 and 9 of the Basel Convention are hardly ever mentioned by scholars discussing conventional provisions on state responsibility or liability.[45]

Whereas most relevant treaty provisions are limited to a general obligation on states to co-operate in the negotiation of rules on responsibility and liability, the relevant provisions of the Basel Convention regime explicitly place responsibility for specifically defined actions of private parties on states, thus establishing a basis on which to build a regime of state responsibility and state liability for damage caused by hazardous wastes. The duty to re-import illegally exported hazardous wastes reaffirms and specifies the existing customary obligation to make reparation. However, the absence of a definition of relevant damage, as well as the failure to impose additional duties of reparation on the states responsible, make it an incomplete basis—a starting point for further negotiations rather than a substantive set of rules. Accordingly, Article 12 of the Basel Convention and Article 12 of the Bamako Convention contain an exhortation to parties to develop relevant rules. In their present form, the provisions are unlikely to contribute significantly to the development of the law in the field of state responsibility, or to the recognition of state liability for damage caused by acts that are not illegal. This will be discussed further in Chapter 7 below.

F. *The Contribution of State Responsibility and Liability to the Achievement of the Objectives: Strengths and Weaknesses*

In practical terms, there are a number of weaknesses inherent in state responsibility that impede its successful application in environmental matters. In addition to specific obstacles, such as difficulties with the valuation of the damage, the identification of the perpetrator, and the establishment of the causal link, the vagueness and generality of the existing rules makes it difficult to predict the outcome of any claims procedure. Procedural obstacles, the complexity, length, and expense of the procedure, diplomatic

[45] See however Abrams, (1990), p. 833 et seq.; also the responses of the USA, Canada and Mexico to a UNEP questionnaire in 1990 (*Secretariat Summary of Responses to UNEP Questionnaire*, 15 May 1990, (Doc. UNEP/CHW/WG.1/INF.2)), describing the equivalent provisions in the North American bilateral agreements as rules on state responsibility and liability.

reasons, and the fear of creating a precedent will often prevent the submission of a claim by the 'victim' state.[46] Partly as a result of these weaknesses, there is a general reluctance on the part of states to resort to state responsibility.[47] None of the recent major environmental disasters gave rise to inter-state litigation based on state responsibility, even where a basis for a claim did in fact exist.[48] Nevertheless, an interesting development can be observed in the context of the recent scandals involving the illegal deposit of hazardous wastes in developing countries, discussed in Chapter 1 above: even though none of these incidents were brought before the ICJ, public outrage and diplomatic pressure did in some cases result in the return of the wastes to the state of export. The best known example is the case of the vessel *Karin B*, where Italy was eventually forced to take back the waste by use of severe diplomatic pressure, which involved the seizure of an Italian ship by Nigeria, and the temporary severance of diplomatic relations between the two countries.[49]

The general reluctance of states to accept state responsibility is reflected in the absence of relevant provisions in international treaties. To a certain extent, this reluctance affected even the comparatively advanced provisions of the Basel Convention: as mentioned in Chapter 2(G) above, there was strong opposition to the inclusion of Articles 8 and 9, and the remaining imperfections of these provisions, discussed above, are largely the result of this opposition. In the present negotiations on a protocol on liability and compensation, state responsibility is envisaged at the most as a subsidiary mechanism (see para. 16 below). The lack of willingness on the part of

[46] On the weaknesses of state responsibility see Boyle, (1989), p. 296 et seq.; idem, in Francioni and Scovazzi, (1991), p. 363 et seq.; Birnie and Boyle, (1992), p. 136 et seq.; Handl, in Magraw, (1991), p. 156 et seq.; Springer, (1983), pp. 31 et seq., 141 et seq.; Kiss, (1989a), p. 106 et seq.; idem, in Brown Weiss, (1992b), p. 329; Orrego Vicuña, ibid, p. 125; also Magraw, in Handl and Lutz, (1989a), ch. 10.

[47] This appears to be the consensus of most writers adressing the issue. See among others Boyle, in Butler, (1991); idem, in Francioni and Scovazzi, (1991), p. 363 et seq.; Francioni, ibid, p. 276; Conforti, ibid, p. 179; Kiss, ibid, p. 3 et seq.; and idem, in Brown Weiss, (1992b), pp. 329–30; Dupuy, in Francioni and Scovazzi, (1991), p. 141 et seq.; idem, in *La réparation des dommages catastrophiques*, (1990), p. 238 et seq.; Politi, ibid, p. 331 et seq.; idem, in OECD, (1977); Rest, (1991), p. 135; idem, (1992), p. 31 et seq. Cf. on the other hand Orrego Vicuña, in Brown Weiss, (1992b), p. 157, maintaining that the law of state responsibility 'is not at all inefficient or ineffective in the environmental field', as it is constantly evolving to adujst to new requirements.

[48] See Dupuy, in *La réparation des dommages catastrophiques*, (1990), p. 222; and Smets, ibid, p. 24 et seq., for an analysis of the recent major environmental disasters; also Rest, (1991), p. 135; Birnie and Boyle, (1992), p. 137; Kiss, (1989a), p. 115; Sand, (1990), p. 30; Handl, (1988), p. 222 et seq.; and idem, in Magraw, (1991), p. 152, discussing international reactions to the Tchernobyl accident. See also Könz, in Brown Weiss, (1992b), p. 168, and McCaffrey, in Handl and Lutz, (1989a), p. 202, both noting that in most of the notorious environmental disasters, seeking legal redress through national courts was the only recourse available to the victims.

[49] See Greenpeace, (1990), in particular p. 94 et seq.; United Nations, (1989); also Abrams, (1990), p. 805 et seq., in particular p. 810 and n. 35; Birnie and Boyle, (1992), p. 337.

states to accept state responsibility may well put into question the serious contemplation of this mechanism in the present context.

In addition, a number of conceptual weaknesses are evident in the use of this mechanism to ensure compliance with modern environmental protection regimes, including that of the Basel Convention and related legal instruments. First, state responsibility is based on the bilateral relationship between sovereign states with certain rights and duties towards each other. Therefore, while it can address environmental provisions which adopt the sovereignty-based approach, i.e. establish rights and duties of states towards each other, it fails to provide a useful enforcement mechanism for holistic obligations, i.e. obligations pertaining to the protection of the global environment as a whole (see Chapter 1(K) above).[50] As we saw in the preceding chapters, the emerging global waste management regime establishes both types of obligations. Holistic obligations, however, include some of its most fundamental concepts, such as the minimization of the generation and transboundary movement of hazardous wastes, the environmentally sound management of hazardous wastes whatever the place of disposal, the cessation or phasing-out of unsound disposal options, the exchange of information, and technical co-operation. This kind of obligation, not being directed at the infringement of the rights of a specific state, cannot be addressed satisfactorily by state responsibility. Similarly, there are problems in the application of state responsibility to damage caused to the global commons (e.g. by dumping or incineration of hazardous wastes on the high seas), even though there is an argument for state responsibility for damage caused to the global commons.[51]

Secondly, state responsibility provides only for remedial but not for preventive action. Thus it can meet only the second of the aims outlined above, i.e. restoration of the environment and compensation of the victim after the damage has already occurred. However, even remedial aims can often not be satisfactorily accomplished through state responsibility.[52] In accordance with the rules of international law, a case can be brought only by the state affected by the wrongful conduct, and the submission of a claim is entirely at the discretion of that state.[53] From the point of view of the actual victims of the pollution, this is a considerable disadvantage: due to the reluctance of states to resort to this mechanism, it can mean that compensation is not available from this source.[54]

[50] Cf. Riphagen, in MacDonald and Johnston, (1983), p. 581 et seq.; also Birnie and Boyle, (1992), p. 136.

[51] For a discussion see Kiss, in Brown Weiss, (1992b), pp. 330–1; Könz, ibid, pp. 172–3; Boyle, in Butler, (1991), p. 72 et seq.

[52] Cf. Springer, (1983), p. 32.

[53] *Barcelona Traction Case*, ICJ Rep. 1970 p. 39 et seq.

[54] Cf. Verdross and Simma, (1984), p. 881, noting that any inequity resulting from the exclusion of the actual victim from the decision is inherent in the inter-state character of claims under state responsibility.

The third aim of directing the costs to the actual polluter is often not met either. The victim state bears the burden of proof in the case of fault-based responsibility. Even if that state succeeds in submitting proof for the responsibility of the perpetrating state, the generally accepted standard of due diligence does not ensure that the burden of reparation is directed to the polluter: reparation has to be made only to the extent that the damage is due to a failure to observe due diligence, and the victim is thus mostly left to bear at least a part of the actual restoration cost.[55]

Despite these shortcomings, state responsibility should not be entirely discarded, especially since relevant rules of the Basel Convention regime provide an unusually strong treaty basis. The allocation of responsibility for environmental damage to states does provide an incentive to states to apply and enforce international rules at the national level. This incentive would not exist if the problem of bearing the consequences of environmental damage were shifted entirely to the private level, e.g. through unification of national rules on civil liability. State responsibility can therefore have the function of ensuring the crucial role of states as guarantors of compliance with international rules by individuals, through the adoption and enforcement of national criminal, administrative and civil legislation. An obvious example of the important role of national measures is the problem of illegal traffic in hazardous wastes, where international control measures must be supplemented with national measures in order to be effective. Article 4(4) of the Basel Convention and the equivalent rule of the Bamako Convention expressly oblige party states to adopt such measures. State responsibility gives them an incentive to comply.

In conclusion, it can be said that due to numerous practical and conceptual weaknesses, state responsibility does not provide in itself an adequate mechanism for ensuring compliance of states and individuals with the emerging global waste management regime. However, within the limits outlined above, it can provide a useful subsidiary mechanism, to be applied where other mechanisms are not available.[56] The objectives would then be met primarily by other enforcement mechanisms, which will be discussed below.

INSTITUTIONAL SUPERVISION

G. *Existing and Emerging Forms of Institutional Supervision: Precedents in Environmental Treaty Systems*

The concept of promoting compliance with international environmental law through institutional supervision, as an alternative to state responsibility,

[55] Cf. Boyle, in Butler, (1991); idem, in Francioni and Scovazzi, (1991), p. 363.

[56] Cf. Birnie and Boyle, (1992), p. 137; Orrego Vicuña, in Brown Weiss, (1992b), p. 143; Handl, in Magraw, (1991), p. 161.

has received some attention in recent academic discussion.[57] Some authors see it as the most important enforcement mechanism for modern international environmental regimes.[58] Practically all of the newer international treaties on environmental protection set up an institutional framework with the functions of administering the treaty, assisting parties in meeting their obligations, facilitating mutual assistance and the exchange of information, and monitoring compliance. This infrastructure usually includes a conference of the parties, which is convened at regular intervals, and in which all parties are represented. As the supreme body, the conference takes the overall policy decisions related to the convention. It adopts amendments to the treaty, as well as subsidiary legal instruments and non-binding resolutions or guidelines of a technical nature, and reviews performance by parties. In some conventions, there is a commission or committee in the place of the conference of the parties, which has similar or stronger functions. Under other treaties, relevant functions are carried out by an international organization.[59]

The conference of the parties is usually assisted by a permanent secretariat, which is in charge of the administration, ensures the flow of information among parties and between the parties and the conference, and carries out any support functions required by the convention. Additional bodies of a special nature, such as financial, scientific or technical committees, are sometimes established.[60] Under some treaties, so-called ad hoc working groups are established on an informal basis, for a limited period of time, and charged with a specific task related to the further development of the treaty or the examination of a particular question. This technique is used extensively by UNEP and the IMO (for examples see Chapters 2 and 5 above).

[57] See Audretsch, (1987), p. 838 et seq.; Boyle, (1991), p. 229 et seq.; Birnie and Boyle, (1992), p. 160 et seq.; Gehring, (1990), p. 35 et seq.; Handl, (1990), p. 3 et seq.; Hurrell and Kingsbury, in Hurrell and Kingsbury, (1992), p. 27; Kimball, (1990); Kiss, (1989a), p. 51 et seq.; idem, in Kalshoven, Kuyper, and Lammers, (1980), p. 100 et seq.; Kummer, (1994b); von Moltke, in Carroll, (1988), p. 87 et seq.; Sachariev, (1991), p. 31 et seq.; Sand, (1990), p. 33 et seq.; Szasz, in Brown Weiss, (1992b), p. 372 et seq.; Timoshenko, in Butler, (1991), p. 51 et seq. See also Sand, (1992), providing an analysis of the effectiveness of some 120 environmental treaties, including an examination of their institutional mechanisms.

[58] Timoshenko, in Butler, (1991), p. 53; Sachariev, (1991), p. 33.

[59] A commission is established under the 1992 Oslo/Paris Convention; the 1992 Helsinki Convention; the 1979 Geneva Convention on Long-Range Tranboundary Air Pollution; the Antarctic Treaty system; and the 1978 Canada–USA Great Lakes Water Quality Agreement. The IMO serves as secretariat to the MARPOL and London Conventions. For further examples see Birnie and Boyle, (1992), p. 165; Kiss, (1989a), p. 57. See also Gehring, (1990), p. 35 et seq.; von Moltke, in Carroll, (1988), p. 87 et seq.

[60] Such bodies exist, for example, under the 1987 Montreal Protocol; the 1979 Geneva Convention on Long-Range Transboundary Air Pollution; the 1973 CITES; the 1992 Framework Convention on Climate Change; and the 1992 Convention on Biological Diversity. See Gehring, (1990), p. 38 et seq., for an analysis of the role of technical bodies within the framework of environmental conventions.

The majority of the environmental conventions provide for some form of compliance monitoring by the conference of the parties, under which party states must submit reports on their performance on a regular basis. These reports are made available to all parties, and are reviewed by the conference.[61] Some treaties establish a formal requirement for periodical review of the treaty's effectiveness, to be performed by a specially designated institution.[62] In some instances, there is a provision for the verification by the competent institution of information supplied by states, or of their conduct, or for the reporting of offenders to the institution by other parties.[63] A small number of existing institutions can adopt decisions on the future conduct of the state that has been found to act in breach of its obligations.[64] Very few institutions also have independent powers of inspection,[65] or the competence to approve in advance potentially harmful activities.[66] Treaties usually establish a procedure for the settlement of disputes regarding the implementation or interpretation of the treaty, through arbitration or similar means, and provide that the dispute shall be submitted to international adjudication in the event of failure of such mechanisms.

For the most part, however, the mandate of institutions established under existing treaties focuses on the facilitation and support of the implementation of the treaty by states, rather than on verification of compliance

[61] e.g. CITES; London Convention; MARPOL Convention; Geneva Convention on Long-Range Transboundary Air Pollution and related protocols; Vienna Convention on the Protection of the Ozone Layer and Montreal Protocol; UN Framework Convention on Climate Change. For an analysis of reporting as an implementation mechanism see Sachariev, (1991), p. 39 et seq.; also Handl, (1990), pp. 16–17; Kiss, in Brown Weiss, (1992b), p. 327 et seq.

[62] See Sand, (1990), p. 35 et seq., quoting the examples of the 1987 Montreal Protocol; the 1988 Sofia Protocol; and the Basel Convention.

[63] The 1978 Great Lakes Water Quality Agreement (repr. in Hohmann, (1992), Vol. 2, p. 1167 et seq.) gives competences of verification to the International Joint Commission (Article 7(5); for a discussion see Boyle, (1991), p. 236). Under the 1987 Montreal Protocol (as amended), the Implementation Committee reviews allegations of non-compliance. Based on its recommendations, the Conference of the Parties may 'decide upon and call for steps to bring out full compliance with the Protocol' (Decision II/5 of the 2nd Meeting of the Parties, and Annex III, repr. in *Handbook for the Montreal Protocol* (UNEP, Nairobi 1991), p. 84 et seq.). See also Handl, (1990), p. 17; and Benedick and Pronove, in Sand, (1992), pp. 140–1.

[64] Cf. the non-compliance procedure of the Montreal Protocol, and Article 23 of the 1992 Oslo/Paris Convention for the Protection of the Marine Environment of the North-East Atlantic.

[65] e.g. the IAEA, although its inspection powers are weakened by the fact that they may only be exercised at the request of a state. Cf. Handl, (1988), p. 211 et seq., for a discussion of post-Tchernobyl developments in this field; also Birnie and Boyle, (1992), pp. 168, 354; Timoshenko, in Butler, (1991), p. 54. Under the Antarctic Treaty System, party states have the right to inspect each other's installations (e.g. Article 24 of CCAMLR; Articles 11, 12 of CRAMRA). Cf. Boyle, (1991), p. 237, for additional examples; Sands, in Verhoeven, Sands and Bruce, (1991), p. 53 et seq.; also Forster and Osterwoldt, in Sand, (1992), p. 67.

[66] This function was accorded to the Oslo Commission under the 1972 Oslo Dumping Convention (cf. OSCOM Decision 89/1), and, in a more far-reaching form, to the Antarctic Mineral Resource Commission to be established under CRAMRA. See Boyle, (1991), pp. 234–5, 240 et seq.

or adoption of sanctions against offenders. The convention secretariat or equivalent body usually acts as a clearing-house for the exchange of information, e.g. on technical matters, relevant scientific data, and the availability of technical expertise. It also supports and co-ordinates mutual technical and financial assistance between parties. In some cases, the secretariat actively assists parties in the fulfilment of their obligations under the convention, e.g. by organizing training seminars, assisting in the solution of concrete technical problems, or helping with the elaboration of relevant national legislation. A particularly powerful incentive for compliance is the establishment of a fund to provide the financial means for national implementation measures.[67]

H. *Institutional Supervision Under the Emerging Global Waste Management Regime*

8. The Basel Convention

The existing and emerging institutional mechanism of the Basel Convention, outlined briefly in Chapter 2 para. 18 above, largely follows the pattern described above.[68]

The main functions of the Conference of the Parties are the continuous evaluation and review of the Convention's effectiveness; the promotion of waste-related policies and strategies; the adoption of amendments to the Convention and its annexes; and the adoption of protocols. In practice, the instrument of Conference Decision is used extensively. As discussed, parties are required to submit yearly reports on their implementation of the Convention to the Conference. These reports are made available to all party states and are discussed by the Conference. The Conference of the Parties may also expand the institutional arrangements by establishing subsidiary bodies.

The functions of the Basel Convention Secretariat are comparatively broad, as mentioned in Chapter 2 para. 18 above. The main co-ordinating function is the channelling of the information exchange required under Article 10. This function, if effectively discharged, can facilitate the implementation of the Convention by ensuring the necessary transparency: it provides the basis for the monitoring of each state's performance by the other states and the Conference of the Parties. The Secretariat also co-ordinates and facilitates co-operation between parties in accordance with Article 13, mainly by identifying sources of technical assistance, training

[67] For a more detailed discussion see Kummer, (1994b), p. 260 et seq.

[68] Cf. Kiss, in Brown Weiss, (1992b), pp. 328–9, describing the Basel Convention's institutional mechanism as one of the most advanced in terms of reporting and exchange of information.

and know-how related to environmentally sound waste management and the handling of the PIC procedure, and by identifying consultants or consulting firms qualified to assist states in the assessment of notifications, hazardous waste shipments and disposal facilities. The Secretariat is required to co-ordinate its activities with those of other international bodies. To this end it may enter into contractual agreements as appropriate. As noted in Chapter 2 para. 18 above, the Secretariat must also assist parties, on request, in identifying cases of illegal traffic, and it is required to co-operate with parties and international organizations in the provision of experts and equipment to assist parties in emergency situations.

Since its inception on an interim basis in November 1989, the Secretariat has been very active in all of these areas, in particular with respect to promoting international co-operation, training, provision of assistance to parties in various fields, and investigating means to combat illegal traffic, as noted in Chapter 2 above. The Secretariat provides substantive input and support to the work of the subsidiary bodies established under the Convention. The Conference of the Parties, besides continuously elaborating on the tasks of the Secretariat, also allocates new tasks to it: an example is the development of an electronic information system and integrated telecommunications network, mentioned in Chapter 2 above. Due to perpetual financial constraints, however, some Secretariat activities are carried out on a restricted basis.[69]

The Convention provides for the possibility of international organizations and NGOs contributing to its implementation, both as observers at meetings of the Conference of the Parties and by co-operation with the Secretariat (Articles 15(6), 16(1.b), (1.d).[70] Both these options are being actively pursued. Many of the activities of the Secretariat are carried out in co-operation with interested organizations. An example is the conclusion in 1994 of a Memorandum of Understanding with UNITAR on co-operation in training activities related to the implementation of the Convention by party states. At the second meeting of the Conference of the Parties, twelve UN agencies, seven international organizations, and fifteen environmental and industrial NGOs were represented as observers. Through aggressive campaigning both within and outside the Conference of the Parties, Greenpeace International played an instrumental part in the adoption, in

[69] For an overview of relevant Secretariat activities see e.g. *Note of the Secretariat to the 1st Conference of the Parties on International Co-operation*, 1 September 1992, (UNEP/CHW.1/15); Docs. UNEP/CHW.1/7 (7 July 1992) and UNEP/CHW.1/7/Add.1 (15 September 1992); *Note of the Secretariat to the 2nd meeting of the Conference of the Parties*, 2 December 1993, (UNEP/CHW.2/20); Conference Decisions I/20 (1992), II/18 and II/20 (1994).

[70] For a discussion of the role of NGOs in the implementation of treaties cf. Handl, (1990), p. 18; Clapp, (1994), p. 18 et seq.

1994, of Decision II/12 banning the transboundary movement of hazardous wastes from OECD to non-OECD countries.

In accordance with its mandate, the Conference of the Parties at its first meeting in November–December 1992 established a number of subsidiary bodies (see Chapter 2 above). The open-ended Ad Hoc Committee on Implementation was set up to develop further the recommendations of the Ad Hoc Working Group on implementation, convened by the (then) Interim Secretariat in early 1992, on the adoption of implementation mechanisms in accordance with Article 15(5.e) and Resolution 1 of the Basel Conference.[71] Among other things, the Committee was mandated to investigate the possibility of establishing regional training centres for hazardous waste management in accordance with Article 14(1) of the Basel Convention. The Committee was also charged with other functions related to the implementation of the Convention, discussed elsewhere in this study, on which it has made significant progress since its inception. The Committee met for the first time in October 1993; its second meeting was held in December 1994.[72]

The Technical Working Group was established primarily to elaborate the Technical Guidelines, discussed in Chapter 2 para. 7 above. It has been allocated other tasks related to technical matters, such as the examination of problems pertaining to transboundary movements of hazardous wastes subject to recycling or recovery, and the question of the inclusion of low-level radioactive waste not covered by other regulatory systems.[73] As of March 1995, the Technical Working Group had held seven meetings.

Other bodies established or confirmed by the Conference include the Bureau, and the second Working Group on liability, which is mandated to finalize the elaboration of a protocol on liability and compensation, and to consider the establishment of international funds for emergency response and compensation (discussed in paras. 16, 19 below). As mentioned in Chapter 2 para. 19 above, a trust fund for the Basel Convention, as well as a technical co-operation trust fund to provide assistance to developing countries in technical fields, have been established.

Most of the functions and activities of the infrastructure established under the Basel Convention focus on assisting states in implementing the Convention and meeting their obligations. They should thus provide an

[71] Conference Decision I/2 (UNEP/CHW. 1/24 (1992)). See also Docs. UNEP/CHW/WG.3/1/2 (*Note of the Executive Director to the Conference*), UNEP/CHW/WG.3/1/3 (*Report on the implementation of Resolution 1*), and UNEP/CHW/WG.3/1/4 (*Report of the Ad Hoc Working Group on implementation*).

[72] On the mandate of the Ad Hoc Committee see Conference Decisions I/3, I/9, I/11, I/13, I/15, and I/19 (UNEP/CHW. 1/24 (1992)); Decisions II/4, II/10, II/16, II/17, II/19, II/26, (1994). See also the *Report of the Committee on its 1st meeting*, October 1993, (UNEP/CHW/C.1/1/9), with Committee Decisions annexed.

[73] Conference Decisions II/11, II/14, (1994).

incentive for adherence to the Convention and compliance with its provisions.

As we saw in Chapter 2(K) above, the Basel Convention does not provide an institutionalized procedure for the verification of states' compliance with their obligations, nor the imposition of sanctions for breach of the Convention, since this was not acceptable to the majority of the negotiating states. The Convention does not in fact address the consequences of such contravention. Instead, it merely gives the Secretariat a very modest competence to monitor instances of non-compliance. This was implicitly criticized by the Commission on Sustainable Development, which issued the cautiously worded suggestion that the Conference of the Parties might consider the development of non-compliance procedures for the Convention.[74]

Under the Basel Convention, national legal systems and institutions also play an important part in compliance monitoring, as we saw in Chapter 2 above. The effectiveness of the PIC system depends to a large extent on its administration by the competent national authorities to be established by parties, as already mentioned. In addition, party states are required by the Convention to adopt and enforce criminal legislation to address illegal traffic. This explicit obligation on states to penalize certain behaviour of their subjects is a rather unusual feature in international conventions on environmental protection.[75] The imposition of criminal sanctions under national law may contribute to the effective enforcement of the Convention at the national level.

9. Regional waste management systems and sectoral pollution control regimes

A virtually identical mechanism is to be established under the Bamako Convention after its entry into force. The functions of the prospective secretariat are somewhat more far-reaching, as we saw in Chapter 3 para. 6 above: they include carrying out hazardous waste audits based on information received from parties, and a stronger monitoring function in the PIC procedure. The institutional mechanisms of the Bamako Convention have not yet been developed as the Convention is not in force. The two North American bilateral agreements and the 1992 Central American

[74] *Report of the Commission on Sustainable Development*, 12 July 1994, (E/CN.17/1994/20), p. 43.

[75] On treaty provisions providing for criminal sanctions by state authorities see Kiss, in Brown Weiss, (1992b), pp. 325–6. Article VIII(1.a) of CITES also includes an obligation on states to penalize activities infringing its provisions. The role of national criminal law in the enforcement of international obligations was endorsed by UNGA Resolution 45/107 on International Co-operation for Crime Prevention and Criminal Justice in the Context of Development, (14 December 1990) (repr. in Kwiatkowska and Soons, (1993), p. 89).

Agreement do not set up an institutional mechanism. Article 39 of Lomé IV operates within the Lomé framework, which is based on the provision of assistance to the ACP states by EU members.

The provision of the Bamako Convention on verification is similar to that of the Basel Convention, as we saw in Chapter 3 para. 6 above. It is, however, somewhat stronger in that it imposes on the Secretariat the duty to 'carry out a verification of the substance of the allegation and submit a report thereof to all the Parties of this Convention' (Article 19). Like the Basel Convention, the Bamako Convention obliges states to adopt and implement criminal legislation to prevent and punish illegal traffic, as does the Central American Agreement. The two North American agreements, although not establishing international bodies with relevant competences, do expressly impose a duty of inspection (spot-checking of waste shipments) on national authorities (see Chapter 3(J) above).

Due to the special nature of the legal system and institutions of the EU, compliance supervision is considerably stronger in the case of the EU's Regulation and Directives. The Commission's functions include the supervision of member states' compliance with the EU legal system. As we saw in Chapter 4 para. 2 above, legislation addressing the hazardous waste cycle imposes extensive duties on states to submit data and reports to the Commission. It also requires national authorities to carry out inspections of installations and operations, and spot-checking of shipments. The competences of the ECJ include finding whether or not a state has complied with its obligations. In the event of alleged non-compliance, action can be brought against the state in question by the Commission, or by other member states.[76] Compliance monitoring within the OECD relies almost exclusively on the exchange of information and scientific data, consultation, and review of states' performance by intergovernmental and subsidiary bodies. There is no judicial review. The emphasis is on mutual assistance and political pressure rather than sanctions.[77]

The institutional mechanisms of the sectoral pollution control treaties also follow the pattern discussed. The institutional mechanism of the London Convention relies to a large extent on subsidiary bodies and working groups. To a varying degree, the conventions concluded within the UNEP Regional Seas Programme establish networks of specialist bodies in addition to the conference of the parties and the secretariat. The most advanced example of this is the Mediterranean Action Plan. The Oslo/Paris and Helsinki Conventions establish Commissions with supervisory and

[76] Treaty of Rome, Articles 155, 169–71. For a detailed discussion of institutional supervision within the EU see Audretsch, (1987), p. 840 et seq. (also discussing the functioning of this system in practice); Krämer, (1992), pp. 218–28 (concluding that compliance monitoring and enforcement is often insufficient in practice); also Mathijsen, (1990), p. 71; Slynn, (1984), p. 409 et seq.

[77] For a discussion see Audretsch, (1987), p. 845 et seq.

advisory functions, in which all parties are represented. As in the case of the Basel Convention regime, the verification procedures are not well developed in the sectoral pollution control treaties. The focus of the institutional frameworks is on facilitation of implementation.

This overview shows that the institutional mechanisms established under the emerging global waste management regime, in common with most other environmental treaty regimes, place the emphasis on the provision of assistance and incentives to states in the implementation of the relevant treaties (notably technical and financial assistance, and training), and the increase of transparency through exchange of information and reporting, rather than on active compliance monitoring and sanctions against parties found to be in breach of the treaties.

I. *The Contribution of Institutional Supervision to the Achievement of the Objectives: Strengths and Weaknesses*

In comparison with state responsibility and state liability, the mechanism of institutional supervision in the form described above has obvious advantages.[78] As a non-confrontational mechanism, it is more easily acceptable to states. This effect is enhanced where the relevant procedure is informal and flexible.[79] The emphasis on transparency as a basis for compliance monitoring, on the one hand, and on the support of states in their efforts to implement the rules, on the other, favours the preventive approach addressed above. This is an advance on state responsibility and civil liability, both of which focus on remedies.[80] Through political pressure, the discussion of reports submitted by states and the adoption of non-binding guidelines and standards of behaviour by the institution can induce compliance by states before damage has been sustained. Such 'collective or community supervision' is enhanced considerably if the meetings of the relevant body are open to IGOs and NGOs.[81] The institution's role of facilitating access to—or actively providing—technical and financial assistance and information can both provide an incentive for compliance, and enhance states' capability to comply. This is especially important in the case of developing countries lacking the necessary infrastructure and expertise.[82]

Institutional supervision is not contingent on the infringement of specific

[78] Cf. Boyle, (1991), p. 230 et seq.

[79] This point is made by Audretsch, (1987), p. 848 et seq., in the context of the OECD's review process.

[80] On this point cf. Sachariev, (1991), p. 32 et seq.; Könz, in Brown Weiss, (1992b), p. 165; Kiss and Hassan, in Sand, (1992), p. 34.

[81] Boyle, (1991), p. 231; also Sachariev, (1991), p. 33. Cf. also Morgenstern, (1986), p. 91 et seq.

[82] For a more thorough discussion of the role of incentives as opposed to sanctions in environmental treaty systems see Kummer, (1994b), p. 259 et seq.

rights of a state or individual: in this sense, it is better adjusted to the implementation of modern environmental regimes than the traditional enforcement mechanisms. Unlike state responsibility and liability, it can address holistic as well as sovereignty-based issues, which is important in the context of the Basel Convention regime. The fulfilment of the obligation of reducing the generation and transboundary movement of hazardous wastes, for example, can be monitored to some extent if states have the obligation to submit annual reports on the amounts of wastes generated and the number of transboundary movements in which they have been involved. At the same time, the problem is not shifted entirely to the level of the individual, and the role of the state as guarantor of private conduct is thus maintained.

At the same time, there are some equally obvious disadvantages. Unlike state responsibility, which is primarily based on customary law, institutional supervision is established exclusively through conventions. It is therefore only effective for those states that have voluntarily submitted to it by becoming parties to the relevant convention, and only to the extent on which the parties have agreed. The competences accorded to international institutions usually represent the lowest common denominator, which accounts for their often very limited extent.[83] The absence or weakness of competences of inspection, verification, independent decision-making, and imposition of sanctions on offenders is the most serious drawback of this mechanism.[84] It is the result of the notorious absence of political will to hand over such powers to international institutions, combined with the fact that institutions having the relevant powers would be very costly to set up and maintain, since they would require extensive personnel, infrastructure, equipment and technical expertise. For this last reason, many industrialized countries and UNEP in fact opposed proposals by African states, during the negotiations on the Basel Convention, to set up an institution with more extensive competence (see Chapter 2 para. 18 above).

As the absence of real enforcement powers may seriously hamper the successful implementation of the global waste management regime, it is regrettable that this issue has not as yet been included in the agenda of the Basel Convention's open-ended Ad Hoc Committee on Implementation (para. 8 above), and it is to be hoped that this will be remedied in the longer term. One option would be the establishment—either within the framework of the Basel Convention, or jointly by the organizations currently administering the legal instruments constituting the emerging global waste management regime—of a new institution, along the lines advocated in the 1989 Hague Declaration in the context of climate change. The prospective institution

[83] See Könz, in Brown Weiss, (1992b), p. 175 et seq.; Teclaff and Teclaff, (1991), p. 211.

[84] Cf. Timoshenko, in Brown Weiss, (1992b), p. 437 et seq.; Springer, (1983), p. 33; also Kiss, in Kalshoven, Kuyper, and Lammers, (1980), pp. 111–12.

was proposed to have the power to adopt, by majority voting, decisions which would be binding on states.[85] Important competences to be accorded to such an institution should include, in particular, the independent inspection of waste carriers and waste disposal sites (e.g. in the form of spot-checking as provided by the two North American agreements and the EU legislation); and the imposition of an obligation to remedy any shortcomings, and/or penalties.[86] It could, of course, be argued that these functions can more easily be carried out by national institutions established by parties in accordance with their own legal systems (e.g. spot-checking by specially trained customs officials). This is the approach taken under CITES.[87] However, in the case of hazardous waste management, this is very difficult for the majority of states, especially developing and transitional countries, due to lack of infrastructure and expertise. Besides, international control would be absent if this function were entrusted entirely to national legal systems. National infrastructures would obviously have to supplement the international body.

If such an institution were to be established, a judicial mechanism should be set up within the framework of the global waste management regime, before which decisions of the institution could be contested. This approach underlies the concept of the International Tribunal for the Law of the Sea, to be established under UNCLOS (Articles 287 et seq, Annex VI), and the proposal of the 1989 Hague Declaration.[88] An alternative could be the establishment of a judicial mechanism for environmental disputes at the global level, to which private operators would have access, similar to the existing human rights courts. The establishment of an international court competent for environmental matters, either in the form of special chambers of the ICJ (in accordance with Article 26 of the ICJ Statute), or of an International Court of Justice for the Environment, has in fact been discussed in various contexts.[89]

Additional shortcomings of the current form of institutional supervision directly concern the reporting procedures. From a practical point of view, such procedures are easy to circumvent. In fact, the record of reporting is

[85] Declaration of the Hague, 10 March 1989 (repr. in Churchill and Freestone, (1991), p. 318).

[86] Cf. Kimball, in ODIL 20(1989), p. 155, quoted by Handl, (1990), p. 19 (suggesting that inspection be entrusted to environmental NGOs); Abrams, (1990), p. 834 (advocating the inclusion of an obligation of spot-checking into the Basel Convention).

[87] Cf. Forster and Osterwoldt, in Sand, (1992), pp. 79, 82.

[88] Cf. Brown Weiss, (1992b), in particular the chapters by Könz and Timoshenko; Magraw, in Magraw, (1991), ch. 1.

[89] See Rest, (1991), p. 135 et seq. (on the relevant discussions of the UN/ECE Task Force on Responsibility and Liability Regarding Transboundary Water Pollution); Szasz, in Brown Weiss, (1992b), p. 368, and Timoshenko, ibid, p. 449 (noting that the ICJ itself considered the establishment of an environmental chamber); also Könz, ibid, p. 167 et seq.; Kiss, ibid, pp. 328–9. On the role of the ICJ in environmental disputes cf. Jennings, (1992), p. 312 et seq.

poor under many of the treaties establishing such a system (including the Basel Convention, as noted above).[90] In addition, the pressure to comply is very limited: the only consequence of non-compliance is a negative impact on public relations. In discussing the reports submitted by party states, the institution will often be reluctant to point out any individual party's failure to comply in too blatant terms, as the party states represented will want to avoid damaging diplomatic relations with the state in question. This shortcoming is somewhat mitigated if the meetings of the institution are open to NGOs, who are independent of states and are therefore more critical. A better way of addressing this problem would be to entrust compliance monitoring to an institution with greater independence from the party states than is given to the typical conference of the parties.[91]

In conclusion, it can be said that institutional supervision in its present predominant form favours the first of the aims set out above: the prevention of damage. In this, it provides a new and important approach, as opposed to traditional mechanisms focusing on remedy for breach of obligations. Unless institutions are given real enforcement powers, it does not, however, address at all the issues of remedying the situation and compensating the victims, which is the second aim; or of directing the costs to the actual or potential polluter, which is the third aim. Thus, like state responsibility and liability, this mechanism on its own would hardly provide a useful solution to the problem. Combined with other mechanisms, however, it can make an important contribution to the achievement of the first aim, i.e. the prevention of damage.

CIVIL LIABILITY AND COMPULSORY INSURANCE

J. *The Emergence of International Civil Liability Regimes: Precedents for the Global Waste Management Regime*

International rules on civil liability for environmental damage amount to a unification of national law through international treaties.[92] By providing a regulatory framework for the liability of private operators for damage caused to individuals in other states, the issue is transferred from the inter-

[90] e.g. CITES (see Forster and Osterwoldt, in Sand, (1992), p. 82), the London Convention, and MARPOL (Boyle, Freestone, Kummer, and Ong, ibid, p. 156). See also Sachariev, (1991), p. 41 et seq., and sources quoted there.

[91] Boyle, (1991), p. 245; Sachariev, (1991), p. 33 et seq.; also von Moltke, in Carroll, (1988), p. 90 et seq.

[92] The following information on regimes of civil liability and compulsory insurance is drawn in part from an unpublished consultant's report on the establishment of an international fund, submitted to the Interim Secretariat of the Basel Convention in 1991 (on file with the author) (*Consultant's Report on a Compensation Fund*, (1991)).

state level to the private level.[93] At the same time, such unification serves to overcome procedural and substantive obstacles to the submission of claims in the national courts of the 'source' state by victims resident in the 'recipient' state; such obstacles necessarily arise out of differences between the national legal systems.[94] Significant progress has been made in the adoption of international conventions on civil liability in the last decades,[95] particularly in the fields of the management of radioactive substances[96] and marine pollution by oil.[97] More recent efforts have been aimed at the development of international legal instruments on civil liability for damage caused by the transport of dangerous goods, and for environmental damage in general: negotiations are in progress within the framework of the IMO on an International Convention on Liability and Compensation for Damage in Connection with the Carriage of Hazardous and Noxious Substances by Sea (HNS Convention). In October 1989, the Convention on Civil Liability for Damage Caused during the Carriage of Dangerous Goods by Road, Rail and Inland Navigation Vessels (CRTD Convention) was adopted under the auspices of the UN/ECE, and the Lugano Convention on Civil Liability for Damage Resulting from Activities Dangerous to the Environment was adopted under the auspices of the Council of Europe in June 1993. Neither of these legal instruments had entered into force as of November 1994.[98] A meeting of legal experts was convened in November 1994 to discuss the development of civil liability rules under the 1991 Protocol on environmental protection in the Antarctic. The Commission of the EU in May 1993 submitted a Green Paper on

[93] Cf. Kiss, (1989a), pp. 117–18; Boyle, in Francioni and Scovazzi, (1991), p. 367 et seq.

[94] For a discussion of these obstacles cf. Kiss, (1989a), pp. 118–22; McCaffrey, in Handl and Lutz, (1989a), p. 199 et seq.

[95] For an overview of existing legal instruments cf. *La réparation des dommages catastrophiques*, (1990), Annexes. Cf. also Roelants du Vivier, ibid, p. 417 et seq.; Kiss, (1989a), p. 122 et seq.; Rest, (1992), p. 32. An analysis of the effectiveness of the most important liability conventions is given by Doeker and Gehring, in Sand, (1992), p. 392 et seq.

[96] 1960 Paris Convention on Third Party Liability in the Field of Nuclear Energy; 1963 Vienna Convention on Civil Liability for Nuclear Damage (and 1988 Joint Protocol); 1971 Brussels Convention Relating to Civil Liability in the Field of Maritime Carriage of Nuclear Material; 1962 Brussels Convention on the Liability of Operators of Nuclear Ships (all repr. in *Selected Multilateral Treaties in the Field of the Environment*, Vols. 1, 2). For a discussion see Politi, in *La réparation des dommages catastrophiques*, (1990), pp. 319–37, in particular p. 330.

[97] 1969 Brussels Convention on Civil Liability for Oil Pollution Damage (as amended); 1971 Fund Convention; 1977 London Convention on Civil Liability for Damage Resulting from Exploration and Exploitation of Seabed Mineral Resources (all repr. in *Selected Multilateral Treaties in the Field of the Environment*, Vol. 1). On the 1969 and 1971 Conventions see Kiss, (1989a), p. 123; also Redgwell, (1992), p. 90 et seq.

[98] Draft HNS Convention, 18 May 1993, (IMO Doc. LEG69/3) (see also the report of the IMO Legal Committee on its 71st session, 13 October 1994, (IMO Doc. LEG71/WP.1); CRTD Convention, 10 October 1989, (Doc. ECE/TRANS/79) (see the discussion by Lang, in Lang, Neuhold, and Zemanek, (1991), p. 158 et seq.); Lugano Convention, 21 June 1993, (*European Treaty Series* no. 150).

Remedying Environmental Damage.[99] In addition, many environmental treaties as well as non-binding rules call upon states to develop rules on civil liability in an international context.[100]

The concepts and structure of the existing and proposed treaties on civil liability are very similar. They set out fairly concise and comprehensive rules. Practically all liability conventions include the following concepts: strict liability, channelling of liability, a financial limitation and a time limitation of liability, a requirement of compulsory insurance, and a procedure for civil claims in national courts.[101]

10. Strict or absolute liability

Under a strict liability regime, as adopted by most existing conventions, an operator or other person is liable for damage regardless of whether or not he is at fault. Most conventions provide the possibility of exoneration for all or several of the following reasons: *force majeure*; distress; act of war, insurrection, or hostilities; intentional or negligent conduct of the victim as sole cause of the damage; wilful act of a third person as sole cause of the damage. A small number of conventions establish a regime of absolute liability, not providing for exoneration, or only to a very limited extent. From the point of view of the victims of pollution, this approach is a strong point of the existing civil liability conventions. Strict or absolute liability favours the position of the victim of pollution, as opposed to fault-based liability: in addition to the existence of the damage and the causal link with the operator's action, the victim must, under a regime of fault-based liability, prove a fault on the part of the operator. Failure to provide such proof results in the victim effectively bearing the costs of reparation.

11. Channelling of liability or joint and several liability

In the allocation of liability, there are two basic options: channelling the liability to one person, or establishing joint and several liability of several persons. Practically all existing conventions opt for the first solution. Liability is channelled to a single clearly identifiable person, who is usually

[99] Communication from the Commission to the Council and Parliament and the Economic and Social Committee: Green Paper on Remedying Environmental Damage, May 1993, (COM(93)47) (EU Green Paper).

[100] e.g. Principle 22 of the Stockholm Declaration, Principle 13 of the Rio Declaration, and various UNEP Guidelines and Principles, UNCLOS, Article 235(2), as well as most sectoral treaties dealing with marine pollution. For examples see Boyle, in Francioni and Scovazzi, (1991), p. 367.

[101] A detailed overview of the ruling principles of existing liability conventions and important draft conventions is given in UNEP, *Annotations to the elements to be included in a protocol on liability under the Basel Convention*, 15 May 1990, (UNEP/CHW/WG.1/INF.3) (UNEP, Annotations); see also EU Green Paper, May 1993, (COM(93)47).

also in control of the activity, and has the strongest economic interest in it. That person has recourse to other operators under certain circumstances. In the case of waste management and transport, the person liable could be the generator, the exporter, the carrier, the importer, the disposer, or the person having control of the waste at a given moment. Channelling has the advantage of greater clarity and simplicity, and is in most cases consistent with the polluter pays principle. On the other hand, it has the disadvantage of allowing the claimant to address only one potentially liable person. This is especially problematic if that person proves to be elusive, or unable to raise the funds to provide compensation. In the context of hazardous waste management, this is quite probable in cases of illegal traffic. In this instance, joint and several liability of the operators listed above would more adequately ensure compensation of the victim.

12. Definition of damage

An increasing number of relevant conventions adopt a fairly comprehensive definition of damage, including not only quantifiable economic loss, but also damage to the environment.[102] The latter usually covers the costs of measures of reinstatement, sometimes extending to monetary compensation in cases where reinstatement is not possible or practical. It also covers preventive measures taken to prevent further deterioration of the affected ecosystem.

13. Limitations of liability

A financial ceiling is a common feature in existing liability conventions, even though a few treaties provide for unlimited liability. This concept is also adhered to by a number of national liability regimes, particularly in European countries.[103] In order to prevent the ceiling from becoming impracticably low due to inflation, a flexible system based on the Special Drawing Right defined by the IMF is often used. Some conventions admit the operator's right to limit his liability only under certain conditions (e.g. if the damage is not the result of his personal act or omission), or make it contingent upon his establishing a fund in the total amount for which he is potentially liable in accordance with the financial limit.[104]

By establishing an upper financial limit to the compensation to be paid

[102] See for example the 1989 CRTD Convention; the 1993 Lugano Convention; and the draft HNS Convention.

[103] Examples of conventions providing for unlimited liability are the 1972 Convention on International Liability for Damage caused by Space Objects (cf. Spinedi, in Francioni and Scovazzi, (1991), p. 104); and the 1993 Lugano Convention. On national regimes see *Responses to UNEP Questionnaire*, 15 May 1990, (UNEP/CHW/WG.1/INF.1).

[104] e.g. the 1969 Brussels Convention and the 1989 CRTD Convention.

by the polluter, the interests of persons carrying out potentially hazardous but economically desirable activities are protected: the ceiling averts the possibility of the consequences of the activity becoming so expensive as to be virtually prohibitive. It also makes it easier for the operator to obtain insurance coverage. From the point of view of the victim, this has a problematical aspect: any damage that goes beyond the ceiling will be borne by the victim, in particular if the ceiling is set considerably lower than the potential amount of compensation necessary.[105]

Most conventions also provide a time limit beyond which a claim against the operator is no longer admissible.

14. Compulsory insurance or other financial guarantee

The obligation on persons carrying out a potentially dangerous activity to obtain insurance coverage or other financial guarantee is set out in a number of liability conventions. The provisions usually specify a minimum amount of coverage (floor). The choice of the form of financial security to be provided is sometimes left to the potentially liable operator so as to impinge on his economic freedom as little as possible. Some conventions set out an obligation on the state to verify insurance coverage as a condition for the authorization of the hazardous activity.[106]

The ratio of requiring compulsory insurance is clearly to give substance to the operator's obligation of providing financial compensation in the event of damage being caused by his activities, by assuring the availability of sufficient financial means. At the same time, the floor allows the expenditure to be kept within certain limits. As in the case of financial limitation of liability, this may mean that part of the costs will be borne by the victim. A possible side-effect of this form of regulation is the provision of an incentive to operators to comply with the applicable national or international safety standards: in order to obtain insurance on reasonable terms, the operator must demonstrate to the insurer that he has minimized the risks by adhering to the applicable standards.

15. Unified procedural rules, equal access, and mutual recognition of court decisions

The conventions provide that the national courts of the parties are competent for the adjudication of claims, and establish a unified procedure. They

[105] Cf. Springer, Commentary on the chapter by Zemanek, in Lang, Neuhold, and Zemanek, (1991), p. 201.

[106] e.g. the 1989 CRTD Convention, the draft HNS Convention, the 1993 Lugano Convention; and the draft Directive on liability for damage caused by waste, proposed by the EU Commission (para. 17 below). On the function of insurance in international conventions see Deprimoz, in *La réparation des dommages catastrophiques*, (1990), p. 103 et seq. Cf. Saxer, (1990), p. 175 et seq.; Krämer, in *La réparation des dommages catastrophiques*, (1990), p. 413.

either provide for exclusive jurisdiction of one state (usually either the state where the incident occurred, or the state where the damage was sustained), or give a choice of fora in which the claim can be submitted. From the point of view of the victim, this latter solution is undoubtedly the most advantageous, as it provides the option of seeking out the state whose legislation is the most favourable. The conventions provide for equal access to the courts of the parties by nationals of other party states,[107] and mutual recognition and enforcement of judgments among the parties. These elements of civil liability conventions are very important in overcoming otherwise significant procedural obstacles to the submission of a claim by an individual in a foreign court.

K. *Civil Liability Under the Global Waste Management Regime*

16. The proposed liability protocol to the Basel Convention

In accordance with Article 12 of the Basel Convention, work is underway to develop a global civil liability regime for transboundary movements of hazardous wastes.[108] In response to Resolution 3 of the 1989 Basel Conference and a 1989 Resolution of the UN General Assembly,[109] a first Working Group of experts was convened in 1990 under the auspices of UNEP to elaborate draft elements for inclusion in a protocol on liability and compensation. This Working Group held two sessions in 1990 and 1991, attended by experts from sixty one countries.[110] Based on the draft elements elaborated by the Group, the (then) Interim Secretariat of the Basel Convention prepared a set of draft articles of a liability protocol,[111] which was discussed by the first meeting of the Conference of the Parties in November–December 1992. The Conference established a second Working

[107] For a definition of the right of equal access see the OECD Council Recommendation on Equal Right of Access in Relation to Transfrontier Pollution (C(76)55 final), and the *OECD Environment Committee's Report on the right of equal access*; also OECD Council Recommendations C(74)224 and C(77)28 (all repr. in OECD, (1977)). A far-reaching system of equal access is provided by the 1974 Nordic Convention on the Protection of the Environment.

[108] For an overview of this work see the relevant *Report by the Executive Director of UNEP to the 1st Conference of the Parties to the Basel Convention*, 7 July 1992, (UNEP/CHW.1/2); the *Note of the Executive Director on the Implementation of Resolution 3*, 7 July 1992, (UNEP/CHW.1/4), and the *Note by the Secretariat to the 2nd meeting of the Conference of the Parties*, 1 December 1993 (UNEP/CHW.2/3).

[109] UNGA Resolution 44/226 on Traffic in and Disposal, Control and Transboundary Movements of Toxic and Dangerous Products and Wastes, 22 December 1989, (repr. in Kwiatkowska and Soons, (1993), p. 84).

[110] *Report on the 1st session*, Geneva, 2–6 July 1990 (UNEP/CHW/WG.1/3 (6 July 1990)); *Report on the 2nd session*, Nairobi, 6–9 March 1991 (UNEP/CHW/WG.1/2/3 (14 March 1991)).

[111] *Note of the Secretariat*, 7 July 1992, (UNEP/CHW.1/5). Cf. also Conference Docs. UNEP/CHW/WG.1/2, UNEP/CHW/WG. 1/4, UNEP/CHW/WG.1/8, (1992).

Group to continue and complete the work.[112] As of March 1995, this Group had held three meetings (September 1993, October 1994, and February 1995). Work is progressing slowly due to controversies over numerous issues. It is clear at this point that the tentative aim of finalizing the protocol by the autumn of 1995, set by the Conference of the Parties at its second meeting in March 1994, will not be met.[113] Work will have to continue after the third meeting of the Conference of the parties in September 1995.

When elaborating the draft liability elements, the first Working Group relied strongly on the concepts of existing liability conventions, as well as on elements contained in national legislation. It also decided to co-ordinate its work with that of other organizations, in particular the Council of Europe and the IMO (see paras. 10–15 above). Accordingly, most of the above concepts were included in the draft elements elaborated by the Group. The draft protocol in its present form, provisionally agreed by the second Working Group at its third session, leaves open many of the crucial issues. It can therefore hardly be considered indicative of the final outcome. A brief outline of emerging trends is given in the following paragraphs.

The objective of the future protocol is determined in Article 1 of the draft as follows: 'to provide for a comprehensive regime for liability and for adequate and prompt compensation, including reinstatement of the environment, for damage resulting from the transboundary movement of hazardous wastes and other wastes and their disposal'. In addition to loss of life, personal injury, and loss of or damage to property, 'damage' as defined by the draft protocol includes impairment of the environment, and loss of profit due to such impairment. It also includes the costs of preventive measures, and loss resulting from such measures. The future protocol should cover damage caused by hazardous wastes from the moment the transboundary movement commences to the completion of their disposal. Compensation is to be limited to the costs of reinstatement measures actually undertaken. The situation with regard to irreparable environmental damage remains to be determined.

Regarding the person liable, the current preference is for joint and several liability of various operators, with the right of recourse expressly reserved. The principal options under consideration place liability either on all persons involved in a transaction, or on the principal operators, including the generator and the exporter. In this context, a number of problems remain to be resolved, including the allocation of damages where more than

[112] Conference Decision I/5 (UNEP/CHW.1/24 (1992)).

[113] Conference Decision II/1 (1994); *Report of the 2nd Working Group on Liability on its 1st meeting*, 16 September 1993, (UNEP/CHW.1/WG.1/1/5); and *Report on its 2nd meeting*, 24 October 1994, (UNEP/CHW.1/WG.1/2/4); *Report on its 3rd meeting*, 3 March 1995 (UNEP/CHW.1/WG.1/3/2, with draft protocol as Annex).

one person is liable, and liability for damage caused by a mixture of wastes subject to the protocol and wastes not subject to the protocol.

The draft protocol proposes a regime of strict liability: exoneration clauses include armed conflict, civil war or insurrection that was not reasonably foreseeable; natural phenomena of an exceptional, inevitable and irresistible character; and wrongful intentional conduct of a third party as the sole cause of damage. Additional exclusion clauses are under consideration. Compensation may be reduced or disallowed if the victim has caused or contributed to the damage by his own fault. It has been proposed that if the damage is due to illegal traffic, no exoneration is to be permitted, but there is as yet no agreement on this point. The issue of public interest litigation is not under consideration.

Unlike the majority of the existing conventions, the proposed protocol does not at present provide for a financial ceiling on liability; this is not uncontested, however. A time limit is envisaged but remains to be determined. It has been proposed that no time limit should apply in the case of damage resulting from illegal traffic. Compulsory insurance is envisaged, as already called for in the Basel Convention (Article 6(11)). The determination of a floor and a ceiling is under discussion.

Subsidiary mechanisms are provisionally envisaged to ensure the availability of resources to the extent that compensation under the civil liability regime is insufficient or unavailable: on the one hand, state responsibility or liability is being considered as a subsidiary mechanism,[114] and on the other, the establishment of an international hazardous waste compensation fund and an emergency fund are under discussion (see below). Both these options are very contentious, however.

The draft protocol provisionally provides for a choice of forum to be given to the claimant, equal access to national courts, and mutual recognition of judgments. Matters of substance and procedure are to be governed by national law. A number of procedural questions are still under discussion. Efforts have been made to determine the relationship between the future protocol and other pertinent international agreements, with various alternatives under consideration.

As is evident from this brief overview, work on a civil liability protocol to the Basel Convention is still at an early stage, and many questions remain to be resolved. Since the discussion on some of the more contentious issues has started in earnest only within the framework of the second Working Group, the current draft is in some ways more undetermined than the previous ones. This situation is by no means exceptional, however: practically all treaties on civil liability for environmental damage that were negotiated in the 1980s and 1990s took years to complete, and none of them

[114] See *Note of the Secretariat on state liability as a possible element of a regime on civil liability*, 12 July 1993, (UNEP/CHW.1/WG.1/1/3).

has as yet entered into force. In view of this, the fairly ambitious schedule envisaged by the Conference of the Parties will have to be subject to adjustment.

17. Other existing and emerging liability provisions under the global waste management regime

The two North American bilateral agreements do not address the question of civil liability, apart from the provision of the USA–Mexico agreement, already mentioned, which requires the state of export to endeavour to ensure remedial action or payment of compensation by the operator. However, an interesting feature of these agreements in the present context is that they allow the state of import to require evidence of insurance coverage as a condition of entry (USA–Mexico agreement, Article XIV; Canada–USA agreement, Article 9).

The Bamako Convention requires parties to impose 'unlimited as well as joint and several liability on hazardous waste generators' in the context of waste transactions within Africa, and calls for the establishment of a working group to develop relevant rules, similar to the Basel Convention (Articles 4(3), 12). This has not been followed up, as the Convention is not yet in force.

Within the EU, a draft Directive on civil liability for damage caused by waste is under consideration,[115] although relevant work seems to have come to a standstill since 1991. The focus is now on the elaboration of civil liability rules in a wider context, with the Commission's Green Paper, referred to above, as a basis for discussion. The draft liability Directive for waste is worth a short analysis, however. Its declared aims are to apply the polluter pays principle, and to harmonize national rules within the EU in order to avoid market distortions. The draft Directive envisages strict liability of the waste producer from the moment of the generation of the wastes to the time of the lawful transfer to an authorized treatment or disposal facility, with the usual exonerations. Subsidiary liability of other operators is envisaged under certain circumstances, e.g. if the generator cannot be identified within a reasonable period of time. In such cases, joint and several liability is proposed. The concept of damage is limited to damage to persons and property, but is supplemented by a separate concept, 'impairment of the environment', which is defined as 'any significant physical, chemical or biological deterioration of the environment . . .'.

[115] *Commission Proposal for a Council Directive on Civil Liability for Damage Caused by Waste*, 15 September 1989, (COM(89)282 final–SYN217); and amended proposal, 27 June 1991, (COM(91) 219 final–SYN217 (EU Draft Liability Directive, (1991)); see in particular the *Explanatory Memorandum*. See also Krämer, in *La réparation des dommages catastrophiques*, (1990), p. 407.

Preventive measures are not included in either concept. There is to be no financial ceiling to liability, as this was considered by the Commission to be contrary to the polluter pays principle. A requirement for insurance or other financial security was introduced in 1991 pursuant to a proposal by the European Parliament. The form of such guarantee may be chosen by the producer. A significant advance on other civil liability regimes is the proposed establishment of a form of public interest litigation: the right to institute proceedings is to be accorded not only to victims in the traditional sense, but also to common interest groups whose object is environmental protection, provided that they satisfy criteria to be determined by the member states.

Under the sectoral pollution control regimes discussed in Chapter 5 above, little concrete work has yet been done in the area of civil liability. A Task Force established by the UN/ECE has elaborated Guidelines on Responsibility and Liability Regarding Transboundary Water Pollution.[116] Progress on the draft HNS Convention has been rather slow, although it is now hoped to be finalized in 1996.[117] Plans to develop a liability protocol to the London Convention in accordance with the mandate contained in that treaty have been postponed pending the completion of the work on the Basel Convention protocol and the 1993 Lugano Convention, in order to ensure co-ordination with those instruments.[118]

L. *The Contribution of the Civil Liability Regimes to the Achievement of the Objectives: Strengths and Weaknesses*

In comparison with the mechanisms that rely chiefly on the role of the state as guarantor of private conduct, civil liability regimes have the advantage of giving the victim a direct influence on the proceedings, and transferring at least some of the financial consequences of environmental damage from states to private parties who have direct control over the hazardous activities, as well as an economic interest in them.[119] This can, to a certain extent, serve as an incentive for private operators to minimize the risks by compliance with the relevant rules, and thus further the first aim outlined above.[120] On the other hand, the focus on the obligations of private

[116] Repr. in Hohmann, (1992), Vol. 1, p. 310; discussed by Rest, in EPL 21/3/4(1991) p. 135, and idem, in EPL 22/1(1992) p. 31 et seq.

[117] *Report of the IMO Legal Committee on its 71st session*, October 1994, (IMO Doc. LEG71/WP.1), p. 24.

[118] *Report of the 14th Consultative Meeting of the Contracting Parties to the London Convention*, November 1991, (IMO Doc. LDC14/16); and *Report of the 5th Meeting of the Ad Hoc Group of Legal Experts on Dumping* (IMO Doc. LDC/LG5/10, (1991)), p. 9. See also Doeker and Gehring, in Sand, (1992), pp. 429–30.

[119] See Boyle, in Francioni and Scovazzi, (1991), p. 368; also Könz, in Brown Weiss, (1992b), p. 168.

[120] Könz, in Brown Weiss, (1992b), p. 167. For an opposing view see Kiss, (1989a), p. 131.

operators can diminish the incentive to states to comply with their international obligations. It is for this reason that some regimes, among them the proposed liability protocol to the Basel Convention, consider state responsibility as a subsidiary mechanism to civil liability.

To a certain extent, the use of national legal institutions and procedures, combined with the establishment of uniform international rules, gives the state a role in ensuring compliance by individuals, while at the same time taking account of national differences. However, the reliance on national legal institutions and procedures can also prove a weakness: procedural obstacles and the costs of litigation can make it difficult for the victim to obtain compensation, even though this problem is to a certain extent remedied by the civil liability conventions.[121] Long delays in national judicial procedures can result in considerable financial loss. In the case of the *Amoco Cadiz* oil spill in 1978, for example, compensation was awarded by the court over 10 years after the accident occurred.[122] As in the case of state responsibility, procedural problems can thus impede or delay remedial action. This problem is aggravated if the defendant is a multinational enterprise, as in the case of the Bhopal disaster.[123] Also, as with institutional supervision, civil liability regimes only apply if the states involved in an incident are parties to the legal instruments in question. In a case where parties and non-party states are involved, the applicability of a civil liability convention can depend on the forum in which a claim is submitted.

From a conceptual viewpoint, civil liability regimes also share some of the weaknesses inherent in state responsibility: they focus on the relationship between 'polluter' and 'victim', and they can only address situations where there is clearly defined damage, and a victim whose rights have been infringed. Compliance with holistic obligations, such as waste minimization or environmentally sound waste management, cannot be addressed through civil liability regimes, nor can damage to global commons be redressed.[124] This defect could be remedied to a certain extent by the introduction of public interest litigation, as proposed by the draft EU Directive discussed above. Also, despite providing a certain incentive to private operators to

[121] Kiss, (1989a), p. 118 et seq. A thorough analysis not only of procedural but also of factual obstacles to the provision of timely and adequate compensation of victims is given by McCaffrey, in Handl and Lutz, (1989a), p. 199 et seq., using the Bhopal disaster as an example. See also Könz, in Brown Weiss, (1992b), p. 168 et seq., noting that differences in the judicial systems can lead to 'forum shopping', as happened in the *Bhopal* and *Amoco Cadiz* cases.

[122] Kiss, (1989a), pp. 127–30, giving a detailed anaylsis of the *Amoco Cadiz* case; also Smets, in *La réparation des dommages catastrophiques*, (1990), pp. 26, 29–30.

[123] Cf. Könz, in Brown Weiss, (1992b), p. 169 et seq.

[124] Cf. the EU Green Paper, May 1993, (COM(93)47), giving an interesting analysis of this problem; also Kiss, (1989a), p. 131; Könz, in Brown Weiss, (1992b), pp. 162–3. For an extensive analysis of the weaknesses inherent in resorting to national civil liability rules, and proposals to strengthen this remedy, cf. McCaffrey, in Handl and Lutz, (1989a), p. 199 et seq.

comply with relevant rules, civil liability focuses strongly on remedial rather than preventive action, as does state responsibility.

Civil liability regimes generally balance the aim of protecting the victim (and, more indirectly, the environment) against that of enabling the hazardous activity, which is usually economically beneficial, to take place.[125] The concept of strict or absolute liability, possibly with a financial ceiling, coupled with compulsory insurance and the duty of the state to verify insurance coverage, clearly shows this duality of aims. On the one hand, it is a particularly useful tool for ensuring the availability of financial means to compensate the victims, and directing the costs to the potential or actual polluter, thus supporting the second and third aims outlined above.[126] Strict or absolute liability saves the victim from having to prove the polluter's failure to observe a standard of due diligence. Through compulsory insurance, it is possible to avoid a situation where financial compensation is unavailable, and the victim is left to bear the costs of reparation. The requirement of verification of insurance could easily be introduced into the Basel Convention system, e.g. by making insurance coverage a condition of authorization of a transboundary waste movement. As already mentioned, this approach is adopted by the two North American bilateral agreements. Compulsory insurance also supports the aim of spreading the costs equally among persons carrying out a hazardous activity such as the transport and management of hazardous wastes. It has been suggested that civil liability systems with a limitation of liability, and with a requirement for insurance or other financial security, do not fully implement the polluter pays principle, as they divide the costs among the industry concerned or even the victims, instead of directing them to the actual polluter.[127] As far as the victims are concerned, this is certainly true. In the case of industry sharing the costs through insurance or other compensation mechanisms, it can be argued that spreading the costs of reparation of a given damage between operators whose activities entail an equal risk to that which caused the damage is not contrary to the polluter pays principle, especially since this ensures the availability of funds for compensation of the victims.[128]

On the negative side, a financial ceiling of liability and/or a floor to compulsory insurance coverage, especially if these are unrealistically low, can mean that a substantial part of the cost is borne by the victim or by third parties. This is dramatically illustrated by the *Amoco Cadiz* oil spill: the 1969 Brussels Convention on Civil Liability for Oil Pollution Damage, in its contemporary form, would have limited the shipowner's liability to the equivalent of 77 million French francs, whereas the actual damage was estimated as exceeding one billion francs. This prompted the victims to avoid

[125] See Doeker and Gehring, in Sand, (1992), p. 393.
[126] Birnie and Boyle, (1992), p. 201.
[127] Boyle, in Francioni and Scovazzi, (1991), pp. 374–6.
[128] Cf. Saxer, (1990), p. 177.

the application of the Brussels Convention altogether by submitting their claims to an American court (the USA being the country of domicile of the shipowner, and a non-party to the Brussels Convention).[129] This weakness could be substantially reduced by establishing unlimited liability of the operator, as considered by the Basel Convention Working Group on liability and compensation, and by the EU Commission.

Finally, a practical weakness is the difficulty of reconciling conflicting interests in negotiating liability regimes, and subsequently obtaining sufficient support from states for the treaties to enter into force. This is illustrated not only by the difficult negotiations of the liability Working Group under the Basel Convention, but also by the fact that none of the recent efforts have as yet resulted in a functioning international civil liability regime, as mentioned above.

In conclusion, it can be said that civil liability regimes, especially if they provide for compulsory insurance, support the aims of reparation and ensuring availability of financial means by spreading the costs among potential polluters. Despite the limitations discussed, this is an advance on state responsibility and institutional supervision. On the other hand, they do little to further the aim of prevention, which is an important element of the Basel Convention regime.

ESTABLISHMENT OF AN INTERNATIONAL HAZARDOUS WASTE COMPENSATION FUND

M. *The Functioning of an International Fund: Precedents for the Global Waste Management Regime*

The concept of a fund, financed by contributions from potential polluters, to provide for emergency response and/or reparation of damage, exists at the international as well as the national levels.[130] At the international level, the International Oil Pollution Compensation Fund (IOPC), established under the 1971 Convention on the Establishment of an International Fund for Compensation for Oil Pollution Damage (Fund Convention), has been operational since 1978.[131] The establishment of a fund is to be considered by the contracting parties of the 1988 CRAMRA in accordance with

[129] On the *Amoco Cadiz* case see n. 122 above. See also Boyle, in Francioni and Scovazzi, (1991), p. 374 et seq.

[130] A substantive part of the following information on the concept of a compensation fund, as well as numerous ideas, are drawn from the *Consultant's Report on a Compensation Fund* (1991); see n. 92 above. For an overview of existing and proposed international funds and their characteristics see Magraw, in Handl and Lutz, (1989a), pp. 263–4; McCaffrey, ibid, pp. 233–4; Orrego Vicuña, in Brown Weiss, (1992b), pp. 156–7. See also the 1982 UNEP Guidelines on Offshore Mining and Drilling (para. 41).

[131] See Kiss, (1989a), p. 126 et seq.; also Redgwell, (1992), p. 90 et seq.

Article 8(7.c.iii). It is also envisaged under the draft HNS Convention mentioned above, with the IOPC serving as a model for a number of draft provisions. In the field of oil processing, industry has in addition set up its own funds: the 1969 Tanker Owners Voluntary Agreement Concerning Liability for Oil Pollution (TOVALOP), which covers some 90 per cent of the world's tanker fleet, and the 1971 Contract Regarding an Interim Supplement to Tanker Liability for Oil Pollution (CRISTAL).[132] The 1963 Convention Supplementary to the Paris Convention provides for the establishment by the contracting parties, at the national level, of public funds to provide compensation for nuclear damage.[133] An important example of a fund established at the national level is the United States Hazardous Substance Response Trust Fund (Superfund) established under the Comprehensive Environmental Response, Compensation and Liability Act (CERCLA), which pays response costs incurred by the Federal and State governments. Under a number of other national systems, there are similar funds.[134]

The existing and proposed international funds are established and operate in conjunction with a civil liability regime. They are either governed by the same or by a separate international legal instrument: the first of these options was chosen, for example, in the 1971 Fund Convention, the second for the Financial Scheme to be established under the draft HNS Convention. Their main objectives are to ensure adequate compensation of the victims of pollution, and to spread the financial burden among polluters.[135] They cover the same types of damage as the corresponding civil liability convention. The funds have a legal personality, which must be recognized under the national jurisdiction of all party states, and an institutional framework. In accordance with a predetermined assessment system, contributions are made to the funds by operators who are potentially liable for damage caused by the hazardous activity. States act as intermediaries by collecting and forwarding these contributions. The funds pay compensation to victims of environmental damage to the extent that this is not available under the corresponding liability regime. This can be the case if the operator's identity is not known, if he cannot be held liable, if the damage sustained exceeds the financial ceiling of the civil liability regime and/or

[132] TOVALOP, repr. in 8 ILM (1969); p. 497, CRISTAL, repr. in 10 ILM (1971) p. 137. See Doeker and Gehring, in Sand, (1992), p. 418; Kiss, (1989a), pp. 126–7.

[133] Repr. in *Selected Multilateral Treaties*, Vol. 1, p. 171.

[134] CERCLA, 42 U.S.C. para. 6901 et seq. See the American response to the UNEP questionnaire on liability and compensation, in *Responses to UNEP Questionnaire*, 15 May 1990, (UNEP/CHW/WG.1/INF.1), p. 88. See also the summaries by the Basel Convention Secretariat of government replies to various questionnaires on this subject (Docs. UNEP/CHW/WG.1/INF.2, (15 May 1990), p. 21; UNEP/CHW.1/WG.1/2/2, (12 July 1994), p. 7; UNEP/CHW/WG.1/2/INF.3, (15 September 1994)). Cf. Krämer, in *La réparation des dommages catastrophiques*, (1990), p. 409.

[135] e.g. the 1971 Fund Convention; see Doeker and Gehring, in Sand, (1992), p. 414.

the amount covered by compulsory insurance, or if the operator liable is unable to meet his financial obligations. Thus the funds provide an alternative or supplementary source of compensation. A maximum limit of compensation payable by the fund is usually determined. However, as the fund supplements civil liability, this limit is considerably higher than that of the corresponding civil liability convention. This is illustrated by the oil pollution compensation regime: the 1984 Protocol amending the 1969 Brussels Convention limits the operator's liability to 59.7 units of account per incident, whereas the amount payable by the fund is limited to 135 million (or exceptionally, 200 million) units of account per incident under the 1984 Protocol amending the 1971 Fund Convention.[136] In some cases, the funds are exonerated from their obligation to pay compensation, but exoneration is more restricted than in the case of civil liability. The conditions for payments to be made by the fund, compensation to be paid by it, and the claims procedure, are determined by the constituting legal instrument.

In addition to compensation, the funds may be given the task of providing rapid assistance in the case of environmental emergencies. Existing funds have this function to a very limited extent.[137] Similar functions are carried out by specialized institutions within the UN system, for example the UN Centre for Urgent Environmental Assistance (UNCUEA), which was incorporated into the UN Department of Humanitarian Affairs (UN/DHA) in July 1994.

N. *Establishment of a Fund Under the Basel Convention Regime*

The establishment of a 'revolving fund' to provide emergency response in the event of an accident involving hazardous wastes is based on Article 14(2) of the Basel Convention. In addition, the idea of establishing a hazardous waste compensation fund within the framework of the Basel Convention was conceived during the negotiations on the liability protocol within the first Working Group.[138] Both concepts were developed further by the (then) Interim Secretariat.[139] The first meeting of the Conference of the Parties in November–December 1992 entrusted the second Working Group on liability with the further development of these concepts.[140] Little progress on this issue has been made by the Working Group to date, and

[136] See UNEP, Annotations, (UNEP/CHW.1/INF.3).

[137] Fund Convention, Article 4(7), (8); draft HNS Convention, Article 13(k).

[138] *Report of the 1st Working Group on liability on its 2nd session*, March 1991, (UNEP/CHW/WG.1/2/3), pp. 5–6, Annex.

[139] *Note of the Executive Director on the establishment of a revolving fund to assist on an interim basis in case of an emergency situation to minimize the damage from accidents arising from transboundary movements of hazardous wastes* (UNEP/CHW.1/6); *Note of the Executive Director on the establishment of an international fund for compensation for damage resulting from the transboundary movement of hazardous wastes and their disposal* (UNEP/CHW.1/11).

[140] Conference Decisions I/5 and I/14 (UNEP/CHW.1/24 (1992)).

the proposals are still at a preliminary and incomplete stage. This is in part due to the fact that the Group devoted most of its time and effort to the elaboration of the liability protocol. It is also due to far-reaching controversies over the concept and modalities of a fund, and to the reluctance on the part of a number of states to support such a concept.[141]

Accordingly, the concept of a fund has not as yet been agreed, and it has not been decided whether it would be desirable to establish two separate funds, or whether the functions of emergency response and compensation should be carried out by the same fund. On the basis of pertinent consultations in 1991 and 1992, the Basel Convention Secretariat proposed that two funds be established initially, but that the emergency fund should operate on an interim basis, its functions later to be taken over by the compensation fund. As a basis for discussion, it also made proposals regarding the modalities.[142] The ratio of establishing two separate funds is that a fund for emergency response should become operational as soon as possible; this is more easily achieved if its functions are limited. Nevertheless, there are some disadvantages to this solution, mainly a duplication of administration and costs. Both the 1971 Fund Convention and the draft HNS Convention take the opposite approach.

18. Basel Convention emergency fund ('revolving fund')

The establishment of an emergency fund has a basis in the Basel Convention, as noted above. The Conference of the Parties has expressly mandated the second Working Group on liability to pursue this issue.[143] To facilitate this work and avoid duplication with existing mechanisms, the Secretariat prepared a study on the modalities of the establishment and functioning of a future emergency fund, and an assessment of existing international capacities in this field.[144] The establishment of the emergency fund is provisionally included in Article 8 of the draft liability protocol.

In accordance with current proposals, the emergency fund would be set up under Secretariat auspices. Its task would be to provide rapid assistance

[141] *Report of the 2nd Working Group on liability on its 1st meeting*, September 1993, (UNEP/CHW.1/WG.1/1/5), p. 5 et seq.; *Note of the Secretariat to the Conference of the Parties on an emergency fund*, 1 December 1993, (UNEP/CHW.2/4).

[142] See the *Consultant's Report on a Compensation Fund* (1991), n. 92 above, and the conclusions of a meeting of Senior Advisors to the Executive Director of UNEP in August 1992 (*Notes of the Executive Director to the Senior Advisors on the establisment of a compensation fund and an emergency fund* (dated 23 June, 30 July, 10 August, and 17 August 1992, respectively) (*Executive Director's Notes on a Compensation Fund*); *Executive Director's Note to the 1st meeting of the Conference of the Parties on an emergency fund* (Doc. UNEP/CHW. 1/6) and *Note on a compensation fund* (Doc. UNEP/CHW. 1/11).

[143] Conference Decisions I/14 (1992), II/2 (1994).

[144] *Report of the Secretariat on an emergency fund*, 12 July 1993, (UNEP/CHW.1/WG.1/1/4); *Report of the Secretariat on the assessment of existing capacities in the field of emergency assistance*, 19 July 1994, (UNEP/CHW.1/WG.1/2/3).

in the event of an accident occurring during the handling of hazardous wastes. It would intervene at the request of a state affected by an emergency situation created by an accident involving hazardous wastes. Action to be taken by the fund would include assessment of the situation as well as identification, provision, and mobilization of experts, equipment, and financial resources. In this it would enhance the role of the Secretariat, which already has this duty. In addition, the fund could provide credit facilities to affected states. Contributions to the fund would be made by party states in accordance with a scale of assessment, and would be derived from such sources as each party state would determine. In the event that its means were insufficient, the emergency fund could call for additional contributions from parties. The fund could claim reimbursement of its expenditures from states or individuals, or from the compensation fund.

19. Basel Convention compensation fund

Unlike the emergency fund, the compensation fund does not have a clear basis in the Basel Convention. The second Working Group on liability is to decide on its establishment and modalities. The tendency at present is to defer decision on this issue pending the conclusion of the work on the liability protocol.[145]

According to Secretariat proposals, the compensation fund would be set up in close connection with the civil liability regime. It could either operate under the responsibility of the Basel Convention Secretariat, or have its own institutional mechanism. Its main features would be similar to those of equivalent schemes, as outlined above. Its principal purpose would be to ensure adequate compensation in the event that compensation under the civil liability rules was unavailable or insufficient for the legal and practical reasons discussed. The grounds for exoneration are to be more restricted than in comparable schemes. Thus the fund would provide compensation even in cases of *force majeure* or act of war. Compensation would not, however, be available from the fund if the damage was not caused by a transboundary movement of hazardous wastes in the narrow sense defined by the Basel Convention, or if it was caused intentionally by the victim. The liability of the operator would not be affected, and the fund would have recourse to any person liable under the civil liability protocol. For practical reasons, a maximum limit of compensation to be obtained from the compensation fund is proposed. Contributions to the compensa-

[145] Conference Decision I/5, (1992); *Report of the 2nd Working Group on Liability on its 1st session*, September 1993, (UNEP/CHW.1/WG.1/1/5) and *Report on its 3rd session*, February 1995, (UNEP/CHW.1/WG.1/3/2). See also the *Executive Director's Notes on a Compensation Fund* 23 June, 30 July, 10 August, and 17 August 1992, and Conference Doc. UNEP/CHW. 1/11 (1992).

tion fund would come from two sources: from states, and from private operators who are potentially liable under the civil liability rules. Both contributions should be forwarded by the states in order not to burden the fund with this task. The contributions from states could be financed through fees charged under national licensing systems to operators handling hazardous wastes (Article 4(7.a) of the Basel Convention). The direct contributions from operators would be based on an assessment system, which according to the current Secretariat proposals should take into account such criteria as the quantity and hazard potential of the wastes handled. In the author's view, the security record of the operator should also play a role, although this has not as yet been discussed. The position of operators domiciled in states not members to the scheme will have to be addressed: it will be necessary to find a way to impose levies on them, or alternatively prohibit them from operating in party states.

A claims procedure would be established, which should be sufficiently simple to allow for an expeditious decision on any claim submitted. For the same reason, it has been proposed that minor claims could be decided on an ad hoc basis by the fund administrator. Disagreements between the fund and any claimant would have to be referred to a national court. For this reason, the fund as a legal person must have standing in national courts. An alternative solution, not under consideration at this stage, would be the referral of disputes to an international body established within the institutional framework of the emerging global waste management regime, or to a future international court of justice for the environment (see para. (I) above). It has been proposed to give the fund the right to take legal action against any state that fails to pay its contribution.

20. Establishment of regional waste compensation funds?

Similar proposals do not as yet exist under any of the regional waste management systems, or under sectoral pollution control regimes. The Bamako Convention does envisage the establishment of a revolving fund to assist in emergency situations (Article 14(3)), as does the Basel Convention. However, this has not been followed up as the Convention is not yet in force. The EU Commission decided to defer decision on the inclusion of such a mechanism in the draft Directive on liability for damage caused by wastes. The draft Directive provides, however, that the Commission should study the feasibility of the establishment of a 'European Fund for Compensation for Damage and Impairment of the Environment caused by Waste' at a later stage.[146]

Consideration of the concept of a fund is thus at present limited to

[146] EU Draft Liability Directive (see n. 115 above), Amended Proposal, COM(91)219 (1991), and *Explanatory Memorandum*; EU Green Paper, May 1993, (COM(93)47).

transactions covered by the Basel Convention. This narrows its scope of application considerably, since the Convention covers a limited range of transactions. Depending on the success of the future Basel funds, this mechanism could be considered also for other elements of the emerging global waste management regime.

O. *Contribution of the Hazardous Waste Funds to the Achievement of the Objectives: Strengths and Weaknesses*

The concept of an international fund for compensation and/or emergency response is a very interesting one. It could offset some of the weaknesses of the enforcement mechanisms discussed above, and combine some of their strengths.[147] While avoiding the two-dimensional, confrontational approach of both state responsibility and civil liability, it gives more attention to the concerns of the victims of pollution than does institutional supervision. Unlike any of the other mechanisms discussed, it contains no element of penalization, being based entirely on financial contributions levied in accordance with objective criteria. This might contribute to its acceptance by states and industry, as no stigma is attached to this mechanism.

In common with state responsibility and civil liability, the fund focuses on remedial rather than preventive action, and adopts the sovereignty-based rather than the holistic approach. The extent to which damage prevention is addressed and obligations of a holistic nature are taken into account will depend to a large extent on the assessment system for contributions to the fund. Herein lies a significant potential for inducing compliance: the contributions could be designed in such a way that they influence the behaviour of the individual operator. Making the amount of the operator's contribution dependent on the amount and hazard potential of the waste handled would provide a strong incentive towards waste minimization. In order to promote the minimization of transboundary waste movement, a significantly higher levy could be imposed on wastes crossing national boundaries than on wastes disposed of domestically. If the operator's security record or some other measure of environmental safety were included in the criteria, there would also be a direct incentive for environmentally sound waste management. One possibility for achieving this would be to allow companies to make deductions for security measures they have adopted. All of these issues remain to be addressed by the second Working Group on liability established under the Basel Convention. If such criteria were adopted, the fund would probably strike a more convincing balance between the three aims outlined on pages 212 and 213 above than any other enforcement mechanism.

[147] For a discussion of the strengths and weaknesses of international funds in the context of hazardous technologies and substances cf. Magraw, in Handl and Lutz, (1989a), ch. 10.

In furthering the second aim of safeguarding the interests of the victim, restoring the environment, and providing rapid emergency response, a fund is a more effective tool than the other mechanisms discussed. In this context, the following advantages are worth pointing out.

By avoiding a situation of confrontation between 'victim' and 'polluter' (whether a state or a private operator) in a judicial procedure, the fund can circumvent some of the problems pertaining to that situation, e.g. the reluctance of victims to submit a claim for fear of creating a precedent or of damaging relations with the 'polluter'. Through the establishment of a simplified claims procedure combined with the fund's right of recourse, the procedural obstacles inherent in state responsibility and civil liability can be circumvented, and compensation can be provided with much less delay. Likewise, a fund accorded the relevant competences can ensure that emergency response measures are taken immediately after an accident occurs. No other available mechanism can provide this.

As is the intention, a fund can effectively complement and strengthen the protection of the victim, and the environment, under the systems of civil liability and compulsory insurance. Its function of providing an alternative or supplementary source of compensation is particularly strong if, as is being considered under the Basel Convention, the fund cannot refuse to pay compensation except where the damage was caused intentionally by the victim, or where it was not caused by hazardous wastes subject to transboundary movement. Thus the position of the victim is much stronger than under a system of even absolute liability. This aspect is especially important in the case of damage caused by illegal traffic in hazardous wastes, where the operator responsible is often elusive.

The fund can offset the limitations imposed by a financial ceiling and/or a floor of compulsory insurance as provided by some civil liability regimes. This advantage is however qualified by the introduction of an upper limit to the financial responsibilities of the fund itself, which may again mean that the victim is left to bear part of the financial burden. In order to minimize that risk, the fund's financial limit must be set considerably higher than the ceiling of the operator's liability. This is a viable solution, as the burden of payment, unlike in the case of civil liability, is not placed on an individual with possibly insufficient means.

As financial means are provided exclusively through contributions from potential polluters, a fund also supports the polluter pays principle more effectively than other mechanisms. Even more than the requirement of compulsory insurance, a fund can ensure that the financial burden of meeting environmental costs is spread out between numerous polluters. A system of contributions that takes into account the hazard potential of the operator's activities and his security record would contribute to the equitable allocation of these costs: an operator who invested in safety measures would have the benefit of lower contributions. Predetermined contributions or levies would also allow enterprises to 'internalize' the environmental costs of their activities by including them in the production costs of relevant goods or services.

Compared to civil liability, the concept of a compensation fund administered by an international body is a more effective way of avoiding crippling financial burdens on individual operators while safeguarding the interests of the victims: instead of protecting the operator by limiting his obligations at the expense of the victim, the burden is spread among many potential polluters. Lastly, by establishing the party states' duty to collect and forward contributions to the fund, the role of the state in ensuring compliance by individuals is somewhat stronger than under the civil liability regimes.

In addition to this impressive list of advantages, there are also a number of weaknesses.[148] Foremost of these, as in the case of other mechanisms, is a strong reluctance on the political front to accept the type of commitment required by a fund, namely establishing a fairly independent international mechanism, and imposing levies on industry.[149] The entry into force of the 1971 Convention establishing the IOPC Fund was considerably hampered by this problem.[150] As mentioned above, the deliberations of both Working Groups on liability established under the Basel Convention on this issue are very contentious, and it is by no means certain that this concept will eventually be accepted. It has indeed been suggested to elaborate a separate protocol for the establishment of the compensation fund rather than including the relevant provisions in the liability protocol, so as not to jeopardize the entry into force of the liability regime, which was considered likely to get far more support than the concept of a fund.[151]

As in the case of institutional supervision and civil liability, a fund can only be effective for those states that are parties to the relevant legal instrument. In order to function, the scheme must be adhered to by a reasonably large number of states to ensure the availability of sufficient financial means.[152] These states must have the capability and the will to ensure that the agreed contributions are made to the fund. Such a system thus presupposes a strong and efficient national infrastructure. In common with the PIC procedure, it will therefore be difficult to implement in states lacking the necessary resources and expertise (see Chapter 2 above, Chapter 3 above). Lack

[148] For a discussion of problematical aspects of a fund see Magraw, in Handl and Lutz, (1989a), pp. 265–6. In the author's view, many of the points raised by Magraw constitute deficiencies not in the concept of the fund as such, but more generally in the legal regulation of the issues involved.

[149] Cf. Handl and Lutz, in Handl and Lutz, (1989a), p. 59.

[150] Doeker and Gehring, in Sand, (1992), p. 418.

[151] Cf. *Executive Director's Notes on a Compensation Fund* 23 June, 30 July, 10 August, and 17 August 1992; and *Executive Director's Notes on a Compensation Fund to the 1st Conference of the Parties* (UNEP/CHW.1/6; UNEP/CHW.1/11, (1992)).

[152] Cf. Magraw, in Handl and Lutz, (1989a), pp. 265–6.

of funds, however, can effectively prevent the functioning of the scheme.[153]

Another disadvantage is that because the system depends on operators of hazardous wastes being registered and licensed in their state of domicile, and making correct and complete statements regarding the types and quantities of hazardous wastes they handle, illegal operators would not come within its purview.

It has been argued that the administrative problems and expenditure of operating a compensation fund or an emergency fund might be substantial.[154] This obviously depends on the way in which the fund is set up. Costs can be minimized if the fund operates within the framework of an existing body. The Secretariat of the IOPC Fund, for example, rents accommodation from the IMO and utilizes that organization's infrastructure, thus being able to operate with a professional staff of five persons.[155] In fulfilling functions that require special expertise and equipment (e.g. valuation of damage, or carrying out emergency response measures), the services of consultants or industrial companies specialized in the relevant field could be used. This was the approach taken by the UNCUEA during its pilot phase: operating with a small staff, it focused among other things on maintaining a roster of consultants who could be mobilized by the Centre at short notice in the event of an emergency. A similar approach is taken by the Environment Unit of the UN/DHA.[156]

As in the case of civil liability, the incentive for the state itself to comply with international rules is not very strong, its role being limited to the collection and forwarding of the contributions. Also, sanctions against states that do not fulfil their obligations towards the fund are not provided, unless the fund is given the right to take legal action against states that fail to contribute. The incentives for private operators to fulfil their obligations are also considerably weaker than in the case of civil liability.

The above analysis shows that a fund can be very effective in supporting the second and third aims, whereas its contribution to the achievement of the first aim is more limited. It can function most effectively in conjunction with a civil liability regime which it supplements and enhances.

CONCLUSIONS

The examination of the existing and emerging international mechanisms designed to ensure compliance with international rules shows that none of

[153] Doeker and Gehring, in Sand, (1992), p. 414, discussing the example of the IOPC Fund.

[154] Krämer, in *La réparation des dommages catastrophiques*, (1990), pp. 408–11.

[155] *Consultant's Report on a Compensation Fund*, (1991), n. 92 above.

[156] Cf. *Report of the Secretatiat on the Assessment of Existing Capacities in the Field of Emergency Assistance*, 19 July 1994, (UNEP/CHW.1/WG.1/2/3); also Basel Convention Conference Doc. UNEP/CHW.1/6, (1992).

the relevant concepts can, on its own, provide a satisfactory enforcement mechanism. Each is subject to the general problem that it is up to states to determine the extent to which they are willing to subject themselves to relevant mechanisms, thus making compliance monitoring a question of political will rather than of the form of the legal rules.[157] With this reservation, it can nevertheless be said that between them the mechanisms examined do have a potential to further the aims outlined in the first paragraph above, i.e. promoting the preventive approach, protecting the victim, and applying the polluter pays principle. Institutional supervision is the only mechanism that focuses on the preventive approach, whereas civil liability regimes and an international fund are useful tools for providing remedial action and applying the polluter pays principle. The holistic approach is supported by institutional supervision, while state responsibility and civil liability focus on the traditional sovereignty-based approach. The concept of a fund reflects both these approaches to a certain extent. A combination of the different mechanisms should therefore be envisaged for the enforcement of the global waste management regime. Such a combination is envisaged also in other international environmental regimes: the 1988 CRAMRA, for example, provides for strict civil liability with a financial ceiling, subsidiary responsibility of the sponsoring state, and the creation of an international fund.[158]

The concept of an international fund is a particularly interesting and innovative approach. Accordingly, the rapid establishment of the funds considered under the Basel Convention should be promoted. The assessment procedure for contributions to be made by industry should provide an incentive to comply with environmental standards. The establishment of funds should be considered also for regional waste management systems and sectoral pollution control treaties. Likewise, the further development of the civil liability regime, which should provide for unlimited liability and include compulsory insurance, should be promoted, especially in the context of sectoral pollution control regimes where relevant efforts have to date been rather modest. Institutional supervision should be further developed to include allocating independent supervisory powers, and the power to impose sanctions, to relevant international bodies.[159] State responsibility can fulfil a useful subsidiary function by providing a direct incentive to the state to comply with its obligations.

[157] Cf. Könz, in Brown Weiss, (1992b), p. 165.

[158] Cf. *La réparation des dommages catastrophiques*, (1990), in particular the contributions by Deprimoz (p. 103), Jessurun d'Oliveira (p. 164), Politi (p. 319), and Zuleeg (pp. 373–5). See also Rest, (1992), p. 34 et seq.

[159] Cf. Könz, in Brown Weiss, (1992b), pp. 176–8.

7

The Contribution of the Basel Convention and Related Rules to an Emerging Global Waste Management System

INTRODUCTION

In Chapter 1 above, the need for a comprehensive international regime for the control of transboundary movements of hazardous wastes was established. It was submitted that the Basel Convention could serve as a basis for the future regime, with other relevant international rules as component elements. The main characteristics of the future regime were outlined. Chapter 2 above discussed the fundamental principles and rules of the Basel Convention. In Chapters 3 and 4 above, the rules and principles of the existing regional waste management systems were examined, and it was established that the Basel Convention can serve as an umbrella for these systems, forming the 'Basel Convention regime' for transboundary movements of hazardous wastes. In Chapter 5 above, proposals were made for the harmonization of sectoral pollution control treaties with the Basel Convention regime which can lead to the formation of a global regime to address the hazardous waste cycle. Finally, Chapter 6 above proposed ways of ensuring compliance with the rules discussed in the preceding chapters.

This chapter will set out the conclusions of the study, examining in particular the submissions made in Chapter 1 above. Accordingly, the following questions will be addressed.

First, what fundamental principles for the regulation of the hazardous waste cycle can be derived from the legal instruments examined in this work, and to what extent do these principles contribute to the further development of the body of customary law discussed in Chapter 1 above? In particular, to what extent do the legal instruments establish new rules, and to what extent are existing or emerging rules enhanced and confirmed? Which of the rules are relevant to pollution control in general, and which ones specifically address transboundary movements of hazardous wastes as an aspect of pollution source transfer?

Secondly, to what extent do these rules contribute to the formation of a global, holistic and integrated regime for the control of the hazardous waste cycle, as advocated in Chapter 1 above? To what extent do they reflect the emerging concepts discussed in Chapter 1 above?

Thirdly, what are the strengths and weaknesses of the emerging regime? What additional measures would be required to make it more effective?

THE CONTRIBUTION OF THE BASEL CONVENTION AND RELATED LEGAL INSTRUMENTS TO EMERGING RULES AND CONCEPTS RELEVANT TO THE HAZARDOUS WASTE CYCLE

The analysis of the relevant legal instruments in the preceding chapters shows that a number of fundamental concepts are common to all or most of them. As discussed in Chapter 4 above, this is in part the result of the closely interdependent elaboration of the legal instruments in question. The pivotal point in this development is the Basel Convention, which took up and developed further the fundamental rules already incorporated in older legal instruments, and subsequently—by virtue of its global scope—influenced the development of later instruments. This is evident in particular in the legal instruments forming the Basel Convention regime, which, as we have seen, conform to the fundamental rules of the Basel Convention to a large extent. It is also evident, albeit to a lesser degree, in some sectoral pollution control treaties, where the incorporation of some of the fundamental concepts of the Basel Convention is under consideration.

Shortly after the adoption of the Basel Convention, Günther Handl noted that the participation of over 100 states in the Convention's elaboration made it 'a likely catalyst in the evolution of concordant state practice and the crystallization of customary international law'.[1] Six years later, with the Basel Convention in force and a number of pertinent regional agreements and arrangements in place, this suggestion is worth further examination.

The Basel Convention and the related legal instruments have in the interim received widespread support. As noted in Chapter 2(B) above, the ratification process of the Basel Convention, initially slow, accelerated significantly after entry into force. The Convention now has over eighty parties, including most of the world's industrialized nations. The EU and virtually all of its members have acceded, and the USA as the world's largest waste generator is in the process of developing implementing legislation with a view to ratifying the Basel Convention.[2] With the OAU no longer fundamentally opposing the Basel Convention, twelve African states have thus far become parties. The Bamako Convention, which embodies

[1] Handl, (1989), p. 368.

[2] On relevant legislative efforts in the USA see e.g. Abrams, (1990), p. 842; Cusack, (1990), p. 397 et seq.; Hackett, (1990), p. 298 et seq.; Mounteer, (1991), p. 10085 et seq.; Murphy, (1992), p. 9 et seq.; Seigler, (1992); Walsh, (1992); Rosenthal, (1992).

the concepts of the Basel Convention and introduces stricter rules in some areas, has received widespread political support, not only in Africa but also in other developing countries and the NGO community. As mentioned in Chapter 3 above, it has had a catalytic effect and provides a model for similar regional treaties, mainly in the developing world. Its significance is thus considerable, despite the fact that it has not as yet entered into force. Its aims are supported by the relevant provisions of the Lomé IV and Abuja Conventions (see Chapter 3 above). The relevant legislation of the EU and the OECD is indicative of prevailing opinions of the world's industrialized states (see Chapter 4 above). Lomé IV has entered into force and has the support of the EU members and the vast majority of the ACP states (see Chapter 3(H) above). The London Convention, with its significant number of parties and after nearly 20 years of operation, is widely recognized as representing commonly accepted standards in the field of ocean dumping and incineration of wastes (see Chapter 5(A) above). Since the mid-1980s, a large number of states have enacted national legislation addressing the hazardous waste cycle, often taking into account the fundamental principles of one or more of the international legal instruments mentioned above.[3] To assist states in this task, the Secretariat of the Basel Convention organizes workshops and seminars (Chapter 6 para. 8 above), and has developed model national legislation on the management of hazardous wastes in general, and on transboundary hazardous waste traffic in particular.[4]

It can be argued, therefore, that rules or principles embodied or advocated consistently in the above international legal instruments and supported by national policy, legislation, and practice can now be considered customary law in the field of management and transboundary movements of hazardous wastes. If a rule is not new, but merely extends, reaffirms or specifies existing customary law, its incorporation in only a part of the relevant legal instruments may be considered sufficient.

A. *Principles of Waste Minimization and Proximity of Disposal*

These principles advocate the reduction of the generation of hazardous wastes to a minimum, on the one hand, and the disposal of such wastes as

[3] *Compilation of the Provisions of National Legislation Related to the Control of Transboundary Movements of Hazardous Wastes and their Disposal*, Basel Convention Series/SBC no 94/002 (January 1994). See also greenpeace, (1990), outlining the national policies of a large number of developing and industrialized countries. For an overview of the waste management policy and legislation in selected Eastern and Western European countries, see Sander and Küppers, (1993). For an overview of national legislation in Asia see Spitalnik, (1992). A sophisticated example is the Japanese legislation implementing the Basel Convention (March 1994).

[4] *Revised Draft Model Legislation on the Management of Hazardous Wastes*, Basel Convention Series/SBC no 94/003 (Geneva, April 1994). See also Conference Decisions I/12 (1992) and II/5 (1994); Conference Doc. UNEP/CHW.2/5 (8 Decmber 1993).

close as possible to the source of generation, on the other. They are indicative of the 'cleaner production approach' discussed in Chapter 1(J), (L) above. They can be considered a further development of the existing customary rule that limits the 'freedom to pollute', examined in Chapter 1 para. 4 above), in a form that specifically addresses the hazardous waste cycle. In this respect, the principle of proximity is especially interesting because it addresses traffic in hazardous wastes as an aspect of pollution source transfer as defined in Chapter 1(E) above), thus going beyond the previous preoccupation of customary law with transboundary pollution in the traditional sense.

As we have seen in the preceding chapters, these principles are supported by virtually all relevant legal instruments constituting the emerging Basel Convention regime.[5] The Basel Convention and the guidelines and strategy elaborated within its framework not only incorporate these principles, but also provide guidance to parties as to how they should be implemented (see Chapter 2 above, in particular para. 7), as does the Bamako Convention (see Chapter 3(F) above). The Bamako Convention and the Central American Agreement expressly endorse the concept of cleaner production. These principles are embodied in the Cairo Guidelines (see Chapter 2(A) above) and in the relevant policy and legal instruments of the EU and the OECD, which also clarify and develop them further (see Chapter 4 above). The related but broader concept of rectification of environmental damage at source is embodied in Article 130r of the SEA.[6] The EU legislation has developed the concept of self-sufficiency in waste disposal within the EU as a variant of the principle of proximity. The principle of waste minimization is embodied in the Environmental Protocol to the Antarctic Treaty (see Chapter 5(E) above). Both principles have also been advocated, subsequent to the adoption of the Basel Convention, within the framework of the London Convention (see Chapter 5(A) above). Other sectoral pollution control regimes discussed in Chapter 5 above do not as yet expressly incorporate these principles, beyond providing a general obligation to prevent or reduce the relevant forms of pollution to the extent practicable. A notable exception is the 1992 UN/ECE Convention on international waterways (Article 3(1.a)). In addition to the binding legal instruments analysed in the preceding chapters, a significant number of statements issued by international organizations reaffirm these principles.[7] Most importantly, Chapters

[5] See also Birnie and Boyle, (1992), p. 302 et seq.

[6] Krämer, (1990), p. 62.

[7] e.g. UNGA Resolution 42/183, 20 December 1988; UNEP Governing Council Decisions SS.II/4/B of 3 August 1990, and Decision 16/30 of 31 May 1991 (all repr. in Kwiatkowska and Soons, (1993)); Resolution WHA 43.25 of the World Health Assembly (17 May 1990); Resolution on Environment, Development, Employment and the Role of ILO adopted by the International Labour Conference at its 77th Session, June 1990 (relevant paras. repr. in Basel Conference Doc. UNEP/CHW.1/7 (7 July 1992); UN/ECE Declaration on Low-and Non-Waste Technology and Re-utilization and Recycling of Wastes (1979); repr. in Hohmann,

17, 20 and 21 of UNCED's Agenda 21, which deal with waste management and marine pollution, advocate the principle of waste minimization. Chapter 20 also supports the principle of proximity by encouraging the development of domestic disposal options for hazardous wastes.

The incorporation of the principles of waste minimization and proximity of disposal in virtually all international legal instruments relevant to the hazardous waste cycle may be considered an indication of their emergence as customary law rules.[8] The fact that these rules are but a logical extension of the existing customary rule which limits the 'freedom to pollute' lends some support to this argument. However, this can be said unequivocally only in the case of hazardous wastes not having economic value which are intended for final disposal. As we have seen in Chapter 4 above, the principle of proximity is not fully supported by the relevant policy and legislation of the EU and the OECD in the case of hazardous wastes which have economic value and are intended for recycling or recovery operations. In that case, there is some support for the concept of subjecting the transfer of the substances in question to the mechanisms of the free market, or at least applying laxer control mechanisms.

B. *Prohibition or Restriction of Hazardous Waste Disposal Outside the Generating State*

Conceptually, the restriction or ban of exports of hazardous wastes for disposal outside the state of generation is a logical consequence and an extension of the principle of proximity of disposal, discussed in the previous paragraph. In common with that principle, it constitutes an innovation insofar as it does not address transboundary pollution in the traditional sense, but transboundary movements of hazardous wastes as an aspect of pollution source transfer.

As we have seen in the previous chapters, there is as yet no international legal instrument that advocates or incorporates a general prohibition of every form of disposal of hazardous wastes outside the territory of the generating state. There is, however, very widespread support in recent international policy and law for different forms of restrictions or conditional bans on such exports. Of the emerging concepts discussed here, the restriction or conditional prohibition of hazardous waste exports—as opposed to mere monitoring—has probably gained the most rapid acceptance within the past few years. In addition to environmental treaties, this concept is

(1992), Vol. 1 p. 338); Ministerial Declaration on Environment and Development of the 4th South Pacific Forum (Noumea, July 1991) (repr. in UN Doc. A/CONF.151/PC/87); 1992 Manaus Declaration on UNCED adopted by the Presidents of the Amazonian States (repr. in Kwiatkowska and Soons, (1993), p. 1077).

[8] Cf. Boyle, (1990a), p. 151.

endorsed by numerous non-binding statements.[9] As we have seen in Chapter 2 above, the Basel Convention restricts the export of hazardous wastes in certain cases, and requires its parties to reconsider periodically the adoption of a complete or partial ban on hazardous waste traffic in the light of the latest available information. All regional hazardous waste management systems discussed in this study feature some form of restriction on traffic in hazardous wastes. In addition, state practice lends support to the argument that there is an emerging customary law rule restricting hazardous waste exports: since the mid-1980s, numerous states have enacted national legislation on the subject. In particular, a large number of developing countries have adopted import bans for hazardous wastes.[10] The majority of the OECD member states now strongly restrict the export of hazardous wastes outside the OECD area, and some states have adopted general or conditional export bans.[11]

The total or conditional ban on transboundary movements of hazardous wastes, or even their restriction, inevitably leads to interference with free trade and can result in trade discrimination against certain states. This raises important questions regarding the compatibility of such measures with the provisions of GATT. The problems that arise in this context are

[9] E.g. UNGA Resolutions 42/183 of 20 December 1988 and 44/226 of 22 December 1989; UN/ECOSOC Resolution 1989/62 of 24 May 1989; UNHCR Resolution 1989/42 of 6 March 1989; Tlatelolco Platform of the UN/ECLAC Preparatory Meeting for UNCED (1991); Cairo and Abidjan Declarations of the two UN/ECA Preparatory Meetings for UNCED (all repr. in Kwiatkowska and Soons, (1993)); *Action Plan for the Environment* adopted by the 7th Meeting of Environment Ministers (October 1990); *Statement of the Non-Aligned Movement Summit Meeting*, September 1989, (Doc. NAC9/EC/Doc.8/Rev.4); Port of Spain Accord of the Caribbean Community Summit (July 1989); Langkawi Declaration on the Environment, adopted by the Commonwealth Heads of Government (October 1989); Ministerial Declaration on Environment and Development of the 4th South Pacific Forum, Noumea, July 1991, (repr. in UN Doc. A/CONF.151/PC/87); Resolution on Environment, Development, Employment and the Role of ILO, adopted by the International Labour Conference at its 77th Session, June 1990 (relevant paras. repr. in Doc. UNEP/CHW.1/7 (7 July 1992)); Declaration of the Nordic Council of Ministers on the Minimizing and Disposal of Hazardous Wastes (March 1994); *Report of the Commission on Sustainable Development*, 12 July 1994, (Doc. E/CN.17/1994/20). For an extensive overview see Kwiatkowska and Soons, (1993), Editors' Introduction, p. LXII et seq.; also Greenpeace, (1991a), pp. 11–14; idem, (1990), p. 17 et seq.; Birnie and Boyle, (1992), p. 333 et seq.

[10] See Kiss and Shelton, (1991), p. 321; Greenpeace, (1991c), Table III (listing eighty six developing countries prohibiting the import of hazardous wastes). See also Birnie and Boyle, (1992), p. 332, n. 122.

[11] See e.g. the Italian Law on the transfrontier disposal of industrial waste, 9 November 1988, in force as of June 1989 (28 ILM (1990) p. 393), subjecting the export of industrial wastes to non-EU and non-OECD countries to restrictions (on this see Barozzi, in Sander and Küppers, (1993)). In August 1992, France adopted an import ban for household and similar waste (*Agence Europe*, 21 August 1992; also Rosencranz and Eldridge, (1992), p. 320). In Switzerland, exports of hazardous wastes are subject to prior authorization by the competent government agency in accordance with the Ordinance on Traffic in Special Waste of 1986 (SR814.014). Waste exports to non-OECD countries were phased out by 1 January 1993. See *Report of the Secretariat to the Ad Hoc Committee on Implementation*, 30 September 1994, (UNEP/CHW/C.1/2/5).

to some extent the same as those resulting from restrictions on movements of hazardous wastes subject to recycling within the EU, discussed in Chapter 4 para. 5.3 above. The issue is under discussion within a number of international organizations, including UNCTAD, UNEP, the OECD, and the WTO Committee on Trade and Environment, established in 1994.[12] A full analysis of this problem is beyond the scope of this study; it is discussed elsewhere by the author.[13] Reference also can be made to the numerous works devoted to the relationship between trade and environmental measures in general, an issue attracting increasing interest.[14] Following is a brief outline of the pertinent problems.

Article XI of GATT prohibits import and export restrictions in principle. Article XX provides for an exception to this in certain cases, which are enumerated in the provision. They include measures adopted for the protection of the health of humans, animals or plants (Article XX(b)). Article XX imposes three cumulative requirements for trade restrictions permissible as an exception: first, any export or import ban, or related measure, must be introduced for one of the purposes listed in the provision; secondly, the measure must be necessary for the purpose in question; and thirdly, the measure must be non-discriminatory in practice.

Articles XI and XX are applicable to the Basel Convention and related international legal rules only insofar as the wastes covered by them are considered products. An internationally agreed definition of this term does not exist within the GATT context, nor indeed within the context of international management of hazardous wastes, as we saw in the previous chapters.

To the extent that wastes are considered products, some of the restrictions imposed by the global waste management regime could be considered discriminatory in accordance with the criteria of Article XX. This applies in particular to the prohibition of waste trade with states not members of the OECD, and with non-parties to a particular international agreement: under the GATT perspective, it may constitute an arbitrary trade restriction against countries where conditions are otherwise the same. A similar problem exists in the context of the Montreal Protocol and CITES, both of which provide for restrictions on trade with non-parties. In these cases, the provisions are considered by many to be non-discriminatory and thus in conformity with Article XX(b) of GATT: the provisions prohibiting trade with non-parties are modified insofar as they do allow such trade if the

[12] Decision on Trade and the Environment (repr. in Doc. MTN.TNC/W/141 (29 March 1994)).

[13] Kummer, (1994a), p. 67 et seq.

[14] See among others Rublack, (1993), p. 262 et seq.; GATT, (1992); Arden-Clarke, (1991); Sorsa, (1992); Schoenbaum, (1992), p. 700; Brown Weiss, (1992a), p. 728; Charnowitz, (1993), p. 155 et seq.; Temple Lang, Commentary on Chapter 6, in Lang, Neuhold, and Zemanek, (1991), p. 179 et seq.

states in question fulfil the same requirements or adhere to the same standards as party states. The provisions therefore do not discriminate against non-parties (Montreal Protocol Article 4(8); CITES Article 10). The same can be argued for some types of restrictions currently imposed under the Basel Convention regime. There does, however, remain room for dispute.

The WTO Committee on Trade and Environment is considering the possibility of adjusting the GATT provisions to the requirements of multilateral environmental agreements featuring potential trade restrictions. Two options are under discussion: first, a collective interpretation of Article XX by the GATT parties, which would determine criteria and conditions under which trade measures could be used to achieve the aims of the environmental treaty; and secondly, a waiver of the GATT rules for individual multilateral environmental agreements, in accordance with Article XXV of GATT, where this is considered necessary. The discussion is continuing.

1. Prohibition of export of hazardous wastes to states that have banned their import

This concept is supported by the Basel and Bamako Conventions (see Chapter 2 para. 9 and Chapter 3 para. 4 above), and by EU legislation (see Chapter 4 para. 2 above). It is considered for inclusion in various regional agreements currently under discussion (see Chapter 3 above). It is also advocated in Chapters 20 and 21 of UNCED's Agenda 21, which include the elimination of waste exports to states having enacted import bans in the overall target of a future waste management policy. In Chapter 1 para. 5 above, it was argued that the right of every state to ban the import of hazardous wastes is a logical consequence of its right to control activities in its own territory, and therefore already based in customary law. If we follow this argument, the prohibition of waste exports to states exercizing this right adds nothing to the rule in question. It does, however, have the useful role of affirming and clarifying this right, and emphasizing the obligation of other states to respect it.

2. Prohibition of traffic in hazardous wastes from developed to developing and transitional countries

As we have seen in Chapter 2(B) above, this concept was endorsed by Decision II/12 of the Conference of the Parties to the Basel Convention in 1994, after being hotly debated for a number of years. It had appeared on the agenda since the beginning of the negotiations on the Convention, and had received increasing support within political fora and from the NGO community. It was endorsed by numerous policy statements and by UNCED's Agenda 21 (Chapter 20, para. 20.34(b)). In Africa, it was supported by pertinent resolutions of the OAU and other bodies since the late 1980s, and was subsequently embodied in strong terms in the Bamako, Lomé IV, and Abuja Conventions (Chapter 3 above). The emerging regional treaties on the management of hazardous wastes are unanimous in their support of this concept, as noted in Chapter 3 above. The concept is also incorporated in the legislation of the EU and the OECD, initially by placing restrictions on North-South traffic, and subsequently, in the case of the EU legislation, by banning it completely (see Chapter 4 above). These developments undoubtedly had an influence on the Basel parties' decision to ban all traffic in hazardous wastes from OECD to non-OECD countries.

In the context of the regulation of the hazardous waste cycle, this concept is an innovation in that it expressly acknowledges the existence of differences in technical, legal, institutional and financial capacities within the different groups of countries, and establishes a clear double standard in favour of developing and transitional countries. It is contrary to the initial approach of the Basel Convention, and of the early international legal instruments on hazardous waste management. As late as 1989, Handl and Lutz maintained that a double standard based on the 'development status' of a country was not desirable in the context of the management of hazardous wastes and substances.[15] As noted in Chapter 2 above, the virtually universal support for this concept since the beginning of the 1990s indicates a rapid policy shift, and provides an impressive example of a significant change in perception within a very short period of time.

In a broader context, the endorsement of a double standard in favour of developing and transitional countries follows a trend which is already evident in earlier treaties such as UNCLOS (Articles 194, 203), and is reaffirmed in most of the recent environmental treaties of global scope adhered to by both developed and developing countries, as well as in the 1992 Rio Declaration and other international policy statements. This trend has probably found its strongest expression in the 1992 Framework Convention on Climate Change, which is based on the concept of 'common but differentiated responsibility' of states at different stages of development.[16] The 1987 Montreal Protocol on Substances that Deplete the Ozone Layer (as amended and adjusted) and the 1992 UN Convention on Biological Diversity also establish dual standards in favour of developing and transitional countries.

In view of the strong support recently afforded to the prohibition of traffic in hazardous wastes from industrialized to developing and transitional countries—enhanced, as we have seen, by relevant national policy and legislation—it can justifiably be argued that it is an emerging customary law rule addressing hazardous waste management. As in the case of proximity of disposal, this applies unequivocally only to hazardous wastes that have

[15] Handl and Lutz, in Handl and Lutz, (1989a), pp. 50–1.

[16] See Bodansky, (1993), p. 453 et seq., in particular p. 479 et seq.

no positive economic value and are subject to final disposal. As we have seen in Chapter 4 above, the question of the extent to which the international transfer of hazardous wastes subject to recycling or recovery operations should be restricted has not as yet been resolved at all levels. The controversy surrounding the justification of hazardous waste transfer for the purpose of recycling, outlined in Chapter 1 above, continues. While the environmental and economic merits of recycling are generally acknowledged, concern is often expressed that the relevant operations generate new toxic residues, and that fewer restrictions on international transfer of wastes subject to recycling might provide an incentive for abuse, i.e. wastes being exported for the purpose of illicit disposal under the pretext of recycling. This is illustrated by the controversy over the introduction of less stringent rules for recyclable wastes into the relevant legislation of the EU and the OECD (see Chapter 4 above), and by the relevant discussions of the Conference of the Parties to the Basel Convention in the context of the adoption of Decision II/12 and its proposed inclusion into the Convention: the controversy concerns not the fundamental need to protect developing and transitional countries against imports of hazardous wastes, but the question to what extent recyclable wastes should be included in a ban, and the definition of the wastes to be included.

3. Prohibition of hazardous waste trade with states that are not parties to a particular treaty or other waste control system

The concept of a limited ban, i.e. the notion of a legal instrument prohibiting its parties from trading in hazardous wastes with states that do not adhere to its fundamental principles, was first incorporated into the Basel Convention (Chapter 2 para. 10 above). Subsequently, it was taken up by other legal instruments, namely the Bamako Convention (Chapter 3 para. 5 above); the 1992 Central American Agreement (Chapter 3 above); the 1990 Resolution of the Consultative Meeting of the Contracting Parties to the London Convention (Chapter 5(B) above); and the 1993 EU Council Regulation on waste shipments (see Chapter 4 para. 2.4 above).

The reasoning behind this concept was discussed in Chapters 2 and 3 above. It is not so much a substantive rule providing for an outright ban on certain transactions, as a legal technique which is used to ensure compliance with the standards set by the relevant legal instrument by its parties, and to provide an incentive to non-party states to accede to the instrument in question. This technique is also used in the Montreal Protocol, which prohibits trade in ozone-depleting substances and technologies with non-parties unless they apply standards accepted by the Conference of the Parties. If an emerging customary rule could be derived from this, it would be a prohibition of transboundary movement of hazardous waste unless certain fundamental rules, established by the pertinent legal instruments, are observed. If the rules in question are themselves recognized as customary law, the prohibition of transactions involving hazardous wastes that do not conform to them is in any event prohibited, and the rule under discussion adds nothing in the way of substance. It does, however, have the important function of facilitating the enforcement of the fundamental rules by enabling states that observe the relevant standards to put pressure on those that do not, as noted above. As discussed in Chapter 2 para. 10 above, the effectiveness of this pressure is dependent on the number of states that adhere to the relevant standards, and on their collective significance as trading partners.

4. Prohibition of waste export for disposal in parts of the global commons considered particularly vulnerable

As we have seen in Chapter 5 above, two areas of the global commons have been designated by the legal instruments under consideration as requiring special protection against the deliberate disposal of hazardous wastes: the oceans, and the Antarctic region.

The Bamako Convention (Chapter 3 above), the 1972 London Convention, the 1992 Oslo/Paris Convention, and the 1992 Helsinki Convention all expressly provide for the phasing-out of ocean dumping and incineration at sea of certain types of hazardous wastes (Chapter 5 above). A number of states have enacted national legislation prohibiting or restricting ocean dumping of certain substances. There appears to be a consensus that a customary law rule is emerging which prohibits these practices.[17]

As discussed in Chapter 5(E) above, the status of the Antarctic region as an area worthy of special protection is long established and acknowledged by the various components of the Antarctic Treaty system, as well as a number of other international legal instruments. Annex III of the 1991 Environment Protocol to the Antarctic Treaty supports this concept in the context of the waste cycle, by providing for minimization and environmentally sound disposal of wastes generated in the Antarctic. Under the MARPOL Convention, Antarctica has been designated as a Special Area in which every discharge of wastes is prohibited.[18] The Basel Convention and the Bamako Convention prohibit the import of hazardous wastes into Antarctica, regardless of whether or not these wastes are subject to transboundary movement as defined by those Conventions.

[17] Birnie and Boyle, (1992), pp. 322, 343. See IMO, *Evaluation of National Dumping Instruments: Note by the Secretariat*, 17 October 1990, (Doc. LDC13/INF.35), in particular Table 3, p. 13, analysing pertinent legislation of eighteen industrialized states parties to the London Convention.

[18] IMO News No. 1/1991, p. 16.

C. *Environmentally Sound Management of Hazardous Wastes and the Principle of Non-Discrimination*

Since, as we have seen, the export of hazardous wastes is not banned completely, there is room for the concept of 'environmentally sound management of hazardous wastes, whatever the place of disposal', discussed in Chapters 2 para. 5 and 3(B) above. This has two aspects. The principle of environmentally sound management of hazardous wastes provides that the wastes must be managed in such a way as not to endanger human health and the environment. Whereas it is embodied in most relevant international legal instruments in a fairly vague and unspecified form, it is increasingly given concrete content by reference to standards established by non-binding technical guidelines or codes of conduct in the field. Depending on the wording of the pertinent provisions, the standards in question may thus become binding on the parties to the relevant treaty. As we have seen, this technique is used in the Basel and Bamako Conventions (see Chapters 2 and 3 above), and in the 1993 EU Regulation as well as the 1984 Directive preceding it (see Chapter 4 para. 2 above). The principle of non-discrimination, originally developed in the context of transboundary pollution,[19] provides that the principle of environmentally sound management must be applied equally to wastes that remain within the territory of the generating state and wastes that are exported. In more concrete terms, this means that the same standards must be applied in both cases.

These principles, in common with the principles of waste minimization and proximity, are an extension of the established customary law rule which limits the 'freedom to pollute', discussed in Chapter 1 para. 4 above. The principle of environmentally sound management gives concrete content, in the context of waste management, to the customary law obligation to observe the standard of due diligence.[20] The principle of non-discrimination, in common with the principles already discussed, specifically addresses the issue of transboundary movements of hazardous wastes as an aspect of pollution source transfer. Moreover, it extends the obligation of due diligence to hazardous wastes subject to transboundary movement, since it expressly addresses the treatment of wastes which are exported outside the state of origin. This is an innovative concept, since, as was argued in Chapter 1 para. 4 above, the traditional customary obligation to observe the standard of due diligence is limited to activities taking place in the perpetrating state's own territory, or under its jurisdiction or control.

[19] See the definition in OECD Council Recommendation C(74)224 on Principles Concerning Transfrontier Pollution. Cf. Council Recommendations C(76)55 and C(77)28 (all repr. in OECD, (1977)). See the discussion in OECD, (1977), in particular the articles by Bischoff, Sand, Pacteen, and the OECD Secretariat. See also Kiss and Shelton, (1991), p. 143.

[20] See also Birnie and Boyle, (1992), p. 339.

The principles of environmentally sound waste management and non-discrimination have received widespread support. They are embodied in the Basel Convention and the Technical Guidelines and Strategy elaborated within its framework (see Chapter 2 para. 7 above); the Bamako Convention (see Chapter 3 para. 5 above), and the relevant policy and more recent legislation of the EU and the OECD, which gives fairly specific content to these principles (see Chapter 4 above). The Environment Protocol to the Antarctic Treaty supports the concept of environmentally sound waste management, and the 1992 Central American Agreement refers to UNEP standards and principles in this field. The sectoral treaties addressing marine pollution, even though not expressly advocating the principle of environmentally sound waste management, give some support to it by establishing standards for the discharge of hazardous substances. In addition, the most recent regional pollution control regimes adopted by European states, namely the 1992 Oslo/Paris Convention; the 1992 Helsinki Convention, and the 1992 UN/ECE Convention on international watercourses, advocate and develop the concepts of 'best environmental practices' and 'best available technology' (see Chapter 5 above). The Cairo Guidelines also embody the concepts of environmentally sound management of hazardous wastes and non-discrimination, providing fairly detailed rules (see Chapter 2(A) above). As already noted, the numerous non-binding technical rules establishing safety standards for the handling and transport of dangerous substances also give concrete content to this rule, thus contributing to its development. Finally, the concept of environmentally sound management is included in the overall objective of the waste management strategy advocated in Chapters 20 and 21 of UNCED's Agenda 21, and endorsed by declarations of international organizations.[21] The principle of non-discrimination is also incorporated into legal instruments addressing forms of pollution other than that caused by hazardous wastes, such as the 1974 Nordic Environmental Protection Convention, and the 1978 UNEP Guidelines on Shared Natural Resources.

Since the principles of environmentally sound management and non-discrimination are advocated by most relevant legal instruments, there is a basis for the argument that they constitute emerging customary law obligations. As in the case of the principles of waste minimization and proximity, this view can be supported by the argument that these principles are in effect an extension and clarification of the established customary limitation of the 'freedom to pollute' and the obligation to exercise due diligence, as applied to the control of transboundary movement of hazardous waste as

[21] e.g. Resolution WHA 43.25 of the World Health Assembly, 17 May 1990; Resolution on Environment, Development, Employment and the Role of ILO, adopted by the International Labour Conference at its 77th Session, June 1990 (relevant paras. repr. in Doc. UNEP/CHW.1/7 (7 July 1992)).

an aspect of pollution control. With respect to the principle of non-discrimination, this view is not generally accepted, however.[22]

As regards the principle of environmentally sound management, a special problem emerges in the context of hazardous wastes subject to recycling or recovery operations. The application of this principle to hazardous wastes that have economic value and are destined for recycling or recovery does appear to be generally accepted. The policy and legislation of the EU and, even more clearly, the OECD, go one step further: they specifically advocate recycling and similar operations as a fundamental principle of waste management. The relevant legal instruments consider recycling a means of minimizing waste disposal as well as an environmentally sound management option (see Chapter 4 above). This is supported in part by Chapter 20 of Agenda 21, which endorses recycling as a part of the 'waste management hierarchy'. The hierarchy encompasses, in order of priority, waste minimization; reduction of quantities and toxicity at source; recycling or re-use; and environmentally sound disposal. It is also embodied in the Framework Document on the Preparation of Technical Guidelines, elaborated by the Technical Working Group of the Basel Convention (Chapter 2 para. 7 above). Chapter 20 of Agenda 21 specifies that the wastes should be recycled 'at the source of generation, or as close as possible thereto' (para. 20.13 (f)). The role of recycling in environmentally sound waste management is also emphasized by the 1979 UN/ECE Declaration on Low- and Non-Waste Technology and Re-utilization and Recycling of Wastes.[23]

However, for the reasons mentioned in para. 2 above, the view of recycling as a fundamental element of environmentally sound waste management is not shared by all international legal instruments constituting the Basel Convention regime, particularly where hazardous wastes subject to transboundary movement are concerned. Apart from those of the OECD and the EU, none of the legal instruments constituting the Basel Convention regime explicitly endorse recycling or recovery as a means of ensuring environmentally sound waste management. It can therefore not be considered a universally accepted principle.

D. *Control System Including Prior Notification and PIC*

The emergence of an obligation in customary law to provide prior notification to states that are likely to be affected by a hazardous activity, and to obtain their prior consent, was discussed in Chapter 1 para. 6 above. The obligation of prior notification is generally accepted in the context of transboundary pollution but is contested by some authors if applied to pollution

[22] Cf. Dupuy, in Magraw, (1991), pp. 67–9, arguing that the principle of non-dicrimination is not yet recognized as customary law.

[23] Repr. in Hohmann, (1992), Vol. 1, p. 338.

source transfer. The obligation of PIC, on the other hand, has no basis in customary law as far as transboundary pollution is concerned. In the case of pollution source transfer, there are strong arguments in favour of its customary law status, but this is not generally accepted.

The principles of prior notification and PIC were already gaining recognition prior to the emergence of the Basel Convention regime in the late 1980s and early 1990s, but this was basically limited to the field of trade in hazardous chemicals. This field, in common with transboundary movements of hazardous wastes, constitutes an aspect of pollution source transfer. As early as 1975, the principles of prior notification and PIC were reflected in the WHO Certification Scheme on the Quality of Pharmaceutical Products Moving in International Commerce. They are embodied in UNEP's amended London Guidelines for the Exchange of Information on Chemicals in International Trade (1989), and in the FAO's amended International Code of Conduct on the Distribution and Use of Pesticides (1989). Their significance was enhanced by the establishment of the UNEP/FAO Joint Group of Experts on Prior Informed Consent.[24] However, since none of these instruments are legally binding, and since they apply only to one aspect of pollution source transfer, they were considered by some writers to be insufficient to consolidate their status as customary law, as mentioned in Chapter 1 para. 6 above.

With the adoption of the legal instruments constituting the Basel Convention regime, and the pertinent development of some sectoral pollution control treaties, this situation has changed drastically. As we have seen in the preceding chapters, the legal instruments constituting the Basel Convention regime—with the exception of those that do not provide for any permissible transfer of hazardous wastes—consistently incorporate or advocate a control system based on prior notification and PIC for hazardous wastes subject to transboundary movement. PIC is a cornerstone of the Basel and Bamako Conventions (see Chapter 2(F) above; Chapter 3 para. 5 above), of the 1993 Regulation of the EU, and of the 1992 Decision of the OECD (see Chapter 4 paras. 2, 9 above). It is incorporated, albeit in an incomplete form, into the two North American agreements on hazardous wastes (see Chapter 3(J) above). It is also supported by the Cairo Guidelines (Chapter 2(A) above), and the 1988 Resolution of the UN General Assembly on hazardous wastes.[25] Some states have enacted national legislation incorporating prior notification and PIC. Two examples are the United States Resource Conservation and Recovery Act (RCRA),

[24] See Gündling, in Handl and Lutz, (1989a), p. 65 et seq.; also Pallemaerts, in YBIEL 2(1991), p. 170. The relevant legal instruments are repr. in Kwiatkowska and Soons, (1993), and in Hohmann, (1992), Vol. 1. See also the *Report on the 6th meeting of the Joint Committee*, June–July 1993.

[25] UNGA Resolution 43/212, 20 December 1988 (repr. in Kwiatkowska and Soons, (1993), p. 81).

as amended by the Hazardous and Solid Waste Act (HSWA); and the Japanese Law of March 1994 on the control of export and import of hazardous wastes. The concept of PIC is also gaining support in the area of dumping and incineration at sea: it is advocated in UNCLOS (Article 210(5)); in the Noumea Protocol on Dumping; and in the relevant resolutions of the Consultative Meeting of the Contracting Parties to the London Convention (see Chapter 5(A) above). In the light of these developments, it can be argued that the requirements of prior notification and PIC now have a firm basis in customary law in the context of pollution source transfer.[26] This applies to recyclable as well as non-recyclable wastes, even though there is a tendency in the relevant legislation of the EU and the OECD to modify these requirements for the transfer of wastes destined for recycling or recovery operations (see Chapter 4 above).

Two other concepts, somewhat less far-reaching than PIC, are also used increasingly in the context of pollution source transfer: the requirement of obtaining the prior consent of an international body (see Chapter 6(G) above), and the requirement of obtaining the consent of a national authority of the source state, used in the sectoral treaties on dumping and in some of the regional treaties on marine pollution from land-based sources (see Chapter 5 above).

E. *Duty to Ensure Environmentally Sound Disposal of Hazardous Wastes that were Illegally Exported or Cannot be Disposed of in the State of Import*

This principle, discussed in Chapters 2(G) and 6(E) above, has two aspects. On the one hand, states must ensure the environmentally sound disposal of illegally exported hazardous wastes, if necessary by re-importing them into the state of origin. This duty is allocated to the state of export or import, whichever is considered responsible for the illegality under the terms of the relevant legal instrument. On the other hand, the state of export must arrange or allow re-import if the wastes were legally exported but cannot be disposed of in an environmentally sound manner in the state of destination. Both these rules specifically allocate obligations of reparation to states in the context of pollution source transfer. Thus, in common with the other rules discussed in this chapter, they broaden the traditional perspective which focuses on the duties of states in the context of transboundary pollution.

The duty to prevent illegal traffic in hazardous wastes has received particularly strong international support, in view of the seriousness of this

[26] Cf. Birnie and Boyle, (1992), p. 343.

problem (see Chapter 1 above).[27] It is embodied in the Basel and Bamako Conventions, both of which oblige their parties to adopt relevant criminal legislation. The Central American Agreement includes a similar provision (see Chapter 6(H) above). As discussed in Chapter 2 above, the obligation on states to ensure environmentally sound disposal of wastes subject to illegal traffic, and to re-import legally exported wastes that cannot be properly disposed of, was included in the Basel Convention after considerable debate, but now constitutes one of its fundamental principles. The relevant provisions of the Basel Convention subsequently served as a model for equivalent provisions in the Bamako Convention and the 1993 EU Regulation. The two North American agreements of 1986 also feature these obligations (see Chapter 6(E) above). In addition, the duty to re-import is advocated in the non-binding part of the relevant OECD Council Decision-Recommendation of 1984 (see Chapter 4 para. 8 above), and is supported by the UN General Assembly's 1988 Resolution on hazardous wastes.[28] The Cairo Guidelines incorporate this concept in a modified form: if the state of import has objected to the transaction, and the wastes have already left the exporting state, that state may not object to re-import (see Chapter 2(A) above).

In Chapter 6 para. 3 above, it was argued that the exporting state's duty to re-import hazardous wastes subject to illegal traffic is an aspect of that state's duty to make reparation for breach of an international obligation, and therefore has a basis in customary law. This argument is supported by recent state practice: in some of the cases of attempted or completed disposal of hazardous wastes in states that had not previously been informed nor given their consent to the transaction, the state of origin was eventually compelled to take the wastes back (see Chapter 6(F) above). In this instance, the consistent support of this rule by the Basel Convention regime reaffirms and strengthens an already existing customary rule and adjusts it to the specific issue of transboundary movement of hazardous waste as an aspect of pollution source transfer. Therefore, even if the relevant rule does not contribute significantly to the further development of the law of state responsibility, as concluded in Chapter 6 para. 7 above, it does consolidate the duty to re-import as one particular aspect of reparation.

The duty of the importing state to which the illegality is attributed to ensure the environmentally sound disposal of illegally imported hazardous wastes, on the other hand, is an innovation with respect to existing customary law: this cannot be considered an aspect of the customary duty to

[27] UNGA Resolutions 42/183 of 20 December 1988; 44/226 of 22 December 1989; UNECOSOC Resolution 1989/62 of 24 May 1989 (all repr. in Kwiatkowska and Soons, (1993)); UNCED Agenda 21, Chapter 20 (para. 20.45). For an overview cf. the *Note by the Executive Director of UNEP on Illegal Traffic in Hazardous Wastes*, 15 September 1992, (Basel Conference Doc. UNEP/CHW.1/19).

[28] UNGA Resolution 43/212 (1988).

make reparation since in this case the state responsible for the illegality and the 'victim' state are one and the same. Likewise, the exporting state's duty to re-import hazardous wastes that were legally exported but cannot be properly disposed of in the state of import has no customary law basis, as discussed in Chapter 6 para. 5 above. Unlike the other rules discussed in this chapter, these obligations cannot therefore be considered an extension of existing customary law rules. At the time of their incorporation into the component elements of the Basel Convention regime, their acceptance was by no means universal and undisputed, as discussed. Also, they are not reflected in any legal regime addressing environmental issues other than the hazardous waste cycle. It is therefore doubtful whether their incorporation into the instruments constituting the Basel Convention regime, all of which are fairly recent, will suffice in itself for the consolidation of pertinent customary law. These principles could, however, provide the basis for customary rules if supported by additional international legal instruments and state practice in the years to come.

F. *Conclusions*

The above analysis shows that the fundamental principles of the Basel Convention regime and the pertinent sectoral legal instruments, namely the principles of waste minimization and proximity of disposal; restriction or conditional ban of waste exports and unsound disposal options, environmentally sound waste management and non-discrimination, prior notification and PIC, and the duty to re-import illegally exported hazardous wastes, form the basis of a framework of emerging customary law rules. These and related principles have also received support during the UNCED preparatory process and in Chapters 20 and 21 of Agenda 21, and have been advocated in the academic discussion as the most feasible solution to the waste problem.[29] In their majority, they are not entirely new, but constitute a logical consequence and further development of the existing customary law rules discussed in Chapter 1(F) above. Thus the main merit of these rules is that they adapt existing customary rules to the specific issue of pollution source transfer, and give them more precise content in that context.

Interestingly, the requirement of prior EIA hardly features in the legal instruments constituting the Basel Convention regime, even though it would appear to be an important component of an international waste management system, and would, in particular, give more concrete content to the concept of environmentally sound management of hazardous

[29] *Environmentally Sound Management of Solid Wastes and Sewage-Related Issues: Options for Agenda 21* (A/CONF.151/PC/WG.II/Rev.1); Lang, in Lang, Neuhold, and Zemanek, (1991), p. 149.

wastes.[30] Chapter 21 of Agenda 21 merely endorses the facilitation of impact assessment in rather vague terms. In this respect, the Basel Convention regime adds nothing to the development of the relevant emerging customary rule (see Chapter 1 para. 5 above). In particular, it does not give any guidance with respect to the important issue of the duties and rights of the states concerned with respect to prior EIA of prospective disposal facilities for hazardous wastes imported from abroad. An important aspect of pollution source transfer is thus left open, and it is necessary to resort to the emerging customary rule on this point. The concept of EIA receives more support from the sectoral legal instruments on marine pollution: it is embodied in the 1992 Helsinki Convention and the more recent UNEP Regional Seas Conventions (see Chapter 1 para. 5 and Chapter 5 above), and in Chapter 17 of Agenda 21. In addition, the work carried out under the auspices of the IMO to develop a New Assessment Procedure for wastes is likely to contribute to the development of this rule.[31] It is also embodied in the 1992 UN/ECE Convention on international waterways (see Chapter 5(D) above). However, even in these fields the concept is not consistently endorsed, and the instruments that do support it focus on transboundary pollution rather than pollution source transfer.

THE EMERGENCE OF A GLOBAL, HOLISTIC, AND INTEGRATED REGIME FOR THE CONTROL OF THE HAZARDOUS WASTE CYCLE

The analysis undertaken in this study of the international legal rules that directly or indirectly address the hazardous waste cycle shows that a two-level regime for the control of this cycle is emerging.

At the first level, the Basel Convention and the related regional rules adopted under its umbrella, analysed in Chapters 3 and 4 above, form a control system for the transboundary movement of hazardous wastes in the narrow sense defined by the Basel Convention, i.e. the transfer of the wastes between two or more sovereign states. This control system, which has been termed the 'Basel Convention regime' in this study, is already well developed, the regional waste management systems generally being in line with the Basel Convention.

At the second level, the Basel Convention regime and the sectoral pollution control treaties analysed in Chapter 5 above have the potential to form a wider control system, denoted as the 'global waste management regime', which addresses the management and international transfer of hazardous wastes, and their release into the different spheres of environment,

[30] Cf. Rublack, (1993), p. 173.
[31] Cf. IMO Docs. LDC14/INF.18 and LDC 14/INF.19, (1991).

regardless of whether or not the wastes are subject to transboundary movement within the meaning of the Basel Convention. As noted in Chapter 5 above, this global waste management regime is not as yet fully developed. It can only be realized in a satisfactory manner if the relevant rules are harmonized with the Basel Convention, and with each other. In particular, the concepts embodied in the stronger treaties must be taken up by those which are, at present, less stringent.

The emerging global waste management regime meets the requirement of addressing every stage of the hazardous waste cycle, outlined in Chapter 1(C) above, to a large extent. As mentioned in Chapter 5 above, the Basel Convention regime addresses all stages of the hazardous waste cycle but focuses on the problems of international transfer and management, while the sectoral treaties deal almost exclusively with disposal. The weakest point in the regime is the regulation of the first stage of the cycle, namely waste generation. This stage is addressed by the emerging global waste management regime only in terms of general principles such as waste minimization. This weakness is indirectly addressed by a number of policy statements, which call for the strengthening of mechanisms that promote waste avoidance through alternative cleaner production methods.[32] It could be remedied to some extent by the completion of the proposed waste strategies, discussed in Chapter 2 para. 5 above and Chapter 5 above.

The following paragraphs address the question whether the emerging regime displays the fundamental characteristics set out in Chapter 1 above.

G. *Uniform Global Standards and Regional Rules*

As we saw in Chapter 3 above, the Basel Convention strikes a balance between a so-called 'framework' treaty, which would lay down the fundamental principles only and leave the regulation of details to regional agreements, and a detailed global regime leaving no room for divergent regional regulation. While establishing fairly detailed global standards, it allows for regional regulation taking into account the specific situations and needs of individual groups of countries. These regional rules do not have to conform to the provisions of the Basel Convention in every detail, but they may not derogate from its fundamental concepts, as we have seen in Chapter 3 above. The balance between global and regional regulation, advocated in Chapter 1 above, is thus successfully achieved by the Basel Convention regime.

The conclusions of Chapter 3 above show the different ways in which regional regulation can be used to address specific regional concerns under the umbrella of the Basel Convention. One approach is for regional con-

[32] Cf. UNEP Governing Council Decisions SS.II/4/B (3 August 1990) and 16/30 (31 May 1991).

ventions or other regulatory systems adopted by parties to the Basel Convention to establish independent comprehensive and detailed regimes which conform to the global treaty, and set up their own institutional infrastructure. This approach is taken by the Bamako Convention as well as the legal instruments of the EU and the OECD. In all probability, it will also be followed by the hazardous waste protocols currently under negotiation within the various Regional Seas Programmes of UNEP. Alternatively, regional regulation can be limited to those areas in which the states concerned wish to differ from the global treaty. If they are also parties to the Basel Convention, these states can then rely on the rules and infrastructure of the global regime in all other respects. This concept, which requires much less expenditure and capacities on the part of the states adhering to the regional system, underlies Article 39 of the Lomé IV Convention, and Article 59 of the Abuja Convention.

Outside the Basel Convention regime, the technique of combining global and regional regulation is also used in UNCLOS and the sectoral treaties on ocean dumping, as mentioned in Chapter 1(I) and Chapter 5 above. However, the provisions in question do not lay down the requirements to be met by regional rules in as much detail as the Basel Convention, nor do they address the relationship between the global treaty and the regional agreements concluded within its framework. The UN/ECE Convention on the protection of international waterways also provides for regional regulation, laying down the requirements to be embodied into regional agreements in more detail. As discussed in Chapter 5 above, the relationship of the Basel Convention regime with regional sectoral treaties does not differ substantially from its relationship with global sectoral treaties.

H. *Sectoral and Integrated Regulation*

As we have seen in Chapters 2–4 above, the component parts of the Basel Convention regime are to a large extent based on the integrated approach. The principles of waste minimization, proximity, and environmentally sound waste management, discussed above, generally support the concepts of 'cleaner production' and 'integrated pollution control' which are indicative of an integrated approach, as discussed in Chapter 1(J) above. The principles of PIC and the requirements of full documentation of every waste transaction, incorporated in virtually all component parts of the Basel Convention regime, support the concept of 'cradle-to-grave' monitoring of hazardous wastes, which is also an expression of the integrated approach. The sectoral rules which are part of the emerging global waste management regime can supplement the integrated rules by affording protection to each sphere of the environment in accordance with the special characteristics of the individual spheres, if they are adjusted to the Basel

Convention regime and to each other as discussed. The global waste management regime thus strikes a useful balance between the two approaches, as advocated in Chapter 1(J) above.

I. *Sovereignty-Based and Holistic Rules*

As noted in Chapters 2 and 6 above, the Basel Convention and the legal instruments constituting the global waste management regime feature both sovereignty-based and holistic rules. Of the fundamental obligations discussed above, the duties of waste minimization, proximity, and environmentally sound management reflect the holistic approach, whereas the sovereignty-based approach is reflected in the principles of non-discrimination, prior notification, PIC, and the obligation to re-import wastes under certain circumstances. The concept of restriction or conditional prohibition of waste exports and unsound disposal options lends support to both approaches: while aiming to protect the interests of individual states, it also recognizes the need to protect the environment against pollution by hazardous wastes independently of national interests. Since the Basel Convention regime focuses on transboundary movements of hazardous wastes in the narrow sense, i.e. between two or more states (see Chapter 2 para. 4 above, Chapter 3 above), it generally leans more towards the sovereignty-based approach, whereas the sectoral treaties on marine pollution, aiming to protect areas beyond national jurisdiction against pollution (see Chapter 5 above), tend to be more supportive of the holistic approach. The waste management legislation of the EU and the OECD is an exception to this: aiming to establish comprehensive systems for waste management within their respective areas rather than addressing the mutual rights and obligations of their members, the legal instruments of the EU and the OECD show much stronger support of the holistic approach than other component elements of the Basel Convention regime (see Chapter 4 above).

As discussed in Chapter 6 above, the mechanisms for ensuring compliance also reflect both concepts, albeit to a different extent. The traditional mechanisms, state responsibility and liability as well as civil liability, are based on the sovereignty-based approach, whereas institutional supervision and, to some extent, international compensation funds support the holistic approach.

We can thus conclude that the global waste management regime meets the need for a balance between the sovereignty-based and the holistic approach, established in Chapter 1(K) above.

J. *The Preventive and the Remedial Approach*

The examination of the relevant legal instruments in the preceding chapters shows that the preventive approach determines the characteristics of the emerging global waste management regime to a great extent. This is evident in three respects. First, the fundamental rules developed or enhanced by the regime, discussed above, all support the preventive approach. Secondly, most of the methods of regulation which are indicative of the preventive approach, discussed in Chapter 1(L) above, are used consistently in the legal instruments which constitute the emerging global waste management regime. This applies notably to the restriction or conditional prohibition of hazardous activities, the requirement of PIC or another form of prior authorization, the requirements of information exchange as well as financial and technical co-operation, and the application of technical norms setting qualitative and quantitative standards. Thirdly, the mechanisms to ensure compliance discussed in Chapter 6 above support the preventive approach. This is true especially for institutional supervision, but also for the other mechanisms insofar as they provide an incentive for compliance with primary rules.

The precautionary principle, as an expression of the preventive approach, is advocated either expressly or implicitly in most of the legal instruments constituting the emerging global waste management regime.[33] The Bamako Convention devotes an entire paragraph to this concept (Article 4(3.f)). The Basel Convention, and more specifically the Technical Guidelines and the elements of a Waste Management Strategy elaborated within its framework, strongly support this concept. The Lomé IV Convention, the legislation of the EU and the OECD, the Helsinki Convention (Article 3(2)), the Paris/Oslo Convention (Article 2(2.a)), the UN/ECE Convention on international waterways (Article 4(5)), and Resolution 44(14) of the 14th Consultative Meeting of the Contracting Parties to the London Convention, all incorporate this principle.

The remedial approach is supported by the traditional enforcement mechanisms: state responsibility and liability, and civil liability. Thus, despite their shortcomings discussed in Chapter 6 above, these mechanisms fulfil the important function of ensuring remedy where prevention has failed. The remedial approach is also supported to a certain extent by the establishment of international funds for compensation and emergency response. Both types of funds aim for restoration and reparation, but the time-scale is different: while remedies envisaged by the emergency fund are rapid but provisional, those envisaged by the compensation fund may be longer in materializing but permanent.

[33] Cf. Freestone, in Churchill and Freestone, (1991), p. 37.

As we saw in Chapter 6 above, civil liability and compulsory insurance, as well as the international funds for emergency response and compensation, also favour the polluter pays principle. Conventions on civil liability usually aim to strike a balance between supporting the polluter pays principle and not impeding an economically beneficial activity. The concepts of compulsory insurance and the establishment of an international compensation fund aim to spread the financial burden of remedy to a sufficiently large number of actual and potential polluters so as to guarantee the availability of financial means to restore the environment and compensate the victims. Of the legal instruments constituting the Basel Convention regime, the polluter pays principle has found particularly strong expression in the waste legislation of the EU (see Chapter 4 para. 2 above), and in the Technical Guidelines and the elements of a strategy for waste management elaborated within the framework of the Basel Convention (see Chapter 2 para. 7 above). Of the sectoral pollution control regimes, it is embodied in the 1992 Oslo/Paris Convention (Article 2(2.b)), the 1992 Helsinki Convention (Article 3(4)), and the 1992 UN/ECE Convention on international waterways (Article 2(5.b)) (see Chapter 5 above).

As advocated in Chapter 1(L) above, the global waste management regime is thus based mainly on the preventive approach, but provides adequate remedial mechanisms as a subsidiary option.

K. *Conclusions*

The above analysis justifies the conclusion that a global regime for the management of hazardous wastes is emerging, with the Basel Convention as a basis and regional waste management systems and sectoral pollution control treaties as constituent elements. The regime displays the main characteristics outlined in Chapter 1 above, and therefore has the potential to address successfully the hazardous waste cycle at the international level. Due to the fact that the elaboration of the different component elements of this emerging regime are within the areas of competence of different international organizations or other bodies, each of which has it own methods and practices with regard to the development of international legal rules,[34] this regime is likely to evolve in a slightly haphazard way, instead of following the more systematic approach taken, for example, by the Antarctic Treaty system. As we have seen, the rules are at present at different stages of development, and show considerable differences in their level of detail and stringency. However, the common fundamental principles and concepts adhered to by the relevant legal instruments, and the increasing willingness of the international organizations concerned to co-operate in the

[34] Cf. Birnie, in Hurrell and Kingsbury, (1992), p. 62 et seq.; von Moltke, in Carroll, (1988), p. 87 et seq.

development of these rules, provide a sufficient basis for the emergence of a regime as opposed to a haphazard collection of unrelated and possibly conflicting legal rules.

OUTLOOK

As we have seen, not all problems posed by the hazardous waste cycle are addressed in a satisfactory manner by the emerging global waste management regime. Some weaknesses were pointed out in the preceding chapters, and suggestions for possible improvements were made. Following is a brief summary of these points.

The fairly consistent endorsement, since the early 1990s, of a ban on traffic in hazardous wastes from industrialized to less industrialized nations for disposal constitutes an important step forward in the development of the Basel Convention regime. It also indicates a tendency to differentiate between the different causes of hazardous waste transfer, discussed in Chapter 1 above.

The issue of recyclable hazardous wastes subject to transboundary movement remains, however. The discussion should now focus on the question whether different standards and different levels of restrictions and control should apply to hazardous wastes with merely negative value which are subject to final disposal, and hazardous wastes which have positive economic value and are intended for recycling or recovery operations. As we have seen in earlier chapters, this question, which has considerable practical significance due to the large amounts and the significant value of hazardous wastes exported for recycling or recovery, and their importance for relevant industries in different groups of countries, has not been answered conclusively. It seems clear from the discussion in the preceding chapters that any double standard in favour of wastes destined for recycling or recovery operations would have to be very carefully balanced in order to avoid abuse and illicit practices. A practicable solution could possibly be achieved at the level of technical regulation: the elaboration of clear and internationally recognized definitions of some of the key concepts would provide the basis for a more sophisticated system of restriction or permission of operations involving recyclable wastes. These key concepts include that of recycling and related operations (as opposed to disposal), and that of hazardous wastes subject to control. A classification system for hazardous wastes should ideally extend to the introduction of limit values of concentration, and the specification of testing methods. This should then lead to the elaboration of criteria to distinguish between recyclable hazardous wastes with primarily negative effects, where the risks outweigh any environmental or economic benefit and which should therefore not be subject to international transfer; and secondary products with a positive economic value and a low hazard potential, which could be excluded from pertinent export prohibitions.

In any event, the fundamental principles of hazardous waste management should not be abandoned in the regulation of recyclable hazardous wastes. Agenda 21 of UNCED gives an indication of a possible approach to this problem. Chapter 20 (para. 20.13), which deals with hazardous wastes, recommends the establishment of 'standards or purchasing specifications to avoid discrimination against recycled materials, provided that those materials are environmentally sound', and prescribes environmentally sound management of all hazardous wastes, including recyclable wastes. A certain level of control for recyclable wastes is therefore advocated. By contrast, Chapter 21 (para. 21.17 et seq.), addressing wastes that are not hazardous, endorses recycling without reservations.

Other issues that should be addressed in the future development of the global waste management regime, addressed only summarily in this study, are a more precise definition of the groups of countries between which the general ban on hazardous waste transfer should apply, and the relationship between the waste management regime and the regional and global free trade regimes. This should include the distinction of wastes from 'products' subject to the trade regimes.

As regards the possible further development of the Basel Convention regime, additional regional treaties could be adopted along the lines of the Lomé IV Convention. By enabling more groups of states, especially developing and transitional countries, to adopt stronger rules in specific areas while relying on the fundamental principles and the infrastructure of the Basel Convention, this concept would help to promote progressive strengthening of the fundamental rules of Basel. In order to further develop and enhance the role of the sectoral pollution control treaties in the global waste management regime, these treaties should be strengthened, and harmonized with each other and with the Basel Convention regime, as discussed. Finally, the mechanisms for compliance monitoring and enforcement should be strengthened along the lines discussed in Chapter 6 above, namely by giving international institutions more competence and more independence from states, and by considering the establishment of an international judicial mechanism to which states and individuals would have access. The co-operation of the Basel Secretariat with specialized organizations such as the Customs Co-operation Council and Interpol to combat illegal traffic represents a useful practical approach to this issue.

The developments during the six years since the adoption of the Basel Convention have, to a considerable extent, justified initial hopes that the Convention would provide a starting point for tackling the hazardous waste cycle at a global level. As we saw in the preceding chapters, it has generated or influenced significant global and regional developments in the relevant field, which have led to the emergence of a new regime. This regime has contributed substantially to the further development of international legal principles and concepts, and is continuing to do so. If developments continue in this direction, and if the current shortcomings of the emerging regime can be remedied, it will have an important role to play in the future development of international environmental law in the relevant field. It is in line with current predominant trends in international law and policy addressing environmental protection, and may provide a model for future regimes to be established on the basis of more recent global treaties addressing environmental issues. Undoubtedly, the emerging global waste management regime will not provide the ultimate solution to the complex problems posed by the hazardous waste cycle, but it can make an important contribution. In the light of this, it seems appropriate to conclude with the words of the former Executive Director of UNEP, Mostafa Tolba, after the adoption of the Basel Convention:

> Our agreement has not halted the commerce in poison. But it has signalled the international resolve to eliminate the menace hazardous wastes pose to the welfare of our shared environment and to the health of all the world's peoples.[35]

[35] *Closing Remarks* by Dr. Mostafa K. Tolba, Executive Director of UNEP, to the Conference of Plenipotentiaries on a Global Convention on the Control of Transboundary Movements of Hazardous Wastes, 22 March 1989, (UNEP Information 89/03).

Appendix I

Basel Convention on the Control of Transboundary Movements of Hazardous Wastes and their Disposal (22 March 1989).

PREAMBLE

The Parties to this Convention,

Aware of the risk of damage to human health and the environment caused by hazardous wastes and other wastes and the transboundary movement thereof,

Mindful of the growing threat to human health and the environment posed by the increased generation and complexity, and transboundary movement of hazardous wastes and other wastes,

Mindful also that the most effective way of protecting human health and the environment from the dangers posed by such wastes is the reduction of their generation to a minimum in terms of quantity and/or hazard potential,

Convinced that States should take necessary measures to ensure that the management of hazardous wastes and other wastes including their transboundary movement and disposal is consistent with the protection of human health and the environment whatever the place of disposal,

Noting that States should ensure that the generator should carry out duties with regards to the transport and disposal of hazardous wastes and other wastes in a manner that is consistent with the protection of the environment, whatever the place of disposal.

Fully recognizing that any State has the sovereign right to ban the entry or disposal of foreign hazardous wastes and other wastes in its territory,

Recognizing also the increasing desire for the prohibition of transboundary movements of hazardous wastes and their disposal in other States, especially developing countries,

Convinced that hazardous wastes and other wastes should, as far as is compatible with environmentally sound and efficient management, be disposed of in the State where they were generated,

Aware also that transboundary movements of such wastes from the State of their generation to any other State should be permitted only when conducted under conditions which do not endanger human health and the environment, and under conditions in conformity with the provisions of this Convention,

Considering that enhanced control of transboundary movement of hazardous wastes and other wastes will act as an incentive for their environmentally sound management and for the reduction of the volume of such transboundary movement,

Convinced that States should take measures for the proper exchange of information on and control of the transboundary movement of hazardous wastes and other wastes from and to those States,

Noting that a number of international and regional agreements have addressed the issue of protection and preservation of the environment with regard to the transit of dangerous goods,

Taking into account the Declaration of the United Nations Conference on the Human Environment (Stockholm, 1972), the Cairo Guidelines and Principles for the Environmentally Sound Management of Hazardous Wastes adopted by the Governing Council of the United Nations Environment Programme (UNEP) by decision 14/30 of 17 June 1987, the Recommendations of the United Nations Committee of Experts on the Transport of Dangerous Goods (formulated in 1957 and updated biennially), relevant recommendations, declarations, instruments and regulations adopted within the United Nations system and the work and studies done within other international and regional organizations,

Mindful of the spirit, principles, aims and functions of the World Charter for Nature adopted by the General Assembly of the United Nations at is thirty-seventh session (1982) as the rule of ethics in respect of the protection of the human environment and the conservation of natural resources.

Affirming that States are responsible for the fulfilment of their international obligations concerning the protection of human health and protection and preservation of the environment, and are liable in accordance with international law,

Recognizing that in the case of a material breach of the provisions of this Convention or any protocol thereto the relevant international law of treaties shall apply,

Aware of the need to continue the development and implementation of environmentally sound low-waste technologies, recycling options, good house-keeping and management systems with a view to reducing to a minimum the generation of hazardous wastes and other wastes,

Aware also of the growing international concern about the need for stringent control of transboundary movement of hazardous wastes and other wastes, and of the need as far as possible to reduce such movement to a minimum,

Concerned about the problem of illegal transboundary traffic in hazardous wastes and other wastes,

Taking into account also the limited capabilities of the developing countries to manage hazardous wastes and other wastes,

Recognizing the need to promote the transfer of technology for the sound management of hazardous wastes and other wastes produced locally, particularly to the developing countries in accordance with the spirit of the Cairo Guidelines and decision 14/16 of the Governing Council of UNEP on Promotion of the transfer of environmental protection technology,

Recognizing also that hazardous wastes and other wastes should be transported in accordance with relevant international conventions and recommendations,

Convinced also that the transboundary movement of hazardous wastes and other wastes should be permitted only when the transport and the ultimate disposal of such wastes is environmentally sound, and

Determined to protect, by strict control, human health and the environment against the adverse effects which may result from the generation and management of hazardous wastes and other wastes,

HAVE AGREED AS FOLLOWS:

Article 1

Scope of the Convention

1. The following wastes that are subject to transboundary movement shall be 'hazardous wastes' for the purposes of this Convention:

(a) Wastes that belong to any category contained in Annex I, unless they do not possess any of the characteristics contained in Annex III; and

(b) Wastes that are not covered under paragraph (1) but are defined as, or are considered to be, hazardous wastes by the domestic legislation of the Party of export, import or transit.

2. Wastes that belong to any category contained in Annex II that are subject to transboundary movement shall be 'other wastes' for the purposes of this Convention.

3. Wastes which, as a result of being radioactive, are subject to other international control systems, including international instruments, applying specifically to radioactive materials, are excluded from the scope of this Convention.

4. Wastes which derive from the normal operations of a ship, the discharge of which is covered by another international instrument, are excluded from the scope of this Convention.

Article 2

Definitions

For the purposes of this Convention:

1. 'Wastes' are substances or objects which are disposed of or are intended to be disposed of or are required to be disposed of by the provisions of national law;

2. 'Management' means the collection, transport and disposal of hazardous wastes or other wastes, including after-care of disposal sites;

3. 'Transboundary movement' means any movement of hazardous wastes or other wastes from an area under the national jurisdiction of one State to or through an area under the national jurisdiction of another State or to or through an area not under the national jurisdiction of any State, provided at least two States are involved in the movement;

4. 'Disposal' means any operation specified in Annex IV to this Convention;

5. 'Approved site or facility' means a site or facility for the disposal of hazardous wastes or other wastes which is authorized or permitted to operate for this purpose by a relevant authority of the State where the site or facility is located;

6. 'Competent authority' means one governmental authority designated by a Party to be responsible, within such geographical areas as the Party may think fit, for receiving the notification of a transboundary movement of hazardous wastes or other wastes, and any information related to it, and for responding to such a notification, as provided in Article 6;

7. 'Focal point' means the entity of a Party referred to in Article 5 responsible for receiving and submitting information as provided for in Articles 13 and 16;

8. 'Environmentally sound management of hazardous wastes or other wastes' means taking all practicable steps to ensure that hazardous wastes or other wastes are managed in a manner which will protect human health and the environment against the adverse effects which may result from such wastes;

9. 'Area under the national jurisdiction of a State' means any land, marine area or air space within which a State exercises administrative and regulatory responsibility in accordance with international law in regard to the protection of human health or the environment;
10. 'State of export' means a Party from which a transboundary movement of hazardous wastes or other wastes is planned to be initiated or is initiated;
11. 'State of import' means a Party to which a transboundary movement of hazardous wastes or other wastes is planned or takes place for the purpose of disposal therein or for the purpose of loading prior to disposal in an area not under the national jurisdiction of any State;
12. 'State of transit' means any State, other than the State of export or import, through which a movement of hazardous wastes or other wastes is planned or takes place;
13. 'States concerned' means Parties which are States of export or import, or transit States, whether or not Parties;
14. 'Person' means any natural or legal person;
15. 'Exporter' means any person under the jurisdiction of the State of export who arranges for hazardous wastes or other wastes to be exported;
16. 'Importer' means any person under the jurisdiction of the State of import who arranges for hazardous wastes or other wastes to be imported;
17. 'Carrier' means any person who carries out the transport of hazardous wastes or other wastes;
18. 'Generator' means any person whose activity produces hazardous wastes or other wastes or, if that person is not known, the person who is in possession and/or control of those wastes;
19. 'Disposer' means any person to whom hazardous wastes or other wastes are shipped and who carries out the disposal of such wastes;
20. 'Political and/or economic integration organization' means an organization constituted by sovereign States to which its member States have transferred competence in respect of matters governed by this Convention and which has been duly authorized, in accordance with its internal procedures, to sign, ratify, accept, approve, formally confirm or accede to it;
21. 'Illegal traffic' means any transboundary movement of hazardous wastes or other wastes as specified in Article 9.

Article 3

National Definitions of Hazardous Wastes

1. Each Party shall, within six months of becoming a Party to this Convention, inform the Secretariat of the Convention of the wastes, other than those listed in Annexes I and II, considered or defined as hazardous under its national legislation and of any requirements concerning transboundary movement procedures applicable to such wastes.
2. Each Party shall subsequently inform the Secretariat of any significant changes to the information it has provided pursuant to paragraph 1.
3. The Secretariat shall forthwith inform all Parties of the information it has received pursuant to paragraphs 1 and 2.

4. Parties shall be responsible for making the information transmitted to them by the Secretariat under paragraph 3 available to their exporters.

Article 4

General Obligations

1. (a) Parties exercising their right to prohibit the import of hazardous wastes or other wastes for disposal shall inform the other Parties of their decision pursuant to Article 13.

(b) Parties shall prohibit or shall not permit the export of hazardous wastes and other wastes to the Parties which have prohibited the import of such wastes, when notified pursuant to subparagraph (a) above.

(c) Parties shall prohibit or shall not permit the export of hazardous wastes and other wastes if the State of import does not consent in writing to the specific import, in the case where that State of import has not prohibited the import of such wastes.

2. Each Party shall take the appropriate measures to:

(a) Ensure that the generation of hazardous wastes and other wastes within it is reduced to a minimum, taking into account social, technological and economic aspects;

(b) Ensure the availability of adequate disposal facilities, for the environmentally sound management of hazardous wastes and other wastes, that shall be located, to the extent possible, within it, whatever the place of their disposal;

(c) Ensure that persons involved in the management of hazardous wastes or other wastes within it take such steps as are necessary to prevent pollution due to hazardous wastes and other wastes arising from such management and, if such pollution occurs, to minimize the consequences thereof for human health and the environment;

(d) Ensure that the transboundary movement of hazardous wastes and other wastes is reduced to the minimum consistent with the environmentally sound and efficient management of such wastes, and is conducted in a manner which will protect human health and the environment against the adverse effects which may result from such movement;

(e) Not allow the export of hazardous wastes or other wastes to a State or group of States belonging to an economic and/or political integration organization that are Parties, particularly developing countries, which have prohibited by their legislation all imports, or if it has reason to believe that the wastes in question will not be managed in an environmentally sound manner, according to criteria to be decided on by the Parties at their first meeting.

(f) Require that information about a proposed transboundary movement of hazardous wastes and other wastes be provided to the States concerned, according to Annex VA, to state clearly the effects of the proposed movement on human health and the environment;

(g) Prevent the import of hazardous wastes and other wastes if it has reason to believe that the wastes in question will not be managed in an environmentally sound manner;

(h) Co-operate in activities with other Parties and interested organizations, directly and through the Secretariat, including the dissemination of information on the transboundary movement of hazardous wastes and other wastes, in order to improve the environmentally sound management of such wastes and to achieve the prevention of illegal traffic.

3. The Parties consider that illegal traffic in hazardous wastes or other wastes is criminal.

4. Each Party shall take appropriate legal, administrative and other measures to implement and enforce the provisions of this Convention, including measures to prevent and punish conduct in contravention of the Convention.

5. A Party shall not permit hazardous wastes or other wastes to be exported to a non-Party or to be imported from a non-Party.

6. The Parties agree not to allow the export of hazardous wastes or other wastes for disposal within the area south of 60° South latitude, whether or not such wastes are subject to transboundary movement.

7. Furthermore, each Party shall:

(a) Prohibit all persons under its national jurisdiction from transporting or disposing of hazardous wastes or other wastes unless such persons are authorized or allowed to perform such types of operations;

(b) Require that hazardous wastes and other wastes that are to be the subject of a transboundary movement be packaged, labelled, and transported in conformity with generally accepted and recognized international rules and standards in the field of packaging, labelling, and transport, and that due account is taken of relevant internationally recognized practices;

(c) Require that hazardous wastes and other wastes be accompanied by a movement document from the point at which a transboundary movement commences to the point of disposal.

8. Each Party shall require that hazardous wastes or other wastes, to be exported, are managed in an environmentally sound manner in the State of import or elsewhere. Technical guidelines for the environmentally sound management of wastes subject to this Convention shall be decided by the Parties at their first meeting.

9. Parties shall take the appropriate measures to ensure that the transboundary movement of hazardous wastes and other wastes only be allowed if:

(a) The State of export does not have the technical capacity and the necessary facilities, capacity or suitable disposal sites in order to dispose of the wastes in question in an environmentally sound and efficient manner; or

(b) The wastes in question are required as a raw material for recycling or recovery industries in the State of import; or

(c) The transboundary movement in question is in accordance with other criteria to be decided by the Parties, provided those criteria do not differ from the objectives of this Convention.

10. The obligation under this Convention of States in which hazardous wastes and other wastes are generated to require that those wastes are managed in an environmentally sound manner may not under any circumstances be transferred to the States of import or transit.

11. Nothing in this Convention shall prevent a Party from imposing additional requirements that are consistent with the provisions of this Convention, and are in accordance with the rules of international law, in order better to protect human health and the environment.

12. Nothing in this Convention shall affect in any way the sovereignty of States over their territorial sea established in accordance with international law, and the sovereign rights and the jurisdiction which States have in their exclusive economic zones and their continental shelves in accordance with international law, and the exercise by ships and aircraft of all States of navigational rights and freedoms as provided for in international law and as reflected in relevant international instruments.
13. Parties shall undertake to review periodically the possibilities for the reduction of the amount and/or the pollution potential of hazardous wastes and other wastes which are exported to other States, in particular to developing countries.

Article 5

Designation of Competent Authorities and Focal Point

To facilitate the implementation of this Convention, the Parties shall:
1. Designate or establish one or more competent authorities and one focal point. One competent authority shall be designated to receive the notification in case of a State of transit.
2. Inform the Secretariat, within three months of the date of the entry into force of this Convention for them, which agencies they have designated as their focal point and their competent authorities.
3. Inform the Secretariat, within one month of the date of decision, of any changes regarding the designation made by them under paragraph 2 above.

Article 6

Transboundary Movement between Parties

1. The State of export shall notify, or shall require the generator or exporter to notify, in writing, through the channel of the competent authority of the State of export, the competent authority of the States concerned of any proposed transboundary movement of hazardous wastes or other wastes. Such notification shall contain the declarations and information specified in Annex VA, written in a language acceptable to the State of import. Only one notification needs to be sent to each State concerned.
2. The State of import shall respond to the notifier in writing, consenting to the movement with or without conditions, denying permission for the movement, or requesting additional information. A copy of the final response of the State of import shall be sent to the competent authorities of the States concerned which are Parties.
3. The State of export shall not allow the generator or exporter to commence the transboundary movement until it has received written confirmation that:

(a) The notifier has received the written consent of the State of import; and

(b) The notifier has received from the State of import confirmation of the existence of a contract between the exporter and the disposer specifying environmentally sound management of the wastes in question.

4. Each State of transit which is a Party shall promptly acknowledge to the notifier receipt of the notification. It may subsequently respond to the notifier in writ-

ing, within 60 days, consenting to the movement with or without conditions, denying permission for the movement, or requesting additional information. The State of export shall not allow the transboundary movement to commence until it has received the written consent of the State of transit. However, if at any time a Party decides not to require prior written consent, either generally or under specific conditions, for transit transboundary movements of hazardous wastes or other wastes, or modifies its requirements in this respect, it shall forthwith inform the other Parties of its decision pursuant to Article 13. In this latter case, if no response is received by the State of export within 60 days of the receipt of a given notification by the State of transit, the State of export may allow the export to proceed through the State of transit.

5. In the case of a transboundary movement of wastes where the wastes are legally defined as or considered to be hazardous wastes only:

(a) By the State of export, the requirements of paragraph 9 of this Article that apply to the importer or disposer and the State of import shall apply *mutatis mutandis* to the exporter and State of export, respectively;

(b) By the State of import, or by the States of import and transit which are Parties, the requirements of paragraphs 1, 3, 4 and 6 of this Article that apply to the exporter and State of export shall apply *mutatis mutandis* to the importer or disposer and State of import, respectively; or

(c) By any State of transit which is a Party, the provisions of paragraph 4 shall apply to such State.

6. The State of export may, subject to the written consent of the States concerned, allow the generator or the exporter to use a general notification where hazardous wastes or other wastes having the same physical and chemical characteristics are shipped regularly to the same disposer via the same customs office of exit of the State of export via the same customs office of entry of the State of import, and, in the case of transit, via the same customs office of entry and exit of the State or States of transit.

7. The States concerned may make their written consent to the use of the general notification referred to in paragraph 6 subject to the supply of certain information, such as the exact quantities or periodical lists of hazardous wastes or other wastes to be shipped.

8. The general notification and written consent referred to in paragraphs 6 and 7 may cover multiple shipments of hazardous wastes or other wastes during a maximum period of 12 months.

9. The Parties shall require that each person who takes charge of a transboundary movement of hazardous wastes or other wastes sign the movement document either upon delivery or receipt of the wastes in question. They shall also require that the disposer inform both the exporter and the competent authority of the State of export of receipt by the disposer of the wastes in question and, in due course, of the completion of disposal as specified in the notification. If no such information is received within the State of export, the competent authority of the State of export or the exporter shall so notify the State of import.

10. The notification and response required by this Article shall be transmitted to the competent authority of the Parties concerned or to such governmental authority as may be appropriate in the case of non-Parties.

11. Any transboundary movement of hazardous wastes or other wastes shall be covered by insurance, bond or other guarantee as may be required by the State of import or any State of transit which is a Party.

Article 7

Transboundary Movement from a Party through States which are not Parties

Paragraph 2 of Article 6 of the Convention shall apply *mutatis mutandis* to transboundary movement of hazardous wastes or other wastes from a Party through a State or States which are not Parties.

Article 8

Duty to Re-import

When a transboundary movement of hazardous wastes or other wastes to which the consent of the States concerned has been given, subject to the provisions of this Convention, cannot be completed in accordance with the terms of the contract, the State of export shall ensure that the wastes in question are taken back into the State of export, by the exporter, if alternative arrangements cannot be made for their disposal in an environmentally sound manner, within 90 days from the time that the importing State informed the State of export and the Secretariat, or such other period of time as the States concerned agree. To this end, the State of export and any Party of transit shall not oppose, hinder or prevent the return of those wastes to the State of export.

Article 9

Illegal Traffic

1. For the purpose of this Convention, any transboundary movement of hazardous wastes or other wastes:

(a) without notification pursuant to the provisions of this Convention to all States concerned; or

(b) without the consent pursuant to the provisions of this Convention of a State concerned; or

(c) with consent obtained from States concerned through falsification, misrepresentation or fraud; or

(d) that does not conform in a material way with the documents; or

(e) that results in deliberate disposal (e.g. dumping) of hazardous wastes or other wastes in contravention of this Convention and of general principles of international law,

shall be deemed to be illegal traffic.

2. In case of a transboundary movement of hazardous wastes or other wastes deemed to be illegal traffic as the result of conduct on the part of the exporter or generator, the State or export shall ensure that the wastes in question are:

(a) taken back by the exporter or the generator or, if necessary, by itself into the State of export, or, if impracticable,

(b) are otherwise disposed of in accordance with the provisions of this Convention, within 30 days from the time the State of export has been informed about the illegal traffic or such other period of time as States concerned may agree. To this end the Parties concerned shall not oppose, hinder or prevent the return of those wastes to the State of export.

3. In the case of a transboundary movement of hazardous wastes or other wastes deemed to be illegal traffic as the result of conduct on the part of the importer or disposer, the State of import shall ensure that the wastes in question are disposed of in an environmentally sound manner by the importer or disposer or, if necessary, by itself within 30 days from the time the illegal traffic has come to the attention of the State of import or such other period of time as the States concerned may agree. To this end, the Parties concerned shall co-operate, as necessary, in the disposal of the wastes in an environmentally sound manner.

4. In cases where the responsibility for the illegal traffic cannot be assigned either to the exporter or generator or to the importer or disposer, the Parties concerned or other Parties, as appropriate, shall ensure, through co-operation, that the wastes in question are disposed of as soon as possible in an environmentally sound manner either in the State of export or the State of import or elsewhere as appropriate.

5. Each Party shall introduce appropriate national/domestic legislation to prevent and punish illegal traffic. The Parties shall co-operate with a view to achieving the objects of this Article.

Article 10

International Co-operation

1. The Parties shall co-operate with each other in order to improve and achieve environmentally sound management of hazardous wastes and other wastes.

2. To this end, the Parties shall:

(a) Upon request, make available information, whether on a bilateral or multilateral basis, with a view to promoting the environmentally sound management of hazardous wastes and other wastes, including harmonization of technical standards and practices for the adequate management of hazardous wastes and other wastes;

(b) Co-operate in monitoring the effects of the management of hazardous wastes on human health and the environment;

(c) Co-operate, subject to their national laws, regulations and policies, in the development and implementation of new environmentally sound low-waste technologies and the improvement of existing technologies with a view to eliminating, as far as practicable, the generation of hazardous wastes and other wastes and achieving more effective and efficient methods of ensuring their management in an environmentally sound manner, including the study of the economic, social and environmental effects of the adoption of such new or improved technologies;

(d) Co-operate actively, subject to their national laws, regulations and policies, in the transfer of technology and management systems related to the environmentally sound management of hazardous wastes and other wastes. They shall also co-operate in developing the technical capacity among Parties, especially those which may need and request technical assistance in this field;

(e) Co-operate in developing appropriate technical guidelines and/or codes of practice.

3. The Parties shall employ appropriate means to co-operate in order to assist developing countries in the implementation of subparagraphs a, b, c and d of paragraph 2 of Article 4.
4. Taking into account the needs of developing countries, co-operation between Parties and the competent international organizations is encouraged to promote, *inter alia*, public awareness, the development of sound management of hazardous wastes and other wastes and the adoption of new low-waste technologies.

Article 11

Bilateral, Multilateral and Regional Agreements

1. Notwithstanding the provisions of Article 4 paragraph 5, Parties may enter into bilateral, multilateral, or regional agreements or arrangements regarding transboundary movement of hazardous wastes or other wastes with Parties or non-Parties provided that such agreements do not derogate from the environmentally sound management of hazardous wastes and other wastes as required by this Convention. These agreements or arrangements shall stipulate provisions which are not less environmentally sound than those provided for by this Convention in particular taking into account the interests of developing countries.
2. Parties shall notify the Secretariat of any bilateral, multilateral or regional agreements or arrangements referred to in paragraph 1 and those which they have entered into prior to the entry into force of this Convention for them, for the purpose of controlling transboundary movements of hazardous wastes and other wastes which take place entirely among the Parties to such agreements. The provisions of this Convention shall not affect transboundary movements which take place pursuant to such agreements provided that such agreements are compatible with the environmentally sound management of hazardous wastes and other wastes as required by this Convention.

Article 12

Consultations on Liability

The Parties shall co-operate with a view to adopting, as soon as practicable, a protocol setting out appropriate rules and procedures in the field of liability and compensation for damage resulting from the transboundary movement and disposal of hazardous wastes and other wastes.

Article 13

Transmission of Information

1. The Parties shall, whenever it comes to their knowledge, ensure that, in the case of an accident occurring during the transboundary movement of hazardous wastes or other wastes or their disposal, which are likely to present risks to human health and the environment in other States, those states are immediately informed.
2. The Parties shall inform each other, through the Secretariat, of:

(a) Changes regarding the designation of competent authorities and/or focal points, pursuant to Article 5;

(b) Changes in their national definition of hazardous wastes, pursuant to Article 3;

and, as soon as possible,

(c) Decisions made by them not to consent totally or partially to the import of hazardous wastes or other wastes for disposal within the area under their national jurisdiction;

(d) Decisions taken by them to limit or ban the export of hazardous wastes or other wastes;

(e) Any other information required pursuant to paragraph 4 of this Article.

3. The Parties, consistent with national laws and regulations, shall transmit, through the Secretariat, to the Conference of the Parties established under Article 15, before the end of each calendar year, a report on the previous calendar year, containing the following information:

(a) Competent authorities and focal points that have been designated by them pursuant to Article 5;

(b) Information regarding transboundary movements of hazardous wastes or other wastes in which they have been involved, including:

(i) The amount of hazardous wastes and other wastes exported, their category, characteristics, destination, any transit country and disposal method as stated on the response to notification;

(ii) The amount of hazardous wastes and other wastes imported, their category, characteristics, origin, and disposal methods;

(iii) Disposals which did not proceed as intended;

(iv) Efforts to achieve a reduction of the amount of hazardous wastes or other wastes subject to transboundary movement;

(c) Information on the measures adopted by them in implementation of this Convention;

(d) Information on available qualified statistics which have been compiled by them on the effects on human health and the environment of the generation, transportation and disposal of hazardous wastes or other wastes;

(e) Information concerning bilateral, multilateral and regional agreements and arrangements entered into pursuant to Article 11 of this Convention;

(f) Information on accidents occurring during the transboundary movement and disposal of hazardous wastes and other wastes and on the measures undertaken to deal with them;

(g) Information on disposal options operated within the area of their national jurisdiction;

(h) Information on measures undertaken for development of technologies for the reduction and/or elimination of production of hazardous wastes and other wastes; and

(i) Such other matters as the Conference of the Parties shall deem relevant.

4. The Parties, consistent with national laws and regulations, shall ensure that copies of each notification concerning any given transboundary movement of hazardous wastes or other wastes, and the response to it, are sent to the Secretariat when a Party considers that its environment may be affected by that transboundary movement has requested that this should be done.

Article 14

Financial Aspects

1. The Parties agree that, according to the specific needs of different regions and subregions, regional or sub-regional centres for training and technology transfers regarding the management of hazardous wastes and other wastes and the minimization of their generation should be established. The Parties shall decide on the establishment of appropriate funding mechanisms of a voluntary nature.
2. The Parties shall consider the establishment of a revolving fund to assist on an interim basis in case of emergency situations to minimize damage from accidents arising from transboundary movements of hazardous wastes and other wastes or during the disposal of those wastes.

Article 15

Conference of the Parties

1. A Conference of the Parties is hereby established. The first meeting of the Conference of the Parties shall be convened by the Executive Director of UNEP not later than one year after the entry into force of this Convention. Thereafter, ordinary meetings of the Conference of the Parties shall be held at regular intervals to be determined by the Conference at its first meeting.
2. Extraordinary meetings of the Conference of the Parties shall be held at such other times as may be deemed necessary by the Conference, or at the written request of any Party, provided that, within six months of the request being communicated to them by the Secretariat, it is supported by at least one third of the Parties.
3. The Conference of the Parties shall by consensus agree upon and adopt rules of procedure for itself and for any subsidiary body it may establish, as well as financial rules to determine in particular the financial participation of the Parties under this Convention.
4. The Parties at their first meeting shall consider any additional measures needed to assist them in fulfilling their responsibilities with respect to the protection and the preservation of the marine environment in the context of this Convention.
5. The Conference of the Parties shall keep under continuous review and evaluation the effective implementation of this Convention, and, in addition, shall:

(a) Promote the harmonization of appropriate policies, strategies and measures for minimizing harm to human health and the environment by hazardous wastes and other wastes;

(b) Consider and adopt, as required, amendments to this Convention and its annexes, taking into consideration, *inter alia*, available scientific, technical, economic and environmental information.

(c) Consider and undertake any additional action that may be required for the achievement of the purposes of this Convention in the light of experience gained in its operation and i the operation of the agreements and arrangements envisaged in Article 11;

(d) Consider and adopt protocols as required; and

(e) Establish such subsidiary bodies as are deemed necessary for the implementation of this Convention.

6. The United Nations, its specialized agencies, as well as any State not Party to this Convention, may be represented as observers at meetings of the Conference of the Parties. Any other body or agency, whether national or international, governmental or non-governmental, qualified in fields relating to hazardous wastes or other wastes which has informed the Secretariat of its wish to be represented as an observer at a meeting of the Conference of Parties, may be admitted unless at least one third of the Parties present object. The admission and participation of observers shall be subject to the rules of procedure adopted by the Conference of the Parties.

7. The Conference of the Parties shall undertake three years after the entry into force of this Convention, and at least every six years thereafter, an evaluation of its effectiveness and, if deemed necessary, to consider the adoption of a complete or partial ban of transboundary movements of hazardous wastes and other wastes in light of the latest scientific, environmental, technical and economic information.

Article 16

Secretariat

1. The functions of the Secretariat shall be:
   (a) To arrange for and service meetings provided for in Articles 15 and 17;
   (b) To prepare and transmit reports based upon information received in accordance with Articles 3, 4, 6, 11 and 13 as well as upon information derived from meetings of subsidiary bodies established under Article 15 as well as upon, as appropriate, information provided by relevant intergovernmental and non-governmental entities;
   (c) To prepare reports on its activities carried out in implementation of its functions under this Convention and present them to the Conference of the Parties;
   (d) To ensure the necessary coordination with relevant international bodies, and in particular to enter into such administrative and contractual arrangements as may be required for the effective discharge of its function;
   (e) To communicate with Focal Points and Competent Authorities established by the Parties in accordance with Article 5 of this Convention;
   (f) To compile information concerning authorized national sites and facilities of Parties available for the disposal of their hazardous wastes and other wastes and to circulate this information among Parties;
   (g) To receive and convey information from and to Parties on:
   — sources of technical assistance and training;
   — available technical and scientific know-how;
   — sources of advice and expertise; and
   — availability of resources
   with a view to assisting them, upon request, in such areas as:
   — the handling of the notification system of this Convention;
   — the management of hazardous wastes and other wastes;
   — environmentally sound technologies relating to hazardous wastes and other wastes, such as low- and non-waste technology;
   — the assessment of disposal capabilities and sites;

— the monitoring of hazardous wastes and other wastes; and
— emergency responses;

(h) To provide Parties, upon request, with information on consultants or consulting firms having the necessary technical competence in the field, which can assist them to examine a notification for a transboundary movement, the concurrence of a shipment of hazardous wastes or other wastes with the relevant notification, and/or the fact that the proposed disposal facilities for hazardous wastes or other wastes are environmentally sound, when they have reason to believe that the wastes in question will not be managed in an environmentally sound manner. Any such examination would not be at the expense of the Secretariat;

(i) To assist Parties upon request in their identification of cases of illegal traffic and to circulate immediately to the Parties concerned any information it has received regarding illegal traffic;

(j) To co-operate with Parties and with relevant and competent international organizations and agencies in the provision of experts and equipment for the purpose of rapid assistance to States in the event of an emergency situation; and

(k) To perform such other functions relevant to the purposes of this Convention as may be determined by the Conference of the Parties.

2. The Secretariat functions will be carried out on an interim basis by UNEP until the completion of the first meeting of the Conference of the Parties held pursuant to Article 15.

3. At its first meeting, the Conference of the Parties shall designate the Secretariat from among those existing competent intergovernmental organizations which have signified their willingness to carry out the Secretariat functions under this Convention. At this meeting, the Conference of the Parties shall also evaluate the implementation by the interim Secretariat of the functions assigned to it, in particular under paragraph 1 above, and decide upon the structures appropriate for those functions.

Article 17

Amendment of the Convention

1. Any Party may propose amendments to this Convention and any Party to a protocol may propose amendments to that protocol. Such amendments shall take due account, *inter alia*, of relevant scientific and technical considerations.

2. Amendments to this Convention shall be adopted at a meeting of the Conference of the Parties. Amendments to any protocol shall be adopted at a meeting of the Parties to the protocol in question. The text of any proposed amendment to this Convention or to any protocol, except as may otherwise be provided in such protocol, shall be communicated to the Parties by the Secretariat at least six months before the meeting at which it is proposed for adoption. The Secretariat shall also communicate proposed amendments to the Signatories to this Convention for information.

3. The parties shall make every effort to reach agreement on any proposed amendment to this Convention by consensus. If all efforts at consensus have been

exhausted, and no agreement reached, the amendment shall as a last resort be adopted by a three-fourths majority of the Parties present and voting at the meeting, and shall be submitted by the Depositary to all Parties for ratification, approval, formal confirmation or acceptance.

4. The procedure mentioned in paragraph 3 above shall apply to amendments to any protocol, except that a two-thirds majority of the Parties to that protocol present and voting at the meeting shall suffice for their adoption.

5. Instruments of ratification, approval, formal confirmation or acceptance of amendments shall be deposited with the Depositary. Amendments adopted in accordance with paragraphs 3 or 4 above shall enter into force between Parties having accepted them on the ninetieth day after the receipt by the Depositary of their instrument of ratification, approval, formal confirmation or acceptance by at least three-fourths of the Parties who accepted the amendments to the protocol concerned, except as may otherwise be provided in such protocol. The amendments shall enter into force for any other Party on the ninetieth day after that Party deposits its instrument of ratification, approval, formal confirmation or acceptance of the amendments.

6. For the purpose of this Article, 'Parties present and voting' means Parties present and casting an affirmative or negative vote.

Article 18

Adoption and Amendment of Annexes

1. The annexes to this Convention or to any protocol shall form an integral part of this Convention or of such protocol, as the case may be and, unless expressly provided otherwise, a reference to this Convention or its protocols constitutes at the same time a reference to any annexes thereto. Such annexes shall be restricted to scientific, technical and administrative matters.

2. Except as may be otherwise provided in any protocol with respect to its annexes, the following procedure shall apply to the proposal, adoption and entry into force of additional annexes to this Convention or of annexes to a protocol:

(a) Annexes to this Convention and its protocols shall be proposed and adopted according to the procedure laid down in Article 17, paragraphs 2, 3 and 4;

(b) Any Party that is unable to accept an additional annex to this Convention or an annex to any protocol to which it is party shall so notify the Depositary, in writing, within six months from the date of the communication of the adoption by the Depositary. The Depositary shall without delay notify all Parties of any such notification received. A Party may at any time substitute an acceptance for a previous declaration of objection and the annexes shall thereupon enter into force for that Party;

(c) On the expiry of six months from the date of the circulation of the communication by the Depositary, the annex shall become effective for all Parties to this Convention or to any protocol concerned, which have not submitted a notification in accordance with the provision of subparagraph (b) above.

3. The proposal, adoption and entry into force of amendments to annexes to this

Convention or to any protocol shall be subject to the same procedure as for the proposal, adoption and entry into force of annexes to the Convention or annexes to a protocol. Annexes and amendments thereto shall take due account, *inter alia*, of relevant scientific and technical considerations.
4. If an additional annex or an amendment to an annex involves an amendment to this Convention or to any protocol, the additional annex or amended annex shall not enter into force until such time the amendment to this Convention or to the protocol enters into force.

Article 19

Verification

Any Party which has reason to believe that another Party is acting or has acted in breach of its obligations under this Convention may inform the Secretariat thereof, and in such an event, shall simultaneously and immediately inform, directly or through the Secretariat, the Party against whom the allegations are made. All relevant information should be submitted by the Secretariat to the Parties.

Article 20

Settlement of Disputes

1. In case of a dispute between Parties as to the interpretation or application of, or compliance with, this Convention or any protocol thereto, they shall seek a settlement of the dispute through negotiation or any other peaceful means of their own choice.
2. If the Parties concerned cannot settle their dispute through the means mentioned in the preceding paragraph, the dispute, if the Parties to the dispute agree, shall be submitted to the International Court of Justice or to arbitration under the conditions set out in Annex VI on Arbitration. However, failure to reach common agreement on submission of the dispute to the International Court of Justice or to arbitration shall not absolve the Parties from the responsibility of continuing to seek to resolve it by the means referred to in paragraph 1.
3. When ratifying, accepting, approving, formally confirming or acceding to this Convention, or at any time thereafter, a State or political and/or economic integration organization may declare that it recognizes as compulsory *ipso facto* and without special agreement, in relation to any Party accepting the same obligation:
   (a) submission of the dispute to the International Court of Justice; and/or
   (b) arbitration in accordance with the procedures set out in Annex VI.

Such declaration shall be notified in writing to the Secretariat which shall communicate it to the Parties.

Article 21

Signature

This Convention shall be open for signature by States, by Namibia, represented by the United Nations Council for Namibia, and by political and/or economic integration organizations, in Basel on 22 March 1989, at the Federal Department of

Foreign Affairs of Switzerland in Berne from 23 March 1989 to 30 June 1989 and at United Nations Headquarters in New York from 1 July 1989 to 22 March 1990.

Article 22

Ratification, Acceptance, Formal Confirmation or Approval

1. This Convention shall be subject to ratification, acceptance or approval by States and by Namibia, represented by the United Nations Council for Namibia, and to formal confirmation or approval by political and/or economic integration organizations. Instruments of ratification, acceptance, formal confirmation, or approval shall be deposited with the Depositary.
2. Any organization referred to in paragraph 1 above which becomes a Party to this Convention without any of its members States being a Party shall be bound by all the obligations under the Convention. In the case of such organizations, one or more of whose member States is a Party to the Convention, the organization and its member States shall decide on their respective responsibilities for the performance of their obligations under the Convention. In such cases, the organization and the member States shall not be entitled to exercise rights under the Convention concurrently.
3. In their instruments of formal confirmation or approval, the organizations referred to in paragraph 1 above shall declare the extent of their competence with respect to the matters governed by the Convention. These organizations shall also inform the Depositary, who will inform the Parties of any substantial modification in the extent of their competence.

Article 23

Accession

1. This Convention shall be open for accession by States, by Namibia, represented by the United Nations Council for Namibia, and by political and/or economic integration organizations from the day after the date on which the Convention is closed for signature. The instruments of accession shall be deposited with the Depositary.
2. In their instruments of accession, the organizations referred to in paragraph 1 above shall declare the extent of their competence with respect to the matters governed by the Convention. These organizations shall also inform the Depositary of any substantial modification in the extent of their competence.
3. The provisions of Article 22, paragraph 2, shall apply to political and/or economic integration organizations which accede to this Convention.

Article 24

Right to Vote

1. Except as provided for in paragraph 2 below, each Contracting Party to this Convention shall have one vote.
2. Political and/or economic integration organizations, in matters within their competence, in accordance with Article 22, paragraph 3, and Article 23, paragraph 2, shall exercise their right to vote with a number of votes equal to the number of

their member States which are Parties to the Convention or the relevant protocol. Such organizations shall not exercise their right to vote if their member States exercise theirs, and vice versa.

Article 25

Entry into Force

1. This Convention shall enter into force on the ninetieth day after the day of deposit of the twentieth instrument of ratification, acceptance, formal confirmation, approval or accession.
2. For each State or political and/or economic integration organization which ratifies, accepts, approves or formally confirms this Convention or accedes thereto after the date of the deposit of the twentieth instrument of ratification, acceptance, approval, formal confirmation or accession, it shall enter into force on the ninetieth day after the date of deposit by such State or political and/or economic integration organization of its instrument of ratification, acceptance, approval, formal confirmation or accession.
3. For the purpose of paragraphs 1 and 2 above, any instrument deposited by a political and/or economic integration organization shall not be counted as additional to those deposited by member States of such organization.

Article 26

Reservations and Declarations

1. No reservation or exception may be made to this Convention.
2. Paragraph 1 of this Article does not preclude a State or political and/or economic integration organization, when signing, ratifying, accepting, approving, formally confirming or acceding to this Convention, from making declarations or statements, however phrased or named, with a view, *inter alia*, to the harmonization of its laws and regulations with the provisions of this Convention, provided that such declarations or statements do not purport to exclude or to modify the legal effects of the provisions of the Convention in their application to that State.

Article 27

Withdrawal

1. At any time after three years from the date on which this Convention has entered into force for a Party, that Party may withdraw from the Convention by giving written notification to the Depositary.
2. Withdrawal shall be effective one year from receipt of notification by the Depositary, or on such later date as may be specified in the notification.

Article 28

Depository

The Secretary-General of the United Nations shall be the Depository of this Convention and of any protocol thereto.

Article 29

Authentic texts

The original Arabic, Chinese, English, French, Russian and Spanish texts of this Convention are equally authentic.

Annex I

Categories of Wastes to be Controlled

Waste Streams

Y1 Clinical wastes from medical care in hospitals, medical centers and clinics
Y2 Wastes from the production and preparation of pharmaceutical products
Y3 Waste pharmaceuticals, drugs and medicines
Y4 Wastes from the production, formulation and use of biocides and phytopharmaceuticals
Y5 Wastes from the manufacture, formulation and use of wood preserving chemicals
Y6 Wastes from the production, formulation and use of organic solvents
Y7 Wastes from heat treatment and tempering operations containing cyanides
Y8 Waste mineral oils unfit for their originally intended use
Y9 Waste oils/water, hydrocarbons/water mixtures, emulsions
Y10 Waste substances and articles containing or contaminated with polychlorinated biphenyls (PCBs) and/or polychlorinated terphenyls (PCTs) and/or polybrominated biphenyls (PBBs)
Y11 Waste tarry residues arising from refining, distillation and any pyrolytic treatment
Y12 Wastes from production, formulation and use of inks, dyes, pigments, paints, lacquers, varnish
Y13 Wastes from production, formulation and use of resins, latex, plasticizers, glues/adhesives
Y14 Waste chemical substances arising from research and development or teaching activities which are not identified and/or are new and whose effects on man and/or the environment are not known
Y15 Wastes of an explosive nature not subject to other legislation
Y16 Wastes from production, formulation and use of photographic chemicals and processing materials
Y17 Wastes resulting from surface treatment of metals and plastics
Y18 Residues arising from industrial waste disposal operations

Wastes having as constituents:

Y19 Metal carbonyls
Y20 Beryllium; beryllium compounds
Y21 Hexavalent chromium compounds
Y22 Copper compounds
Y23 Zinc compounds
Y24 Arsenic; arsenic compounds
Y25 Selenium; selenium compounds

Y26 Cadmium; cadmium compounds
Y27 Antimony; antimony compounds
Y28 Tellurium; tellurium compounds
Y29 Mercury; mercury compounds
Y30 Thallium; thallium compounds
Y31 Lead; lead compounds
Y32 Inorganic fluorine compounds excluding calcium fluoride
Y33 Inorganic cyanides
Y34 Acidic solutions or acids in solid form
Y35 Basic solutions or bases in solid form
Y36 Asbestos (dust and fibres)
Y37 Organic phosphorus compounds
Y38 Organic cyanides
Y39 Phenols; phenol compounds including chlorophenols
Y40 Ethers
Y41 Halogenated organic solvents
Y42 Organic solvents excluding halogenated solvents
Y43 Any congenor of polychlorinated dibenzo-furan
Y44 Any congenor of polychlorinated dibenzo-p-dioxin
Y45 Organohalogen compounds other than substances referred to in this Annex (e.g. Y39, Y41, Y42, Y43, Y44)

Annex II

Categories of Wastes Requiring Special Consideration

Y46 — Wastes collected from households
Y47 — Residues arising from the incineration of household wastes

Annex III

List of Hazardous Characteristics

UN Class[1]	*Code*	*Characteristics*
1	H1	Explosive An explosive substance or waste is a solid or liquid substance or waste (or mixture of substances or wastes) which is in itself capable by chemical reaction of producing gas at such a temperature and pressure and at such speed as to cause damage to the surroundings.
3	H3	Flammable liquids The word 'flammable' has the same meaning as 'inflammable.' Flammable liquids are liquids, or mixtures of liquids, or liquids containing solids in solution or suspension (for example, paints, varnishes, lacquers, etc., but not including substances or wastes otherwise classified on account of their dangerous characteristics) which give off a flammable vapour at temperatures of not more than 60.5° C, closed-cup test, or not more than 65.6° C, open-cup test. (Since the results of open-cup

		tests and of closed-cup tests are not strictly comparable and even individual results by the same test are often variable, regulations varying from the above figures to make allowance for such differences would be within the spirit of this definition.)
4.1	H4.1	Flammable solids Solids, or waste solids, other than those classed as explosives, which under conditions encountered in transport are readily combustible, or may cause or contribute to fire through friction.
4.2	H4.2	Substances or wastes liable to spontaneous combustion Substances or wastes which are liable to spontaneous heating under normal conditions encountered in transport, or to heating up on contact with air, and being then liable to catch fire.
4.3	H4.3	Substances or wastes which, in contact with water emit flammable gases Substances or wastes which, by interaction with water, are liable to become spontaneously flammable or to give off flammable gases in dangerous quantities.
5.1	H5.1	Oxidizing Substances or wastes which, while in themselves not necessarily combustible, may, generally by yielding oxygen cause, or contribute to, the combustion of other materials.
5.2	H5.2	Organic Peroxides Organic substances or wastes which contain the bivalent-O-O-structure are thermally unstable substances which may undergo exothermic self-accelerating decomposition.
6.1	H6.1	Poisonous (Acute) Substances or wastes liable either to cause death or serious injury or to harm health if swallowed or inhaled or by skin contact.
6.2	H6.2	Infectious substances Substances or wastes containing viable micro organisms or their toxins which are known or suspected to cause disease in animals or humans.
8	H8	Corrosives Substances or wastes which, by chemical action, will cause severe damage when in contact with living tissue, or, in the case of leakage, will materially damage, or even destroy, other goods or the means of transport; they may also cause other hazards.
9	H10	Liberation of toxic gases in contact with air or water Substances or wastes which, by interaction with air or water, are liable to give off toxic gases in dangerous quantities.
9	H11	Toxic (Delayed or chronic) Substances or wastes which, if they are inhaled or ingested or if they penetrate the skin, may involve delayed or chronic effects, including carcinogenicity.

9 H12 Ecotoxic
Substances or wastes which if released present or may present immediate or delayed adverse impacts to the environment by means of bioaccumulation and/or toxic effects upon biotic systems.

9 H13 Capable, by any means, after disposal, of yielding another material, e.g., leachate, which possesses any of the characteristics listed above.

Tests

The potential hazards posed by certain types of wastes are not yet fully documented; tests to define quantitatively these hazards do not exist. Further research is necessary in order to develop means to characterize potential hazards posed to man and/or the environment by these wastes. Standardized tests have been derived with respect to pure substances and materials. Many countries have developed national tests which can be applied to materials listed in Annex I, in order to decide if these materials exhibit any of the characteristics listed in this Annex.

Annex IV

DISPOSAL OPERATIONS

A. *Operations which do not lead to the possibility of resource recovery, recycling, reclamation, direct re-use or alternative use*

Section A encompasses all such disposal operations which occur in practice.

D1 Deposit into or onto land, (e.g., landfill, etc.)
D2 Land treatment, (e.g., biodegradation of liquid or sludgy discards in soils, etc.)
D3 Deep injection, (e.g., injection of pumpable discards into wells, salt domes of naturally occurring repositories, etc.)
D4 Surface impoundment, (e.g., placement of liquid or sludge discards into pits, ponds or lagoons, etc.)
D5 Specially engineered landfill, (e.g., placement into lined discrete cells which are capped and isolated from one another and the environment, etc).
D6 Release into a water body except seas/oceans
D7 Release into seas/oceans including sea-bed insertion
D8 Biological treatment not specified elsewhere in this Annex which results in final compounds or mixtures which are discarded by means of any of the operations in Section A
D9 Physico chemical treatment not specified elsewhere in this Annex which results in final compounds or mixtures which are discarded by means of any of the operations in Section A, (e.g., evaporation, drying, calcination, neutralization, precipitation, etc.)
D10 Incineration on land
D11 Incineration at sea
D12 Permanent storage (e.g., emplacement of containers in a mine, etc.)
D13 Blending or mixing prior to submission to any of the operations in Section A

D14 Repackaging prior to submission to any of the operations in Section A
D15 Storage pending any of the operations in Section A

B. *Operations which may lead to resource recovery, recycling reclamation, direct re-use or alternative uses*

Section B encompasses all such operations with respect to materials legally defined as or considered to be hazardous wastes and which otherwise would have been destined for operations included in Section A

R1 Use as a fuel (other than in direct incineration) or other means to generate energy
R2 Solvent reclamation/regeneration
R3 Recycling/reclamation of organic substances which are not used as solvents
R4 Recycling/reclamation of metals and metal compounds
R5 Recycling/reclamation of other inorganic materials
R6 Regeneration of acids or bases
R7 Recovery of components used for pollution abatement
R8 Recovery of components from catalysts
R9 Used oil re-refining or other reuses of previously used oil
R10 Land treatment resulting in benefit to agriculture or ecological improvement
R11 Uses of residual materials obtained from any of the operations numbered R1–R10
R12 Exchange of wastes for submission to any of the operations numbered R1–R11
R13 Accumulation of material intended for any operation in Section B

Annex VA

Information to be provided on notification

1. Reason for waste export
2. Exporter of the waste *1/*
3. Generator(s) of the waste and site of generation *1/*
4. Disposer of the waste and actual site of disposal *1/*
5. Intended carrier(s) of the waste or their agents, if known *1/*
6. Country of export of the waste
   Competent authority *2/*
7. Expected countries of transit
   Competent authority *2/*
8. Country of import of the waste
   Competent authority *2/*
9. General or single notification
10. Projected date(s) of shipment(s) and period of time over which waste is to be exported and proposed itinerary (including point of entry and exit) *3/*
11. Means of transport envisaged (road, rail, sea, air, inland waters)
12. Information relating to insurance *4/*

13. Designation and physical description of the waste including Y number and UN number and its composition *5/* and information on any special handling requirements including emergency provisions in case of accidents
14. Type of packaging envisaged (e.g. bulk, drummed, tanker)
15. Estimated quantity in weight/volume *6/*
16. Process by which the waste is generated *7/*
17. For wastes listed in Annex I, classifications from Annex III: hazardous characteristic, H number, and UN class
18. Method of disposal as per Annex IV
19. Declaration by the generator and exporter that the information is correct
20. Information transmitted (including technical description of the plant) to the exporter or generator from the disposer of the waste upon which the latter has based his assessment that there was no reason to believe that the wastes will not be managed in an environmentally sound manner in accordance with the laws and regulations of the country of import.
21. Information concerning the contract between the exporter and disposer.

Notes

1/ Full name and address, telephone or telefax number and the name, address, telephone, telex or telefax number of the person to be contacted.

2/ Full name and address, telephone, telex or telefax number.

3/ In the case of a general notification covering several shipments, either the expected dates of each shipment or, if this is not known, the expected frequency of the shipments will be required.

4/ Information to be provided on relevant insurance requirements and how they are met by exporter, carrier and disposer.

5/ The nature and the concentration of the most hazardous components, in terms of toxicity and other dangers presented by the waste both in handling and in relation to the proposed disposal method.

6/ In the case of a general notification covering several shipments, both the estimated total quantity and the estimated quantities for each individual shipment will be required.

7/ Insofar as this is necessary to assess the hazard and determine the appropriateness of the proposed disposal operation.

Annex VB

Information to be provided on the movement document

1. Exporter of the waste *1/*
2. Generator(s) of the waste and site of generation *1/*
3. Disposer of the waste and actual site of disposal *1/*
4. Carrier(s) of the waste *1/* or his agent(s)
5. Subject of general or single notification
6. The date the transboundary movement started and date(s) and signature on receipt by each person who takes charge of the waste

7. Means of transport (road, rail, inland waterway, sea, air) including countries of export, transit and import, also point of entry and exit where these have been designated
8. General description of the waste (physical state, proper UN shipping name and class, UN number, Y number and H number as applicable)
9. Information on special handling requirements including emergency provision in case of accidents
10. Type and number of packages
11. Quantity in weight/volume
12. Declaration by the generator or exporter that the information is correct
13. Declaration by the generator or exporter indicating no objection from the competent authorities of all States concerned which are Parties
14. Certification by disposer of receipt at designated disposal facility and indication of method of disposal and of the approximate date of disposal.

Notes

The information required on the movement document shall where possible be integrated in one document with that required under transport rules. Where this is not possible the information should complement rather than duplicate that required under the transport rules. The movement document shall carry instructions as to who is to provide information and fill-out any form.

1/ Full name and address, telephone or telefax number and the name, address, telephone, telex or telefax number of the person to be contacted in case of emergency.

Annex VI

Arbitration

Article 1

Unless the agreement referred to in Article 20 of the Convention provides otherwise, the arbitration procedure shall be conducted in accordance with Articles 2 to 10 below.

Article 2

The claimant party shall notify the Secretariat that the Parties have agreed to submit the dispute to arbitration pursuant to paragraph 2 or paragraph 3 of Article 20 and include, in particular, the Articles of the Convention the interpretation or application of which are at issue. The Secretariat shall forward the information thus received to all Parties to the Convention.

Article 3

The arbitral tribunal shall consist of three members. Each of the Parties to the dispute shall appoint an arbitrator, and the two arbitrators so appointed shall designate by common agreement the third arbitrator, who shall be the chairman of the tribunal. The latter shall not be a national of one of the Parties to the dispute, nor have his usual place of residence in the territory of one of these Parties, nor be employed by any of them, nor have dealt with the case in any other capacity.

Article 4

1. If the chairman of the arbitral tribunal has not been designated within two months of the appointment of the second arbitrator, the Secretary-General of the United Nations shall, at the request of either Party, designate him within a further two months period.
2. If one of the Parties to the dispute does not appoint an arbitrator within two months of the receipt of the request, the other Party may inform the Secretary-General of the United Nations who shall designate the chairman of the arbitral tribunal within a further two months' period. Upon designation, the chairman of the arbitral tribunal shall request the Party which has not appointed an arbitrator to do so within two months. After such period, he shall inform the Secretary-General of the United Nations, who shall make this appointment within a further two months' period.

Article 5

1. The arbitral tribunal shall render its decision in accordance with international law and in accordance with the provisions of this Convention.
2. Any arbitral tribunal constituted under the provisions of this Annex shall draw up its own rules of procedure.

Article 6

1. The decisions of the arbitral tribunal both on procedure and on substance, shall be taken by majority vote of its members.
2. The tribunal may take all appropriate measures in order to establish the facts. It may, at the request of one of the Parties, recommend essential interim measures of protection.
3. The Parties to the dispute shall provide all facilities necessary for the effective conduct of the proceedings.
4. The absence or default of a Party in the dispute shall not constitute an impediment to the proceedings.

Article 7

The tribunal may hear and determine counter-claims arising directly out of the subject-matter of the dispute.

Article 8

Unless the arbitral tribunal determines otherwise because of the particular circumstances of the case, the expenses of the tribunal, including the remuneration of its members, shall be borne by the Parties to the dispute in equal shares. The tribunal shall keep a record of all its expenses, and shall furnish a final statement thereof to the Parties.

Article 9

Any Party that has an interest of a legal nature in the subject-matter of the dispute which may be affected by the decision in the case, may intervene in the proceedings with the consent of the tribunal.

Article 10

1. The tribunal shall render its award within five months of the date on which it is established unless it finds it necessary to extend the time-limit for a period which should not exceed five months.
2. The award of the arbitral tribunal shall be accompanied by a statement of reasons. It shall be final and binding upon the Parties to the dispute.
3. Any dispute which may arise between the Parties concerning the interpretation or execution of the award may be submitted by either Party to the arbitral tribunal which made the award or, if the latter cannot be seized thereof, to another tribunal constituted for this purpose in the same manner as the first.

Appendix II

Decision II/12 of the Conference of the Parties to the Basel Convention, (2nd Meeting, 25 March 1994).

Decision II/12

The Conference,

Recalling the request of the G-77 countries at the First Meeting of the Conference of the Parties to the Basel Convention in Uruguay, 30 November–4 December 1992, for the total ban on all exports of hazardous wastes from OECD countries to non-OECD countries;

Recognizing that transboundary movements of hazardous wastes from OECD to non-OECD States have a high risk of not constituting an environmentally sound management of hazardous wastes as required by the Basel Convention;

1. *Decides* to prohibit immediately all transboundary movements of hazardous wastes which are destined for final disposal from OECD to non-OECD States;
2. *Decides also* to phase out by 31 December 1997, and prohibit as of that date, all transboundary movements of hazardous wastes which are destined for recycling or recovery operations from OECD to non-OECD States;
3. *Decides further* that any non-OECD State, not possessing a national hazardous wastes import ban and which allows the import from OECD States of hazardous wastes for recycling or recovery operation until 31 December 1997, should inform the Secretariat of the Basel Convention that it would allow the import from an OECD State of hazardous wastes for recycling or recovery operations by specifying the categories of hazardous wastes which are acceptable for import; the quantities to be imported; the specific recycling/recovery process to be used; and the final destination/disposal of the residues which are derived from recycling/recovery operations;
4. *Requests* the Parties to report regularly to the Secretariat on the implementation of this decision, including details of the transboundary movements of hazardous wastes allowed under paragraph 3 above. Further requests the Secretariat to prepare a summary and to compile these reports for consideration by the Open-ended Ad Hoc Committee. After considering these reports, the Open-ended Ad Hoc Committee will submit a report based on the input provided by the Secretariat to the Conference of the Parties of the Convention;
5. *Requests* further the Parties to cooperate and work actively to ensure the effective implementation of this decision.

Appendix III

Bamako Convention on the Ban of the Import into Africa and the Control of Transboundary Movement and Management of Hazardous Wastes Within Africa (30 January 1991).

PREAMBLE

The Parties to this Convention,

1. Mindful of the growing threat to human health and the environment posed by the increased generation and the complexity of hazardous wastes,

2. Further mindful that the most effective way of protecting human health and the environment from the dangers posed by such wastes is the reduction of their generation to a minimum in terms of quantity and/or hazard potential,

3. Aware of the risk of damage to human health and the environment caused by transboundary movements of hazardous wastes,

4. Reiterating that States should ensure that the generator should carry out his responsibilities with regard to the transport and disposal of hazardous wastes in a manner that is consistent with the protection of human health and environment, whatever the place of disposal,

5. Recalling relevant chapters of the Charter of the Organisation of African Unity (OAU) on environmental protection, the African Charter for Human and Peoples' Rights, Chapter IX of the Lagos Plan of Action and other Recommendations adopted by the Organisation of African Unity on the environment,

6. Further recognizing the sovereignty of States to ban the importation into, and the transit through, their territory, of hazardous wastes and substances for human health and environmental reasons,

7. Recognizing also the increasing mobilization in Africa for the prohibition of transboundary movements of hazardous wastes and their disposal in African countries,

8. Convinced that hazardous wastes should, as far as is compatible with environmentally sound and efficient management, be disposed in the State where they were generated,

9. Convinced that the effective control and minimization of transboundary movements of hazardous wastes will act as an incentive, in Africa and elsewhere, for the reduction of the volume of the generation of such wastes,

10. Noting that a number of international and regional agreements deal with the problem of the protection and preservation of the environment with regard to the transit of dangerous goods,

11. Taking into account the Declaration of the United Nations Conference on the Human Environment (Stockholm, 1972), the Cairo Guidelines and Principles for the Environmentally Sound Management of Hazardous Wastes adopted by the Governing Council of the United Nations Environment Programme (UNEP) by Decision 14/30 of 17 June, 1987, the Recommendations of the United Nations

Committee of Experts on the Transport of Dangerous Goods (formulated in 1957 and updated biennially), the Charter of Human Rights, relevant recommendations, declarations, instruments and regulations adopted within the United Nations System, the relevant articles of the 1989 Basel Convention on the Control of Transboundary Movements of Hazardous Wastes and their Disposal which allow for the establishment of regional agreements which may be equal to or stronger than its own provisions, Article 39 of the Lomé IV Convention relating to the international movement of hazardous wastes and radioactive wastes, African intergovernmental organisations and the work and studies done within other international and regional organisations,

12. Mindful of the spirit, principles, aims and functions of the African Convention on the Conservation of Nature and Natural Resources adopted by the African Heads of State and Government in Algiers (1968) and the World Charter for Nature adopted by the General Assembly of the United Nations at its Thirty-seventh Session (1982) as the rule of ethics in respect of the protection of the human environment and the conservation of natural resources,

13. Concerned by the problem of transboundary traffic in hazardous wastes,

14. Recognizing the need to promote the development of clean production methods, including clean technologies, for the sound management of hazardous wastes produced in Africa, in particular, to avoid, minimize and eliminate the generation of such wastes,

15. Recognizing also that where necessary hazardous wastes should be transported in accordance with relevant international conventions and recommendations,

16. Determined to protect, by strict control, the human health of the African population and the environment against the adverse effects which may result from the generation of hazardous wastes,

17. Affirming a commitment also to responsibly address the problem of hazardous wastes originating within the Continent of Africa,

HAVE AGREED AS FOLLOWS:

Article 1

Definitions

For the purpose of this Convention:

1. 'Wastes' are substances or materials which are disposed of, or are intended to be disposed of, or are required to be disposed of by the provisions of national law;
2. 'Hazardous wastes' means wastes as specified in Article 2 of this Convention;
3. 'Management' means the prevention and reduction of hazardous wastes and the collection, transport, storage, and treatment either for the reuse or disposal, of hazardous wastes including after-care of disposal sites;
4. 'Transboundary movement' means any movement of hazardous wastes from an area under the national jurisdiction of any State to or through an area under the national jurisdiction of another State, or to or through an area not under the national jurisdiction of another State, provided at least two States are involved in the movement;
5. 'Clean production methods' means production or industrial systems which

avoid, or eliminate the generation of hazardous wastes and hazardous products in conformity with Article 4, section 3(f) and (g) of this Convention;
6. 'Disposal' means any operation specified in Annex III to this Convention;
7. 'Approved site or facility' means a site or facility for the disposal of hazardous wastes which is authorised or permitted to operate for this purpose by a relevant authority of the State where the site or facility is located;
8. 'Competent authority' means one governmental authority designated by a Party to be responsible, within such geographical areas as the Party may think fit, for receiving the notification of a transboundary movement of hazardous wastes and any information related to it, and for responding to such a notification, as provided in Article 6 of this Convention;
9. 'Focal point' means the entity of a Party referred to in Article 5 of this Convention responsible for receiving and submitting information as provided for in Articles 13 and 16;
10. Environmentally sound management of hazardous wastes' means taking all practicable steps to ensure that hazardous wastes are managed in a manner which will protect human health and the environment against the adverse effects which may result from such wastes;
11. 'Area under the national jurisdiction of a State' means any land, marine area or airspace within which a State exercises administrative and regulatory responsibility in accordance with international law in regard to the protection of human health or the environment;
12. 'State of export' means a State from which a transboundary movement of hazardous wastes is planned to be initiated or is initiated;
13. 'State of import' means a State to which a transboundary movement is planned or takes place for the purpose of disposal therein or for the purpose of loading prior to disposal in an area not under the national jurisdiction of any State;
14. 'State of transit' means any State, other than the State of export or import, through which a movement of hazardous wastes is planned or takes place;
15. 'States concerned' means States of export or import, or transit states, whether or not parties;
16. 'Person' means any natural or legal person;
17. 'Exporter' means any person under the jurisdiction of the State of export who arranges for hazardous wastes to be exported;
18. 'Importer' means any person under the jurisdiction of the State of import who arranges for hazardous wastes to be imported;
19. 'Carrier' means any person who carries out the transport of hazardous wastes;
20. 'Generator' means any person whose activity produces hazardous wastes, or, if that person is not known, the person who is in possession and/or control of those wastes;
21. 'Disposer' means any person to whom hazardous wastes are shipped and who carries out the disposal of such wastes;
22. 'Illegal traffic' means any transboundary movement of hazardous wastes as specified in Article 9 of this Convention;
23. 'Dumping at sea' means the deliberate disposal of hazardous wastes at sea from vessels, aircraft, platforms or other man-made structures at sea, and includes ocean incineration and disposal into the seabed and sub-seabed.

Article 2

Scope of the Convention

1. The following substances shall be 'hazardous wastes' for the purposes of this convention:

(a) Wastes that belong to any category contained in Annex I of this Convention;

(b) Wastes that are not covered under paragraph (a) above but are defined as, or are considered to be, hazardous wastes by the domestic legislation of the State of export, import or transit;

(c) Wastes which possess any of the characteristics contained in Annex II of this Convention;

(d) Hazardous substances which have been banned, cancelled or refused registration by government regulatory action, or voluntarily withdrawn from registration in the country of manufacture, for human health or environmental reasons.

2. Wastes which, as a result of being radioactive, are subject to any international control systems, including international instruments, applying specifically to radioactive materials, are included in the scope of this Convention.

3. Wastes which derive from the normal operations of a ship, the discharge of which is covered by another international instrument, shall not fall within the scope of this convention.

Article 3

National Definitions of Hazardous Wastes

1. Each State shall, within six months of becoming a Party to this Convention, inform the Secretariat of the Convention of the wastes, other than those listed in Annex I of this Convention, considered or defined as hazardous under its national legislation and of any requirements concerning transboundary movement procedures applicable to such wastes.

2. Each party shall subsequently inform the Secretariat of any significant changes to the information it has provided pursuant to Paragraph 1 of this Article.

3. The Secretariat shall forthwith inform all Parties of the information it has received pursuant to paragraphs 1 and 2 of this Article.

4. Parties shall be responsible for making the information transmitted to them by the Secretariat under Paragraph 3 of this Article available to their exporters and other appropriate bodies.

Article 4

General Obligations

1. Hazardous Waste Import Ban

All Parties shall take appropriate legal, administrative and other measures within the area under their jurisdiction to prohibit the import of all hazardous wastes, for any reason, into Africa from non-Contracting Parties. Such import shall be deemed illegal and a criminal act. All Parties shall:

(a) Forward as soon as possible, all information relating to such illegal hazardous waste import activity to the Secretariat who shall distribute the information to all Contracting Parties;

(b) Co-operate to ensure that no imports of hazardous wastes from a non-Party enter a Party to this Convention. To this end, the Parties shall, at the Conference of the Contracting Parties, consider other enforcement mechanisms.

2. Ban on Dumping of Hazardous Wastes at Sea and Internal Waters

(a) Parties in conformity with related international conventions and instruments shall, in the exercise of their jurisdiction within their internal waters, territorial seas, exclusive economic zones and continental shelf, adopt legal, administrative and other appropriate measures to control all carriers from non-Parties, and prohibit the dumping at sea of hazardous wastes, including their incineration at sea and their disposal in the seabed and sub-seabed. Any dumping of hazardous wastes at sea, including incineration at sea as well as seabed and sub-seabed disposal, by Contracting Parties, whether in internal waters, territorial seas, exclusive economic zones or high seas shall be deemed to be illegal;

(b) Parties shall forward, as soon as possible, all information relating to dumping of hazardous wastes to the Secretariat which shall distribute the information to all Contracting Parties.

3. Waste Generation in Africa

Each Party Shall:

(a) Ensure that hazardous waste generators submit to the Secretariat reports regarding the wastes that they generate in order to enable the Secretariat of the Convention to produce a complete hazardous waste audit;

(b) Impose strict, unlimited liability as well as joint and several liability on hazardous waste generators;

(c) Ensure that the generation of hazardous wastes within the area under its jurisdiction is reduced to a minimum taking into account social, technological and economic aspects;

(d) Ensure the availability of adequate treatment and/or disposal facilities, for the environmentally sound management of hazardous wastes which shall be located, to the extent possible, within its jurisdiction;

(e) Ensure that persons involved in the management of hazardous wastes within its jurisdiction take such steps as are necessary to prevent pollution arising from such wastes and, if such pollution occurs, to minimize the consequence thereof for human health and the environment;

The Adoption of Precautionary Measures:

(f) Each Party shall strive to adopt and implement the preventive, precautionary approach to pollution problems which entails, inter-alia, preventing the release into the environment of substances which may cause harm to humans or the environment without waiting for scientific proof regarding such harm. The Parties shall co-operate with each other in taking the appropriate measures to implement the precautionary principle to pollution prevention through the application of clean production methods, rather than the pursuit of a permissible emissions approach based on assimilative capacity assumptions;

(g) In this respect Parties shall promote clean production methods applicable to entire product life cycles including:
— raw material selection, extraction and processing;
— product conceptualisation, design, manufacture and assemblage;
— materials transport during all phases;
— industrial and household usage;
— reintroduction of the product into industrial systems or nature when it no longer serves a useful function;
Clean production shall not include 'end-of-pipe' pollution controls such as filters and scrubbers, or chemical, physical or biological treatment. Measures which reduce the volume of waste by incineration or concentration, mask the hazard by dilution, or transfer pollutants from one environmental medium to another, are also excluded;

(h) The issue of preventing the transfer to Africa of polluting technologies shall be kept under systematic review by the Secretariat of the Conference and periodic reports shall be made to the Conference of the Parties;

Obligations in the Transport and Transboundary Movement of Hazardous Wastes from Contracting Parties:

(i) Each party shall prevent the export of hazardous wastes to States which have prohibited by their legislation or international agreement all such imports, or if it has reason to believe that the wastes in question will not be managed in an environmentally sound manner, according to criteria to be decided on by the Parties at their first meeting;

(j) A Party shall not permit hazardous wastes to be exported to a State which does not have the facilities for disposing of them in an environmentally sound manner;

(k) Each Party shall ensure that hazardous wastes to be exported are managed in an environmentally sound manner in the State of import and transit. Technical guidelines for the environmentally sound management of wastes subject to this Convention shall be decided by the Parties at their first meeting;

(l) The Parties agree not to allow the export of hazardous wastes for disposal within the area South of 60 degrees South Latitude, whether or not such wastes are subject to transboundary movement;

(m) Furthermore, each Party shall:
(i) Prohibit all persons under its national jurisdiction from transporting, storing or disposing of hazardous wastes unless such persons are authorized or allowed to perform such operations;
(ii) Ensure that hazardous wastes that are to be the subject of a transboundary movement are packaged, labelled, and transported in conformity with generally accepted and recognized international rules and standards in the field of packaging, labelling, and transport, and that due account is taken of relevant internationally recognized practices;
(iii) Ensure that hazardous wastes be accompanied by a movement document, containing information specified in Annex IVB, from the point at which a transboundary movement commences to the point of disposal;

(n) Parties shall take the appropriate measures to ensure that the transboundary movements of hazardous wastes only are allowed if:
   (i) The State of export does not have the technical capacity and the necessary facilities, capacity or suitable disposal sites in order to dispose of the wastes in question in an environmentally sound and efficient manner; or
   (ii) The transboundary movement in question is in accordance with other criteria to be decided by the Parties, provided those criteria do not differ from the objectives of this Convention;

(o) Under this Convention, the obligation of States in which hazardous wastes are generated, requiring that those wastes are managed in an environmentally sound manner, may not under any circumstances be transferred to the States of import or transit;

(p) Parties shall undertake to review periodically the possibilities for the reduction of the amount and/or the pollution potential of hazardous wastes which are exported to other States;

(q) Parties exercising their right to prohibit the import of hazardous wastes for disposal shall inform the other Parties of their decision pursuant to Article 13 of this Convention;

(r) Parties shall prohibit or shall not permit the export of hazardous wastes to States which have prohibited the import of such wastes, when notified by the secretariat or any competent authority pursuant to sub-paragraph (q) above;

(s) Parties shall prohibit or shall not permit the export of hazardous wastes if the State of import does not consent in writing to the specific import, in the case where that State of import has not prohibited the import of such wastes;

(t) Parties shall ensure that the transboundary movement of hazardous wastes is reduced to the minimum consistent with the environmentally sound and efficient management of such wastes, and is conducted in a manner which will protect human health and the environment against the adverse effects which may result from such movement;

(u) Parties shall require that information about a proposed transboundary movement of hazardous wastes be provided to the States concerned, according to Annex IVA of this Convention, and clearly state the potential effects of the proposed movement on human health and the environment.

4. Furthermore

(a) Parties shall undertake to enforce the obligations of this Convention against offenders and infringements according to relevant national laws and/or international law;

(b) Nothing in this Convention shall prevent a Party from imposing additional requirements that are consistent with the provisions of this Convention, and are in accordance with the rules of international law, in order to better protect human health and the environment;

(c) This Convention recognizes the sovereignty of States over their territorial sea, waterways, and air space established in accordance with international law, and jurisdiction which States have in their exclusive economic zone and their continental shelves in accordance with international law, and the exercise by ships and aircraft of all States of navigation rights and freedoms as provided for in international law and as reflected in relevant international instruments.

Article 5

Designation of Competent Authorities, Focal Point and Dumpwatch

To facilitate the implementation of this Convention, the Parties shall:
1. Designate or establish one or more competent authorities and one focal point. One competent authority shall be designated to receive the notification in case of a State of transit.
2. Inform the Secretariat, within three months of the date of the entry into force of this Convention for them, which agencies they have designated as their focal point and their competent authorities.
3. Inform the Secretariat, within one month of the date of decision, of any changes regarding the designations made by them under paragraph 2 above.
4. Appoint a national body to act as a Dumpwatch. In such capacity as a Dumpwatch, the designated national body only will be required to co-ordinate with the concerned governmental and non-governmental bodies.

Article 6

Transboundary Movement and Notification Procedures

1. The State of export shall notify, or shall require the generator or exporter to notify, in writing, through the channel of the competent authority of the State of export, the competent authority of the States concerned of any proposed transboundary movement of hazardous wastes. Such notification shall contain the declarations and information specified in Annex IVA of this Convention, written in a language acceptable to the State of import. Only one notification needs to be sent to each State concerned.
2. The Party of import shall respond to the notifier in writing consenting to the movement with or without conditions, denying permission for the movement, or requesting additional information. A copy of the final response of the State of import shall be sent to the competent authorities of the States concerned that are Parties to this Convention.
3. The State of export shall not allow the transboundary movement until it has received:
   (a) written consent of the State of import; and
   (b) from the State of import, written confirmation of the existence of a contract between the exporter and the disposer specifying environmentally sound management of the wastes in question.
4. Each State of transit which is a Party to this Convention shall promptly acknowledge to the notifier receipt of the notification. It may subsequently respond to the notifier in writing, within 60 days, consenting to the movement with or without conditions, denying permission for the movement, or requesting additional information. The State of export shall not allow the transboundary

movement to commence until it has received the written consent of the State of transit.

5. In the case of a transboundary movement of hazardous wastes where the wastes are legally defined as or considered to be hazardous wastes only:

(a) By the State of export, the requirements of paragraph 8 of this Article that apply to the importer or disposer and the State of import shall apply *mutatis mutandis* to the exporter and State of export, respectively;

(b) By the Party of import, or by the States of import and transit which are Parties to this Convention, the requirements of paragraphs 1, 3, 4 and 6 of this Article that apply to the exporter and State of export shall apply *mutatis mutandis* to the importer or disposer and Party of import, respectively; or

(c) By any State of transit which is a Party to this Convention, the provisions of paragraph 4 of this Article shall apply to such State.

6. The State of export shall use a shipment specific notification even where hazardous wastes having the same physical and chemical characteristics are shipped regularly to the same disposer via the same customs office of entry of the State of import, and in the case of transit, via the same customs office of entry and exit of the State or States of transit; specific notification of each and every shipment shall be required and contain the information in Annex IVA of this Convention.

7. Each party to this Convention shall limit their points or ports of entry and notify the Secretariat to this effect for distribution to all Contracting Parties. Such points and ports shall be the only ones permitted for the transboundary movement of hazardous wastes.

8. The Parties to this Convention shall require that each person who takes charge of a transboundary movement of hazardous wastes sign the movement document either upon delivery or receipt of the wastes in question. They shall also require that the disposer inform both the exporter and the competent authority of the State of export of receipt by the disposer of the wastes in question and, in due course, of the completion of disposal as specified in the notification. If no such information is received within the State of export, the competent authority of the State of export or the exporter shall so notify the State of import.

9. The notification and response required by this Article shall be transmitted to the competent authority of the States concerned.

10. Any transboundary movement of hazardous wastes shall be covered by insurance, bond or other guarantee as may be required by the State of import, or any State of transit which is a Party to this Convention.

Article 7

Transboundary Movement from a Party through States which are not Parties

Paragraph 2 and 4 of Article 6 of this Convention shall apply *mutatis mutandis* to transboundary movements of hazardous wastes from a Party through a State or States which are not Parties.

Article 8

Duty to Re-import

When a transboundary movement of hazardous wastes to which the consent of the States concerned has been given, subject to the provisions of this Convention, cannot be completed in accordance with the terms of the contract, the State of export shall ensure that the wastes in question are taken back into the State of export, by the exporter, if alternative arrangements cannot be made for their disposal in an environmentally sound manner within a maximum of 90 days from the time that the importing State informed the State of export and the Secretariat. To this end, the State of export and any State of transit shall not oppose, hinder or prevent the return of those waste to the State of export.

Article 9

Illegal traffic

1. For the purpose of this Convention, any transboundary movement of hazardous wastes under the following situations shall be deemed to be illegal traffic:
   (a) if carried out without notification, pursuant to the provisions of this Convention, to all States concerned; or
   (b) if carried out without the consent, pursuant to the provisions of this Convention, of a State concerned; or
   (c) if consent is obtained from States concerned through falsification, misrepresentation or fraud; or
   (d) if it does not conform in a material way with the documents; or
   (e) if it results in deliberate disposal of hazardous wastes in contravention of this Convention and of general principles of international law.
2. Each Party shall introduce appropriate national legislation for imposing criminal penalties on all persons who have planned, carried out, or assisted in such illegal imports. Such penalties shall be sufficiently high to both punish and deter such conduct.
3. In case of a transboundary movement of hazardous wastes deemed to be illegal traffic as the result of conduct on the part of the exporter or generator, the State of export shall ensure that the wastes in question are taken back by the exporter or generator or if necessary by itself into the State of export, within 30 days from the time the State of export has been informed about the illegal traffic. To this end the States concerned shall not oppose, hinder or prevent the return of those wastes to the State of export and appropriate legal action shall be taken against the contravenor(s).
4. In the case of a transboundary movement of hazardous wastes deemed to be illegal traffic as the result of conduct on the part of the importer or disposer, the State of import shall ensure that the wastes in question are returned to the exporter by the importer and that legal proceedings according to the provisions of this Convention are taken against the contravenor(s).

Article 10

Intra-African Co-operation

1. The parties to this Convention shall co-operate with one another and with relevant African organizations, to improve and achieve the environmentally sound management of hazardous wastes.
2. To this end, the Parties shall:
   (a) Make available information, whether on a bilateral or multilateral basis, with a view to promoting clean production methods and the environmentally sound management of hazardous wastes, including harmonization of technical standards and practices for the adequate management of hazardous wastes;
   (b) Co-operate in monitoring the effects of the management of hazardous wastes on human health and the environment;
   (c) Co-operate, subject to their national laws, regulations and policies, in the development and implementation of new environmentally sound clean production technologies and the improvement of existing technologies with a view to eliminating, as far as practicable, the generation of hazardous wastes and achieving more effective and efficient methods of ensuring their management in an environmentally sound manner, including the study of the economic, social and environmental effects of the adoption of such new and improved technologies;
   (d) Co-operate actively, subject to their national laws, regulations and policies, in the transfer of technology and management systems related to the environmentally sound management of hazardous wastes. They shall also co-operate in developing the technical capacity among Parties, especially those which may need and request technical assistance in this field;
   (e) Co-operate in developing appropriate technical guidelines and/or codes of practice;
   (f) Co-operate in the exchange and dissemination of information on the movement of hazardous wastes in conformity with Article 13 of this Convention.

Article 11

International Co-operation
Bilateral, Multilateral and Regional Agreements

1. Parties to this Convention may enter into bilateral, multilateral, or regional agreements or arrangements regarding the transboundary movement and management of hazardous wastes generated in Africa with Parties or non-Parties provided that such agreements or arrangements do not derogate from the environmentally sound management of hazardous wastes as required by this Convention. These agreements or arrangements shall stipulate provisions which are no less environmentally sound than those provided for by this Convention.
2. Parties shall notify the Secretariat of any bilateral, multilateral or regional agreements or arrangements referred to in paragraph 1 of this Article and those which they have entered into prior to the entry into force of this Convention for

them, for the purpose of controlling transboundary movements of hazardous wastes which take place entirely among the Parties to such agreements. The provisions of this Convention shall not affect transboundary movements of hazardous wastes generated in Africa which take place pursuant to such agreements provided that such agreements are compatible with the environmentally sound management of hazardous wastes as required by this Convention.

3. Each Contracting Party shall prohibit vessels flying its flag or aircraft registered in its territory from carrying out activities in contravention of this Convention.

4. Parties shall use appropriate measures to promote South–South co-operation in the implementation of this Convention.

5. Taking into account the needs of developing countries, co-operation between international organizations is encouraged in order to promote, among other things, public awareness, the development of rational management of hazardous waste, and the adoption of new and non/less polluting technologies.

Article 12

Liabilities and Compensation

The Conference of Parties shall set up an Ad Hoc expert organ to prepare a draft Protocol setting out appropriate rules and procedures in the field of liabilities and compensation for damage resulting from the transboundary movement of hazardous wastes.

Article 13

Transmission of Information

1. The Parties shall ensure that in the case of an accident occurring during the transboundary movement of hazardous wastes or their disposal which is likely to present risks to human health and the environment in other States, those States are immediately informed.

2. The States shall inform each other, through the Secretariat, of:
   - (a) Changes regarding the designation of competent authorities and/or focal points, pursuant to Article 5 of this Convention;
   - (b) Changes in their national definition of hazardous wastes, pursuant to Article 3 of this Convention;
   - (c) Decisions made by them to limit or ban the import of hazardous wastes;
   - (d) Any other information required pursuant to paragraph 4 of this Article.

3. The Parties, consistent with national laws and regulations, shall set up information collection and dissemination mechanisms on hazardous wastes. They shall transmit such information through the Secretariat, to the Conference of the parties established under Article 15 of this Convention, before the end of each calendar year, in a report on the previous calendar year, containing the following information:
   - (a) Competent authorities, Dumpwatch, and focal points that have been designated by them pursuant to Article 5 of this Convention;
   - (b) Information regarding transboundary movements of hazardous wastes in which they have been involved, including:

(i) The quantity of hazardous wastes exported, their category, characteristics, destination, any transit country and disposal method as stated in the notification;
(ii) The amount of hazardous wastes imported, their category, characteristics, origin, and disposal methods;
(iii) Disposals which did not proceed as intended;
(iv) Efforts to achieve a reduction of the amount of hazardous wastes subject to transboundary movement;

(c) Information on the measures adopted by them in the implementation of this Convention;
(d) Information on available qualified statistics—which have been compiled by them on the effects on human health and the environment of the generation, transportation, and disposal of hazardous wastes—as part of the information required in conformity with Article 4 Section 3(a) of this Convention;
(e) Information concerning bilateral, multilateral and regional agreements and arrangements entered into pursuant to Article 11 of this Convention;
(f) Information on accidents occurring during the transboundary movements, treatment and disposal of hazardous wastes and on the measures undertaken to deal with them;
(g) Information on treatment and disposal options operated within the area under their national jurisdiction;
(h) Information on measures undertaken for the development of clean production methods, including clean production technologies, for the reduction and/or elimination of the production of hazardous wastes; and
(i) Such other matters as the Conference of the Parties shall deem relevant.

4. The Parties, consistent with national laws and regulations, shall ensure that copies of each notification concerning any given transboundary movement of hazardous wastes, and the response to it, are sent to the Secretariat.

Article 14

Financial Aspects

1. The regular budget of the Conference of Parties, as required in Article 15 and 16 of this Convention, shall be prepared by the Secretariat and approved by the Conference.
2. Parties shall, at the first meeting of the Conference of the Parties, agree on a scale of contributions to the recurrent budget of the Secretariat.
3. The Parties shall also consider the establishment of a revolving fund to assist, on an interim basis, in case of emergency situations to minimize damage from disasters or accidents arising from transboundary movements of hazardous wastes or during the disposal of such wastes.
4. The parties agree that, according to the specific needs of different regions and sub-regions, regional or sub-regional centres for training and technology transfers regarding the management of hazardous wastes and the minimization of their generation should be established, as well as appropriate funding mechanisms of a voluntary nature.

Article 15

Conference of the Parties

1. A Conference of the Parties, made up of Ministers having the environment as their mandate, is hereby established. The first meeting of the Conference of the Parties shall be convened by the Secretary-General of the OAU not later than one year after the entry into force of this Convention. Thereafter, ordinary meetings of the Conference of the Parties shall be held at regular intervals to be determined by the Conference at its first meeting.
2. The Conference of the Parties to this Convention shall adopt Rules of Procedure for itself and for any subsidiary body it may establish, as well as financial rules to determine in particular the financial participation of the Parties to this Convention.
3. The Parties to this Convention at their first meeting shall consider any additional measures needed to assist them in fulfilling their responsibilities with respect to the protection and the preservation of the marine and inland waters environments in the context of this Convention.
4. The Conference of the Parties shall keep under continued review and evaluation the effective implementation of this Convention, and in addition, shall:
   (a) promote the harmonization of appropriate policies, strategies and measures for minimizing harm to human health and the environment by hazardous wastes;
   (b) consider and adopt amendments to this Convention and its annexes, taking into consideration, inter alia, available scientific, technical, economic and environmental information;
   (c) consider and undertake any additional action that may be required for the achievement of the purpose of this Convention in the light of experience gained in its operation and in the operation of the agreements and arrangements envisaged in Article 11 of this Convention;
   (d) consider and adopt protocols as required;
   (e) establish such subsidiary bodies as are deemed necessary for the implementation of this Convention; and
   (f) make decisions for the peaceful settlement of disputes arising from the transboundary movement of hazardous wastes, if need be, according to international law.
5. Organizations may be represented as observers at meetings of the Conference of the Parties. Any body or agency, whether national or international, governmental or non-governmental, qualified in fields relating to hazardous wastes which has informed the Secretariat, may be represented as an observer at a meeting of the Conference of the Parties. The admission and participation of observers shall be subject to the rules of procedure adopted by the Conference of the Parties.

Article 16

Secretariat

1. The functions of the Secretariat shall be:
   (a) To arrange for, and service, meetings provided for in Article 15 and 17 of this Convention;
   (b) To prepare and transmit reports based upon information received in accordance with Articles 3, 4, 6, 11, and 13 of this Convention as well as upon information derived from meetings of subsidiary bodies established under Article 15 of this Convention as well as upon, as appropriate, information provided by relevant intergovernmental and non-governmental entities;
   (c) To prepare reports on its activities carried out in the implementation of its functions under this Convention and present them to the Conference of the Parties;
   (d) To ensure the necessary co-ordination with relevant international bodies, and in particular to enter into such administrative and contractual arrangements as may be required for the effective discharge of its functions;
   (e) To communicate with focal points, competent authorities and Dumpwatch established by the Parties in accordance with Article 5 of this Convention as well as appropriate inter-governmental and non-governmental organizations which may provide assistance in the implementation of this Convention;
   (f) To compile information concerning approved national sites and facilities of Parties to this Convention available for the disposal and treatment of their hazardous wastes and to circulate this information;
   (g) To receive and convey information from and to Parties on:
   — sources of technical assistance and training;
   — available technical and scientific know-how;
   — sources of advice and expertise; and
   — availability of resources;
   This information will assist them in,
   — the management of the notification system of this Convention;
   — the management of hazardous wastes;
   — environmentally sound clean production methods relating to hazardous wastes, such as clean production technologies;
   — the assessment of disposal capabilities and sites;
   — the monitoring of hazardous wastes; and
   — emergency responses;
   (h) To provide Parties to this Convention with information on consultants or consulting firms having the necessary technical competence in the field, which can assist them with examining a notification for a transboundary movement, the concurrence of a shipment of hazardous wastes with the relevant notification, and/or whether the proposed disposal facilities for hazardous wastes are environmentally sound, when they have reason to believe that the wastes in question will not be managed in an environmentally sound manner. Any such examinations would not be at the expense of the Secretariat;

(i) To assist Parties to this Convention in their identification of cases of illegal traffic and to circulate immediately to the Parties concerned any information it has received regarding illegal traffic;

(j) To co-operate with Parties to this Convention and with relevant and competent international organizations and agencies in the provision of experts and equipment for the purpose of rapid assistance to States in the event of an emergency situation; and

(k) To perform such other functions relevant to the purposes of this Convention as may be determined by the Conference of the Parties to this Convention.

2. The Secretariat's functions shall be carried out on an interim basis by the Organization of African Unity (OAU) jointly with the United Nations Economic Commission for Africa (ECA) until the completion of the first meeting of the Conference of the Parties held pursuant to Article 15 of this Convention. At this meeting, the Conference of the Parties shall also evaluate the implementation by the interim Secretariat of the functions assigned to it, in particular under paragraph 1 above, and decide upon the structures appropriate for those functions.

Article 17

Amendment of the Convention and of Protocols

1. Any Party may propose amendments to this Convention and any party to a Protocol may propose amendments to that Protocol. Such amendments shall take due account, inter alia, of relevant scientific, technical, environmental and social considerations.

2. Amendments to this Convention shall be adopted at a meeting of the Conference of the Parties. Amendments to any Protocol shall be adopted at a meeting of the Parties to the Protocol in question. The text of any proposed amendment to this Convention or to any Protocol, except as may otherwise be provided in such Protocol, shall be communicated to the Parties by the Secretariat at least six months before the meeting at which it is proposed for adoption. The Secretariat shall also communicate proposed amendments to the Signatories to this Convention for their information.

3. The Parties shall make every effort to reach agreement on any proposed amendment to this Convention by consensus. If all efforts at consensus have been exhausted, and no agreement reached, the amendment shall, as a last resort, be adopted by a two-thirds majority vote of the Parties present and voting at the meeting. It shall then be submitted by the Depository to all Parties for ratification, approval, formal confirmation or acceptance.

Amendment of Protocols to this Convention

4. The procedure specified in paragraph 3 above shall apply to amendments to any protocol, except that a two-thirds majority of the Parties to that Protocol present and voting at the meeting shall suffice for their adoption.

General Provisions

5. Instruments of ratification, approval, formal confirmation or acceptance of amendments shall be deposited with the Depository. Amendments adopted in accordance with paragraph 3 or 4 above shall enter into force between Parties having accepted them, on the ninetieth day after the receipt by the Depository of the instrument of ratification, approval, formal confirmation or acceptance by at least two-thirds of the Parties who accepted the amendments to the Protocol concerned, except as may otherwise be provided in such Protocol. The amendments shall enter into force for any other Party on the ninetieth day after that Party deposits its instrument of ratification, approval, formal confirmation or acceptance of the amendments.
6. For the purpose of this Article, 'Parties present and voting' means Parties present and casting an affirmative or negative vote.

Article 18

Adoption and Amendment of Annexes

1. The annexes to this Convention or to any Protocol shall form an integral part of this Convention or of such Protocol, as the case may be and, unless expressly provided otherwise, a reference to this Convention or its Protocols constitutes at the same time a reference to any annexes thereto. Such annexes shall be restricted to scientific, technical and administrative matters.
2. Except as may be otherwise provided in any Protocol with respect to its annexes, the following procedures shall apply to the proposal, adoption and entry into force of additional annexes to this Convention or of annexes to a protocol:
   (a) Annexes to this Convention and its Protocols shall be proposed and adopted according to the procedure laid down in Article 17, paragraphs 1, 2, 3, and 4 of this Convention;
   (b) Any Party that is unable to accept an additional annex to this Convention or an annex to any Protocol to which it is Party shall so notify the Depository, in writing, within six months from the date of the communication of the adoption by the Depository. The Depository shall without delay notify all Parties of any such notification received. A Party may at any time substitute an acceptance for a previous declaration of objection and the annexes shall thereupon enter into force for that Party;
   (c) Upon the expiration of six months from the date of the circulation of the communication by the Depository, the annex shall become effective for all Parties to this Convention or to any Protocol concerned, which have not submitted a notification in accordance with the provision of sub-paragraph (b) above.
3. The proposal, adoption and entry into force of amendments to annexes to this Convention or to any Protocol shall be subject to the same procedure as for the proposal, adoption and entry into force of annexes to the Convention or annexes to a Protocol. Annexes and amendments thereto shall take due account, inter alia, of relevant scientific and technical considerations.
4. If an additional annex or an amendment to an annex involves an amendment to this Convention or to any Protocol, the additional annex or amended annex shall

not enter into force until such time as the amendment to this Convention or to the Protocol enters into force.

Article 19

Verification

Any Party which has reason to believe that another Party is acting or has acted in breach of its obligations under this Convention must inform the Secretariat thereof, and in such an event, shall simultaneously and immediately inform, directly or through the Secretariat, the Party against whom the allegations are made. The Secretariat shall carry out a verification of the substance of the allegation and submit a report thereof to all the Parties to this Convention.

Article 20

Settlement of Disputes

1. In case of dispute between Parties as to the interpretation or application of, or compliance with, this Convention or any Protocol thereto, the Parties shall seek a settlement of the dispute through negotiations or any other peaceful means of their own choice.
2. If the Parties concerned cannot settle their dispute as provided in paragraph 1 of this Article, the dispute shall be submitted either to an Ad Hoc organ set up by the Conference for this purpose, or to the International Court of Justice.
3. The conduct of arbitration of disputes between Parties by the Ad Hoc organ provided for in paragraph 2 of this Article shall be as provided in Annex V of this Convention.

Article 21

Signature

This Convention shall be open for signature by Member States of the OAU in Bamako and Addis Ababa for a period of six months from 30 January 1991 to 31 July 1991.

Article 22

Ratification, Acceptance, Formal Confirmation or Approval

1. This Convention shall be subject to ratification, acceptance, formal confirmation, or approval by Member States of the OAU. Instruments of ratification, acceptance, formal confirmation, or approval shall be deposited with the Depository.
2. Parties shall be bound by all obligations of this Convention.

Article 23

Accession

This Convention shall be open for accession by Member States of the OAU from the day after the date on which the Convention is closed for signature. The instruments of accession shall be deposited with the Depository.

Article 24

Right to Vote

Each Contracting Party to this Convention shall have one vote.

Article 25

Entry into Force

1. This Convention shall enter into force on the ninetieth day after the date of deposit of the tenth instrument of ratification from Parties signatory to this Convention.
2. For each State which ratifies this Convention or accedes thereto after the date of the deposit of the tenth instrument of ratification, it shall enter into force on the ninetieth day after the date of deposit by such State of its instrument of accession or ratification.

Article 26

Reservations and Declarations

1. No reservations or exception may be made to this Convention.
2. Paragraph 1 of this Article does not preclude a State when signing, ratifying, or acceding to this Convention, from making declarations or statements, however phrased or named, with a view, inter alia, to the harmonization of its laws and regulations with the provisions of this Convention, provided that such declarations or statements do not purport to exclude or to modify the legal effects of the provisions of the Convention in their application to that State.

Article 27

Withdrawal

1. At any time after three years from the date on which this Convention has entered into force for a Party, that Party may withdraw from the Convention by giving written notification to the Depository.
2. Withdrawal shall be effective one year after receipt of notification by the Depository, or on such later date as may be specified in the notification.
3. Withdrawal shall not exempt the withdrawing Party from fulfilling any obligations it might have incurred under this Convention.

Article 28

Depository

The Secretary-General of the Organization of African Unity shall be the Depository for this Convention and of any Protocol thereto.

Article 29

Registration

This Convention, as soon as it enters into force, shall be registered with the Secretary-General of the United Nations Organization (UNO) in conformity with Article 102 of the Charter of the UNO.

Article 30

Authentic Texts

The Arabic, English, French and Portuguese texts of this Convention are equally authentic.

Annex I

Categories of Wastes which are Hazardous Wastes

Waste Streams:

Y0 All wastes containing or contaminated by radionuclides, the concentration or properties of which result from human activity

Y1 Clinical wastes from medical care in hospitals, medical centers and clinics

Y2 Wastes from the production and preparation of pharmaceutical products

Y3 Waste pharmaceuticals, drugs and medicines

Y4 Wastes from the production, formulation and use of biocides and phytopharmaceuticals

Y5 Wastes from the manufacture, formulation and use of wood preserving chemicals

Y6 Wastes from the production, formulation and use of organic solvents

Y7 Wastes from heat treatment and tempering operations containing cyanides

Y8 Waste mineral oils unfit for their originally intended use

Y9 Waste oils/water, hydrocarbons/water mixtures, emulsions

Y10 Waste substances and articles containing or contaminated with polychlorinated biphenyls (PCBs) and/or polychlorinated terphenyls (PCTs) and/or polybrominated biphenyls (PBBs)

Y11 Waste tarry residues arising from refining, distillation and any pyrolytic treatment

Y12 Wastes from production, formulation and use of inks, dyes, pigments, paints, lacquers, varnish

Y13 Wastes from production, formulation and use of resins, latex, plasticizers, glues/adhesives

Y14 Waste chemical substances arising from research and development or teaching activities which are not identified and/or are new and whose effects on man and/or the environment are not known

Y15 Wastes of an explosive nature not subject to other legislation

Y16 Wastes from production, formulation and use of photographic chemicals and processing materials

Y17 Wastes resulting from surface treatment of metals and plastics

Y18 Residues arising from industrial waste disposal operations

Y46 Wastes collected from households, including sewage and sewage sludges
Y47 Residues arising from the incineration of household wastes

Wastes having as constituents:
Y19 Metal carbonyls
Y20 Beryllium; beryllium compounds
Y21 Hexavalent chromium compounds
Y22 Copper compounds
Y23 Zinc compounds
Y24 Arsenic; arsenic compounds
Y25 Selenium; selenium compounds
Y26 Cadmium; cadmium compounds
Y27 Antimony; antimony compounds
Y28 Tellurium; tellurium compounds
Y29 Mercury; mercury compounds
Y30 Thallium; thallium compounds
Y31 Lead; lead compounds
Y32 Inorganic fluorine compounds excluding calcium fluoride
Y33 Inorganic cyanides
Y34 Acidic solutions or acids in solid form
Y35 Basic solutions or bases in solid form
Y36 Asbestos (dust and fibres)
Y37 Organic phosphorous compounds
Y38 Organic cyanides
Y39 Phenols; phenolcompounds including chlorophenols
Y40 Ethers
Y41 Halogenated organic solvents
Y42 Organic solvents excluding halogenated solvents
Y43 Any congener of polychlorinated dibenzo-furan
Y44 Any congener of polychlorinated dibenzo-p-dioxin
Y45 Organohalogen compounds other than substances referred to in this Annex (e.g., Y39, Y41, Y42, Y43, Y44).

Annex II

List of Hazardous Characteristics

*UN Class**	*Code*	*Characteristics*
1	H1	Explosive An explosive substance or waste is a solid or liquid substance or waste (or mixture of substances or wastes) which is in itself capable by chemical reaction or producing gas at such a temperature and pressure and at such a speed as to cause damage to the surroundings.

* Corresponds to the hazardous classification system included in the United Nations Recommendations on the transport of Dangerous Goods (ST/SG/AC.10/1/Rev.5, United Nations, New York, 1988).

UN Class	*Code*	*Characteristics*
3	H3	Flammable liquids The word 'flammable' has the same meaning as 'inflammable'. Flammable liquids are liquids, or mixtures of liquids, or liquids containing solids in solution or suspension (for example paints, varnishes, lacquers, etc., but not including substances or wastes otherwise classified on account of their dangerous characteristics) which give off a flammable vapour at temperatures of not more than 60.5 degrees C, closed-cup test, or not more than 65.6 degrees C, open-cup test. (Since the results of open-cup tests and of closed-cup tests are not strictly comparable and even individual results by the same test are often variable, regulations varying from the above figures to make allowance for such difference would be within the spirit of this definition).
4.1	H4.1	Flammable solids Solids, or waste solids, other than those classed as explosives, which under conditions encountered in transport are readily combustible, or may cause or contribute to fire through friction.
4.2	H4.2	Substances or wastes liable to spontaneous combustion Substances or wastes which are liable to spontaneous heating under normal conditions encountered in transport, or to heating up on contact with air, and being then liable to catch fire.
4.3	H4.3	Substances or wastes which, in contact with water emit flammable gases Substances or wastes which, by interaction with water, are liable to become spontaneously flammable or to give off flammable gases in dangerous quantities.
5.1	H5.1	Oxidizing Substances or wastes which, while in themselves not necessarily combustible, may, generally by yielding oxygen, cause or contribute to the combustion of other materials.
5.2	H5.2	Organic peroxides Organic substances or wastes which contain the bivalent-O-O-structure are thermally unstable substances which may undergo exothermic self-accelerating decomposition.
6.1	H6.1	Poisonous (Acute) Substances or wastes liable either to cause death or serious injury or to harm human health if swallowed or inhaled or by skin contact.
6.2	H6.2	Infectious substances Substances or wastes containing viable micro organisms or their toxins which are known or suspected to cause disease in animals or humans.
8	H8	Corrosives Substances or wastes which, by chemical action, will cause severe damage when in contact with living tissue, or in the case of

*UN Class**	*Code*	*Characteristics*
		leakage, will materially damage, or even destroy, other goods or the means of transport; they may also cause other hazards.
9	H10	Liberation of toxic gases in contact with air or water Substances or wastes which, by interaction with air or water, are liable to give off toxic gases in dangerous quantities.
9	H11	Toxic (Delayed or chronic) Substances or wastes which, if they are inhaled or ingested or if they penetrate the skin, may involved delayed or chronic effects, including carcinogenicity.
9	H12	Ecotoxic Substances or wastes which if released present or may present immediate or delayed adverse impacts to the environment by means of bioaccumulation and/or toxic effects upon biotic systems.
9	H13	Capable, by any means, after disposal, of yielding another material, e.g., leachate, which possesses any of the characteristics listed above.

Annex III

Disposal Operations

D1 Deposit into or onto land, (e.g., landfill, etc.)
D2 Land treatment, (e.g., biodegradation of liquid or sludgy discards in soils, etc.)
D3 Deep injection, (e.g., injection of pumpable discards into wells, salt domes or naturally occurring repositories, etc.)
D4 Surface impoundment, (e.g., placement of liquid or sludge discards into pits, ponds, or lagoons, etc.)
D5 Specially engineered landfill, (e.g., placement into lined discrete cells which are capped and isolated from one another and the environment, etc.)
D6 Release into a water body except seas/oceans
D7 Release into seas/oceans including sea-bed insertion
D8 Biological treatment not specified elsewhere in this Annex which results in final compounds or mixtures which are discarded by means of any of the operations in Annex III
D9 Physico-chemical treatment not specified elsewhere in this Annex which results in final compounds or mixtures which are discarded by means of any of the operations in Annex III, (e.g., evaporation, drying, calcination, neutralisation, precipitation, etc.)
D10 Incineration on land
D11 Incineration at sea
D12 Permanent storage, (e.g., emplacement of containers in a mine, etc.)
D13 Blending or mixing prior to submission to any of the operations in Annex III
D14 Repackaging prior to submission to any of the operations in Annex III
D15 Storage pending any of the operations in Annex III
D16 Use as a fuel (other than in direct incineration) or other means to generate energy

D17 Solvent reclamation/regeneration
D18 Recycling/reclamation of organic substances which are not used as solvents
D19 Recycling/reclamation of metals and metal compounds
D20 Recycling/reclamation of other inorganic materials
D21 Regeneration of acids and bases
D22 Recovery of components used for pollution abatement
D23 Recovery of components from catalysts
D24 Used oil re-refining or other reuses of previously used oil
D25 Land treatment resulting in benefit to agriculture or ecological improvement
D26 Uses of residual materials obtained from any of the operations numbered D1–D25
D27 Exchange of wastes for submission to any of the operations numbered D1–D26
D28 Accumulation of material intended for any operation in Annex III

Annex IVA

Information to be Provided on Notification

1. Reason for waste export
2. Exporter of the waste *1/*
3. Generator(s) of the waste and site of generation *1/*
4. Importer and Disposer of the waste and actual site of disposal *1/*
5. Intended carrier(s) of the waste or their agents, if known *1/*
6. Country of export of the waste
   Competent authority *2/*
7. Countries of transit
   Competent authority *2/*
8. Country of import of the waste
   Competent authority *2/*
9. Projected date of shipment and period of time over which waste is to be exported and proposed itinerary (including point of entry and exit)
10. Means of transport envisaged (road, rail, sea, air, inland waters)
11. Information relating to insurance *3/*
12. Designation and physical description of the waste including Y number and UN number and its composition *4/* and information on any special handling requirements including emergency provisions in case of accidents
13. Type of packaging envisaged (e.g., bulk, drummer, tanker)
14. Estimated quantity in weight/volume
15. Process by which the waste is generated *5/*
16. Waste classifications from Annex II of this Convention: Hazardous characteristics, H number, and UN class
17. Method of disposal as per Annex III of this Convention
18. Declaration by the generator and exporter that the information is correct
19. Information transmitted (including technical description of the plant) to the exporter or generator from the disposer of the waste upon which the latter has based his assessment that there was no reason to believe that the wastes will not be managed in an environmentally sound manner in accordance with the laws and regulations of the country of import

20. Information concerning the contract between the exporter and disposer.

Notes

1/ Full name and address, telephone, telex or telefax number and the name, address, telephone, telex, or telefax number of the person to be contacted.
2/ Full name and address, telephone, telex or telefax number.
3/ Information to be provided on relevant insurance requirements and how they are met by exporter, carrier, and disposer.
4/ The nature and the concentration of the most hazardous components, in terms of toxicity and other dangers presented by the waste both in handling and in relation to the proposed disposal method.
5/ Insofar as this is necessary to assess the hazard and determine the appropriateness of the proposed disposal operation.

Annex IVB

Information to be Provided on the Movement Document

1. Exporter of the waste *1/*
2. Generator(s) of the waste and site of generation *1/*
3. Disposer of the waste and actual site of disposal *1/*
4. Carrier(s) of the waste *1/* or his agent(s)
5. The date the transboundary movement started and date(s) and signature on receipt by each person who takes charge of the waste
6. Means of transport (road, rail, inland waterway, sea, air) including countries of export, transit and import, also point of entry and exit where these have been designated
7. General description of the waste (physical state, proper UN shipping name and class, UN number, Y number and H number as applicable)
8. Information on special handling requirements including emergency provisions in case of accidents
9. Type and number of packages
10. Quantity in weight/volume
11. Declaration by the generator or exporter that the information is correct.
12. Declaration by the generator or exporter indicating no objection from the competent authorities of all States concerned
13. Certification by disposer of receipt at designated disposal facility and indication of method of disposal and of the appropriate date of disposal.

Notes

The information required on the movement document shall where possible be integrated into one document with that required under transport rules. Where this is not possible, the information should complement rather than duplicate that required under the transport rules. The movement document shall carry instructions as to who is to provide information and fill-out any form.

1/ Full name and address, telephone, telex or telefax number and the name, address, telephone, telex or telefax number of the person to be contacted in case of emergency.

Annex V

Arbitration

Article 1

Unless the agreement referred to in Article 20 of the Convention provides otherwise, the arbitration procedure shall be conducted in accordance with Articles 2 to 10 below.

Article 2

The claimant Party shall notify the Secretariat that the Parties have agreed to submit the dispute to arbitration pursuant to paragraph 1 or paragraph 2 of Article 20 of this Convention and include, in particular, the Articles of the Convention, and the interpretation or application of which are at issue. The Secretariat shall forward the information thus received to all Parties to the Convention.

Article 3

The arbitral tribunal shall consist of three members. Each of the Parties to the dispute shall appoint an arbitrator, and the two arbitrators so appointed shall designate by common agreement the third arbitrator, who shall be the chairman of the tribunal. The latter shall not be a national of one of the parties to the dispute, nor have his usual place of residence in one of the Parties, nor be employed by any of them, nor have dealt with the case in any other capacity.

Article 4

1. If the chairman of the arbitral tribunal has not been designated within two months of the appointment of the second arbitrator, the Secretary-General of the OAU shall, at the request of either Party, designate him within a further two months period.
2. If one of the Parties to the dispute does not appoint an arbitrator within two months of the receipt of the request, the other Party may inform the Secretary-General of the OAU who shall designate the chairman of the arbitral tribunal within a further two months period. Upon designation, the chairman of the arbitral tribunal shall request the Party which has not appointed an arbitrator to do so within two months. After such period, he shall inform the Secretary-General of the OAU who shall make this appointment within a further two month's period.

Article 5

1. The arbitral tribunal shall render its decision in accordance with international law and in accordance with the provisions of this Convention.
2. Any arbitral tribunal constituted under the provisions of this Annex shall draw up its own rules of procedure.

Article 6

1. The decisions of the arbitral tribunal both on procedure and on substance, shall be taken by majority vote of its members.
2. The tribunal may take all appropriate measures in order to establish the facts. It may, at the request of one of the Parties, recommend essential interim measures of protection.
3. The Parties to the dispute shall provide all facilities necessary for the effective conduct of the proceedings.
4. The absence or default of a Party in the dispute shall not constitute an impediment to the proceedings.

Article 7

The tribunal may hear and determine counter-claims arising directly out of the subject-matter of the dispute.

Article 8

Unless the arbitral tribunal determines otherwise because of the particular circumstances of the case, the expenses of the tribunal, including the remuneration of its members, shall be borne by the Parties to the dispute in equal shares. The tribunal shall keep a record of all its expenses, and shall furnish a final statement thereof to the Parties.

Article 9

Any Party that has an interest of a legal nature in the subject-matter of the dispute which may be affected by the decision in the case, may intervene in the proceedings with the consent of the tribunal.

Article 10

1. The tribunal shall render its award within five months of the date on which it is established unless it finds it necessary to extend the time-limit for a period which should not exceed five months.
2. The award of the arbitral tribunal shall be accompanied by a statement of reasons. It shall be final and binding upon the Parties to the dispute.
3. Any dispute which may arise between the Parties concerning the interpretation or execution of the award may be submitted by either Party to the arbitral tribunal which made the award or, if the latter cannot be seized thereof, to another tribunal constituted for this purpose in the same manner as the first.

Appendix IV

Lomé IV Convention (15 December 1989), Article 39 and Annexes VIII–X

Article 39

1. The Contracting Parties undertake, for their part, to make every effort to ensure that international movements of hazardous waste and radioactive waste are generally controlled, and they emphasize the importance of efficient international cooperation in this area.

With this in view, the Community shall prohibit all direct or indirect export of such waste to the ACP States while at the same time the ACP States shall prohibit the direct or indirect import into their territory of such waste from the Community or from any other country, without prejudice to specific international undertakings to which the Contracting Parties have subscribed or may subscribe in the future in these two areas within the competent international fora.

These provisions do not prevent a Member State to which an ACP State has chosen to export waste for processing from returning the processed waste to the ACP State of origin.

The Contracting Parties shall expedite adoption of the necessary internal legislation and administrative regulations to implement this undertaking. At the request of one of the Parties, consultations may be held if delays are encountered. At the conclusion of such consultations each Party may take appropriate steps in the light of the situation.

2. The Parties undertake to monitor strictly the implementation of the prohibition measures referred to in the second paragraph of paragraph 1. Should difficulties arise in this respect, consultations may be held subject to the same conditions as those provided for in the second paragraph of paragraph 1 and with the same effect.

3. The term 'hazardous waste' within the meaning of this Article shall cover categories of products listed in Annexes 1 and 2 to the Basle Convention on the Control of Transboundary Movements of Hazardous Wastes and their Disposal.

As regards radioactive waste, the applicable definitions and thresholds shall be those which will be laid down in the framework of the IAEA. In the meantime, the said definitions and thresholds shall be those specified in the declaration in Annex VIII to this Convention.

Annex VIII

Joint declaration on Article 39 on movements of hazardous waste or radioactive waste

Keenly aware of the specific risks attaching to radioactive waste, the Contracting Parties will refrain from any practice of discharging such waste which would encroach upon the sovereignty of States or threaten the environment or public health in other countries. They attach the greatest importance to developing international cooperation to protect the environment and public health against such risks. They accordingly affirm their determination to play an active part in the work being done in the IAEA to produce an internationally approved code of good practice.

Until such time as a more precise definition is formulated in that framework, the term 'radioactive waste' will be taken to mean any material for which no further use is envisaged and which contains or is contaminated by radionuclides of which the levels of radioactivity or the concentrations exceed the limits which the Community has set itself for protecting its own population in Article 4(a) and (b) of Directive 80/836 EURATOM, as last amended by Directive 84/467/EURATOM. As regards levels of radioactivity, these limits range from 5×10^3 becquerel for nuclides of very high radiotoxicity to 5×10^3 becquerel for those of low radiotoxicity. As regards concentrations, these limits are 100 $Bq.g^{-1}$ and 500 $Bq.g^{-1}$ for solid natural radioactive substances.

Annex IX

Joint declaration on Article 39 on movements of hazardous waste and radioactive waste

The Contracting Parties shall make every effort to sign and ratify as quickly as possible the Basle Convention on the Control of Transboundary Movements of Hazardous Wastes and their Disposal.

Annex X

ACP declaration on hazardous and nuclear and other radioactive waste

The ACP States are seriously concerned about environmental problems in general and the transboundary movement of hazardous, nuclear and other radioactive wastes in particular.

In interpreting and implementing the provisions of the third and fourth subparagraphs of Article 39(1) of the Convention, the ACP States have expressed their determination to be guided by the principles and the provisions of the OAU Resolution on the Control of Transboundary Movements of Hazardous Wastes and their Disposal in Africa as contained in Doc. AHG 182 (XXV).

Appendix V

Agreement Between the Government of Canada and the Government of the United States of America Concerning the Transboundary Movement of Hazardous Waste (28 October 1986, as amended).

The Government of Canada (Canada), and the Government of the United States of America (the United States), hereinafter called 'The Parties':

RECOGNIZING that severe health and environmental damage may result from the improper treatment, storage, and disposal of hazardous waste;

SEEKING to ensure that the treatment, storage, and disposal of hazardous waste are conducted so as to reduce the risks to public health, property, and environmental quality;

RECOGNIZING that the close trading relationship and the long common border between the United States and Canada engender opportunities for a generator of hazardous waste to benefit from using the nearest appropriate disposal facility, which may involve the transboundary shipment of hazardous waste;

RECOGNIZING further that the most effective and efficient means of achieving environmentally sound management procedures for hazardous waste crossing the United States–Canada border is through cooperative efforts and coordinated regulatory schemes;

BELIEVING that a bilateral agreement is needed to facilitate the control of transboundary shipments of hazardous waste between the United States and Canada;

REAFFIRMING Principle 21 of the 1972 Declaration of the United Nations Conference on the Human Environment, adopted at Stockholm, which asserts that states have, in accordance with the Charter of the United Nations and the principles of international law, the sovereign right to exploit their own resources pursuant to their own environmental policies and the responsibility to ensure that activities within their jurisdiction or control do not cause damage to the environment of other states or of areas beyond the limits of national jurisdiction;

TAKING into account OECD Council Decisions and Recommendations on transfrontier movements of hazardous wastes, the UNEP Cairo Guidelines and Principles for the Environmentally Sound Management of Hazardous Waste, and resolutions of the London Dumping Convention,

Have agreed as follows:

Article 1

Definitions

For the purposes of this Agreement:

(a) 'Designated Authority' means, in the case of the United States of America, the Environmental Protection Agency and, in the case of Canada, the Department of the Environment.

(b) 'Hazardous Waste' means with respect to Canada, hazardous waste, and with respect to the United States, hazardous waste subject to a manifest requirement in the United States, as defined by their respective national legislations and implementing regulations.
(c) 'Country of Export' means the country from which the shipment of hazardous waste and other waste originated.
(d) 'Country of Import' means the country to which hazardous waste and other waste is sent for the purpose of treatment, storage (with the exception of short-term storage incidental to transportation) or disposal.
(e) 'Country of Transit' means the country which is neither the country of export nor the country of import, through whose land territory or internal waters hazardous waste and other waste is transported, or in whose ports such waste is unloaded for further transportation.
(f) 'Consignee' means the treatment, storage (with the exception of short-term storage incidental to transportation) or disposal facility in the country of import and the name of the person operating the facility.
(g) 'Exporter' means, in the case of the United States, the person defined as exporter, and in the case of Canada, the person defined as consignor, under their respective national laws and regulations governing hazardous waste and other waste.
(h) 'Other waste' means municipal solid waste that is sent for final disposal or for incineration with energy recovery, and residues arising from the incineration of such waste, as defined by the Parties' respective national legislations and implementing regulations, but excluding waste covered under paragraph (b) of this Article.

Article 2

General Obligation

The Parties shall permit the export, import, and transit of hazardous waste and other waste across their common border for treatment, storage, or disposal pursuant to the terms of their domestic laws, regulations and administrative practices, and the provisions of this Agreement.

Article 3

Notification to the Importing Country

(a) The designated authority of the country of export shall notify the designated authority of the country of import of proposed transboundary shipments of hazardous waste and other waste.
(b) The notice referred to in paragraph (a) of this article may cover an individual shipment or a series of shipments extending over a twelve month or lesser period and shall contain the following information:
   (i) The exporter's name, address and telephone number, and if required in the country of export, the identification number.
   (ii) for each hazardous waste and other waste type and for each consignee:
      (1) A description of the hazardous waste and other waste to be exported,

as identified by the waste identification number, the classification and the shipping name as required on the manifest in the country of export;

(2) The estimated frequency or rate at which such waste is to be exported and the period of time over which such waste is to be exported;

(3) The estimated total quantity of the hazardous waste and other waste in units as specified by the manifest required in the country of export;

(4) The point of entry into the country of import;

(5) The name and address of the transporter(s) and the means of transportation, such as the mode of transportation (air, highway, rail, water, etc.) and type(s) of container (drums, boxes, tanks, etc.);

(6) A description of the manner in which the waste will be treated, stored or disposed of in the importing country;

(7) The name and site address of the consignee;

(8) An approximate date of the first shipment to each consignee, if available.

(c) The designated authority of the country of import shall have 30 days from the date of receipt of the notice provided pursuant to paragraphs (a) and (b) of this article to respond to such notice, indicating its consent (conditional or not) or its objection to the export. Such response will be transmitted to the designated authority of the country of export. The date of receipt of the notice will be identified in an acknowledgement of receipt made immediately by the designated authority of the country of import to the country of export.

(d) If no response is received by the designated authority of the country of export within the 30 day period referred to in paragraph (c) of this article, the country of import shall be considered as having no objection to the export of hazardous waste and other waste described in the notice and the export may take place conditional upon the persons importing the hazardous waste and other waste complying with all the applicable laws of the country of import.

(e) The country of import shall have the right to amend the terms of the proposed shipment(s) as described in the notice.

(f) The consent of the country of import, whether express, tacit, or conditional, provided pursuant to paragraphs (c) and (d) of this article, may be withdrawn or modified for good cause. The Parties will withdraw or modify such consent insofar as possible at the most appropriate time for the persons concerned.

(g) For the purpose of this Article and Article 5, manifest-related requirements may, with respect to other waste, be substituted by alternative tracking requirements.

Article 4

Notification to the Transit Country

(a) The designated authority of the country of export shall notify the designated authority of the country of transit of the proposed shipment of hazardous waste and other waste at least 7 days prior to the date of the shipment. The notice shall include the information specified in paragraph (b) of Article 3, with the following exceptions:

(i) The points of entry into and departure from the country of transit shall be provided in lieu of the entry point(s) into the country of import; and

(ii) A description of the approximate length of time the hazardous waste and other waste will remain in the country of transit and the nature of its handling while there shall be submitted instead of a description of the treatment, storage, or disposal of the waste in the country of import.

Article 5

Cooperative Efforts

1. The Parties will cooperate to ensure, to the extent possible, that all transboundary shipments of hazardous waste and other waste comply with the manifest requirements of both countries.
2. The Parties will cooperate in monitoring and spot-checking transboundary shipments of hazardous waste and other waste to ensure, to the extent possible, that such shipments conform to the requirements of the applicable legislation and of this Agreement.
3. To the extent any implementing laws and regulations are necessary to comply with this Agreement, the Parties will act expeditiously to issue such laws and regulations consistent with domestic law. Pending such issuance, the Parties will make best efforts to provide notification in accordance with this Agreement where current regulatory authority is insufficient. The Parties will provide each other with a diplomatic note upon the issuance and the coming into effect of any such laws and regulations.

Article 6

Readmission of Exports

The country of export shall readmit any shipment of hazardous waste and other waste that may be returned by the country of import or transit.

Article 7

Enforcement

The Parties shall ensure, to the extent possible, that within their respective jurisdictions, their domestic laws and regulations are enforced with respect to the transportation, storage, treatment and disposal of transboundary shipments of hazardous waste and other waste.

Article 8

Protection of Confidential Information

If the provision of technical information pursuant to articles 3 and 4 would require the disclosure of information covered by agreement(s) of confidentiality between a Party and an exporter, the country of export shall make every effort to obtain the consent of the concerned person for the purpose of conveying any such information to the country of import or transit. The country of import or transit shall make every effort to protect the confidentiality of such information conveyed.

Article 9

Insurance

The Parties may require, as a condition of entry, that any transboundary movement of hazardous waste and other waste be covered by insurance or other financial guarantee in respect to damage to third parties caused during the entire movement of hazardous waste and other waste, including loading and unloading.

Article 10

Effects on International Agreements

Nothing in this Agreement shall be deemed to diminish the obligations of the Parties with respect to disposal of hazardous waste and other waste at sea contained in the 1972 London Dumping Convention.

Article 11

Domestic Law

The provisions of this Agreement shall be subject to the applicable laws and regulations of the Parties.

Article 12

Amendment

This Agreement may be amended by mutual written consent of the Parties or their authorized representatives.

Article 13

Entry into Force

This Agreement shall enter into force on November 8, 1986 and continue in force for five years. It will automatically be renewed for additional five year periods unless either Party gives written notice of termination to the other at least three months prior to the expiration of any five year period. In any five year period, this Agreement may be terminated upon one year written notice given by one Party to the other.

Appendix VI

Agreement of Co-operation Between the United States of America and the United Mexican States Regarding the Transboundary Shipments of Hazardous Wastes and Hazardous Substances (12 November 1986)

PREAMBLE

The Government of the United States of America ('the United States'), and the Government of the United Mexican States ('Mexico'), ('the Parties'),

Recognizing that health and environmental damage may result from improper activities associated with hazardous waste;

Realizing the potential risks to public health, property and the environment associated with hazardous substances;

Seeking to ensure that activities associated with the transboundary shipment of hazardous waste are conducted so as to reduce or prevent the risks to public health, property and environmental quality, by effectively cooperating in regard to their export and import;

Seeking also to safeguard the quality of public health, property and environment from unreasonable risks by effectively regulating the export and import of hazardous substances;

Considering that transboundary shipments of hazardous waste and hazardous substances between the Parties, if carried out illegally and thus without the supervision and control of the competent authorities, or if improperly managed could endanger the public health, property and environment, particularly in the United States/Mexico border area;

Recognizing that the close trading relationship and the long common border between the Parties make it necessary to cooperate regarding transboundary shipments of hazardous waste and hazardous substances without unreasonably affecting the trade of goods and services;

Reaffirming Principle 21 of the 1972 Declaration of the United Nations Conference on the Human Environment, adopted at Stockholm, which provides that States have, in accordance with the Charter of the United Nations and the principles of international law, the sovereign right to exploit their own resources pursuant to their own environmental policies and the responsibility to ensure that activities within their jurisdiction or control do not cause damage to the environment of other States or of areas beyond the limits of national jurisdiction;

Recognizing that Article 3 of the Agreement between the Parties on Cooperation for the Protection and Improvement of the Environment in the Border Area of 1983 provides that the Parties may conclude specific arrangements for the solution of common problems in the border area as annexes to that Agreement;

Have agreed as follows:

Article I

Definitions

1. 'Designated Authority' means, in the case of the United States, the Environmental Protection Agency and, in the case of Mexico, the Secretariat of Urban Development and Ecology through the Subsecretariat of Ecology.
2. 'Hazardous waste' means any waste, as designated or defined by the applicable designated authority pursuant to national policies, laws or regulations, which if improperly dealt with in activities associated with them, may result in health or environmental damage.
3. 'Hazardous substance' means any substance, as designated or defined by the applicable national policies, laws or regulations, including pesticides or chemicals, which when improperly dealt with in activities associated with them, may produce harmful effects to public health, property or the environment, and is banned or severely restricted by the applicable designated authority.
4. 'Activities' associated with hazardous waste or hazardous substances means, as applicable, their handling, transportation, treatment, recycling, storage, application, distribution, reuse or other utilization.
5. 'Country of export' means the Party from which the transboundary movement of hazardous waste or hazardous substances is to be initiated.
6. 'Country of import' means the Party to which the hazardous waste or hazardous substances are to be sent. This does not include 'transit', as meaning transport of hazardous waste or hazardous substances through the territory of a Party without being imported through its Customs under applicable laws and regulations.
7. 'Consignee' means the facility in the country of import which will ultimately receive the hazardous waste or hazardous substances.
8. 'Exporter' means the physical or juridical person whether public or private, acting on his behalf or as a contractor or subcontractor expressly or implicitly defined as exporter under the national laws and regulations of the country of export which specifically govern hazardous waste or hazardous substances.
9. 'Banned or severely restricted' means final regulatory action, as designated or defined by the applicable designated authority, pursuant to national policies, laws or regulations:
   (a) Prohibiting, cancelling or suspending all or virtually all registered uses of a pesticide for human health or environmental reasons.
   (b) Prohibiting or severely limiting the manufacture, processing, distribution or use of a chemical for human health or environmental reasons.

Article II

General Obligations

1. Transboundary shipments of hazardous waste and hazardous substances across the common border of the Parties shall be governed by the terms of this Annex and their domestic laws and regulations.
2. Each Party shall ensure, to the extent practicable, that its domestic laws and regulations are enforced with respect to transboundary shipments of hazardous

waste and hazardous substances, and other substances as the Parties may mutually agree through appendices to this Annex, that pose dangers to public health, property and the environment.

3. Each Party shall cooperate in monitoring and spot-checking transboundary shipments across the common border of hazardous waste and hazardous substances to ensure, to the extent practicable, that such shipments conform to the requirements of this Annex and its national laws and regulations. To this effect, a program of cooperation in this area should be concluded through an Appendix to this Annex, including the exchange of information resulting from the monitoring and spot-checking of transboundary shipments which may be useful to the other Party.

Hazardous Waste

Article III

Notification to the Importing Country

1. The designated authority of the country of export shall notify the designated authority of the country of import of transboundary shipments of hazardous waste for which the consent of the country of import is required under the laws or regulations of the country of export, with a copy of the notification simultaneously sent through diplomatic channels.

2. The notification referred to in paragraph 1 of this Article shall be given at least 45 days in advance of the planned date of export and may cover an individual shipment or a series of shipments extending over a twelve-month or lesser period, and shall contain the following information for each shipment:

(a) The exporter's name, address, telephone number, identification number and other relevant data required in the country of export.

(b) By consignee, for each hazardous waste type:

(i) A description of the hazardous waste to be exported, as identified by the waste identification number(s) and the shipping description(s) required in the country of export.

(ii) The estimated frequency or rate at which such waste is to be exported and the period time over which such waste is to be exported.

(iii) The estimated total quantity of the hazardous waste in units as specified by the manifest or documents required in the country of export.

(iv) The point of entry into the country of import.

(v) The means of transportation, including the mode of transportation and the type of container involved.

(vi) A description of the treatment or storage to which the waste will be subjected in the country of import.

(vii) The name and site address of the consignee.

3. In order to facilitate compliance with the requirements of the importing country for the exporter to provide information and documents additional to those described in paragraph 2 of this Article, the designated authority of the exporting country will cooperate by making such requirements for information and documents known to the exporter. To that end, the country of import may list such additional required information and documents in appendices to this Annex.

4. The designated authority of the country of import shall have 45 days from the date of acknowledgement of receipt of the notification provided in paragraph 1 of this Article within which to respond to such notification, indicating its consent, with or without conditions, or its objection to the export.
5. The country of import shall have the right to amend the terms of the proposed shipment contained in the notification in order to give its consent.
6. The consent of the country of import provided pursuant to paragraphs 4 and 5 of this Article, may be withdrawn or modified at any time, pursuant to the national policies, laws or regulations of the country of import.
7. Whenever the designated authority of a country of export requires notification of or is otherwise aware of a transboundary shipment that will be transported through the territory of the other Party, it shall, in accordance with its national laws and regulations, notify that party.

Article IV

Readmission of Exports

The country of export shall readmit any shipment of hazardous waste that may be returned for any reason by the country of import.

Hazardous Substances

Article V

Notification of Regulatory Actions

1. When a Party has banned or severely restricted a pesticide or chemical, its designated authority shall notify the designated authority of the other Party that such action has been taken either directly or through an appropriate intergovernmental organization.
2. The notice referred to in paragraph 1 of this Article shall contain the following information, if available:
   (a) the name of the pesticide or chemical that is the object of the regulatory action;
   (b) a concise summary of the regulatory action taken including the timetable for any further actions that are planned. If the regulatory action bans or restricts certain uses but allows other uses, such information should be included;
   (c) a concise summary of the reason for the regulatory action, including an indication of the potential risks to human health or the environment that are the grounds for the action;
   (d) information concerning registered pesticides or substitute chemicals that could be used in lieu of the banned or severely restricted pesticide or chemical;
   (e) the name and address of the contact point to which a request for further information should be addressed.

Article VI

Notification of Exports

1. If the country of export becomes aware that an export of a hazardous substance to the country of import is occurring, the designated authority of the country of export shall notify the designated authority of the country of import.
2. The purpose of such notice shall be to remind the country of import of the notification regarding regulatory action provided pursuant to Article 5 and to alert it to the fact that the export is occurring.
3. The notice referred to in paragraph 1 of this Article shall contain the following information, if available:
   (a) the name of the exported hazardous substance;
   (b) for banned or severely restricted chemicals, approximate date(s) of the export;
   (c) a copy of, or reference to, the information provided at the time of the notification of the regulatory action;
   (d) name and address of the contact point for further information.

Article VII

Timing of the Notifications

1. Notification of regulatory actions, required pursuant to Article 5, shall be transmitted as soon as practicable after the regulatory action has been taken, and in any event not later than 90 days following the taking of such action.
2. When a Party has banned or severely restricted chemicals or pesticides prior to the entry into force of this Annex, its designated authority shall provide an inventory of such prior regulatory actions to the designated authority of the other Party.
3. Notification of exports required pursuant to Article 6, shall be provided at the time the first export of a hazardous substance is occurring to the Country of import following the regulatory action and should recur at the time of the first export of the hazardous substance each subsequent year to that country.
4. When the hazardous substance being exported has been banned or severely restricted prior to the entry into force of this Annex, the first export following the regulatory action shall be considered to be the first export following the provision of the inventory referred to in paragraph 2 of this Article.

Article VIII

Compliance with Requirements in the Importing Country

In order to facilitate compliance with the requirements in the importing country for the import of hazardous substances, the designated authority of the country of export will cooperate by making such requirements, including expected information and documents, known to the exporter. To that end, the country of import may list such requirements, information and documents in appendices to this Annex.

Article IX

Readmission of Exports

The country of export shall readmit any shipment of hazardous substances that was not lawfully imported into the country of import.

General Provisions

Article X

Additional Arrangements

1. The Parties shall consider and, as appropriate, establish additional arrangements to mitigate or avoid adverse effects on health, property and the environment from improper activities associated with hazardous waste and hazardous substances. Such arrangements may include the sharing of research data as well as the definition of criteria regarding imminent and substantial endangerment and emergency responses, and may be included in appendices to this Annex.
2. The Parties shall consult regarding experience with transboundary shipments of hazardous wastes and hazardous substances and, as problems are identified in the special circumstances of the United States–Mexico border relationship may include through appendices to this Annex, additional cooperation and mutual obligations aimed at achieving when necessary a more stringent control of transboundary shipments, such as provisions to bring uniformity in those relating to both hazardous wastes and hazardous substances regarding compulsory notification to and consent by the importing country for each transboundary shipment, as may become permitted by new national laws and regulations adopted by the Parties.

Article XI

Hazardous Waste Generated From Raw Materials Admitted In-Bond

Hazardous waste generated in the processes of economic production, manufacturing, processing or repair, for which raw materials were utilized and temporarily admitted, shall continue to be readmitted by the country of origin of the raw materials in accordance with applicable national policies, laws and regulations.

Article XII

Information Exchange and Assistance

1. The parties shall, to the extent practicable, provide to each other mutual assistance designed to increase the capability of each Party to enforce its laws applicable to transboundary shipments of hazardous waste or hazardous substances and to take appropriate action with respect to violations of its laws.
   (a) Such assistance may generally include:
      (i) the exchange of information;
      (ii) the provision of documents, records and reports;
      (iii) the facilitating of on-site visits to treatment, storage, or disposal facilities;

(iv) assistance provided or required pursuant to any international agreements or treaties in force with respect to the Parties, or pursuant to any arrangement or practice that might otherwise be applicable;
(v) emergency notification of hazardous situations; and
(vi) other forms of assistance mutually agreed upon by the Parties.

(b) Save in exceptional circumstances, requests for assistance made pursuant to this Article shall be submitted in writing and translated into the language of the requested State.
(c) The requested State shall provide the requesting State with copies of publicly available records of government departments and agencies in the requested State.
(d) The requested State may provide any record or information in the possession of a government office or agency, but not publicly available, to the same extent and under the same conditions as it would be available to its own administrative, law enforcement, or judicial authorities.

2. The Parties may establish in an appendix to this Annex a cooperative program relating to the exchange of scientific, technical, and other information for purposes of the development of their own respective regulatory mechanisms controlling hazardous waste and hazardous substances.

Article XIII

Protection of Confidential Information

The Parties shall adopt procedures to protect the confidentiality of proprietary or sensitive information conveyed pursuant to this Annex, when such procedures do not already exist.

Article XIV

Damages

1. The country of import may require, as a condition of entry, that any transboundary shipment of hazardous waste or hazardous substances be covered by insurance, bond or other appropriate and effective guarantee.

2. Whenever a transboundary shipment of hazardous waste or hazardous substances is carried out in violation of this Annex, of the national laws and regulations of the Parties, or of the conditions to which the authorization for import was subject, or whenever the hazardous waste or hazardous substances produce damages to public health, property or the environment in the country of import, the competent authorities of the country of export shall take all practicable measures and initiate and carry out all pertinent legal actions that they are legally competent to undertake, so that when applicable in accordance with its national laws and regulations the physical or juridical persons involved;

(a) return the hazardous waste or hazardous substances to the country of export:
(b) return in as much as practicable the *status quo ante* of the affected ecosystem;
(c) repair, through compensation, the damages caused to persons, property or the environment.

The country of import shall also take, for the same purposes, all practicable measures and initiate and carry out all pertinent legal actions that its authorities are legally competent to undertake.

The country of export shall report to the country of import all measures and legal actions undertaken in the framework of this paragraph, and shall cooperate with the country of import, on the basis of this Annex or of other bilateral treaties and agreements in force between the Parties, and to the extent permitted by its national laws and regulations, to seek in its courts the satisfaction of those matters covered in subparagraphs (a) to (c) of this paragraph.

3. The provisions of this Annex shall not be deemed to abridge or prejudice the Parties' national laws concerning transboundary shipments, or liability or compensation for damages resulting from activities associated with hazardous waste and hazardous substances.

Article XV

Effect On Other Instruments

1. Nothing in this Annex shall be construed to prejudice other existing or future agreements concluded between the Parties, or affect the rights or obligations of the Parties under international agreements to which they are Party.
2. The provision of this Annex shall, in particular, not be deemed to prejudice or otherwise affect the functions entrusted to the International Boundary and Water Commission, in accordance with the 1944 Treaty on the Utilization of Waters of the Colorado and Tijuana Rivers and of the Rio Grande.

Article XVI

Appendices

Any appendices to this Annex may be added through an exchange of diplomatic notes and shall form an integral part of this Annex.

Article XVII

Amendment

This Annex, and any appendices added hereto, may be amended by mutual agreement of the Parties through an exchange of diplomatic notes.

Article XVIII

Review

The Parties shall meet at least every two years from the date of entry into force of this Annex, at a time and place to be mutually agreed upon, in order to review the effectiveness of its implementation and to agree on whatever individual and joint measures are necessary to improve such effectiveness.

Article XIX

Entry into Force

This Annex shall enter into force upon an exchange of diplomatic notes between the Parties stating that each Party has completed its necessary internal procedures.

Article XX

Termination

This Annex shall remain in force indefinitely, unless one of the Parties notifies the other in writing through diplomatic channels of its desire to terminate it, in which case the Annex shall terminate six months after the date of such written notification. Unless otherwise agreed, such termination shall not affect the validity of any agreements made under this Annex.

Appendix VII

EC Council Regulation on the Supervision and Control of Shipments of Waste within, into and out of the European Community (No 259/93, 1 February 1993)

THE COUNCIL OF THE EUROPEAN COMMUNITIES,

Having regard to the Treaty establishing the European Economic Community, and in particular Article 130s thereof,

Having regard to the proposal from the Commission,

Having regard to the opinion of the European Parliament,

Having regard to the opinion of the Economic and Social Committee,

Whereas the Community has signed the Basle Convention of 22 March 1989 on the control of transboundary movements of hazardous wastes and their disposal;

Whereas provisions concerning waste are contained in Article 39 of the ACP–EEC Convention of 15 December 1989;

Whereas the Community has approved the Decision of the OECD Council of 30 March 1992 on the control of transfrontier movements of wastes destined for recovery operations;

Whereas, in the light of the foregoing, Directive 84/631/EEC, which organizes the supervision and control of transfrontier shipments of hazardous waste, needs to be replaced by a Regulation;

Whereas the supervision and control of shipments of waste within a Member State is a national responsibility; whereas, however, national systems for the supervision and control of shipments of waste within a Member State should comply with minimum criteria in order to ensure a high level of protection of the environment and human health;

Whereas it is important to organize the supervision and control of shipments of wastes in a way which takes account of the need to preserve, protect and improve the quality of the environment;

Whereas Council Directive 75/442/EEC of 15 July 1975 on waste lays down in its Article 5(1) that an integrated and adequate network of waste disposal installations, to be established by Member States through appropriate measures, where necessary or advisable in cooperation with other Member States, must enable the Community as a whole to become self-sufficient in waste disposal and the Member States to move towards that aim individually, taking into account geographical circumstances or the need for specialized installations for certain types of waste; whereas Article 7 of the said Directive requests the drawing up of waste management plans, if appropriate in cooperation with the Member States concerned, which shall be notified to the Commission, and stipulates that Member States may take measures necessary to prevent movements of waste which are not in accordance with their waste management plans and that they shall inform the Commission and the other Member States of any such measures;

Whereas it is necessary to apply different procedures depending on the type of waste and its destination, including whether it is destined for disposal or recovery;

Whereas shipments of waste must be subject to prior notification to the competent authorities enabling them to be duly informed in particular of the type, movement and disposal or recovery of the waste, so that these authorities may take all necessary measures for the protection of human health and the environment, including the possibility of raising reasoned objections to the shipment;

Whereas Member States should be able to implement the principles of proximity, priority for recovery and self-sufficiency at Community and national levels—in accordance with Directive 75/442/EEC—by taking measures in accordance with the Treaty to prohibit generally or partially or to object systematically to shipments of waste for disposal, except in the case of hazardous waste produced in the Member State of dispatch in such a small quantity that the provision of new specialized disposal installations within that State would be uneconomic; whereas the specific problem of disposal of such small quantities requires cooperation between the Member States concerned and possible recourse to a Community procedure;

Whereas exports of waste for disposal to third countries must be prohibited in order to protect the environment of those countries; whereas exceptions shall apply to exports to EFTA countries which are also Parties to the Basle Convention;

Whereas exports of waste for recovery to countries to which the OECD Decision does not apply must be subject to conditions providing for environmentally sound management of waste;

Whereas agreements or arrangements on exports of waste for recovery with countries to which the OECD Decision does not apply must be subject to periodic review by the Commission leading, if appropriate, to a proposal by the Commission to reconsider the conditions under which such exports take place, including the possibility of a ban;

Whereas shipments of waste for recovery listed on the green list of the OECD Decision shall be generally excluded from the control procedures of this Regulation since such waste should not normally present a risk to the environment if properly recovered in the country of destination; whereas some exceptions to this exclusion are necessary in accordance with Community legislation and the OECD Decision; whereas some exceptions are also necessary in order to facilitate the tracking of such shipments within the Community and to take account of exceptional cases; whereas such waste shall be subject to Directive 75/442/EEC;

Whereas exports of waste for recovery listed on the OECD green list to countries to which the OECD Decision does not apply must be subject to consultation by the Commission with the country of destination; whereas it may be appropriate in the light of such consultation that the Commission make proposals to the Council;

Whereas exports of waste for recovery to countries which are not parties to the Basle Convention must be subject to specific agreements between these countries and the Community; whereas Member States must, in exceptional cases, be able to conclude after the date of application of this Regulation bilateral agreements for the import of specific waste before the Community has concluded such agreements, in the case of waste for recovery in order to avoid any interruption of waste treatment and in the case of waste for disposal where the country of dispatch does not have or cannot reasonably acquire the technical capacity and necessary facilities to dispose of the waste in an environmentally sound manner;

Whereas provision must be made for the waste to be taken back or to be disposed of or recovered in an alternative and environmentally sound manner if the shipment cannot be completed in accordance with the terms of the consignment note or the contract;

Whereas, in the event of illegal traffic, the person whose action is the cause of such traffic must take back and/or dispose of or recover the waste in an alternative and environmentally sound manner; whereas, should he fail to do so, the competent authorities of dispatch or destination, as appropriate, must themselves intervene;

Whereas it is important for a system of financial guarantees or equivalent insurance to be established;

Whereas Member States must provide the Commission with information relevant to the implementation of this Regulation;

Whereas the documents provided for by this Regulation must be established and the Annexes adapted within a Community procedure,

HAS ADOPTED THIS REGULATION:

Title I

Scope and Definitions

Article 1

1. This Regulation shall apply to shipments of waste within, into and out of the Community.
2. The following shall be excluded from the scope of this Regulation:
   (a) the offloading to shore of waste generated by the normal operation of ships and offshore platforms, including waste water and residues, provided that such waste is the subject of a specific binding international instrument;
   (b) shipments of civil aviation waste;
   (c) shipments of radioactive waste as defined in Article 2 of Directive 92/3/Euratom of 3 February 1992 on the supervision and control of shipments of radioactive waste between Member States and into and out of the Community;
   (d) shipments of waste mentioned in Article 2(1)(b) of Directive 75/442/EEC, where they are already covered by other relevant legislation;
   (e) shipments of waste into the Community in accordance with the requirements of the Protocol on Environmental Protection to the Antarctic Treaty.
3. (a) Shipments of waste destined for recovery only and listed in Annex II shall also be excluded from the provisions of this Regulation except as provided for in subparagraphs (b), (c), (d) and (e), in Article 11 and in Article 17(1), (2) and (3).
   (b) Such waste shall be subject to all provisions of Directive 75/442/EEC. It shall in particular be:
   — destined for duly authorized facilities only, authorized according to Article 10 and 11 of Directive 75/442/EEC,
   — subject to all provisions of Articles 8, 12, 13 and 14 of Directive 75/442/EEC.
   (c) However, certain wastes listed in Annex II may be controlled, if, among other reasons, they exhibit any of the hazardous characteristics listed in

Annex III of Council Directive 91/689/EEC, as if they had been listed in Annex III or IV.
These wastes and the decision about which of the two procedures should be followed shall be determined in accordance with the procedure laid down in Article 18 of Directive 75/442/EEC. Such wastes shall be listed in Annex II(a).

(d) In exceptional cases, shipments of wastes listed in Annex II may, for environmental or public health reasons, be controlled by Member States as if they had been listed in Annex III or IV.
Member States which make use of this possibility shall immediately notify the Commission of such cases and inform other Member States, as appropriate, and give reasons for their decision. The Commission, in accordance with the procedure laid down in Article 18 of Directive 75/442/EEC, may confirm such action including, where appropriate, by adding such wastes to Annex II.A.

(e) Where waste listed in Annex II is shipped in contravention of this Regulation or of Directive 75/442/EEC, Member States may apply appropriate provisions of Articles 25 and 26 of this Regulation.

Article 2

For the purposes of this Regulation:

(a) *waste* is as defined in Article 1(a) of Directive 75/442/EEC;
(b) *competent authorities* means the competent authorities designated by either the Member States in accordance with Article 36 or non-Member States;
(c) *competent authority of dispatch* means the competent authority, designated by the Member States in accordance with Article 36, for the area from which the shipment is dispatched or designated by non-Member States;
(d) *competent authority of destination* means the competent authority, designated by the Member States in accordance with Article 36, for the area in which the shipment is received, or in which waste is loaded on board before disposal at sea without prejudice to existing conventions on disposal at sea or designated by non-Member States;
(e) *competent authority of transit* means the single authority designated by Member States in accordance with Article 36 for the State through which the shipment is in transit;
(f) *correspondent* means the central body designated by each Member State and the Commission, in accordance with Article 37;
(g) *notifier* means any natural person or corporate body to whom or to which the duty to notify is assigned, that is to say the person referred to hereinafter who proposes to ship waste or have waste shipped:
   (i) the person whose activities produced the waste (original producer); or
   (ii) where this is not possible, a collector licensed to this effect by a Member State or a registered or licensed dealer or broker who arranges for the disposal or the recovery of waste; or
   (iii) where these persons are unknown or are not licensed, the person having possession or legal control of the waste (holder); or

(iv) in the case of import into or transit through the Community of waste, the person designated by the laws of the State of dispatch or, when this designation has not taken place, the person having possession or legal control of the waste (holder);

(h) *consignee* means the person or undertaking to whom or to which the waste is shipped for recovery or disposal;

(i) *disposal* is as defined in Article 1(e) of Directive 75/442/EEC;

(j) *authorized centre* means any establishment or undertaking authorized or licensed pursuant to Article 6 of Directive 75/439/EEC, Articles 9, 10 and 11 of Directive 75/442/EEC and Article 6 of Directive 76/403/EEC;

(k) *recovery* is as defined in Article 1(f) of Directive 75/442/EEC;

(l) *State of dispatch* means any State from which a shipment of waste is planned or made;

(m) *State of destination* means any State to which a shipment of waste is planned or made for disposal or recovery, or for loading on board before disposal at sea without prejudice to existing conventions on disposal at sea;

(n) *State of transit* means any State, other than the State of dispatch or destination, through which a shipment of waste is planned or made;

(o) *consignment note* means the standard consignment note to be drawn up in accordance with Article 42;

(p) *the Basle Convention* means the Basle Convention of 22 March 1989 on the control of transboundary movements of hazardous wastes and their disposal;

(q) *the fourth Lomé Convention* means the Lomé Convention of 15 December 1989;

(r) *the OECD Decision* means the decision of the OECD Council of 30 March 1992 on the control of transfrontier movements of wastes destined for recovery operations.

Title II

Shipments of Waste Between Member States

Chapter A

Waste for disposal

Article 3

1. Where the notifier intends to ship waste for disposal from one Member State to another Member State and/or pass it in transit through one or several other Member States, and without prejudice to Articles 25(2) and 26(2), he shall notify the competent authority of destination and send a copy of the notification to the competent authorities of dispatch and of transit and to the consignee.
2. Notification shall mandatorily cover any intermediate stage of the shipment from the place of dispatch to its final destination.
3. Notification shall be effected by means of the consignment note which shall be issued by the competent authority of dispatch.
4. In making notification, the notifier shall complete the consignment note and shall, if requested by competent authorities, supply additional information and documentation.

5. The notifier shall supply on the consignment note information with particular regard to:

— the source, composition and quantity of the waste for disposal including, in the case of Article 2(g)(ii), the producer's identity and, in the case of waste from various sources a detailed inventory of the waste and, if known, the identity of the original producers,
— the arrangements for routing and for insurance against damage to third parties,
— the measures to be taken to ensure safe transport and, in particular, compliance by the carrier with the conditions laid down for transport by the Member States concerned,
— the identity of the consignee of the waste, the location of the disposal centre and the type and duration of the authorization under which the centre operates. The centre must have adequate technical capacity for the disposal of the waste in question under conditions presenting no danger to human health or to the environment,
— the operations involving disposal as referred to in Annex ILA to Directive 75/442/EEC.

6. The notifier must make a contract with the consignee for the disposal of the waste.

The contract may include some or all of the information referred to in paragraph 5.

The contract must include the obligation:

— of the notifier, in accordance with Articles 25 and 26(2), to take the waste back if the shipment has not been completed as planned or if it has been effected in violation of this Regulation,
— of the consignee, to provide as soon as possible and no later than 180 days following the receipt of the waste a certificate to the notifier that the waste has been disposed of in an environmentally sound manner.

A copy of this contract must be supplied to the competent authority on request. Should the waste be shipped between two establishments under the control of the same legal entity, this contract may be replaced by a declaration by the entity in question undertaking to dispose of the waste.

7. The information given in accordance with paragraphs 4 to 6 shall be treated confidentially in accordance with existing national regulations.

8. A competent authority of dispatch may, in accordance with national legislation, decide to transmit the notification itself instead of the notifier to the competent authority of destination, with copies to the consignee and to the competent authority of transit.

The competent authority of dispatch may decide not to proceed with notification if it has itself immediate objections to raise against the shipment in accordance with Article 4(3). It shall immediately inform the notifier of these objections.

Article 4

1. On receipt of the notification, the competent authority of destination shall, within three working days, send an acknowledgement to the notifier and copies thereof to the other competent authorities concerned and to the consignee.

2. (a) The competent authority of destination shall have 30 days following dispatch of the acknowledgement to take its decision authorizing the shipment, with or without conditions, or refusing it. It may also request additional information.

It shall give its authorization only in the absence of objections on its part or on the part of the other competent authorities. The authorization shall be subject to any transport conditions referred to in (d).

The competent authority of destination shall take its decision not earlier than 21 days following the dispatch of the acknowledgement. It may, however, take its decision earlier if it has the written consent of the other competent authorities concerned.

The competent authority of destination shall send its decision to the notifier in writing, with copies to the other competent authorities concerned.

(b) The competent authorities of dispatch and transit may raise objections within 20 days following the dispatch of the acknowledgement. They may also request additional information. These objections shall be conveyed in writing to the notifier, with copies to the other competent authorities concerned.

(c) The objections and conditions referred to in (a) and (b) shall be based on paragraph 3.

(d) The competent authorities of dispatch and transit may, within 20 days following the dispatch of the acknowledgement, lay down conditions in respect of the transport of waste within their jurisdiction.

These conditions must be notified to the notifier in writing, with copies to the competent authorities concerned, and entered in the consignment note. They may not be more stringent than those laid down in respect of similar shipments occurring wholly within their jurisdiction and shall take due account of existing agreements, in particular relevant international conventions.

3. (a) (i) In order to implement the principles of proximity, priority for recovery and self-sufficiency at Community and national levels in accordance with Directive 75/442/EEC, Member States may take measures in accordance with the Treaty to prohibit generally or partially or to object systematically to shipments of waste. Such measures shall immediately be notified to the Commission, which will inform the other Member States.

(ii) In the case of hazardous waste (as defined in Article 1(4) of Directive 91/689/EEC) produced in a Member State of dispatch in such a small quantity overall per year that the provision of new specialized disposal installations within that State would be uneconomic, (i) shall not apply.

(iii) The Member State of destination shall cooperate with the Member State of dispatch which considers that (ii) applies, with a view to resolving the issue bilaterally. If there is no satisfactory solution, either Member State may refer the matter to the Commission, which will determine the issue in accordance with the procedure laid down in Article 18 of Directive 75/442/EEC.

(b) The competent authorities of dispatch and destination, while taking into account geographical circumstances or the need for specialized installations for certain types of waste, may raise reasoned objections to planned shipments if they are not in accordance with Directive 75/442/EEC, especially Articles 5 and 7:
   (i) in order to implement the principle of self-sufficiency at Community and national levels;
   (ii) in cases where the installation has to dispose of waste from a nearer source and the competent authority has given priority to this waste;
   (iii) in order to ensure that shipments are in accordance with waste management plans.

(c) Furthermore, the competent authorities of dispatch, destination and transit may raise reasoned objections to the planned shipment if:
   — it is not in accordance with national laws and regulations relating to environmental protection, public order, public safety or health protection,
   — the notifier or the consignee was previously guilty of illegal trafficking.

In this case, the competent authority of dispatch may refuse all shipments involving the person in question in accordance with national legislation, or
   — the shipment conflicts with obligations resulting from international conventions concluded by the Member State or Member States concerned.

4. If, within the time limits laid down in paragraph 2, the competent authorities are satisfied that the problems giving rise to their objections have been solved and that the conditions in respect of the transport will be met, they shall immediately inform the notifier in writing, with copies to the consignee and to the other competent authorities concerned.

If there is subsequently any essential change in the conditions of the shipment, a new notification must be made.

5. The competent authority of destination shall signify its authorization by appropriately stamping the consignment note.

Article 5

1. The shipment may be effected only after the notifier has received authorization from the competent authority of destination.
2. Once the notifier has received authorization, he shall insert the date of shipment and otherwise complete the consignment note and send copies to the competent authorities concerned three working days before the shipment is made.
3. A copy or, if requested by the competent authorities, a specimen of the consignment note, together with the stamp of authorization, shall accompany each shipment.
4. All undertakings involved in the operation shall complete the consignment note at the points indicated, sign it and retain a copy thereof.
5. Within three working days following receipt of the waste for disposal, the consignee shall send copies of the completed consignment note, except for the certificate referred to in paragraph 6, to the notifier and the competent authorities concerned.

6. As soon as possible and not later than 180 days following the receipt of the waste, the consignee shall, under his responsibility, send a certificate of disposal to the notifier and the other competent authorities concerned. This certificate shall be part of or attached to the consignment note which accompanies the shipment.

Chapter B

Waste for recovery

Article 6

1. Where the notifier intends to ship waste for recovery listed in Annex III from one Member State to another Member State and/or pass it in transit through one or several other Member States, and without prejudice to Articles 25(2) and 26(2), he shall notify the competent authority of destination and send copies of the notification to the competent authorities of dispatch and transit and to the consignee.
2. Notification shall mandatorily cover any intermediary stage of the shipment from the place of dispatch to its final destination.
3. Notification shall be effected by means of the consignment note which shall be issued by the competent authority of dispatch.
4. In making notification, the notifier shall complete the consignment note and shall, if requested by competent authorities, supply additional information and documentation.
5. The notifier shall supply on the consignment note information with particular regard to:
— the source, composition and quantity of the waste for recovery, including the producer's identity and, in the case of waste from various sources, a detailed inventory of the waste and, if known, the identity of the original producer,
— the arrangements for routing and for insurance against damage to third parties,
— the measures to be taken to ensure safe transport and, in particular, compliance by the carrier with the conditions laid down for transport by the Member States concerned,
— the identity of the consignee of the waste, the location of the recovery centre and the type and duration of the authorization under which the centre operates. The centre must have adequate technical capacity for the recovery of the waste in question under conditions presenting no danger to human health or to the environment,
— the operations involving recovery as contained in Annex II.B to Directive 75/442/EEC,
— the planned method of disposal for the residual waste after recycling has taken place,
— the amount of the recycled material in relation to the residual waste,
— the estimated value of the recycled material.
6. The notifier must conclude a contract with the consignee for the recovery of the waste.

The contract may include some or all of the information referred to in paragraph 5.

The contract must include the obligation:
— of the notifier, in accordance with Articles 25 and 26(2), to take the waste back

if the shipment has not been completed as planned or if it has been effected in violation of this Regulation,

— of the consignee to provide, in the case of retransfer of the waste for recovery to another Member State or to a third country, the notification of the initial country of dispatch,

— of the consignee to provide, as soon as possible and not later than 180 days following the receipt of the waste, a certificate to the notifier that the waste has been recovered in an environmentally sound manner.

A copy of this contract must be supplied to the competent authority on request.

Should the waste be shipped between two establishments under the control of the same legal entity, this contract may be replaced by a declaration by the entity in question undertaking to recover the waste.

7. The information given in accordance with paragraphs 4 to 6 shall be treated confidentially in accordance with existing national regulations.

8. A competent authority of dispatch may, in accordance with national legislation, decide to transmit the notification itself instead of the notifier to the competent authority of destination, with copies to the consignee and to the competent authority of transit.

Article 7

1. On receipt of the notification the competent authority of destination shall send, within three working days, an acknowledgement to the notifier and copies thereof to the other competent authorities and to the consignee.

2. The competent authorities of destination, dispatch and transit shall have 30 days following dispatch of the acknowledgement to object to the shipment. Such objection shall be based on paragraph 4. Any objection must be provided in writing to the notifier and to other competent authorities concerned within the 30-day period.

The competent authorities concerned may decide to provide written consent in a period less than the 30 days.

Written consent or objection may be provided by post, or by telefax followed by post. Such consent shall expire within one year unless otherwise specified.

3. The competent authorities of dispatch, destination and transit shall have 20 days following the dispatch of the acknowledgement in which to lay down conditions in respect of the transport of waste within their jurisdiction.

These conditions must be notified to the notifier in writing, with copies to the competent authorities concerned, and entered in the consignment note. They may not be more stringent than those laid down in respect of similar shipments occurring wholly within their jurisdiction and shall take due account of existing agreements, in particular relevant international conventions.

4. (a) The competent authorities of destination and dispatch may raise reasoned objections to the planned shipment:

— in accordance with Directive 75/442/EEC, in particular Article 7 thereof, or

— if it is not in accordance with national laws and regulations relating to environmental protection, public order, public safety or health protection, or

— if the notifier or the consignee has previously been guilty of illegal trafficking. In this case, the competent authority of dispatch may refuse all shipments involving the person in question in accordance with national legislation, or
— if the shipment conflicts with obligations resulting from international conventions concluded by the Member State or Member States concerned, or
— if the ratio of the recoverable and non-recoverable waste, the estimated value of the materials to be finally recovered or the cost of the recovery and the cost of the disposal of the non recoverable fraction do not justify the recovery under economic and environmental considerations.

(b) The competent authorities of transit may raise reasoned objections to the planned shipment based on the second, third and fourth indents of (a).

5. If within the time limit laid down in paragraph 2 the competent authorities are satisfied that the problems giving rise to their objections have been solved and that the conditions in respect of the transport will be met, they shall immediately inform the notifier in writing, with copies to the consignee and to the other competent authorities concerned.

If there is subsequently any essential change in the conditions of the shipment, a new notification must be made.

6. In case of prior written consent, the competent authority shall signify its authorization by appropriately stamping the consignment note.

Article 8

1. The shipment may be effected after the 30-day period has passed if no objection has been lodged. Tacit consent, however, expires within one year from that date.

Where the competent authorities decide to provide written consent, the shipment may be effected immediately after all necessary consents have been received.

2. The notifier shall insert the date of shipment and otherwise complete the consignment note and send copies to the competent authorities concerned three working days before the shipment is made.

3. A copy or, if requested by the competent authorities, a specimen of the consignment note shall accompany each shipment.

4. All undertakings involved in the operation shall complete the consignment note at the points indicated, sign it and retain a copy thereof.

5. Within three working days following receipt of the waste for recovery, the consignee shall send copies of the completed consignment note, except for the certificate referred to in paragraph 6, to the notifier and to the competent authorities concerned.

6. As soon as possible and not later than 180 days following receipt of the waste the consignee, under his responsibility, shall send a certificate of recovery of the waste to the notifier and the other competent authorities concerned. This certificate shall be part of or attached to the consignment note which accompanies the shipment.

Article 9

1. The competent authorities having jurisdiction over specific recovery facilities may decide, notwithstanding Article 7, that they will not raise objections concerning shipments of certain types of waste to a specific recovery facility. Such decisions may be limited to a specific period of time; however, they may be revoked at any time.
2. Competent authorities which select this option shall inform the Commission of the recovery facility name, address, technologies employed, waste types to which the decision applies and the period covered. Any revocations must also be notified to the Commission.

The Commission shall send this information without delay to the other competent authorities concerned in the Community and to the OECD Secretariat.
3. All intended shipments to such facilities shall require notification to the competent authorities concerned, in accordance with Article 6. Such notification shall arrive prior to the time the shipment is dispatched.

The competent authorities of the Member States of dispatch and transit may raise objections to any such shipment, based on Article 7(4), or impose conditions in respect of the transport.
4. In instances where competent authorities acting under terms of their domestic laws are required to review the contract referred to in Article 6(6), these authorities shall so inform the Commission. In such cases, the notification plus the contracts or portions thereof to be reviewed must arrive seven days prior to the time the shipment is dispatched in order that such review may be appropriately performed.
5. For the actual shipment, Article 8(2) to (6) shall apply.

Article 10

Shipments of waste for recovery listed in Annex IV and of waste for recovery which has not yet been assigned to Annex II, Annex III or Annex IV shall be subject to the same procedures as referred to in Article 6 to 8 except that the consent of the competent authorities concerned must be provided in writing prior to commencement of shipment.

Article 11

1. In order to assist the tracking of shipments of waste for recovery listed in Annex II, they shall be accompanied by the following information, signed by the holder:
   (a) the name and address of the holder;
   (b) the usual commercial description of the waste;
   (c) the quantity of the waste;
   (d) the name and address of the consignee;
   (e) the operations involving recovery, as listed in Annex II.B to Directive 75/442/EEC;
   (f) the anticipated date of shipment.
2. The information specified in paragraph 1 shall be treated confidentially in accordance with existing national regulations.

Chapter C

Shipment of waste for disposal and recovery between Member States with transit via third States

Article 12

Without prejudice to Articles 3 to 10, where a shipment of waste takes place between Member States with transit via one or more third States,

(a) the notifier shall send a copy of the notification to the competent authority(ies) of the third State(s);

(b) the competent authority of destination shall ask the competent authority in the third State(s) whether it wishes to send its written consent to the planned shipment:

— in the case of parties to the Basle Convention, within 60 days, unless it has waived this right in accordance with the terms of that Convention, or

— in the case of countries not parties to the Basle Convention, within a period agreed between the competent authorities.

In both cases the competent authority of destination shall, where appropriate, wait for consent before giving its authorization.

Title III

Shipments of Waste within Member States

Article 13

1. Titles II, VII and VIII shall not apply to shipments within a Member State.
2. Member States shall, however, establish an appropriate system for the supervision and control of shipments of waste within their jurisdiction. This system should take account of the need for coherence with the Community system established by this Regulation.
3. Member States shall inform the Commission of their system for the supervision and control of shipments of waste. The Commission shall inform the other Member States thereof.
4. Member States may apply the system provided for in Titles II, VII and VIII within their jurisdiction.

Title IV

Exports of Waste

Chapter A

Waste for disposal

Article 14

1. All exports of waste for disposal shall be prohibited, except those to EFTA countries which are also parties to the Basle Convention.

2. However, without prejudice to Articles 25(2), and 26(2), exports of waste for disposal to an EFTA country shall also be banned:

(a) where the EFTA country of destination prohibits imports of such wastes or where it has not given its written consent to the specific import of this waste;

(b) if the competent authority of dispatch in the Community has reason to believe that the waste will not be managed in accordance with environmentally sound methods in the EFTA country of destination concerned.

3. The competent authority of dispatch shall require that any waste for disposal authorized for export to EFTA countries be managed in an environmentally sound manner throughout the period of shipment and in the State of destination.

Article 15

1. The notifier shall send the notification to the competent authority of dispatch by means of the consignment note in accordance with Article 3(5), with copies to the other competent authorities concerned and to the consignee. The consignment note shall be issued by the competent authority of dispatch.

On receipt of the notification, the competent authority of dispatch shall within three working days send the notifier a written acknowledgement of the notification, with copies to the other competent authorities concerned.

2. The competent authority of dispatch shall have 70 days following dispatch of the acknowledgement to take its decision authorizing the shipment, with or without conditions, or refusing it. It may also request additional information.

It shall give its authorization only in the absence of objections on its part or on the part of the other competent authorities and if it has received from the notifier the copies referred to in paragraph 4. The authorization shall, where applicable, be subject to any transport conditions referred to in paragraph 5.

The competent authority of dispatch shall take its decision no earlier than 61 days following the dispatch of the acknowledgement.

It may, however, take its decision earlier if it has the written consent of the other competent authorities.

It shall send a certified copy of the decision to the other competent authorities concerned, to the customs office of departure from the Community and to the consignee.

3. The competent authorities of dispatch and transit in the Community may, within 60 days following the dispatch of the acknowledgement, raise objections based on Article 4(3). They may also request additional information. Any objection must be provided in writing to the notifier, with copies to the other competent authorities concerned.

4. The notifier shall provide to the competent authority of dispatch a copy of:

(a) the written consent of the EFTA country of destination to the planned shipment;

(b) the confirmation from the EFTA country of destination of the existence of a contract between the notifier and the consignee specifying environmentally sound management of the waste in question; a copy of the contract must be supplied, if requested.

The contract shall also specify that the consignee be required to provide:

— within three working days following the receipt of the waste for disposal, copies of the fully completed consignment note, except for the certification referred to in the second indent, to the notifier and to the competent authority concerned,

— as soon as possible and not later than 180 days following the receipt of the waste, a certificate of disposal under his responsibility to the notifier and to the competent authority concerned. The form of this certificate shall be part of the consignment note which accompanies the shipment.

The contract shall, in addition, stipulate that if a consignee issues an incorrect certificate with the consequence that the financial guarantee is released he shall bear the costs arising from the duty to return the waste to the area of jurisdiction of the competent authority of dispatch and its disposal in an alternative and environmentally sound manner;

(c) written consent to the planned shipment from the other State(s) of transit, unless this (these) State(s) is (are) a Party (Parties) to the Basle Convention and has (have) waived this in accordance with the terms of that Convention.

5. The competent authorities of transit in the Community shall have 60 days following the dispatch of the acknowledgement in which to lay down conditions in respect of the shipments of waste in their area of jurisdiction.

These conditions,which shall be forwarded to the notifier, with copies to the other competent authorities concerned, may not be more stringent than those laid down in respect of similar shipments effected wholly within the area of jurisdiction of the competent authority in question.

6. The competent authority of dispatch shall signify its authorization by appropriately stamping the consignment note.

7. The shipment may be effected only after the notifier has received authorization from the competent authority of dispatch.

8. Once the notifier has received authorization, he shall insert the date of shipment and otherwise complete the consignment note and send copies to the competent authorities concerned three working days before the shipment is made. A copy or, if requested by the competent authorities, a specimen of the consignment note, together with the stamp of authorization, shall accompany each shipment.

All undertakings involved in the operation shall complete the consignment note at the points indicated, sign it and retain a copy thereof.

A specimen of the consignment note shall be delivered by the carrier to the last customs office of departure when the waste leaves the Community.

9. As soon as the waste has left the Community, the customs office of departure shall send a copy of the consignment note to the competent authority which issued the authorization.

10. If, 42 days after the waste has left the Community, the competent authority which gave the authorization has received no information from the consignee about his receipt of the waste, it shall inform without delay the competent authority of destination.

It shall take action in a similar way if, 180 days after the waste has left the Community, the competent authority which gave the authorization has not received from the consignee the certificate of disposal referred to in paragraph 4.

11. A competent authority of dispatch may, in accordance with national legisla-

tion, decide to transmit the notification itself instead of the notifier, with copies to the consignee and the competent authority of transit.

The competent authority of dispatch may decide to proceed with any notification if it has itself immediate objections to raise against the shipment in accordance with Article 4(3). It shall immediately inform the notifier of these objections.

12. The information given in paragraphs 1 to 4 shall be treated confidentially in accordance with existing national regulations.

Chapter B

Waste for recovery

Article 16

1. All exports of waste for recovery shall be prohibited except those to:
   (a) countries to which the OECD decision applies;
   (b) other countries:
   — which are Parties to the Basle Convention and/or with which the Community, or the Community and its Member States, have concluded bilateral or multilateral or regional agreements or arrangements in accordance with Article 11 of the Basle Convention and paragraph 2, or
   — with which individual Member States have concluded bilateral agreements and arrangements prior to the date of application of this Regulation, in so far as these are compatible with Community legislation and in accordance with Article 11 of the Basle Convention and paragraph 2. These agreements and arrangements shall be notified to the Commission within three months of the date of application of this Regulation or of their date of application, whichever is the earlier, and shall expire when agreements or arrangements are concluded in accordance with the first indent.

2. The agreements and arrangements referred to in paragraph 1(b) shall guarantee an environmentally sound management of the waste in accordance with Article 11 of the Basle Convention and shall, in particular:
   (a) guarantee that the recovery operation is carried out in an authorized centre which complies with the requirements for environmentally sound management;
   (b) fix the conditions for the treatment of the non-recoverable components of the waste and, if appropriate, oblige the notifier to take them back;
   (c) enable, if appropriate, the examination of the compliance of the agreements on the spot in agreement with the countries concerned;
   (d) be subject to periodic review by the Commission and for the first time not later than 31 December 1996, taking into account the experience gained and the ability of the countries concerned to carry out recovery activities in a manner which provides full guarantees of environmentally sound management. The Commission shall inform the European Parliament and the Council about the results of this review. If such a review leads to the conclusion that environmental guarantees are insufficient, the continuation of waste exports under such terms shall, on a proposal from the Commission, be reconsidered, including the possibility of a ban.

3. However, without prejudice to Article 25(2) and 26(2), exports of waste for recovery to the countries referred to in paragraph 1 shall be prohibited:
   (a) where such a country prohibits all imports of such wastes or where it has not given its consent to their specific import;
   (b) if the competent authority of dispatch has reason to believe that the waste will not be managed in accordance with environmentally sound methods in such a country.

4. The competent authority of dispatch shall require that any waste for recovery authorized for export be managed in an environmentally sound manner throughout the period of shipment and in the State of destination.

Article 17

1. In respect of waste listed in Annex II, the Commission shall notify prior to the date of application of this Regulation to every country to which the OECD Decision does not apply the list of waste included in that Annex and request written confirmation that such waste is not subject to control in the country of destination and that the latter will accept categories of such waste to be shipped without recourse to the control procedures which apply to Annex III or IV or that it indicate where such waste should be subject to either those procedures or the procedure laid down in Article 15.

If such confirmation is not received six months before the date of application of this Regulation, the Commission shall make appropriate proposals to the Council.

2. Where waste listed in Annex II is exported, it shall be destined for recovery operations within a facility which under applicable domestic law is operating or is authorized to operate in the importing country. Furthermore, a surveillance system based on prior automatic export licensing shall be established in cases to be determined in accordance with the procedure laid down in Article 18 of Directive 75/442/EEC.

Such a system shall in each case provide that a copy of the export licence be forwarded without delay to the authorities of the country in question.

3. Where such waste is subject to control in the country of destination or upon request of such a country in accordance with paragraph 1 or where a country of destination has notified under Article 3 of the Basle Convention that it regards certain kinds of waste listed in Annex II as hazardous, exports of such waste to that country shall be subjected to control. The Member State of export or the Commission shall notify all such cases to the committee established pursuant to Article 18 of Directive 75/442/EEC; the Commission shall determine in consultation with the country of destination which of the control procedures shall apply, that is those applicable to Annex III or IV or the procedure laid down in Article 15.

4. Where waste listed in Annex III is exported from the Community for recovery to countries and through countries to which the OECD Decision applies, Articles 6, 7, 8 and 9(1), (3), (4) and (5) shall apply, the provisions concerning the competent authorities of dispatch and transit applying only to the competent authorities in the Community.

5. In addition, the competent authorities of the exporting and Community-transit countries shall be informed of the decision referred to in Article 9.

6. Where the waste for recovery listed in Annex IV and waste for recovery which has not yet been assigned to Annex II, III or IV is exported for recovery to countries and through countries to which the OECD Decision applies, Article 10 shall apply by analogy.

7. In addition, where waste is exported in accordance with paragraphs 4 to 6:

— a specimen of the consignment note shall be delivered by the carrier to the last customs office of departure when the waste leaves the Community,
— as soon as the waste has left the Community, the customs office of departure shall send a copy of the consignment note to the competent authority of export,
— if, 42 days after the waste has left the Community, the competent authority of export has received no information from the consignee about this receipt of the waste, it shall inform without delay the competent authority of destination.
— the contract shall stipulate that, if a consignee issues an incorrect certificate with the consequence that the financial guarantee is released, he shall bear the costs arising from the duty to return the waste to the area of jurisdiction of the competent authority of dispatch and its disposal or recovery in an alternative and environmentally sound manner.

8. Where waste for recovery listed in Annex III and IV and waste for recovery which has not yet been assigned to Annex II, III or IV is exported to and through countries to which the OECD Decision does not apply:

— Article 15, except for paragraph 3, shall apply by analogy,
— reasoned objections may be raised in accordance with Article 7(4) only,

save as otherwise provided for in bilateral or multilateral agreements entered into in accordance with Article 16(1)(b) and on the basis of the control procedure of either paragraph 4 or 6 of this Article or Article 15.

Chapter C

Export of waste to ACP States

Article 18

1. All exports of waste to ACP States shall be prohibited.

2. This prohibition does not prevent a Member State to which an ACP State has chosen to export waste for processing from returning the processed waste to the ACP State of origin.

3. In case of re-export to ACP States, a specimen of the consignment note, together with the stamp of authorization, shall accompany each shipment.

Title V

Imports of Waste into the Community

Chapter A

Imports of waste for disposal

Article 19

1. All imports into the Community of waste for disposal shall be prohibited except those from:

(a) EFTA countries which are Parties to the Basle Convention;
(b) other countries:
— which are Parties to the Basle Convention, or
— with which the Community, or the Community and its Member States, have concluded bilateral or multilateral agreements or arrangements compatible with Community legislation and in accordance with Article 11 of the Basle Convention guaranteeing that the disposal operations carried out in an authorized centre and complies with the requirements for environmentally sound management, or
— with which individual Member States have concluded bilateral agreements or arrangements prior to the date of application of this Regulation, compatible with Community legislation and in accordance with Article 11 of the Basle Convention, containing the same guarantees as referred to above and guaranteeing that the waste originated in the country of dispatch and that disposal will be carried out exclusively in the Member State which has concluded the agreement or arrangement. These agreements or arrangements shall be notified to the Commission within three months of the date of application of the Regulation or of their date of application, whichever is the earlier, and shall expire when agreements or arrangements are concluded in accordance with the second indent, or
— with which individual Member States conclude bilateral agreements or arrangements after the date of application of this Regulation in the circumstances of paragraph 2.

2. The Council hereby authorizes individual Member States to conclude bilateral agreements and arrangements after the date of application of this Regulation in exceptional cases for the disposal of specific waste, where such waste will not be managed in an environmentally sound manner in the country of dispatch. These agreements and arrangements shall comply with the conditions set out in paragraph 1(b), third indent and shall be notified to the Commission prior to their conclusion.

3. The countries referred to in paragraph 1(b) shall be required to present a duly motivated request beforehand to the competent authority of the Member State of destination on the basis that they do not have and cannot reasonably acquire the technical capacity and the necessary facilities in order to dispose of the waste in an environmentally sound manner.

4. The competent authority of destination shall prohibit the bringing of waste into its area of jurisdiction if it has reason to believe that the waste will not be managed in an environmentally sound manner in its area.

Article 20

1. Notification shall be made to the competent authority of destinations by means of the consignment note in accordance with Article 3(5) with copies to the consignee of the waste and to the competent authorities of transit. The consignment note shall be issued by the competent authority of destination.

On receipt of the notification, the competent authority of destination shall, within three working days, send a written acknowledgement to the notifier, with copies to the competent authorities of transit in the Community.

2. The competent authority of destination shall authorize the shipment only in the absence of objections on its part or from the other competent authorities concerned. The authorization shall be subject to any transport conditions referred to in paragraph 5.

3. The competent authorities of destination and transit in the Community may, within 60 days of dispatch of the copy of the acknowledgement, raise objections based on Article 4(3).

They may also request additional information. These objections shall be conveyed in writing to the notifier, with copies to the other competent authorities concerned in the Community;

4. The competent authority of destination shall have 70 days following dispatch of the acknowledgement to take its decision authorizing the shipment, with or without conditions, or refusing it. It may also request additional information.

It shall send certified copies of the decision to the competent authorities of transit in the Community, the consignee and the customs office of entry into the Community.

The competent authority of destination shall take its decision no earlier than 61 days following the dispatch of the acknowledgement. It may, however, take its decision earlier if it has the written consent of the other competent authorities.

The competent authority of destination shall signify its authorization by appropriately stamping the consignment note.

5. The competent authority of destination and transit in the Community shall have 60 days following dispatch of the acknowledgement to lay down conditions in respect of the shipment of the waste. These conditions, which must be conveyed to the notifier, with copies to the competent authorities concerned, may not be more stringent than those laid down in respect of similar shipments occurring wholly within the jurisdiction of the competent authority in question.

6. The shipment may be effected only after the notifier has received authorization from the competent authority of destination.

7. Once the notifier has received authorization, he shall insert the date of the shipment and otherwise complete the consignment note and send copies to the competent authorities concerned three working days before the shipment is made. A specimen of the consignment note shall be delivered by the carrier to the customs office of entry into the Community.

A copy or, if requested by the competent authorities, a specimen of the consignment note, together with the stamp of authorization, shall accompany each shipment.

All undertakings involved in the operation shall complete the consignment note at the points indicated, sign it and retain a copy.

8. Within three working days following receipt of the waste for disposal, the consignee shall send copies of the completed consignment note, except for the certificate referred to in paragraph 9, to the notifier and the competent authorities concerned;

9. As soon as possible and not later than 180 days following the receipt of the waste, the consignee shall, under his responsibility, send a certificate of disposal to

the notifier and the other competent authorities concerned. This certificate shall be part of or attached to the consignment note which accompanies the shipment.

Chapter B

Imports of waste for recovery

Article 21

1. All imports of waste for recovery into the Community shall be prohibited, except those from:

(a) countries to which the OECD decision applies;

(b) other countries:

— which are Parties to the Basle Convention and/or with which the Community, or the Community and its Member States, have concluded bilateral or multilateral or regional agreements or arrangements compatible with Community legislation and in accordance with Article 11 of the Basle Convention, guaranteeing that the recovery operation is carried out in an authorized centre and complies with the requirements for environmentally sound management, or

— with which individual Member States have concluded bilateral agreements or arrangements prior to the date of application of this Regulation, where these are compatible with Community legislation and in accordance with Article 11 of the Basle Convention, containing the same guarantees as referred to above. These agreements or arrangements shall be notified to the Commission with three months of the date of application of this Regulation or of their date of application, whichever is the earlier, and shall expire when agreements or arrangements are concluded in accordance with the first indent, or

— with which individual Member States conclude bilateral agreements or arrangements after the date of application of this Regulation in the circumstances of paragraph 2.

2. The Council hereby authorizes individual Member States to conclude after the date of applications of this Regulation bilateral agreements and arrangements in exceptional cases for the recovery of specific waste, where a Member State deems such agreements or arrangements necessary to avoid any interruption of waste treatment before the Community has concluded those agreements and arrangements. Such agreements and arrangements shall also be compatible with Community legislation and in accordance with Article 11 of the Basle Convention; they shall be notified to the Commission prior to their conclusion and shall expire when agreements or arrangements are concluded in accordance with paragraph 1(b), first indent.

Article 22

1. Where waste is imported for recovery from countries and through countries to which the OECD Decision applies, the following control procedures shall apply by analogy:

(a) for waste listed in Annex III: Articles 6, 7, 8, 9(1), (3), (4) and (5), and 17(5);

(b) for waste listed in Annex IV and waste which has not yet been assigned to Annex II, III or IV: Article 10.

2. Where waste for recovery listed in Annexes III and IV and waste which has not yet been assigned to Annex II, III or IV is imported from and through countries to the OECD Decision does not apply:

— Article 20 shall apply by analogy,

— reasoned objections may be raised in accordance with Article 7(4) only,

save as otherwise provided for the bilateral or multilateral agreements entered into in accordance with Article 21(1)(b) and on the basis of the control procedures of either paragraph 1 of this Article or Article 20.

Title VI

Transit of Waste from Outside and Through the Community for Disposal or Recovery Outside the Community

Chapter A

Waste for disposal and recovery (except transit covered by Article 24)

Article 23

1. Where waste for disposal and, except in cases covered by Article 24, recovery is shipped through (a) Member State(s), notification shall be effected by means of the consignment note to the last competent authority of transit within the Community, with copies to the consignee, the other competent authorities concerned and the customs offices of entry into and departure from the Community.

2. The last competent authority of transit within the Community shall promptly inform the notifier of receipt of the notification. The other competent authorities in the Community shall, on the basis of paragraph 5, convey their reactions to the last competent authority of transit in the Community, which shall then respond in writing to the notifier within 60 days, consenting to the shipment with or without reservations; or imposing, if appropriate, conditions laid down by the other competent authorities of transit, or withholding information. Any refusal or reservations must be justified. The competent authority shall send a certified copy of the decision to both the other competent authorities concerned and the customs offices of entry into and departure from the Community.

3. Without prejudice to Articles 25(2) and 26(2), the shipment shall be admitted into the Community only if the notifier has received the written consent of the last competent authority of transit. This authority shall signify its consent by appropriately stamping the consignment note.

4. The competent authorities of transit within the Community shall have 20 days following notification to lay down, if appropriate, any conditions attached to the transport of the waste.

These conditions, which must be conveyed to the notifier, with copies to the competent authorities concerned, may not be more stringent than those laid down in respect of similar shipments occurring wholly within the jurisdiction of the competent authority in question.

5. The consignment note shall be issued by the last competent authority of transit within the Community.

6. Once the notifier has received authorization, he shall complete the consignment note and send copies to the competent authorities concerned three working days before the shipment is made.

A specimen of the consignment note, together with the stamp of authorization, shall accompany each shipment.

A specimen of the consignment note shall be supplied by the carrier to the customs office of departure when the waste leaves the Community.

All undertakings involved in the operation shall complete the consignment note at the points indicated, sign it and retain a copy thereof.

7. As soon as the waste has left the Community, the customs office of departure shall send a copy of the consignment note to the last competent authority of transit within the Community.

Furthermore, at the latest 42 days after the waste has left the Community, the notifier shall declare or certify to that competent authority, with copies to the other competent authorities of transit, that it has arrived at its intended destination.

Chapter B

Transit of waste for recovery from and to a country to which the OECD Decision applies

Article 24

1. Transit of waste for recovery listed in Annexes III and IV from a country and transferred for recovery to a country to which the OECD Decision applies through (a) Member State(s) requires notification to all competent authorities of transit of the Member State(s) concerned.
2. Notification shall be effected by means of the consignment note.
3. On receipt of the notification the competent authority(ies) of transit shall send an acknowledgement to the notifier and to the consignee within three working days.
4. This competent authority(ies) of transit may raise reasoned objections to the planned shipment based on Article 7(4). Any objection must be provided in writing to the notifier and to the competent authorities of transit of the other Member States concerned within 30 days of dispatch of the acknowledgement.
5. The competent authority of transit may decide to provide written consent in less than 30 days.

In the case of transit of waste listed in Annex IV and waste which has not yet been assigned to Annex II, III or IV, consent must be given in writing prior to commencement of the shipment.

6. The shipment may be effected only in the absence of any objection.

Title VII

Common Provisions

Article 25

1. Where a shipment of waste to which the competent authorities concerned have consented cannot be completed in accordance with the terms of the consignment note or the contract referred to in Articles 3 and 6, the competent authority of dis-

patch shall, within 90 days after it has been informed thereof, ensure that the notifier returns the waste to its area of jurisdiction or elsewhere within the State of dispatch unless it is satisfied that the waste can be disposed of or recovered in an alternative and environmentally sound manner.
2. In cases referred to in paragraph 1, a further notification shall be made. No Member State of dispatch or Member State of transit shall oppose the return of this waste at the duly motivated request of the competent authority of destination and with an explanation of the reason.
3. The obligation of the notifier and the subsidiary obligation of the State of dispatch to take the waste back shall end when the consignee has issued the certificate referred to in Articles 5 and 8.

Article 26

1. Any shipment of waste effected:
   (a) without notification to all competent authorities concerned pursuant to the provisions of this Regulation; or
   (b) without the consent of the competent authorities concerned pursuant to the provisions of this Regulation; or
   (c) with consent obtained from the competent authorities concerned through falsification, misrepresentation or fraud; or
   (d) which is not specified in a material way in the consignment note; or
   (e) which results in disposal or recovery in contravention of Community or international rules; or
   (f) contrary to Articles 14, 15, 19 and 21

shall be deemed to be illegal traffic.
2. If such illegal traffic is the responsibility of the notifier of the waste, the competent authority of dispatch shall ensure that the waste in question is:
   (a) taken back by the notifier or, if necessary, by the competent authority itself, into the State of dispatch, or if impracticable;
   (b) otherwise disposed of or recovered in an environmentally sound manner, within 30 days from the time when the competent authority was informed of the illegal traffic or within such other period of time as may be agreed by the competent authorities concerned.

In this case a further notification shall be made. No Member State of dispatch or Member State of transit shall oppose the return of this waste at the duly motivated request of the competent authority of destination and with an explanation of the reason.
3. If such illegal traffic is the responsibility of the consignee, the competent authority of destination shall ensure that the waste in question is disposed of in an environmentally sound manner by the consignee or, if impracticable, by the competent authority itself within 30 days from the time it was informed of the illegal traffic or within any such other period of time as may be agreed by the competent authorities concerned. To this end, they shall cooperate, as necessary, in the disposal or recovery of the waste in an environmentally sound manner.
4. Where responsibility for the illegal traffic cannot be imputed to either the notifier or the consignee, the competent authorities shall cooperate to ensure that the

waste in question is disposed of or recovered in an environmentally sound manner. Guidelines for this cooperation shall be established in accordance with the procedure laid down in Article 18 of Directive 75/442/EEC.

5. Member States shall take appropriate legal action to prohibit and punish illegal traffic.

Article 27

1. All shipments of waste covered within the scope of this Regulation shall be subject to the provision of a financial guarantee or equivalent insurance covering costs for shipment, including cases referred to in Articles 25 and 26, and for disposal or recovery.

2. Such guarantees shall be returned when proof has been furnished, by means of:
— the certificate of disposal or recovery, that the waste has reached its destination and has been disposed of or recovered in an environmentally sound manner,
— Control copy T5 drawn up pursuant to Commission Regulation (EEC) No 2823/87 that, in the case of transit through the Community, the waste has left the Community.

3. Each Member State shall inform the Commission of the provision which it makes in national law pursuant to this Article. The Commission shall forward this information to all Member States.

Article 28

1. While respecting the obligations imposed on him by the applicable Articles 3, 6, 9, 15, 17, 20, 22, 23 and 24, the notifier may use a general notification procedure where waste for disposal or recovery having the same physical and chemical characteristics is shipped periodically to the same consignee following the same route. If, in the case of unforeseen circumstances, this route cannot be followed, the notifier shall inform the competent authorities concerned as soon as possible or before the shipment starts if the need for route modification is already known at this time.

Where the route modification is known before the shipment starts and this involves other competent authorities than those concerned in the general notification, this procedure shall not be used.

2. Under a general notification procedure, a single notification may cover several shipments of waste over a maximum period of one year. The indicated period may be shortened by agreement between the competent authorities concerned.

3. The competent authorities concerned shall make their agreement to the use of this general notification procedure subject to the subsequent supply of additional information. If the composition of the waste is not as notified or if the conditions imposed on its shipment are not respected, the competent authorities concerned shall withdraw their consent to this procedure by means of official notice to the notifier. Copies of this notice shall be sent to the other competent authorities concerned.

4. General notification shall be made by means of the consignment note.

Article 29

Wastes which are the subject of different notifications shall not be mixed during shipment.

Article 30

1. Member States shall take the measures needed to ensure that waste is shipped in accordance with the provisions of this Regulation. Such measures may include inspections of establishments and undertakings, in accordance with Article 13 of Directive 75/442/EEC, and spot checks of shipments.
2. Checks may take place in particular:
— at the point of origin, carried out with the producer, holder or notifier,
— at the destination, carried out with the final consignee,
— at the external frontiers of the Community,
— during the shipment within the Community.
3. Checks may include the inspection of documents, the confirmation of identity and, if appropriate, the physical control of the waste.

Article 31

1. The consignment note shall be printed and completed and any further documentation and information referred to in Article 4 and 6 shall be supplied in a language which is acceptable to the competent authority of:
— dispatch, as referred to in Articles 3, 7, 15 and 17, in the case of both a shipment of waste within the Community and the export of waste,
— destination, as referred to in Articles 20 and 22, in the case of the import of waste,
— transit, as referred to in Articles 23 and 24.
A translation shall be supplied by the notifier at the request of the other competent authorities concerned in a language acceptable to them.
2. Further details may be determined in accordance with the procedure laid down in Article 18 of Directive 75/442/EEC.

Title VIII

Other Provisions

Article 32

The provisions of the international transport conventions listed in Annex I to which the Member States are parties shall be complied with in so far as they cover the waste to which this Regulation refers.

Article 33

1. Appropriate administrative costs of implementing the notification and supervision procedure and usual costs of appropriate analyses and inspections may be charged to the notifier.
2. Costs arising from the return of waste, including shipment, disposal or recovery of the waste in an alternative and environmentally sound manner pursuant to Articles 25(1) and 26(2), shall be charged to the notifier or, if impracticable, to the Member States concerned.
3. Costs arising from disposal or recovery in an alternative and environmentally sound manner pursuant to Article 26(3) shall be charged to the consignee.

4. Costs arising from disposal or recovery, including possible shipment pursuant to Article 26(4), shall be charged to the notifier and/or the consignee depending upon the decision by the competent authorities involved.

Article 34

1. Without prejudice to the provisions of Article 26 and to Community and national provisions concerning civil liability and irrespective of the point of disposal or recovery of the waste, the producer of that waste shall take all the necessary steps to dispose of or recover or to arrange for disposal or recovery of the waste so as to protect the quality of the environment in accordance with Directives 75/442/EEC and 91/689/EEC.
2. Member States shall take all necessary steps to ensure that the obligations laid down in paragraph 1 are carried out.

Article 35

All documents sent to or by the competent authorities shall be kept in the Community for at least three years by the competent authorities, the notifier and the consignee.

Article 36

Member States shall designate the competent authority or authorities for the implementation of this Regulation. A single competent authority of transit shall be designated by each Member State.

Article 37

1. Member States and the Commission shall each designate at least one correspondent responsible for informing or advising persons or undertakings who or which make enquiries. The Commission correspondent shall forward to the correspondents of the Member States any questions put to him which concern the latter, and *vice versa*.
2. The Commission shall, if requested by Member States or if otherwise appropriate, periodically hold a meeting of the correspondents to examine with them the questions raised by the implementation of this Regulation.

Article 38

1. Member States shall notify the Commission not later than three months before the date of application of this Regulation of the name(s), address(es) and telephone and telex/telefax number(s) of the competent authorities and of the correspondents, together with the stamp of the competent authorities.

Member States shall notify the Commission annually of any changes in this information.
2. The Commission shall send the information without delay to the other Member States and to the Secretariat of the Basle Convention.

The Commission shall furthermore send to Member States the waste management plans referred to in Article 7 of Directive 75/442/EEC.

Article 39

1. Member States may designate customs offices of entry into and departure from the Community for shipments of waste entering and leaving the Community and inform the Commission thereof.

The Commission shall publish the list of these offices in the *Official Journal of the European Communities* and, if appropriate, update this list.

2. If Member States decide to designate the custom offices referred to in paragraph 1, no shipment of waste shall be allowed to use any other frontier crossing points within a Member State for entering or leaving the Community.

Article 40

Member States, as appropriate and necessary in liaison with the Commission, shall cooperate with other parties to the Basle Convention and inter-State organizations directly or through the Secretariat of the Basle Convention, *inter alia*, via the exchange of information, the promotion of environmentally sound technologies and the development of appropriate codes of good practice.

Article 41

1. Before the end of each calendar year, Member States shall draw up a report in accordance with Article 13(3) of the Basle Convention and send it to the Secretariat of the Basle Convention and a copy thereof to the Commission.

2. The Commission shall, based on these reports, establish every three years report on the implementation of this Regulation by the Community and its Member States. It may request to this end additional information in accordance with Article 6 of Directive 91/692/EEC.

Article 42

1. The Commission shall draw up not later than three months before the date of application of this Regulation and adapt if appropriate afterwards, in accordance with the procedure laid down in Article 18 of Directive 75/442/EEC, the standard consignment note, including the form of the certificate of disposal and recovery (either integral to the consignment note or, meanwhile, attached to the existing consignment note under Directive 84/631/EEC) taking account in particular of:

— the relevant Articles of this Regulation,

— the relevant international Conventions and agreements.

2. The existing form of the consignment note shall apply by analogy until the new consignment note has been drawn up. The form of the certificate of disposal and recovery to be attached to the existing consignment note shall be drawn up as soon as possible.

3. Without prejudice to the procedure laid down in Article 1(3)(c) and (d) regarding Annex II.A, Annexes II, III and IV shall be adapted by the Commission in accordance with the procedure laid down in Article 18 of Directive 75/442/EEC only to reflect changes already agreed under the review mechanism of the OECD.

4. The procedure referred to in paragraph 1 shall apply also to define

environmentally sound management, taking into account the relevant international conventions and agreements.

Article 43

Directive 84/631/EEC is hereby repealed with effect from the date of application of this Regulation. Any shipment pursuant to Articles 4 and 5 of that Directive shall be completed not later than six months from the date of application of this Regulation.

Article 44

This Regulation shall enter into force on the third day following its publication in the *Official Journal of the European Communities.*

It shall apply 15 months after publication.

This Regulation shall be binding in its entirety and directly applicable in all Member States.

Annex I

List of International Transport Conventions Referred to in Article 32

1. ADR:
   European Agreement concerning the international carriage of dangerous goods by road (1957).
2. Cotif:
   Convention concerning the international carriage of dangerous goods by rail (1985).
   RID:
   Regulation on the international carriage by rail of dangerous goods (1985).
3. Solas Convention:
   International Convention for the safety of life at sea (1974).
4. IMDG Code:
   International maritime dangerous goods code.
5. Chicago Convention:
   Convention on international civil aviation (1944), Annex 18 to which deals with the carriage of dangerous goods by air (TI: Technical instructions for the safe transport of dangerous goods by air).
6. Marpol Convention:
   International Convention for the prevention of pollution from ships (1973 to 1978).
7. ADNR:
   Regulations of the carriage of dangerous substances on the Rhine (1970).

Annex II

*Green List of Wastes**

Regardless of whether or not wastes are included on this list, they may not be moved as green wastes if they are contaminated by other materials to an extent which (a) increases the risks associated with the waste sufficiently to render it appropriate for inclusion in the amber or red lists, or (b) prevents the recovery of the waste in an environmentally sound manner.

GA. *Metal and Metal-Alloy Wastes in Metallic, Non-Dispersible Form***

The following waste and scrap of precious metals and their alloys:

GA 010 ex	7112 10	— Of gold
GA 020 ex	7112 20	— Of platinum (the expression 'platinum' includes platinum, iridium, osmium, palladium, rhodium and ruthenium)
GA 030 ex	7112 90	— Of other precious metal, e.g., silver NB: 1. Mercury is specifically excluded as a contaminant of these metals or their alloys or amalgams. The following ferrous waste and scrap of iron or steel:
GA 040	7204 10	— Waste and scrap of cast iron
GA 050	7204 21	— Waste and scrap of stainless steel
GA 060	7204 29	— Waste and scrap of other alloy steels
GA 070	7204 30	— Waste and scrap of tinned iron or steel
GA 080	7204 41	— Turnings, shavings, chips, milling waste, filings, trimmings and stampings, whether or not in bundles
GA 090	7204 49	— Other ferrous waste and scrap
GA 100	7204 50	— Remelting scrap ingots
GA 110 ex	7302 10	— Used iron and steel rails

The following waste and scrap of non-ferrous metals and their alloys:

GA 120	7404 00	— Copper waste and scrap
GA 130	7503 00	— Nickel waste and scrap
GA 140	7602 00	— Aluminium waste and scrap
GA 150 ex	7802 00	— Lead waste and scrap
GA 160	7902 00	— Zinc waste and scrap
GA 170	8002 00	— Tin waste and scrap

* Wherever possible, the code number of the Harmonized Commodity Description and Coding System, established by the Brussels Convention of 14 June 1983 under the auspices of the Customs Cooperation Council (Harmonized System) is listed opposite an entry. This code may apply to both wastes and products. This Regulation does not include items which are not wastes. Therefore, the code—used by customs officials in order to facilitate their procedures as well as by others—is only provided here to help in identifying wastes that are listed and subject to this Regulation. However, corresponding official Explanatory Notes as issued by the Customes Cooperation Council should be used as interpretative guidance to identify wastes covered by generic headings. The indicative 'ed' identifies a specific item contained within a heading of the Harmonized System code.

The code in bold in the first column is the OECD code: it consists of two letters (one for the list: Green, Amber or Red and one for the category of waste: A, B, C, . . .) followed by a number.

** 'Non-dispersible' does not include any wastes in the form of powder, sludge, dust or solid items containing encased hazardous waste liquids.

GA 180	ex 8101 91	— Tungsten waste and scrap
GA 190	ex 8102 91	— Molybdenum waste and scrap
GA 200	ex 8103 10	— Tantalum waste and scrap
GA 210	8104 20	— Magnesium waste and scrap
GA 220	ex 8105 10	— Cobalt waste and scrap
GA 230	ex 8106 00	— Bismuth waste and scrap
GA 240	ex 8107 10	— Cadmium waste and scrap
GA 250	ex 8108 10	— Titanium waste and scrap
GA 260	ex 8109 10	— Zirconium waste and scrap
GA 270	ex 8110 00	— Antimony waste and scrap
GA 280	ex 8111 00	— Manganese waste and scrap
GA 290	ex 8112 11	— Beryllium waste and scrap
GA 300	ex 8112 20	— Chromium waste and scrap
GA 310	ex 8112 30	— Germanium waste and scrap
GA 320	ex 8112 40	— Vanadium waste and scrap
	ex 8112 91	Wastes and scrap of:
GA 330		— Hafnium
GA 340		— Indium
GA 350		— Niobium
GA 360		— Rhenium
GA 370		— Gallium
GA 380		— Thallium
GA 390	ex 2805 30	Thorium waste and scrap
GA 400	ex 2804 90	Selenium waste and scrap
GA 410	ex 2804 50	Tellurium waste and scrap
GA 420	ex 2805 30	Rare earths waste and scrap

GB. *Metal Bearing Wastes Arising from Melting, Smelting and Refining of Metals*

GB 010	2620 11	Hard zinc spelter
GB 020		Zinc containing drosses:
GB 021		— Galvanizing slab zinc top dross (> 90% Zn)
GB 022		— Galvanizing slab zinc bottom dross (> 92% Zn)
GB 023		— Zinc die cast dross (> 85% Zn)
GB 024		— Hot dip galvanizers slab zinc dross (batch) (> 92% Zn)
GB 025		— Zinc skimmings
GB 030		Aluminium skimmings
GB 040	ex 2620 90	Slags from precious metals and copper processing for further refining
GB 050		Tantalum bearing tin slags with less than 0.5% tin

GC. *Other Wastes Containing Metals*

GC 010	Electrical assemblies consisting only of metals or alloys
GC 020	Electronic scrap (e.g. printed circuit boards, electronic components, wire, etc.) and reclaimed electronic components suitable for base and precious metal recovery

GC 030	ex 8908 00	Vessels and other floating structures for breaking up, properly emptied of any cargo and other materials arising from the operation of the vessel which may have been classified as a dangerous substance or waste
GC 040		Motor vehicle wrecks, drained of liquids
GC 050		Spent catalysts:
GC 051		— Fluid catalytic cracking (FCC) catalysts
GC 052		— Precious metal bearing catalysts
GC 053		— Transition metal catalysts (e.g. chromium, cobalt, copper, iron, nickel, managanese, molybdenum, tungsten, vanadium, zinc)
GC 060	2618 00	Granulated slag arising from the manufacture of iron and steel
GC 070	ex 2619 00	Slag arising from the manufacture of iron and steel*

GD. *Wastes from Mining Operations: These Wastes to be in Non-Dispersible Form*

GD 010	ex 2504 90	Natural graphite waste
GD 020	ex 2514 00	Slate waste, whether or not roughly trimmed or merely cut, by sawing or otherwise
GD 030	2525 30	Mica waste
GD 040	ex 2529 30	Leucite, nepheline and nepheline syenite waste
GD 050	2529 10	Feldspar waste
GD 060	2529 21	Fluospar waste
	ex 2529 22	
	ex 2811 22	Silica wastes in solid form excluding those used in foundry operations

GE. *Class Waste in Non-Dispersible Form*

GE 010	ex 7001 00	Cullet and other waste and scrap of glass except for glass from cathode-ray tubes and other activated glasses
GE 020		Fibre glass wastes

GF. *Ceramic Wastes in Non-Dispersible Form*

GF 010		Ceramic wastes which have been fired after shaping, including ceramic vessels (before and/or after use)
GF 020	ex 8113 00	Cermet waste and scrap (metal ceramic composites)
GF 030		Ceramic based fibres not elsewhere specified or included

GG. *Other Wastes Containing Principally Inorganic Constituents, which may Contain Metals and Organic Materials*

GG 010		Partially refined calcium sulphate produced from flue gas desulphurization (FGD)
GG 020		Waste gypsum wallboard or plasterboard arising from the demolition of buildings

* This entry covers the use of such slags as a source of titanium dioxide and vanadium.

GG 030 ex 2621	Bottom ash and slag tap from coal-fired power plants
GG 040 ex 2621	Coal-fired power plants fly ash
GG 050	Anode butts of petroleum coke and/or bitumen
GG 060 ex 2803	Spent activated carbon
GG 070 3103 20	Basic slag arising from the manufacture of iron or steel suitable for phosphate fertiliser and other use
GG 080 ex 2621 00	Slag from copper production, chemical stabilized, having a high iron content (above 20%) and processed according to industrial specifications (e.g. DIN 4301 and DIN 8201) mainly for construction and abrasive applications
GG 090	Sulphur in solid form
GG 100	Limestone from the production of calcium cyanamide (having a pH less than 9)
GG 110 ex 2621 00	Neutralized red mud from alumina production
GG 120	Sodium, potassium, calcium chlorides
GG 130	Carborundum (silicon carbide)
GG 140	Broken concrete
GG 150 ex 2620 90	Lithium-tantalum and lithium-niobium containing glass scraps

GH. *Solid Plastic Wastes*

Including, but not limited to:

GH 010 3915	Waste, parings and scrap of plastics:
GH 011 3915 10	— Polymers of ethylene
GH 012 3915 20	— Polymers of styrene
GH 013 3915 30	— Polymers of vinyl chloride
GH 014 3915 90	Polymerized or co-polymers for example:
	— Polypropylene
	— Polyethylene terephthalate
	— Acrylonitrile copolymer
	— Butadiene copolymer
	— Styrene copolymer
	— Polyamides
	— Polybutylene terephthalates
	— Polycarbonates
	— Polyphenylene sulphides
	— Acrylic polymers
	— Paraffins (C10–C13)
	— Polyurethane (not containing chlorofluorocarbons)
	— Polysiloxalanes (silicones)
	— Polymethyl methacrylate
	— Polyvinyl alcohol
	— Polyvinyl butyral
	— Polyvinyl acetate
	— Polymers of fluorinated ethylene (Teflon, PTFE)
GH 015 ex 3915 90	Resins or condensation products, for example:
	— Urea formaldehyde resins
	— Phenol formaldehyde resins

— Melamine formaldehyde resins
— Epoxy resins
— Alkyd resins
— Polyamides

GI. *Paper, Paperboard and Paper Product Wastes*

GI 010	4707	Waste and scrap of paper or paperboard:
GI 011	4707 10	— Of unbleached kraft paper or paperboard or of corrugated paper or paperboard
GI 012	4707 20	— Of other paper or paperboard made mainly of bleached chemical pulp, not colored in the mass
GI 013	4707 30	— Of paper or paperboard made mainly of mechanical pulp (for example, newspapers, journals and similar printed matter)
GI 014	4707 90	— Other, including but not limited to: 1. Laminated paperboard 2. Unsorted waste and scrap

GJ. *Textile Wastes*

GJ 010	5003	Silk waste (including cocoons unsuitable for reeling, yarn waste and garnetted stock):
GJ 011	5003 10	— Not carded or combed
GJ 012	5003 90	— Other
GJ 020	5103	Waste of wool or of fine or coarse animal hair, including yarn waste but excluding garnetted stock:
GJ 021	5103 10	— Noils of wool or of fine animal hair
GJ 022	5103 20	— Other waste of wool or of fine animal hair
GJ 023	5103 30	— Waste of coarse animal hair
GJ 030	5202	Cotton waste (including yarn waste and garnetted stock):
GJ 031	5202 10	— Yarn waste (including thread waste)
GJ 032	5202 91	— Garnetted stock
GJ 033	5202 99	— Other
GJ 040	5301 30	Flax tow and waste
GJ 050 ex	5302 90	Tow and waste (including yarn waste and garnetted stock) of true hemp (*Cannabis sativa L.*)
GJ 060 ex	5303 90	Tow and waste (including yarn waste and garnetted stock) of jute and other textile bast fibres (excluding flax, true hemp and ramie)
GJ 070 ex	5304 90	Tow and waste (including yarn waste and garnetted stock) of sisal and other textile fibres of the genus Agave
GJ 080 ex	5305 19	Tow, noils and waste (including yarn waste and garnetted stock) of coconut
GJ 090 ex	5305 29	Tow, noils and waste (including yarn waste and garnetted stock) of abaca (Manila hemp or *Musa textilis Nee*)
GJ 100 ex	5305 99	Tow, noils and waste (including yarn waste and garnetted stock) of ramie and other vegetable textile fibres, not elsewhere specified or included

GJ 110	5505	Waste (including noils, yarn waste and garnetted stock) of man-made fibres
GJ 111	5505 10	— Of synthetic fibres
GJ 112	5505 20	— Of artificial fibres
GJ 120	6309 00	Worn clothing and other worn textile articles
GJ 130 ex	6310	Used rags, scrap twine, cordage, rope and cables and worn out articles of twine, cordage, rope or cables of textile materials
GJ 131 ex	6310 10	— Sorted
GJ 132 ex	6310 90	— Other

GK. *Rubber Wastes*

GK 010	4004 00	Waste, parings and scrap of rubber (other than hard rubber) and granules obtained therefrom
GK 020	4012 20	Used pneumatic tyres
GK 030 ex	4017 00	Waste and scrap of hard rubber (for example, ebonite)

GL. *Untreated Cork and Wood Wastes*

GL 010 ex	4401 30	Wood waste and scrap, whether or not agglomerated in logs, briquettes, pellets or similar forms
GL 020	4501 90	Cork waste; crushed, granulated or ground cork

GM. *Wastes Arising from Agro-Food Industries*

GM 070 ex	2307	Wine lees
GM 080 ex	2308	Dried and sterilized vegetable waste, residues and by-products, whether or not in the form of pellets, of a kind used in animal feeding, not elsewhere specified or included
GM 090	1522	Degras; residues resulting from the treatment of fatty substances or animal or vegetable waxes
GM 100	0506 90	Waste of bones and horn-cones, unworked, defatted, simply prepared (but not cut to shape), treated with acid or degelatinized
GM 110 ex	0511 91	Fish waste
GM 120	1802 00	Cocoa shells, husks, skins and other cocoa waste
GM 130		Waste from the agro-food industry excluding by-products which meet national and international requirements and standards for human or animal consumption

GN. *Wastes Arising from Tanning and Fellmongery Operations and Leather Use*

GN 010 ex	0502 00	Waste of pigs', hogs' or boars' bristles and hair or of badger hair and other brush-making hair
GN 020 ex	0503 00	Horsehair waste, whether or not put up as a layer with or without supporting material

GN 030 ex 0505 90		Waste of skins and other parts of birds, with their feathers or down, of feathers and parts of feathers (whether or not with trimmed edges) and down, not further worked than cleaned, disinfected or treated for preservation
GN 040 ex 4110 00		Parings and other waste of leather or of composition leather, not suitable for the manufacture of leather articles, excluding leather sludges

GO. *Other Wastes Containing Principally Organic Constituents, Which May Contain Metals and Inorganic Materials*

GO 010 ex 0501 00	Waste of human hair
GO 020	Waste straw
GO 030	Deactivated fungus mycelium from penicillin production to be used as animal feed
GO 040	Waste photographic film base and waste photographic film not containing silver
GO 050	Single-use cameras without batteries

Annex III

*Amber List of Wastes**

Regardless of whether or not wastes are included on this list, they may not be moved as amber wastes if they are contaminated by other materials to an extent which (a) increases the risks associated with the waste sufficiently to render it appropriate for inclusion in the red list, or (b) prevents the recovery of the waste in an environmentally sound manner.

AA. *Metal Bearing Wastes*

AA 010 ex	2619 00	Dross, scalings and other wastes from the manufacture of iron and steel
AA 020	2620 19	Zinc ashes and residues**
AA 030	2620 20	Lead ashes and residues**

* Wherever possible, the code number of the Harmonized Commodity Description and Coding System, established by the Brussels Convention of 14 June 1983 under the auspices of the Customs Cooperation Council (Harmonized System) is listed opposite an entry. This code may apply to both wastes and products. This Regulation does not include items which are not wastes. Therefore, the code—used by customs officials in order to facilitate their procedures as well as by others—is only provided here to help in identifying wastes that are listed and subject to this Regulation.

However, corresponding official Explanatory Notes as issued by the Customs Cooperation Council should be used as interpretative guidance to identify wastes covered by generic headings.

The indicative 'ex' identifies a specific item contained within a heading of the Harmonized System code.

The code in bold in the first column is the OECD; it consists of two letters (one for the list: Green; Amber or Red and one for the category of waste: **A, B, C**, . . .) followed by a number.

** This listing includes wastes in the form of ash, residue, slag, dross, skimming, scaling, dust, powder, sludge and cake, unless a material is expressly listed elsewhere.

AA 040 ex 2620 30		Copper ashes and residues**
AA 050 ex 2620 40		Aluminium ashes and residues**
AA 060 ex 2620 50		Vanadium ashes and residues**
AA 070	2620 90	Ashes and residues** containing metals or metal compounds not elsewhere specified or included
AA 080		Thallium waste and residues**
AA 090 ex 2804 80		Arsenic waste and residues**
AA 100 ex 2620 90		Mercury waste and residues**
AA 110		Residues from alumina production not elsewhere specified or included
AA 120		Galvanic sludges
AA 130		Liquors from the pickling of metals
AA 140		Leaching residues from zinc processing, dusts and sludges such as jarosite, hematite, goethite, etc.
AA 150		Precious metal bearing residues in solid form which contain traces of inorganic cyanides
AA 160		Precious metal ash, sludge, dust and other residues such as:
AA 161		— Ash from incineration of printed circuit boards
AA 162		— Photographic film ash
AA 170		Lead-acid batteries, whole or crushed
AA 180		Used batteries or accumulators, whole or crushed, other than lead-acid batteries, and waste and scrap arising from the production of batteries and accumulators, not otherwise specified or included

AB. *Wastes Containing Principally Inorganic Constituents, Which May Contain Metals and Organic Materials*

AB 010	2621 00	Slag, ash and residues**, not elsewhere specified or included
AB 020		Residues arising from the combustion of municipal/household wastes
AB 030		Wastes from non-cyanide based systems which arise from surface treatment of metals
AB 040 ex 7001 00		Glass waste from cathode-ray tubes and other activated glasses
AB 050 ex 2529 21		Calcium fluoride sludge
AB 060		Other inorganic fluorine compounds in the form of liquids or sludges
AB 070		Sands used in foundry operations
AB 080		Waste catalysts not on the green list
AB 090		Waste hydrates of aluminium
AB 100		Waste alumina
AB 110		Basic solutions
AB 120		Inorganic halide compounds, not elsewhere specified or included
AB 130		Used blasting grit
AB 140		Gypsum arising from chemical industry processes
AB 150		Unrefined calcium sulphite and calcium sulphate from flue gas desulphurization (FGD)

AC. *Wastes Containing Principally Organic Constituents, Which May Contain Metals and Inorganic Materials*

AC 010 ex 2713 90	Waste from the production/processing of petroleum coke and bitumen, excluding anode butts
AC 020	Asphalt cement wastes
AC 030	Waste oils unfit for their originally intended use
AC 040	Leaded petrol (gasoline) sludges
AC 050	Thermal (heat transfer) fluids
AC 060	Hydraulic fluids
AC 070	Brake fluids
AC 080	Antifreeze fluids
AC 090	Waste from production, formulation and use of resins, latex, plasticizers, glues and adhesives
AC 100 ex 3915 90	Nitrocellulose
AC 110	Phenols, phenol compounds including chlorophenol in the form of liquids or sludges
AC 120	Polychlorinated naphtalenes
AC 130	Ethers
AC 140	Triethylamine catalyst for setting foundry sands
AC 150	Chlorofluorocarbons
AC 160	Halons
AC 170	Treated cork and wood wastes
AC 180 ex 4110 00	Leather dust, ash, sludges and flours
AC 190	Fluff—light fraction from automobile shredding
AC 200	Organic phophorous compounds
AC 210	Non-halogenated solvents
AC 220	Halogenated solvents
AC 230	Halogenated or unhalogenated non-aqueous distillation residues arising from organic solvent recovery operations
AC 240	Wastes arising from the production of aliphatic halogenated hydrocarbons (such as chloromethanes, dichloro-ethane, vinyl chloride, vinylidene chloride, allyl chloride and epichlohydrin)
AC 250	Surface active agents (surfactants)
AC 260	Liquid pig manure; faeces
AC 270	Sewage sludge

AD. *Wastes Which May Contain Either Inorganic or Organic Constituents*

AD 010	Wastes from the production and preparation of pharmaceutical products
AD 020	Wastes from the production, formulation and use of biocides and phytopharmaceuticals
AD 030	Wastes from the manufacture, formulation and use of wood preserving chemicals

	Wastes that contain, consist of or are contaminated which any of the following:
AD 040	— Inorganic cyanides, excepting precious metal-beraring residues in solid form containing traces of inorganic cyanides
AD 050	— Organic cyanides
AD 060	Waste oils/water, hydrocarbons/water mixtures, emulsions
AD 070	Wastes from production, formulation and use of inks, dyes, pigments, paints, lacquers, varnish
AD 080	Wastes of an explosive nature, when not subject to specific other legislation
AD 090	Wastes from production, formulation and use of reprographic and photographic chemicals and materials not elsewhere specified or included
AD 100	Wastes from non-cyanide based systems which arise from surface treatment of plastics
AD 110	Acidic solutions
AD 120	Ion exchange resins
AD 130	Single-use cameras with batteries
AD 140	Wastes from industrial pollution control devices for cleaning of industrial off-gases, not elsewhere specified or included
AD 150	Naturally occuring organic material used as a filter medium (such as bio-filters)
AD 160	Municipal/household wastes

Annex IV

Red List of Wastes

'Containing' or 'contained with', when used in this list, means that the substance referred to is present to an extent which (a) renders the waste hazardous, or (b) renders it not suitable for suitable for submission to a recovery operation.

RA. *Wastes Containing Principally Organic Constituents, Which May Contain Metals and Inorganic Materials*

RA 010	Wastes, substances and articles containing, consisting of or contaminated with polychlorinated biphenyl (PCB) and/or polychlorinated terphenyl (PCT) and/or polybrominated biphenyl (PBB), including any other polybrominated analogues of these compounds, at a concentration level of 50 mg/kg or more
RA 020	Waste tarry residues (excluding asphalt cements) arising from refining, distillation and any pyrolitic treatment

RB. *Wastes Containing Principally Inorganic Contaminants, Which May Contain Metals and Organic Materials*

RB 010	Asbestos (dusts and fibres)
RB 020	Ceramic-based fibres of physic co-chemical characteristics similar to those of asbestos

RC. *Wastes Which May Contain Either Inorganic or Organic Constituents*

	Wastes that contain, consist of or are contaminated with any of the following:
RC 010	— Any congenor of polychlorinated dibenzo-furan
RC 020	— Any congenor of polychlorinated dibenzo-dioxin
RC 030	Leaded anti-knock compounds sludges
RC 040	Peroxides other than hydrogen peroxide

Appendix VIII

OECD Council Decision Concerning the Control of Transfrontier Movements of Wastes Destined for Recovery Operations (C(92)39, 30 March 1992)

THE COUNCIL,

Having regard to Article 5(a) of the Convention on the Organisation for Economic Co-operation and Development of 14 December 1960;

Having regard to the Decision and Recommendation of the Council of 1 February 1984 on Transfrontier Movements of Hazardous Waste [C(83)180(Final)] which requires Member countries to control transfrontier movements of hazardous wastes;

Having regard to the Decision of the Council of 27 May 1988 on Transfrontier Movements of Hazardous Wastes [C(88)90(Final)] which defines 'wastes', identifies those wastes referred to as hazardous wastes in relevant Council Acts, and sets out a classification system for wastes subject to transfrontier movements;

Having regard to the Decision–Recommendation of the Council of 31 January 1991 on the Reduction of Transfrontier Movements of Wastes [C(90)178/FINAL] which, inter alia, calls for delineation of such controls as may be appropriate for the transfrontier movement of wastes destined for recovery operations, clarification of the definition of such wastes and characterization of those wastes which may require differing levels of control;

Having regard to the Basel Convention on the Control of Transboundary Movements of Hazardous Wastes and their Disposal, adopted on 22 March 1989, and noting that most Member countries and the European Economic Community have become signatories to this Convention;

Desiring to conclude an arrangement or agreement under Article 11 of that Convention;

Noting that recovery of valuable raw materials from wastes has been an integral part of the international economic system and that well established international markets exist for the collection and processing of such wastes;

Noting further that many industrial sectors are already implementing waste recovery techniques in an economically and environmentally satisfactory manner, thus protecting limited virgin sources of raw materials, and convinced that further efforts in this direction are necessary and should be encouraged;

Recognising that efficient and environmentally sound management of wastes may justify some transfrontier movements of such wastes in order to make use of adequate recovery facilities in other countries;

Convinced however that, pursuant to the obligations set forth in the relevant Council Acts and compatible with the provisions of the Basel Convention, an appropriate system should be implemented to control transfrontier movements of those wastes destined for recovery operations;

Convinced that all persons involved in any contracts or arrangements for transfrontier movements of wastes destined for recovery operations must have the appropriate legal status to ensure environmentally sound management of these wastes; and

Recognizing that work is now in progress within the United Nations Environment Programme concerning the environmentally sound management of hazardous wastes.

On the proposal of the Environment Committee:

I. DECIDES that Member countries shall control transfrontier movements of wastes destined for recovery operations within the OECD area as specified in Annex 1 which is an integral part of this Decision.

II. INSTRUCTS the Environment Committee in co-operation with other relevant OECD bodies, in particular the Trade Committee, to review periodically the control system and the lists of wastes set out in Annex 1, taking into account the criteria listed in Annex 2, and to make any proposals it deems necessary for revisions of Annex 1.

III. INSTRUCTS the Environment Committee in co-operation with other relevant OECD bodies to review annually action taken by Member countries in pursuance of this Decision.

IV. REQUESTS the Secretary General to transmit this Decision to the Executive Director of the United Nations Environment Programme and the Interim Secretariat of the Basel Convention.

Annex 1

I. *Definitions*

For the purposes of this Decision:

WASTES are as defined in OECD Council Decision C(88)90(Final) of 27 May 1988.

RECOVERY OPERATIONS mean activities leading to resource recovery, recycling, reclamation, direct re-use or alternative uses as listed in Table 2B of the Annex of OECD Council Decision C(88)90(Final) of 27 May 1988.

TRANSFRONTIER MOVEMENT means any shipment of wastes destined for recovery operations from an area under the national jurisdiction of one OECD Member country to an area under the national jurisdiction of another OECD Member country.

RECOVERY FACILITY means an entity which, under applicable domestic law, is operating or is authorized to operate in the importing country to receive wastes and to perform recovery operations on them.

INTERNATIONAL WASTE IDENTIFICATION CODE ('IWIC') is the classification system specified and described in OECD Council Decision C(88)90(Final) of 27 May 1988.

EXPORTING COUNTRY means any OECD Member country from which a transfrontier movement of wastes is planned or has commenced.

IMPORTING COUNTRY means any OECD Member country to which a transfrontier movement of wastes is planned or takes place for the purpose of submitting the wastes to recovery operations therein.

COUNTRY OF TRANSIT means any OECD Member country other than the exporting or importing country across which a transfrontier movement of wastes is planned or takes place.

CONCERNED COUNTRIES means the exporting and importing OECD Member countries and any OECD Member countries or transit.
OECD AREA means all land or marine areas under the national jurisdiction of any OECD Member country.
COMPETENT AUTHORITIES means the regulatory authorities of concerned countries having jurisdiction over transfrontier movements of wastes destined for recovery operations.
PERSON means any natural or legal person whether public or private.
NOTIFIER means the person under the jurisdiction of the exporting country who has, or will have at the time the planned transfrontier movement commences, possession or other forms of legal control of the wastes and who proposes their transfrontier movement for the ultimate purpose of submitting them to recovery operations.
CONSIGNEE means the person to whom possession or other form of legal control of the waste is assigned at the time the waste is received in the importing country.
RECOGNISED TRADER means a person who, with appropriate authorisation of concerned countries, acts in the role of principal to purchase and subsequently sell wastes; this person has legal control of such wastes from time of purchase to time of sale; such a person may act to arrange and facilitate transfrontier movements of wastes destined for recovery operations.
GENERATOR means a person whose activities create wastes.

II. *General Provisions*

(1) All of the following conditions shall apply to transfrontier movements of wastes subject to this Decision:

(a) The wastes shall be destined for recovery operations within a facility which, under applicable domestic law, is operating or is authorized to operate in the importing country;

(b) The transfrontier movements shall be carried out under terms of applicable international transport agreements. (Appendix 1 contains an illustrative list of such agreements);

(c) Any transit of wastes through a non-member country shall be subject to all applicable international and national laws and regulations.

(2) A three-tiered system serves to delineate controls to be applied to such transfrontier movements:

(a) *'Green' tier*

Wastes destined for recovery operations included on the green list shall move among OECD Member countries toward recovery operations subject to all existing controls normally applied in commercial transactions. These provisions shall not apply to wastes on this list which are contaminated by other materials to an extent which increases the risks associated with the wastes sufficiently to render them appropriate for inclusion in the amber or red lists, when taking into account the criteria in Annex 2.

(b) *'Amber' tier*

Wastes destined for recovery operations included in the amber list shall be subject to the control system set out in Section IV of this Annex.

(c) *'Red' tier*

Wastes destined for recovery operations included in the red list shall be subject to the controls indicated in Section V of this Annex.

(3) The criteria listed in Annex 2 must be taken into account for evaluating wastes for inclusion on the green, amber or red lists. In accord with provisions of this Decision, items may be added, altered or deleted periodically. Subject to Section III(2) no single criterion shall be used in isolation in assigning wastes to the lists.

(4) While the lists are intended to be exclusive, a specific waste included in either the amber or red lists might not be legally defined or considered to be a hazardous waste in the exporting country because the competent authorities of that country are satisfied that it does not exhibit any of the hazardous characteristics listed in Table 5 of OECD Council Decision C(88)90(Final) as determined using national procedures*. If, however, this waste is legally defined or considered to be a hazardous waste by the importing country, then all of the requirements set forth in Section IV or Section V—whichever is applicable—shall apply as follows: the importing country shall assume the obligations of the exporting country under these Sections, in particular as regards the notification requirements. A copy of the notification form must be transmitted to the competent authorities of the exporting country. Member countries operating under provisions of this paragraph shall promptly inform the OECD Secretariat of the waste(s) involved and applicable legislative requirements.

(5) Member countries who prescribe the use of certain tests and testing procedures in order to determine whether a waste exhibits one or more of the hazardous characteristics listed in Table 5 of OECD Council Decision C(88)90(Final) shall inform the OECD Secretariat concerning which tests and testing procedures are being so utilized; and, if possible, which wastes would or would not be legally defined or considered to be hazardous wastes based upon application of these national procedures.

(6) This Decision does not prejudice the right of Member countries to control certain wastes which have been assigned to the green list as if those wastes had been assigned to one of the other lists, in conformity with domestic legislation and the rules of international law, in order to protect human health and the environment. In such cases, Member countries exercising this right shall immediately inform the OECD secretariat citing the specific waste(s) and applicable legislative requirements.

(7) Wastes which are destined for recovery operations but have not yet been assigned to the green, amber or red lists shall be eligible for transfrontier movements pursuant to this Decision subject to the following conditions:

i) Member countries shall identify such wastes and bring them to the attention of the review mechanism established by operative paragraphs II and III of this Decision;

* The potential hazards posed by certain types of wastes are not yet fully documented; tests to define quantitatively these hazards do not exist. Further research is necessary in order to develop means to characterise potential hazards posed to man and/or the environment by these wastes. Standardized tests have been derived with respect to pure substances and materials. Many Member countries have developed tests which can be applied to materials destined for disposal by means of operations listed in Table 2 of OECD Council Decision C(88)90(Final) in order to decide if these materials exhibit any of the hazardous characteristics listed in Table 5 of that Decision.

ii) such wastes shall be promptly examined by the Review Mechanism in order to assign them to the appropriate list;

iii) pending assignment to a list, such wastes shall be subject to the controls required for the transfrontier movements of wastes by the domestic legislation of the concerned countries in order that no country is obliged to enforce laws other than its own;

iv) however, if such wastes exhibit a hazardous characteristic listed in Table 5 of OECD Council Decision C(88)90(Final) as determined using national procedures and any applicable international agreements, such wastes shall be subject to controls applicable to the red tier.

(8) If two or more lots of wastes are mixed and/or otherwise subjected to physical or chemical transformation operations, the person who performs these operations shall be deemed to be the generator of the new wastes resulting from these operations.

III. *Green Tier*

(1) Specific items included in the green list are shown under their corresponding main categories. Only the items specified under a main category and not the main categories themselves are part of the green list.

(2) Wastes may not be included in the green list if they exhibit any of the hazardous characteristics listed in Table 5 of OECD Council Decision C(88)90(Final). The procedures in force in each Member country for determining whether a specific waste does or does not exhibit one or more of these characteristics are taken into account in placing or not placing a waste onto the green list.

(3) If green list wastes are re-exported, responsibilities of the exporting country under other relevant agreements or conventions shall transfer to the country initiating the re-export, and shall not apply to the original exporting country.

(4) *Green list of wastes*

The green list of wastes is set out at Appendix 3.

IV. *Amber Tier*

(1) *Conditions*

Transfrontier movements of wastes under the amber control system may only occur under the terms of a valid written contract, or chain of contracts, or equivalent arrangements between facilities controlled by the same legal entity, starting with the notifier and terminating at the recovery facility. All persons involved in the contracts, or arrangements shall have appropriate legal status.

Such contracts shall include provisions for financial guarantees in accordance with applicable national or international law requirements. Financial guarantees so required are intended to provide for alternate recycling, disposal or other means of sound management of the wastes in cases where arrangements for the shipment and the recovery operations cannot be carried out as foreseen. These contracts shall also specify which party to the contract shall assume responsibility for alternate management of the wastes. These contracts shall also specify and, as the case may be, require from the consignee the notification required in 3(a) below (Re-export to a Third Country).

In such cases:

i) the person having actual possession or physical control over the wastes shall immediately inform the notifier and the competent authorities of the exporting and importing countries and, if the wastes are located in a country of transit, the competent authorities of that country;

ii) the person specified in the contract shall assume responsibility for the adequate management of the wastes in compliance with applicable laws and regulations including, if necessary, their return. The competent authorities of the concerned countries shall require that the necessary actions are carried out within a limited period of time, and shall not oppose, hinder or prevent the return of those wastes to the exporting country.

(2) *Control System*

Procedures are provided under the amber control system for the following two cases:

i) transactions which require consent for specific shipments to a recovery facility; and

ii) transactions involving specific recovery facilities to which the competent authorities having jurisdiction over such recovery facilities have granted general pre-consent concerning the reception of certain wastes.

Case (1): Provisions concerning transactions requiring specific consent.

(a) Prior to commencement of the transfrontier movement, the notifier shall provide written notification to the competent authorities of the concerned countries; this notification shall include all of the information listed in Appendix 2.A. The competent authorities of the exporting country may, in accord with domestic laws, decide to transmit this notification instead of the notifier.

(b) The competent authorities of the importing country, upon receipt of the completed notification referred to in paragraph (a) above, shall transmit an acknowledgement to the notifier with a copy to the competent authorities of other concerned countries within three (3) working days of their receiving the notification.

(c) The competent authorities of the exporting and importing countries shall have thirty (30) days to object in accord with their respective domestic laws to the proposed transfrontier movement. The 30-day period shall commence upon issuance of the acknowledgement referred at paragraph (b) above.

(d) Countries of transit may, in accord with domestic laws, object to the transfrontier movement entering their territory.

(e) Any objection by any of the concerned countries must be provided in writing to the notifier and to the competent authorities of other concerned countries within the 30-day period.

(f) If no objection has been lodged, the transfrontier movement may commence after the 30-day period has passed. Tacit consent, however, expires within one (1) calendar year from that date.

(g) The competent authorities of the concerned countries may decide to provide written consent in a period less than the 30 days. The transfrontier movement may commence immediately after all necessary consents are received.

(h) Written consent or objection may be provided by post, or by telefax followed by post. Such consent shall expire within one (1) calendar year unless otherwise specified.

(i) Each transfrontier movement shall be accompanied by a tracking document which includes the information listed in Appendix 2.

(j) Within three (3) days of the receipt of the wastes by the recovery facility, the recovery facility shall provide a signed copy of the tracking document to the notifier and to the competent authorities of the concerned countries. The recovery facility shall retain the original of the tracking document for three (3) years.

(k) In cases where essentially similar wastes (e.g. those having essentially similar physical and chemical characteristics) are to be sent periodically to the same recovery facility by the same notifier, the competent authorities of the concerned countries may elect to accept one notification for these wastes for a period of up to one year:

i) Such acceptance may be renewed for further periods of up to one year each;

ii) Revocation of this acceptance may be accomplished by means of official notice to the notifier from any of the competent authorities of the concerned countries. Notice of revocation of acceptance for shipments previously granted under this provision shall be given to the competent authorities of all concerned countries by the competent authorities of the country that revokes such acceptance.

Case (2): Provisions relating to pre-consent by competent authorities for shipments to specific recovery facilities.

(a) Competent authorities having jurisdiction over specific recovery facilities may decide not to raise objections concerning shipments of certain types of wastes to a specific recovery facility. Such decisions can be limited to a specified period of time; however, they may be revoked at any time.

(b) Competent authorities who elect this option shall inform the OECD Secretariat of the recovery facility name, address, technologies employed, waste types to which the pre-consent applies, and the period covered. Any revocations must also be notified to the OECD Secretariat.

(c) All proposed transfrontier movements to such facilities shall require notification; the notifier shall provide to the competent authorities of the concerned countries the information listed in Appendix 2.A. Such notification shall arrive prior to the time the shipment is dispatched.

(d) The competent authorities of the exporting and transit country may, in accord with their domestic laws, prohibit or otherwise restrict any such transfrontier movement.

(e) In instances where competent authorities acting under terms of their domestic laws are required to review the contracts referred to in (1) above (Conditions), these authorities shall so inform the OECD Secretariat. In such cases, the notification information plus the contract(s) or portions thereof to be reviewed must arrive seven (7) days prior to the time the shipment is dispatched in order that such review may be appropriately performed.

(f) Paragraphs (i), (j) and (k) of Case (1) shall apply.

(3) *Additional provisions relating to re-export to a third country*

(a) Re-export from an importing country of wastes subject to the amber control system may only occur following notification by a notifier in the importing country to the competent authorities of the initial exporting country, which shall be acknowledged within three (3) working days of receipt. The competent authorities of the initial exporting country shall have thirty (30) days to object to the proposed movement. The 30-day period shall commence upon issue of the acknowledgement referred to above. If no objection has been lodged, the transfrontier movement may commence after the 30-day period has passed. The competent authorities may decide to provide written consent in a period of less than 30 days. The transfrontier movement may commence immediately after such consent is received. Written consent may be provided by telefax in the first instance, followed by post if required.

(b) Re-export to a country outside the OECD area shall be fully subject to, and in accord with, all international agreements and arrangements to which the importing OECD Member country is a party.

(4) *Provisions relating to recognised traders*

(a) A recognised trader who takes physical custody of the wastes and intends to perform any of the operations in Table 2B of OECD Council Decision C(88)90(Final) shall require appropriate authorisation from its competent authorities to act as a recovery facility.

(b) A recognised trader may act as a notifier or consignee for wastes with all the responsibilities associated with being a notifier or consignee.

(c) The contracts referred to in (1) above (Conditions) shall:

i) clearly identify: the generator of each type of waste; each person who shall have physical custody of the wastes; each person who shall have legal control of the wastes; and the recovery facility;

ii) provide that all requirements of this Decision are taken into account and are legally binding on all parties to the contracts.

(d) The notification information called for at Appendix 2A shall include a signed declaration by the notifier that the appropriate contracts are in place and are legally enforceable in all concerned countries.

(e) Competent authorities of the exporting and importing countries may under terms of their domestic laws require the notifier to provide copies of such contracts or portions thereof.

(f) Any information contained in the contracts provided under terms of paragraph (e) above shall be held as strictly confidential in accordance with, and to the extent allowable by, domestic laws.

(5) *Provisions relating to wastes designated for exchange or accumulation prior to submission to recovery operations designated R1–R11 in Table 2B of OECD Council Decision C(88)90(Final)*

(a) The notification information included in Appendix 2A shall also indicate that exchange or storage is foreseen for the wastes covered by the notification.

(b) The competent authorities of concerned countries may request that the recovery facility where operations designated R1–R11 in Table 2B of Council Decision C(88)90(Final) will occur be identified.

(c) The tracking document referred to in Appendix 2B shall accompany the wastes to the recovery facility noted in paragraph (b) above which shall then comply with paragraph (j) of (2) above (Control System).

(6) *Amber list of wastes*
The amber list of wastes is set out at Appendix 4.

V. *Red Tier*

(1) The red list represents certain specific substances which, even moved in an adequately managed way, nevertheless must be controlled in a more stringent way than provided for by the amber control system. Wastes included in the red list shall be subject to the same controls as applied to wastes included in the amber list (see Section IV), and shall move in accord with Case (1), except that the importing and any transit countries must provide written consent prior to commencement of the transfrontier movement.

(2) *Red list of wastes*
The red list of wastes is set out at Appendix 5.

VI. *Actions to Promote Harmonised Implementation*

(1) Member countries individually, and as a group acting through the Review Mechanism established in this Decision, shall take appropriate steps toward improving the green, amber and red lists of wastes and toward uniform application of this Decision.

(2) Member countries shall cooperate in efforts aimed at:
- i) developing procedures for evaluating the criteria in Annex 2 to determine to which list a waste should be assigned; and
- ii) harmonising procedures for determining whether a waste exhibits any of the hazardous characteristics listed in Table 5 of OECD Council Decision C(88)90(Final).

(3) Member countries shall cooperate to identify and assess steps taken toward optimization of environmentally sound and economically efficient practices for recovery operations of each waste.

(4) When Sections II(4), II(6) and II(7) must be resorted to, Member countries shall cooperate to ensure that the provisions of this Decision are fully complied with.

(5) The OECD Secretariat shall circulate to all Member countries the information provided in accordance with this Decision, in particular under Sections II(4), II(5), II(6) and II(7).

Appendix 1

International Transport Agreements

1. Chicago Convention:
   Convention on International Civil Aviation (1944) Annex 18 which deals with the carriage of dangerous goods by air
   (T.I.: Technical Instructions for the Safe Transport of Dangerous Goods by Air);

2. ADR:
European Agreement concerning the International Carriage of Dangerous Goods by Road (1957);
3. ADNR:
Regulations of the Carriage of Dangerous Substances on the Rhine (1970).
4. MARPOL Convention:
International Convention for the Prevention of Pollution from Ships (1973/1978);
5. SOLAS Convention:
International Convention for the Safety of Life at Sea (1974);
6. IMDG Code:
International Maritime Dangerous Goods Code; (incorporated into SOLAS since 1985);
7. COTIF:
Convention concerning the International Carriage of Goods by Rail (1985);
8. RID:
Regulation on the International Carriage by Rail of Dangerous Goods (1985) [Annex I to COTIF];

Appendix 2

Notification and Tracking Information

A. *Information to be submitted upon notification*
1) Serial number or other accepted identifier of notification form.
2) Notifier name, address, telephone, telefax.
3) Recovery facility name, address, telephone, telefax, and technologies employed.
4) Consignee if not the recovery facility, address, telephone, telefax.
5) Intended carrier(s) and/or their agents.
6) Country of export and relevant competent authority.
7) Countries of transit and relevant competent authorities.
8) Country of import and relevant competent authority.
9) Is this a single notification or a general notification? If general, period of validity requested.
10) Date foreseen for commencement of transfrontier movement.
11) Certification that any applicable insurance or other financial guarantee is or shall be in force covering the transfrontier movement.
12) Designation of waste type(s) on the appropriate list (amber or red) and their description(s), probable total quantity of each, and an accepted uniform classification code (such as the IWIC) for each.
13) Certification of the existence of written contract or chain of contracts or equivalent arrangement as required by this Decision.
14) Certification by notifier that the information is complete and correct to the best of his knowledge.

B. *Tracking Document*
Include all information at A. above plus

(a) Date shipment was dispatched.
(b) Shipper (if not notifier), address, telephone, telefax.
(c) Actual carrier(s).
(d) Means and mode of transport including types of packaging.
(e) Any special precautions to be taken by carrier(s).
(f) Declaration by notifier that no objection has been lodged by the competent authorities of all concerned countries. This declaration requires signature of the notifier.
(g) Appropriate signatures for each custody transfer.

C. *All of this Information shall be Provided on a Form to be Developed for Use Within the OECD Area*

D. *Note.* Under terms of domestic legislation, some Member countries require information in addition to that included in A and B above in order to assess aspects of the environmentally sound management of wastes. Affected countries shall inform the OECD Secretariat and provide a list of the additional information needed.

Appendix 3

Green List of Wastes†

Regardless of whether or not wastes are included on this list, they may not be moved as Green Tier wastes if they are contaminated by other materials to an extent which (a) increases the risks associated with the waste sufficiently to render it appropriate for inclusion in the amber or red lists, when taking into account the criteria in Annex 2, or (b) prevents the recovery of the waste in an environmentally sound manner.

GA. *Metal and Metal-Alloy Wastes in Metallic, Non Dispersible Form*‡

The following waste and scrap of precious metals and their alloys:

GA 010 ex 711210 — of gold

GA 020 ex 711220 — of platinum (the expression 'platinum' includes platinum, iridium, osmium, palladium, rhodium and ruthenium)

GA 030 ex 711290 — of other precious metal, e.g., silver
N.B. Mercury is specifically excluded as a contaminant of these metals or their alloys or amalgams

† Whenever possible, the code number of the Harmonized Commodity Description and Coding System, established by the Brussels Convention of 14th June 1983 under the auspices of the Customs Co-operation Council (Harmonized System Code) is listed opposite an entry. This code may apply to both wastes and products. This Decision does not include items which are not wastes. Therefore, the code—used by customs officials in order to facilitate their procedures as well as by others—is only provided here to help in identifying wastes that are listed and subject to this Decision. However, corresponding official Explanatory Notes as issued by the Customs Co-operation Council should be used as interpretative guidance to identify wastes covered by generic headings. The indicative 'ex' identifies a specific item contained within a heading of the Harmonized System Code.

‡ 'Non-dispersible' does not include any wastes in the form of powder, sludge, dust or solid items containing encased hazardous waste liquids.

The following ferrous waste and scrap of iron or steel;

GA 040	720410	— Waste and scrap of cast iron
GA 050	720421	— Waste and scrap of stainless steel
GA 060	720429	— Waste and scrap of other alloy steels
GA 070	720430	— Waste and scrap of tinned iron or steel
GA 080	720441	— Turnings, shavings, chips, milling waste, filings, trimmings and stampings, whether or not in bundles
GA 090	720449	— Other ferrous waste and scrap
GA 100	720450	— Remelting scrap ingots
GA 110	ex 730210	— Used iron and steel rails

The following waste and scrap of non-ferrous metals and their alloys:

GA 120	740400	Copper waste and scrap
GA 130	750300	Nickel waste and scrap
GA 140	760200	Aluminium waste and scrap
GA 150	780200	Lead waste and scrap
GA 160	790200	Zinc waste and scrap
GA 170	800200	Tin waste and scrap
GA 180	ex 810191	Tungsten waste and scrap
GA 190	ex 810291	Molybdenum waste and scrap
GA 200	ex 810310	Tantalum waste and scrap
GA 210	810420	Magnesium waste and scrap
GA 220	ex 810510	Cobalt waste and scrap
GA 230	ex 810600	Bismuth waste and scrap
GA 240	ex 810710	Cadmium waste and scrap
GA 250	ex 810810	Titanium waste and scrap
GA 260	ex 810910	Zirconium waste and scrap
GA 270	ex 811000	Antimony waste and scrap
GA 280	ex 811100	Manganese waste and scrap
GA 290	ex 811211	Beryllium waste and scrap
GA 300	ex 811220	Chromium waste and scrap
GA 310	ex 811230	Germanium waste and scrap
GA 320	ex 811240	Vanadium waste and scrap
	ex 811291	Wastes and scrap of
GA 330		— Hafnium
GA 340		— Indium
GA 350		— Niobium
GA 360		— Rhenium
GA 370		— Gallium
GA 380		— Thallium
GA 390	ex 284430	Thorium waste and scrap
GA 400	ex 280490	Selenium waste and scrap
GA 410	ex 280450	Tellurium waste and scrap
GA 420	ex 280530	Rare earths waste and scrap

GB. *Metal Bearing Wastes Arising from Melting, Smelting and Refining of Metals*

GB 010	262011	Hard zinc spelter
GB 020		Zinc containing drosses:
GB 021		— Galvanizing slab zinc top dross (> 90% Zn)
GB 022		— Galvanizing slab zinc bottom dross (> 92% Zn)
GB 023		— Zinc die casting dross (> 85% Zn)
GB 024		— Hot dip galvanizers slab zinc dross (batch) (> 92% Zn)
GB 025		— Zinc skimmings
GB 030		Aluminium skimmings
GB 040	ex 262090	Slags from precious metals and copper processing for further refining
GB 040	ex 262090	Tantalum bearing tin slags with less than 0.5% tin

GC. *Other Wastes Containing Metals*

GC 010		Electrical assemblies consisting only of metals or alloys
GC 020		Electrical scrap (e.g. printed circuit boards, electronic components, wire, etc.) and reclaimed electronic components suitable for base and precious metal recovery
GC 030	ex 890800	Vessels and other floating structures for breaking up, properly emptied of any cargo and other materials arising from the operation of the vessel which may have been classified as a dangerous substance or waste
GC 040		Motor vehicle wrecks, drained of liquids
GC 050		Spent catalysts:
GC 051		— fluid catalytic cracking (FCC) catalysts
GC 052		— precious metal bearing catalysts
GC 053		— transition metal catalysts (e.g. chromium, cobalt, copper, iron, nickel, manganese, molybdenum, tungsten, vanadium, zinc).
GC 060	261800	Granulated slag arising from the manufacture of iron and steel.
GC 070	ex 261900	Slag arising from the manufacture of iron and steel.*

GD. *Wastes from Mining Operations: These Wastes to be in Non-Dispersible Form*

GD 010	ex 250490	Natural graphite waste
GD 020	ex 251400	Slate waste, whether or not roughly trimmed or merely cut, by sawing or otherwise
GD 030	252530	Mica waste
GD 040	ex 252930	Leucite, nepheline and nepheline syenite waste
GD 050	ex 252910	Feldspar waste
GD 060	ex 252910 ex 252922	Fluospar waste
GD 070	ex 281122	Silica wastes in solid form excluding those used in foundry operations

* This entry covers the use of such slags as a source of titatium dioxide and vanadium.

GE. *Glass Waste in Non-Dispersible Form*

GE 010 ex 700100 Cullet and other waste and scrap of glass except for glass from cathode-ray tubes and other activated glasses
GE 020 Fibre glass wastes

GF. *Ceramic Wastes in Non-Dispersible Form*

GF 010 ex Ceramic wastes which have been fired after shaping, including ceramic vessels (before and/or after use)
GF 020 ex 811300 Cermet wastes and scrap (metal ceramic composites)
GF 030 Ceramic based fibres not otherwise specified

GG. *Other Wastes Containing Principally Inorganic Constituents, Which May Contain Metals and Organic Materials*

GG 010 Partially refined calcium sulphate produced from flue gas desulphurisation (FGD)
GG 020 Waste gypsum wallboard or plasterboard arising from the demolition of buildings
GG 030 ex 2621 Bottom ash and slag tap from coal fired power plants
GG 040 ex 2621 Coal fired power plants fly ash
GG 050 Anode butts of petroleum coke and/or bitumen
GG 060 ex 2803 Spent activated carbon
GG 070 310320 Basic slag arising from the manufacture of iron or steel suitable for phosphate fertiliser and other use
GG 070 ex 262100 Slag from copper production, chemically stabilized, having a high iron content (above 20%) and processed according to industrial specification (e.g. DIN 4301 and DIN 8201) mainly for construction and abrasive applications
GG 090 Sulphur in solid form
GG 100 Limestone from the production of calcium cyanamide (having a pH less than 9)
GG 110 ex 262100 Neutralized red mud from alumina production
GG 120 Sodium, potassium, calcium chlorides
GG 130 Carborundum (silicon carbide)
GG 140 Broken concrete
GG 150 ex 262090 Lithium-Tantalum and Lithium-Niobium containing glass scraps

GH. *Solid Plastic Wastes*

Including, but not limited to:
GH 010 3915 Waste, parings and scrap of plastics
GH 011 ex 391510 — polymers of ethylene
GH 012 ex 391520 — polymers of styrene
GH 013 ex 391530 — polymers of vinyl chloride

GH 014	ex 391590	polymers or co-polymers e.g.: — polypropylene — polyethylene terephthalate — acrylonitrile copolymer — butadiene copolymer — styrene copolymer — polyamides — polybutylene terephthalates — polycarbonates — polyphenylene sulphides — acrylic polymers — paraffins (C10–C13)* — polyurethane (not containing chlorofluorocarbons) — polysiloxalanes (silicones) — polymethyl methacrylate — polyvinyl alcohol — polyvinyl butyral — polyvinyl acetate — polymers of fluorinated ethylene (Teflon, PTFE)
GH 015	ex 391590	resins or condensation products e.g.: — urea formaldehyde resins — phenol formaldehyde resins — melamine formaldehyde resins — epoxy resins — alkyd resins — polyamides

GI. *Paper, Paperboard and Paper Product Wastes*:

GI 010	4707	Waste and scrap of paper or paperboard:
GI 011	470710	— of unbleached kraft paper or paperboard or of corrugated paper or paperboard
GI 012	470720	— of other paper or paperboard, made mainly of bleached chemical pulp, not colored in the mass
GI 013	470730	— of paper or paperboard made mainly of mechanical pulp (for example, newspapers, journals and similar printed matter)
GI 014	470790	— other, including but not limited to: 1) laminated paperboard 2) unsorted waste and scrap

GJ. *Textile Wastes*

GJ 010	5003	Silk waste (including cocoons unsuitable for reeling, yarn waste and garnetted stock)
GJ 011	500310	— not carded or combed

* These cannot be polymerised and are used as plasticisers.

GJ 012	500390	— other
GJ 020	5103	Waste of wool or of fine or coarse animal hair, including yarn waste but excluding garnetted stock
GJ 021	510310	— noils of wool or of fine animal hair
GJ 022	510320	— other waste of wool or of fine animal hair
GJ 023	510330	— waste of coarse animal hair
GJ 030	5202	Cotton waste (including yarn waste and garnetted stock)
GJ 031	520210	— yarn waste (including thread waste)
GJ 032	520291	— garnetted stock
GJ 033	520299	— other
GJ 040	530130	Flax tow and waste
GJ 050 ex	530290	Tow and waste (including yarn waste and garnetted stock) of true hemp (*Cannabis sativa L.*)
GJ 060 ex	530390	Tow and waste (including yarn waste and garnetted stock) of jute and other textile bast fibres (excluding flax, true hemp and ramie)
GJ 070 ex	530490	Tow and waste (including yarn waste and garnetted stock) of sisal and other textile fibres of the genus Agave
GJ 080 ex	530519	Tow, noils and waste (including yarn waste and garnetted stock) of coconut
GJ 090 ex	530529	Tow, noils and waste (including yarn waste and garnetted stock) of abaca (Manila hemp or *Musa textilis Nee*)
GJ 100 ex	530599	Tow, noils and waste (including yarn waste and garnetted stock) of ramie and other vegetable textile fibres, not elsewhere specified or included
GJ 110	5505	Waste (including noils, yarn waste and garnetted stock) of man-made fibres
GJ 111	550510	— of synthetic fibres
GJ 112	550520	— of artificial fibres
GJ 120	630900	Worn clothing and other worn textile articles
GJ 130	6310	Used rags, scrap twine, cordage, rope and cables and worn out articles of twine, cordage, rope or cables of textile materials
GJ 131	631010	— sorted
GJ 132	631090	— other

GK. *Rubber Wastes*

GK 010 ex	400400	Waste, parings and scrap of rubber (other than hard rubber) and granules obtained therefrom
GK 020	401220	Used pneumatic tyres
GK 030 ex	401700	Waste and scrap of hard rubber (for example, ebonite)

GL. *Untreated Cork and Wood Wastes*

GL 010 ex	440130	Wood waste and scrap, whether or not agglomerated in logs, briquettes, pellets or similar forms
GL 020 ex	450190	Cork waste; crushed, granulated or ground cork

GM. *Wastes Arising from Agro-Food Industries*

GM 070 ex 2307		Wine lees
GM 080	2308	Dried and sterilized vegetable waste, residues and by-products, whether or not in the form of pellets, of a kind used in animal feeding, not elsewhere specified or included
GM 090	152200	Degras; residues resulting from the treatement of fatty substances or animal or vegetable waxes
GM 100	050609	Waste of bones and horn-cores, unworked, defatted, simply prepared (but not cut to shape), treated with acid or degelatinised
GM 110 ex 051191		Fish waste
GM 120 ex 180200		Cocoa shells, husks, skins and other cocoa waste
GM 130		Wastes from the agro-food industry excluding by-products which meet national and international requirements and standards for human or animal consumption

GN. *Wastes Arising from Tanning and Fellmongery Operations and Leather Use*

GN 010 ex 050200	Waste of pigs', hogs' or boars' bristles and hair or of badger hair and other brush making hair
GN 020 ex 050300	Horsehair waste, whether or not put up as a layer with or without supporting material
GN 030 ex 050590	Waste of skins and other parts of birds, with their feathers or down, of feathers and parts of feathers (whether or not with trimmed edges) and down, not further worked than cleaned, disinfected or treated for preservation
GN 040 ex 411000	Parings and other waste of leather or of composition leather, not suitable for the manufacture of leather articles, excluding leather sludges

GO. *Other Wastes*

GO 010 ex 050100	Waste of human hair
GO 020	Waste straw
GO 030	Deactivated fungus mycelium from penicillin production to be used as animal feed
GO 040	Waste photographic film base and waste photographic film not containing silver
GO 050	Single use cameras without batteries

Appendix 4

*Amber List of Wastes**

Regardless of whether or not wastes are included on this list, they may not be moved as Amber Tier wastes if they are contaminated by other materials to an extent which (a) increases the risks associated with the waste sufficiently to render it appropriate for inclusion in the red list, when taking into account the criteria in Annex 2, or (b) prevents the recovery of the waste in an environmentally sound manner.

AA. *Metal Bearing Wastes*

AA 010 ex 261900	Dross, scalings and other wastes from the manufacture of iron and steel**
AA 020 ex 262019	Zinc ashes and residues**
AA 030 ex 262020	Lead ashes and residues**
AA 040 ex 262030	Copper ashes and residues**
AA 050 ex 262040	Aluminium ashes and residues**
AA 060 ex 262050	Vanadium ashes and residues**
AA 070 ex 262090	Ashes and residues** containing metals or metal compounds not elsewhere specified or included
AA 080	Thallium waste and residues**
AA 090 ex 280480	Arsenic waste and residues**
AA 100 ex 280540	Mercury waste and residues**
AA 110	Residues from alumina production not elsewhere specified or included
AA 120	Galvanic sludges
AA 130	Liquors from the pickling of metals
AA 140	Leaching residues from zinc processing, dusts and sludges such as jarosite, hematite, goethite, etc.
AA 150	Precious metal bearing residues in solid form which contain traces of inorganic cyanides
AA 160	Precious metal ash, sludge, dust and other residues such as:
AA 161	— ash from incineration of printed circuit boards

* Whenever possible, the code number of the Harmonized Commodity Description and Coding System, established by the Brussels Convention of 14th June 1983 under the auspices of the Customs Co-operation Council (Harmonized System Code) is listed opposite an entry. This code may apply to both wastes and products. This Decision does not include items which are not wastes. Therefore, the code—used by customs officials in order to facilitate their procedures as well as by others—is only provided here to help in identifying wastes that are listed and subject to this Decision. However, corresponding official explanatory notes as issued by the Customs Co-operation Council should be used as interpretative guidance to identify wastes covered by generic headings. The indicative 'ex' identifies a specific item contained within a heading of the Harmonized System Code

The code in bold in the first column is the OECD code: it consists of two letters (one for the list Green, Amber or Red and one for the category of waste **A**, **B**, **C** . . .) followed by a number.

** This listing includes wastes in the form of ash, residue, slag, dross, skimming, scaling, dust, powder, sludge and cake, unless a material is expressly listed elsewhere.

AA 162		— photographic film ash
AA 170		Lead-acid batteries, whole or crushed
AA 180		Used batteries or accumulators, whole or crushed, other than lead-acid batteries, and waste and scrap arising from the production of batteries and accumulators, not elsewhere specified or included

AB. *Wastes Containing Principally Inorganic Constituents, Which May Contain Metals and Organic Materials*

AB 010	261900	Slag, ash and residues**, not elsewhere specified or included
AB 0200		Residues arising from the combustion of municipal/household wastes
AB 030		Wastes from non-cyanide based systems which arise from surface treatment of metals
AB 040	ex 700100	Glass waste from cathode-ray tubes and other activate glasses
AB 050	ex 252921	Calcium fluoride sludge
AB 060		Other inorganic fluorine compounds in the form of liquid or sludges
AB 070		Sands used in foundry operations
AB 080		Waste catalysts not on the green list
AB 090		Waste hydrates of aluminium
AB 100		Waste alumina
AB 110		Basic solutions
AB 120		Inorganic halide compounds, not elsewhere specified or included
AB 130		Used blasting grit
AB 140		Gypsum arising from chemical industry processes
AB 150		Unrefined calcium sulphite and calcium sulphate from flue gas desulphurisation (FGD)

AC. *Wastes Containing Principally Organic Constituents, Which May Contain Metals and Inorganic Materials*

AC 010	ex 271390	Waste from the production/processing of petroleum coke and bitumen, excluding anode butts
AC 020		Asphalt cement wastes
AC 030		Waste oils unfit for their originally intended use
AC 040		Leaded petrol (gasoline) sludges
AC 050		Thermal (heat transfer) fluids
AC 060		Hydraulic fluids
AC 070		Brake fluids
AC 080		Antifreeze fluids
AC 090		Wastes from production, formulation and use of resins latex, plasticisers, glues and adhesives
AC 100	ex391590	Nitrocellulose
AC 110		Phenols, phenol compounds including chlorophenol in the form

of liquids or sludges

AC 120	Polychlorinated naphthalenes
AC 130	Ethers
AC 140	Triethylamine catalysts for setting foundry sands
AC 150	Chlorofluorocarbons
AC 160	Halons
AC 170	Treated cork and wood wastes
AC 180 ex 411000	Leather dust, ash, sludges and flours
AC 190	Fluff—light fraction from automobile shredding
AC 200	Organic phosphorous compounds
AC 210	Non-halogenated solvents
AC 220	Halogenated solvents
AC 230	Halogenated or unhalogenated non-aqueous distillation residues arising from organic solvent recovery operations
AC 240	Wastes arising from the production of aliphatic halogenated hydrocarbons (such as chloromethanes, allyl chloride and epichlorhydrin)
AC 250	Surface active agents (surfactants)
AC 260	Liquid pig manure; faeces
AC 270	Sewage sludge

AD. *Wastes Which May Contain Either Inorganic or Organic Constituents*

AD 010	Wastes from the production and preparation of pharmaceutical products
AD 020	Wastes from the production formulation and use of biocides and phytopharmaceuticals
AD 030	Wastes from the manufacture, formulation and use of wood preserving chemicals
	Wastes that contain, consist of or are contaminated with any of the following:
AD 040	— inorganic cyanides, excepting precious metal-bearing residues in solid form containing traces of inorganic cyanides
AD 050	— organic cyanides
AD 060	Waste oils/water, hydrocarbons/water mixtures, emulsions
AD 070	Wastes from production, formulation an duse of inks, dyes, pigments, paints, lacquers, varnish
AD 080	Wastes of an explosive nature, when not subject to specific other legislation
AD 090	Wastes from production, formulation and use of reprographic and photographic chemicals and materials not elsewhere specified or included
AD 100	Wastes from non-cyanide based systems which arise from surface treatment of plastics
AD 110	Acidic solutions
AD 120	Ion exchange resins
AD 130	Single use cameras with batteries

AD 140	Wastes from industrial pollution control devices for cleaning of industrial off-gases, not elsewhere specified or included
AD 150	Naturally occuring organic material used as a filter medium (such as bio-filters)
AD 100	Municipal/household wastes*

Appendix 5

Red List of Wastes

'Containing' or 'contaminated with', when used in this list, mean that the substance referred to is present to an extent which (a) renders the waste hazardous when taking into account the criteria in Annex 2, or (b) renders it not suitable for submission to a recovery operation.

RA. *Wastes Containing Principally Organic Constituents, Which May Contain Metals and Inorganic Materials*

RA 010	Wastes, substances and articles containing, consisting of or contaminated with polychlorinated biphenyl (PCB) and/or polychlorinated terphenyl (PCT) and/or polybrominated biphenyl (PBB), including any other polybrominated analogues of these compounds, at a concentration level of 50 mg/kg or more
RA 020	Waste tarry residues (excluding asphalt cements) arising from refining, distillation and any pyrolitic treatment of organic materials

RB. *Wastes Containing Principally Inorganic Constituents, Which May Contain Metals and Inorganic Materials*

RB 010	Asbestos (dusts and fibres)
RB 020	Ceramic based fibres of physico-chemical characteristics similar to those of asbestos

RC. *Wastes Which May Contain Either Inorganic or Organic Constituents*

	Wastes that contain, consist of or are contaminated with any of the following:
RC 010	— any congenor of polychorinated dibenzo-furan
RC 020	— any congenor of polychorinated dibenzo-dioxin
RC 030	Leaded anti-knock compound sludges
RC 040	Peroxides other than hydrogen peroxide

* In the Basel Convention household wastes—defined as an 'other waste'—are controlled when they are subject to transfrontier movements. Therefore under this Decision all household wastes (and *not* just those which exhibit a hazardous characteristic) will be subject to the procedures in Section IV (Amber Tier). Until exporting countries have the legal authority to control transfrontier movements of household wastes, the provisions in Section II(4) will be applied.

Appendix IX

London Convention on the Prevention of Marine Pollution by Dumping of Wastes and Other Matter (29 December 1972, as amended)

The Contracting Parties to this Convention,

Recognizing that the marine environment and the living organisms which it supports are of vital importance to humanity, and all people have an interest in assuring that it is sc managed that its quality and resources are not impaired;

Recognizing that the capacity of the sea to assimilate wastes and render them harmless, and its ability to regenerate natural resources, is not unlimited;

Recognizing that States have, in accordance with the Charter of the United Nations and the principles of international law, the sovereign right to exploit their own resources pursuant to their own environmental policies, and the responsibility to ensure that activities within their jurisdiction or control do not cause damage to the environment of other States or of areas beyond the limits of national jurisdiction;

Recalling Resolution 2749(XXV) of the General Assembly of the United Nations on the principles governing the sea-bed and the ocean floor and the subsoil thereof, beyond the limits of national jurisdiction;

Noting that marine pollution originates in many sources, such as dumping and discharges through the atmosphere, rivers, estuaries, outfalls and pipelines, and that it is important that States use the best practicable means to prevent such pollution and develop products and processes which will reduce the amount of harmful wastes to be disposed of;

Being convinced that international action to control the pollution of the sea by dumping can and must be taken without delay but that this action should not preclude discussion of measures to control other sources of marine pollution as soon as possible; and

Wishing to improve protection of the marine environment by encouraging States with a common interest in particular geographical areas to enter into appropriate agreements supplementary to this Convention;

Have agreed as follows:

Article I

Contracting Parties shall individually and collectively promote the effective control of all sources of pollution of the marine environment, and pledge themselves especially to take all practicable steps to prevent the pollution of the sea by the dumping of waste and other matter that is liable to create hazards to human health, to harm living resources and marine life, to damage amenities or to interfere with other legitimate uses of the sea.

Article II

Contracting Parties shall, as provided for in the following Articles, take effective measures individually, according to their scientific, technical and economic capabilities, and collectively, to prevent marine pollution caused by dumping and shall harmonize their policies in this regard.

Article III

For the purpose of the Convention:

1. (a) 'Dumping' means:
   (i) any deliberate disposal at sea of wastes or other matter from vessels, aircraft, platforms or other man-made structures at sea;
   (ii) any deliberate disposal at sea of vessels, aircraft, platforms or other man-made structures at sea.
   (b) 'Dumping' does not include:
   (i) the disposal at sea of wastes or other matter incidental to, or derived from the normal operations of vessels, aircraft, platforms or other man-made structures at sea and their equipment, other than wastes or other matter transported by or to vessels, aircraft, platforms or other man-made structures at sea, operating for the purpose of disposal of such matter or derived from the treatment of such wastes or other matter on such vessels, aircraft, platforms or structures;
   (ii) placement of matter for a purpose other than the mere disposal thereof, provided that such placement is not contrary to the aims of this Convention.
   (c) The disposal of wastes or other matter directly arising from, or related to the exploration, exploitation and associated off-shore processing of sea-bed mineral resources will not be covered by the provisions of this Convention.

2. 'Vessels and aircraft' means waterborne or airborne craft of any type whatsoever. This expression includes air cushioned craft and floating craft, whether self-propelled or not.

3. 'Sea' means all marine waters other than the internal waters of States.

4. 'Wastes or other matter' means material and substance of any kind, form or description.

5. 'Special permit' means permission granted specifically on application in advance and in accordance with Annex II and Annex III.

6. 'General permit' means permission granted in advance and in accordance with Annex III.

7. 'The Organisation' means the Organisation designated by the Contracting Parties in accordance with Article XIV(2).

Article IV

1. In accordance with the provisions of this Convention Contracting Parties shall prohibit the dumping of any wastes or other matter in whatever form or condition except as otherwise specified below:

(a) the dumping of wastes or other matter listed in Annex I is prohibited;
(b) the dumping of wastes or other material listed in Annex II requires a prior special permit;
(c) the dumping of all other wastes or matter requires a prior general permit.

2. Any permit shall be issued only after careful consideration of all the factors set forth in Annex III, including prior studies of the characteristics of the dumping site as set forth in Sections B and C of that Annex.

3. No provision of this Convention is to be interpreted as preventing a Contracting Party from prohibiting, insofar as that Party is concerned, the dumping of wastes or other matter not mentioned in Annex I. That Party shall notify such measures to the Organisation.

Article V

1. The provisions of Article IV shall not apply when it is necessary to secure the safety of human life or of vessels, aircraft, platforms or other man-made structures at sea in cases of *force majeure* caused by stress of weather, or in any case which constitutes danger to human life or a real threat to vessels, aircraft, platforms or other man-made structures at sea, if dumping appears to be the only way of averting the threat and if there is every probability that the damage consequent upon such dumping will be less than would otherwise occur. Such dumping shall be so conducted as to minimise the likelihood of damage to human or marine life and shall be reported forthwith to the Organisation.

2. A Contracting Party may issue a special permit as an exception to Article IV(1)(a), in emergencies, posing unacceptable risk relating to human health and admitting no other feasible solution. Before doing so the Party shall consult any other country or countries that are likely to be affected and the Organisation which, after consulting other Parties, and international organisations as appropriate, shall in accordance with Article XIV promptly recommend to the party the most appropriate procedures to adopt. The Party shall follow these recommendations to the maximum extent feasible consistent with the time within which action must be taken and with the general obligation to avoid damage to the marine environment and shall inform the Organisation of the action it takes. The Parties pledge themselves to assist one another in such situations.

3. Any Contracting Party may waive its rights under paragraph (2) at the time of, or subsequent to ratification of, or accession to this Convention.

Article VI

1. Each Contracting Party shall designate an appropriate authority or authorities to:

(a) issue special permits which shall be required prior to, and for, the dumping of matter listed in Annex II and in the circumstances provided for in Article V(2);
(b) issue general permits which shall be required prior to, and for, the dumping of all other matter;
(c) keep records of the nature and quantities of all matter permitted to be dumped and the location, time and method of dumping;

(d) monitor individually, or in collaboration with other Parties and competent International Organisations, the condition of the seas for the purposes of this Convention.

2. The appropriate authority or authorities of a Contracting Party shall issue prior special or general permits in accordance with paragraph (1) in respect of matter intended for dumping:

(a) loaded in its territory;

(b) loaded by a vessel or aircraft registered in its territory or flying its flag, when the loading occurs in the territory of a State not party to this Convention.

3. In issuing permits under sub-paragraphs (1)(a) and (b) above, the appropriate authority or authorities shall comply with Annex III, together with such additional criteria, measures and requirements as they may consider relevant.

4. Each Contracting Party, directly or through a Secretariat established under a regional agreement, shall report to the Organisation, and where appropriate to other Parties, the information specified in sub-paragraphs (c) and (d) of paragraph (1) above, and the criteria, measures and requirements it adopts in accordance with paragraph (3) above. The procedure to be followed and the nature of such reports shall be agreed by the Parties in consultation.

Article VII

1. Each Contracting Party shall apply the measures required to implement the present Convention to all:

(a) vessels and aircraft registered in its territory or flying its flag;

(b) vessels and aircraft loading in its territory or territorial seas matter which is to be dumped;

(c) vessels and aircraft and fixed or floating platforms under its jurisdiction believed to be engaged in dumping.

2. Each Party shall take in its territory appropriate measures to prevent and punish conduct in contravention of the provisions of this Convention.

3. The Parties agree to co-operate in the development of procedures for the effective application of this Convention particularly on the high seas, including procedures for the reporting of vessels and aircraft observed dumping in contravention of the Convention.

4. This Convention shall not apply to those vessels and aircraft entitled to sovereign immunity under international law. However each Party shall ensure by the adoption of appropriate measures that such vessels and aircraft owned or operated by it act in a manner consistent with the object and purpose of this Convention, and shall inform the Organisation accordingly.

5. Nothing in this Convention shall affect the right of each Party to adopt other measures, in accordance with the principles of international law, to prevent dumping at sea.

Article VIII

In order to further the objectives of this Convention, the Contracting Parties with common interests to protect in the marine environment in a given geographical area shall endeavour, taking into account characteristic regional features, to enter into regional agreements consistent with this Convention for the prevention of pollution, especially by dumping. The Contracting Parties to the present Convention shall endeavour to act consistently with the objectives and provisions of such regional agreements, which shall be notified to them by the Organisation. Contracting Parties shall seek to co-operate with the Parties to regional agreements in order to develop harmonized procedures to be followed by Contracting Parties to the different conventions concerned. Special attention shall be given to co-operation in the field of monitoring and scientific research.

Article IX

The Contracting Parties shall promote, through collaboration within the Organisation and other international bodies, support for those Parties which request it for:

(a) the training of scientific and technical personnel;
(b) the supply of necessary equipment and facilities for research and monitoring;
(c) the disposal and treatment of waste and other measures to prevent or mitigate pollution caused by dumping;

preferably within the countries concerned, so furthering the aims and purposes of this Convention.

Article X

In accordance with the principles of international law regarding State responsibility for damage to the environment of other States or to any other area of the environment, caused by dumping of wastes and other matter of all kinds, the Contracting Parties undertake to develop procedures for the assessment of liability and the settlement of disputes regarding dumping.

Article XI

The Contracting Parties shall at their first consultative meeting consider procedures for the settlement of disputes concerning the interpretation and application of this Convention.

Article XII

The Contracting Parties pledge themselves to promote, within the competent specialised agencies and other international bodies, measures to protect the marine environment against pollution caused by:

(a) hydrocarbons, including oil, and their wastes;
(b) other noxious or hazardous matter transported by vessels for purposes other than dumping;
(c) wastes generated in the course of operation of vessels, aircraft, platforms and other man-made structures at sea;
(d) radio-active pollutants from all sources, including vessels;
(e) agents of chemical and biological warfare;
(f) wastes or other matter directly arising from, or related to the exploration, exploitation and associated off-shore processing of sea-bed mineral resources.

The Parties will also promote, within the appropriate international organisation, the codification of signals to be used by vessels engaged in dumping.

Article XIII

Nothing in this Convention shall prejudice the codification and development of the law of the sea by the United Nations Conference on the Law of the Sea convened pursuant to Resolution 2750C(XXV) of the General Assembly of the United Nations nor the present or future claims and legal views of any State concerning the law of the sea and the nature and extent of coastal and flag State jurisdiction. The Contracting Parties agree to consult at a meeting to be convened by the Organisation after the Law of the Sea Conference, and in any case not later than 1976, with a view to defining the nature and extent of the right and the responsibility of a coastal State to apply the Convention in a zone adjacent to its coast.

Article XIV

1. The Government of the United Kingdom of Great Britain and Northern Ireland as a depositary shall call a meeting of the Contracting Parties not later than three months after the entry into force of this Convention to decide on organisational matters.
2. The Contracting Parties shall designate a competent Organisation existing at the time of that meeting to be responsible for Secretariat duties in relation to this Convention. Any Party to this Convention not being a member of this Organisation shall make an appropriate contribution to the expenses incurred by the Organisation in performing these duties.
3. The Secretariat duties of the Organisation shall include:
   (a) the convening of consultative meetings of the Contracting Parties not less frequently than once every two years and of special meetings of the Parties at any time on the request of two-thirds of the Parties;
   (b) preparing and assisting, in consultation with the Contracting Parties and appropriate International Organisations, in the development and implementation of procedures referred to in sub-paragraph (4)(e) of this Article;
   (c) considering enquiries by, and information from the Contracting Parties, consulting with them and with the appropriate International Organisations, and providing recommendations to the Parties on questions related to, but not specifically covered by the Convention;
   (d) conveying to the Parties concerned all notifications received by the Organisation in accordance with Articles IV(3), V(1) and (2), VI(4), XV, XX and XXI.

Prior to the designation of the Organisation these functions shall, as necessary, be performed by the depositary, who for this purpose shall be the Government of the United Kingdom of Great Britain and Northern Ireland.

4. Consultative or special meetings of the Contracting Parties shall keep under continuing review the implementation of this Convention and may, *inter alia*:
   (a) review and adopt amendments to this Convention and its Annexes in accordance with Article XV;
   (b) invite the appropriate scientific body or bodies to collaborate with and

advise the Parties or the Organisation on any scientific or technical aspect relevant to this Convention, including particularly the content of the Annexes;

(c) receive and consider reports made pursuant to Article VI(4);

(d) promote co-operation with and between regional organisations concerned with the prevention of marine pollution;

(e) develop or adopt, in consultation with appropriate International Organisations, procedures referred to in Article V(2) including basic criteria for determining exceptional and emergency situations, and procedures for consultative advice and the safe disposal of matter in such circumstances, including the designation of appropriate dumping areas, and recommend accordingly;

(f) consider any additional action that may be required.

5. The Contracting Parties at their first consultative meeting shall establish rules of procedure as necessary.

Article XV

1. (a) At meetings of the Contracting Parties called in accordance with Article XIV amendments to this Convention may be adopted by a two-thirds majority of those present. An amendment shall enter into force for the Parties which have accepted it on the sixtieth day after two-thirds of the Parties shall have deposited an instrument of acceptance of the amendment with the Organisation. Thereafter the amendment shall enter into force for any other Party 30 days after that Party deposits its instrument of acceptance of the amendment.

(b) The Organisation shall inform all Contracting Parties of any request made for a special meeting under Article XIV and of any amendments adopted at meetings of the Parties and of the date on which each such amendment enters into force for each Party.

2. Amendments to the Annexes will be based on scientific or technical considerations. Amendments to the Annexes approved by a two-thirds majority of those present at a meeting called in accordance with Article XIV shall enter into force for each Contracting Party immediately on notification of its acceptance to the Organisation and 100 days after approval by the meeting for all other Parties except for those which before the end of the 100 days make a declaration that they are not able to accept the amendment at that time. Parties should endeavour to signify their acceptance of an amendment to the Organisation as soon as possible after approval at a meeting. A Party may at any time substitute an acceptance for a previous declaration of objection and the amendment previously objected to shall thereupon enter into force for that Party.

3. An acceptance or declaration of objection under this Article shall be made by the deposit of an instrument with the Organisation. The Organisation shall notify all Contracting Parties of the receipt of such instruments.

4. Prior to the delegation of the Organisation, the Secretarial functions herein attributed to it, shall be performed temporarily by the Government of the United Kingdom of Great Britain and Northern Ireland, as one of the depositaries of this Convention.

Article XVI

This Convention shall be open for signature by any State at London, Mexico City, Moscow and Washington from 29 December 1972 until 31 December 1973.

Article XVII

This Convention shall be subject to ratification. The instruments of ratification shall be deposited with the Governments of Mexico, the Union of Soviet Socialist Republics, the United Kingdom of Great Britain and Northern Ireland, and the United States of America.

Article XVIII

After 31 December 1973, this Convention shall be open for accession by any State. The instruments of accession shall be deposited with the Governments of Mexico, the Union of Soviet Socialist Republics, the United Kingdom of Great Britain and Northern Ireland, and the United States of America.

Article XIX

1. This Convention shall enter into force on the thirtieth day following the date of deposit of the fifteenth instrument of ratification or accession.
2. For each Contracting Party ratifying or acceding to the Convention after the deposit of the fifteenth instrument of ratification or accession, the Convention shall enter into force on the thirtieth day after deposit by such Party of its instrument of ratification or accession.

Article XX

The depositaries shall inform Contracting Parties:

(a) of signatures to this Convention and of the deposit of instruments of ratification, accession or withdrawal, in accordance with Articles XVI, XVII, XVIII and XXI, and
(b) of the date on which this Convention will enter into force, in accordance with Article XIX.

Article XXI

Any Contracting Party may withdraw from this Convention by giving six months' notice in writing to a depositary which shall promptly inform all Parties of such notice.

Article XXII

The original of this Convention of which the English, French, Russian and Spanish texts are equally authentic, shall be deposited with the Governments of Mexico, the Union of Soviet Socialist Republics, the United Kingdom of Great Britain and Northern Ireland and the United States of America who shall send certified copies thereof to all States.

In Witness Whereof the undersigned Plenipotentiaries, being duly authorised thereto by their respective Governments have signed the present Convention.

Done in quadruplicate at London, Mexico City, Moscow and Washington, this twenty-ninth day of December, 1972.

Annex I

1. Organohalogen compounds.
2. Mercury and mercury compounds.
3. Cadmium and cadmium compounds.
4. Persistent plastics and other persistent synthetic materials, for example, netting and ropes, which may float or may remain in suspension in the sea in such a manner as to interfere materially with fishing, navigation or other legitimate uses of the sea.
5. Crude oil and its wastes, refined petroleum products, petroleum, distillate residues, and any mixtures containing any of these, taken on board for the purpose of dumping.
6. Radioactive wastes or other radioactive matter.
7. Materials in whatever form (e.g. solids, liquids, semi-liquids, gases or in a living state) produced for biological and chemical warfare.
8. With the exception of paragraph 6 above, the preceding paragraphs of this Annex do not apply to substances which are rapidly rendered harmless by physical, chemical or biological processes in the sea provided they do not:
   (i) make edible marine organisms unpalatable, or
   (ii) endanger human health or that of domestic animals.

   The consultative procedure provided for under Article XIV should be followed by a Party if there is doubt about the harmlessness of the substance.
9. Except for industrial waste as defined in paragraph 11 below, this Annex does not apply to wastes or other materials (e.g. sewage sludge and dredged material) containing the matters referred to in paragraphs 1–5 above as trace contaminants. Such wastes shall be subject to the provisions of Annexes II and III as appropriate.

   Paragraph 6 does not apply to wastes or other materials (e.g. sewage sludge and dredged material) containing de minimis (exempt) levels of radioactivity as defined by the IAEA and adopted by the Contracting Parties. Unless otherwise prohibited by Annex I, such wastes shall be subject to the provisions of Annexes II and III as appropriate.
10. (a) Incineration at sea of industrial waste, as defined in paragraph 11 below, and sewage sludge is prohibited.
    (b) The incineration at sea of any other wastes or other matter requires the issue of a special permit.
    (c) In the issue of special permits for incineration at sea Contracting Parties shall apply regulations as are developed under this Convention.
    (d) For the purpose of this Annex:
        (i) 'Marine incineration facility' means a vessel, platform, or other man-made structure operating for the purpose of incineration at sea.
        (ii) 'Incineration at sea' means the deliberate combustion of wastes or

other matter on marine incineration facilities for the purpose of their thermal destruction. Activities incidental to the normal operation of vessels, platforms or other man-made structures are excluded from the scope of this definition.

11. Industrial waste as from 1 January 1996.
For the purpose of this Annex:
'Industrial waste' means waste materials generated by manufacturing or processing operations and does not apply to:
(a) dredged material;
(b) sewage sludge;
(c) fish waste, or organic materials resulting from industrial fish processing operations;
(d) vessels and platforms or other man-made structures at sea, provided that material capable of creating floating debris or otherwise contributing to pollution of the marine environment has been removed to the maximum extent;
(e) uncontaminated inert geological materials the chemical constituents of which are unlikely to be released into the marine environment;
(f) uncontaminated organic materials of natural origin.
Dumping of wastes and other matter specified in subparagraphs (a)–(f) above shall be subject to all other provisions of Annex I, and to the provisions of Annexes II and III.
This paragraph shall not apply to the radioactive wastes or any other radioactive matter referred to in paragraph 6 of this Annex.

12. Within 25 years from the date on which the amendment to paragraph 6 enters into force and at each 25 year interval thereafter, the Contracting Parties shall complete a scientific study relating to all radioactive wastes and other radioactive matter other than high level wastes or matter, taking into account such other factors as the Contracting Parties consider appropriate, and shall review the position of such substances on Annex I in accordance with the procedures set forth in Article XV.

Annex II

The following substances and materials requiring special care are listed for the purposes of Article VI(1)(a).

A Wastes containing significant amounts of the matters listed below:

arsenic, beryllium, chromium, copper, lead, nickel, vanadium, zinc — and their compounds

organosilicon compounds
cyanides
fluorides

pesticides and their by-products not covered in Annex I.

B Containers, scrap metal and other bulky wastes liable to sink to the sea bottom which may present a serious obstacle to fishing or navigation.

C In the issue of special permits for the incineration of substances and materials listed in this Annex, the Contracting Parties shall apply the Regulations for the Control of Incineration of Wastes and Other Matter at Sea set forth in the Addendum to Annex I and take full account of the Technical Guidelines on the Control of Incineration of Wastes and Other Matter at Sea adopted by the Contracting Parties in consultation, to the extent specified in these Regulations and Guidelines.

D Materials which, though of a non-toxic nature, may become harmful due to the quantities in which they are dumped, or which are liable to seriously reduce amenities.

Annex III

Provisions to be considered in establishing criteria governing the issue of permits for the dumping of matter at sea, taking into account Article IV(2), include:

A. *Characteristics and composition of the matter*

1 Total amount and average composition of matter dumped (e.g. per year).
2 Form, e.g. solid, sludge, liquid, or gaseous.
3 Properties: physical (e.g. solability and density), chemical and biochemical (e.g. oxygen demand, nutrients) and biological (e.g. presence of viruses, bacteria, yeasts, parasites).
4 Toxicity.
5 Persistence: physical, chemical and biological.
6 Accumulation and biotransformation in biological materials or sediments.
7 Susceptibility to physical, chemical and biochemical changes and interaction in the aquatic environment with other dissolved organic and inorganic materials.
8 Probability of production of taints or other changes reducing marketability of resources (fish, shellfish, etc.).
9 In issuing a permit for dumping, Contracting Parties should consider whether an adequate scientific basis exists concerning characteristics and composition of the matter to be dumped to assess the impact of the matter on marine life and on human health.

B. *Characteristics of dumping site and method of deposit*

1 Location (e.g. co-ordinates of the dumping area, depth and distance from the coast), location in relation to other areas (e.g. amenity areas, spawning, nursery and fishing areas and exploitable resources).
2 Rate of disposal per specific period (e.g. quantity per day, per week, per month).
3 Methods of packaging and containment, if any.
4 Initial dilution achieved by proposed method of release.
5 Dispersal characteristics (e.g. effects of currents, tides and wind on horizontal transport and vertical mixing).

6 Water characteristics (e.g. temperature, pH, salinity, stratification, oxygen indices of pollution-dissolved oxygen (DO), chemical oxygen demand (COD), biochemical oxygen demand (BOD)—nitrogen present in organic and mineral form including ammonia, suspended matter, other nutrients and productivity).
7 Bottom characteristics (e.g. topography, geochemical and geological characteristics and biological productivity).
8 Existence and effects of other dumpings which have been made in the dumping area (e.g. heavy metal background reading and organic carbon content).
9 In issuing a permit for dumping. Contracting Parties should consider whether an adequate scientific basis exists for assessing the consequences of such dumping, as outlined in this Annex, taking into account seasonal variations.

C. *General considerations and conditions*

1 Possible effects on amenities (e.g. presence of floating or stranded material, turbidity, objectionable odour, discolouration and foaming).
2 Possible effects on marine life, fish and shellfish culture, fish stocks and fisheries, seaweed harvesting and culture.
3 Possible effects on other uses of the sea (e.g. impairment of water quality for industrial use, underwater corrosion of structures, interference with ship operations from floating materials, interference with fishing or navigation through deposit of waste or solid objects on the sea floor and protection of areas of special importance for scientific or conservation purposes).
4 The practical availability of alternative land-based methods of treatment, disposal or elimination, or of treatment to render the matter less harmful for dumping at sea.

Bibliography

ABRAMS, David J. (1990), 'Regulating the International Hazardous Waste Trade: A Proposed Global Solution', in Colum. J. Transnat'l. L. 28(1990) pp. 801–45.

ADEDE, A.O., 'International Environmental Law from Stockholm to Rio: An Overview of Past Lessons and Future Challenges', in EPL 22/2(1992) p. 88 et seq.

AKEHURST, M.B., 'International Liability for Injurious Consequences Arising out of Acts not Prohibited in International Law', in 16 NYIL(1985) p. 3 et seq.

ARDEN-CLARKE, Charles, *The General Agreement on Tariffs and Trade, Environmental Protection and Sustainable Development* (WWF, 1991).

ATKINSON, Nicola, 'The Regulatory Lacuna: Waste Disposal and the Clean-Up of Contaminated Sites', in J Env L 3/2(1991) p. 265 et seq.

AUDRETSCH, H.A.H, 'Supervision in the EEC, OECD, and Benelux—a Difference in Degree, but also in Kind?', in ICLQ 36(1987) p. 838 et seq.

AUST, Anthony, 'The Theory and Practice of Informal International Instruments', in ICLQ 35(1986) pp. 786–812.

BARENTS, René, 'The International Market Unlimited: Some Observations on the Legal Basis of Community Legislation', in *Common Market Law Review* 30(1993), p. 85 et seq.

BARTRAM, Berit and ENGEL, Bruno, 'Ende des "Giftmüllkolonialismus"?', in *Vereinte Nationen* 4/1989, pp. 115–21.

BERNSTORFF, Andreas, 'Stellungnahme der Umweltschutzorganisation Greenpeace zur Basler Konvention', in *Müllmagazin* 3(1989) pp. 8–11.

BIRNIE, Patricia W. and BOYLE, Alan E., *International Law and the Environment* (Clarendon Press, Oxford 1992).

BLAY, S.K.N., 'New Trends in the Protection of the Antarctic Environment: The 1991 Madrid Protocol', in AJIL 86(1992) p. 377 et seq.

BODANSKY, Daniel, 'The United Nations Framework Convention on Climate Change: A Commentary', in Yale J. Int'l. L. 18/2(1993), pp. 451–557.

BOEHMER-CHRISTIANSEN, Sonja, 'An end to radioactive waste "at sea"?', in *Marine Policy* 10/2, April 1986, pp. 119–31.

BOTHE, Michael, 'International Regulation of Transboundary Movement of Hazardous Waste', in GYIL 33(1990) p. 422.

BOURNE, C.B., 'International Law and Pollution of International Rivers and Lakes', in U. Brit. Colum. L. Rev. 6(1971) pp. 115–36.

BOYLE, Alan E. (1992a), 'Land-Based Sources of Marine Pollution', in *Marine Policy* (January 1992), p. 20 et seq.

—— (1992b), 'Protecting the Marine Environment: Some Problems and Developments in the Law of the Sea', in *Marine Policy* (March 1992), p. 79 et seq.

—— (1991), 'Saving the World? Implementation and Enforcement of International Environmental Law through International Institutions', in J. Env. L. 3/2(1991).

—— (1990a), 'The Law of the Sea and International Watercourses: An Emerging Cycle', in *Marine Policy* (March 1990), p. 151 et seq.

BOYLE, Alan E. (1990b), 'State Responsibility and International Liability for Injurious Consequences of Acts Not Prohibited by International Law: A Necessary Distinction?', in ICLQ 39/1(1990), pp. 1–26.

—— (1989), 'Nuclear Energy and International Law: An Environmental Perspective', in BYIL (1989), p. 257 et seq.

—— (1985), 'Marine Pollution under the Law of the Sea Convention', in AJIL 79/2(1985), p. 347 et seq.

BROMM, Susan E., 'Creating a Hazardous Waste Management Program in a Developing Country', in Am. U. J. Int'l. L. & Pol'y 5/2(1990), p. 325 et seq.

BROWN WEISS, Edith (1992a), 'Environment and Trade as Partners in Sustainable Development: A Commentary', in AJIL 86(1992) p. 728 et seq.

—— (Ed.) (1992b), *Environmental Change and International Law: New Challenges and Dimensions* (United Nations University Press, Tokyo 1992).

BROWNLIE, Ian (1990), *Principles of Public International Law* (4th Ed., Clarendon Press, Oxford 1990).

—— (1983), *System of the Law of Nations, State Responsibility, Part I* (Clarendon Press, Oxford 1983).

—— (1973), 'A Survey of International Customary Rules of Environmental Protection', in 13 Nat. Res. J. (1973) p. 179 et seq.

BRÜCKNER, Peter, 'The European Community and the United Nations', in Europ. J. Int'l. L. 1(1990), pp. 174–92.

BRUSASCO-MACKENZIE, Margaret and KISS, Alexandre, 'Les relations extérieures des Communautés Européennes en matière de protection de l'environnement', in *Annuaire Français de Droit International* XXXV(1989) p. 702 et seq.

BUREAU DE LA GESTION DES DÉCHETS, Environnement Canada, 'Synthèse et analyse des politiques et pratiques de gestion des déchets domestiques dangereux dans les pays de l'OCDE' (Doc. WM-16F, Ottawa 1993).

BUTLER, W.E. (Ed.) (1991), *Control over Compliance with International Law* (Kluwer Academic Publishers, 1991).

—— (Ed.) (1990), *Perestroika and International Law* (Kluwer Academic Publishers, 1990).

CAFLISCH, Lucius, 'La Convention des Nations Unis sur le droit de la mer adoptée le 30 avril 1982', in Swiss YIL 39(1983) pp. 39–104.

CALDWELL, Lynton Keith, *International Environmental Policy* (2nd Ed., Duke University Press, Durham/London 1990).

CAMERON, James, 'The Constraints on European Community Institutions Acting in the Field of Environmental Protection arising from International Agreements' (paper presented at the Research Centre for International Law, University of Cambridge, October 1992; unpublished).

CARROLL, John E. (Ed.), *International Environmental Diplomacy* (Cambridge University Press, Cambridge 1988).

CARTIER, Barry E. and TRIMBLE, Philip R. (Eds.), *International Law: Selected Documents* (1991).

CASSESE, Antonio, *International Law in a Divided World* (Clarendon Press, Oxford 1986).

CHARNOWITZ, Steve, 'Environmental Trade Measures: Multilateral or Unilateral?', in EPL 23/3/4(1993) p. 155 et seq.

CHURCHILL, Robin and FREESTONE, David (Eds.), *International Law and Climate Change* (Graham & Trotman, London 1991).

—— and LOWE, A.V., *The Law of the Sea* (3rd ed., Manchester University Press, Manchester 1988).

CLAPP, Jennifer, 'Dumping on the Poor: the Toxic Waste Trade to Developing Countries', University of Cambridge, Faculty of Political Sciences, Global Security Programme, Occasional Paper no. 5 (August 1994).

CLERC, Alain, 'The Basel Convention: Origins, Development, and Potential Impact on Health and the Human Environment', in *International Digest of Health Legislation* 40/4(1990), p. 904 et seq.

1990 Commission Proposal: EU Commission Proposal for a Council Regulation on the supervision and control of shipments of waste within, into and out of the European Community, 26 October 1990, (COM(90)415 final SYN 305).

CREMONA, Marise, 'The Doctrine of Exclusivity and the Position of Mixed Agreements in the External Relations of the European Community', in *Oxford Journal of Legal Studies* 2/1982, pp. 393–428.

CUSACK, Marguerite M., 'International Law and the Transboundary Shipment of Hazardous Waste to the Third World: Will the Basel Convention Make a Difference?', in Am. U. J. Int'l. L. & Pol'y 5/2(1990), p. 393 et seq.

DONALD, J.W., 'The Bamako Convention as a Solution to the Problem of Hazardous Waste Exports to Less Developed Countries', in Colum. J.Env.L.17/2(1992) pp. 419–58.

DUPUY, Pierre, 'Due Diligence in the International Law of Liability', in OECD, *Legal Aspects of Transfrontier Pollution* (Paris 1977).

Executive Director's Basel Proposals: Proposals by the Executive Director for Consideration by the Ad Hoc Working Group at its 5th Session, 12–13 March 1989 (UNEP/WG.191/3, 191/3/Add.1–7).

Executive Director's Luxembourg Note: Note by the Executive Director of UNEP on Some Points of the Hazardous Wastes Convention Which Were Not Resolved at the 4th Session of the Ad Hoc Working Group, 10 February 1989 (UNEP/WG.191/2).

Executive Director's Report to the 1st Conference of the Parties: Report by the Executive Director to the 1st Meeting of the Conference of the Parties to the Basel Convention: Implementation of the Resolutions Adopted by the Conference of Plenipotentiaries on the Global Convention on the Control of Transboundary Movements of Hazardous Wastes and their Disposal, 7 July 1992 (UNEP/CHW.1/2).

FATHALLA, Ahmed, 'Work on Liability within UNEP', in International Bar Association (Ed.), *Environmental Liability*, p. 26 et seq. (Graham & Trotman, London 1991).

FITZMAURICE, Malgosia, *International Legal Problems of the Environmental Protection of the Baltic Sea* (Graham & Trotman, London 1992).

FLUCK, Jürgen, 'The Term "Waste" in EU Law', in EELR 3(1994) p. 79 et seq.

DA FONSECA-WOLLHEIM, Hermann, 'The European Community and the Law of the Sea Convention' (paper given at the Law of the Sea Institute Conference, Genova, June 1992).

FORSTER, Malcolm J., 'London Dumping Convention: In the Ranks of Tuscany?', in EPL 16/1(1986), p. 7 et seq.

FRANCIONI, Francesco (1994), 'From Sovereignty to Common Governance: the EC and Environmental Policy', in Markesinis (Ed.), *The Gradual Convergence: Foreign Ideas, Foreign Influences and English Law on the Eve of the 21st Century* (Oxford University Press, 1994).

—— (Ed.)(1992), *International Environmental Law for Antarctica* (Giuffrè Publishing, Milan 1992).

—— (1983), 'Sharing of Community and Member States' Powers in the Field of Foreign Policy', in Collana di Studi No. 1, Istituto di Diritto Pubblico e Internazionale, Facoltà di Giurisprudenza (Proceedings of the Siena-Bonn Seminar, March–June 1983).

—— and SCOVAZZI, Tullio (Eds.), *International Responsibility for Environmental Harm* (Graham & Trotman, London 1991).

GADE, Mary A., 'Exporting Trouble: The Case for a U.S. Ban on Hazardous Waste Exports', in Canadian Council on International Law, Proceedings of the XVIIIth Annual Conference (1989), p. 321 et seq.

GAJA, G., 'Sull'interpretazione di accordi misti da parte della Corte di guistizia', in *Rivista di Diritto Internazionale* (1988), p. 605 et seq.

GATT, *International Trade 1990–91: Trade and the Environment* (1992).

GEHRING, Thomas, 'International Environmental Regimes: Dynamic Sectoral Legal Systems', in YBIEL 1(1990), p. 35 et seq.

GLAZEWSKI, Jan I., 'Regulating Transboundary Movements of Hazardous Waste: International Developments and Implications for South Africa', in *Comparative and International Law Journal of Southern Africa* XXVI/2(1993), pp. 234–49.

GOLD, Edgar, 'Legal Aspects of the Transportation of Dangerous Goods at Sea', in *Marine Policy* (July 1986), p. 186 et seq.

GREENPEACE (1994), Database of Known Hazardous Waste Exports from OECD to non-OECD Countries 1989–March 1994 (1994).

—— (1992), 'When Green is Not', Technical Paper 07/92.

—— (1991a), *Critique of the Proposal for a Council Regulation on the Supervision and Control of Shipments of Wastes within, into and out of the European Community* (1991).

—— (1991b), *The Single European Dump: Free Trade in Hazardous and Nuclear Wastes in the New Europe* (1991).

—— (1991c), *Preventing the Transboundary Movement of Hazardous Wastes in the Mediterranean Region* (1991).

—— (1990), *The International Trade in Wastes: A Greenpeace Inventory* (5th Ed. 1990).

GREFE, Christiane and BERNSTORFF, Andreas, *Zum Beispiel Giftmüll* (Lamuv, Göttingen 1991).

GRÖBL, Wolfgang, 'Stellungnahme des Bundesumweltministeriums zur Basler Konvention', in *Müllmagazin* 3(1989) pp. 6–8.

GÜNDLING, Lothar, 'The Precautionary Principle', in Int'l. J. of Est. & Coastal L. 5(1990), p. 23 et seq.

HAAS, Peter M., *Saving the Mediterranean: The Politics of International Co-operation* (Columbia University Press, New York 1990).

HACKETT, David P., 'An Assessment of the Basel Convention on the Control of

Transboundary Movements of Hazardous Wastes and Their Disposal', in Am. U. J. Int'l. L. & Pol'y 5/2(1990), p. 291 et seq.

HAIGH, Nigel, 'The European Community and International Environmental Policy', in *International Environmental Affairs* 3/3(1991), p. 163 et seq.

HANDL, Günther (1990), 'Environmental Security and Global Change: The Challenge to International Law', in YBIEL 1(1990), pp. 3–33.

—— (1989), 'The 1989 Basel Convention on the Transboundary Movement of Hazardous Waste: A Preliminary Assessment', in Canadian Council on International Law, Proceedings of the XVIIIth Annual Conference (1989), p. 367 et seq.

—— (1988), 'Transboundary Nuclear Accidents: The Post-Chernobyl Multilateral Legislative Agenda', in *Ecology Law Quarterly* 15/2(1988), p. 203 et seq.

—— (1985), 'Liability as an Obligation Established by a Primary Rule of International Law', in 16 NYIL (1985), pp. 49–79.

—— (1980), 'State Liability for Accidental Transnational Environmental Damage by Private Persons', in AJIL 74(1980), p. 525 et seq.

—— (1975), 'Balancing of Interests and International Liability for the Pollution of International Watercourses: Customary Principles of Law Revisited', in CYIL 13(1975), pp. 156–94.

—— and LUTZ, Robert E. (Eds.) (1989a), *Transferring Hazardous Technologies and Substances: The International Legal Challenge* (Graham & Trotman, London/Dordrecht/Boston 1989).

—— and —— (1989b), 'An International Policy Perspective on the Trade of Hazardous Materials and Technologies', in Harvard Int'l. L. J. 30/2(1989), p. 351 et seq.

HANDLEY, F.J. (1990), 'Export of Wastes from the U.S. to Canada', in Env. L. Rep. 20(1990).

—— (1989), 'Hazardous Waste Exports: A Leak in the System of International Legal Controls', in Env. L. Rep.19/4(1989), p. 10171 et seq.

VAN HEIJNSBERGEN, P., 'The "Pollution" Concept in International Law', in EPL 5(1979), p. 11 et seq.

HILF, Meinrad, 'The Single European Act and 1992: Legal Implications for Third Countries', in Europ. J. Int'l. L. 1(1990), pp. 89–117.

HILZ, Christoph, *The International Toxic Waste Trade* (Van Nostrano, New York 1992).

—— 'Toxic Waste Exports to the Third World: An Analysis of Policy Options and Recommendations for an International Protocol to Protect the Global Environment', (Massachusetts Institute of Technology Thesis; Paper no. HSMP 16, 1990).

—— and RADKA, Mark, 'Environmental Negotiation and Policy: The Basel Convention on Transboundary Movement of Hazardous Wastes and their Disposal', in *International Journal of Environment and Pollution* 1/2(1991), pp. 55–72.

HOHMANN, Harald (Ed.)(1992), *Basic Documents of International Environmental Law, Vols. 1–3* (Graham & Trotman/Martinus Nijhoff, London 1992).

—— (1990), 'Suche nach nationalen und internationalen Regelungen eines modernen Meeresumweltschutzes', in Natur + Recht 2/12(1990), p. 49 et seq.

—— (1989), 'Massnahmen zur Bekämpfung der Meeresverschmutzung: Völkerrechtliche Regelungen und Suche nach Massnahmen, die einer modernen

Konzeption des Meeresumweltschutzes entsprechen', in Donner et al. (Eds.), *Umweltschutz zwischen Staat und Markt: Moderne Konzeptionen im Umweltschutz* (Nomos Verlagsgesellschaft, Baden-Baden 1989).

HUNTOON, Barbara D., 'Emerging Controls on Transfers of Hazardous Waste to Developing Countries', in *Law and Policy in International Business* 21(1989), pp. 247–71.

HURRELL, Andrew and KINGSBURY, Benedict (Eds.), *The International Politics of the Environment* (Clarendon Press, Oxford 1992).

INTERNATIONAL LAW COMMISSION, 'Commentary on the Draft Articles on the Law of Treaties', *Yearbook of the International Law Commission* II(1966) (ILC Commentary).

INTERNATIONAL MARITIME ORGANIZATION (1991), *Focus on IMO: The Safe Transport of Dangerous, Hazardous and Harmful Cargoes Including Environmentally Hazardous Substances (Marine Pollutants) and Wastes, by Sea* (London 1991).

—— (1989), *Focus on IMO: Dumping at Sea—IMO and the Convention on the Prevention of Marine Pollution by Dumping of Wastes and Other Matter* (London 1989).

INTERNATIONAL MONETARY FUND (1993), *World Economic Outlook: A Survey by the Staff of the IMF* (October 1993).

JENNINGS, Sir Robert, 'Need for Environmental Court?', in EPL 122/5/6(1992), p. 312 et seq.

JIMÉNEZ DE ARÉCHAGA, Eduardo (1978), 'International Law in the Past Third of a Century', in *Recueil des Cours,* Vol. 1 (1978).

—— (1968), 'International Responsibility', in Sørensen (Ed.), *Manual of Public International Law* (Macmillan, London/Melbourne/Toronto 1968), p. 531 et seq.

JOHNSON, Stanley P. and CORCELLE, Guy, *The Environmental Policy of the European Communities* (Graham & Trotman, London/Dordrecht/Boston 1989).

JONES, Wordsworth F., 'The Evolution of the Bamako Convention: An African Perspective', in *Colorado Journal of International Environmental Law & Policy* 4(1993), pp. 324–42.

KALSHOVEN, F., KUYPER, P.J. and LAMMERS, J.G. (Eds.), *Essays on the Development of the International Legal Order* (Sijthoff & Nordhoff, Alphen an den Rijn (Netherlands) 1980).

KELLY, Mary Elizabeth, 'International Regulation of Transfrontier Hazardous Waste Shipments: A New EEC Environmental Directive', in Tex. Intl. L. J. 21(1986) p. 90 et seq.

KEMPEL, Willy, 'Transboundary Movements of Hazardous Wastes', in Sjöstedt (Ed.), *International Environmental Negotiation* (Sage, Newbury Park/London 1993).

KIMBALL, Lee, *Forging International Agreement: Strengthening Inter-Governmental Institutions for Environment and Development* (World Resources Institute, Washington D.C. 1990).

KISS, Alexandre (1991), 'The International Control of Transboundary Movement of Hazardous Waste', in Tex. Int'l. Law J. 26(1991), p. 521 et seq.

—— (1989a), *Droit international de l'environnement* (Pédone, Paris 1989).

—— (1989b), 'Nouvelles tendances en droit international de l'environnement', in GYIL 32(1989), pp. 241–63.

—— (1983), 'The International Protection of the Environment', in MacDonald and Johnston (Eds.), *The Structure and Process of International Law: Essays in Legal Philosophy, Doctrine and Theory* (Martinus Nijhoff, The Hague/ Boston/Lancaster 1983).

—— and SHELTON, Dinah, *International Environmental Law* (Transnational Publishers, New York 1991).

KRÄMER, Ludwig (1993), 'Environmental Protection and Article 30 EEC Treaty', in *Common Market Law Review* 30(1993) pp. 111–43.

—— (1992), *Focus on European Environmental Law* (Sweet & Maxwell, London 1992).

—— (1990), *EEC Treaty and Environmental Protection* (Sweet & Maxwell, London 1990).

KUMMER, Katharina (1994a), 'Transboundary Movements of Hazardous Wastes at the Interface of Environment and Trade' (UNEP Environment and Trade Monograph no. 7, Nairobi 1994).

—— (1994b), 'Providing Incentives to Comply with Multilateral Environmental Agreements: An Alternative to Sanctions?', in EELR 3/9(1994), p. 256 et seq.

—— (1992), 'The International Regulation of Transboundary Traffic in Hazardous Wastes: the 1989 Basel Convention', in ICLQ 41/3(1992), p. 530 et seq.

—— and RUMMEL-BULSKA, Iwona, 'The Basel Convention on the Control of Transboundary Movements of Hazardous Wastes and their Disposal' (UNEP, Environmental Law Library no. 2, Nairobi 1990).

KWIATKOWSKA, Barbara and SOONS, Alfred H.A. (Eds.), *Transboundary Movement and Disposal of Hazardous Wastes in International Law: Basic Documents* (Martinus Nijhoff/Graham & Trotman, Dordrecht/Boston/London 1993).

La réparation des dommages catastrophiques: Les risques technologiques majeurs en droit international et en droit communautaire, Travaux des XIIIes Journées d'Études Juridiques Jean Dabin, Université Catholique de Louvain (Establissements Emile Bruylant, Brussels 1990).

LANG, Winfried, NEUHOLD, Hanspeter and ZEMANEK, Karl (Eds.), *Environmental Protection and International Law* (Graham & Trotman, London 1991).

VON LERSNER, Heinrich, 'Requirements on Waste Disposal in Europe', in EPL 20/6(1990), p. 211 et seq.

LESTER, Anthony P., 'River Pollution in International Law', in AJIL 57(1963), pp. 828–53.

DI LEVA, Charles E., 'Trends in International Environmental Law: A Field With Increasing Influence', in 21 Env. L. Rep. (2–1991), p. 10076.

LONG, William L., 'Economic Aspects of Transport and Disposal of Hazardous Waste', in *Marine Policy* 14/3(1990), p. 198 et seq.

LOUIS, Jean-Victor, *The Community Legal Order* (2nd Ed., EC Office for Official Publications, Brussels 1990).

LOUKA, Elli, *Overcoming National Barriers to International Waste Trade* (Martinus Nijhoff/Graham & Trotman 1994).

LUKASIK, Lucjan, *Report on Resolution 2 of the 1989 Basel Conference* (unpublished consultant's report submitted to the Environmental Law and Institutions Unit of UNEP in 1989).

LUMSDAINE, J.S., 'Ocean Dumping Regulation: An Overview', in Ecology Law Quarterly 5(1976) p. 753 et seq.

MacDonald, R.S.J. and Johnston, Douglas M. (Eds.), *The Structure and Process of International Law: Essays in Legal Philosophy, Doctrine and Theory* (Martinus Nijhoff, The Hague/Boston/Lancaster 1983).

Magraw, Daniel B. (Ed.) (1991), *International Law and Pollution* (University of Pennsylvania Press, Philadelphia 1991).

—— (1986), 'Transboundary Harm: the International Law Commission's Study of "International Liability",' in AJIL 80(1986) p. 305 et seq.

Marin, Manuel, 'Lomé IV—The Scope of a New Convention', in *The Courier*, Africa/Caribbean/Pacific—European Community 120(1990) p. 14 et seq.

Mathijsen, P.S.R.F., *A Guide to European Community Law* (5th Ed., Sweet & Maxwell, London 1990).

McCaffrey, Stephen, 'Current Developments: The 42nd Session of the ILC', in AJIL 84(1990), p. 940.

Meng Qing-Nan, *Land-Based Marine Pollution* (1987).

van der Mensbrugghe, Yves (1990), 'La Convention de Bâle du 22 Mars 1989 sur le contrôle des mouvements transfrontières de déchets dangereux et de leur élimination', in *European Transport Law* 25/3(1990), pp. 267–77.

—— (1989), 'Les frontières maritimes de la CEE: Observations à propos de la directive 84/631 sur les transferts transfrontaliers de déchets dangereux', in *Revue du Marché Commun* 328(1989), p. 360.

Moisé, Evdokia, 'La Convention de Bâle sur les mouvements transfrontières des déchets dangereux (22 mars 1989)', in *Revue Générale du Droit Public* 93(1989), p. 899 et seq.

Montgomery, Mark A., 'Travelling Toxic Trash: An Analysis of the 1989 Basel Convention', in *The Fletcher Forum of World Affairs* 14/2(1990), p. 313 et seq.

Morgenstern, Felice, *Legal Problems of International Organizations* (Grotius, Cambridge 1986).

Mounteer, Thomas R., 'Codifying Basel Convention Obligations into U.S. Law: The Waste Export Control Act', in Env. L. Rep. 21(1991) p. 10085.

Müller, Jörg Paul, *Vertrauensschutz im Völkerrecht* (Bern 1971).

—— and Wildhaber, Luzius (Eds.), *Praxis des Völkerrechts* (Stämpfli, Bern 1977).

Murphy, Sean D., 'The Future of Transboundary Hazardous Waste Movements', in *International Practitioner's Notebook* 55(1992), p. 9 et seq.

Ndi, George K., 'Africa and Lomé IV, Cooperation Towards Sustainable Development in the African ACPs', in EPL 23/1(1993), p. 19 et seq.

Nollkaemper, André (1991), 'Laws of the Sea: Transboundary Movement of Hazardous Wastes', in *Marine Pollution Bulletin* 22/9(1991) p. 428 et seq.

—— (1987), 'The European Community and International Environmental Co-operation: Legal Aspects of External Community Powers', in *Legal Issues of European Integration* 2/1987, pp. 55–91.

O'Connell, D.P., *The International Law of the Sea, Vols. 1 and 2* (Oxford University Press, Oxford 1982/1984).

OECD (1993a), 'Monitoring and Control of Transfrontier Movements of Hazardous Wastes', OECD Environment Monograph no. 34, Document OCDE/GD (93)151 (updated version, Paris 1993).

—— (1993b), *Transfrontier Movements of Hazardous Wastes 1989–90* (Paris 1993).

—— (1991), *Environmental Data* (Paris 1991).

—— (1987), 'Improving the Enforcement of Environmental Policies', OECD Environment Monograph no. 8 (Paris 1987).

—— (1986a), *OECD and the Environment* (Paris 1986).

—— (1986b), 'Fate of Small Quantities of Hazardous Waste', OECD Environment Monograph no. 6 (Paris 1986).

—— (1977), *Legal Aspects of Transfrontier Pollution* (Paris 1977).

OTT, David H., *Public International Law in the Modern World* (Pitman Publishing, London 1987).

PALLEMAERTS, Marc, 'The North Sea Ministerial Declarations from Bremen to The Hague: Does the Process Generate Substance?', in Int'l. J. of Est. & Coastal L. 7/1(1992), pp. 1–26.

PETSONK, Carol A., 'The Role of the United Nations Environment Programme (UNEP) in the Development of International Environmental Law', in Am. U. J. Int'l. L. & Pol'y 5/2(1990), p. 351 et seq.

PLANT, Glen, 'Legal Environmental Restraints Post-Braer', in *Oil & Gas Law and Taxation Review* 10/9/10(1993), p. 1 et seq.

PORTEOUS, Andrew (Ed.), *Hazardous Waste Management Handbook* (Butterworth & Co., London 1985).

RAFTOPOULOS, Evangelos, 'The Barcelona Convention System for the Protection of the Mediterranean Sea against Pollution: An International Trust at Work', in Int. J. of Est. & Coastal L. 7/1(1992), pp. 27–41.

REDGWELL, Catherine, 'Compensation for Oil Pollution Damage: Quantifying Environmental Harm', in *Marine Policy* (March 1992), p. 90 et seq.

REPETTO, Robert, 'Trade and Sustainable Development', UNEP Environment and Trade Monograph no. 1 (1994).

REST, Alfred (1992), 'Ecological Damage in Public International Law', in EPL 22/1(1992) p. 31 et seq.

—— (1991), 'New Tendencies in Environmental Responsibility and Liability Law', in EPL 21/3/4(1991), p. 135 et seq.

REUTER, Paul, *Introduction to the Law of Treaties* (Pinter Publishers, London/New York 1989).

RICHTER, Roland, *Giftmüllexporte nach Afrika: Ueberblick, Zusammenhänge, Perspektiven* (Stiftung Wissenschaft und Politik, Ebenhausen (Germany) 1989).

RIPA DI MEANA, Carlo, 'Hazardous Waste Shipments: Regulation within the EC', in *Marine Policy* 14/3(1990), p. 271 et seq.

RIPHAGEN, Willem, 'State Responsibility: New Theories of Obligation in State Practice', in MacDonald and Johnston (Eds.), *The Structure and Process of International Law: Essays in Legal Philosophy, Doctrine and Theory* (Martinus Nijhoff, The Hague/Boston/Lancaster 1983).

ROBINSON, Jonathan, 'The Legal Basis of EC Environmental Law (analysis of the Titanium Dioxide Case, 1991)', in J. Env. L. 4/1(1992), p. 112 et seq.

ROSENCRANZ, Armin and ELDRIDGE, Christopher L., 'Hazardous Wastes: Basel after Rio', in EPL 22/5/6(1992), p. 318.

ROSENNE, Shabtai (Ed.) (1991), *The International Law Commission's Draft Articles on State Responsibility, Part I, Articles 1–35* (Martinus Nijhoff, Dordrecht 1991).

—— (1985), *Breach of Treaty* (Grotius, Cambridge 1985).

ROSENTHAL, Robert M., 'Ratification of the Basel Convention: Why the United States Should Adopt the *No Less Environmentally Sound* Standard', in *Temple Environmental Law and Technology Journal* XI/1(1992), pp. 61–78.

RUBLACK, Susanne (1994), 'Völkerrecht und Umweltrisikenexport', in *Archiv des Völkerrechts* 32/1(1994), pp. 54–98.

—— (1993), *Der grenzüberschreitende Transfer von Umweltrisiken im Völkerrecht* (Nomos Verlagsgesellschaft, Baden-Baden 1993).

—— (1989), 'Fighting Transboundary Waste Streams: Will the Basel Convention Help?', in *Verfassung und Recht in Uebersee—Law and Politics in Africa, Asia and Latin America* 22/4(1989), p. 386 et seq.

SACHARIEV, Kamen, 'Promoting Compliance with International Environmental Legal Standards: Reflections on Monitoring and Reporting Mechanisms', in YBIEL 2(1991), pp. 31–52.

SAND, Peter H. (Ed.) (1992), *The Effectiveness of International Environmental Agreements* (Grotius, Cambridge 1992).

—— (1990), *Lessons Learned in Global Environmental Governance* (World Resources Institute, 1990).

SANDER, Andrea and KÜPPERS, Peter (Eds.), *Environmentally Sound Waste Management? Current Legal Situation and Practical Experience in Europe* (Peter Lang, Frankfurt a.M. 1993).

SAXER, Otto, 'Kernenergie und Versicherung: Risikoanalyse und Risikobewältigung', in *Schweiz. Versicherungszeitschrift* 58/7/8(1990), pp. 175–80.

SCHMIDT, Alke, 'Transboundary Movements of Waste under EC Law: The Emerging Regulatory Framework', in J. Env. L. 4/1(1992), pp. 57–80.

SCHNEIDER, Jan (1981), 'Codification and Progressive Development of International Environmental Law at the 3rd UNCLOS: The Environmental Aspects of the Treaty Review', in 20 Colum. J. Transnat'l. L. (1981), p. 243 et seq.

—— (1979), *World Public Order of the Environment: Towards an International Ecological Law and Organization* (Stevens & Sons, London 1979).

SCHOENBAUM, Thomas J., 'Free International Trade and Protection of the Environment: Irreconcilable Conflict?', in AJIL 86(1992), p. 700 et seq.

SCHRÖDER, Meinhard, 'Aktuelle Konflikte zwischen europäischem und deutschem Abfallrecht', in *Die öffentliche Verwaltung* 21(1991), pp. 910–15.

SCISO, Elena, *Gli accordi internazionali confliggenti* (Cacucci Editore, Bari (Italy) 1986).

SEBEK, Viktor, 'International Legal Regulation of Trade in Toxic Waste, its Transport and Disposal', in Postiglione, *Per un tribunale internazionale dell'ambiente* (Milan 1990), pp. 285–301.

SEIGLER, Jane, 'An U.S. Perspective on the Import of Hazardous Wastes: Towards More Effective International Control', in *Canada–United States Law Journal* 18(1992), p. 115 et seq.

Selected Multilateral Treaties in the Field of the Environment, Vol. 1 (Ed. by A. Kiss, UNEP, Nairobi 1983); Vol. 2 (Ed. by I. Rummel-Bulska and S. Osafo, Grotius, Cambridge 1991).

SINCLAIR, Ian, *The Vienna Convention on the Law of Treaties* (2nd ed., Manchester 1984).

SKJAERSETH, Jon Birger, 'Towards the End of Dumping in the North Sea: An Example of Effective International Problem Solving?', in *Marine Policy* (March 1992).

SLYNN, Gordon, 'The Court of Justice of the European Communities', in ICLQ 33/2(1984), p. 409 et seq.

SMETS, Henri (1991), 'Quelques problèmes relatifs aux mouvements transfrontières de déchets dangereux', in EPL 21/3/4(1991), p. 141 et seq.

—— (1985), 'Transfrontier Movements of Hazardous Wastes: An Examination of the OECD Council Decision and Recommendation', in EPL 14(1985), p. 16 et seq.

SMITH, John Thomas, 'The Challenges of Environmentally Sound and Efficient Regulation of Waste—The Need for Enhanced International Understanding', in J. Env. L. 5/1(1993), pp. 91–107.

SOHN, Louis, 'The Stockholm Declaration on the Human Environment', in Harv. Int'l. L. J. 14(1973), p. 423 et seq.

SORSA, Piritta, 'Environment—A New Challenge to GATT?' (World Development Report 1992, Background Paper no. 4).

SPITALNIK, Ellen R., 'Hazardous Waste Management Legislation in Asia' (Paper presented at the International Chemical Regulation Briefing, Washington DC, November 1992).

SPRINGER, Allen L., *The International Law of Pollution: Protecting the Global Environment in a World of Sovereign States* (1983).

STOCKER, Werner, 'Das Prinzip des Common Heritage of Mankind als Ausdruck des Staatsgemeinschaftsinteresses im Völkerrecht', *Schweizer Studien zum Internationalen Recht*, Vol. 81 (Schulthess Polygraphischer Verlag, Zürich 1993).

STROHM, Laura A., 'The Environmental Politics of the International Waste Trade', in *Journal of Environment and Development* 2/2(1993), pp. 129–53.

TECLAFF, Ludvik A. and TECLAFF, Eileen (1991), 'Transfer of Pollution and the Marine Environment Conventions', in Nat. Res. J. 31(1991), p. 187 et seq.

—— and —— (1985), 'Transboundary Toxic Pollution and the Drainage Basin Concept', in Nat. Res. J. 25(1985), p. 589 et seq.

TOLBA, Mostafa K., 'The Global Agenda and the Hazardous Waste Challenge', in *Marine Policy* 14(1990), p. 205 et seq.

—— and EL-KHOLY, Osama A., *The World Environment 1972–1992* (Chapman & Hall, London 1992).

UNITED NATIONS (1989), Report of the UN Secretary-General to the General Assembly on Illegal Traffic in Toxic and Dangerous Wastes, 18 July 1989 (UN Doc. A/44/362).

UNITED NATIONS ENVIRONMENT PROGRAMME (UNEP) (1993), *Environmental Data Report 1993–94* (Blackwell, Oxford 1993).

—— (1991), *Environmental Law in UNEP* (UNEP Environmental Law Library no. 1, Nairobi 1991).

—— (1989a), *Proposals and Position of the African States during the Negotiations on the Basel Convention on the Control of Transboundary Movements of Hazardous Wastes and their Disposal and the Status of their Incorporation into the Basel Convention* (Nairobi 1989).

—— (1989b), *Directory of organizations and organizational units co-ordinating or contributing to the co-ordination of Action Plans related to the Regional Seas Programme*, (Rev. 2, Nairobi 1989).

—— (1988), *Status of regional agreements negotiated in the framework of the Regional Seas Programme* (Rev.1, Nairobi 1988).

United Nations Environment Programme (UNEP) Joint Group of Experts on the Scientific Aspects of Marine Pollution (GESAMP) (UNEP/GESAMP 1991), 'Global Strategies for Marine Environmental Protection' (GESAMP Reports and Studies No. 45, 1991).

—— —— (UNEP/GESAMP 1990), 'The State of the Marine Environment' (UNEP Regional Seas Reports and Studies No. 115, Nairobi 1990).

Utton, Albert E., 'International Water Quality Law', in Nat. Res. J. 13(1973) pp. 282–313.

Verdross, Alfred and Simma, Bruno, *Universelles Völkerrecht* (3rd ed., Duncker & Humblot, Berlin 1984).

Verhoeven, J., Sands, P. and Bruce, M. (Eds.), *The Antarctic Environment and International Law* (Graham & Trotman, London 1991).

de Villeneuve, Carel, 'Les mouvements transfrontières des déchets dangereux (Convention de Bâle et droit communautaire)', in *Revue du Marché Commun* (1990) pp. 568–77.

Walsh, Maureen T., 'The Global Trade in Hazardous Wastes: Domestic and International Attempts to Cope with a Growing Crisis in Waste Management', in *Catholic University Law Review* 42(1992), pp. 103–41.

Watts, Sir Arthur, *International Law and the Antarctic Treaty System* (Grotius, Cambridge 1992).

Watts, K.G., *Global Garbage* : *Exporting Trash and Toxic Waste* (1992).

Weinstein, Elaine B., 'The Impact of Regulation of Transport of Hazardous Waste on Freedom of Navigation', in IJMCL 9/2(1994) pp. 135–72.

Wilkinson, David, 'Maastricht and the Environment: The Implications for the EC's Environment Policy of the Treaty of European Union', J. Env. L. 4/2(1992), p. 221 et seq.

Williamson, Gabrielle H., 'Regulation of the Transfrontier Shipment of Hazardous Waste: A European Community Perspective', in Canadian Council on International Law, Proceedings of the XVIIIth Annual Conference (1989), p. 346 et seq.

von Wilmowsky, Peter, 'Waste Disposal in the International Market: The State of Play after the ECJ's Ruling on the Walloon Import Ban', in *Common Market Law Review* 30(1993) pp. 541–70.

World Bank, 'The Safe Disposal of Hazardous Wastes: The Special Needs and Problems of Developing Countries', Vols. I–III (World Bank Technical Paper no. 93, 1989).

World Commission on Environment and Development (WCED), *Our Common Future* (Oxford University Press, Oxford 1987).

World Resources Report 1990–91.

Wynne, Brian, 'The Toxic Waste Trade: International Regulatory Issues and Options', in *Third World Quarterly* 11/3(1989) pp. 120–47.

Ydhego, M., 'Cleaner Production in Tanzania', in *Industry and Environment* No. 16/3 (July–September 1993).

Zacklin, Ralph and Caflisch, Lucius (Eds.), *The Legal Regime of International Rivers and Lakes* (London 1981).

Index

The manufacturer's authorised representative in the EU for product safety is Oxford University Press España S.A. of el Parque Empresarial San Fernando de Henares, Avenida de Castilla, 2 – 28830 Madrid (www.oup.es/en or product.safety@oup.com). OUP España S.A. also acts as importer into Spain of products made by the manufacturer.

www.ingramcontent.com/pod-product-compliance
Ingram Content Group UK Ltd.
Pitfield, Milton Keynes, MK11 3LW, UK
UKHW020850150926
475595UK00003B/112

9780198259947